A More Perfect Union

Introduction to American Government

The Dorsey Series in Political Science

Photo by Chris Davidson

Samuel C. Patterson

The University of Iowa

Samuel C. Patterson is professor of political science at the University of Iowa. He received his undergraduate education at the University of South Dakota and in 1959 received his Ph.D. from the University of Wisconsin. He has been a visiting professor at the University of Wisconsin, the University of Oklahoma, and the University of Essex in England. He was editor of the *American Journal of Political Science* from 1971 to 1973 and has served on the editorial boards of several scholarly journals. In 1985 he became editor of *The American Political Science Review*. He was chairman of the Department of Political Science at the University of Iowa from 1973 to 1976. He has co-authored *The Legislative Process in the United States* (4th ed., 1985); *Comparative Legislative Behavior: Frontiers of Research* (1972); *Representatives and Represented* (1975); and *Comparing Legislatures* (1979). From 1975 to 1983 he served as consulting editor of The Dorsey Press. In 1980–81, he was president of the Midwest Political Science Association. He was a Guggenheim Fellow during 1984–85.

Roger H. Davidson

Congressional Research Service
U.S. Library of Congress

Roger H. Davidson is senior specialist in American government and public administration for the Congressional Research Service, where he conducts research and advises members and committees concerning congressional operations. He also serves as adjunct professor of government and politics at the University of Maryland, College Park. He received his B.A. from the University of Colorado and his Ph.D from Columbia University. He began his teaching career at Dartmouth College and then became a member of the political science faculty at the University of California, Santa Barbara, where he also served as department chair and associate dean of letters and science. He has served as special research consultant to the U.S. Senate's Select Committee on Committees and earlier played a similar role with its House counterpart. His books include *Congress and its Members* (with Walter J. Oleszek, 2nd ed., 1985), *The Politics of Comprehensive Manpower Legislation* (1972), *The Role of the Congressman* (1969), and numerous articles and monographs.

Randall B. Ripley

The Ohio State University

Randall B. Ripley received his B.A. from DePauw University in Indiana and his M.A. and Ph.D. from Harvard University. He served as an intern in the office of the Majority Whip in the United States House of Representatives in 1963, and from 1963 to 1967 he was on the staff of the Brookings Institution in Washington, D.C. In 1967 he became a member of the political science faculty at The Ohio State University, and since 1969 he has served as chairperson of his department. He is the author of numerous articles and has written and edited a number of books. Among his recent books are *Congress: Process and Policy* (3d ed., 1983), *Congress, the Bureaucracy, and Public Policy* (with Grace A. Franklin, 3d ed., 1984), and *Bureaucracy and Policy Implementation* (with Grace A. Franklin, 1982). He has served as a consultant to the Department of Labor and the Department of Housing and Urban Development, as well as to several congressional committees and governmental commissions.

A More Perfect Union

Introduction to American Government

Third Edition
1985

THE DORSEY PRESS
Homewood, Illinois 60430

ISBN 0-256-03240-8
Library of Congress Catalog Card No. 84-71432

Printed in the United States of America

1 2 3 4 5 6 7 8 9 0 V 2 1 0 9 8 7 6 5

Prologue

The year 1987 marks the bicentennial of the Constitution of the United States. This bicentennial will be celebrated across the land in a wide variety of ways— in commemorative books and documents, in theater and in exhibits, and in festivals, forums, conferences, and workshops. The National Endowment for the Humanities, an agency of the federal government, has created a special office to promote and support the celebration of the bicentennial. And in 1983, Congress established a Commission on the Bicentennial of the Constitution, consisting of 23 members directed "to promote and coordinate activities" for the commemoration of the Constitution.

This bicentennial promises to be celebrated far differently than the 1976 gala commemorating the 200th anniversary of the Declaration of Independence, with its fireworks and sailing ships. It will be marked not only by admiration for the Founders' achievements, but also by sober reflection on the adequacy of the Constitution for the years ahead. In March 1984, for example, 150 Virginians gathered in the historic House of Burgesses chamber at Williamsburg, Virginia, to begin discussing specific constitutional provisions. Their deliberations will be duplicated throughout the country during the bicentennial season. An impressive potpourri of lectures, programs, debates, symposia, and forums will be staged during that season, allowing a broad array of Americans to participate in reflection about our constitutional system.

This celebration of the 200th birthday of the adoption of the Constitution recalls the struggles of the early days of the republic, the trials and difficulties faced by the leaders of the new nation as they sought to establish national sovereignty and a new constitutional order. It highlights, as well, the durability of the work they accomplished. Little could those leaders have imagined that their handiwork would, in its fundamentals, last 200 years.

This book portrays in detail the government which grew up from the Constitution, and which still takes its basic authority from the Constitution. The Constitutional document is printed in an appendix at the end of the book. You should read it carefully. The 55 men who participated in the Constitutional Convention which met in Philadelphia from late May until mid-September 1787, crafted the document with great care and thorough deliberation. To justify its provisions, the Founders wrote a Preamble to the seven articles of the Constitution. That Preamble said:

> We, the People of the United States, in order to form a more perfect Union, establish Justice, insure domestic Tranquility, provide for the common Defence, promote the General Welfare, and secure the Blessings of Liberty to Ourselves and our Posterity, do ordain and establish this Constitution of the United States of America.

In this single sentence, the Preamble expresses with clarity and eloquence the purposes of government. In simple words it declares those purposes to be the establishment of *justice*, the guarantee of domestic peace and *tranquility*, the *defense* of the nation from aggression, the advancement of the *general welfare* of the people, and the protection of the blessings of *liberty* both for those living then and for future generations.

At the time the Constitution was being written, the United States was governed by the Articles of Confederation. Under these Articles, the national government consisted of a loose confederation of states, each retaining a great deal of independence. The Founders, working on the new Constitution in 1787, strongly desired a fresh system of national government, which would be grounded in the loyalties and support of, and dependent on the consent of, the people generally, not merely the state governments. This matter came up explicitly during the drafting of the Constitution, when it was determined to put aside the language of the Articles of Confederation, which had referred to itself as an agreement "between the States of New Hampshire, Massachusetts, Rhode Island, . . ." and the others, and instead begin with, "We the People of the States. . . ."

In September 1787, a committee on style was selected by the Constitutional Convention to polish up the language of the draft document, in order to make it ready for final approval. Gouverneur Morris of Pennsylvania, a member of the committee on style, found the draft language wanting. He took the leadership within the committee to see to it that the Preamble resonated the nationalist image which he and others believed the new constitution required.

And so the list of states in the draft proposal was replaced with "We the People of the United States, . . ." These opening words probably would not have been agreed to by the delegates in the early days of the Constitutional Convention. After all, they had come to Philadelphia mandated only to revise the Articles of Confederation. The Convention delegates, representing Americans from all of the 13 original states, were much more national in their outlooks than most of their fellow citizens. But it was the intensive deliberation and debate of the Convention which convinced these delegates that the nation required a stronger constitution than mere revision of the Articles of Confederation would permit. By the end of the Convention, they had framed an entirely new instrument of government, the Constitution of the United States, which rested on the authority of all the people.

No one knew in those days of the late 1780s, when the new instrument of government was being formulated and ratified, what "a more perfect union" would be like. They did know that functioning as 13 largely independent states only loosely banded together was not working very well. They intended the new Constitution to forge a stronger unity among the states and their people. They did not want to destroy the states—far from it. They did want to invent a system in which strong and vibrant states could be blended in harmony and strength to create a new balance, so that states and nation could pull together in union.

The Founders surely understood better than any of their fellow Americans that forming a more perfect union was going to be an ongoing process, not something which would be conceived in a moment or born full-grown. Indeed, these people of practical political sense showed a deeply mature perception of the difficult and often frustrating experience that lay ahead for the new union. No one understood this better than Benjamin Franklin, who made a brief speech to the delegates as the Convention concluded its work. "I agree to this constitution with all its faults," Franklin said. Although he doubted whether any other convention of political leaders could "make a better Constitution," he did not think it was perfect.

> For when you assemble a number of men to have the advantage of their joint wisdom, you inevitably assemble with those men all their prejudices, their passions, their errors of opinion, their local interests and their selfish views. From such an assembly can a perfect production be expected? It therefore astonishes me . . . to find this system approaching so near to perfection as it does.

So, said Franklin, "I consent . . . to this Constitution because I expect no better, and because I am not sure it is not the best."

The bicentennial gives us an opportunity to go beyond merely reflecting on the Founders' wisdom. It stimulates us to take stock of the adequacy of their charter for the 21st century ahead. It may be that the Constitution has endured more because of its flexibility and pliability than because its inventors were prescient. The development of the American government after the Constitution was in place was inconceivable, in many ways, without things that were not in the Constitution at all, or even contemplated by its authors. Political parties, judicial review of congressional and administrative acts, intricate legislative-executive arrangements, the cabinet, universal adult suffrage—these matters were not addressed in the Constitution.

Some Americans today are wondering whether changes in the Constitution would foster more effective government. Should members of Congress be allowed to serve in the president's cabinet in order to bond the legislative and executive branches more closely together? Should the president be permitted to dissolve Congress and call new elections if there were a stalemate between the two? Should Congress be allowed to remove a president more easily than the present impeachment process makes possible? Should candidates for president and for Congress be required to run as a political party slate so as to build in closer ties between them? Should the terms of office of president and member of the House of Representatives be longer? Should the president have the power of the "item veto" so he or she could annul specific provisions of legislation without vetoing it entirely? These are the kinds of questions about the Constitution which can stimulate a healthy and constructive debate as we mark its 200th birthday.

The Constitution's opening words are a statement of goals and ideals. As ideals, the purposes of the new nation were not likely to be realized quickly or easily, and perhaps never perfectly. But a constitution of government needs, first and foremost, to set forth its ideals in order for the people to give it their respect and trust, and in order for politicians and statesmen to be inspired to hold up a standard for their own performance. Because they understood that the ideals of the Preamble to the Constitution would take time to reach, the Founders created a Constitution not just for those who were alive in the late 18th century, but for posterity. And that Preamble enjoins Americans to form "a more perfect union." Debate about the contemporary meaning of the Constitution and discussion of constitutional change is invaluable to the search for better ways to make government work.

The 200th birthday of the Constitution occasions many retrospectives about American political and governmental life. Assessments of the Constitution and the governing institutions it spawned will be more useful and interesting to those who are well-informed about how the American political system works. This book contributes to that end.

Acknowledgments

A textbook is never the product of its authors alone. This is especially true when the book has reached its third manifestation. For this edition and its predecessors, we have benefited from the advice and criticism of many of our colleagues around the country.

For help with this third edition, we especially thank the following people:

John Bibby, University of Wisconsin-Milwaukee

Christopher Deering, George Washington University

Calvin Mackenzie, Colby College

William McCoy, University of North Carolina

Alan Monroe, Illinois State University

Robert Murphy, St. Louis Community College at Florissant Valley

Walter Rosenbaum, University of Florida

Robert Salisbury, Washington University, St. Louis

Hugh Stephens, University of Houston

We are also grateful for the continuing help of Grace Franklin and Grier E. Patterson. And to all those instructors and students who have used this book, who have found value in its approach and emphases, who have encouraged us to undertake a new edition (and who have not hesitated to suggest specific changes)—to all of them we convey our deepest thanks. You are the real reason for this enterprise, and you make it all worthwhile.

For helping us with the first and second editions of this text, we thank the following people: Timothy Almy, University of Georgia; Lawrence Baum, Ohio State University; William E. Bicker, University of California, Berkeley; Harvey Boulay, Boston University; David Brady, Rice University; James E. Gregg, California State University, Chico; Margaret A. Hunt, University of North Carolina, Greensboro; William R. Keech, University of North Carolina, Chapel Hill; William J. Keefe, University of Pittsburgh; Lyman Kellstedt, University of Illinois, Chicago Circle; Henry C. Kenski, University of Arizona; Michael R. King, Pennsylvania State University; James Klonoski, University of Oregon; Robert D. McClure, Syracuse University; Richard H. Payne, Sam Houston State University; Ronald B. Rapoport, College of William and Mary; Wilber C. Rich, Columbia University; Wayne Shannon, University of Connecticut; Elliot E. Slotnick, Ohio State University; Dale Vinyard, Wayne State University; Stephen L.

Wasby, State University of New York, Albany; and David Yamada, Monterey Peninsula College. Our earlier efforts were also helped by Joe Cantor, Paul Dwyer, Louis Fisher, Virginia Graham, Clark Norton, Edward M. Davis III, and Harold Relyea of the Congressional Research Service; Gregory A. Caldeira and Peter G. Snow of the University of Iowa; and Grace Franklin and Richard S. Stoddard, Ohio State University.

Samuel C. Patterson
Roger H. Davidson
Randall B. Ripley

Contents

Part Three

THE MOBILIZATION OF POLITICAL FORCES

Part Four

GOVERNMENT POLICYMAKERS

Part Five

POLITICAL PROCESSES AND PUBLIC POLICY

A More Perfect Union
Introduction to American Government

PART 1

The Context of
American Politics

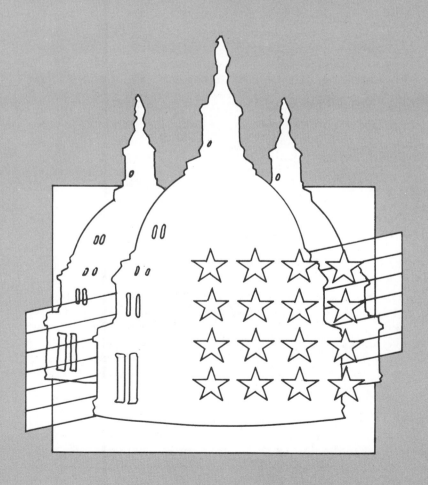

1
Origins of the American Polity

As soon as it was clear in 1788 that enough states would ratify the Constitution of the United States to make it the new fundamental law of the land, in state after state there were elaborate celebrations of the new regime. Historian Catherine Drinker Bowen has artfully described this in her book, *Miracle at Philadelphia* (1966: 306–10). The centerpieces of these state festivities were parades in major cities. In Philadelphia, the "federal procession" to celebrate the new Constitution was held on July 4, 1788. At sunrise, the bells tolled at Christ Church, and the ship, *Rising Sun*, lying in the harbor, fired a salute from her cannon. At 9:30, the parade began, led by the soldiers of the First City Troop of Light Dragoons. The parade included bands, horse-drawn floats, and marchers of all kinds. The most elaborate float was called the Grand Federal Edifice. It was mounted on a carriage pulled by 10 white horses. This magnificent float was a large dome held up by 13 Corinthian columns and decorated with 13 stars. On top of the dome was a statue of the figure *Plenty* holding a cornucopia, and around the pedestal were the words "In Union the Fabric stands firm." Ten men sat inside this dazzling edifice; they represented citizens of the new nation to whom the Constitution had been given for ratification.

Following the Edifice came the marchers—450 architects and house carpenters, saw makers and file cutters, members of the Agricultural Society, brick makers and clock makers, saddlers and boat builders, coopers, blacksmiths, gunsmiths and brewers, and clergy of all denominations. The 20-gun federal ship *Union*, mounted on a wagon, was drawn by horses with signs attached to their harnesses bearing the names of the ratifying states. The parade ended at a park named Union Green in honor of the occasion. There, James Wilson made a speech, and many toasts were offered to the new Union, "each toast being announced by a trumpet and answered by a discharge of artillery from the *Rising Sun*. The crowd drank to "The people of the United States." They toasted "Honor and Immortality to the Members of the late Convention." Lastly, with a large benevolence, they drank to "The Whole Family of Mankind." And, after the festivities were over, Benjamin Rush, a Philadelphia physician and signer of the Declaration of Independence, wrote: "Tis done. We have become a nation."

* * * * *

Parades and speeches celebrate important events. The men and women who celebrated the birth of the nation in Philadelphia nearly 200 years ago had a good time. But celebrations do not make nations and governments—these grow up over a long period. Dr. Rush's crowning words were only a start.

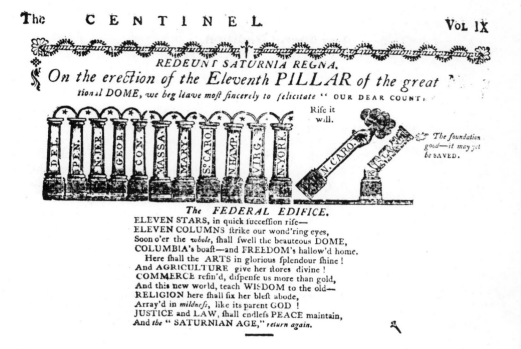

The CENTINEL VoL IX

REDEUNT SATURNIA REGNA.
On the erection of the Eleventh PILLAR of the great *
tional DOME, we beg leave most sincerely to felicitate " OUR DEAR COUNT
Rise it will.
* The foundation good—it may yet be SAVED.

The FEDERAL EDIFICE.
ELEVEN STARS, in quick succession rise—
ELEVEN COLUMNS strike our wond'ring eyes,
Soon o'er the *whole*, shall swell the beauteous DOME,
COLUMBIA's boast—and FREEDOM's hallow'd home.
Here shall the ARTS in glorious splendour shine !
And AGRICULTURE give her stores divine !
COMMERCE refin'd, dispense us more than gold,
And this new world, teach WISDOM to the old—
RELIGION here shall fix her blest abode,
Array'd in *mildness*, like its parent GOD !
JUSTICE and LAW, shall endless PEACE maintain,
And *the* " SATURNIAN AGE," *return again.*

Ratification of the Constitution occasioned patriotic celebration. This cartoon was printed in the Massachusetts *Centinel* to celebrate New York's ratification of the Constitution on July 26, 1788. The Constitution went into effect after New Hampshire ratified, but the importance of New York and Virginia made their approval essential. The new government was elected in the fall of 1788, although North Carolina did not ratify until 1789, and Rhode Island did not ratify until 1790.

All political systems are rooted in their pasts; that of the United States is no exception. Many of our political beliefs and practices grew out of our colonial experience. We cannot understand American politics today without reflecting on our history.

The United States has a rich and exciting history, worth studying in detail. We cannot tell here the full story of the birth of the nation and its early years— that is the province of the historian. But in this chapter we point out the main characteristics of the emerging American republic. We explain that many features of American politics came from Europe and evolved under the conditions life in the New World made possible. We describe the main outlines of colonial politics to show how early practices began to shape the political future of the country. We take stock of the most important ways the American Revolution reflected our independence and aroused the nation's spirit. Finally, we look at the Constitution of the United States, which was meant to foster "a more perfect union."

AMERICA AND EUROPE

It is easy to forget the small scale on which colonial life was organized. By 1700 the colonies had only about a quarter of a million people—fewer than present-day Des Moines, Iowa. By the time of the Revolution, they had about 2.75 mil-

Newspaperman, printer, inventor, diplomat—Benjamin Franklin represented the United States in London during the Revolution and was the oldest, most experienced statesman at the Constitutional Convention.

Author of the Declaration of Independence—Thomas Jefferson served as ambassador to France during the time the new Constitution was being written in Philadelphia, but he returned afterward to serve as Washington's secretary of state and then organized the political movement which elected him president in 1800.

lion. Although there were centers of Germans in Pennsylvania and of Dutch in New York, most people were British. Only a few thousand Indians were left in the settled areas. By 1765, about 20 percent of the people were blacks. Most of these were slaves, and most lived in the southern colonies. Slavery and the place of blacks in American life later were momentous issues. But their status as slaves in the early days made blacks almost completely irrelevant in politics.

The liberal tradition

Like other colonial peoples—the Spanish and Portuguese in Latin America, the Dutch in South Africa, the French in Canada, and the British in Australia—the people who first settled the American colonies were a "fragment society" (Hartz, 1964). They were a fragment of Europe, like the seeds of a maple tree carried far away to grow up in new and different soil. This fragment was detached at a time when Europeans, particularly the British, were starting to strongly assert and put into practice the ideals of individual freedom and liberty. Most of the colonists brought with them British ways of thinking and political values. But they faced very new experiences in settling a wilderness far from the strong reach of British authority.

The ideas of John Locke   The political outlooks of the colonists varied in many ways. However, the main theme of British political thought they brought with them was the "liberal tradition." This was a bundle of political ideas argued by the 17th-century English philosopher John Locke (Hartz, 1955). Locke studied philosophy and medicine at Oxford University; after completing his degrees he occasionally practiced medicine. His real interests were in philosophy and politics, and he spent a good deal of his time advising British officials. He helped the Earl of Shaftesbury, one of the king's ministers, draft a constitution for the colony of Carolina. He also wrote essays intended to help Shaftesbury campaign for religious toleration and civil liberties and against the "divine right" of kings to rule as absolute monarchs.

Locke most fully developed his political ideas in his *Two Treatises on Government*, first published in 1689 and in a number of subsequent editions. People in Europe and America read and discussed his writings. His ideas about politics and government greatly influenced colonial leaders such as Benjamin Franklin, Thomas Jefferson, and James Madison. Americans of the 18th century so widely accepted Locke's political ideas that they came to be the "textbook of the American Revolution" (Parrington, 1954: I, 193).

Locke made three central arguments, one following from the other, which deeply influenced the Founders of the American republic. First, he argued that human beings in a natural state—without government—have inalienable rights to life, liberty, and property. However, in the "state of nature," there is no way to protect the rights of the weak against infringements by the strong. Second, Locke argued that people instinctively establish government to protect their rights. Locke thought of this as quite a rational and practical step. For the sake of self-preservation, people band together and draw up a governing contract. This contract, or constitution, would spell out the rights and duties of members of the polity; it also set forth the responsibilities of and limitations on the government. Third, Locke believed that government must be strong enough to protect citizen's rights, but not so strong as to threaten their freedoms. So, he

THE MAYFLOWER COMPACT, 1620

We whose names are underwritten, . . . having undertaken . . . a voyage to plant the first colony in the northern parts of Virginia, do by these presents solemnly and mutually in the presence of God, and of one another, covenant and combine ourselves together into a civil body politic; . . . and by such virtue hereof, to enact, constitute, and frame such just and equal laws, ordinances, acts, constitutions, and offices from time to time, as shall be thought most meet and convenient for the general good of the colony unto which we promise all due submission and obedience.

Political theorist and congressional leader—James Madison wrote the most lasting numbers of *The Federalist* papers advocating the ratification of the Constitution. Although he served masterfully as a leader in the newly formed House of Representatives, he did not enjoy a successful presidency after his election in 1808.

stressed limiting the powers of government in the constitution, assuring that government could be held accountable to the people. He thought the people could rightly overthrow government if it failed to protect and defend their natural and inalienable rights.

Locke's ideas in America   To the little groups who struggled to create a European society in America, especially those in New England, Locke's ideas seemed more to describe reality than to state profound new truths. Had not the early settlers established a government by agreeing to the Mayflower Compact? The Puritans, seeking to practice their religion freely, left England on the ship *Mayflower* in 1620. After a very rough voyage of more than two months, they landed at Plymouth in Massachusetts. This was far from their intended destination south of the Hudson River, where the Virginia Company in London had granted them land. Before leaving the ship, the group's leaders met to draw up an agreement which would be the basis for their self-government. Several other New England colonies owed the establishment of their first governments to contracts among the settlers such as the one drawn up on the *Mayflower*.

The liberal tradition in America grew strongest in New England in those early years. Alexis de Tocqueville, the famous French observer of American life and politics in the 1830s, was to say in *Democracy in America* that "the civilization of New England has been like a beacon lit upon a hill, after it has diffused its warmth around, tinges the distant horizon with its glow."

Individual freedom and equality seemed very natural in the New World; there newness, abundance, and a fresh start gave a sense of practicality to Locke's political ideas. And to the Americans of the 18th century, Locke's ideas seemed consistent with American colonial experience. As a result, the liberal tradition was very well received. It became the basis both for America's claim to independence and for the constitution of the new nation. "To this day," one student of American politics has concluded, "we are largely Lockeans. . . . In the sense of adherence to the central doctrines of Locke, we are all 'little liberals' " (Mitchell, 1962: 108).

Escape from Europe

English liberties   Americans in the 1700's had about a century of colonial history and culture behind them; but they remained very much a part of British culture and politics. The life in Britain which the colonists had escaped was often savage and unpleasant. Here is how it has been described by a British historian (Plumb, 1963: 9–10):

John Locke (1632–1704) was an English philosopher whose ideas greatly influenced those who wrote the American Constitution. Locke's essays—*Two Treatises on Government, Essay Concerning Human Understanding*, and *A Letter Concerning Toleration* had a major impact on political thinking in the 1680s and 1690s.

The placid countryside and sleepy market towns witnessed rick burnings, machine-smashing, hunger-riots. The starving poor were run down by the yeomanry, herded into jails, strung up on gibbets, transported to the colonies. No one cared. This was a part of life like the seasons, like the deep-drinking, meat-stuffing orgies of the good times and bumper harvests. The wheel turned, some were crushed, some favoured. Life was cheap enough. Boys were urged to fight. Dogs baited bulls and bears. Cocks slaughtered each other for trivial wagers. . . . Death came so easily. A stolen penknife and a boy of ten was strung up at Norwich; a handkerchief, taken secretly by a girl of fourteen, brought her the noose. Every six weeks London gave itself to a raucous fête as men and women were dragged to Tyburn to meet their end at the hangman's hands. The same violence, the same cruelty, infused all ranks of society. . . . Jails and workhouses resembled concentration camps; starvation and cruelty killed the sick, the poor, and the guilty. . . . Vile slums in the overcrowded towns bred violent epidemics; typhoid, cholera, smallpox ravaged the land.

Yet at the same time, England had become triumphant in warfare, in commerce, and in statecraft. While life there was often cruel, many Englishmen, other Europeans, and Americans admired England for the freedom of its people. English freedoms were the result, it was believed, of the peculiarly mixed character of the English constitution. The constitution mixed monarchy in the crown, aristocracy in the House of Lords, and democracy in the House of Commons. This "balance of power" was thought to protect Englishmen from arbitrary government power.

Why they came to America   People left England to settle the Atlantic seaboard for a variety of reasons. Some sought to improve their economic condition, lured by the prospect of free land and a good business venture. Some were recruited by those who saw that colonial development could add to the power of the mother country; such recruits shared the vision of building a great colonial empire. Some sought freedom from religious persecution. The Puri-

Early immigrants. Most of the first European immigrants to America were English like these pilgrims leaving Plymouth, England, for the hazardous sailing to the New World.

A colonial town meeting. In colonial New England towns where all the adult male citizens met together to govern the community, politics was not free of vigorous, sometimes violent, conflict.

tans who migrated to Massachusetts in the early 1600s were among them; they were filled with religious zeal and unhappy with the restrictions England placed on their religious practices.

As the colonies grew and developed, the British government made more and more laws regulating them. (By 1760, there were some 100 new laws. Most concerned military and economic affairs.) Although many were good for the colonists, some were regarded as arbitrary and restrictive. Particularly disliked were trade restrictions requiring, among other things, that goods shipped to and from the colonies pass through British ports. Many colonists resented what they saw as Britain exploiting them. Widespread evasion of British economic regulations fostered a spirit of independence and disobedience in the colonists.

The colonists felt the English constitution protected liberty and individual freedom, but they were not being allowed these rights in full measure. They often argued that the corruption of British officials explained the gap between their rights under the English constitution and what was being done to restrict and exploit the colonists.

Opposition to authority   In reality, the political stability of 18th-century Britain flowed largely from the power of the king and his government; plus, there was the strong British tradition of deference to political authority. The king's ministers could readily control a large number of seats in Parliament through malapportionment (so-called rotten boroughs), control of elections, and patronage. As a result, loud opposition plagued the government, both in England and in America. This opposition accused the government of corruption and condemned it for letting the exercise of power overcome the protection of liberty.

Admiration of the British constitution as a system of mixed government was widespread among 18th-century Americans. But so was the belief that the excessive growth of power and the taint of corruption had been subverting it more and more. As a result, in the "fragment society" of the colonies, ideas about public affairs were very British; however, they had been given a distinctive slant by the colonists' ready acceptance of criticisms of British government made in England. As an American historian has said, "the opposition vision of English politics . . . was determinative of the political understanding of 18th-century Americans" (Bailyn, 1968: 56).

The colonists widely accepted the idea that political power was, by nature, likely to be used to suppress liberty. They believed that "threats to free government . . . lurked everywhere, but nowhere more dangerously than in the designs of ministers in office to aggrandize power by the corrupt use of influence, and by this means ultimately to destroy the balance of the constitution." Political corruption "was as universal a cry in the colonies as it was in England, and with it the same sense of despair at the state of the rest of the world, the same belief that tyranny, already dominant over most of the earth, was continuing to spread its menace and was threatening even that greatest bastion of liberty, England itself" (Bailyn, 1968: 56–57).

The wide acceptance of the liberal tradition together with fears that it was being corrupted in England made for a distinctive pattern of colonial politics.

THE PATTERN OF COLONIAL POLITICS

Three political trends stood out during colonial times—the emergence of representative government; persistent political conflict, especially between the executive and the legislature; and growth of a sense of national community.

The colonial legislatures and representation

One of the most notable features of American politics is its legislative assemblies. These came to have an important role even in colonial times. The Virginia House of Burgesses first met in 1619; this was only 12 years after the colony of Virginia was founded in Jamestown. These assemblies were set up on the initiative of authorities in London who assumed that they would add to political stability. By the middle of the 18th century, they had survived for 100 years or more. So, representative government was a part of everyday political life for Americans long before the Revolution.

By 18th-century standards, these legislatures were remarkable. First, they were much more democratically apportioned than legislatures anywhere else. The members were closely tied to their constituents. Second, a kind of two-party politics gradually developed in them. A "country" party drew inland farmers and a "commercial" party attracted businessmen in the coastal towns. Third, people voted in numbers unequaled by any standards of the time. Taxpaying and property qualifications for voting did exist. But, since most people owned land, voting rights were broader in the colonies than elsewhere—certainly they were broader than in Britain. Voting laws differed from one colony to the next; however, between 50 and 75 percent of adult male whites were eligible to vote. (Fewer actually did.) Finally, the assemblies had important legislative power. Laws were needed to regulate distribution of land and provide for construction of public facilities, such as wharfs, roads, ferries, and public buildings; towns and schools had to be established; provision had to be made for death and inheritance. In England, these issues had been settled so gradually that the government did not play an active role. In America, the situation demanded rapid development through the public sector. As a result, active colonial legislatures were the setting for vigorous political controversies.

Colonial legislatures versus British governors

The major political conflicts in the colonies came to revolve around the executive—governors appointed by officials in London. The British thought the colonies should have mixed governments like the British one. The crown was represented by the governor, the aristocracy by the upper house (council), and the people by the popular house of the legislature. In practice, this system worked out much differently in the colonies. Although governors had great formal powers in relation to the assemblies, these powers were, in practice, ineffective.

The patronage that the king used to manipulate Parliament was not so available to the governors. This was because the legislatures had convinced officials in London who made colonial policies to give them important appointive powers. Manipulation of legislative elections also was not so possible for the governors as for the king and his supporters. Governors were in office only a short time, and the colonists could appeal directly to London. There was not much of a colonial aristocracy, particularly in New England. Its ability to support the governors' elitist leadership or to provide "natural" leaders for the colonies was small.

As a result, leadership in the colonies was uncertain, factional, and often highly contentious. Governors had wide authority but lacked the influence to enforce it. This uncertainty of authority meant the colonies did not become stable political systems. Rather, colonial governments "bred belief that faction was seditious, a menace to government itself, and the fear . . . that the government was corrupt and a threat to the survival of Liberty" (Bailyn, 1968: 105).

The colonial political situation gave legislatures great opportunities to capture real power from the governors. In the power of the purse, through which they were able to control colonial finances, the legislatures had a powerful weapon. By the mid-18th century, they were politically dominant in almost every colony.

A sense of American community

Another development in colonial politics was the growth of a sense of community. Before the mid-1700s, most colonists thought of themselves as British subjects. But more and more, and especially after the 1760s, they came to see themselves as Americans. They thought in continental terms rather than identifying just with their own colony. This shift has been demonstrated in an interesting way by analyzing British, American, and continental symbols in the colonial newspapers of the 18th century. The overall results of this analysis are shown in Figure 1–1. The trace lines in this figure show the percentage of the content of the colonial press with American, as opposed to British, references. Notice the slow but steady increase in American community awareness until the mid-1760s; then note the explosion of American identity as Britain sought to tighten control over the colonies through new regulations many colonists saw as repressive.

The more restrictive British policies helped arouse the growing sense of American community. Americans clung together in their hostility to distant British authority. More soldiers were sent to America. The colonists were forbidden to settle beyond the Appalachian Mountains. Their trade with the Indians was restricted. (Partly because the colonists often cheated them.) New customs duties were levied. The colonial assemblies were prohibited from making their paper currency legal tender. New taxes were imposed; the Stamp Act, for example, required the purchase of a stamp for use on legal documents, newspapers, and licenses.

Bostonians protesting the Stamp Act. [left] Protests like this one against British authority helped to forge a sense of common identity among Americans.

The Boston Tea Party. [right] Some Bostonians dressed as Indians and dumped chests of British tea into the harbor as a protest against commercial restrictions.

FIGURE 1–1

The Growth of American Community Awareness in the 1700s

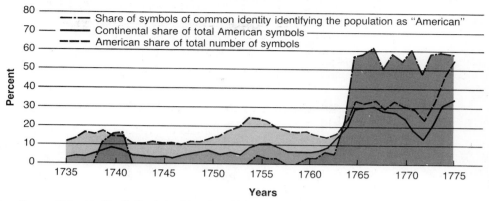

Source: Richard L. Merritt, *Symbols of American Community, 1735–1775* (New Haven, Conn.: Yale University Press, 1966), p. 144.

New taxes on imports brought about acts of resistance. The most famous was the Boston Tea Party. In the fall of 1773, some Boston townsmen dressed up as Mohawk Indians and dumped 342 chests of tea into Boston harbor. The British repaid this kind of resistance with punitive laws. Such laws closed the harbor; they also set new requirements on quarters for British troops and changed the constitution of the colony of Massachusetts. These "Intolerable Acts," as the colonists called them, encouraged wider resistance to British authority.

As resistance spread, so did the belief that there was an American community whose interests differed from those of Britain. Certainly by the early 1770s, "the colonists were sufficiently different from their English contemporaries that they comprised a political community—embryonic in some respects, perhaps, but nonetheless a distinct American political community" (Merritt, 1966: 182). Revolution was not far off.

WHAT DID THE AMERICAN REVOLUTION MEAN?

Many colonists were fierce individualists, opposed to unchecked power, ready to fight to protect their liberty. Numerous times throughout the colonial era, mob violence and rioting broke out against what were seen as oppressive government acts. One historian noted that "in the period from 1645 to 1760 there were 18 insurgent movements directed by white Americans toward the overthrow of colonial governments" (quoted in Kurtz and Hutson 1973: 85). One of these, Bacon's Rebellion in Virginia in the 1670s, led to major violence. Politics "out-of-doors" as another historian has called it, has always been a periodic American pastime.

At one time or another, action outside the legislative realm, often in the form of mob violence, virtually paralyzed all major cities of the colonies. Farmers and settlers on the frontier also protested from time to time. Their protests closed the local courts, destroyed property, and stopped local government. These actions were not the work of the poor and the downtrodden. Rather, historians tell us, "they represented a common form of political protest and political action in both England and the colonies during the 18th century by groups who could find no alternative institutional expression for their demands and grievances, which were more often than not political" (Wood, 1969: 320).

Starting in the 1740s, determined efforts by the British to bring the colonies under firmer control brought growing political protest. A series of urban riots and violence runs from the Stamp Act riots of 1765 through the Boston Massacre, the Boston Tea Party, and to the fighting at Lexington and Concord in 1775.

What caused the Revolution?

What caused the colonists to rebel against British rule? Until the 1760s, this rule was not very oppressive—it was not even especially effective. The colonies had achieved a great degree of self-government. Freedom and equality, at least among whites, were widely accepted. There was no feudal system to destroy, as in the case of the French and Russian revolutions. British control of commerce and trade in the colonies, epitomized by the Intolerable Acts, was greatly resented. But economic causes are not enough to explain the Revolution.

Many Americans thought that they were entitled to a larger political role in the British empire after their extensive involvement in the war between England and France which ended in 1763. (This war was called the Seven Years' War in Europe and the French and Indian War in the colonies.) But British policies toward the colonies, far from giving them a greater role, were meant to subordinate them further. British colonial policies in the two decades before the Revolution were often poorly conceived. These "policy blunders" contributed to the colonists' growing support of independence and home rule.

Ideological and social conflicts caused general feelings of discontent in the colonies. Leaders of colonial thought were split between conservatives who believed in elitist rule and feared the democratic "rabble" and populists who favored complete democracy. This is shown by the political tracts, pamphlets, and newspaper editorials that poured forth in the 1760s and 1770s. Intense political conflict developed in some colonies between the well-to-do—the mer-

THE CONTINENTAL CONGRESS

Legislatures played a central part in the early political development of the United States. The first national legislature was the Continental Congress. The First Continental Congress met in Philadelphia in September and October 1774. Its 56 delegates had been chosen by either the legislatures or revolutionary conventions in the states. John and Samuel Adams of Massachusetts were there, and George Washington, Richard Henry Lee, and Patrick Henry of Virginia. In all, "It was a notable body of men; with a few exceptions, probably the pick of the colonies" (Burnett, 1964: 31).

On October 14, 1774, the Congress adopted a Declaration of Rights, a 10-point statement of the rights of colonists that was similar in many respects to the Declaration of Independence adopted in 1776. Congress also approved a plan called "the Association" which was intended to bring about a boycott of English products until colonial grievances were redressed.

By the time the Second Continental Congress met, in May 1775, the Revolution was under way—there was fighting in Massachusetts and New Hampshire, and Ethan Allen's troops, the Green Mountain Boys, had captured Fort Ticonderoga on Lake Champlain in New York. The Second Continental Congress appointed George Washington commander of the colonial forces and was mainly preoccupied with matters of defense.

What began as an extralegal assembly became the Congress of the United States when the Articles of Confederation went into effect in 1781 (see Henderson, 1974).

chants and lawyers of the middle class—and poor farmers and merchant seamen. Among these farmers and seamen, according to historian James Truslow Adams, "there was a vast mass of smouldering discontent" (in Wahlke, 1973: 108). The leaders of the Revolution—such as George Washington, Thomas Jefferson, Thomas Paine, Richard Henry Lee, and Samuel Adams—did fairly well in channeling social class conflicts and fears into zeal for rebellion against the British.

The causes of the Revolution were complex and numerous. But the short answer to the question, "What caused the Revolution?" is that the colonists revolted against arbitrary British rule. They feared that the leadership of the British government meant to destroy the delicate fabric of their liberties. That this fear was not groundless was proved by Britain's sustained efforts to tighten controls over colonial affairs. They believed that the only way to protect their freedom was through organized resistance.

Declaring independence

The colonial assemblies sent delegates to a Continental Congress in 1774. Among other things, this Congress adopted a Declaration of Rights which claimed that the colonists were entitled to all the rights of Englishmen. It cited times when these rights had been violated over the last decade. The British had closed the port at Boston and greatly restricted trade by the four New England colonies. Massachusetts virtually declared its independence. On the morning of April 19, 1775, the minutemen exchanged shots with British soldiers at Lexington. The Revolution had started. For a little more than a year, the colonists skirmished with British redcoats, struggled to raise an army, and tried to reach an understanding with British authorities. King George III and Parliament rejected colonial peacemaking efforts. Finally, on the evening of July 4, 1776, the Continental Congress adopted the Declaration of Independence. Drafted by Thomas Jefferson, the Declaration gave formal notice of the independence of the colonies. It is most unique for its statement of basic principles which had come to be deeply believed by many of the colonists. The key paragraph of the Declaration reads:

> We hold these truths to be self-evident, that all men are created equal, that they are endowed by their Creator with certain unalienable rights, that among these are life, liberty, and the pursuit of happiness; that to secure these rights, governments are instituted among men, deriving their just powers from the consent of the governed; that whenever any form of government becomes destructive of these ends, it is the right of the people to alter or to abolish it, and to institute new government, laying its foundation on such principles, and organizing its powers in such form, as to them shall seem most likely to effect their safety and happiness.

John Locke's political philosophy and the liberal tradition of the colonies were never better stated. It is certainly true that the signers of the Declaration did not mean to include women, blacks, or Indians as having inalienable rights, at least not in the same sense as white men had them. That was more than the belief system of the late 18th century could manage. In its own time, however, the Declaration was a ringing statement of freedom. Rights for women, blacks, native Americans and others required time and struggle, as the meaning of the Declaration came more and more to embrace all persons.

Hard-fought battles of the Revolutionary War. At the Battle of Cowpens, fought in South Carolina in 1781 [upper left], John Eager Howard of Maryland became one of the first to be awarded the Congressional Medal of Honor. Hugh Mercer, a physician and soldier, became a heroic Continental Army general. He was killed at the Battle of Princeton (New Jersey, 1777) [upper right]. At the Battle of King's Mountain, fought in South Carolina in 1780 [lower left], Colonel William Campbell's militiamen defeated an army of American Loyalists, heeding Campbell's battle cry: "Shout like hell and fight like devils." Major Joseph Eggleston, a daring cavalry officer, boldly led his troops of the Lighthorse Cavalry against the British in the Battle of Eutaw Springs, South Carolina, in 1781 [lower right].

After the Revolution

The Revolutionary War did not bring sweeping social and economic changes as followed the great revolutions in France and Russia. It rid the colonies of one set of authorities and replaced them with another. That "long, straggling, often disruptive and sometimes atrocious war," as one historian called it, had the effect of politicizing communities and individuals. "After the fortunes and pressures of war had destroyed his other alternatives, each member of a large majority could claim his tiny but concrete share in the creation of the United States" (in Kurtz and Hutson, 1973: 155).

The Revolution was revolutionary in yet another way: it gave rise to what has been called a "revolutionary syndrome"—to ideas very much like those expressed in other revolutions in Western history. In the American revolutionary syndrome can be found "the same general disgust with a chaotic and corrupt

Thomas Jefferson presents the Declaration of Independence to John Hancock, the president of the Continental Congress. This mural shows the artist's idealized version of the scene.

world, the same anxious and angry bombast, the same excited fears of conspiracies by depraved men, the same utopian hopes for the construction of a new and virtuous order" as in revolutions in other times and places (Gordon S. Wood in Wahlke, 1973: 238).

But the most tangible result of the Revolution was, of course, that independent American governments were set up. The new state governments were much like the colonial ones, but most did away with the office of governor. Late in 1777, the Continental Congress approved the final draft of a national constitution; these Articles of Confederation were not ratified by all the states until March 1781. The Articles set up a confederation of states and gave Congress quite a bit of national power (including that to conduct foreign policy and war). But they stressed in no uncertain terms the independence of the states, and they made no provision for a national court system or a chief executive. Our first constitution did little more than legalize what the Continental Congress had been doing. Congress did gain the power to create executive departments; it promptly set up departments of foreign affairs, finance, war, admiralty, and post office.

The Revolution and the adoption of the Articles of Confederation did not put an end to discontent. Hard times after the war, especially for farmers, led to protests against mortgage foreclosure and jailing when people could not pay debts and taxes. The most serious of these protests was Shays' Rebellion in Massachusetts in 1787. The prevailing discontent led many to believe that the federal government should be strengthened.

Congress sought to do this, but with no real success. Meanwhile, to improve the flow of trade, Virginia and Maryland signed an agreement dealing with commercial traffic on the Potomac River. The arrangements seemed to work out so well that the Virginians proposed holding a general commercial conference in Annapolis, Maryland. The Annapolis Convention did not have great success. But its moving spirits—Alexander Hamilton and James Madison—used the occasion to urge the convening of another meeting of state delegates; this new conference would deal with pressing constitutional and economic problems. A number of state legislatures endorsed this suggestion. Congress then passed a resolution calling for a meeting to consider needed changes in the Articles of Confederation. It was to be held in Philadelphia in 1787.

Drafting a new constitution. Delegates from the thirteen states gathered at the Pennsylvania statehouse in 1787 to "revise" the Articles of Confederation.

THE FIRST NEW NATION

The 55 leaders who met at this Constitutional Convention had been commissioned by their states to revise the Articles of Confederation. Instead, most of them agreed that a wholly new constitution was required—required to provide more effective central government as well as protection (among other things, for property) against unchecked majority rule.

Adoption of the constitution

Compromise politics The political skills of these leaders were shown in the shrewd compromises and the spirit of trying new things found in the constitution they drafted. These leaders have been called a "reform caucus in action" for the political imaginativeness and sensitivity that they showed. They framed

DANIEL SHAYS' REBELLION, 1787

Economic conditions were not good in the New England states in the 1780s. In some states, if farmers fell on hard times, the law postponed collection of debts and mortgages and was otherwise lenient with debtors. But Massachusetts took a hard line; many farmers landed in jail as a result of judgments for overdue taxes and debts made by Massachusetts courts. Farmers not in jail began to protest and riot, preventing the state courts from sitting in western Massachusetts. The governor called out the militia to put down the demonstrations. One protester, Revolutionary War veteran Daniel Shays, emerged as the leader of the rebels. Shays

and 1,100 of his men attacked Springfield, Massachusetts, to keep the state's highest court from sitting and to get arms from the federal arsenal there. The Massachusetts militia, equipped with artillery, soon defeated Shays' rebels, and Shays escaped to Vermont. Mercifully, the rebel leaders who were caught were either pardoned or given brief prison terms; the newly elected legislature adopted measures relieving the economic plight of farmers and merchants. But more important, Shays' Rebellion worried leaders in every state and convinced many Americans that a stronger federal government was necessary.

George Washington served as presiding officer of the Constitutional Convention which drafted the Constitution of the United States in 1787.

a constitution reflecting both their shared political experience and many compromises among different points of view. If they could not compromise on an issue, as was true for slavery, they did not confront it directly. Other issues, such as the scope of the executive's powers, they resolved by using language that could be understood in more than one way. Yet other issues involved straightforward compromises. Whether the states or the people directly should be represented in the new union was resolved by inventing a two-house Congress: the states were represented in one (the Senate) and the people directly in the other (the House of Representatives).

And so "the Constitution . . . was a patchwork sewn together under the pressure of both time and events by a group of extremely talented democratic politicians" (Roche, 1961: 151). These politicians did not create a centralized national government based on the principle of legislative supremacy for the very good reason that the people would not have accepted it. But they did greatly strengthen the national government because they were convinced that the existing government was a failure. In the words of a close student of the Constitutional Convention (Roche, 1961: 152): "For over three months, in what must have seemed to the faithful participants an endless process of give-and-take, they reasoned, cajoled, threatened, and bargained amongst themselves. The result was a Constitution which the people, in fact, by democratic processes, did accept, and a far better national government was established."

Ratification   Once the Constitution had been drafted, it had to be ratified by the states. The issue sparked one of the most interesting constitutional debates ever. Such men as George Washington, James Madison, Alexander Hamilton, and John Jay were Federalists. They defended the Constitution and skillfully maneuvered for ratification. Their chief propaganda tool was a series of newspaper articles together called *The Federalist* papers. It set out powerful arguments in support of the new Constitution. Almost at once, it came to be viewed as the most important statement of American political theory. The Anti-Federalists were not as well organized, but many opposed to the new Constitution made strong arguments against it. The opposition argued that the new system was the handiwork of a few prominent leaders. Many felt the government would not be democratic enough. Ratification was debated with vigor in most states and adopted with reluctance in some of them.

The Bill of Rights   The contest over ratification was won in several states by promising that a bill of rights would be added through amendments as soon as the new government was in business. When the First Congress met, many of its members felt there was a moral obligation to keep these commitments; they felt that the new system would be more strongly supported if a bill of rights were added to the Constitution. The first president, George Washington, backed this addition in his inaugural speech.

Congress debated proposed amendments which were ultimately to become the Bill of Rights. Some of the proposed amendments failed in the House of Representatives. One of these would have guaranteed the people the right to give binding instructions to their congressmen on public issues. Some proposals were killed in the Senate. These included a clause which would have exempted conscientious objectors from compulsory military service. At last, in the fall of 1789, Congress submitted 12 amendments to the states for ratification.

Of the 12 proposed, only 10 were ratified by enough states to become part of the Constitution. One of the two which failed would have guaranteed that there should be no less than one congressman for every 50,000 people; the other would have prohibited changing the salaries of members of Congress until after an election. The 10 successful amendments became the federal Bill of Rights. They did not change the federal powers set forth in the Constitution itself. But they did give formal recognition and standing to rights and liberties taken for granted by 18th-century Americans and written into many state constitutions.

Adoption of the Constitution was the climax of the revolutionary era; it pointed up American belief in reform, American acceptance of political change as an effective course. The old political order in Europe had been fairly static; the Revolution, and at last the Constitution of 1787, gave proof of the sharp American change in the art and practice of government. An eminent historian of the period in which the Constitution was made has said (Wood, 1969: 614):

> The Americans of the Revolutionary generation believed that they had made a momentous contribution to the history of politics. They had for the first time demonstrated to the world how a people could diagnose the ills of its society and work out a peaceable process of cure. They had, and what is more significant they knew they had, broken through the conceptions of political theory that had imprisoned men's minds for centuries and brilliantly reconstructed the framework for a new republican polity, a reconstruction that radically changed the future discussion of politics.

Thus was created the "first new nation" (Lipset, 1963). The United States was the first major colonial region to gain its independence through revolution and create its own system of government.

The new American government

When the first federal census was taken in 1790, there were fewer than 4 million people living in the 13 states. These people were scattered over quite a

George Washington, the nation's first president, was said to be "first in war, first in peace, and first in the hearts of his countrymen."

large territory. It is likely that most were absorbed with the protection of their lives and property under hard conditions. If their lives were unsettled, all the more frail and fragile was the new national government the Constitution had set up. It is hard now to imagine how experimental the government was; no federal, republican government had ever worked on such a large scale. George Washington, the first president, told a friend that he faced "an ocean of difficulties, without that competency of political skill, abilities, and inclinations which is necessary to manage the helm" (in Morison, 1965: 317).

Most successful revolutionaries in modern times inherited a government machinery which could be turned to the aims of the new regime. In the first new nation, the apparatus of the central government had to be built virtually from scratch. Most important, the new government had to establish its authority as an effective instrument and provide the basis on which Americans could identify themselves as a nation.

George Washington's leadership A national government establishes its authority when its existence and functioning are widely accepted. That is, the government has the authority to govern, not just the power to do so, when it is seen as *legitimate*. In its early days, the new government's authority flowed mainly from two springs: there was the personal role of George Washington as our first chief executive; and there was the government's success in dealing with key economic and political problems.

Washington's role as "the father of his country" has often been overdrawn. But his part in establishing national political authority was of the highest importance. S. M. Lipset (1963: 22–23) neatly summed up Washington's role in this regard:

1. His prestige was so great that he commanded the loyalty of the leaders of the different factions as well as the general populace. Thus, in a political entity marked by much cleavage he, in his own person, provided a basis for unity.
2. He was strongly committed to the principles of constitutional government and exercised a paternal guidance upon those involved in developing the machinery of government.
3. He stayed in power long enough to permit the crystallization of factions into embryonic parties.
4. He set a precedent as to how the problem of succession should be managed, by voluntarily retiring from office.

Alexander Hamilton, revolutionary soldier, delegate to the Constitutional Convention, and first secretary of the treasury, might have been president had he not been killed in a duel with Vice President Aaron Burr in 1804. Hamilton's major contribution lay in the establishment of a more effective fiscal system for the new nation.

Political and economic effectiveness Of equal importance, the new government was fairly successful. Under the leadership of Alexander Hamilton, the first Secretary of the Treasury, a sound financial plan was put into effect. The new program drew the support of state governments; provisions for federal assumption of state debts and refinancing debts owed to foreign governments such as France won their confidence in the new regime. The Bank of the United States provided a means for national investment in economic development. More and more in the 19th century, the federal government (as well as the states) intervened in the economy to foster rapid economic growth.

The new system proved to be successful politically, as well. Thomas Jefferson's election as president in 1800 was the first case of the succession of one party over another. It showed that peaceful succession in party control of the government was workable. Further, that election showed how two national parties competing for office could bring politics to the grass roots, providing a link between the ordinary citizen and the nation's leaders.

American national identity

National identity took root in the 1760s, and more Americans were politicized by the Revolution. Without a doubt, the leadership of such nationalists as George Washington, John Adams, James Madison, and Thomas Jefferson helped to firm up our sense of being a nation. But the early national government was not highly visible. It did not have a fixed site until it was settled in Washington, D.C. in 1800. (Washington was created as a federal territory out of land ceded by Virginia and Maryland.) Previously, Congress met in Philadelphia and New York (and before that, in other towns). Even with a fixed capital, the government was not a vital center of national political life or a major focal point of identification with the nation. Small and remote, it had very little impact on the everyday lives of most citizens. In our own time, we are used to big government and large bureaucracies; it is not so easy to imagine how small the early government was. Two years after it had been settled in Washington, it was made up of a mere 291 officials. At the end of the Jefferson era, 27 years later, the "headquarters establishment" had only a little more than doubled in size. Said one student of the Washington community in the early 1800s, "Some establishment for the government of a nation; some government to inspire a mass trek to Washington!" (Young, 1966: 28).

National authority and identity did grow in the early years of the nation, but only slowly and unevenly. Their uncertain nature was shown in the strongest possible terms by the Civil War. Still, the setting in which the new government grew up had advantages that helped it to establish its identity and authority. There was enough time to develop, and only moderate urgency about national mobilization. The country was isolated from outside forces and influences; it could therefore develop on its own. There was abundance, especially in the open frontier.

WHAT DOES THE CONSTITUTION SAY?

The United States was the first nation to have a written constitution. This seems quite commonplace today; 200 years ago it was remarkable. That ours is the oldest written constitution in the world is extraordinary even today. Despite sharp debate over ratification, it was widely accepted almost from the start, and its virtues have often been praised. In a speech to the House of Representatives in 1805, a Maryland congressman said (quoted in Hyneman and Carey, 1967: 36): "How different, how honorably different, is the American Constitution! With us it is reduced to writing. It is in every man's hand; it is known to the whole world, and every citizen agrees in its true and legitimate meaning." The basic principles of the Constitution have to be understood to make any sense of American politics. We should, therefore, describe briefly what these basics are.

Rule by the people

The Constitution contains the principle of **popular sovereignty.** This means rule by the people, government based on the consent of the governed. In the Declaration of Independence, it had been proclaimed that governments derive "their just powers from the consent of the governed." No such language appears in the Constitution. But the Preamble does say, "We the people of the United States . . . do ordain and establish this Constitution for the United States of America." James Fenimore Cooper reached the conclusion in 1838 that these words were "a naked and vague profession" (Cooper, 1956: 18). But popular rule in the Constitution does not stand or fall on the language of the Preamble. Article I requires that members of the House of Representatives shall be "chosen every second year by the people of the several states." It was the intent of the founders that direct popular participation would be limited to the election of members of the House.

In an important case decided in 1964, the U.S. Supreme Court held that the meaning of "the people" in Article I includes the notion of "one person, one vote" in elections for the House. In this court case, *Wesberry* v. *Sanders* (1964), the Georgia legislature was required to draw congressional district lines so that the districts would be as equal in population as possible. Mr. Justice Black, who gave the opinion of the Court, said that "it would defeat the principle solemnly embodied in the Great Compromise—equal representation in the House of equal numbers of people—for us to hold that [state] legislatures may draw the lines of congressional districts in such a way as to give some voters a greater voice in choosing a congressman than others."

Senators were chosen indirectly by the state legislatures until 1913. In that year, the 17th Amendment, which provided for direct election of senators, was approved. The president is officially elected by electoral votes; these are cast by electors chosen in a popular election. Federal judges and officials of the federal administrative departments are, of course, appointed. (They are appointed by the president with the advice and consent of the Senate.) Thus, the role of the people is not pervasive, though it is clearly present.

Representative government

The principle of **representative government** is firmly built into the Constitution. Although direct rule by the people, as in New England town meetings, may be possible in small communities, it is not feasible on a large scale. A vital part of our concept of government has been that the people rule through representatives chosen in free elections and accountable to them. These representatives meet in a legislative assembly; there they deliberate, debate, and compromise to make laws for all, which, ideally, are in the public interest. In an imperfect world, there will always be debate and strife over what laws are in the public interest and how well elected representatives enact them. The U.S. Congress is, with all its imperfections, a highly representative lawmaking body.

Our concept of representation has included the belief that a legislature is representative of the people only if the members of its houses have an equal number of people in their districts. The Senate is exempted from this because of its special federal character—the Constitution gives each state two senators, no matter what the state populations. **Malapportionment** is the term for a situation in which the populations of legislative districts are grossly unequal. By the 1960s, many state legislatures were malapportioned—some districts were far too large, some far too small. For instance, the Tennessee legislature had not been reapportioned for 60 years. This was despite the fact that the state constitution required representation based on the number of qualified voters in each county. One county with 2,340 voters chose one representative, while another county with 312,245 chose only seven. Because of this kind of gross malapportionment, a voter named Baker brought suit against Tennessee's Secretary of State, Carr. He claimed that his constitutional rights had been violated. In the case of *Baker* v. *Carr* (1962), the U.S. Supreme Court held that boundary lines must be drawn so that state legislative districts are reasonably equal in population.

Limitations on government

The principle of **limited government** simply means that the powers of government are limited by the Constitution. It is sometimes called **constitutionalism,** which is a confusing name. These limits are reflected in the specific grants of power to government. For example, in Article I, Section 8, the powers of Congress are given: "The Congress shall have power to lay and collect taxes . . ., borrow money . . ., regulate commerce . . ., establish post offices . . ., declare war . . .," and so forth. They are also reflected in the Constitution's specific bans against government action. For instance, Congress is banned from enacting **ex post facto laws** or **bills of attainder.** The former are retroactive criminal laws; the latter, in effect, declare a person to be convicted of a crime without benefit of a trial. The Bill of Rights explicitly limits the power of the government. Thus, the First Amendment says that "Congress shall make no law respecting an establishment of religion, or prohibiting the free exercise thereof; or abridging the freedom of speech, or of the press; or the right of the people peaceably to assemble and to petition the government for a redress of grievances."

Such constitutional limits have not, of course, always worked. This is partly because of abuse and partly because much of the language of the Constitution is vague. An especially difficult problem has been in the area of the limits of executive power; the vagueness of Article II leaves much room for interpretation. Most recently, former President Richard M. Nixon (1969–74) seems to have believed that otherwise illegal acts (such as burglary or obstruction of justice) could be deemed legal if, in the president's judgment, such acts were in the national interest. Very few of us accept this exotraordinary reading of the Constitution.

Separation of powers

The Constitution includes the principle of **separation of powers.** Dear to the heart of its framers was the belief that freedom and liberty depended on two things: one was dividing legislative, executive, and judicial powers; the other was providing for checks and balances among these powers. The principle of separation of powers is shown by the way the Constitution is organized. Article I says that "all legislative powers herein granted shall be vested in a Congress of the United States"; Article II provides that "the executive powers shall be vested in a President of the United States"; and Article III says that "the judicial power of the United States shall be vested in one supreme court, and in such inferior courts as the Congress may from time to time ordain and establish."

Separation of powers carries the corollary of checks and balances; each branch

Separation of powers. The three branches of the federal government—Congress, the presidency, and the Supreme Court, occupy separate buildings. The houses of Congress meet in the Capitol [top]. The President often works in the Oval Office in the White House [middle]. The Supreme Court holds its sessions in the stately "marble palace" built for it in the 1930s [bottom].

of government is to balance the power of the others, and check their actions. The Constitution provides explicit checks one branch of government might exert over another. Congress is empowered to enact laws; the president can exercise a veto. In turn, Congress can, by a two-thirds vote, override a veto. The president can propose legislation to Congress, which might refuse to enact the proposals. The Supreme Court can scrutinize the constitutionality of laws passed by Congress and signed by the president; but court justices are appointed by the president, with the agreement of the Senate. Moreover, the power of the Supreme Court to hear appeals from lower courts is subjected to limitations passed by Congress and approved by the president. Even within Congress, the power of the states, equally represented in the Senate, is balanced with the power of the people, directly represented in the House; and the agreement of both houses is required to pass legislation.

These provisions of the Constitution do not mean that *only* Congress is involved in lawmaking; they do not mean that the president does *nothing* but exercise executive powers; and they do not mean that judicial powers are exercised *only* by the courts. The three branches of the government *share* lawmaking, executive, and judicial powers. Congress shares in executive power when it enacts laws setting up executive departments such as Health and Human Services or Agriculture. It shares in judicial power when it sets up or reorganizes the lower federal court system (the courts below the U.S. Supreme Court). The president shares in legislative power in suggesting laws to Congress or vetoing acts of Congress. The Supreme Court can declare an act of Congress unconstitutional if it finds that the law is not consistent with the meaning of the Constitution; in doing so, the Court has a kind of veto. Beyond this negative power, the Court interprets the meaning of laws passed by Congress as they are applied to particular circumstances. Executive agencies make laws when they draw up the regulations needed to put into effect policies adopted by Congress. Making laws, executing them, and judging are intertwined functions of government. As a result, the principle of separation of powers, along with checks and balances, really means separate institutions *sharing powers.*

Federalism

Yet another basic principle of the Constitution is **federalism.** This is the division of political power between the national government and the states. The United States is, of course, a federal system; it is made up of 50 states which are, in many ways, independent. The federal principle is best shown in the Constitution by the equal representation given to each state in the Senate, regardless of population. It can also be seen in the provision that states cannot be divided or combined without the approval of their legislatures. And it is evident in the requirement that constitutional amendments be approved by three fourths of the states.

The Constitution, of course, stresses the wide powers granted to the national government. Over 200 years of use, the Constitution has come to be seen as granting far greater power to the national government than the framers could have imagined. At the same time, important government powers are still held by the states. Some, such as the power to tax, are held by both the states and the federal government.

Capitols of the little republics. Federalism is not merely an abstract principle of the Constitution. It can be observed with the naked eye in the capitols of the 50 states. New York's capitol in Albany [upper left], completed in 1898, was distinctive both because its French Second Empire architecture made it look like no other and because it was the most costly capitol built in the 19th century. The capitols of Iowa (in Des Moines) and Illinois (in Springfield) were built at the same time and designed by the same architects. Iowa's capitol [upper right] is a splendid specimen, its dome patterned after St. Peter's in Rome. It was completed in the late 1880s. California's capitol in Sacramento [lower left], begun during the Civil War and completed in 1878, like many state capitols sports a cast iron dome similar to that of the federal capitol in Washington. The newer state houses are skyscrapers, like Nebraska's in Lincoln or Louisiana's in Baton Rouge [lower right], both built in the 1930s.

The states today perform many government functions largely by themselves. Public education, although federally subsidized and run in accordance with some federal standards, is largely a state function. Laws concerning birth, death, marriage, and divorce are state laws, and most of the criminal and civil law of the United States is state law. Running elections is a state function, although the electoral rules are affected by federal regulations. The states are solely responsible for setting up local governments. The hundreds of cities, counties, and special-purpose districts, the governmental units that most directly affect us, operate under state laws. Finally, the states wield so-called police powers—to protect and nurture the health, safety, welfare, and morals of their people.

Federal supremacy

In those realms where the federal government has power, its law is supreme. The principle of **federal supremacy** is clearly stated in Article VI: "This Constitution, and the laws of the United States which shall be made in pursuance thereof; and all treaties made, or which shall be made, under the authority of the United States, shall be the supreme law of the land." Therefore, provisions of state constitutions and state laws which are not consistent with the federal Constitution are invalid; they may be declared so by the U.S. Supreme Court.

The Civil War settled the question of whether a state could defy federal authority when the Constitution gives the federal government power. But issues still come up involving federal versus state authority. In 1970, Congress amended the Voting Rights Act by lowering the voting age in both state and federal elections to 18. President Nixon signed the bill, but voiced doubts about the constitutionality of a federal law that changed the state voting age. The Constitution clearly gives Congress the power to regulate elections for Congress and the presidency; but its framers intended that qualifications for voting for state offices should be left to the states. Could the federal government now exercise control over state elections by requiring an overall voting age of 18?

In the case of *Oregon* v. *Mitchell* (1970), the Supreme Court held that Congress could fix the voting age in national elections—but it invalidated the requirement that at age 18 people also be granted the right to vote in state elections. This prompted Congress to approve, and the states to ratify, the 26th Amendment. It provides that "the right of citizens of the United States, who are 18 years of age or older, to vote shall not be denied or abridged by the United States or by any State on account of age." State voting laws then had to be brought into line with the new constitutional requirement.

Judicial review

Finally, the Constitution contains the seeds of the principle of **judicial review.** This is the authority of the highest court—the Supreme Court of the United States—to declare laws and actions of public officials invalid if they conflict with the Constitution. Article III, which provides for federal courts, implies this principle. It states that these courts have the power to judge cases "arising under this Constitution" and to consider the validity of laws made under its authority. But judicial review is not expressly spelled out in the Constitution. Rather, it was asserted in a landmark decision of the Supreme Court, the case of *Marbury* v. *Madison* (1803).

Thomas Jefferson was elected President in 1800. The race between Jefferson and the Federalist candidate, incumbent President John Adams, had been bitter. Between the election and the inauguration, "lame-duck" President Adams appointed his Secretary of State, John Marshall, to the post of Chief Justice of the Supreme Court. The lame-duck Congress, which was controlled by the Federalists, passed a law giving Adams the power to appoint new justices of the peace for the District of Columbia. Adams named loyal Federalists to these positions. Because of the pressures of time, however, some of the commissions for these justiceships were not signed by Adams until the night before Jefferson's inauguration; thus, they did not arrive on the desk of Secretary of State Marshall, soon to be chief justice, until after Jefferson became president. Jeffer-

John Marshall served as a Federalist congressman from Virginia and secretary of state before being appointed chief justice of the United States Supreme Court by President John Adams. He served as chief justice from 1801 until his death in 1835. More than any other member of the Supreme Court, his decisions fundamentally shaped the development of the federal government.

son then ordered his new Secretary of State, James Madison, not to make good on them.

One of the midnight appointees whose commission Madison did not deliver was William Marbury. Marbury asked the Supreme Court, whose chief justice was now Marshall, to issue an order requiring Madison to deliver his commission as justice of the peace. The Judiciary Act of 1789 had given the Supreme Court the power to issue orders requiring public officers to perform their duties. It was on the strength of this act that Marbury made his request to the Court.

At the same time, the Court was under attack by the Jeffersonian majority in Congress. This majority threatened to weaken Federalist dominance of the Court and impeach Federalist judges for alleged misconduct. Chief Justice Marshall wished to strengthen and protect the Court as an instrument of national power. He saw in this case a politically acceptable way to do so. In his opinion on behalf of the Court Marshall held that Madison could not be required to deliver Marbury's commission. The reason, he said, was that the provision of the Judiciary Act giving the Court the power to require such action was unconstitutional. The jurisdiction of the Court was provided in the Constitution and could not, said Marshall, be enlarged by Congress—Congress could not give the Court the power which it had been granted.

In *Marbury* v. *Madison*, for the first time, the Supreme Court declared a law made by Congress unconstitutional. This was a momentous decision because it established the principle of judicial review. It involved an odd set of circumstances—as Chief Justice, John Marshall wrote a Court decision concerning an appointment he had been unable to deliver as Secretary of State. Marbury's problem was small compared to the great constitutional issue involved.

No law made by Congress was held unconstitutional after that for more than half a century. The Supreme Court cannot invalidate state and and federal laws willy-nilly; but when a specific case is brought before it through the regular judicial procedure, it may sit as an arbiter of the meaning of the Constitution; then, if need be, it may declare that a law is unconstitutional.

AMENDING THE CONSTITUTION

These principles of the Constitution are not absolute; instead, they have had to be shaped and interpreted as circumstances changed. Not all provisions of the original Constitution worked out. For example, the provisions for election of the president and vice president turned out to be inconsistent with the emerging system of party politics; they had to be changed in 1803 with the 12th Amendment. Other amendments reflected calls for changes and additions to the Constitution. And the meaning of the Constitution has changed as the courts, executive agencies, president, and Congress have faced changing times and conditions over the years.

The Constitution provides two ways of proposing amendments and two ways of ratifying them. These are shown in Figure 1–2. Amendments can be proposed in a resolution passed by a two-thirds vote of both houses of Congress; or they can be proposed by a national convention called if Congress is asked to do so by two thirds of the state legislatures. All 26 amendments added to the Constitution since 1789 have been proposed by a vote of the houses of Congress; none has been proposed by the convention method.

FIGURE 1—2

Methods of Amending the Constitution

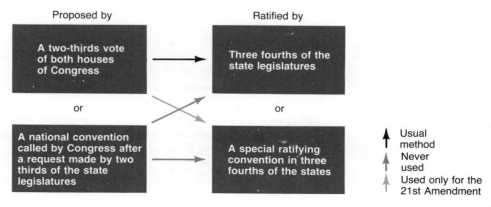

Proposed by

Ratified by

A two-thirds vote of both houses of Congress

Three fourths of the state legislatures

or

or

A national convention called by Congress after a request made by two thirds of the state legislatures

A special ratifying convention in three fourths of the states

↑ Usual method
↑ Never used
⇑ Used only for the 21st Amendment

"FIRST THING TO DO IS TOSS OUT A LOT OF THIS STUFF ADOPTED BY THE PREVIOUS CONVENTION"

After amendments have been proposed, they must be approved by three fourths of the states. This can be done by the state legislatures or by special ratifying conventions in the states. Only the 21st Amendment, which repealed the 18th Amendment banning "the manufacture, sale, or transportation of intoxicating liquors," was ratified by state conventions; the others were ratified by the state legislatures.

Of late, the state legislatures have considered the Equal Rights Amendment (ERA), which was proposed by Congress in 1972. It provides that "equality of rights under the law shall not be denied or abridged by the United States or by any State on account of sex." The amendment won the approval of 35 of the 38 states needed for ratification. When it looked as if it would not be ratified by the March 1979 deadline, Congress extended the deadline to June 30, 1982. This marked the first time Congress had granted such an extension since time limits for the approval of amendments were first set in 1917. When the second deadline passed, and no additional states had ratified, the amendment effort died. But pro-ERA forces promptly began a new campaign for ratification by reintroducing the amendment in Congress.

In August 1978, Congress proposed yet another amendment. This one would repeal the 23rd Amendment, which provides for three presidential electoral votes for the District of Columbia. Instead, it would give the seat of government the same status as a state for purposes of representation in Congress or electing the president. This change would give the District two senators and representation in the House of Representatives commensurate with its population. (See Appendix B at the end of the book for the full text.) This proposed amendment has not met with success in attracting approval from state legislatures and expires in 1985.

Other constitutional amendments are frequently under discussion. In recent years there has been support for amendments to prohibit abortions and to allow prayers in public schools. Conservative organizations have lobbied for both, and both received support from President Ronald Reagan.

More concerted political effort has gone into a proposed amendment requiring a balanced federal budget. This amendment would require Congress to adopt a budget in which spending and revenues were balanced; deficit spending would be allowed only by a 3/5 majority vote. The Senate approved a balanced budget amendment in 1982, but it was rejected by the House. Thirty-two state legislatures have passed resolutions asking Congress to call a constitutional convention to consider an amendment requiring a balanced federal budget (if 34 states act, Congress must call such a convention), although there are legal clouds over some of the state resolutions. President Reagan campaigned in favor of the balanced budget amendment in 1984.

Another Reagan proposal which would require amending the Constitution is the notion of giving the president veto power over specific programs or items in bills passed by Congress. Now the president must accept or reject bills *in toto*; if the proposed amendment were adopted, he would have an item veto akin to the veto power of most state governors.

CIVIL RIGHTS AND LIBERTIES

In our earlier discussion of the ratification struggle we pointed out that there was much criticism of the original Constitution because it did not have a bill of rights. Alexander Hamilton expressed the view of many Federalists when he argued that a bill of rights was not needed, that it would only limit national powers which, in his view, the national government did not have to begin with. But other leaders, including many Anti-Federalists, but also Thomas Jefferson, argued that a bill of rights should be added to the Constitution. This came to be a major part of the business of the first Congress. In June 1789, Congressman James Madison, who became the fourth President, spoke as follows on the floor of the House of Representatives (in Hyneman and Carey, 1967: 260–61):

> It cannot be a secret to the gentlemen in this House that, not withstanding the ratification of this system of Government by 11 of 13 United States, in some cases unanimously, in others by large majorities, yet still there is a great number of our constituents who are dissatisfied with it, among whom are many respectable for their talents and patriotism and respectable for the jealousy they have for their liberty, which, though mistaken in its object, is laudable in its motive. . . . We ought not to disregard their inclination but, on principles of amity and moderation, conform to their wishes and expressly declare the great rights of mankind secured under this Constitution.

Soon, the first 10 amendments, which we call the Bill of Rights, were approved by Congress. Three fourths of the states ratified them by the end of 1791.

The first 10 amendments mainly concern two kinds of rights: rights of individual liberty and rights of persons accused of crimes. The first kind includes freedom of religion, speech, press, and assembly and the right to privacy, property, and petition. The second kind includes such things as the right to trial by jury and protection against "unreasonable searches and seizures," self-incrimination, excessive bail, and "cruel and unusual punishments." The Bill of Rights' protections of freedom of expression and of the rights of persons accused of crimes have a long and quite distinguished history in our constitutional law. Many Supreme Court decisions, acts of Congress, and administrative regulations are relevant to a full understanding of our constitutional rights. In Chapter 13, we will discuss our rights and liberties more thoroughly.

The first 10 amendments applied only to the national government. Most state constitutions, though, guarded the rights of citizens from encroachment by the state government. But the 14th Amendment, which was added in 1868, prohibited each of the states from depriving "any person of life, liberty, or property, without due process of law" and from denying "to any person within its jurisdiction the equal protection of the laws." In effect, it applied most of the Bill of Rights in the federal Constitution to the states. Interpretation in the courts to this effect came slowly. Now, though, virtually all of the provisions of the Bill of Rights protect all people in the United States against infringements of their rights either by the states or by the national government.

The "equal protection" clause of the 14th Amendment has come to play a vital role in the legal guarantee of equal treatment for all Americans. It bans only states, not the federal government, from denying any person equality under the law. But the Supreme Court has, in effect, made it apply to the federal government, as well. In the case of *Bolling* v. *Sharpe* (1954), the Court ruled that the right to equal treatment guaranteed against state infringement by the 14th Amendment, was so basic to the concept of "due process of law" in the 5th Amendment that this right limited federal as well as state power. From these provisions protecting equal treatment have come major movements since World War II by groups which have been discriminated against. Blacks, women, Indians, Chicanos, and others have taken legal action and sought passage of new laws to ensure equal treatment. Starting in the 1950s, new public policies regarding equality have come from the Supreme Court and from Congress in the form of civil rights acts. These momentous changes in public policy have had a large role in reshaping human relations in the United States. Analyzing the adoption of these policies, and their implications, will be the purpose of Chapter 13 of this book.

The longevity of the Constitution has been due largely to its flexibility as the basic law of the nation. Its vagueness on many questions and its silence on others left it open to interpretations which made it workable in changing times; the amending process, though cumbersome and difficult, allowed formal changes where they were needed. On the average, the Constitution has been amended about every 12 years, if we count the first 10 amendments as one change (they were ratified as a group). The most recent amendment, the 26th, which set 18 as the voting age, was approved in 1971. But the Constitution has changed as a matter of practice, too, as Congress, the presidents, and the courts have shaped its meaning over the years.

ERA—THE EQUAL RIGHTS AMENDMENT

The Equal Rights Amendment was proposed by Congress in 1972. To be added to the Constitution, the proposed amendment needed the approval of 38 states. By early in 1977, 35 legislatures had ratified ERA (shown on the map in light brown), although 4 legislatures later rescinded their approval (shown on the map in dark brown). No states ratified after 1977, although Congress gave them an opportunity to do so by extending the deadline from March 1979 to June 1982. Having failed to get ratification, proponents of ERA plan to seek congressional approval again by initiating a new round of consideration by the states.

THE BILL OF RIGHTS

The first 10 amendments to the United States Constitution make up what is called the Bill of Rights. Here the amendments are abbreviated and grouped by major purpose. The full text of the Bill of Rights can be found in Appendix B at the end of the book.

Freedom of expression

Amendment 1 Protection against a government-established religion, freedom of religious expression, freedom of speech and press, right of assembly and petitioning the government.

Arms and troops

Amendment 2 Right to bear arms.

Amendment 3 In peacetime, troops may not be quartered in citizens' homes.

Rights of accused persons

Amendment 4 Protection against unreasonable searches and seizures.

Amendment 5 Indictment by grand jury in prosecutions of persons for serious crimes; trial twice for the same offense prohibited (double jeopardy); cannot be required to be a witness against oneself; prohibits loss of life, liberty, or property without due process; prohibits government taking private property for public use without fair compensation.

Amendment 6 Speedy and public jury trial for crimes; right to be informed of accusation, confront witnesses, cross-examine witnesses, have legal counsel for defence.

Amendment 7 Right to jury trial in civil cases involving more than $20.

Amendment 8 Prohibition against excessive bail or fines, and the infliction of cruel and unusual punishments.

Rights of people and states

Amendment 9 Because rights are listed in the Constitution does not mean the people may not have other unspecified rights.

Amendment 10 Powers which are neither granted to the federal government nor prohibited to the states are reserved to states.

A CHANGING FEDERAL SYSTEM

One especially important constitutional change has had to do with *federalism*. The Civil War settled the question of whether states could go their separate ways in the negative. But federal systems everywhere—in Canada, Australia, West Germany, Switzerland, or wherever—have a kind of tension between national and state power which is never fully relaxed. This dynamic relationship between nation and states has a profound effect on the making and implementation of public policy.

In the United States, the nation and the states share functions to a degree unimaginable by the framers of the Constitution. They share functions so much so that we often use the term **intergovernmental relations** as a synonym for federalism. State government activities have increased by leaps and bounds in the last 20 years. Per capita state and local expenditures have more than tripled since 1960; the number of state and local government employees has more than doubled.

Much of this growth has been fostered by federal dollars, about one fifth of state and local income comes from the federal government. Part of this is **revenue sharing;** the federal government collects tax dollars and transfers money to the states and localities according to an allocation formula. Most federal assistance to the states, though, comes in the form of grants-in-aid that finance specific programs enacted by the national government but run by the states.

It is hard to exaggerate the influence of federalism on public policy in the United States. Today, states may not be as autonomous as they once were, but they play a major role in implementing public policies. Whether in public education, medical care, highways, urban renewal, housing, environmental protection, or many other government programs, state and federal government are close collaborators. Because federalism has such an important impact upon the formulation of public policies, and such a vital effect on how policies are carried out, it must be analyzed as a central feature of the American policy process. For this reason, we defer further discussion until we deal with the policy process in Chapter 14.

Thus, a highly decentralized polity has been more or less able to cope with the vast policy demands made on government in a 20th-century urban, industrial society. The virtue of a federal system is that it allows combining a national response to national problems with decentralization which fosters local differences and attachments. Accordingly, "the American political tradition and the Constitution embodying it . . . remain viable because neither Capitol Hill nor the 50 state houses have been able to serve all the variegated interests on the American scene without working in partnership" (Elazar, 1972: 226).

CONCLUSIONS

In this chapter, we have dealt with important aspects of the background of our political institutions and processes. We can draw the following conclusions.

1 The American colonies as a "fragment society" developed a political tradition that was partly grounded in British ideas of rights and freedoms of the individual on which government could not infringe, and partly in Americans' own experience with their emerging democratic, representative politics.

2 The colonial experience permitted the development of representative assemblies in America and created the conditions for national independence and national community.

3 The American Revolution politicized and nationalized the colonial people; independence gave them the luxury of a unique experiment in representative government on a larger scale than had previously been thought possible.

4 The Constitution was widely accepted as the fundamental law of the land. The legitimacy of the new regime was fostered by both the "charismatic" leadership of George Washington and the effective performance of the new system.

5 The Constitution is a remarkable expression of the American political tradition. Its flexibility made it a workable constitution as the United States underwent the extraordinary transformation from a small, largely rural national community to a huge urban, industrial society.

FURTHER READING

LIPSET, SEYMOUR MARTIN (1963) The First New Nation. New York: Basic Books. An inquiry into the conflicting values of achievement and equality in America, with an excellent analysis of American character as it emerged from our early national experience.

SCHWARTZ, BERNARD (1977) The Great Rights of Mankind: A History of the American Bill of Rights. New York: Oxford University Press. An engrossing history of how the Bill of Rights came to be added to the U.S. Constitution.

WILLS, GARRY (1978) Inventing America. Garden City, N.Y.: Doubleday Publishing. A detailed dissection of the origins of the Declaration of Independence as it was formulated by Thomas Jefferson.

WOOD, GORDON S. (1969) The Creation of the American Republic, 1776–1787. New York: W. W. Norton. The most exhaustive and distinguished history of the early, formative years of the American nation.

2
Political Development of the Nation

The plan for our capital—Washington, D.C.—was made by Major Pierre Charles L'Enfant, an architect and engineer. He was hired by President George Washington in 1791 to plan a federal city on the Potomac River. L'Enfant was born and educated in France; he emigrated to the United States and joined the Revolutionary army in 1776. After the Revolution, he lived in New York. There, among other jobs, he remodeled the building used for sessions of Congress.

L'Enfant's plan for the capital was based on the Constitution. There is no central plaza, no central focus of activity. Rather, there are several centers of attention. The three main centers are for the Congress, the president, and the Supreme Court.

But the capital of the new nation got off to a pretty poor start. It was hard to sell land for commercial development in the new federal district. Yet money from private sales was needed to finance the construction of government buildings. Attracting people to the new city, especially construction workers, also was hard. Measures to attract businesses to the district were not very successful. Construction of the Capitol and the White House progressed at a snail's pace. L'Enfant's imaginative city took a long time to build.

The new capital was forbidding and dismal in the early 1800s, just as the new government itself was small and sometimes ineffectual. Like Washington, D.C., our government took time to establish.

* * * * *

Our political system as we know it took a long time to develop. It is still changing. The country began as a rural and agricultural society. It became a mixed, mostly urban, technologically advanced, and industrialized society. The United States was not much involved in world affairs until the 1900s—it pursued mainly isolationist policies. But in this century, it has become an awesome military and industrial power. Its mainly British people became a highly diverse population. From 13 sparsely populated territories clinging to the eastern seaboard, Americans settled a large continent. In the 1800s, Americans left their tracks across the prairies of the West; in this century, they left their tracks on the moon.

A country is politically developed if, over time, it sets up and maintains political institutions able to govern. **Political development** refers to changes in a country's institutions. It occurs when government organizations become differentiated and specialized. By differentiated, we mean more distinct or independent. In the hunter-gatherer groups of old, laws were made by common consent of the tribe. As such groups became larger, more far-flung, and more

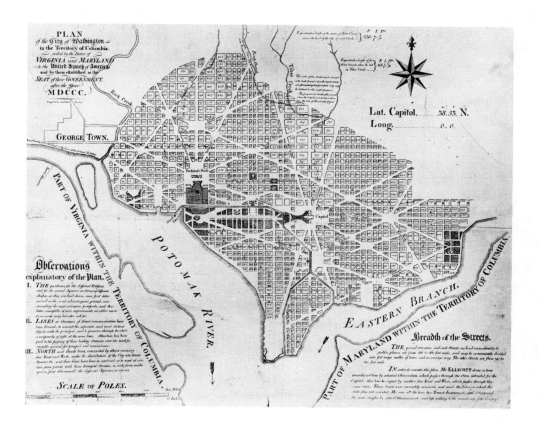

L'Enfant's plan for the new national capital. Major streets were laid out so as to focus attention on the three major branches of the federal government—the executive, the legislative, and the judicial.

complex, their laws were made by a council of elders. The elders were a group of lawmakers distinct from the population in general. As a nation's political structures, like its lawmaking bodies, become increasingly differentiated and specialized, they govern more effectively.

All societies are developing countries in the sense that their political institutions are changing. In some, like those of the Third World (Africa, Latin America, and some parts of Asia), political changes are rapid. In contrast, politically "developed" countries like the United States have reached a point where their governments are highly differentiated and specialized. The governments of developed countries are therefore very stable. To be sure, our political institutions are changing. Over the last 200 years, many leaders have worked and struggled to change our politics for the better. At the same time, our political institutions have been notably stable and workable in many ways. Dramatic changes have occurred here in the last 200 years, so that the United States has become very modern. But our political institutions have developed slowly and have kept many of their original features.

In this chapter, we will characterize major features of U.S. political development over the 200 plus years of the national history. Although this may seem easy, in fact it is very hard to explain completely. Political scientists do not yet have concise theories about how political systems develop. History shows that as political institutions grow, they have to face hurdles at various stages. These hurdles, or "growing pains," are problems developing countries have to solve. One way to look at the political development of the United States is to ask, "What are the main problems of our political development?" We begin this chapter with what political scientists think are the most pressing development problems for growing nations like the United States. Then we turn to more specific questions: "How have political parties and government institutions evolved?" "How did the government develop?" "How have changes in our economy and society affected our political institutions and processes?"

PROBLEMS OF AMERICAN POLITICAL DEVELOPMENT

Political scientists, looking mostly at developing countries of the Third World, have tried to find the most important problems political systems face as their institutions evolve, stabilize, and adapt to changing conditions. Five major problems have been analyzed: (1) identity, (2) legitimacy, (3) penetration, (4) participation, and (5) distribution of opportunities and rewards. These are problems political systems have to cope with as they develop. Under some circumstances, one or more of these problems may become a serious crisis (Binder et al., 1971).

Developing national identity

The problem of identity means the degree to which people think they are members of the political community. In many less-developed countries, large numbers of people do not have a strong sense of national awareness and attachment. Early in our history, as we saw in Chapter 1, the colonists identified as American rather than British. At least 10 years before the Revolution, a majority of Americans had an American identity. This identity both deepened and grew in the 1800s. Our most serious identity crisis came with the Civil War of the 1860s, when loyalties were torn between the North and the South. As President Abraham Lincoln told Congress in 1862, "that portion of the earth's surface which is owned and inhabited by the people of the United States is well adapted to be the home of one national family, and it is not well adapted for two or more." Reconstruction, restoring the "national family," was slow and painful.

The scope and strength of a nation's identity are found in its national symbols. George Washington symbolized our nation to many people—he was "first in peace, first in war, and first in the hearts of his countrymen." The Constitution, the flag, the national anthem, and the Capitol are important symbols of our national identity.

A legitimate government

The problem of legitimacy concerns who makes governmental decisions and how they are made. Decisions are accepted and obeyed because people think

A flag for the new nation. In 1777, the Continental Congress resolved "The flag of the United States shall be thirteen stripes, alternate red and white, with a union of thirteen stars of white on a blue field, representing a new constellation." Seamstress Betsy Ross is shown presenting one of the new flags to George Washington, but the belief that she made the first Stars and Stripes did not develop until 1870 and probably is not authentic.

they are made in a right and proper way by those in authority. The "rule of law" was the standard expectation well before the Constitution was adopted. But more than anything else, the Constitution gave legitimacy to our government.

The rift between the North and the South over slavery caused a breach in the legitimacy of the Constitution. A long, bloody Civil War finally restored the union. After the Civil War, the Constitution was amended in several important ways; the first changes in the Constitution since 1804. The 13th Amendment (1865) abolished slavery. The 14th Amendment (1868) said that no states could "deprive any person of life, liberty, or property, without due process of law; nor deny to any person within its jurisdiction the equal protection of the laws." The 15th Amendment (1870) banned racial discrimination in voting rights. These were historic changes, but the Constitution's basic provisions are largely intact. The lasting character of the Constitution demonstrates that our system has generally had a very high degree of legitimacy.

Penetrating the countryside

New governments often face problems in effectively controlling their territory and, more important, in bringing government protection and services to their people. Much of U.S. history concerns expanding territory and incorporating new people into the citizenry. In 1803, the Jefferson administration negotiated the so-called Louisiana Purchase, which more than doubled the size of the country. Eventually, there was a problem governing such a vast continent. New territories, once adequately settled, became new states—the Constitution provided a ready means of expansion. But setting up government, state or federal, was a long, difficult process on the frontier.

More basic to "law and order" in the West was the emerging political party system which shaped national politics and pulled the system together. Grass-roots competition for public office linked people and government together and mobilized people in a national constituency. When political parties began, Washington, Hamilton, and Madison thought they were destructive rather than helpful. However, "as the party system linked men and groups from region to region and state to state, providing a national framework for political expression within which both Massachusetts men and South Carolinians could be Federalists, and both New Yorkers and Virginians could be Republicans, it served to advance the process of national integration" (Chambers and Burnham, 1975: 20).

This happened while the United States was mostly rural. Now, almost three fourths of the people live in 318 standard metropolitan areas, that is, areas that include a city and its suburbs. In 1980, there were 226 million Americans, a 56-fold increase over the 4 million recorded in the 1790 census. There are 23 million more Americans today than there were in 1970. The population is expected to grow by 50 million people by 2000. Keeping a link between government and citizen in a country with a large, growing, urban, and highly mobile population is a basic political problem.

Participating in the political system

Participation refers to those who take part in choosing political leaders and influencing government decisions. The electoral history of the United States has shown an increase in the proportion of potential voters.

Problems of participation   The first major extension of political participation was the elimination of property and taxpaying qualifications for voting. These were all but abolished by the mid-1840s. The second major problem was black voting rights. These were assured by the 15th Amendment but were not fully effective until passage of the Voting Rights Act of 1965.

On November 19, 1863, President Abraham Lincoln delivered an address at the federal cemetery in Gettysburg, Pennsylvania. This was where so many Union and Confederate soldiers had died in a huge battle the previous July. In this "Gettysburg Address," Lincoln said, in part:

> Four score and seven years ago our Fathers brought forth on this continent a new nation, conceived in liberty and dedicated to the proposition that all men are created equal.
> Now we are engaged in a great civil war testing whether that nation or any nation so conceived and so dedicated can long endure. We are met on a great battlefield of that war. We have come to dedicate a portion of that field as a final resting place for those who here gave their lives that that nation might live . . .
> . . . we here highly resolve that these dead shall not have died in vain—that this nation under God

shall have a new birth of freedom—and that government of the people, by the people, for the people shall not perish from the earth.

Distinguished antislavery leader Frederick Douglass escaped slavery and lectured in the North and in Europe in behalf of the efforts of the Massachusetts Antislavery Society. He was one of the most effective orators in American history.

The third problem arose between the Civil War and the 1920s, with alien voting and electoral corruption. There was widespread fraud in elections; to counteract corruption, states passed voting reforms. Voting was restricted to people who could prove they intended to become citizens, so that newly arrived immigrants could not be manipulated. Today, all states permit only citizens of the United States to vote.

After the Civil War, laws were also passed in the states to counter corruption. They required voter registration, a secret ballot (the so-called Australian ballot), and regulation of election practices to ensure honesty. At the same time, poll taxes and other devices to restrict black voting were used in the South to discourage black participation. In 1964, the 24th Amendment to the Constitution was ratified. It prohibited payment of a poll tax as a condition for voting.

A fourth important problem came up over women's right to vote. After a long struggle dating back to the 1840s, the 19th Amendment was ratified in 1920. It prohibited the denial of the right to vote on account of sex. Finally, after World War II, the issue of voting rights for 18- to 20-year-olds arose. In 1971, the 26th Amendment gave voting rights to all citizens 18 years of age or older.

Suffrage and turnout Changes in the Constitution and laws have expanded political participation. As we shall see in Chapter 4, many factors affect how much people participate in politics. Eligibility to vote in elections has changed dramatically. By the 1840s, all white males in the United States could vote; by 1971, most all people over 18 could vote. And participation in elections has also grown in the long run. Figure 2–1 shows the proportion of the total population voting in presidential elections since 1824. Note the effect of granting women the right to vote for the first time in the presidential election of 1920.

But if the number of potential voters in the United States has grown since the early 1800s, actual voting turnout has declined (Burnham, 1965). Figure 2–2 shows the proportion of eligible people who voted in presidential elections. Sharp declines in voter turnout beginning in the 1890s reflect the wholesale denial of voting rights to blacks in the South and the passing of state residency and ballot reform laws aimed at reducing corruption. Although women's suf-

THE POLL TAX

The word *poll* is derived from the Old English word *polle*, which meant "a head." Thus, a poll tax was a uniform payment made by each person, or "head." This kind of tax was used in England from the 14th to the 17th centuries to raise money.

In this country, poll taxes have been levied mainly as a way to keep black people from voting. In Southern states, a person had to pay a $1 to $2 tax to qualify to vote. This sum was enough to keep many blacks and poor whites from voting. In some states, a person had to pay not just this year's poll tax but unpaid poll taxes for all previous years.

In 1937, the Supreme Court upheld the constitutionality of the poll tax in Georgia. By the 1950s, it had been abolished in several Southern states. But it remained in Virginia, Arkansas, Texas, Alabama, and Mississippi. By the 1960, the $1 or $2 poll tax probably did not disenfranchise many people. But it remained a symbol of discrimination against blacks.

In 1964, the 24th Amendment to the Constitution was ratified. This prohibited the requirement of a poll tax for federal elections. Then, in 1966, the Supreme Court held that a poll tax requirement for voting in any election, including state and local elections, violated the "equal protection" clause of the 14th Amendment. At long last, the poll tax was dead.

Victory for the 19th Amendment. Alice Paul, leader of the National Woman's Party, receives the congratulations of her followers on the occasion of the passage of the women's suffrage amendment.

frage greatly increased the number of potential voters, its immediate effect was to drastically reduce the percent of people who voted (especially in 1920 and 1924). Only since the 1970s has female voting been about the same as male voting. Finally, the inclusion of 18-year-olds in the 1972 election mainly accounts for the drop in recent turnout (Converse, 1972).

Although the drop in the proportion of eligible voters who cast ballots has been a result of changes in election laws and the increase in population, other factors are involved. Politics were more entertaining in the later 1800s than today. Voting turnout is stimulated by certain candidates and issues (for example, Al Smith in 1928 and Dwight Eisenhower in 1952). Sometimes certain events (such as the Vietnam War or the Watergate crisis of 1973 which precipitated President Nixon's resignation) cause political apathy, indifference, and estrangement.

Distributing opportunities and rewards

The problem of **distribution** involves how government distributes or redistributes benefits in the society. In the early 1800s, Congress spent money to spur economic development. These funds helped to build roads and canals. They also spurred private enterprise. More important, federal land policies in the 1800s

FIGURE 2–1

Growth in the Electorate since 1824

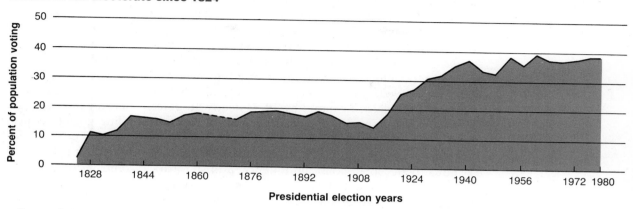

Sources: Robert E. Lane, *Political Life* (Glencoe, Ill.: Free Press, 1959), p. 20; *Statistical Abstract of the United States,* various years.

FIGURE 2–2

Turnout in Presidential Elections since 1824

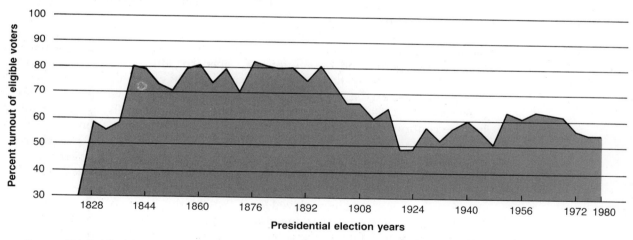

Sources: *Historical Statistics of the United States* (Washington, D.C.: U.S. Government Printing Office, 1975), pp. 1071–72; *Statistical Abstract of the United States* (Washington, D.C.: U.S. Government Printing Office, various years).

distributed vast tracts of land, first to private speculators and then to home-steaders. The Homestead Act of 1862 gave 160 acres of free land in the West to anyone who would settle on and improve them within five years. This huge land giveaway drew thousands of poor farmers and their families. Also in 1862, Congress gave land grants of up to 100 million acres to help build transcontinental railroads.

If handing out western land played a vital role in the physical development of the country, education helped develop the American character. Public schools have been the hallmark of our educational system since colonial times. In the

1830s the French observer de Tocqueville said, "It is by the attention it pays to Public Education that the original character of American civilization is at once placed in the clearest light." Public education has grown remarkably, especially in the 20th century. Now, almost all children go to school, usually to public schools. In 1870, only 2 percent of 18-year-olds were high school graduates; since the mid-1960s, three fourths of 18-year-olds are high school graduates. In the last generation, the proportion of adults who have a college degree has doubled. In 1960, about 8 percent of those 25 years old or older had finished four years of college or more; by 1978, nearly 16 percent had finished college. Now, most state spending and a large part of federal spending goes to education.

Just as those who get high school diplomas or college degrees are rewarded by status (better jobs, political influence, and so forth), income and wealth distribution helps some and hinders others. As a country grows, political power may be used to distribute economic resources among the people. The problem of distribution comes up when the government is pressured to change how the economic system works.

In our early days, a large amount of personal wealth was in land, and many people owned land. The practice of political equality which grew during the 19th century is often attributed to the relative equality of economic condition. Government policies that regulated inheritance helped distribute property more widely; the open frontier in the West made cheap land abundant.

As time passed and an industrial economy replaced subsistence agriculture, money became more important than land. In the 1800s, there were alternating times of prosperity and depression. But even so, affluence has usually prevailed. In recent years, family incomes have steadily grown for Americans as a group. But there is still a gap in the average incomes of whites and blacks (Thurow, 1975). Despite high inflation in the 1970s and 1980s, average family income continues to rise in constant dollars (correcting for inflation).

In 1913, the 16th Amendment was added to the Constitution. This cleared the way for Congress to pass income tax legislation. By taking a larger proportion from high-income people than from low-income people, tax policy can help redistribute wealth. Social welfare programs also move funds from the government to the poor, the unemployed, and the elderly. Even so, the overall distribution of income has not changed much in the last 50 years. The top 20 percent of American families receive about 40 percent of total income; the lowest 20 percent receive only about 5 percent. But the huge expansion of welfare programs in the last 20 years has redistributed economic resources. This is best shown in the percentage of people whose incomes are below poverty level. The Congressional Budget Office said that 27 percent of Americans were below the poverty level in 1976 if only cash income were counted. But if so-called transfer payments (social security, pensions, aid to families with dependent children, food stamps, housing assistance, medicare) were counted, the proportion of families below the poverty level shrank to about 8 percent. But, since the mid-1970's, the percent of Americans below the poverty level has grown somewhat to about 9 percent (taking noncash transfers into account).

The problems of political development are never really solved. They are ongoing. Sometimes, as during the Civil War, problems of legitimacy, identity, or participation become massive crises. Now problems of distribution are acute, especially since the New Deal of the 1930s and '40s ushered in the welfare state.

DIVERSITY AND UNITY

If you look closely at a U.S. coin, you will see the expression *E Pluribus Unum.* This Latin phrase means "One from many." It stands for the intention of our constitutional system that national unity can come from a diverse group of people living throughout a large country that is governed by many state and local bodies. A major theme in our political development, as we cope with national identity, legitimacy, penetration, participation, and distribution, is to forge unity out of increasing diversity.

A federal union

American politics has always been a politics of territory. The 13 original states were locked in a fight over how to combine strong national government with state independence. The Constitution bound the states together in a federal union. But for a long time, the states were the most important part. The same Constitution provided for adding new states. Under these provisions, the Union moved steadily west in the 1800s and early 1900s. Arizona entered the Union as the 48th state in 1912. Then, after World War II, Alaska (January 1959) and Hawaii (August 1959) became states.

Federalism was a means both to expand the nation across the continent and to develop a system that could benefit from diversity (Elazar, 1972). But federalism also resulted in a major, continuing tension that still persists in politics. New states brought new problems and needs to the national government. They also allowed, even encouraged, distinct political practices, new ways of governing, state loyalty and pride, and a sense of independence. The secession of the South in the 1860s over slavery and growing economic dominion by the North were vivid lessons in tensions between nation and states. It required a bloody civil war to resolve the issues.

As the Union grew, much of federal-state relations was political, involving constitutional powers and how to allocate functions between the nation and states. But after the Civil War, federal-state relations became more fiscal (Reagan and Sanzone, 1981). This started with federal grants-in-aid to the states (money payments for specific purposes). The grants are spent subject to certain laws or regulations. The grants-in-aid system began in the 1880s with agricultural experiment stations set up by the states with federal grants. The system is now a major part of our government. Grants-in-aid helped avoid the question, "Which level of government should carry out a function?" Usually state functions (like public education) continue to be run at that level. But pressing fiscal problems can be resolved with federal financial aid. Government programs can expand and grow without kindling the historic tensions between federal and state levels.

Fiscal federalism, as it is called, has become a very large enterprise, especially since 1960. In 1980, 23 percent of state spending was federally collected money supplied through grant programs. Today there are about 500 different grant-in-aid programs, so diverse that together they touch almost all areas of state and local government. In the past, most federal grant-in-aid programs gave funds to the states. But in recent years, more programs bypass the states and give money to local governments. In 1980, a fourth of all federal grant money went straight to cities. The enormous scope of the federal role in local government can be seen even more strikingly. Federal aid now goes to nearly four

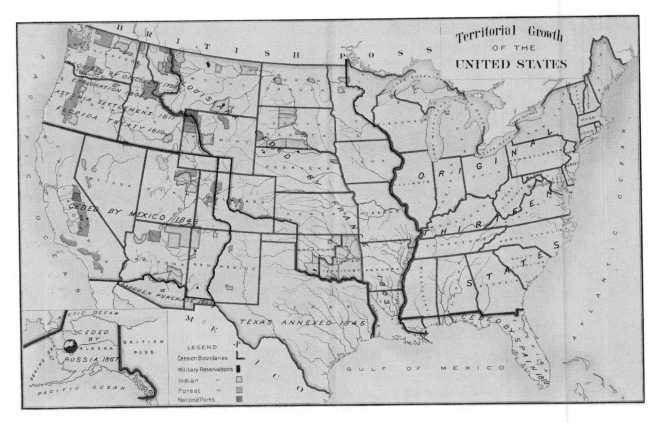

Westward expansion. Much of American history is a story of the addition of new states to the federal union.

fifths of the 80,000 subnational government units in the United States—cities, counties, school districts, other special districts, and states. And, when this money comes, federal regulations come, too. In 1980, there were 1,259 different conditions for receiving grants-in-aid or direct orders about how to spend aid. In the past 20 years, the federal government's role has grown but without much increase in its own bureaucracy. Rather, this expansion has occurred through financing programs run by the states, cities, and other local bodies.

The current federal system tries to keep at least some local diversity while ensuring that national goals are reached. It allows unobtrusive growth of federal purposes, programs, and standards. But the grant-in-aid system has become very large and complex. Critics now find it too congested, too confusing, and too regulated. Recently a federal agency, the Advisory Commission on Intergovernmental Relations, complained that "the federal government's role in the federal system has become more pervasive, more intrusive, more unmanageable, more ineffective, more costly, and more unaccountable."

Growing more urban

When the nation was founded, it was mostly rural. The first census in 1790 counted no city larger than 50,000 people. New York City had 49,400; less than 30,000 lived in Philadelphia; Boston and Baltimore had less than 20,000; and the 10th largest city, Alexandria, Virginia, totaled only 2,700. To some early leaders, such as Thomas Jefferson, rural, small-town America was a blessing.

Jefferson's vision of the future saw a pastoral, plantation society, free of Europe's urban and industrial problems. Let factories and cities grow in Europe, Jefferson thought, not here. He believed the new nation should avoid the problems brought about by urban growth. But other leaders, such as Alexander Hamilton, had a different view. Hamilton foresaw a growing, expanding, industrializing, urban society, and he thought the national government should foster such growth.

Hamilton was right. In the 1800s, America became more urban. By the 1920 census, more people were living in towns and cities than in rural areas. Today, three fourths of us live in urban areas. Twelve of the world's 60 largest urban areas are in the United States. Vast urban regions stretch from Boston to Richmond on the East Coast, from Chicago to Detroit in the Midwest, and from San Francisco to San Diego on the West Coast. Urban growth meant many things— expansion, building, opportunity, excitement, cultural richness, prosperity, complexity, and many peoples. It also meant harder, more complex, and challenging problems of government.

Americans have always been on the move. In the 1800s, they moved west; in the 1900s, they moved to cities. We are still moving. The Census Bureau estimates that, between 1975 and 1979, nearly two thirds of 20- to 24-year-olds and three fourths of 25- to 29-year-olds changed their residence. The 1980 census shows that the population has grown by about 11 percent since 1970. It has also moved to the South and West. The Sunbelt states—Florida, Arizona, California, Nevada, and Texas—have had dramatic growth. At the same time, the population of some north central and northeastern states grew only slightly. New York and Rhode Island actually declined. This shift foreshadows a major change in the regional basis of political power. This can be seen in the changes the 1980 census is bringing to representation in Congress.

The number of representatives a state has in the House of Representatives is based on its population counted by the federal census taken every 10 years. Therefore, these recent shifts mean less representation for states in the Northeast and Midwest and more for Western and Sunbelt states. As Figure 2–3 shows, the big loser is New York. The big winners are Florida, California, and Texas.

Urban growth means government growth. In rural areas or small towns, people can do much for themselves. Urban dwellers need more government. They cannot get rid of garbage, get water, walk to work, or provide fire protection. The interdependence and complexity of urban life require government help in many areas: housing, health, sanitation, fire and police protection, poverty, unemployment, traffic and parking, urban renewal, water supply, treatment of the elderly and minorities, and so on. Urban growth has greatly expanded government activities and programs at all levels. Since 1960, the role of the federal government in handling urban problems has grown rapidly. Also, population shifts, as seen in the 1980 census, deeply affect our politics. The special growing pains of Sunbelt states overshadow the problems of the older, industrial Northeast.

Racial and ethnic diversity

The United States has absorbed large tides of immigrants and many racial and ethnic groups. While native Americans now number about 800,000, more than ever before and more than double the number in 1940, most U.S. citizens have

FIGURE 2–3

Gains and Losses of Seats in the U.S. House of Representatives after the 1980 Census

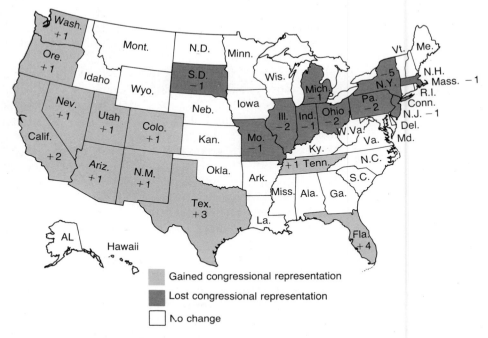

Source: Bureau of the Census, 1980.

come here from somewhere else, mostly Europe. Several hundred thousand slaves were brought from Africa, most before 1820.

As Figure 2–4 shows, the number of immigrants who flowed into the United States has varied greatly since the 1820s. The influx was large from the 1870s

FIGURE 2–4

Absorption of Immigrants into the United States, 1820–1980

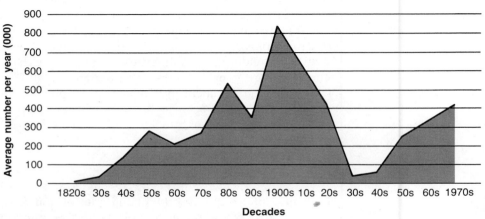

Source: *Historical Statistics of the United States*, 1980, p. 91.

to the 1920s. At that time, new laws were made limiting immigration. In total, more than 49 million people came here between 1820 and 1980.

Immigration has grown since the 1940s; it now averages more than 400,000 a year. More than 10 million people came to this country between 1951 and 1980: 33 percent were Europeans, 19 percent Asians, and 46 percent from the Western Hemisphere (including 1.8 million Mexicans and Cubans). Although many European immigrants have kept an ethnic identity over a long time, the largest single ethnic group in the United States today is blacks. They comprise about 12 percent of the population. Asian Americans, mainly Japanese, Chinese, and Filipinos, now make up about 1 percent. Americans with Spanish surnames, mostly from Mexico, Puerto Rico, and Cuba, comprise more than 6 percent.

The absorption of immigrants did not mean assimilation. Most immigrants did become "Americanized." They learned to speak English, qualified for citizenship, got jobs, and were accepted into the community. But much ethnic diversity was preserved. The pressures on immigrants to "Americanize" shows the strength of our national identity and our mixed feelings about cultural pluralism. As a student of ethnicity (Greeley, 1974: 17) said:

> In America there is a profound distrust of diversity based on anything other than social class, which is the only "rational" diversity. . . . Most Americans feel ambivalent about the fact of diversity and also about their own particular location in ethnic geography. We are torn between pride in the heritage of our own group and resentment at being trapped in that heritage. This ambivalence is probably the result of the agonies of the acculturation experience in which an immigrant group alternately felt shame over the fact that it was different and unwanted and a defensive pride about its own excellence, which the rest of the society seemed neither to appreciate nor understand.

Mixed feelings about Americanization may have been masked and largely overcome. Most immigrants came poor and illiterate and then enjoyed economic success and social mobility. The sharpest exception to this pattern has

A nation of immigrants. Millions of people like these left their native homes in Europe to resettle in the United States, seeking freedom, land, prosperity, and hope for the future for their children.

Ethnic prejudice in the 1920s. The hooded members of the Ku Klux Klan marched in Washington, D.C., in support of racial prejudice and bigotry. Great progress has been made in providing racial justice, but the Klan still survives as an organization even today.

been among blacks and Hispanics. Their share in the "American dream" has certainly not been as great as that of other ethnic groups.

The huge change in the ethnic makeup of our population resulting from immigration fostered new social and political conflicts. Ethnic hostility and prejudice showed up in anti-Semitic and anti-Catholic political movements. The Prohibition amendment—the 18th Amendment, ratified in 1919 and repealed in 1933—banned the making and sale of liquor. But "while the immediate objective was a ban on the sale of alcoholic beverages, the whole struggle was heavily symbolic: the real enemy was the 'different ways' of many of the new Americans" (Ladd, 1970: 145).

The huge influx of immigrants produced strong reactions from some groups. The Ku Klux Klan of the 1920s was the largest nativist movement in our history. For a time it successfully spread its doctrines of white supremacy, religious fundamentalism, and extreme moralism. Moreover, the massive immigration of the late 1800s greatly influenced the political realignment of the Roosevelt era of the 1930s, which made the Democrats the dominant national party.

Diversity and violence

A mobile society, racially and ethnically diverse, urban and industrial, with growing, more difficult governing problems, can erupt in violent conflict. We could write our history as a story of constant violence, but that would be tiresome, overdrawn, and misleading. Nonetheless, political conflicts—often leading to violence—have been a frequent part of our politics. Sometimes the violence was started by challenging groups, sometimes by the governing authorities.

One study of U.S. political violence showed that between 1890 and 1970, 2,861 instances of domestic violence were recorded. They lasted for 3,393 days and resulted in 18,985 arrests and 1,180 deaths. About one fourth of these were triggered by the government or dominant political groups; about 15 percent were started by antisystem groups; and about 60 percent were "clashes" in which it could not be determined who started the violence. More than half of these events were racial. Another 29 percent involved labor-management relations (Stohl, 1976: 80–87).

Most American violence is not particularly political; political violence has rarely focused against our political system or the Constitution. Violence has largely involved immediate grievances or long-term complaints against social or economic conditions. Seldom has it become attacks against constitutional order. Ironically, it has often been hard to change the conditions that produced dissatisfaction because of the great stability of our political system. Witness the passage of 100 years before blacks got voting rights. The system is so stable that it is sometimes slow to change and is out of the reach of small, deprived groups.

The Constitution was supposed to prevent the tyranny of the majority. But it was not enacted in Heaven. The men and women who created our constitutional ideals were imperfect. Thus, the black minority suffered from white oppression. The business class and its many supporters successfully blocked trade union efforts, especially early in this century. As one political scientist shrewdly observed (Lowi, 1971: 53):

The history of the United States is not merely one of mutual accommodation among competing groups under a broad umbrella of consensus. The proper image of our society has never been a melting pot. In bad times, it is a boiling pot; in good times, it is a tossed salad. For those who are *in,* this is all very well. But the price has always been paid by those who are *out,* and when they do get in they do not always get in through a process of mutual accommodation under a broad umbrella of consensus.

In the main, political violence has resulted from impatience over failure to carry out policies or programs, or from strong grievances about specific wrongs or evils. It has not been because of general alienation, frustration, or weakness. Violence has been a political act "aimed at furthering the purposes of the group that uses it when they have some reason to think it will help their cause" (Gamson, 1975: 81). More often than not, violent protest has given new advantages to challenging groups and brought them into the political mainstream.

THE RISE OF POLITICAL PARTIES

It has been said that "the unplanned institution of organized partisanship has been surprisingly successful as a means of furnishing the American people with a more democratic process for the election of presidents than was planned by the framers of the Constitution" (Holcombe, 1950: 107). The framers assumed the president would be elected on a nonpartisan basis. They thought presidents would only be nominated by the electoral college. Normally no candidate would earn a majority of electoral votes. So the usual site of the election would be the House of Representatives. Leaders such as Hamilton, Washington, Madison, and Jefferson felt that political parties (called "factions") would be destructive, divisive forces which would frustrate the public interest. A large portion of Washington's Farewell Address warned against "the baneful effects of the Spirit of Party."

Ironically, Madison and Jefferson were among those who started the first opposition party in the history of democratic governments. Ostensibly on a nature study, the two traveled all over in the 1790s to mobilize the support of "Democratic Societies" in communities. In this way they helped to form a popular political party designed to capture government control from the Federalists (led by Washington, Hamilton, and John Adams). They succeeded. In 1801 Jefferson became president. He was followed in the White House by Madison in 1809. Political participation grew rapidly. Mass political organizations mobilized voters. These developments are the basis for the view that "the distinctive American contributions to politics are in the organization of popular participation," and "the one major political institution invented in America is . . . the political party" (Huntington, 1968: 130).

The founders' main concern was to create a constitution with workable checks on political power. They were not sure that competitive parties would be an adequate check. This certainly is not hard to understand. The modern idea of a competitive party system did not exist in the 1700s. The framers of the Constitution thought that checks on power had to be built into the structure of the Constitution itself. "Their hopes were pinned on a formal, written system of internal checks and balances, the precise enumeration of limited powers, and the explicit statement of constitutional guarantees, such as the opponents of the Constitution insisted on adding to it" (Hofstadter, 1972: 50).

Yet parties played a vital role in fostering the huge growth of participation and in resolving the problem of succession in office. The election of 1800 "was the first election in modern history which, by popular decision, resulted in the quiet and peaceful transition of national power from the hands of one of two embattled parties to another" (Hofstadter, 1972: 128). The rise of opposition, its legitimation, and the two-party system were significant in the development of our political system.

The first party system, 1789–1824

Once it had broken formal ties with England, the new nation faced some crucial, divisive issues: How centralized should the government be? What should its stance be toward such powers as England and France? How should it handle such economic issues as war debts and coinage? The struggle over centralization continued. In the 1790s, rival groups in the new Congress argued over policy questions. Factions clustered around issues and leaders.

Although Washington struggled to stay above the fray, his Secretary of the Treasury, Alexander Hamilton, became the intellectual leader of the Federalists. The Federalists espoused what Hamilton called "energetic government." This meant strong central direction and national solutions to public problems. They tended to be elitists. They feared widespread democratic participation and protected business interests. In 1793, war broke out in Europe between revolutionary France and a coalition of old regimes including England. The Federalists sided with the dependable (and commercially profitable) British against the French "party of humanity."

The rival Republican faction (later to be called the "Democratic-Republicans," and then the "Democrats") looked to Thomas Jefferson as its spiritual leader. It attracted those who opposed the policies of Washington and Adams. These Democratic-Republicans favored local autonomy, weaker national government, lower-class and debtor interests, and "French principles."

Factionalism in the new nation was a kind of half-party system. Neither the Federalists nor the Democratic-Republicans had the broad electoral base of modern parties. The issues were national rather than local. Grass-roots groups were rare. Only a few were interested in such issues, since democratic participation was not fully developed. Foreign policy issues loomed large, as leaders chose sides between the French and British. Both factions saw their own principles and the national interest as the same. They thought their rivals were disloyal and courted foreign (French or British) control. The harsh Alien and Sedition Acts (1798), a last-ditch effort by the fading Federalists to harass their political opponents by threatening fines or imprisonment for criticizing government officials, showed a lack of tolerance for opposition. Such extreme restraints on political criticism have not been imposed since then.

The factional battle lines formed during the 1790s broke apart by the 1800s. The Federalists, who could not compete with the rising Democratic-Republicans, last elected a president in 1796. They dwindled to a New England base after 1800, and disappeared after 1816. The aristocratic Federalists were indifferent organizers; Jefferson and his allies were ceaseless in this area. Issues blurred, declining in fervor after Jefferson's election in 1800. "With each passing year," Goodman writes (1967: 85), "Jefferson's vision was increasingly coming to pass—'We are all republicans, we are all federalists'—although the emphasis fell on the former term." The first era of partisan competition had ended.

During the so-called Era of Good Feelings (which was hardly that), the dominant Democratic-Republicans were torn apart by factionalism. Their congressional caucus picked its presidential candidates, who were assured of election. Maneuvering within the caucus was constant. Caucus leaders were often given cabinet jobs, which caused congressional factionalism in the tiny executive branch. The caucus, never popular, was further hurt by the supposed corrupt bargain that gave John Quincy Adams the 1824 nomination.

Meanwhile, a "hidden revolution" (McCormick, 1967: 102) was taking place in the electorate. Voting rights expanded. State after state dropped property qualifications for voting in favor of universal manhood suffrage. Presidential electors were no longer picked by state legislators; they were chosen by the people on general tickets. For the first time, voters were ready to rally behind a party banner.

The second party system, 1828–1856

The invention of modern American political parties took place between 1824 and 1828. At about that time, Andrew Jackson and his followers burst on the political scene. Ambitious and clever men, they seized on the expanded electorate and mobilized it.

Jackson was the most popular president since George Washington. Presidential voting had lagged before 1828. That year it rose more than threefold with the hero of the Battle of New Orleans on the ballot. To raise popular interest, the Jacksonians and their rivals dropped the discredited caucuses and used conventions to make nominations. The new parties invented the large-scale political campaign, with its colorful blend of cynicism and zeal, hoopla and organization. For better or worse, these forms still survive.

"Old Hickory." Andrew Jackson brought mass appeal to the presidency.

For 30 years after Jackson's election in 1828, the two national parties—Jackson's Democrats and the rival Whigs—were close battlers. The Democrats won a majority of the House seats in most of the elections. Until 1860, they captured the White House all but two times. Yet the Whigs were just as shrewd in campaign techniques, as is shown by their 1840 campaign ("Tippecanoe and Tyler too"). Three times they used the clever minority-party tactic of choosing a popular military man for the presidency; twice (with William Henry Harrison and Zachary Taylor) they elected him.

For the first time, party rivalries extended to state and local contests. Partisans at all levels talked about the same issues. They adopted the same organizations and styles. They rallied to the same party banners. As one historian said (McCormick, 1967: 342), "Voters everywhere thought of themselves as either Whigs or Democrats."

Sorting out the parties' differences is not easy. Like their successors, the Democrats and Whigs were scattered coalitions. Broadly speaking, Jackson's Democrats echoed the Jeffersonians' distrust of central government. They championed the farmers in the West. Based in New England, the Whigs represented business interests and backed stronger nationalism.

Yet neither party fought for big government in today's sense. Neither wished

"TIPPECANOE AND TYLER TOO"

The 1840 presidential campaign was a model of noisy absurdity. It was matched but never surpassed in later years.

The Democratic candidate, incumbent President Martin Van Buren, was a self-made man. He masterminded Andrew Jackson's political career and became Jackson's handpicked successor.

The rival Whigs nominated William Henry Harrison of Ohio for President. Virginia's John Tyler was his running mate. A farmer, military man, and politician of modest achievements, Harrison in 1811 led a combined force of militia and regular troops which defeated a band of Indians in what was later called the Battle of Tippecanoe. The victory was militarily insignificant, but it was destined to become famous in politics. During the War of 1812, Harrison rose to the rank of major general.

The Whigs had few issues to air in 1840. Neither Harrison nor any other Whig leader was to say "a single word about what he thinks now or will do hereafter."

The campaign's theme was provided by a Baltimore Democratic editor. He called Harrison a "log cabin and hard cider" candidate. (Harrison's Ohio farmhouse had once been a log cabin, and he was said to drink cider with his meals.) The Whigs responded by portraying their candidate as a man of the people in contrast to an "aristocratic" Van Buren (whose origins were every bit as humble as Harrison's).

The Whigs' slogan, "Tippecanoe and Tyler too," was emblazoned on flags and posters, as was the log cabin symbol. Rallies, picnics, bonfires, and torchlight parades were staged. Songs were composed ("Farewell, dear Van,/You're not our man;/To guide the ship/We'll try old Tip").

The 1840 campaign set the pattern for political campaigns for more than 100 years. Though an historic event, the campaign had an inconclusive result: Harrison won, but a month after taking office, he died of pneumonia.

to topple established economic and social interests. Pre-Civil War politics were described as a three-sided game: the North wanted high tariffs to protect its growing industries; the South preferred low tariffs to protect its raw materials exports; and the West wanted cheap land to meet the economic needs of its farmers and ranchers. Rival parties maneuvered to form a winning mix of these interests. The issues were not fully resolved until a fourth issue—slavery—split the old party lines and made possible a new, and largely successful, partisan coalition.

The third party system, 1860—1896

By the 1850s, the racial question had become the pivot around which sectional and producer-group alliances shifted (Sundquist, 1983). The abolitionists, who denounced slavery as a moral horror, swept the North, which was outstripping the South in growth. In the ceaseless westward push, the burning question was whether the "peculiar institution" of slavery would extend into the territories.

Inevitably, the Democratic party was proslavery. This was because southerners dominated the party and its congressional ranks. Southern Democrats were aided by the two-thirds rule, whereby convention nominees required two-thirds support rather than a simple majority. This led them to choose such weak neutralist "doughfaces" as Franklin Pierce and James Buchanan as presidential candidates. With a southern-led Congress and a weak presidency, the national government struggled in vain with the slavery problem.

The Whigs dissolved before the slavery issue, only to be reborn as a broader, stronger alliance. Though traditionally nationalist, the Whigs were split over slavery. Yet many astute Whigs cast their lot with a party that was pledged to

Presidential politics, 1840 style. Harrison rally during the noisy campaign between ''Old Tippecanoe'' and incumbent Martin Van Buren.

prevent any spread of slavery. Leaving for a while the economic and social issues that separated Democrats and Whigs, the new partisans rallied behind "free soil, free men." In its second presidential race, the new party's candidate, Abraham Lincoln, won every free state but one. The Democrats, split into proslavery and neutralist wings, captured the Deep South and border states. The collapse of the Whigs, the Republican rise, and the Democratic split shows "the power of a moral issue to disrupt political alignments" (Sundquist, 1983: 88).

The Grand Old Party (as the Republican Party is called) proved to be a strong, lasting alliance. As the party of the Union, it fought the Civil War on behalf of the North. For years thereafter, GOP politicians never tired of "waving the bloody shirt" to remind voters of the war's sacrifices, including the martyred Lincoln, and to condemn the traitorous Democrats. In keeping the war before the people, the GOP was helped by strong Union veterans' groups. For both moral reasons and political gain, Radical Republicans, the congressional faction bent on punishing the South for secession and disloyalty, tried to disfranchise Confederate sympathizers. They tried to install loyalist regimes, including blacks and northern politicians willing to undertake official posts in southern states (sometimes called "carpetbaggers" after their luggage). After this reconstruction policy collapsed in 1876, the minority Democrats were able to compete more equally with the GOP. But by this time, the GOP also embraced westerners,

A new political party. Today, some commentators speak about the possibility of new political parties being formed. In the 1850s the slavery question killed the Whig party. Its place in American politics was taken by the Republican party. In his Emancipation Proclamation, Abraham Lincoln, the first Republican president, declared the black slaves to be free.

who were attracted by a cheap land policy, and new industrial elites brought in by high tariffs and laissez-faire thinking (minimal intervention in the economy). Democrats dominated the post-reconstruction South. They drew scattered strength in the North, especially within the strong urban political machines.

The system of 1896

Post–Civil War America was very different from what went before. In place of a rural, farming society, the North was now urban and industrial. Northern cities teemed with people, fed by growing waves of immigrants. Big businesses, with their newly rich owner-manager class, were the order of the day. It was the golden age of American inventiveness, and economic productivity soared. The Republicans were the party of rapid industrialization. Although professing the doctrine of laissez-faire, the GOP upheld the kind of benign government intervention that the business class welcomed: high protective tariffs, huge land grants to western railroads, and laws ensuring "sound money."

As producers of raw materials, the less built-up regions of the South and West did not share the views of the business class. To export their products, these areas needed low rather than high tariffs; to pay their debts, they preferred inflationary rather than stable money; to market their goods and assure high returns, they wanted protection against the greedy railroads and other trusts. Urban workers organized and struck out against the harsh hidden side of industrial growth—low wages, long hours, and squalid working conditions.

Rebuffed by the GOP, farmer and urban discontent flowed into a series of splinter groups that tried to capture the Democratic party. The "me too" Democrats, hard to single out from their GOP counterparts, won by picking Grover

Campaign poster for William Jennings Bryan, "the great commoner." Poster shows slogans from the populist, free-silver platform he brought to the Democratic party.

Cleveland (1884, 1888, 1892). But in 1896, 1900, and 1908, the reformers prevailed with William Jennings Bryan.

Bryan's nomination proved disastrous for the Democrats. His agrarian populism and favoring of inflationary currency ("free silver") were greeted with horror by the industrial elites. He was even too radical for the urban workers and progressive farmers of the upper Midwest. Guided by a capitalist political mastermind, Marcus Alonzo Hanna, the GOP choice, William McKinley, swept the industrial Northeast, the border states, and the Midwest. Bryan was left with the South and the states west of the Missouri River.

For 35 years, the Democratic party was all but wiped out in the North except in the large cities. Its strength was confined to the underdeveloped areas of the South and West (Burnham, 1970: 34–70). Its image was tarnished. It was the party of rum, Romanism, rebellion, economic recession, and radicalism (Sundquist, 1983: 165). Between 1896 and 1932, the Democrats elected only one president—Woodrow Wilson—and he gained office in 1912 because of a Republican party split.

The New Deal coalition since 1932

The last major reshaping of electoral coalitions came in the 1930s, in the wake of the nation's greatest economic depression. The Democrats had attracted various reform movements, urban and rural. This was not the case in the South. There, the Democrats upheld white supremacy and Republicans were nowhere to be found. Urban voters, schooled by the strong machines, voted Democratic.

The tendency of Democrats to dominate among urban voters was reinforced in 1928 by the nomination of city-dwelling, antiprohibitionist, Catholic, Alfred E. Smith. But their growing support did not make the Democrats the majority party. They needed a crisis such as the slavery issue of the 1850s or the economic upheaval of the 1890s. This event was the Great Depression which not only highlighted the bungling of the industrial elite, but also brought out the unsure response of their politicians, the leaders of the Republican party.

Under the pragmatic leadership of Franklin D. Roosevelt, the Democratic party took on a progressive role. It was sworn to strong, positive government and social welfare programs. Roosevelt's progressivism appealed to the working class in the industrial North. As Sundquist (1983: 215) writes, "Franklin Roosevelt and the issues of the Great Depression completed what Alfred E. Smith and the issue of Prohibition had begun—the transformation of the northern urban centers into the network of Democratic bastions they have since remained." In many urban centers, which already leaned toward the Democrats, the Republicans just ceased to compete. Unemployed workers were strong Roosevelt supporters. So too, were the labor unions—by now a strong national voice.

The shift to the Democrats included minority voters. Immigrants such as the Irish had been pushed into the Democratic ranks by urban machines. Now their party loyalties matured. Other Catholic groups, attracted to the party by Smith in 1928, stayed there. Jewish voters had been mostly Republican until the 1930s. They moved into the Democratic camp with Roosevelt's stand against Fascism in Europe. Blacks (and a lot of them voted in the North), who had been loyal to the party of Lincoln, also joined the Roosevelt alliance. Young people joining the political system after the 1930s were strongly Democratic.

Since the 1930s, the alignment of the two major parties has not basically changed. True, the fights over New Deal programs were fought and forgotten. But the basic battle lines remain. Republicans tend to favor business interests; Democrats are closely tied to labor and social reform groups. During recessions, the old New Deal lines come out. Democrats want strong pump-priming and job-creating programs; Republicans want to stimulate business.

As a majority coalition, Democrats have not sought to make major changes in their appeal to voters. So their leaders try to stifle division and stress the bread-and-butter issues that brought the Democrats victory in the 1930s. The GOP could be helped most by exploiting a cross-cutting issue, but has not found a consistent strategy. However, the post–New Deal electorate is volatile. This has brought about startling shifts in the presidential successes of the parties. Republicans have made gains in the South, which had been a Democratic base. Many southerners returned to the Democrats with Jimmy Carter in 1976. But the 1980 election showed that the Republican party, with an attractive candidate such as Ronald Reagan, could win most of the South. The Republicans used a strong base in the West to offset the usually Democratic northern industrial states. In 1980, Reagan's victory margin was smaller in the East than in other regions. But he still won all but 23 of the eastern states' electoral votes.

THE DEVELOPMENT OF GOVERNING INSTITUTIONS

Ample time was a real advantage in our political development. Nowhere is this clearer than in the evolution of our basic institutions. Today, in developing nations such as in Africa or Asia, pressures on government force the quick establishment of authority. In the United States, on the other hand, institutions evolved more slowly. Although all branches of government were helped by having time to develop, Congress was helped the most. The history of the world's parliaments shows that they, more than any other government agencies, take time to grow.

The growth of Congress

Under the new Constitution, Congress, a frail and fragile institution in many ways, began its work with a certain optimism and zeal. A quorum (the majority of members needed to conduct business) was finally present on April Fool's Day 1789. The House then chose Congressman Frederick A. C. Muhlenberg as its first speaker. He was a Federalist from Pennsylvania. Shortly, the House adopted rules of procedure and began its legislative business. Legislation was needed to establish executive departments (such as War, Treasury, and State), the judicial system, and government for the Northwest Territory. Taxes had to be levied; and appropriations had to be made. Laws were passed regulating patents and copyrights, governing bankruptcies, controlling harbors, and punishing crimes, as well as regulating naturalization, importing of slaves, and relations with Indians. This Congress also also offered the first constitutional amendments—the Bill of Rights—to the state legislatures for ratification.

Busy as this first session was, the House was small and unheralded in its early years. When Congress first met in Federal Hall in New York City, the House had only 59 members. The first Senate had only 22 of its full complement of 26 senators. This was because two of the original 13 states had not yet

A new capitol for a new nation. The national Capitol building in Washington, D.C., symbolizes the unity and sovereignty of the nation. Begun in the 1790s, the Capitol was not completed until after the Civil War. When the Capitol was first occupied by Congress in 1800 [upper left], the House of Representatives shared the first floor with the Supreme Court, while the Senate chamber occupied the second floor. In the middle of the 19th century, new wings of the building were added for the House and Senate. In 1861 [upper right], the new Senate wing was nearly finished, while the House wing and dome were still under construction. Adornments were added to the Capitol from time to time. In 1916, sculptural work was completed. "Hope Protecting Genius," the first figure of the House pediment, is shown being hoisted into position [lower left]. Scaffolding had to be built to complete the House pediment [lower right]. The completed sculptural grouping is known as "The Apotheosis of Democracy."

ratified the Constitution. The Senate first met in secret. Thus, its activities were even more distant to ordinary citizens than were those of the House. In its early days, the Senate was much preoccupied with procedure. And some of this may seem odd today. For instance, Vice President John Adams worried the Senate over what title to use when addressing the President. At one point, "His Highness, the President of the United States and Protector of the Rights of the Same" was seriously proposed! But good sense prevailed; almost all agreed to "George Washington, President of the United States." For his somewhat tiresome preoccupation with this issue, the rather portly Adams was given the title "His Rotundity" by an irreverent Senate colleague.

At first, the House clearly overshadowed the Senate in status and power; it seemed to be the center of emerging national decision making. It was also the focus of attention to the extent Americans took an interest in their nascent national institutions. As the nation grew westward and became more populous, the House grew, as well. There were fewer than 60 at its first sitting. By 1910 the House grew to 435 members but then its size was capped. The preeminence of the House of Representatives did not last long. The smaller Senate, equally representing the large and small states, came to hold the limelight. Here was a center of freewheeling debate and celebrated executive functions: approving treaties; giving or withholding consent to presidential nominees for posts in the executive branch.

There were two characteristics in the evolution of Congress: growth of the committee system, and establishment of political parties and party leadership. The first few Congresses were so small that committees were not seen as necessary. Some temporary committees were appointed; most of the business of the House was conducted without committees. The standing, or permanent, committees of Congress grew up over the years. The House Committee on Interstate and Foreign Commerce was the first major standing committee. It was formed in 1795 and is now called Energy and Commerce. The government moved to the new capital, Washington, D.C., in 1801. At this time, the House began to transform temporary committees into standing committees. Accordingly, Ways and Means, Post Office, Judiciary, Agriculture, military services committees, and Foreign Affairs were all established before the Civil War. With industrialization after the Civil War, new committees came into being—Appropriations, Banking and Currency, Merchant Marine and Fisheries, Education and Labor. It took the Senate a little longer to create a committee system. But by the 1820s it had established many standing committees that paralleled those in the House. The emerging committee system allowed a division of labor. Thus, a rapidly growing workload could be dealt with. Committees allowed individual congressmen and senators to become experts on a limited number of policy issues. With this expertise, the legislature could effectively enact laws.

Political parties are nowhere mentioned in the Constitution. But party divisions arose fairly early in Congress. Policies advocated by Secretary of the Treasury Alexander Hamilton—those providing for payment of federal and state debts and creating a national bank—gained the warm support of business and commercial interests. They also stimulated the opposition of congressmen speaking for farm interests. James Madison became the key House leader opposing the programs of Washington and Hamilton. By 1800, Democratic-Republican Thomas Jefferson was elected president; his followers also captured a majority of both House and Senate from the Federalists. Partisanship became a central feature of congressional life by the end of the 19th century. At this point, especially the House was dominated by unified parties with strong leaders. Speakers like Thomas B. Reed and Joseph G. Cannon had so much influence they were called "czars." Beginning in the 1920s, congressional party battles came to be less fierce. Central questions of public policy—tariffs, taxes, foreign policy, economic regulation, government management—fell into the hands of experts. These specialists on committees and staffs made their policy decisions on the basis of special interests, knowledge, or "scientific" criteria. Partisan political considerations became less important.

By roughly 1900, Congress had a modern form and had become an autonomous body. It had a complex committee system and party leadership. It was also able to operate independently of the president in many ways. Traditions evolved concerning the conduct of members. There were settled rules of the game, written and unwritten. These permitted effective lawmaking; they also gave an air of dignity and formality to the process. The well-developed committee system and stable two-party structure gave coherence to many of the major policy questions facing Congress and the country. Congress had proved to be a durable, resilient, adaptive political body (Jewell and Patterson, 1977:30–59). Today, Congress is a large, highly complex organization. It has more than 300 committees and subcommittees; its members and committees employ more than 16,000 staff people; and it is deeply and innovatively involved in formulating and enacting the laws of the land.

INSTITUTION-ALIZING THE PRESIDENCY

The American government under its first constitution had no chief executive. Advocates of a new constitution believed effective national government required a "vigorous executive." Alexander Hamilton defended the presidency in No. 70 of *The Federalist*. Here, he argued that "energy in the executive is a leading character in the definition of good government," so "a feeble executive implies a feeble execution of the government."

George Washington had great stature as the first president. As we explained, he readily became a national symbol. He also performed the office in such a way that national identity was enhanced and the new government was seen as legitimate. But Washington and the other presidents who served in the early years had no models to follow. They were elected president, limited in term in office and powers, in a free republic. And this was a novelty, a new invention. Moreover, the early presidents were not always the center of attention. Thomas Jefferson walked to his inauguration. Cabinet members and legislators often outshone the president in fame and social prominence. The White House was drafty and uncomfortable. (Until the turn of this century, sheep grazed on the lawn.) Like a pendulum, influence and leadership swung between "weak" and "strong" presidents.

The modern presidency rests on the action of strong leaders. By dint of personality or strong response to crisis, presidents have expanded their powers. In turn, what the public expects of them has grown.

The first of these strong leaders was Andrew Jackson (1829–1837), the first presidential candidate backed by a coherent political party. The Democrats had become a powerful, national force. And the Jacksonians, the party leaders, remade the party system. They began the national nominating convention and the modern campaign with its noise and hoopla. In the 1828 election, the electorate mushroomed; three times more votes were cast for president than four years before.

Jackson used the constitutional and political powers of the presidency in impressive ways. The **spoils system** (patronage) was used to reward the party faithful. The system of "rotation in office" gave loyal partisans government jobs and turned out opponents. Jackson was the first to use the veto extensively to get Congress to accede to his wishes. He used the cabinet more effectively than his predecessors. In it he assembled loyal and trusted friends. He also had an

George Washington was inaugurated the first president of the United States on April 30, 1789. He was sworn in at Federal Hall in New York City, the capital not having been built at Washington, D.C., as yet. Since a chief justice of the Supreme Court had not been appointed, Washington took the oath from Robert R. Livingston, Chancellor of the state of New York.

President Ronald Reagan takes the oath of office as president of the United States. Chief Justice Warren Berger administers the oath.

able corps of informal advisers, known as the "kitchen cabinet." These were the forerunners of today's White House advisers.

Abraham Lincoln (1861–65) was the next person to leave a substantial imprint on the presidency. No president before or since confronted the crisis of civil war; few have managed the office as forcefully or as shrewdly. In the midst of the national emergency, Lincoln demonstrated the outer reaches of the president's "war powers." He took a more forceful role as commander-in-chief than any president. He used the president's power to "take care that the laws be faithfully executed," justifying drastic steps to save the union.

Perhaps Lincoln's most memorable action was the Emancipation Proclamation freeing the slaves. Lincoln called his cabinet to the White House in September 1862 to read them a draft of the proclamation. When the cabinet arrived, Lincoln insisted on reciting a chapter from the book he was reading—a tale by humorist Artemus Ward. Lincoln told his puzzled advisers that the strain of the presidency was so great he needed relief. "If I did not laugh I should die." He then took a paper from his stovepipe hat. It was the proclamation which he read to the cabinet. He formally signed the proclamation on January 1, 1863. Lincoln later described it as "the central act of my administration, and the great event of the 19th century."

After a nearly 40-year eclipse, Theodore Roosevelt (1901–09) brought life back to the presidency. He was probably the most popular president since Jackson. He was strong and vigorous, a sometime cowboy, big game hunter, and war hero (the Battle of San Juan Hill during the Spanish-American War). In domestic politics, Roosevelt stood for trust-busting and wages and hours laws. He also favored government regulation to stop abuses in packinghouses, railroads, and other industries. Roosevelt was an outdoorsman and early conservationist and worked hard for national parks and forests.

In foreign affairs, Roosevelt was an unabashed activist. His motto was that the United States should "speak softly, and carry a big stick." Thus, he acted boldly in construction of the Panama Canal. Despite congressional disapproval, he sent the fleet around the world to show off American seapower. And he helped negotiate an end to the Russo-Japanese War. This last contribution made him the first American president to win the Nobel Peace Prize.

Implementing presidential prerogatives. President Abraham Lincoln meets with his cabinet members for the first reading of the Emancipation Proclamation, a presidential proclamation affirming that slaves in any district of rebellion would be "thenceforward, and forever free."

When the presidency was a fairly leisurely "bully pulpit." As the nation's 26th president (1901–09), Theodore Roosevelt could operate with a small staff and a relaxed schedule. Here "Teddy" Roosevelt confers in the White House Oval Office with one of his handful of assistants, William Loeb.

To back up his wide conception of presidential powers, Roosevelt espoused the so-called **stewardship theory.** In his autobiography (1927: 357), he described the theory. "[E]xecutive power was limited only by specific restrictions and prohibitions appearing in the Constitution or imposed by the Congress under its [c]onstitutional powers."

The modern presidency owes its greatest debt to Theodore Roosevelt's distant cousin, Franklin Delano Roosevelt (1933–45). FDR served in a challenging period that encompassed the Great Depression, and World War II. FDR's administration is called the New Deal because it was a bold experiment with public policies designed to improve the economy and the well-being of citizens. The basic outlines of FDR's program laid the path to today's welfare state. It included social security and industrial legislation. Roosevelt's grand plan for winning World War II and his world view in postwar planning (including the United Nations) were the framework for America's activist role in world affairs.

Since the New Deal, presidents have followed the Roosevelt model, whatever their politics. The public expects presidents to be strong, to exert leadership, to range widely, and to resolve public problems. The common thread of the past 50 years is the institutional nature of the presidency. One precedent set by FDR was categorically rejected: his breaking the "two-term tradition" when he ran for a third term in 1940. (And again when he was elected to a fourth term in 1944.) The two-term limitation on presidential tenure was reinstated with the 22nd Amendment in 1951.

American politics are, after all, remarkably stable. And much of the modern presidency represents continuity with past conceptions and traditions. Accordingly, the Constitution mentions "executive departments" and "heads of departments," but not the president's cabinet. It was just assumed that department secretaries would serve as advisers to the president. Practices have varied and the number of departments has grown. But cabinet customs that started with George Washington persist in great part to this day (Fenno, 1959).

There is more striking change in the staffing of the presidency. Washington had only one assistant, a nephew whom he paid out of his own pocket. Thomas Jefferson managed as president with a messenger and an occasional clerk. More than 100 years later, Woodrow Wilson led the country through World War I with only seven assistants. But in 1939, Franklin D. Roosevelt established the

Symbol of hope. FDR, shown greeting constituents in 1933, was a tireless and skillful campaigner (note his traditional campaign hat) who relished the campaign challenge. He aroused intense feelings among both friends and foes.

FIGURE 2–5

Growth of the Institutionalized Presidency: Roosevelt to Reagan

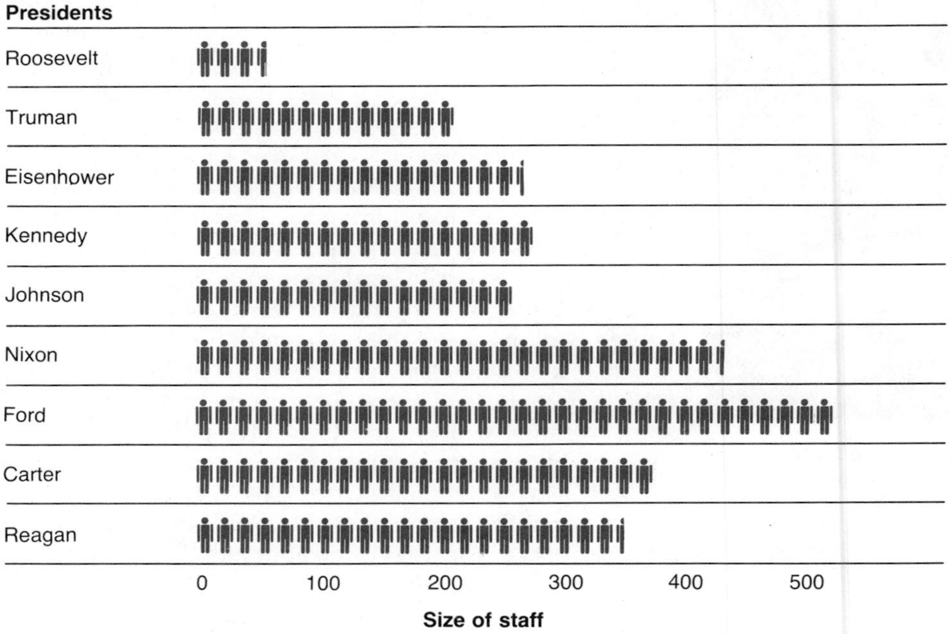

Note: Figures are the average budgeted positions for the White House Office for the years of each respective presidency, beginning with creation of the Executive Office of the President in 1939.

Source: U.S. House of Representatives, Committee On Post Office and Civil Service, Subcommittee on Employee Ethics and Utilization. *Presidential Staffing-A Brief Overview*, committee print (95th Congress, 2nd session, 1978), p. 57. Recent figures are from Budget of the United States (Appendix).

Executive Office of the President to provide effective staff support. As Figure 2–5 shows, since Roosevelt's presidency the White House staff has grown. By the 1980s, about 350 staff people were provided by the budget for the White House Office; others often work for the White House on loan from executive branch agencies. Today, when we speak of the President of the United States we are not referring merely to a lonely figure toiling away in the Oval Office. The institutionalized presidency involves the person of the president, to be sure. But it includes also the advisers, cabinet officers, and staff specialists who constitute the presidential office.

The growth of the court system

The federal judicial body has always been fairly small. The Supreme Court was provided for in Article III of the Constitution. It first met after the passage of the Judiciary Act of 1789. Of the six justices appointed, one turned down the post and one resigned without attending a session. The other four met in the Royal Exchange building in New York City as the first Supreme Court. They started what came to be a very potent part of our constitutional system. This was the role of the Court in interpreting the meaning of a constitution with a good deal of unclear language (McCloskey, 1960).

The size of the Supreme Court changed more than once in the 1800s; today there are nine justices. The 1789 act, much of which is still in force, created 13 district courts and 3 circuit courts. The number of federal judicial jobs was only 115 in 1816. In 1881, the federal court system grew, causing a sudden leap in the number of jobs to about 2,700. From then until 1946, the number stayed under 3,000. Since then, the workload of the federal courts has grown sharply.

There has been enormous growth in the last two decades in requests that the Supreme Court review lower court decisions. However, the number of cases on the Court's docket, or agenda, has grown only gradually. Figure 2–6 shows that in the 1980s the Supreme Court has more than 5,000 cases on its agenda each year. With a continuing membership of only nine justices, the Court's workload must remain fairly constant. But the lower federal courts have grown. Numbers of courts, judges, and other court staff (bailiffs, clerks, and other officers) have increased. Thus, by 1982, the federal courts employed well over 15,000 people. As Figure 2–6 dramatizes, the workload of the federal trial and appeals courts has risen quite steadily for the past 20 years.

Historically, courts have played an important role in the United States. The Supreme Court's power of judicial review gives it a part in adjusting the meaning of the Constitution as historical circumstances change. More broadly, in a society governed by law and insistent upon equality, many will bring their grievances to court. Ours is a litigious society. Citizens are very prone to sue, to take an adversary to court. Thus, we have great need of courts, and a developing judicial system to master an ever-growing demand for justice in court.

FIGURE 2–6

The Mushrooming Workload of the U.S. Courts

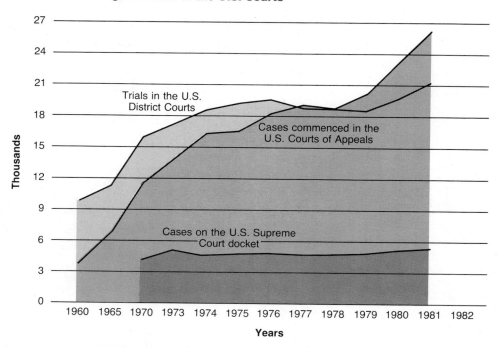

Source: *Statistical Abstract of the United States, 1982–83* (Washington, D.C.: U.S. Government Printing Office, 1982), p. 187.

Delivering the mail. The U.S. Postal Service, one of the largest federal agencies, employs about 660,000 employees.

The burgeoning bureaucracy

The federal government's bureaucracy has mushroomed in size and scope since the departments of State, War, and Treasury were first set up in 1789. Most of its expansion occurred in the 20th century. During the 1800s the bureaucracy grew but slowly. In 1821, there were fewer than 7,000 federal civilian employees; by the 1920s, their number was more than one-half million, with a large increase around the turn of the century (1890–1910). This bureaucratic growth was the government's response to industrialization. It was a reaction to late 19th century demands for government to regulate economic development and facilitate economic expansion. Industrialism fostered the growth of the federal government, "fortified with an independent arm of national administrative action" (Skowronek, 1982: 286). The second great burst of growth in federal bureaucracy came with the New Deal as the government initiated new, large-scale welfare programs and expanded its regulatory activities.

Today, the federal bureaucracy is unquestionably enormous. The executive branch is big, complex, and far-flung. It is made up of 13 cabinet departments; some 60 major agencies, boards, and commissions and 100 smaller units of these types; 850 interagency committees; hundreds of citizens' advisory groups; and dozens of presidential commissions, committees, and task forces. One of the largest federal executive agencies is the U.S. Postal Service. With more than 660,000 employees, it alone is far larger than was the whole federal bureaucracy before the 1890s.

At the same time, there has, in fact, been little growth in the federal establishment since World War II. As Figure 2–7 indicates, direct federal civilian employment actually dropped between 1971 and 1981. But this decline can be misleading. Perhaps 10 to 12 million people are indirectly employed by the federal government as consultants or contractors, or are paid through federal grants.

Today, civilian employment in federal agencies is about 2.9 million. But, as Figure 2–7 shows, total state and local government employment is much larger. It has also grown at a much faster rate. More than 13 million people work for state and local government (more than half of these in public education). And they make up over 82 percent of all government workers. State and local agencies have grown by more than 220 percent in the last 30 years. This has occurred both because of new federal programs that states and localities administer, and because states and localities expanded their own services.

The governing institutions which evolved under the Constitution over the 200-year history of our nation have changed in many ways. They have become larger in scale, and perform more complex functions. Today, the party system and the system of congressional politics are still engaged in adapting to the bureaucratization of government. Considering the enormity of change in modern life, it is perhaps most remarkable that our governing institutions have retained so much of their original form and substance.

CONCLUSIONS

The political development of the United States pinpoints main facets of political stability and change over the past 200 years. In viewing the problems of our political development, we may conclude that:

1 An unmistakable national identity emerged early in the history of the republic. It remained a marked feature of political life except for the major breach brought about by the Civil War. An unprece-

FIGURE 2–7

The Growth of Bureaucracy in the United States

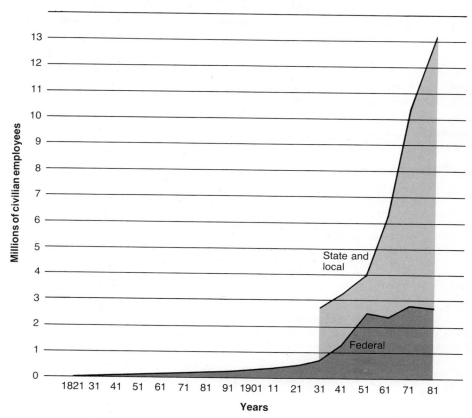

Sources: *Historical Statistics of the United States* (Washington, D.C.: U.S. Government Printing Office, 1975), pp. 1102, 1104; *Statistical Abstract of the United States* (Washington, D.C.: U.S. Government Printing Office, various years).

dented flood of immigrants was absorbed by the system. These new Americans embraced a national identity while often keeping a distinct cultural and ethnic identity.

2 The new American regime gained legitimacy almost at its start. The Constitution was widely accepted. The governing establishment in Washington, centering on Congress, evolved from a very modest start to become complex and extensive. The major governing bodies—Congress, the presidency, the bureaucracy, and the courts—grew in size and in the scope of their powers. But they retained the basic forms set forth for them in the Constitution.

3 Our political system was the first experiment in running democratic government over such a large area. The government reached the countryside because from the start it was active in fostering commerce and industry. The federal system provided an effective means for adding new territory to the union. It took new people into the body politic. The invention of a competitive party system in which political groups sought mass support allowed ordinary citizens into politics and promoted orderly political change. Expansion was by no means easy. But the nation systematicaly did so to govern a continent. It used a system that allowed and even encouraged a great deal of political localism, while at the same time its electoral politics became increasingly nationalized.

4 In modern terms, the republic was hardly democratic at its founding. Constant struggle, even violence, was needed to make it more democratic. But our political system became more and more participatory. The development of political parties and party opposition gave us a mechanism for active political participation in the electoral process.

5 In an environment rich in resources, shrewd people were able to spur rapid economic growth and gain material affluence. This confirms how well the constitutional system can work. Although the benefits of economic growth were not equally dis-

tributed, they were widely distributed. The main distributive principle, equal opportunity, emphasized private initiative and individual productivity in an economy that was almost always richer than those of other nations. Those who did not share in the general wealth—factory workers in the early 1900s and many blacks in recent years—often protested to improve their condition. Because equality is a widely held principle, demands for equality in social, economic, or political benefits have always been on the governing agenda.

FURTHER READING

CHAMBERS, WILLIAM NISBET, and WALTER DEAN BURNHAM, eds. (1975) The American Party Systems. 2d ed. New York: Oxford University Press. Various authors analyze the role of political parties in the development of the American political system, and identify major stages of development.

ELAZAR, DANIEL J. (1972) American Federalism: A View from the States. 2d ed. New York: Thomas Y. Crowell Company. A very perceptive examination of the role of the states in the American federal system featuring an analysis of the effects of differing state political cultures on federal politics.

HOLLINGSWORTH, J. ROGERS (1978) "The United States," in Crises of Political Development in Europe and the United States. Edited by Raymond Grew. Princeton, N. J.: Princeton University Press, pp. 163–195. A unique, if brief, analysis of the importance of "crises" in the political development of the United States.

SKOWRONEK, STEPHEN (1982) Building a New American State. Cambridge: Cambridge University Press. An account of the expansion of the administrative arm of the national government between 1877 and 1920.

YOUNG, JAMES S. (1966) The Washington Community, 1800–1828. New York: Columbia University Press. A fascinating portrayal of life in the nation's capitol in its infancy, including an interesting and controversial analysis of the development of national government beginning with the Jefferson administration.

3
The Political Beliefs of Americans

In 1961, Congress recognized Samuel Wilson as the namesake of a national symbol. His name is not exactly a household word today. But during the War of 1812 he was a major supplier of beef to the U.S. Army. His barrels of beef were marked "U.S." to show they were government property. His nickname, Uncle Sam, came to be identified with the "U.S." stamped on the beef. And so the nickname Uncle Sam came to refer to the U.S. government. Cartoonists such as Thomas Nast, who caricatured Uncle Sam in the 1870s, portrayed him as a tall, thin, craggy old man with goatee, top hat, and striped pants. Later, the stars and stripes of our flag adorned his clothes.

In 1956, Congress changed the name of Bedloe's Island in New York Harbor to Liberty Island. On that island has stood, since 1886, the statue of the Goddess of Liberty, a 151-foot-high, copper-skinned likeness of a lady in flowing robes. She is crowned with a diadem and holds a torch high in her right hand. Cradled in her left arm is a scroll inscribed with the date July 4, 1776. The statue, sculpted by Frédéric Auguste Bartholdi, was a gift to the United States from the people of France. A poem by Emma Lazarus, inscribed inside the pedestal, closes with the famous invitation:

> Give me your tired, your poor,
> Your huddled masses yearning to breathe free,
> The wretched refuse of your teeming shore.
> Send these, the homeless, tempest-tost to me,
> I lift my lamp beside the golden door!

Symbol of freedom and equality. The Statue of Liberty has stood in New York Harbor since 1886.

Uncle Sam symbolizes civic duty and vigilance. He can be stern and demanding; he wants you to serve your country. He has been depicted as being hoodwinked and cheated, as a benefactor, and as a person who fights corruption. The Goddess of Liberty is a symbol of freedom and equality. She is America the Bountiful, America the Land of the Free, America the Land of Opportunity. Uncle Sam and the Goddess of Liberty are symbols of our political culture. They stand for the beliefs, attitudes, and values of our political society.

* * * * *

Americans hold a wide variety of beliefs about how the political system works. They have ideas about the roles of individuals and leaders in the system, values about the nature of political life, and conceptions of what government should

68

Symbol of civic duty. In this famous poster designed to attract army recruits, Uncle Sam sternly calls on Americans to perform their duty as citizens by serving in the armed forces.

and should not do. In this chapter, we draw attention to basic American political beliefs in liberty and equality, religious freedom, and property rights; we discuss the kinds of things Americans know and do not know about their political world, and their degree of awareness of public affairs; we consider the extent of political trust, and of cyncical beliefs about politics; and we assess the place of ideology in American politics. Then we turn to how political beliefs, values, or attitudes are acquired by Americans. We explain how Americans' attitudes toward their nation and government evolve as individuals mature. We discuss beliefs about the president and attitudes toward political parties as outlooks which especially play a role in political life. Then we consider how Americans acquire their particular values, beliefs, attitudes, identities, and attachments. Finally, we take into account some important racial and ethnic variations in acquiring patterns of political beliefs.

BASIC POLITICAL BELIEFS

The American liberal tradition stresses the values of liberty, equality, religious expression, and protection of property. Their most celebrated statement is in the Declaration of Independence. Jefferson wrote: "We hold these truths to be self-evident, that all men are created equal, that they are endowed by their Creator with certain unalienable Rights, that among these are Life, Liberty and the Pursuit of Happiness."

Freedom of expression

Free expression. Americans practice the freedom to dissent, and to organize for the purpose of protecting their interests. Before the 1975 national convention of the Communist Party U.S.A., General Secretary Gus Hall and activist Angela Davis speak at a press conference.

Attitudes toward freedom of speech and press and tolerance of unpopular opinions show the American belief in liberty. Freedom and tolerance are, as a rule, basic to the idea of democracy. Democratic government depends on the freedom of minorities to fault majority decisions and to try to win support for their views. At the same time, we have always known that liberty is not absolute. We are protected from personal damage by libel laws. These laws ban speech or writing that damages one's reputation by making false claims. Moreover, freedom of expression is limited by laws forbidding the violent overthrow of the government.

Most Americans have a basic belief in freedom of speech and other personal liberties. But in practice they often condone the suppression of extremist opinions. In 1965 many upheld the right to demonstrate peaceably against the Vietnam War. But by 1970 most opposed unrestrained freedom to criticize the government if it could damage the national interest. They also opposed the unrestrained freedom of extremist groups to protest. And unrestrained freedom of speech for communists gets little support. In short, we accept the general democratic principle of freedom of expression. But we also believe it cannot be absolute and unrestrained. Unfortunately, many of us are intolerant of unpopular ideas. The ideal of liberty is widely espoused. But it is often not practiced. "What is surprising," according to a recent study, "is the frequency with which many Americans, though endorsing civil liberties in the abstract, reject them in their concrete application" (McClosky and Brill, 1983: 417).

A classic study of Americans' attitudes toward communists and atheists was made in 1954. It showed two thirds of Americans favored removing books by communists from public libraries, not letting someone speak against churches and religion, and forbidding communists to speak publicly (Stouffer, 1966: 32–42). Since then, we seem to have become much more tolerant of nonconformist opinions and their expression (Nunn, Crockett, and Williams, 1978). An inquiry into tolerance of communists and atheists in 1982 can be compared with the attitudes analyzed in 1954 (see Figure 3–1). It shows this marked increase in tolerance.

More people today would allow a communist or an atheist to teach in a college or university than in 1954. A majority, though, still is opposed. Also large numbers of Americans now appear to accept free expression for homosexuals. Although Americans today may be more tolerant of communists or atheists than they were 25 years ago, tolerance of other kinds of nonconformity—antinuclear demonstrators, antiwar radicals, black separatists—may be low. Educated people are much more likely to be tolerant than are the uneducated. To some extent, education measures a person's ability to think abstractly and conceptualize problems. Those with some college education have been taught to "think

FIGURE 3—1

Changes in American Tolerance of Nonconformity

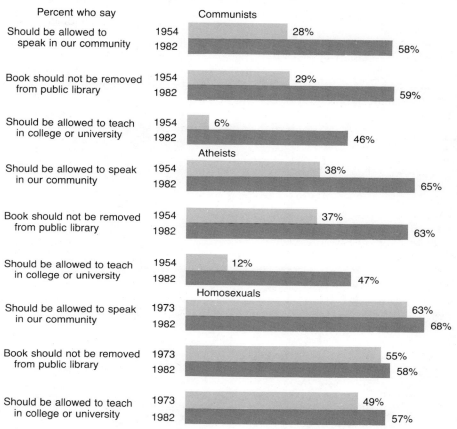

Percent who say

Communists

Should be allowed to speak in our community	1954	28%
	1982	58%
Book should not be removed from public library	1954	29%
	1982	59%
Should be allowed to teach in college or university	1954	6%
	1982	46%

Atheists

Should be allowed to speak in our community	1954	38%
	1982	65%
Book should not be removed from public library	1954	37%
	1982	63%
Should be allowed to teach in college or university	1954	12%
	1982	47%

Homosexuals

Should be allowed to speak in our community	1973	63%
	1982	68%
Book should not be removed from public library	1973	55%
	1982	58%
Should be allowed to teach in college or university	1973	49%
	1982	57%

Sources: Samuel A. Stouffer, *Communism, Conformity, and Civil Liberties* (New York: John Wiley, & Sons. 1966), pp. 32–46; *Public Opinion* 5 (October/November 1982), p. 35.

about the world in a way that those with only an elementary school education cannot" (Jackman, 1972: 769). So, tolerance of nonconformity is likely to grow as more Americans get college educations.

Of course, our belief in liberty often includes much more than freedom of expression and tolerance of nonconformity. For most people, freedom includes freedom of movement, job choice, and privacy. Some believe their liberty should include the right to have an abortion; others think the unborn possess a "right to life." The Gallup poll has shown a sharp split in public attitudes toward abortion. Nearly equal proportions of Americans favor and oppose a constitutional amendment prohibiting abortions except where the life of the mother is in danger. People are more likely to *act* on the basis of intense feelings on issues such as abortion, than on the basis of more casual opinions. Many Catholics intensely oppose abortions; college-educated Protestants intensely favor permitting them (Blake, 1971: 540–49).

Another disputed freedom is the right to own guns. Opinions are also highly intense on this issue. Nearly half of all American families own at least one gun.

Public opinion polls, or surveys, provide a wealth of information about what people think and do. Sometimes it is hard to understand how the thinking of more than 200 million Americans can be estimated accurately by polling. The key to making estimates from these polls is sampling. Modern polls and surveys use what is called **probability sampling.** This draws national samples of 1,200 to 2,000 people in such a way that everyone has a known chance of being chosen as part of the sample.

Poll results are estimates, not precise figures. The **sampling error** of polls such as the Gallup poll, the Harris survey, or those of the Survey Research Center at the University of Michigan is about 3 percent. Say a poll indicates that 18 percent favor complete freedom of speech for Communist party members to speak on the radio. This means that *actual* support for free radio speech for Communists lies between 15 percent and 21 percent. The science of sample surveys is so highly developed now that opinion polls can be very accurate estimates. In fact, much of the official census is taken by polling.

Question wording can make a big difference in poll results. Often the Gallup and Harris polls show differ-ent results because they ask slightly different questions. A good example of this kind of discrepancy occurred when both the Gallup and Harris polls took the public's pulse about former President Jimmy Carter's effectiveness. These polls were taken in 1977. The Gallup poll showed that 59 percent approved of how Carter was handling his job as President; only 24 percent disapproved. In contrast, the Harris survey conducted at the same time showed that 48 percent approved and 48 percent disapproved.

The Gallup poll asked: "Do you approve or disapprove of the way Carter is handling his job as President?" The Harris survey asked people to rate the President's performance on a four-point scale—excellent, pretty good, only fair, and poor. For Harris, "excellent" and "pretty good" ratings constitute approval; "only fair" and "poor" constitute disapproval. It is undoubtedly easier to say that the President's performance is "only fair" than to disapprove of his performance. Indeed, many may regard an "only fair" performance as a positive evaluation, about the best that can be expected.

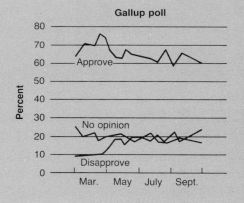

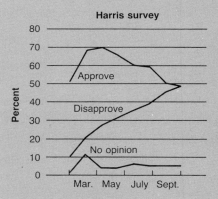

The Gallup poll has shown that about two thirds of Americans (about half of gun owners and three fourths of nonowners) favored gun control laws. However, millions feel strongly that gun ownership is a constitutional right that should not be limited in any way.

Political equality

Like belief in liberty, equality is a part of the liberal tradition in our country. As we saw in Chapter 1, the belief in and practice of equality have been especially pronounced in the American experience. The Constitution was meant to

'I DON'T KNOW ABOUT YOU, BUT I'M GOING BACK TO TEA LEAVES AND EYE OF NEWT.'

enshrine *political* equality—equality before the law, or equal treatment by the government. So we expect equal treatment from government even though we do not always get it. Generally, we are not very deferential to authority. In 1939, when the British king and queen came to the United States, a Gallup poll found that most people approved of the visit. However, two thirds of those polled said they would not curtsy or bow. They would shake hands with the visiting royalty. If such a question were posed today, the results would surely be similar.

In regard to equal treatment under the law—civil rights—the most glaring disparities have existed. The tortured struggle of blacks to gain full civil rights is only too well known. The civil rights movement of the 1960s did make great strides in protecting the rights of blacks. But discrimination lingers. Only a minority of whites see that discrimination against blacks still exists. (An exception is decent housing. More than half of all whites feel that blacks are discriminated against here.) Yet two thirds or more of blacks experience prejudice in housing, jobs, and police treatment. Blacks are four times as likely as whites to feel discrimination in their treatment by the federal government.

Minority rights. In the 1960s, blacks led by Dr. Martin Luther King, Jr. demonstrated in support of civil rights. The civil rights movement championed by Dr. King made a major contribution to the passage of legislation by Congress. In 1983 Dr. King's birthday was made a national holiday by Congress.

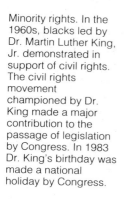

The views of whites toward black civil rights have changed greatly since the 1950s. Whites have become far more supportive of nondiscrimination in race relations. Black views have changed as well. Nevertheless, support for racial integration has declined in some cities with large black populations, such as Detroit (Aberbach and Walker, 1973). This is partly because many whites think black progress in integration has moved too quickly. But it is also partly because black leaders are no longer sure of unified support for integration programs in the black community. Also, many black leaders have moved beyond support for integration to work for improvements in the black community itself. This includes more inner-city jobs for blacks or busing school children to achieve racial balance.

Rights of property

The framers of the Constitution thought human freedom depended on the sanctity of property. They defended the Constitution because it vowed to help protect their property. Under the Constitution, government cannot take private property for public use without fair payment to the owner. It states that "no person shall be deprived of life, liberty, or property without due process of law." Views concerning property are shown in the widely held belief in private property and widespread opposition to government ownership or operation of basic industries (Devine, 1972: 206–11). Also, our feelings about property are shown by emphasis on making money and the high value given work and its rewards.

The government routinely and properly takes part of our property in the form of taxes. Personal income taxes are at least in name, progressive; that is, the percentage of income paid in taxes goes up as income goes up. In contrast, property taxes and sales taxes are regressive; that is, such taxes take more from low-income people than from high-income people. Because of this, one might expect low-income people to favor income taxes, and high-income people to favor property and sales taxes. Surveys concerning forms of taxation do lean very slightly in these directions. But, strangely, Americans' attitudes toward the fairness or unfairness of different forms of taxation do not differ much by income levels.

For at least the last 20 years, we have complained about high taxes. Starting in 1978, this discontent could be seen in several states where laws were passed limiting state and local taxes. The most famous of these "tax revolts" was Proposition 13 in California, which limited property taxes. Recent public opinion polls show that about 80 percent of Americans think our taxes are unreasonable. And many feel the income tax system is unfair. A CBS News/*New York Times* Poll in mid-1978 showed that 55 percent felt that way. The strongest objection to the income tax came from those in the higher-income groups.

Religion in America

Religious ideas are certainly central to our beliefs. These ideas often have political implications. Freedom of religion was fundamental to the colonists and to the founders of the nation. There is little doubt that ours is a religious country. A 1971 Gallup Poll showed that about 9 percent of Americans were agnos-

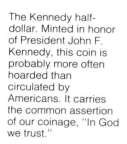

The Kennedy half-dollar. Minted in honor of President John F. Kennedy, this coin is probably more often hoarded than circulated by Americans. It carries the common assertion of our coinage, ''In God we trust.''

tics, 11 percent were atheists, and 77 percent believed in God. Recent Gallup Polls have shown that 9 out of 10 people believe in God or a universal spirit. In 1981, about 70 percent of those polled said they believed there is a Heaven. In 1983, 7 out of 10 Americans claimed to be members of a church or synagogue; 40 percent said they had attended a house of worship in the past seven days. In a 1978 survey, 40 percent said they had ''been 'born again' or had a 'born again' experience, that is, a turning point in your life when you committed yourself to Christ.''

Prayer is an important part of many public events in this country. In 1969, nearly 7 out of 10 Americans favored keeping the words *under God* in the Pledge of Allegiance. These words had been added by Congress in 1954. The words *In God we trust* appear on our coins. Polls have shown that most people believe both in the separation of church and state and in the basic religious character of our political tradition. More broadly, Americans show a large measure of humanitarianism and moralism toward disadvantaged people and in their feelings about the role of their country in world affairs (Almond, 1950).

To say that our political culture is one in which beliefs in liberty, equality, property, and religion are widely shared does not mean America is a democratic paradise. Our basic political beliefs are, in everyday use, disagreed on and sometimes poorly applied. There is always prejudice and bigotry. Even organized bigotry, such as that of the Ku Klux Klan and the American Nazi party, persists and is free to do so. Moreover, democratic values often conflict. Social welfare may conflict with drives to make money. Beliefs in liberty and equality may conflict; busing to promote equality of education for blacks limits the right of parents to choose the schools their children attend. Rights of property and liberty may conflict; an example is when cities take private property for parks and transportation facilities.

Priorities among these basic political beliefs are changing. Property rights have become more regulated as government has sought to cope with the growth and influence of business corporations. The civil rights movement of the last generation brought liberty to the forefront and gave it high priority. Our society now perhaps values liberty over achievement. Tax and welfare policies have, since the New Deal of the '30s, changed the value of equality. Still, in both their constancy and their changes, liberty, equality, property, and religion are at the core of our political beliefs.

WHAT AMERICANS KNOW ABOUT POLITICS

Americans' political awareness

Americans are not true political animals. They do not have much interest in or concern for politics and government in their daily lives. Many Americans know little about political events, officials, and institutions. A *Playboy* poll in 1977 showed that only 35 percent know that "GOP" stands for "Grand Old Party"— the nickname for the Republicans. Other polls have shown that only about one fifth of the people can name the legislative, executive, and judicial branches of the federal government. In 1975, on the eve of our bicentennial, 3 in 10 could not name the important event of 1776. But more than 80 percent knew that in 1492 Columbus discovered America!

Many people do not know the names and parties of major politicians. Of course, the president is highly visible. Most Americans know his name and party. Also, many know who their state governor is. But historical figures and entertainers are, on the whole, much better known than members of Congress.

According to the polls, 92 percent can identify Christopher Columbus, 88 percent know that Joe Namath played football, and more than 80 percent can identify William Shakespeare and Ludwig van Beethoven. Yet, in a *Washington Post*/ABC News poll taken in December 1983, only 10 percent or less could recognize the names of George McGovern, Gary Hart, Reubin Askew, and Ernest Hollings as Democratic candidates for the presidential nomination. Nearly half recognized the candidacy of Walter Mondale, the front runner; two fifths recognized that John Glenn was a candidate; more than a third recognized Jesse Jackson; and 13 percent recognized Alan Cranston.

Fifty percent of those questioned in a 1970 Gallup poll said they had given little or no thought to the congressional election; 38 percent did not know the party of their congressman; and three fourths neither knew how their representative voted on any major bill nor knew of anything their congressman had done for the district in which they lived. In a Harris survey in 1973, 89 percent could name their state's governor. Only 59 percent could name one senator from their state. Only 39 percent could identify both senators. Apparently, more than a third of us do not clearly understand the makeup of Congress. A 1973 Harris survey showed that 62 percent knew that Congress consisted of the House of Representatives and the Senate. But 38 percent did not know. And about half of these thought Congress included the Supreme Court! The University of Michigan's National Election Study found that nearly 60 percent of those polled did not know that more Democrats than Republicans had been elected to the House in 1978. Eleven percent actually thought the Republicans had won more seats in the House than the Democrats that year. After the 1982 congressional election, the Michigan survey showed that only a third of Americans knew the names of candidates for the House and Senate in their locality.

Americans compared to others

These tests seem to show a lack of political awareness. However, it should be said that in America politicians are generally more visible to the public than in

Taking the public's pulse. Much of what we know about political behavior has been learned by polling. Here a Gallup pollster interviews a respondent.

many other countries. In 1968, 51 percent of Americans could not name a congressional candidate or his party. In Italy and the Netherlands the figures were 57 percent and 63 percent, respectively. And in 1967–68 the percentage of Americans who could name their congressman was higher than that of Australians who could name their national legislator. In West Germany in 1972, only 54 percent knew there was a legislator in the parliament who represented them. After the 1969 West German election, 61 percent said they did not know the names of any candidate. In Great Britain, only 49 percent of the voters could identify their member of Parliament in 1969.

Compared to people in other democratic countries, we are quite politically active and aware. In 1959–60, an unusual study undertaken in five democratic countries—the United States, England, West Germany, Italy, and Mexico—assessed the degree of political awareness and knowledge. This study showed that, compared to people in other countries, we have more interest in government and politics and pay more attention to political campaigns. We are more aware of political figures and more likely to have political opinions (Almond and Verba, 1963: 86–97). On balance, we do not go overboard on politics. But neither are we found lacking as citizens. We may not be political animals. But we are generally more politically involved than people in many other nations.

PRIDE, TRUST, AND CHANGE

Some constants and variations in our views toward the political system are especially intriguing. Most of us are proud of our system of government. But in the last 20 years our trust in the government and in our power to influence the system has declined sharply. Still, few of us feel that the system should be basically changed. This may seem to be a paradox. Let us consider pride in government institutions, trust in the government, and attitudes toward constitutional change.

National pride

Almost all observers of our political scene have noted a historically high degree of national pride. One study compared the national pride of Americans and people of four other countries. It showed that 85 percent of Americans expressed pride in their government and political institutions. Only 4 percent said they were proud of nothing. Our national pride was much higher than that in the other countries studied.

A 1972 University of Michigan Survey Research Center study showed that 86 percent of us were "proud of many things about our form of government." Only 14 percent could not "find much about our form of government to be proud of" (Citrin, 1974: 975). However, the level of pride fell after the events of the Nixon administration (the Watergate break-in and cover-up). These nearly brought about Nixon's impeachment and led him to resign—the first president to do so. Thus, in 1976 only 80 percent expressed pride in our form of government. One fifth said that there was little to be proud of. Nearly two thirds of those in the Survey Research Center's 1976 study said their lack of pride in government was a result of the acts of certain people in office. But a third felt there was "something more seriously wrong with government in general and the way it operates."

Although national pride declined in the early 1970s, it remained relatively

Pride in the nation. Max Cleland, legless, one-armed director of the Veterans' Administration during the presidency of Jimmy Carter, salutes during ceremonies commemorating the sacrifices of veterans of the Vietnam War.

high and seems to have increased in the 1980s. Most say they are extremely proud to be Americans and express pride especially in the liberties and freedoms they enjoy.

Americans may take pride in their country and form of government. But they have never been noted for their trust in politicians and government officials. The 19th-century writer Artemus Ward said on one Fourth of July: "I am not a politician, and my other habits are good." The poet e. e. cummings wrote a verse called "One Times One" in 1944. In it he said, "a politician is an arse upon which everyone has sat except a man." In *Pudd'nhead Wilson,* Mark Twain wrote: "It could probably be shown by facts and figures that there is no distinctly native American criminal class except Congress." Many Americans share this kind of cynicism.

Political trust

Americans have always distrusted political authorities. They do so today. Sample survey research now makes possible accurate estimates of how much citizens trust their government. These data point out the high levels of trust in the Eisenhower years and the marked decline since then. However, as Figure 3–2 suggests, political trust may be on the rise—marked by the increase in the percent who were trusting in 1982. The extent of trust in government is closely tied to class differences. Distrust is highest among the working and lower classes. Trust is highest among the middle and upper-middle class. Also, there is a marked difference between whites and blacks. Since the mid-1960s distrust has grown much more among blacks. Finally, Americans' trust in government may depend on their economic outlook; people may trust the government more when it seems to produce favorable economic conditions.

One political sociologist has two thoughts on the effects of political alienation. First, he notes a connection between the actual use of political influence and the belief that one *can* be influential. He concludes that "the alienated are drawn from social groups whose members characteristically participate little in politics, are inactive in political or other voluntary associations, and have little of the money, time, or resources that effective politicking requires." These politically alienated people probably have little effect on the political system as a whole. This is his portrait of the alienated (Wright, 1976: 165):

> The "typical" politically alienated person . . . is aging, poorly educated, and working class, unlikely to attend church, inattentive to the mass media, probably not interested or involved in much of anything outside the family, work, and perhaps a close circle of friends. The common suggestion that political alienation represents a "threat" to democratic regimes seems farfetched in light of these results.

Second, he shows that this alienation is not strongly related to other political feelings or actions. Because of their political isolation, it would be very hard to group the alienated into a mass political movement. Thus, Wright feels they pose little threat.

The decline in trust in government traced in Figure 3–2 could be repeated for most major institutions in the country. It was not only public confidence in government that declined after the mid-1960s. So did public confidence in business, labor, education, religion, the military, and the press. This general decline in confidence in major institutions seems to reflect loss of trust in those

FIGURE 3-2

Trends in Trust in Government

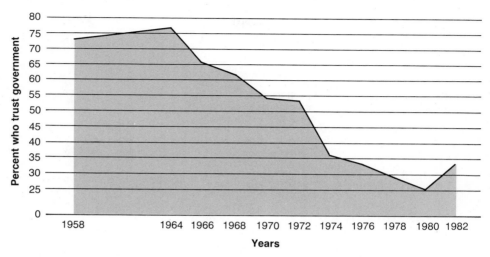

Sources: Paul R. Abramson, *Political Attitudes in America* (San Francisco: W. H. Freeman, 1983), p. 12; Arthur Miller, "Is Confidence Rebounding?" *Public Opinion* 6 (June-July 1983), p. 17.

running the institutions, rather than a crisis of legitimacy for the system as such (Lipset and Schneider, 1983: 375–412).

Attitudes toward change

In our country, distrust of government does not lead to widespread calls for change. The constitutional system has changed since 1790, partly through amendments. But support for basic changes is weak. In the 1940s, more than two thirds of us agreed that "our form of government . . . is as near perfect as it can be and no important changes should be made in it." About a fifth felt that "the Constitution . . . should be thoroughly revised to make it fit present-day needs." But only a small group were willing to act. Sentiments for changes in our form of government have increased since the 1940s. But present-day support for changes is still not great. Even those who distrust the government often express pride in its form, and few advocate major changes.

These facts are borne out by data gathered in the 1970s (see Table 3–1). Note that pride in our form of government and reluctance to change it are very high among those whose trust in it is strong. Even among those low in trust, three fourths express pride in the constitutional system. Only a fourth feel the need for big changes. Watergate and Nixon's downfall in 1974 made more of us feel the need for change in 1976. Forty-seven percent said the system should be kept as it was, compared to 59 percent in 1972. Those wanting big change increased from 15 percent in 1972 to 25 percent in 1976. In the 1980s, substantial proportions of the citizenry continued to favor changes in the governmental process, according to the polls, though most did not advocate changes with strong intensity.

Our political culture is not monolithic. Many express pride in our system of government yet are apt to complain, criticize, and distrust. We are cynical about

TABLE 3—1

Political Trust and Attitudes toward the American Form of Government

Percent who say	Total		Trust in government in 1972		
	1972	1976	High	Medium	Low
Pride in government					
I am proud of many things about our form of government	86	80	97	92	74
I can't find much about our form of government to be proud of	14	20	2	8	26
Change our form of government					
Keep our form of government as is	59	47	81	63	43
Some change needed	26	28	14	28	32
Big change needed	15	25	5	9	25

Source: Jack Citrin, "The Political Relevance of Trust in Government," *American Political Science Review* 68 (September 1974), p. 975; Survey Research Center, University of Michigan.

the system and our role in it. In juggling such feelings, we show that, on the one hand, we are proud of the strength and effectiveness of our constitutional system. On the other hand, like our colonial forebearers, we distrust power and those who have it.

POLITICS AND POLITICIANS

Ambivalent attitudes toward politicians

Americans are ambivalent about political power. This is shown in our views toward politicians. We are typically cynical about politicians and politics as a vocation. A good sample of these views is provided by the Harris survey data reproduced in Table 3–2. Politicians' sacrifices and public-spiritedness have been commended by many (in declining proportions since the 1960s). But cynicism about politicians has been nearly universal. In 1973, more than two thirds of

TABLE 3—2

Americans' Attitudes toward Politicians

Percent who agree	Years		
	1967	1971	1973
Positive statements			
"Most men in public office have little personal privacy and are often unfairly criticized."	88	76	78
"Working in government as a career is one of the most useful and public-spirited professions."	67	55	59
"Many men holding high office make real financial sacrifices to be in public service."	63	49	48
Negative statements			
"Most elected officials promise one thing at election time and do something different once in office."	*	81	82
"Only a few men in politics are dedicated public servants."	58	65	67
"Many politicians take graft."	54	59	65

*Not available.

Source: Harris survey.

those surveyed agreed that most politicians are not committed public servants and that many take graft. The view is that politicians are apt to be corrupt and crooked. Therefore, we rarely wish a political career for our children. The Gallup poll used to ask periodically, "If you had a child, would you like to see him or her go into politics as a life's work?" Here are the percentages of those who said yes:

1945	21%
1953	20
1965	36
1973	23

Except for a brief spurt of spirit in the mid-1960s, only about one fifth of us have desired political careers for our children.

At the same time, we often admire politicians and give high prestige to political occupations (Hodge, Siegel, and Rossi, 1964). When the Gallup poll asks which men and women are admired most, public officials usually dominate. Studies of occupational prestige usually show that a number of political offices are considered among the most prestigious. Of 90 occupations looked at, those of Supreme Court justice, state governor, cabinet secretary, congressman, and big city mayor are among the most highly viewed.

These mixed feelings toward politicians may occur because we expect more than we can get. On the one hand, we believe political leaders should be honest, hardworking, competent, and subservient to the public interest. But on the other hand, graft and corruption among politicians arise often enough to make us suspicious and distrustful. Cynicism toward politics and politicians may help to protect us against excesses of power. But cynicism has its drawbacks. For one thing, public opinion really does not treat politicians very fairly; far fewer politicians are crooked than most people think. For another, cynicism about politicians and a belief that politics is immoral surely discourage civic participation.

Conspiratorial interpretations

A major result of popular cyncism toward politics is belief in conspiracies. We often believe that the many are controlled by the few for evil and immoral reasons (Hofstadter, 1965). Our political history is filled with examples of how we tend to adopt a belief in conspiracies about political movements and events. This is not to say that conspiracies never exist; for instance, there was surely a well-planned plot to kill President Lincoln in 1865. Rather, we are saying that Americans often tend to believe that public affairs are manipulated by conspiracies, whether true or not.

In the 1820s it was widely believed that Freemasons had infiltrated the U.S. government. People thought this Masonic conspiracy planned to subvert orthodox Christian beliefs. A political party, the Anti-Masons, became a strong movement in the 1820s and '30s. In the 1880s and '90s the Populist movement was built around the "widespread Populist idea that all American history since the Civil War could be understood as a sustained conspiracy of the international money power" (Richard Hofstadter in Curry and Brown, 1972: 100).

Fears of a communist conspiracy accompanied the growth of labor unions at the turn of the century. A "red scare" followed the Great Steel strike of 1919. After the Japanese attacked Pearl Harbor in 1941, many feared a subversive

McCARTHYISM

Joe McCarthy was America's most successful national demagogue. In the early 1950s, the Cold WAr between the United States and the Soviet Union made many Americans fear the threat of communism. Joseph R. McCarthy, elected to the U.S. Senate from Wisconsin in 1946, became nationally prominent because of his crusade against communism between 1950 and 1954.

McCarthy claimed the State Department had been infiltrated by Communists. He accused many people in government of being "fellow travelers" and charged leading Army officers and civilian officials of the Army with communist sympathies. Many innocent people were falsely accused. Their reputations were destroyed. As a result, many of them lost their livelihoods as well.

Public fear of communism, sometimes hysterical, made McCarthy's charges seem credible. He was feared by Senators, government officials, and many media people. Even President Eisenhower could not find an effective way to curb McCarthy's reckless and unsupported charges. McCarthy created a climate of fear. Many people were afraid to express opinions, especially about our policies toward Russia or about his assaults on freedom. Finally, McCarthy was brought down by the Senate itself. In 1954, it condemned him for conduct "contrary to Senate traditions."

Herbert Block, the cartoonist for the *Washington Post* who signs himself "Herblock," coined the term *McCarthyism*. It has become a synonym for mudslinging and baselessly defaming a person or a class of people.

conspiracy among Japanese-Americans on the West Coast; 120,000 Americans of Japanese descent, most of them native-born citizens, were interned in relocation centers. This was one of the most glaring deprivations of citizens' rights in our history.

In the 1950s, Senator Joseph McCarthy of Wisconsin led and symbolized what has come to be known as "McCarthyism." He and his supporters attacked what they thought was a communist plot to subvert the government. In the '60s, "corporate imperialism" was a concern of the New Left. They thought democratic institutions had been perverted by a power elite led by a "corporate directorate." When President Kennedy was killed in 1963, many believed the alleged assassin, Lee Harvey Oswald, could not have killed the president alone. No hard evidence of a plot has been found, but efforts to rekindle the probe into Kennedy's assassination have had an effect. Twenty years later, in November 1983, fully 80 percent of Americans told Gallup pollsters they thought there had been a conspiracy.

POLITICAL IDEOLOGY IN AMERICA

Americans rarely voice strong opinions on political issues. It is often said that our politics is not very ideological. We can take **ideology** to mean a set of beliefs that is a tightly organized, logical, and consistent program of action. We may speak of the ideology of socialism, communism, fascism, or nazism. In that strict sense of the term, there are few ideologues in our politics. Many people hold inconsistent attitudes toward political issues. One of the most common is favoring raising government spending and reducing taxes in the same breath! Thus, you can know how an average person stands on, say, welfare. But you cannot predict accurately his or her stand on abortion, busing, or defense spending.

A more ideological politics

Americans have become more sophisticated ideologically since the 1950s. In 1956 a study of the extent of ideology showed that about 12 percent of us could be called **ideologues.** These people held fairly constant stands on policy issues. They had a clear idea of what the labels *liberal* and *conservative* meant. And they could connect their beliefs about issues and their partisan choices in elections. In contrast, about a fifth of the people in the 1956 study seemed to lack any ideological sense. They understood policy issues in only the simplest way. Another fourth showed somewhat more abstract political concerns. They explained their understanding of politics and their partisan choices in terms of "the nature of the times." Finally, 40 percent expressed their view of politics by focusing on "group interests." They showed some grasp of how groups are represented in government. ("The Democrats are the party of working people." Or "the Republican party is the party of business.")

The same analysis was done in 1968. The estimate of the number of ideologues in the electorate had grown to 24 percent. Understanding of political issues had increased. This seemed to be due to increases in education and interest in politics. Yet another repeat of this research in 1972 showed that 27 percent met the standards set for ideologues. Although more than half remained nonideological, the 70s brought a rise in the correlation between ideologues and presidential voting choice. Presidential election politics became more ideological. The reason was partly that candidates took more clear-cut positions on issues. Also, more of the electorate was polarized. Ideological liberals were far more apt to vote Democratic; ideological conservatives were more inclined to vote Republican (Miller and Levitin, 1976: 13–20). In 1976 the lack of a sharp ideological difference between Jimmy Carter and Gerald Ford dampened this kind of voting.

To some extent, a politics of ideology is always at work in elections. But its importance has waxed and waned. During the Great Depression, with millions out of work, leftist ideological voting had some importance. But when our politics has shown a strong ideological flavor, it has more often come from the right than from the left. In 1968, for instance, right-winger George Wallace, with the American Independent party, got nearly 14 percent of the popular vote for president.

To say that only a small group of Americans are political ideologues does not mean we are adrift politically. Few have the sophisticated, coordinated attitudes which would qualify as a full-blown ideology. Many, though, have deep-seated conceptions of their democratic rights. As two keen observers of ideology in U.S. politics point out (Lipset and Raab, 1970: 430), "to say that the large public does not consist of ideologues is not to day that it is feckless." On the contrary, "the American public demonstrably has a strong sense of its own basic democratic rights and has no reluctance to assert itself with respect to those rights."

Most of us have beliefs about freedom and equality. We have ideas about what the government should do and about our roles as citizens (Lane, 1962). Some citizens, and a lot of our political leaders, not only believe strongly in democratic principles, but also practice them. The concrete application of democratic principles "to the matter of balancing these rights under stress calls for

Ideological politics. Reverend Jerry Falwell won public attention in the 1970s and 1980s as a political conservative. As leader of he so-called Moral Majority in America, he is shown here speaking at an "I Love America" rally in front of the Kansas state capitol building in Topeka.

conceptual skills, historical perspective, and wide-based integrated belief systems which for the most part do not exist." So, according to one analysis (Lipset and Raab, 1970: 431),

> massive numbers of Americans who presumably have a ritual attachment to the concept of free speech and would reject any gross attempts to subvert it do not understand or have a commitment to the fine points of that concept when hard-core dissenters intrude upon their sensibilities. The American people would reject any gross attempt to subvert religious freedom, but almost half of them say that if a man does not believe in God, he should not be allowed to run for public office. And a majority of them, while jealous of due process, would throw away the book and resort to the whip when dealing with sex criminals. In short, . . . abstract and complex democratic institutions and practices have stood and flourished in America because some people understood them and most of the rest were loyal to them. This loyalty was based on an inertia of investment in the country, the system, and the traditional political structure.

An eminent political scientist once said: "Democracy is an odd system. It requires that most men tolerate freedom and that some men hold it dear" (Lane, 1962: 39). The primitive political beliefs of most people are not an ideology in the programmatic sense. But being nonideologues does not keep Americans from meaningful citizenship.

Liberals and conservatives

There are liberals and conservatives in American politics. Political leaders, such as state and national officials or party leaders, are far more ideologically oriented than the ordinary person. Some are fiercely liberal or conservative. Well-known conservatives in recent presidential politics included Senator Barry Goldwater of Arizona, unsuccessful Republican candidate for president in 1964. His strategy centered on winning the support of avowed conservatives. That election brought about a heightened ideological response from voters. And, in 1980, a recognized political conservative, Republican Ronald Reagan, won election as president. Perhaps the best known all-around liberal in recent years was Senator Hubert H. Humphrey of Minnesota. He was vice president under Lyndon Johnson and the Democratic presidential choice in 1968. More recently, former Senator George McGovern of South Dakota, the unsuccessful Democratic party candidate for president in 1972, and Senator Edward M. Kennedy, the Massachusetts Democrat who has been a potential presidential candidate in recent years have been among the more notable liberals in politics.

Pollsters periodically ask Americans whether they identify themselves as liberals, conservatives, or moderates. Most people are able to place themselves in one of these categories. And, over the years, the proportion in each classification has been remarkably stable. A 1982 Gallup poll showed that about a fifth were liberal, nearly a third conservative, and almost two fifths "center" or "middle-of-the-road" (*Public Opinion*, 6, April–May 1983: 21). The way Republican and Democrat adherents identify themselves differs. Most Democrats consider themselves liberal or moderate, while a majority of Republicans consider themselves conservative.

Despite widespread use, labels like liberal or conservative have little meaning to most people (Erikson and Luttbeg, 1973: 66–86). Those who say they are "liberal" or "conservative" often cannot explain what that means in terms of public policies. Many Americans are liberal on some things and conservative on others. For instance, many people are politically liberal when it comes to federal programs in welfare, housing, education, poverty, medical care, urban renewal, or unemployment. But they take the conservative side on growth of government or expansion of government activities affecting their daily lives.

POLITICAL SUBCULTURES

Political change in the South

The southern states have a distinct political culture even today. Although they have become more like the rest of the country in many ways, southern politics continues to be somewhat different. And greater political changes have occurred in the South than in any other part of the nation. The civil rights movement brought basic social change. It greatly altered the relations between blacks and whites. Legislative reapportionment brought blacks into state legislatures in most cases for the first time since the 1870s. Urban and industrial growth changed the face of the South—the "bulldozer revolution." Some of the uniqueness of southern politics is gone. Southern political patterns are now more like those of the rest of the nation (Bass and DeVries, 1976). In recent presidential elections, the South has not been solid Democratic. Nixon, a Republican, won the electoral votes of 11 southern states in 1972. In 1976, a representative of the "emerging South," Jimmy Carter, was able to appeal to people outside the South. He won the Democratic presidential nomination and then the presidency itself. But even an incumbent from Georgia could not hold the southern vote in 1980. Ronald Reagan won throughout the Deep South except in Georgia.

Still, the South remains a distinct region. Its black population is three times as large as the black population outside the South; its white population is more Anglo-Saxon and less ethnically diverse than elsewhere. The South's economic growth has been impressive in recent years; educational opportunity has im-

MR. DOOLEY AND THE ETHNIC FACTOR

In the 1890s, an imaginative writer by the name of Finley Peter Dunne invented a homespun Irish-American philosopher called "Mr. Dooley." About ethnic social and political assimilation, Dunne had Mr. Dooley say (Dunne, 1898: 54–56):

An Anglo-Saxon, Hinnissy, is a German that's forgot who was his parents. . . . I'm an Anglo-Saxon. . . . Th' name iv Dooley has been th' County Roscommon f'r many years. . . . Pether Bowbeen down be th' Frinch church is formin' th' Circle Francaize Anglo-Saxon club, an' me ol' frind Domingo . . . will march at th' head iv th' Dago Anglo-Saxons whin th' time comes. There ar're twenty thousan' Rooshian Jews at a quarther a vote in th' Sivinth Ward; an', ar-rmed with rag hoods, they'd be a tur-r-ble thing f'r anny inimy

iv th' Anglo-Saxon 'lieance to face. Th' Bohemians an' Pole Anglo-Saxons may be a little slow in wakin' up to what th' pa-apers calls our common hurtage, but ye may be sure they'll be all r-right whin they're called one. . . . I tell ye, whin th' Clan an' th' Sons iv Sweden an' th' Banana Club an' th' Circle Francaize an th' Pollacky Benivolent Society an' th' Rooshian Sons of Dinnymite an' th' Benny Brith an' th' Coffee Clutch that Schwartzmeister r-runs an' th' Turrnd' yemind an' th' Holland society an' th' Afro-Americans an' th' other Anglo-Saxons begin f'r to raise their Anglo-Saxon battle cry, it'll be all day with th' eight or nin people in th' wurruld that has th' misfortune iv not bein' brought up Anglo-Saxon.

proved. But levels of education and income are still lower in the South than elsewhere. Religion is much more Protestant fundamentalist than in the rest of the country. In short, "perhaps some day the homogenizing forces of the bulldozer revolution will erase the distinctive patterns of regional diversity in the United States, but at least insofar as the South is concerned, that day has not yet arrived" (Bartley and Graham, 1975: 20).

Ethnic cultural diversity

Regional cultural diversity has not yet vanished. Ethnic diversity remains a big part of our political life. Ethnic groups differ in their political participation and styles (Greeley, 1974). For instance, Irish Catholics are much more active politically than other ethnic groups. This is even true when differences in region and social class are accounted for. Many communities have distinct ethnic subcultures—for example, "Chinatowns" and "Little Italys"—with distinct political styles. Northern cities such as Detroit have two separate cultures, black and white, which live apart and sharply differ in their politics. Native Americans maintain a unique political culture in South Dakota, Arizona, New Mexico, and Oklahoma. The political cultures of southwestern cities such as San Antonio reflect the Mexican-American style. Uncle Sam remains a symbol of Yankee Anglo-Saxonism. The Goddess of Liberty beckons the immigrant to share in the national culture of liberty. But America has not been a "melting pot" that erased ethnic cultural diversity, though this may sometimes seem to have been the case.

ACQUIRING A POLITICAL SELF

Human beings are not born political animals. The political self is molded and shaped by the values of family, friends, schoolmates, the community, TV, schools, and major political events. As children mature they acquire more complex political outlooks. At the core of the political self are basic loyalties and attachments and often strong feelings toward the nation and its institutions. When asked who they are, Americans usually respond with such basic attachments as: "I am an American," "I am a Republican," or "I am a Democrat." Also, the political self includes important kinds of political knowledge and evaluation. This consists of some knowledge of how government works, some feeling for the rights and duties of citizens, and judgments about parties and leaders.

Most children form notions about politics before they go to school. In preschool, their most common civic learning deals with basic views about the nation and its symbols, such as the flag. Children also identify with parties to a great extent. Probably half learn to be little Democrats or Republicans by the fourth grade (Dennis, 1973; Easton and Dennis, 1969). At first, these ties to nation and party are just labels without much content. Later, young people become much more sophisticated.

These identifications develop at a time when other kinds of social awareness are also forming. A child gains racial awareness, a religious bent, and a sense of social class identity along with political ties. Thus, a young child becomes aware that he or she is a black, Baptist, working-class Democrat, a white, Anglo-Saxon, Protestant Republican, a middle-class, Jewish Democrat, or a Bos-

ton, Irish-Catholic Democrat. Other views form along with such social and political identifications. The child starts to develop attitudes and views about political leaders and what they do. The first public figure most children know about is the police officer. But they think the president is important, too.

Later in childhood, from about 9 through 13, children move away from notions of politics based largely on feelings and vague ideas. They become more sophisticated and know more about what leaders do and how governments work. By about 13, young people understand politics in much the same way as most adults. But this does not mean that teenagers do not change their beliefs. At this point, young people spend less time with their parents and are swayed more by their peers. They leave home, perhaps to attend college in an area quite different from what they were used to. They work in a service station, a grocery store, or a factory. At work they may meet people whose political beliefs differ greatly from those of the people they knew as children. And teenagers gain political knowledge and understanding, usually in school, and often get involved in some kind of political activity.

Political socialization

Americans do not all come from the same mold. The process of socialization does not mean all people have the same political outlooks. But it is possible to make some statements about the attitudes we learn. The process of acquiring political beliefs, attitudes, or values is **political socialization.** Research on political socialization permits various generalization about this process (from Dawson, Prewitt, and Dawson, 1977: 59–60):

1. Political learning begins early and continues through early childhood, late childhood, and adolescence.
2. Different types of political learning take place at different points over the preadult years.
3. Basic attachments and identifications—those orientations . . . identified . . . as the core components of the political self—are among the first political outlooks to be acquired.
4. Early orientations toward political authorities seem to be indiscriminately positive and benevolent. They become less so as the child moves through late childhood and into adolescence.
5. Early conceptions of politics and government are highly personalized. The government, the president, the mayor, and so on are understood initially in personal terms. This personalization fades and is replaced by more abstract perceptions by late childhood and early adolescence.
6. Affective orientations, or feelings about political objects, seem to be acquired before information or knowledge. One has feelings about the nation and the president (usually positive feelings) before one has much understanding of what they are.

Black mayors lead American cities. In the 1970s and 1980s black politicians were elected mayors of several cities, including Gary, Indiana, Chicago, Birmingham, New Orleans, Los Angeles, Philadelphia, and Detroit. These large-city mayors are [top to bottom] Harold Washington of Chicago, Andrew Young of Atlanta, W. Wilson Goode of Philadelphia, and Tom Bradley of Los Angeles.

Campaigning for the ethnic vote. Presidential candidate Ronald Reagan seeks ethnic support in a speech to the Ukrainian National Association in New York City. The large poster behind candidate Reagan proclaimed support for him by a variety of nationality groups.

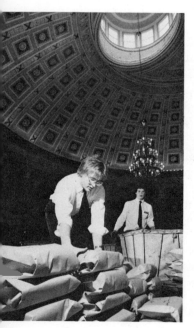

Learning firsthand about politics. These two teenagers serve as pages in the U.S. House of Representatives. Here they begin the delivery of budget documents to House and Senate committees.

7. During late childhood the child acquires information and knowledge about the political world. He or she begins to distinguish between different political roles and to acquire the basic factual information needed to map out the political world.

8. During adolescence the individual increases his or her capacity to deal with abstractions, and to engage in ideological thinking and ends-means analysis. He or she becomes more involved in partisan and electoral politics.

9. Because different types of political learning occur at different points over the preadult years, it is difficult to specify any particular period as the most important or crucial point. If one places importance on the ability of the maturing citizen to understand political roles and relationships, the end of late childhood and early adolescence might be regarded as most significant—roughly the period between ages eleven and fifteen.

10. Political learning seems to coincide with other types of social learning. Political identities are formed during the same period when other social identities are acquired. The development of political thinking follows the capacity of the individual to handle abstractions and engage in the types of thinking necessary for understanding social and political relationships.

11. By the end of the preadult years the political self is well developed. Most of the basic orientations and knowledge about the political world, as well as the capacity to understand political relationships, are acquired or developed as far as they are likely to be.

Early political socialization greatly affects the kinds of citizens we become. But early learning can be changed. Adult experiences, such as an active role in politics, or the effects of events such as war or depression, may cause changes in political beliefs. But many attachments and values acquired early in life have a lasting effect on our political behavior.

IMAGES OF NATION AND GOVERNMENT

What is our country?

A British social psychologist asked an 11-year-old in Glasgow, "What is Britain?" and "What is Scotland?" The lad replied, "Scotland is a country. Britain is a lot of different countries—Glasgow, London, France" (Jahoda, 1963: 58). Young children often have an imperfect idea of their nation. In Britain, which takes in the separate "countries" of England, Scotland, Wales, and Northern Ireland, confusion about country and nation is easy to understand.

You would expect American children to have an easier time. But even here most children do not have a clear idea of nation until about the fifth grade. A few years ago, a researcher interviewed more than 800 school children in Philadelphia. One question he asked was, "What is the name of our country?" Sixty-eight percent of the third graders did not know the right answer; about half said "Philadelphia," and another large group said "Pennsylvania." The vast majority of children in seventh to ninth grade knew the right answer (Greenberg, 1969: 478).

One of the first political ideas children learn is a sense of their country, a national identity, a sense of being part of a political community. This is shown in their ability to identify national symbols. These symbols give them "tangible objects toward which feelings of attachment can be socialized" (Hess and Torney, 1967: 28).

Such symbols are only vaguely understood by very young children. But even they often connect the symbols and the values that go with them. A second-grade boy in Chicago was asked, "What does the Statue of Liberty do?" The child replied, "Well, it keeps liberty." "How does it do that?" "Well, it doesn't do it, but there are some guys that do it." "Some other guys do it for the Statue of Liberty?" "The Statue is not alive." "Well, what does it do?" "It has this torch in its hand, and sometimes they light up the torch. If the statue was gone, there wouldn't be any liberty" (Hess and Torney, 1967: 29). Over the grammar school years, American children acquire a sharply defined notion of their country and of the meaning of its major symbols.

Very young children have a simple notion of the *government* of their country, and it is highly personal. As they mature, however, their ideas become more complex and realistic. Their view includes activities such as voting and giving a central place in the government to the Congress. As people mature, they gain a better understanding of how government works, as well as a better notion of its structure. Many children in the early grades think the president makes laws. By seventh grade, most students know that Congress plays a major part in lawmaking. By the time children leave grammar school, they have some idea of the structure of political leadership.

Students at the University of Iowa got involved in the 1984 caucuses which began the process of choosing delegates to the national party conventions. This student had been able to collect the campaign buttons of most of the contestants.

THE ROLE OF THE PRESIDENT

The president plays a central role in political socialization. The president is a very important and visible political figure and both adults and children know more about the president than about any other public official. Studies showed that by about 13, young people know as much as adults about the president and vice president. But they are not very aware of any other politicians. Almost all children by the end of grammar school know who the president is.

The benevolent leader

Earlier in this chapter, we described the mixed feelings of adults toward political authority. We noted that Americans often see politics as crooked and dirty. Yet they accord great prestige to high political offices. Do we learn negative attitudes toward political leaders early in life? Much evidence shows that, in the main, we do not. Most children have a very positive image of the president—they see him as extremely important and powerful, and they feel kindly toward him. During early childhood feelings about the president are both very personal and highly idealized. As children get older, their positive feelings about the president erode. By adolescence, their attitudes are much like those of adults.

This idealizing of the president does not wholly depend on the fact that some presidents are admired and some scorned. Some attitudes of second and fourth graders were as positive about President Nixon after Watergate as they were toward Presidents Eisenhower and Kennedy. In the post-Watergate early 1970s, decline in positive ideas about the president was much greater than in the 1960s. This suggests that "children appear able—in a wholly un-self-conscious way— to distinguish between roles and the individuals who fill them" (Greenstein, 1975: 1390). That is, children are capable of holding negative attitudes toward a particular president, while at the same time harboring idealized notions of the presidency as a high office.

The benevolent leader. American children very often have an idealized image of the role of the president. President George Washington is depicted here as a sacred, godly figure, in the hands of the angels. Although highly respected by his political associates and revered by the public in his own time, he came to be viewed as more than human by later generations.

Why are young children so positive about the president when adults are often so cynical? In our culture, honesty, trustworthiness, helpfulness, and caring are highly valued. Children expect the president to act like good adults in general. But it is also probable that "highly positive preadult views of the president . . . result from a combination of adult tendencies to cushion children from the more negative aspects of adult perceptions of the political world, and from preadult tendencies to perceive selectively the kindly, supportive aspects of a central figure in the wider environment" (Greenstein, 1974: 130). Parents shield their children from negative and hostile assessments of political leaders, and especially from such assessments of the president.

Reactions to the president's assassination

One event that dramatizes the importance of the president in our political world is his assassination. The killing of John F. Kennedy in Dallas on November 22, 1963, deeply affected both young and old (Crotty, 1971). Shock and disbelief followed the event. People grieved as if a close friend or relative had died (Greenberg and Parker, 1965). A typical reaction came from a seventh-grade boy in New York (Wolfenstein and Kliman, 1965: 224–25):

> I was walking into my homeroom class when I heard that the President of the United States was shot. I just didn't want to believe it. I walked home from school wondering if it was true. Then, I heard another bulletin when I got home. It went, "Ladies and Gentlemen, the President is dead." I was dumbfounded. When I heard the bulletin I couldn't believe it, yet it was true. He died in a Dallas hospital. I never thought I would ever live to hear about an assassination of a President that really happened. I just couldn't believe it. I just couldn't bear the thoughts of having someone take away the life of the heroic John Fitzgerald Kennedy. He was so living at first, and then "poof" he's dead. I was thinking that it isn't even safe to take a walk anymore. I hope I will never have to witness anything like that again.

Adults reacted the same way children did. College-age students reacted as if a member of their own family had died. One student said (Greenberg and Parker, 1965: 229):

> The only experience I've had with death is that my grandfather died after two years of the state that Joseph Kennedy [President Kennedy's father] is in now and it wasn't pleasant. And at the time I vividly recall that I was sorry, but not upset like this, like I was Friday. . . . Somehow I felt when I heard this news like . . . someone real close to me had died. It's something . . . I've tried to explain to myself, and I can't.

The way parents explained the assassination to their children reinforced the children's idealized view of the president. How parents shield their children from the seamier side of politics or from their own cynicism toward politics was shown in how they explained the assassination. Many adults thought there had been a conspiracy, that a lone gunman could not have killed the president. But they apparently kept this view from their children (Orren and Peterson, 1967: 399).

The death of the president creates a crisis of authority. It is shocking for both young and old. The murder of President Kennedy in 1963 was not a unique event. Presidents Abraham Lincoln, James Garfield, and William McKinley were also assassinated. Attempts were made on the lives of Andrew Jackson, Theodore Roosevelt (who was wounded), Franklin D. Roosevelt (the assassin's shot

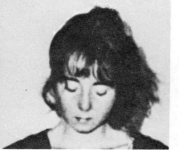

missed FDR but killed Mayor Anton Cermak of Chicago), Harry S Truman, Gerald R. Ford, and Ronald Reagan (who was also wounded). President Ford was attacked twice in September 1975 but was not hurt. Also, William H. Harrison, Zachary Taylor, Warren G. Harding, and Franklin D. Roosevelt died of natural causes while in office. And two other prominent leaders were assassinated in 1968—presidential candidate Robert Kennedy and civil rights leader Martin Luther King, Jr.

Too little is known about how presidential deaths affect attitudes toward political figures. But many patterns are repeated again and again. Deeply felt grief is widespread; the fallen leader is immortalized. However ordinary he was in life, the fallen president becomes a heroic figure. Policies that were not likely to be passed in more normal times may be adopted as part of the dead leader's legacy. Since assassination is an extreme and violent act, it can raise levels of suspicion and distrust of government, perhaps even of political life in general. The death of a great leader surely helps create a benevolent image. But the murder of a prominent figure seems to cause doubt, mistrust, apathy, and estrangement from politics. In short, the killing of the president may make the young despair. It may foster the belief that a good political society is futile. The murders of President John Kennedy, Senator Robert Kennedy, and Reverend Martin Luther King, Jr., between 1963 and 1968 surely contributed to the political apathy and alienation of the 70s.

The effects of scandal

Corruption or improper actions in high places are bound to have a negative effect on political leaders' images. Fraud and corruption during the term of Ulysses S. Grant in the 1870s are the best-known aspects of his presidency. This is so even though Grant was never personally implicated. More devastating scandal struck the presidency of Warren G. Harding in the 1920s. His cabinet secretaries took bribes in connection with developing the Teapot Dome oil reserve in South Dakota. Like Grant, Harding was not personally involved. But his incompetence made corruption by his underlings easier.

There were no studies of political socialization during the Grant presidency or after the Teapot Dome scandal. But the effects of corruption during the presidency of Richard M. Nixon have been studied. Acts of political chicanery and corruption during the 1972 presidential election—called the Watergate affair because the Democratic National Committee's offices in the Watergate building in Washington, D.C., were burglarized—drastically discredited Nixon among adults. Watergate also deeply influenced children's feelings about the president.

However, even the Watergate scandal failed to crush children's idealizing of the president. Post-Watergate studies show that children still have positive at-

Presidential assassins. Lee Harvey Oswald [top] shot President John F. Kennedy in Dallas in November 1963. He was, in turn, murdered by Jack Ruby in the Dallas police station. Leon Czolgosz [second from top] shot President William McKinley to death at the Pan American Exposition in Buffalo in September 1901. He was executed in the electric chair after a brief trial. Giuseppe Zangara attempted to assassinate President Franklin D. Roosevelt in Miami in 1932, but he missed and killed Mayor Anton Cermak of Chicago instead. Zangara died in the electric chair. Lynette Fromme [bottom] tried to shoot President Gerald Ford in Sacramento, California, in 1975, but missed. She is serving a life sentence in a federal prison.

titudes about the president. These studies also show that children here have more idealized views of national leaders than do children in other Western democratic countries (Greenstein, 1975: 1384).

President Nixon was disgraced and forced to resign because of Watergate. But political scandal has a much smaller effect on members of Congress. There, corruption seems to be more widely expected and less disapproved. For example, a study of congressional corruption in 1968–78 showed that charges of wrongdoing had a limited impact on reelection. Of 80 congressmen accused of corruption, 49 were relected in spite of the charges (Peters and Welch, 1980).

No one knows the lasting effects of these events. The national shock of assassination and the anger and cynicism over the Vietnam War and Watergate may have produced a new generation of citizens who will be politically alienated for their whole lives.

ACQUIRING A POLITICAL PARTY IDENTIFI-CATION

Forming party ties is one of the most notable features of early childhood political socialization. By 10 or 12, most children know the terms *Republican* and *Democrat*. They respond in a partisan or independent way when asked about their voting preferences. They identify with parties even before they learn much about the parties themselves or about social and political issues.

From parents to children

Americans tend to adopt the political loyalties of their parents. Studies based upon interviews with high school students and their parents have found, as Table 3–3 illustrates, that Democratic parents tend to have Democratic children; Republican parents tend to have Republican children; and independent parents tend to have independent children. Why are these party loyalties passed from parents to children?

Party loyalty makes it possible for many people to join in the political process without taking the time to master all its complexities. Children hear a lot of political talk in their families. They pick up their parents' attachments to political parties (or their independence) just as they may acquire their parents' religious, ethnic, or class identity. Since parents often discuss politics in front of the children, children are highly aware of their loyalties. For about three fourths of American parents, the husband and wife have the same party alle-

TABLE 3–3

Party Identification of Children and Parents

Percent of children who are	Parents are		
	Democrats	**Independents**	**Republicans**
Democrats	66	29	13
Independents	27	53	36
Republicans	7	17	51
Total	100	100	100

Source: M. Kent Jennings and Richard G. Niemi, *The Political Character of Adolescence: The Influence of Families and Schools* (Princeton, N.J.: Princeton University Press, 1974), p. 41. Copyright © 1974 by Princeton University Press. Reprinted by permission of Princeton University Press.

giance (Niemi, 1974). Where this is so, children strongly tend to adopt their parents' views.

But it is not a law that a person must be loyal to the same party as his or her parents. As Table 3–3 shows, this passing of party loyalty is far from perfect. Some children from Democratic families become Republicans. Some children from Republican families come to be Democrats. In the 1970s, although not many young people took a partisan allegiance opposite that of their parents, a growing proportion were attracted to the "independent" label (Jennings and Niemi, 1981: 89–93).

The decline in the partisanship of youth

Party affiliation has been one of the most stable features of politics in this country. But the proportion of independents has grown in recent years. This increase is largely generational. The youth of the 1970s and 1980s were less inclined than the youth of earlier decades to call themselves Democrats or Republicans. They were also much less inclined to do so than the adults of these decades.

Direct evidence of these trends is found in Michigan Survey Research Center study of parents and high school students in 1965 and 1973. The same parents and students were asked about their party ties in both years. Thus, one may see to what extent changes in party ties are maturational (people identify more or less with a party as they get older) or generational (one generation shows a distinct pattern). Figure 3–3 shows that the pattern of attachment among the

FIGURE 3–3

Party Identification of Parents and High School Students, 1965 and 1973

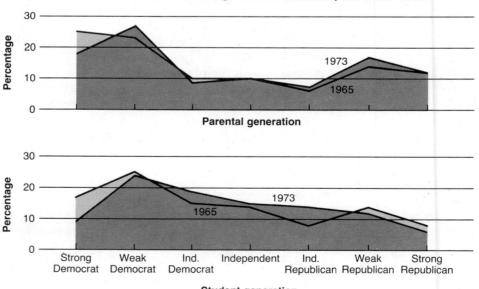

Source: M. Kent Jennings and Richard G. Niemi, *Generations and Politics* (Princeton, N.J.: Princeton University Press, 1981), p. 153.

parents was much the same in 1965 and 1973. In both years, most parents identified themselves as Democrats or Republicans.

In contrast, a large proportion of the students were independents in the mid-1960s, and this percentage increased 11 percent by 1973. The proportion of "strong" identifiers declined. These young people who were high school students in 1965 and young adults in 1973 emerged from the Vietnam War protests and the Watergate scandals politically much like their parents' generation. But they were distinct in their much lower levels of partisan loyalty.

The researchers who did the study concluded: "Although there may be a decline in the proportion of Independents in the future, . . . the rate of decline will not bring the proportion down to levels observed in previous generations for some years, if ever." Rather, they say, "the fact that many of these respondents have felt a degree of independence from parties for several years is . . . likely to make them more resistant to future changes" even though "sustained psychological attachment to the nonentity of 'independence' seems intuitively more difficult than attachment to the entity of a political party" (Jennings and Niemi, 1981: 154–155).

AGENTS OF POLITICAL SOCIALIZATION

Gaining political values, ties, and attitudes is affected by many factors. No easy formula accounts for all aspects of political socialization. But we do know that social experiences as people grow up have important consequences. Among these influences are the family, the school, peer groups, and the mass media.

The political role of the family

The family plays a crucial role in political socialization. This is partly because some political learning takes place very early. The early years are especially important for childrens' growth in every respect, including the political. The family is also central because of the strong bonds that exist there. Where there are strong personal ties, as between parents and children, learning, including political learning, is more likely to be swayed by the relationship.

Partisanship versus opinions   The influence of the family is most important in transmitting norms of behavior and beliefs. This includes basic political identifications. National identity and loyalty are well formed at an early age. And this development takes place almost wholly within the family. In addi-

A highly political family. These three members of the Kennedy family have been highly involved in American politics. Robert (Bobby) Kennedy [left] served as attorney general and U.S. senator from New York in the 1960s; Edward (Ted) Kennedy [center] is U.S. senator from Massachusetts; John (Jack) Kennedy [right] was elected president of the United States in 1960 and served until he was assassinated in November 1963. Their father had served in various offices during the New Deal administration of Franklin D. Roosevelt, and both of their grandfathers had been ardent politicians in Boston.

tion, children gain many loyalties and beliefs early. These include ties to and views toward political leaders. As we saw earlier, attitudes toward the president and party allegiance normally emerge early in childhood, usually with family guidance.

The role of the family in transmitting specific opinions and preferences is not so great. Parents are much more likely to teach children their party ties than their views on issues or candidates. The same is true for nonpolitical values. Children tend to acquire the religious identifications of their parents. But they are much less likely to take on their parents' exact religious beliefs and attitudes. It is easy to see why family socialization is strong in regard to party loyalties but relatively weak in regard to specific views and preferences. Party loyalty is acquired early in life, when family influence is at its peak. People gain political views over their lifetimes in response to changing events, experiences, and political figures.

Of course, all families are not alike. We have noted that children are much more likely to acquire the party ties of their parents if both parents have the same loyalty. One reason so many people share the same party ties as their parents is that so many parents agree about politics. And nowadays many parents have no party attachment, so their children are likely to help maintain the ranks of political independents.

Politicized families   Some families are highly politicized. The parents are interested in politics, participate, talk about it a lot at home, and perhaps even get their children involved. In other families, the parents have no interest in politics. Political socialization is much stronger in politicized families. Where parents have strong ties and take strong stands on issues, children are most likely to adopt these views. One reason party attachment is more influenced by family than are opinions is that the former is more clearly communicated from parents to children.

Politics interest most adults only in passing. Yet the degree of family transmission of political views is impressive. Much of this socialization is not deliberate: "parents socialize their children despite themselves" (Jennings and Niemi, 1974: 61). Most parents probably do not care what their children's views are. They just want those views to be what the parents think of as socially and culturally appropriate. Because families differ in their social, cultural, and political views, family socialization helps to maintain diverse loyalties, attitudes, and perspectives. But children tend to be shaped by their parents' values and to model themselves on their parents. So, family political learning has a conservative effect on the system. Each new generation will, in many ways, reflect the old.

Education and schools

Awareness, skills, and efficacy   Education has a dramatic effect on political behavior. Educated people read and travel. They have many opportunities to gain political knowledge, information, and interests. Their skills and habits make them better organizers than those with less education. They are, therefore, better prepared to take part in civic affairs. Educated people tend to think they can control many events and social processes. They think their efforts can help human progress. So educated people are more confident that their involvement in public affairs can produce some desired result or achieve some goal.

Finally, educated people are relatively high in social and economic status. This gives them reason to think that political outcomes will affect them personally. These attributes of educated people—feelings of effectiveness, confidence, sense of purpose, ability to influence the political process and a belief in a responsive political system—are together called a "sense of political efficacy." Educated people have a strong sense of political efficacy. They are likely to be more active in politics because their own well-being is at stake.

The effects of education on political involvement are huge. In Figure 3–4 we show variations in political interest for people with various levels of schooling. Note that interest tends to grow with age, regardless of the level of education. At the same time, at all ages, the more educated are more interested than the less educated. Also, note that middle-aged high school graduates are at least as interested as younger, college-educated people. But the effects of schooling on political interest, as well as on a wide range of other political leanings and behavior, are quite clear.

Civic education Educated people everywhere are far more politically involved than uneducated people. In the United States, civics has always been taught in the schools. Of the major nations, perhaps only the Soviet Union places a higher priority on educating its people. Unlike the Soviet Union, however, the United States does not plan and coordinate civic training on a national basis. But there are civics programs in nearly all our schools. In grammar schools civic education helps politically socialize children. Patriotic rites in the lower grades, such as the pledge of allegiance and the national anthem, reinforce and symbolize childrens' basic national ties. In grammar schools, children learn about the duties of citizens to the extent that the school, the classroom environment, and the teachers stress compliance with authority and rules. Teachers serve as

FIGURE 3–4

Levels of Political Interest by Education and Age

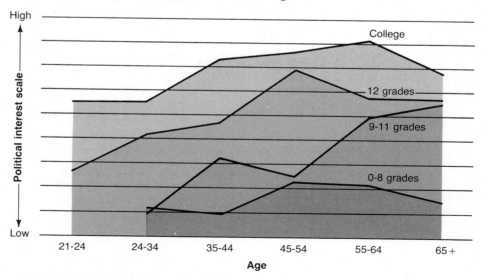

Source: M. Kent Jennings and Richard G. Niemi, *The Political Character of Adolescence: The Influence of Families and Schools* (Princeton, N.J.: Princeton University Press, 1974), p. 257. Reprinted by permission of Princeton University Press.

role models for pupils. Studies show that in many ways children's political views are like those of their teachers.

Much political socialization is established by the end of grammar school. Thus you might think that civic education in high school or college would have less influence on a person. This is largely true. Though high schools stress civic education, the program normally does little to change students' ties or values. The main effect of civics courses at this point is to impart knowledge. The courses aim mostly at those who have not had much previous exposure.

Peer groups and political learning

Most people's behavior, views, and opinions are molded and shaped by their social environment. And most people search out others whose views reinforce their own. As a result, people's opinions are both shaped and strengthened by the social groups they are part of.

Families tend to live in neighborhoods of like-minded people. They live with people of the same general social class, racial or ethnic background, and political leanings. As a result, the school, and especially the grammar school, is likely to strengthen the socialization that takes place in the family. Also, since children's friends tend to be from the same neighborhood, peer groups are likely to share the same outlooks. Thus, many children are socialized in a web with a high degree of sharing and reinforcement of political beliefs.

But we know that American families are quite mobile. When children grow up, they tend to leave the family and move to a different area. They also tend to move several times, especially during early adulthood. This mobility, as well as adulthood itself, brings people into contact with a wide range of social groups and circumstances. The more socially and geographically mobile people are, the more they are influenced by social groups with different views. For instance, a person raised in a Republican family and town (say, Orange City, Iowa) moves to a strongly Democratic town in the South (say, Plains, Georgia). There is a pretty strong chance that he or she will become a Democrat.

Peer groups in which people meet face to face have important socializing effects. This is most true during the time between adolescence and adulthood. Studies of high school students underscore the influence of peer groups on such things as dress, tastes, activities, and attitudes toward authority. But high school students do not make friends because of political leanings. A study of the political views among groups of high school friends showed that they agreed, but not very strongly, about party ties, candidates, issues, and opinions, such as efficacy and trust (Jennings and Niemi, 1974: 234). Teenagers' party and voting choices are much more affected by family than by peer groups. But their stance on issues is swayed more by peers.

The media

Many claims are made about the influence of mass media. No one could deny that the media are important in many ways. But there is not much evidence that the media play a big part in political socialization. Children use the mass media (TV, newspapers, magazines, radio) more and more as they go through the lower grades. But at these ages the media, especially TV, are probably more a source of entertainment than political information. We do know that the use of the media as a news source increases after high school. High school students do use the media for news but far less so than their parents. Parents frequently select the political TV programming (and newspapers, magazines, and radio broadcasts, too) which their children consume. Thus, they indirectly control the effects of the medium on their children.

Research on the impact of the media in political socialization has not been vast. But it does show that (1) the media play a big role in providing political information, but (2) the media have little independent influence on the development of political opinions or political activity. There is serious concern about the media's potential for a kind of mass political thought control. But the media mainly reinforce the views children get from other sources, mostly from the family.

VARIATIONS IN POLITICAL SOCIALIZATION

Social class, racial, ethnic, and sex differences among Americans do not always show up as differences in political socialization. Often where the differences do occur, they are not very great. Social class differences in political learning can be found. However, they loom larger in the advantage middle-class children have in acquiring political interests, knowledge, and skills than they appear in differences in basic class orientations toward political authorities. Middle-class children grow up in more highly polticized families than lower-class children. Thus, they acquire stronger tendencies to participate in politics. As a result, class differences in adult participation persist from one generation to the next.

Gender differences

Theoretically, male control of political offices in the United States might stem from sex differences in childhood political socialization. If, in the process of political learning, children think females have a subordinate role, then the views of boys and girls will be quite different. This may have once been true. But research since the 1960s has shown that now there is only small differences in the socialization of girls and boys. In early childhood, girls have slightly more positive feelings toward government and its leaders. But they are less politically active. Girls seem to be more influenced than boys by their immediate environment. So, in high school, girls are more apt to agree politically with their parents and friends. But sex differences in political participation do not last into the high school years (Jennings and Niemi, 1974: 325–26). And there are few sex differences in adult political behavior.

But so-called gender-role stereotyping is real enough. Many women do learn that, while they can participate in politics, only men can hold office. Many men

First woman elected to the U.S. Congress. For a number of years after she began a career as a social worker in Seattle in 1909, Jeannette Rankin campaigned for women's suffrage in California, Washington, and Montana. She became legislative secretary of the National American Women's Suffrage Association. In 1916 she was elected as a Republican member of Congress from Montana, the first woman elected to a congressional seat. She voted against declaring war against Germany in 1917, and this unpopular vote contributed to her defeat in a bid to capture a U.S. Senate seat in 1918. In 1940 she again won a House seat, and attracted special attention by being the only member to vote against declaring war against Japan after the Japanese attack on Pearl Harbor. She did not run for reelection in 1942.

agree. Many women think their role in society is at home raising children. Women may still feel that public office demands more than their maternal role can permit. In no country do women seek public office as actively as men. But women who are elected are every bit as effective as men (Kirkpatrick, 1974).

The women's movement of the 1960s and '70s brought many reforms. Groups such as the National Organization for Women (NOW) have raised the consciousness of both women and men about sex discrimination. Feelings about the role of women in politics are changing, more so among men than women (Githens and Prestage, 1977).

Racial differences

Blacks and whites are not very different in their political ties or in their mostly positive feelings about our system of government. If anything, black children are slightly more positive toward government than white children. Black children also differ from white children in their feelings toward the president. Black children felt more positive about Presidents Kennedy and Johnson than white children; they had more negative feelings about President Nixon. These and other differences come largely from long deprivation and discrimination against blacks as they tried to exercise their civil and political rights (Orum and Cohen, 1973). Blacks thought Kennedy and Johnson were highly supportive of black rights, but Nixon was not.

Differences in party loyalty   Major black-white differences exist in learning party attachment, in the effect of school socialization, and in feelings about political effectiveness. Since at least the 1960s, black adults have generally agreed that the Democratic party serves black interests more than the Republican party. They feel the Democrats will improve the economic condition of blacks and enforce their rights. This view has meant that more black children by far see themselves as Democrats.

Parental transmission of party ties has been far weaker among blacks than whites. The Democratic party has attracted young blacks, regardless of the party attachment of their parents. Since the 1960s, family socialization has had much less impact on party loyalty for blacks than for whites. Black children seem to respond more to the larger political arena and to racial consciousness in their party ties.

Effects of civic education   On average, black children score lower than white children on questions of political knowledge. This difference stems mainly from the poorer social and educational environment of black children. Black children come to high school with much less political knowledge than whites. So the high school civics course (which has little impact on whites) has a great effect on blacks. Their political *knowledge* is more affected by the course than is that of whites. Civics courses in high school do not change white students' feelings of political effectiveness. But they do enhance the sense of political efficacy among blacks. Blacks, especially from low-status families, are more *politicized* by civics programs.

These effects occur because the information is not as much of a rehash for black students as it is for whites. Blacks, "because of cultural and social status differences, . . . are more likely to encounter new or conflicting perspectives and content" in civics courses. For white students, the program "is a further layering of familiar materials which, by and large, repeat the message from other

FIGURE 3–5

Political Efficacy among Black and White School Children

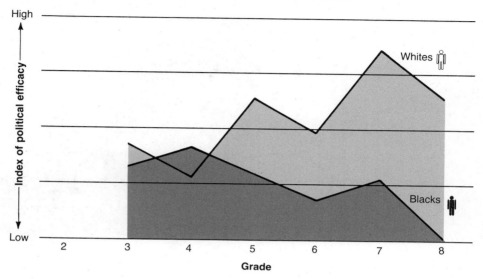

Source: Richard G. Niemi, *The Politics of Future Citizens* (San Francisco: Jossey-Bass, 1974), p. 91.

past and contemporary sources" (Jennings and Niemi, 1974: 206). On the whole, school socialization has a greater impact on blacks than whites.

Political efficacy and trust   Black children have much weaker feelings of political effectiveness and of trust in politicians than white children. Children's sense of effectiveness (efficacy) is shown by asking them how much they agree or disagree with five statements: (1) My family doesn't have any say about what the government does; (2) Citizens don't have a chance to say what they think about running the government; (3) What happens in the government will happen no matter what people do; (4) There are some big powerful men in the government who are running the whole thing, and they don't care about us ordinary people; (5) I don't think people in the government care much what people like my family think. Children's responses to these statements make it possible to set up an "index of political efficacy."

This index was used in a study of black and white students in Rochester, New York. The results are shown in Figure 3–5. Note: (1) black and white children in third and fourth grades show little difference in political efficacy; (2) after fourth grade, white children feel more effective—black children less; and (3) the gap between the white and black children generally grows with each grade level.

Differences between blacks and whites in political trust have fluctuated some in the last 25 years. Generally blacks have had less trust in political leaders than whites. This black-white gap was especially large in the early 1970s. Because trust has declined steadily among whites and has increased recently among blacks, the racial gap did not appear in 1978 or 1980. These trends are shown for one entry in the trust scale in Figure 3–6. It shows the total "always" and "almost always" responses to the statement "The government in Washington can be trusted to do what is right." Black distrust is tied mostly to political events,

FIGURE 3–6

Political Trust among Black and White Adults

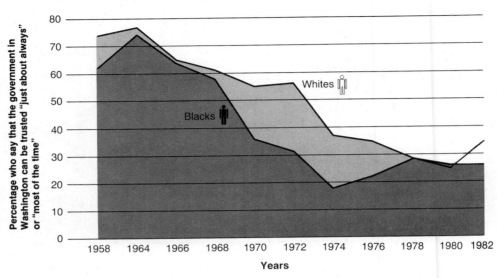

developments in the black community, and a realistic appraisal of the black political condition. The data in Figure 3–6 are for adults. Similar trends are reported, though, for black school children, as well. Young blacks are not hostile because their parents are. They feel that way because both young and adult blacks have less reason than whites to trust politicians.

Ethnic differences

Little is known about the political socialization of white ethnic groups, such as the Irish, the Poles, or the Italians. Scattered evidence suggests that "Americanization" was the major socializing experience for immigrants. It is possible that these groups have a stronger tie to national politics than Americans in general. By and large, these white ethnics were accepted into the mainstream of American life and politics. Other ethnic groups—American Indians, Orientals, Hispanics—have suffered discrimination. The Mexican-Americans, or Chicanos, are the largest of such groups. An in-depth study of the political socialization of Chicanos in California gives us some data (Garcia, 1973).

The California study was based on interviews held in 1970–71 with 1,227 Chicano and "Anglo" school children. The majority of Chicanos have a lower class status and a long history of discrimination. Yet there are very few differences in the socialization of Chicano and Anglo children. Chicano children show a very strong attachment to the political community and remarkably positive feelings toward the government. (Often their feelings are more positive than those of Anglo children.) When social class differences are taken into account, there are no differences between Chicano and Anglo children in these basic

Hispanic schoolchildren. The schools contribute to integrating ethnic minorities into the practices of American citizenship.

political views. Also, Chicano children support democratic procedures and values as much as Anglo children do. And the two groups have very similar ideas about a citizen's duties.

There is some difference between Chicanos and Anglos in idealization of the president. In the California study, third-grade Chicano children were more positive toward the president than third-grade Anglo children. By ninth grade, this was reversed. Positive feelings toward the president (Richard Nixon) declined radically for both groups between third and ninth grade. The differences between the Chicano and the Anglo children were, in any event, not very great. In sharp contrast to blacks, Chicano children do not differ from Anglos in their trust of politicians. On the whole, among both Chicanos and Anglos, the level of cynicism was very high for ninth graders.

The one striking difference between the Chicanos and the Anglos in the California study is their feelings of efficacy. Typically, the Anglo children's sense of political efficacy increased from third to ninth grade. We have seen this tendency earlier (see Figure 3–5). But unlike black children, the Chicano children did not show a decline in their feelings of political effectiveness. Rather, their sense of political efficacy increased, but at a much slower rate than that of the Anglos, as shown in Figure 3–7. Note the same widening gap in the figure between Chicano and Anglo political efficacy as between black and white children.

FIGURE 3–7

Political Efficacy among Chicano and Anglo School Children

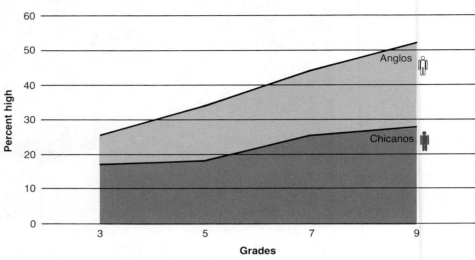

Source: F. Chris Garcia, *Political Socialization of Chicano Children* (New York: Praeger Publishers, 1973), p. 125.

CONCLUSIONS

We can draw several conclusions from this chapter:

1 The world of politics is not highly salient to most people most of the time. Americans have a strong sense of civic duty, but politics is not usually in the front of their minds. People are not highly knowledgeable about politics and government. Sometimes levels of public awareness about political life are disturbingly low. But awareness of political affairs and interest in politics are not particularly common to citizens of other democratic countries, either. And, compared to the people of other democratic countries, Americans are more prone to feel a strong sense of national pride. At the same time, distrust of politics and politicians is endemic among Americans. Americans have ambivalent attitudes toward politics. But their discontents are mainly directed against politicians, and not against the constitutional system.

2 Americans have historically been suspicious of political power. They feel that politics tend to be corrupt and that power is not to be trusted. It appears that American democracy is capable of surviving a large measure of hostility toward political power.

3 Americans' political beliefs include strong attachment to the ideals of liberty, equality, religious faith, and property. Most Americans believe in these as abstract principles. But in some cases, people can be bigoted and intolerant, and discriminate against minorities. The frequent discrepancy between principles and practice is inconsistent with underlying American values.

4 American politics is not very ideological. Strictly defined, only a small proportion of Americans are political ideologues. They seem to care more for what works than for what is ideologically consistent. Americans tend to be pragmatic.

5 Americans agree widely on basic political beliefs and fundamental orientations toward political life. Yet there is a good deal of cultural diversity. Subcultural differences—among religious and ethnic groups—continue, and this diversity enriches the politics of a nation in which much is held in common.

6 The deep commitment of Americans to their nation—the strength of their national identity and their loyalty to the American political community—is acquired in early childhood and reinforced by both family and school socialization.

7 American political socialization distinctly favors a positive, kindly view toward the government and its leaders. As they grow older, children's views become similar to those of adults. The gap between the idealized political world they first learned about and the realities of the actual political world may help to account for widespread cynicism among adults.

8 Political party ties are learned early in life. Children tend to acquire the party loyalties of their parents, if the parents have such ties. And party attachment learned in early childhood tends to persist through life. But, if stability in American partisanship is the most remarkable of its features, changes are far from unusual. In the 1970s and 1980s, more Americans, especially in the younger generation, became political independents than was the case in the two previous decades.

9 The family, the school, peer groups, and the mass media are important agents of political so-

cialization. Of these, the family's influence seems to be the most important. But as they mature, go to school, associate with others, and are exposed to the mass media, people's political attachments and beliefs may and often do change.

10 American political socialization, roughly speaking, tries to give the young some civic competence. The aim is to help new generations become effective citizens in a democratic society. When things go wrong—when riots bring cities to a boil, when a war becomes hopeless and wrong, when social injustices continue, and when scandals raise doublts about the trustworthiness of leaders—many people naturally feel helpless. They have a sense of futility about what their country is doing. Trust in political leaders understandably declines, and restoring it takes time. People do not feel as politically effective as they did in quieter times. In particular, people who are discriminated against, such as blacks and Hispanics, distrust political leaders and feel powerless because of thier very real deprivation.

FURTHER READING

ABRAMSON, PAUL R. (1983) Political Attitudes in America. San Francisco: W. H. Freeman. An analysis of continuities and change in Americans' party loyalties, feelings of political efficacy, political trust, and tolerance.

BROWN, RICHARD M. (1975) Strain of Violence: Historical Studies of American Violence and Vigilantism. New York: Oxford University Press. An excellent history of the role of political violence and vigilante activity in America which attempts to explain why American politics has been so violent.

CURRY, RICHARD O., and THOMAS M. BROWN, eds. (1972) Conspiracy: The Fear of Subversion in American History. New York: Holt, Rinehart & Winston. Various authors deal with important aspects of conspiracy in America and examine the role of conspiratorial groups with an eye to understanding the disturbing tendency of Americans to view the world in conspiratorial terms.

JENNINGS, M. KENT, and RICHARD G. NIEMI (1981) Generations and Politics. Princeton, N.J.: Princeton University

Press. An analysis of persistence and change in the attitudes of parents and their high school age offspring, making comparisons for data gathered in 1965 and 1973.

KIRKPATRICK, JEANE J. (1974) Political Woman. New York: Basic Books. This study helps us understand how political learning takes place among adults by focusing on women serving in state legislatures.

LIPSET, SEYMOUR MARTIN, and WILLIAM SCHNEIDER (1983) The Confidence Gap. New York: Free Press. An exhaustive study of public opinion polls tapping Americans' confidence in a wide range of social, economic, and political institutions. The theme of the analysis is that confidence in institutions has declined across the board since the mid-1960s.

McCLOSKY, HERBERT, and ALIDA BRILL (1983) Dimensions of Tolerance. New York: Russell Sage Foundation. A major study of Americans' beliefs about civil liberties which stresses the view that tolerance is learned behavior and that "tolerance may be harder to learn than intolerance."

PART 2

The Individual in the Political Process

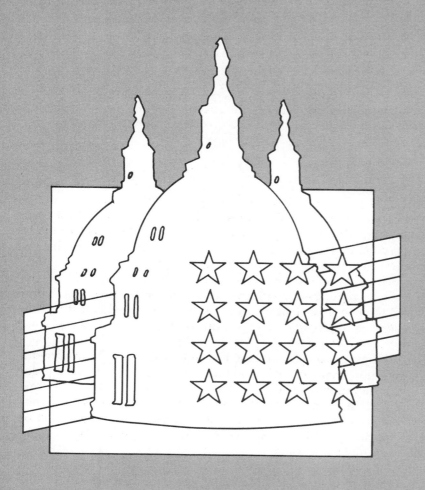

4
Political Participation

In discussing "politics as a calling," Stimson Bullitt (1977: 3–22) has advised that

> to enjoy politics, one must enjoy people; it helps if one likes them as well. A politican wants and tries to like people. He must be with them, and a friendly relationship makes it easier for him to satisfy and please.
>
> An able politician is neither an amateur nor a specialist. He is a general practitioner.
>
> Most American citizens are given better government than they realize, and most politicians are better public servants than many people think.
>
> To enter politics at the bottom is easy and good sense. Competition is mild, and one may practice in an arena where mistaken judgment is not fatal.
>
> To succeed in American politics, one must win the acceptance of many people and the approval of some, but compared to what other fields require, the approval needs to be more widespread and need not be as strong.
>
> To enter politics costs a person little in his vocational progress. The return is the rub. The likelihood that they cannot recover their former private stations deters many good men and women from a whirl at politics.

* * * * *

For Stimson Bullitt, a Seattle lawyer and businessman, politics has been a fascination. He has been active in it all his life, mostly in the state of Washington. He was twice a candidate for Congress; he lost both times. But for him, politics is a calling—not as a vocation, but as a summons to be involved. Politics do not call very loudly for many of us. Yet we have a sense that as citizens we have some duty to take part in the democratic process.

This chapter focuses on how people take part in politics. The standard wisdom holds that active, participating citizens are important to the political process. What would happen if we had elections and no one voted? Or if it were possible everywhere, as in Nevada, to vote "none of the above," and everyone did that?

Taking part and making choices are essential in a democracy. However, no one knows for sure how many citizens must be politically active to keep a democracy healthy. If the reach of such involvement must include every adult, or even all but a few, then no nation could be called fully democratic. It is not realistic to say that a country can be called a democracy only if all or most of its people are highly active politically. But we do expect a large amount of rank-and-file involvement in such a system.

We must know what the record shows about political involvement in this country to take stock of its democratic makeup. What are the various ways people take part in our political process? How active are they in politics? What are the traits of the highly active, compared to those who are only somewhat active or inactive? Under what conditions are people most and least apt to take part in politics? These are the main questions we address in this chapter. We analyze political participation in this chapter with the individual citizen in mind. In Chapter 5, we will consider elections and electoral processes in greater depth.

HOW DO PEOPLE PARTICIPATE?

In a political system as diverse, large scale, open, and equal as ours, there are many ways to take part. Voting is most often discussed. It is, though, only one kind of political activity.

Voting in elections

Americans are called to vote in more elections than people in any other country. The political demands on us as citizens are very heavy indeed. Every four years, we pick a president and a vice president. Every two years, all 435 members of the House of Representatives and a third of the members of the Senate are elected. Governors, state legislators, county and city officials, school board members, and other local officials are elected periodically, often in different elections. Candidates for many offices are picked in primary elections. Moreover, beyond electing public officers, we regularly vote on state constitutional amendments, referenda, and school or municipal bonds to finance public projects. In this country, elections are so frequent that they are large items of public expense. They require a large bureaucracy. And our elections are much more mechanized than those of any other system—mainly in terms of use of voting machines.

Americans vote for many reasons. Many vote as an act of loyalty or patriotism and out of a sense of civic duty. Many find the act of voting satisfying and enjoyable. One survey showed that 71 percent felt a sense of satisfaction in voting; two thirds found election campaigns pleasant and enjoyable (Almond and Verba, 1963: 146). Most people know that one person's vote does not, by itself, have much effect on the outcome of elections. But with the votes of other like-minded people, that vote can help decide who is elected.

The act of voting requires little knowledge or motivation compared to other forms of political activity. Many people who are not politically involved vote in elections. Many who are very active in politics may not bother to vote. There is the story of the lady in her 80s who was to babysit on the night of the first Kennedy-Nixon TV debate in 1960. She urged the parents to pick her up on time so that she would not miss any of the debate. When asked why she was so interested, the lady replied that she had been fascinated with presidential campaigns since Grover Cleveland ran against Benjamin Harrison in 1892. She

Posters proclaim the candidates for public offices and stimulate voting in elections.

109

had followed these campaigns ever since then with great interest. When she was settled in front of the TV set well before the start of the debate, she was asked how she planned to vote. "Why, I've never voted," she said. "I could never bring myself to vote against one of those nice boys."

Yet the act of voting requires something from everyone who goes to the polls. In the first place, it requires some effort: voters have to be registered; they have to take time to go the polls; they may have to stand in line to vote; and they must have confidence in their ability to make choices. To some, it can be intimidating. The often long and complicated ballot can be confusing. Some find that using a voting machine is more than they can cope with. Second, voting requires some kind of a decision. Voters must take a choice—either between parties or between candidates. Third, going to the polls requires a modicum of social consciousness on the part of the voter. He or she must be aware to some degree of what is going on. A voter must at least know that election day is *this* Tuesday and where the polling place is. Fourth, voting requires the play of at least some emotion. That emotion could be an urge to conform, a wish to show party loyalty, support for policies or a program, or ties to a certain candidate. And finally, the act of voting is an affirmation; it expresses a belief that "democracy is not a sham," that voting makes a difference (Lane, 1959: 47).

Party and campaign activity

Even in the age of television, elections involve thousands of people in party organizations and campaign work. These are the precinct committeemen and women who serve as grass-roots party workers. They are the delegates to county and state party conventions, as well as the delegates and alternates to national party conventions. In addition to these activists, campaigns enlist many volunteers. These workers pass out leaflets, posters, and bumper stickers, handle mailings, ring doorbells, work at the polls, and make telephone calls. This work requires more information and motivation than does the mere act of voting. Campaign workers are the "gladiators" who do most of the political work. Most people sit in the "spectator grandstands" and decide the outcome of elections by voting for the candidates of their choice (Milbrath and Goel, 1977: 13).

Community activity

Political activity is not confined to elections. After all, elections occur only at fixed intervals. For instance, a president is elected only in November of every fourth year. Yet thousands of people are active in ongoing public affairs in their communities. They work for bond issues for new schools. They concern themselves about school policies and programs through participation in Parent-Teacher Associations. They work for community beautification through garden clubs. They fight against rezoning the property across the street for use as a service station.

Political issues and problems are often not raised or resolved by elections. Thus, it is common for us to work together in our communities to grapple with public needs that are of direct and immediate concern to us.

Congressman talks to young constituents. [Left] Representative Jim Leach, Republican member of the U.S. House of Representatives from Iowa's 1st District, talks to a high school government class in Burlington, Iowa. Most members of Congress hold regular meetings in their districts, sometimes called "town meetings" or "forums," to keep in touch with their constituents.

Ohio students contact their congressman on a trip to Washington, D.C. [Right] Representative Chalmers P. Wylie, Republican member of Congress from Columbus, Ohio, since 1966, visits in his office with students who are in the nation's capital on a "youth to youth" program.

Contacting officials

We take part in politics by contacting public officials when we are concerned about some issue that affects us directly. In general, public officials are highly accessible to ordinary citizens.

The University of Michigan's Center for Political Studies took a poll after the 1978 congressional elections. Seventy-six percent answered that they had some contact with their congressman. But only 14 percent said they had met their congressman personally. Two thirds said they thought their congressman would help them if contacted about a problem.

Many government services are provided directly to us. Therefore, millions of us have contact with administrative workers. A 1973 study of this kind of contact focused on seven service agencies and showed that 58 percent had contacted a government office. Almost three fourths said their "bureaucratic encounter" had been helpful (Katz et al., 1975).

Moreover, in thousands of localities, people contact state and local politicians and officials. No one has tried to figure the extent of such contact. But the evidence indicates that we are more inclined than people of other democratic countries to be active in our communities and to feel we can influence public affairs (Almond and Verba, 1963).

Millions of people contact public officials by mail, and this kind of contact is growing. Figure 4–1 shows that political letter writing nearly doubled between 1964 and 1976. Those who write to officials are also likely to be politically involved in other ways.

A prominent target of letter writers is congressmen. Handling this great volume of mail is a big part of the work of a congressman's office. In 1981, more than 150 million pieces of mail flowed into congressional offices. Some senators received as many as 10,000 letters a week. The Postal Service figures that 400 to 500 million pieces of mail are sent from Capitol Hill each year.

Protesting

Protest marches and demonstrations are historic forms of political participation in this country. Even before the Revolution, Americans had developed the art and strategy of the demonstration. Conflicts over states' rights, abolition of slavery, women's rights, the tariff, the gold standard, unionization of labor,

FIGURE 4–1

Growth in Letter Writing to Public Officials

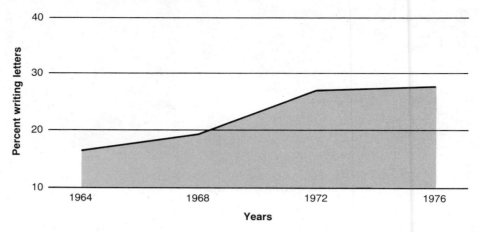

Source: Richard A. Brody, "The Puzzle of Political Participation in America," in *The New American Political System*, ed. Anthony King (Washington, D.C.: American Enterprise Institute, 1978), p. 317.

and war (to name only a few) have historically caused public protests. Public protest has become a potent political technique. Witness the protest marches of the 1960s for civil rights for blacks, demonstrations on college campuses in the early 1970s, and more recently, protests against environmental policies such as killing whales or constructing nuclear power plants.

In his book *The Amateur Democrat*, James Q. Wilson distinguishes deftly between amateur and professional politicians. Here are some exerpts (pp. 2–4):

> By amateur is not meant a dabbler, a dilettante or an inept practitioner of some special skill. . . . Nor does amateur here mean a person who is in politics for fun or as an avocation, rather than for money or as a career.
>
> An amateur is one who finds politics *intrinsically* interesting because it expresses a conception of the public interest. The amateur politician sees the political world more in terms of ideas and principles than in terms of persons. Politics is the determination of public policy, and public policy ought to be set deliberately rather than as the accidental by-product of a struggle for personal and party advantage. . . . He is not oblivious to considerations of partisan or personal advantage in assessing the outcome but (in the pure case) he dwells on the relation of outcome to his conception, be it vague or specific, of the public weal. Although politics may have attractions as a game of skill, it is never simply that.
>
> The professional, on the other hand—even the "professional" who practices politics as a hobby rather than as a vocation—is preoccupied with the outcome of politics in terms of winning and losing. Politics, to him, consists of concrete questions and specific persons who must be dealt with in a manner that will "keep everybody happy" and thus minimize the possibility of defeat at the next election.
>
> The principal reward of politics to the amateur is the sense of having satisfied a felt obligation to "participate," and this satisfaction is greater the higher the value the amateur can attach to the ends which the outcomes of politics serve. The principal reward of the professional is to be found in the extrinsic satisfactions of participation—power, income, status, or the fun of the game.

The politics of protest. Protesting and demonstrating is a timeworn type of political participation in the United States. These demonstrators in New Jersey march on the local electric power company, protesting plans for nuclear power generation. The gas mask is a reminder of the nuclear generator accident at Three Mile Island, Pennsylvania, in 1980.

Most people feel it is all right to go with a group to protest to a public official. But many take a dim view of street demonstrations. An interesting study done in Buffalo, New York, gives some clues to our feelings about protests (see Figure 4–2). One notable finding is that blacks are much more in favor of pro-

FIGURE 4–2

Americans' Attitudes toward Protesting

Percent of Buffalo, New York
citizens who say it is wrong to:

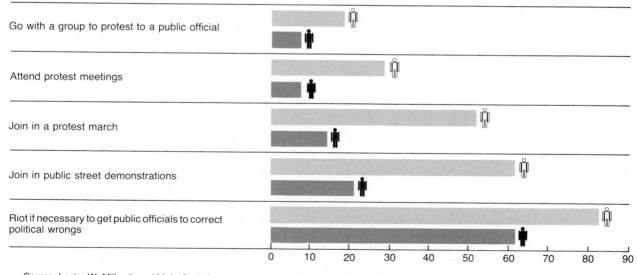

Source: Lester W. Milbrath and M. L. Goel, *Political Participation,* 2d ed. (Chicago: Rand McNally, 1977), p. 15. Reprinted by permission.

tests than whites. This stands to reason. Blacks have suffered greater deprivations than whites, and their protests have more often succeeded in bringing about change. But one should also note that the majority of both blacks and whites think it is wrong to riot.

Running for public office

Few of us try to secure public office—either by election or by appointment. Seeking office may involve deciding to invest much time, money, and energy in public affairs. Some, such as the Kennedys, have huge personal wealth and fame; their commitment to public service seemingly was instilled in them by their parents. But most public officeholders are not wealthy or famous. And campaigning for most offices does not require a lot of money. Moreover, the large number of elective offices provides a fair amount of opportunity to run—there are about 526,000 elected public officials in this country.

HOW MUCH DO AMERICANS PARTICIPATE?

Many Americans engage in some kind of civic activity. But the number varies from one activity to another. Our best estimates of the extent of activity are shown in Figure 4–3. The most widespread activity is voting. Nearly two thirds of us vote in national and local elections with some regularity, while other kinds of political activity draw smaller numbers

The University of Michigan Survey Research Center has conducted National Election Studies since 1952. These surveys regularly include questions asking about election-related political activities. One indicator of political activism used is whether respondents "talked politics." (They are asked, "During the campaign, did you talk to any people and try to show them why they should vote for one of the parties or candidates?") Since 1960, about a third have reported this kind of activity in presidential years. This is more than in the 1950s. In 1976 and 1980, record proportions of Americans reported such "talking politics." (The numbers were 37 percent in 1976 and 36 percent in 1980.) Since 1952, 6 to 10 percent have reported attending political meetings, rallies, and the like. The incidence of such activity has barely changed over the years.

In recent election years, party or candidate work is twice as high as in the 1950s. Nevertheless, the proportions are small—4 to 7 percent report working for a party or candidate in any one election. Fewer people wear a campaign button or put a bumper sticker on their car during an election campaign. The figure is less than 10 percent, fewer than did so in the 1950s and 1960s. These

FIGURE 4–3

How Much Americans Participate in Politics

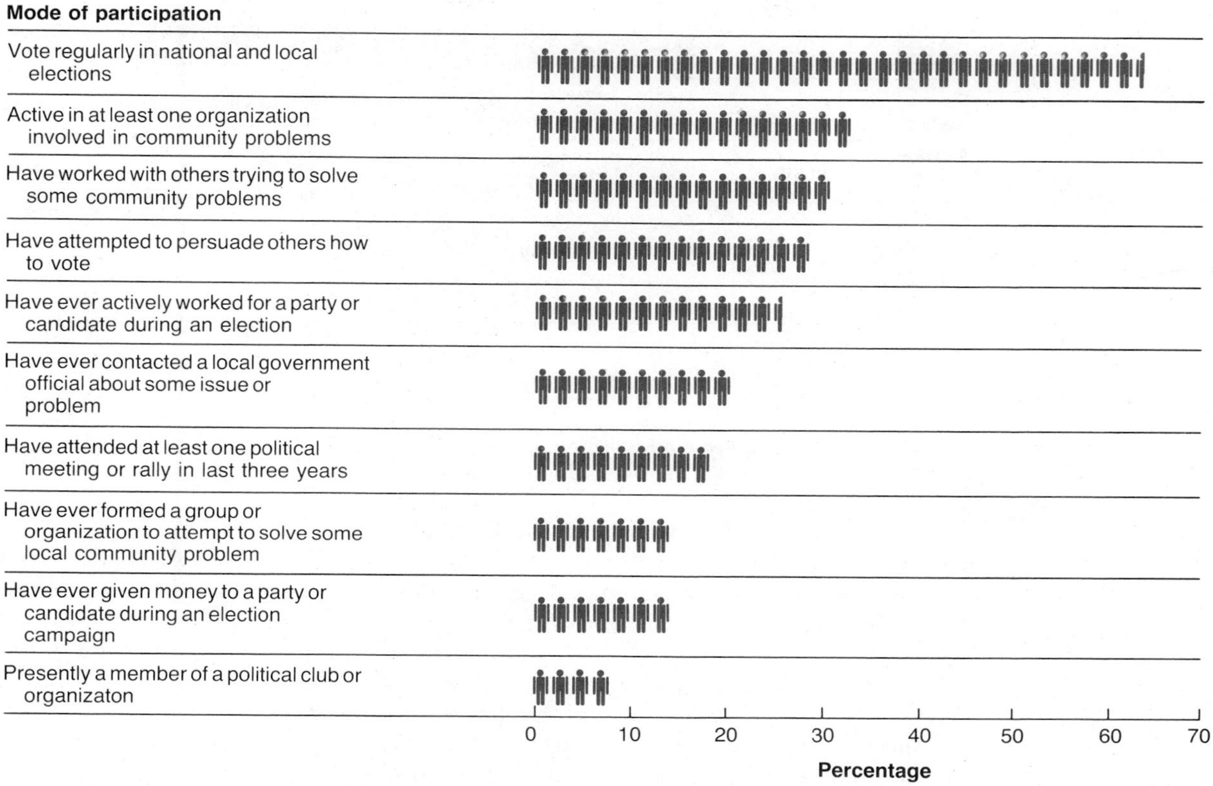

Mode of participation

Sources: Sidney Verba and Norman H. Nie, *Participation in America* (New York: Harper & Row, 1972), p. 31; Lester W. Milbrath and M. L. Goel, *Political Participation*, 2d ed. (Chicago: Rand McNally, 1977), p. 22.

Survey Research Center indicators do not, of course, show, as Figure 4–3 does, the extent of participation in particular activities. Neither do they indicate how much people have been involved over a period of years. Instead, these election-by-election indicators show involvement for a single election campaign.

Is political participation in the United States high or low? The answer requires a comparison. Comparing levels of political activism today with our past suggests that the level of overall activity is higher today. As we saw in Chapter 2, voter turnout in elections has waxed and waned. But other kinds of political activity may well have increased. This could be because such activity is highly correlated with education. Since the ranks of the educated have grown, plausibly, levels of activity have also gone up. And, of course, some explicit evidence points in this direction.

A more precise contrast can be made between political participation in the United States and other democratic countries. Compared with Europe, voter turnout is lower here. But this does not seem to stem from greater political apathy among Americans. In party and campaign activity we compare favorably with Europeans. In community activity, Americans are clearly more involved than Europeans (Nie and Verba, 1975: 24–25).

FIGURE 4—4

Political Involvement Other Than Voting in Five Countries

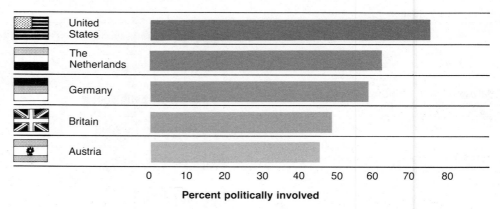

Source: Samuel H. Barnes and Max Kaase, *Political Action: Mass Participation in Five Western Democracies* (Beverly Hills, Calif.: Sage Publications, 1979), p. 169.

A study of political activity in the United States and four European democracies focused on action other than voting (see Figure 4–4). It excluded voting because the nature of elections differs so much in different democracies. Here, the national election is only one of many. European democracies have far fewer elections in a given time. The study showed participation to be fairly high here. The authors note that "political apathy, by a wide margin, is lowest in the United States." They conclude that "the United States can be characterized as a fully developed participant political culture" (Barnes et al., 1979: 168–69). This study found that Americans were more willing to engage in political protests and boycotts, as well as in more conventional actions.

Types of political activity

For a long time political scientists thought that political activity formed a hierarchy. Members of political clubs also engaged in community work, contacted public officials, engaged in party and campaign work, and voted in elections. Now we know there are distinct types of politically active people. Involvement in one aspect of politics does not always mean involvement in another (Verba and Nie, 1972: 79–91).

Some Americans, 20 to 25 percent by the best estimate, are completely inactive. They take no part in political affairs. These *inactives* do not participate in community action or in party and campaign work; they do not contact public officials; and most of them do not vote. They are "out of it." They add very little to the political life of the nation, and they have very little effect on the course of public affairs.

Another group is *voting specialists*. They are not very active politically, but do vote regularly. About one fifth of us are in this category. This is a fairly large group. But note that it is not the case that most people, as often claimed, vote and do nothing else. These voting specialists are far from being a majority.

Community activists engange heavily in community work but are not much involved in partisan political activity. They make up about a fifth of the people.

These activists are found in every community. In contrast, the political *campaigners*, about 15 percent of us, are little involved in community affairs but are heavily engaged in campaign work.

About 1 person in 10 is a *complete activist.* These people engage in all kinds of political activity. They provide much of the personnel and leadership for politics, and doubtless have influence far in excess of their proportion of the population. Of all types, they rank highest in psychological involvement in politics, political skill, partisanship and issue awareness, and civic mindedness.

In our country people are free not to be active in politics and public affairs. A democracy may prefer politically active citizens, but does not demand it. For many, being informed and active in public and civic life does not seem to pay off. They "cling tenaciously to ignorance of public affairs" partly because they can avoid conflicts. Like the Communist who reads only Marxist tracts, these people may avoid politics so as not to threaten their sense of well-being. They may avoid such activity because they do not see it as meeting any of thier needs. Politics seem far from the concerns of their daily lives. They may avoid it partly because they fear it might threaten their social environment; political activity may alienate customers, friends, neighbors, or employers (Lane, 1959: 113–14).

Protest through marches and demonstrations has become both sport and serious business in recent years. A large number of people sympathize with one issue or another. But the number who actually protest is small, only 2 to 3 percent. At the same time, in some locales—especially black city ghettos—a large percentage may engage in protests. The protesting minority has visibility and intensity. Thus, protests tend to have an impact well beyond the number of those involved. Also, as many as a fifth of Americans are potential protesters. They are willing to protest if necessary (Barnes et al., 1979: 155).

WHO ARE THE POLITICALLY ACTIVE?

The truly active people in politics stand out. They have been called the "active minority" or the "politically active subculture." As we have seen, they take part in politics well beyond just voting. They also work in party organizations; they are active in the community; they contact public officials in person and by writing letters; they give money for election campaigns; and some of them become candidates for public office. Who are these highly active people?

Socioeconomic status

Politically active people tend to be well educated, have high-status occupations, and high incomes. And these three traits—education, occupation, and income—indicate a person's socioeconomic status. The strong relationship be-

Citizens participate at the grass roots. At a ward meeting in the office of a Chicago alderman, a policeman speaks to the group about neighborhood crime.

tween socioeconomic status and political activity is shown in Figure 4–5. For the lowest participation group, at the far left of the figure, about 60 percent have low status; about a third have middle status; only about 10 percent have high socioeconomic status. In contrast, in the highest participation group (on the far right of the figure), 57 percent are high-status people; 29 percent have middle status; and 14 percent have low status.

One group stands out for its high rate of action in politics—the college educated. Most public officeholders and most who occupy the higher positions at state and national levels have college degrees. Similarly, among those involved in politics, the college educated dominate. A 1975 Harris survey underscored the role of the college educated in the politically active subculture. About 38 percent of those 18 and over are college educated. They tend to be the most affluent. But they make up 46 percent of the people most likely to vote and 57 percent of the most politically active.

FIGURE 4–5

Socioeconomic Status and Political Participation

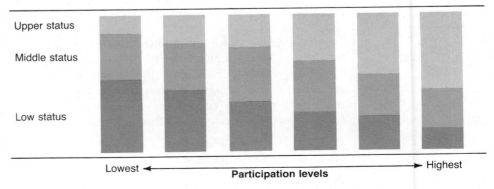

Source: Sidney Verba and Norman H. Nie, *Participation in America* (New York: Harper & Row, 1972), p. 131.

FIGURE 4–6

Age and Political Participation

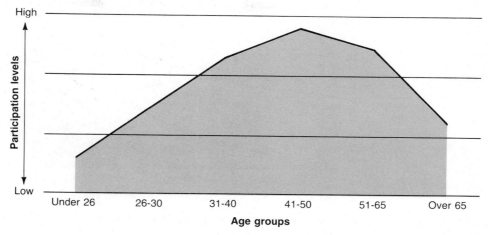

Source: Sidney Verba and Norman H. Nie, *Participation in America* (New York: Harper & Row, 1972), p. 139.

Age and participation

The rate of political involvement grows sharply from youth to middle age. Levels are lowest among those aged 18 to 26 (see Figure 4–6). The young usually have not established themselves in a community. They are apt to move often and to be deeply involved in finding an occupation. For the most part, they have relatively little stake in local affairs. This comes with extended residence, owning a home, forming a family, sending children to school, and taking part in community and job-related groups.

Figure 4–6 tells the story. It shows that participation levels are relatively low in the youngest groups. Rates go up smartly with increasing age to the group in their 40s. Though showing a lower level of involvement than those between 41–50, those in their 50s participate in politics at a relatively high level. Participation drops off for those over 65, undoubtedly partly because of aging itself. People over 65 may lose some of their social interests. Some become physically infirm and unable to take part. They may also withdraw after retirement.

Part of the increase with age surely occurs because older groups have higher average socioeconomic status. And higher status, in turn, enhances the likelihood of political activism. But much of the decline shown in Figure 4–6 occurs because, at present, those over 50 have relatively less education and income. They were raised in an era when education was not so available as today, when job opportunities were meager, and when income levels were lower.

Political participation by blacks

Few political changes are more striking than the closing of the gap in participation of blacks and whites. Traditionally, black participation was much lower. This is not hard to understand. Many blacks have lower socioeconomic status and suffered discrimination. Today, the average black person still takes part in politics less than the average white (see Figure 4–7). But when racial differ-

FIGURE 4–7

The Political Participation of Blacks and Whites

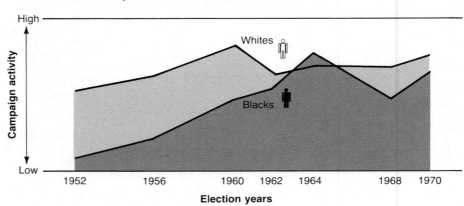

Source: Sidney Verba and Norman H. Nie, *Participation in America* (New York: Harper & Row, 1972), p. 255.

ences in socioeconomic status are considered, blacks actually do as much as, or more than whites.

Black political consciousness increased in the 1960s. This had a good deal to do with increasing black participation in politics. Rising political activism was spearheaded by Dr. Martin Luther King, Jr. and other black leaders. It was also helped by groups such as the Southern Christian Leadership Conference, the National Association for the Advancement of Colored People, the Congress on Racial Equality, and the Urban League.

Equally striking were laws and regulations easing civil and political discrimination against blacks. Especially crucial was the Voting Rights Act of 1965. This guaranteed that legally qualified black citizens could register and vote freely in federal and state elections.

To be legally qualified in most places, a voter must be registered. One common form of discrimination against blacks before 1965, especially in the South, was to deny them, by legal or illegal means, this right. Table 4–1 shows the proportions of whites and blacks registered in the southern states before and after the Voting Rights Act. Black registrations rose sharply between 1960 and 1970 in every southern state, more in some states than in others. In Mississippi, only 5 percent of black adults were registered to vote in 1960; in 1970, 68 percent were registered! Since the act, the numbers of registered whites and blacks in southern states have varied. In 1976, a larger percentage of blacks were registered than whites in Arkansas and Georgia. The denial of blacks' political rights has not been completely eliminated in the United States. But few public policies have been more effective than the Voting Rights Act.

Increases in potential black voters are shown for the South in Figure 4–8. The figure shows the rise in the number of blacks registered to vote in southern states. It also shows a marked decline in the gap between white and black registrations. Registration of blacks was increasing before the mid-1960s, but the Voting Rights Act speeded it up. In the mid 1970s, the gap between white and black registrations for all southern states together was very small. The gap grew somewhat larger in the 1980s. This suggested that efforts are necessary to maintain relatively high rates of voter registration.

TABLE 4–1

Black and White Voter Registration in the South

	Percent of voting age population registered		
State and race	1960	1970	1980
Alabama			
Blacks	14	64	56
Whites	64	96	81
Arkansas			
Blacks	38	72	57
Whites	61	80	77
Florida			
Blacks	39	67	58
Whites	69	94	68
Georgia			
Blacks	29	64	49
Whites	57	90	63
Louisiana			
Blacks	31	62	61
Whites	77	88	75
Mississippi			
Blacks	5	68	62
Whites	64	87	99
North Carolina			
Blacks	39	55	51
Whites	92	80	70
South Carolina			
Blacks	14	57	54
Whites	57	73	59
Tennessee			
Blacks	59	77	64
Whites	73	88	79
Texas			
Blacks	36	85	56
Whites	43	74	75
Virginia			
Blacks	23	61	53
Whites	46	78	62
Total South			
Blacks	29	66	56
Whites	61	83	72

Source: *Statistical Abstract of the United States, 1982–83* (Washington, D.C.: U.S. Government Printing Office, 1982), p. 488.

Gender and political activity

Studies in the 1950s showed men to be more politically active than women. This was largely because women's average education level was lower than that of men. Since then, the education gap between them has closed; so has the gap in political involvement. Men still take part more than women, but in most respects not much more. The remaining differences are shown in Table 4–2. Although participation of women is now about the same as that of men, they actually exercise much less political influence. Women constitute about half of the adult population; but far fewer women than men run for public offices or are elected. There seem to be four main reasons women are less active than men:

1. General social values and norms discourage women from highly active political roles; their socially set roles as housewives and mothers do not encourage them to run for office.

FIGURE 4—8

Black Voter Registration in the South

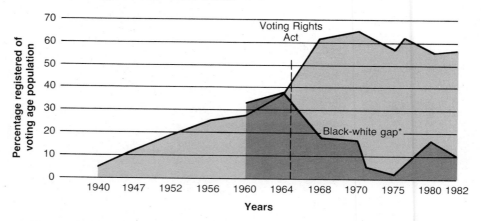

*Percent of whites of voting age who are registered minus the percent of blacks of voting age who are registered.

Sources: Donald R. Matthews and James W. Prothro, *Negroes and the New Southern Politics* (New York: Harcourt, Brace & World, 1966), p. 148; J. R. Feagin and Harlan Hahn, "The Second Reconstruction: Black Political Strength in the South," *Social Science Quarterly* 51 (June 1970), pp. 42–56; *Statistical Abstract of the United States* (Washington, D.C.: U.S. Government Printing Office, various years).

2. Female socialization discourages political activity. Thus, women's motivations for political careers are not as strong as those of men.
3. Political careers are not felt to particularly fit women's family duties.
4. Men discriminate against women.

Exactly what part each reason plays in the lack of highly active women in politics is not certain. The explanations of those who are highly involved provide some clues.

Jeane Kirkpatrick, now Ambassador to the United Nations, studied delegates to the 1972 national party conventions. Her intensive interviews with large samples of delegates included questions about sex roles in politics. Some results of this study are shown in Table 4–3. It gives answers to the question: "In general, there have been fewer women candidates for political office than men. Why do you think this has been the case?" The answers of men and women

Jeane Kirkpatrick, political scientist, has served as Ambassador to the United Nations during the Reagan Administration.

TABLE 4—2

Political Participation of Women Compared to Men

Percentage who	Women	Men
Are definitely registered to vote	77	80
Always vote in presidential elections	48	51
Try to influence others on political issues	26	35
Write public officials	25	29
Wear political buttons or stickers	14	14
Contribute money to campaigns	9	12
Have worked for a candidate	6	4

Source: John W. Soule and Wilma E. McGrath, "A Comparative Study of Male-Female Political Attitudes at Citizen and Elite Levels," in *A Portrait of Marginality: The Political Behavior of the American Woman*, edited by Marianne Githens and Jewel L. Prestage (New York: Longman, Inc., 1977), pp. 178–195. Reprinted by permission.

TABLE 4–3

Why Women Rarely Run for Public Office

There are fewer women candidates for public office because of	Percentage of	
	Women	Men
Society in general	45	47
Lack of motivation	25	21
Family responsibilities	22	25
Male discrimination	8	7

Source: Jeane Kirkpatrick, *The New Presidential Elite: Men and Women in National Politics* (New York; Russell Sage Foundation and Twentieth Century Fund, 1976), p. 455.

were about the same. Most said that social values were the main reason. The fewest blamed male discrimination.

Yet the study gave other evidence about attitudes toward women's failure to seek public office. Most delegates agreed that "men prevent women from seeking political careers." Nearly half disagreed with the claim that "women have just as much opportunity as men to become political leaders." At the same time, many said local party leaders encouraged women to run for political office. As many women reported preferential treatment as those reporting discrimination. Most women delegates denied ever being discriminated against. The political experiences of women differ in different areas and different partisan circumstances. Therefore, it is hard to generalize. Most women still believe men are more suited for political office than women. The best conclusion now seems to be that "women's low participation in power today derives from relatively low political ambition *and* from male prejudice" (Kirkpatrick, 1976: 455, 458, 488).

Organizational involvement

Alexis de Tocqueville, the French observer of our politics in the 1830s, thought a key feature of our democracy was our tendency to be joiners. He thought democracy depended on people with an active voluntary organizational life. His study, done without the help of modern survey research methods, seems largely correct. There is now much evidence that "a rich political participant life" rests on "a rich associational life." Taking part in all kinds of groups is one of the strongest predictors of active political involvement (Verba and Nie, 1972: 175). Americans are not more prone to join groups than people in other societies. But those Americans who are group members are more active than people in other industrial countries.

About two thirds of Americans belong to some social, religious, economic, or professional group; about 40 percent are active members. Active group members are much more politically involved than nonmembers. As Figure 4–9 shows, this strong tie persists even when the effects of socioeconomic status, age, sex, and race are taken into account. (The influences of these factors have been removed to show the "pure" effect of group membership on participation.) Group involvement has an independent effect on political activism. It also enlarges the gap between high and low socioeconomic status. High-status people are more apt to be active in organizations.

Merely being a member of a group does not foster political action. One must

FIGURE 4–9

Organizational Involvement and Political Participation

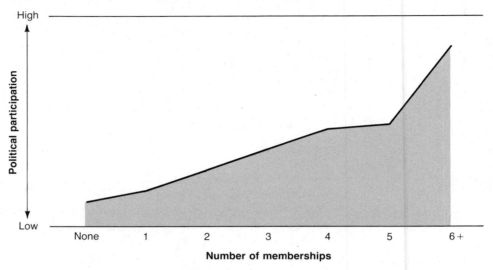

Source: Sidney Verba and Norman H. Nie, *Participation in America* (New York: Harper & Row, 1972), p. 184.

Political women. The League of Women Voters is an organization in which women are politically involved, promoting good government and analyzing political issues as a basis for political action.

be *active.* Inactive members are no more participants in politics than nonmembers. What is more, though blacks are no more active in groups than whites, their participation is more apt to spark political activism. Involved members of groups such as the Elks Club, League of Women Voters, NAACP, American Legion, National Farmers' Union, PTA, or American Medical Association, learn group-related skills. They mix with like-minded people who may come to share their concerns. They learn about public affairs and how to use available resources to reach their goals. Perhaps their sense of civic duty is aroused. The participant, democratic person is clearly one who becomes actively involved in organizations.

Membership in American political parties is unique. Most Americans identify themselves as Republicans or Democrats. But few are members in a strict sense. Being a Democrat is different from being a member of the Rotary Club or Lambda Chi Alpha. In the latter, membership means paying dues, attending meetings, taking part in activities, perhaps even carrying a membership card. Few of us are card-carrying, dues-paying, meeting-attending party members.

There are some organized political clubs in our country. But fewer than 10 percent of Americans belong to such clubs. That is not very many. Membership in other kinds of groups is not very great either. Americans are about as apt to belong to strictly political clubs as they are to veterans', youth, or professional groups. Many more belong to sports, fraternal, school service, or labor groups. However, members of political clubs are usually quite active.

Partisanship

Political parties are, for most people, not membership groups in the strict sense. But millions of us identify with a party. We think of ourselves as Democrats or Republicans (or Communists, Socialists, Prohibitionists, or whatever). Party identification indicates psychological involvement in politics. And about 80

" IF THE 1984 PRESIDENTIAL ELECTION WERE HELD TODAY... WHO WOULD YOU
BE THINKING ABOUT VOTING FOR IN 1988?.."

percent of us are so involved. Does identifying with a party, and the strength of that identification, foster political action?

The short answer is that partisanship does foster political activity. Those who identify with a party are far more politically active than nonidentifiers. What is more, though those of higher status are more apt to identify with a political party than those of lower status, both groups take part in politics more than do independents, regardless of status. Also, political action rises with how strongly partisan people are. This is shown in Figure 4–10. "Strong" Demo-

FIGURE 4–10

Partisanship and Political Participation

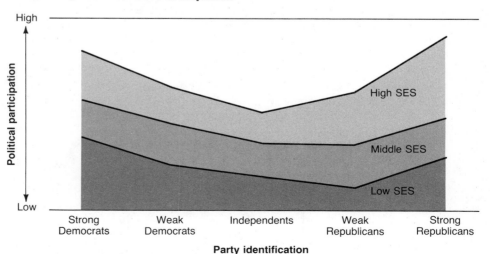

Source: Sidney Verba and Norman H. Nie, *Participation in America* (New York: Harper & Row, 1972), p. 217.

Republican party symbols. Bill Brock, former chairman of the Republican Party, stands in front of a portrait of Teddy Roosevelt, a Republican president. And to his right is a sculpture of an elephant, the famous symbol of the Republican party.

crats and Republicans are more active politically than are "weak" ones or independents in each major socioeconomic status (SES) category.

Notice in Figure 4–10 that Republicans, especially high-status ones, participate more than Democrats. This Republican "hyperactivity" is very large if one looks only at differences between parties. But much of the difference is because there are more high-status Republicans. Even when this fact is considered, that hyperactivity persists. Also Republicans hold political beliefs more strongly than Democrats. Republicans' higher social status and more intensely-held beliefs together help explain why their rate of political activity is higher than for Democrats.

Such factors as socioeconomic status, maturity, group involvement, and partisanship tend to raise political involvement. Also people take part more if their environment is conducive to it. Political activism depends partly on who people are. But it also depends partly on where they live. We would expect, for example, to find levels of political activity higher in areas where political parties are competitive.

Competition and participation

Political participation is greatest when rival parties and candidates compete strongly for public offices. This is easy to show. Thus, another reason for the low levels of activism in the South is that large parts of the area are politically stagnant. One-party, noncompetitive politics breed citizen inertia.

But the tie between competitive environments and involvement is more general. It is well illustrated by checking voter turnout in a congressional election compared to the tightness of contests for congressional seats, illustrated with data from the 1972 election in Table 4–4. In competitive districts (those where the winner got less than 55 percent of the vote), about 65 percent of voters went to the polls. In uncompetitive districts (where the winner got more than 65 percent of the vote), voting participation fell to 50 percent of the voting population.

Why is this so? Election contests may be lopsided and the outcome a foregone conclusion. Then, it is very hard for ordinary citizens to get interested in politics. Something similar occurs if candidates from two parties do not differ on any issues or present voters with any other meaningful choice. Where pol-

TABLE 4—4

Electoral Competition and Political Participation

Winner's share of the popular vote in district (1972)	Percent of average voting participation
Competitive	
Under 55 percent	65
55–59.9 percent	62
60–64.9 percent	59
Uncompetitive	
65 percent and above	50

Source: Kevin P. Phillips and Paul H. Blackman, *Electoral Reform and Voter Participation* (Washington, D.C.: American Enterprise Institute for Public Policy Research, 1975), p. 37.

"Stump speaking" then, and now. Competition for office breeds citizen participation. So, contenders have traditionally gone "on the stump" to vie for voters' support. In the 1800s, candidates aroused public interest by talking at public meetings [left]. By the same token, in 1983 Senator John Glenn (D–Ohio) literally stood on a stump to speak to a rally in Houston during his bid for the Democratic presidential nomination.

itics is "Tweedledum and Tweedledee," voter reaction is apt to be "ho hum." Where it is only "Tweedledum," voters are not likely to find it at all interesting. Another consideration has to do with organized party activity. Where parties do not compete vigorously for office, grass-roots party work is likely to be sparse. Workers will not contact voters, proselytize, stimulate interest, or work to get voters to the polls. People who are contacted by party workers in election campaigns are more likely to vote than those who are not contacted. Therefore, in noncompetitive environments with little or no campaigning, low participation is likely.

CONCLUSION

In the United States, politics is not the foremost concern of many citizens. People are free to take part in politics or not; many choose to have little to do with it. Legal restrictions, such as registration for voting, may discourage some. The extent of political inactivity is far greater, however, than could result from legal limitations. In this chapter we have explored the key elements of political activity in the United States. We have shown that:

1 People may take part in politics in many ways. They may vote; engage in party and campaign activity; involve themselves in community affairs; contact public officials; take part in marches, demonstrations, and other protests; run for political office; or be active party members. Those active in politics are likely to have more influence over the course of public affairs than those not active.

2 Those who take part in politics are by no means a random sample of the general adult population. They form an elite in the sense that they are better educated and have higher incomes and higher-status occupations. Thus, ironically, those needing the greatest public or government help are the least active in politics.

3 Political activity is fostered by several factors. The most important is probably organizational involvement. People who are most involved in social, economic, religious, civic, and other groups are most likely to take part in politics. Political participation grows with age. This is partly because increasing age is accompanied by increasing involvement in organizations. But psychological factors such as group consciousness and partisan ties can cause political activity, too. This is well illustrated by the political activism of blacks whose racial consciousness has been raised and by the heightened political involvement of those who have strong ties to a political party.

4 Where politics is competitive, people take part more actively. Competition sparks interest in politics. It also creates incentive for parties and their leaders to organize and mobilize people for political involvement.

Political participation does make a difference. Those who are active in politics have more access to the political leadership. The policy positions and attitudes of leaders are more likely to coincide with those of politically active people than with those of inactives. Political and government decisions are very responsive to the beliefs and preferences of people in the politically active subculture. And de-cisions about who is nominated and elected to public office are greatly influenced by politically active people. "Government for the people" may well involve accounting for the opinions and needs of the politically inactive; inactives may be represented because of their social and economic needs. But "government by the people" is very largely government by the politically active. Except for voting in elections, the politically involved are an active minority.

FURTHER READING

LANE, ROBERT E. (1959) Political Life: Why People Get Involved in Politics. Glencoe, Ill.: Free Press. A classic study explaining the social, political, and psychological factors which influence people to participate in politics.

MILBRATH, LESTER W., and M. L. GOEL (1977) Political Participation, 2d ed. Chicago: Rand McNally. An examination of the factors affecting political participation which draws its evidence from a large number of countries.

VERBA, SIDNEY, and NORMAN H. NIE (1972) Participation in America. New York: Harper & Row. Based on sample survey data, this study distinguishes various ways of participating in politics, examines why people participate in different ways and to different degrees, and assesses whether or not participation has important consequences.

5

National Elections

On election day America is Republican until five or six in the evening. It is in the last few hours of the day that working people and their families vote on their way home from work or after supper; it is then, at evening, that America goes Democratic if it goes Democratic at all. All of this is invisible, for it is the essence of the act that as it happens it is a mystery in which millions of people each fit one fragment of a total secret together, none of them knowing the shape of the whole.

Theodore H. White (1961)

* * * * *

Candidates and voters are the leading actors in the quadrennial drama of American presidential politics. They hold the same role in congressional, state, and local elections, as well. In 1980, thousands of candidates and 87 million citizens took a direct part in the electoral process. The outcome of elections—who wins and who loses—is affected not only by voters choosing candidates. It is also affected by the electoral situation itself. These include such things as the turnout at the polls, campaign features, the voting situation, and how the popular votes are translated into electoral decisions.

In Chapter 4, our attention was drawn to the involvement of individuals in the political process. In this chapter, we focus on elections as aggregate national political events. First, we ask "What is the context of voting?" The electoral verdict depends upon how people vote. When the votes are counted, those who win the most are elected. But the verdict of the electorate is shaped by many factors beyond the control of individual voters. These factors are part of the context of voting. The voter is an actor on the electoral stage; the context includes the stage itself, the props, the script, and dialogue of the other actors, and the stage directions. The electoral context includes levels of voter turnout, the nature of the ballot, the conduct and administration of elections, and the biases of the electoral system.

There is a second closely related question. "How does the American electoral system work?" We have a complex system for electing officers in this country. There are many elections and many offices. Also, we elect the president by means of the complex **electoral college system.** Understanding our elections requires a good grasp of the way our electoral system works.

Election defeat is no fun. President Gerald Ford stands between his son, Steve, and his daughter, Susan, listening grimly as his wife, Betty, reads a congratulatory message he sent to the newly-elected president, Jimmy Carter. President Ford could not read the message because he had lost his voice through the rigors of the 1976 presidential campaign.

Our third question is, "Who are the Democratic and Republican voters?" In Chapter 4 we discussed political participation in general. Here we want to take special note of those who vote in elections. Their role is especially important. They determine which candidates will hold public offices. We present a profile of the voters for the two major parties. Prominent traits are highlighted. They include socioeconomic status, race, ethnic and religious background, sex, age, trade union membership, and residence.

Fourth, we ask, "What factors explain the voting behavior of Americans?" Everyone knows it is hard to explain why people do what they do. People often do not act as expected or do what they say they will. Human behavior is highly complex; it cannot be "explained" by any simple set of factors. Let's say how you vote depends on what you had for breakfast. Then a social scientist will have trouble using data from national samples to discover that cause of your behavior. Your behavior is *idiosyncratic*—unique to you as an individual. However, certain factors that affect how people vote can be analyzed in a systematic way since they pertain to millions of voters. These factors—party ties, candidate appeal, campaign issues—have a predictable effect on many people.

We close this chapter by painting the shape of American elections on a large canvas. We classify elections and show that these periodic political events have different forms. Some elections have been "repeats" of previous events. Voting patterns and election results repeat what occurred in the previous election. Some elections are "test patterns" for future changes. They show changing voter alignments, which forecast changes in political leadership. Some elections reflect sharp changes in voting patterns. They produce new and different leaders. The 1984 presidential race shows how such an election can both continue and depart from past trends. We will discuss it as a case study.

THE ELECTORAL CONTEXT OF VOTING

American elections are conducted in accord with laws, rules, and practices. These affect who votes and can affect the outcome of elections. The scholar who told Charlemagne that the voice of the people was the voice of God may have been right. But that voice is rarely a clarion call unchanged by humans. Our electoral process is conducted on a vast scale. No one understands all the factors that affect its outcome. Nevertheless, many of these factors have been observed. One is voter turnout.

Voter turnout

As noted before, election turnout is rather low in this country. The average in presidential elections has been about 60 percent over the last 25 years. In many European countries, turnout in national elections is between 75 and 90 percent. This kind of comparison is tricky, though. Europeans as a rule must be registered, a process entrusted to the government. Election turnout figures are based on the number of registered voters, not on the total voting-age population. And the total voting-age population may include aliens, illiterates, the mentally disabled, prisoners, and other ineligibles.

In contrast, registration is voluntary here. Those who do not want to take part in elections are free not to register. Also, registration requires personal initiative. Going to the appropriate office to register could be inconvenient.

Getting out the vote. During 1983 and 1984, many efforts were made to register voters so they would be eligible to vote on election day. In Chicago, mobile registrars went to unusual places to find prospective voters. Here, Democratic presidential candidate Jesse Jackson looks on as registrars sign up voters in the Cook County Jail!

Even taking into account only those who are registered, Americans simply do not turn out to vote in national elections in the same measure as in other democracies. The exception is Switzerland, a very model of grass-roots democracy, with voter turnout lower than in the United States (Glass, Squire, and Wolfinger, 1984).

Voter registration   Seventy-two percent of those interviewed by the University of Michigan Survey Research Center before the 1980 presidential election said they were registered. A smaller number really were; more people think they are registered than in fact are. Of those who thought they were registered, 50 percent said they were registered Democrats; 27 percent, registered Republicans; and 23 percent, registered with no party preference.

The main purpose of registration has been to prevent fraud in elections. It is now required by law in every state except North Dakota. Without registration, it is easy for a dishonest person to vote several times in different precincts. One person wrote to ask his congressman for a favor; he said he was a loyal supporter who had voted for the congressman several times; "the several times I voted for you were in the election of 1966."

State voter registration laws always involve residence requirements of some kind. By federal law, these may not exceed 30 days' residence for presidential elections or 50 days for state and local elections. Also, federal law forbids the states to use literacy or "good character" tests for registration. Otherwise, all U.S. citizens who are at least 18 years of age and not mentally incompetent or in prison are generally eligible to vote.

Drive to register Hispanic voters. This poster says, "The hope of the future. . . . Our children deserve a better life. Register and vote. . . . Your vote is your voice."

The registration requirement and the qualifications to register disenfranchise many persons of voting age. In 1980 5.4 million resident aliens reported to the federal government. And there is good reason to think that many more resident aliens fail to report, although they are required to. Over 2 million people are in institutions. This includes prisons, mental hospitals, homes for the mentally retarded, or homes for the aged and dependent. Many of these people are part of the voting-age population. But they are for the most part not eligible to be registered voters.

Residence rules are designed to permit proper personal identification of voters and prevent voting fraud. But they disenfranchise many people who might have registered and voted had they not moved just before election day. No one knows for sure how extensive this is. It is easy, though, to forget how mobile our population is. The Census Bureau found that, on the average, Americans make 12 moves in their lifetimes. Between 1975 and 1980, more than 45 percent of the nation's people moved to a different house or apartment—over 90 million people! In short, voter registration without doubt keeps highly mobile people from voting. Also, many do not register because it is too much bother and they are not interested.

Some effects of registration and population mobility on voter turnout are shown in Table 5–1. (Figures are for the 1974 congressional election, not a presidential election.) Notice that the proportion of adults registered to vote is very low among those whose length of residence is less than a year. It is higher, though, for people with longer residence. Of those with less than a one-year residence, many were not eligible to register. Voter turnout in general was low. But high proportions of those registered went to the polls, regardless of their length of residence.

Registration requirements have stirred much controversy (Crotty, 1977: 72–100). Some favor ending voter registration completely. North Dakota has no registration. But vote fraud has been rare there, and voter turnout is among the highest of all the states. However, North Dakota is hardly typical. How would not having registration work in states or localities with long histories of corruption? Some would retain registration but make it more convenient. Registration by mail has been adopted in 20 states; door-to-door registration cam-

TABLE 5–1

Residence, Registration, and Voter Turnout

Length of residence	Percent of population	Percent registered to vote	Percent of voting-age population who voted in 1974	Percent of registered who voted in 1974
Less than one year	17	38	22	60
One–two years	16	52	36	69
Three–five years	16	66	47	71
Six years or more	48	78	58	75
Total	97*	62	45	72

*Not reported for 3 percent.

Source: *Statistical Abstract of the United States* (Washington, D.C.: U.S. Governmental Printing Office, 1977), p. 468.

paigns are done in some states. On the whole, these devices appear to have distressingly little effect on how many voters take part (Phillips and Blackman, 1975: 14–22).

Minnesota and Wisconsin adopted election-day registration after the 1972 election. As a result, voter turnout was 1 or 2 percent higher in 1976 in these two states. But the costs of this system can be large. Experiences in these states suggest that voters are encouraged to wait until election day to register. That causes confusion and long waiting lines at the polls. It makes possible registration errors that allow hundreds to vote in the wrong place. And it opens the door for vote fraud in states where the honesty of elections is not taken for granted (Smolka, 1977).

Many elections   Voter turnout usually is discussed in relation to presidential elections. But there are many elections in the country. Voters are called upon regularly to vote for candidates for Congress, governor, state legislator, county and local offices, and referenda issues. If we limit analysis of turnout to the presidential contests, we understate voting participation. Consider these facts based on surveys conducted from 1972 to 1976, shown in Figure 5–1. During this period, the average adult voted 3.4 times; the average registered voter voted 4.5 times. On the one hand, only about a fourth of all Americans, and 5 percent of registered voters, failed to vote in any election. On the other hand, a third of all adults and 45 percent of those registered voted in five elections or more. So voting is much more intense among Americans than it seems from presidential turnout alone.

Variations in turnout   Figuring voter turnout on the basis of the voting-age population gives a low estimate. The voting-age population includes many who are ineligible or unable to vote. Although a higher proportion of those able and eligible to vote did so in 1980, the total was only 53 percent of the voting-age population. However, voter turnout in 1976 and 1980 was lower than in any presidential election since Truman ran against Dewey in 1948. One cause

FIGURE 5–1

The Extent of Voting by Americans

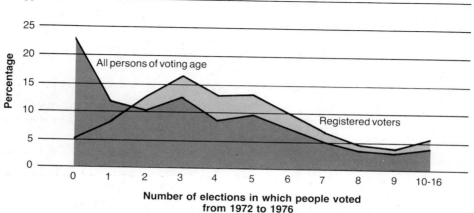

Number of elections in which people voted
from 1972 to 1976

Source: Richard W. Boyd, "Decline of U.S. Voter Turnout: Structural Explanations," *American Politics Quarterly* 9 (April 1981), p. 148.

" I THINK VOTER APATHY IS TERRIBLE... EVERYBODY SHOULD COME OUT AND VOTE FOR EITHER WHAT'S-HIS-NAME OR YOU-KNOW-WHO! "

of this was the addition of 18-to-20-year-olds to the electorate. This age group is noted for low turnout. Also, disenchantment with politics and loss of interest in elections have contributed to lower turnout.

Only 53 to 54 percent of those of voting age voted in the 1976 and 1980 presidential elections. But this national average covers up wide variations among states (see Table 5–2). In 1980, more than 65 percent of those of voting age voted in Maine, Minnesota, South Dakota, Wisconsin, Idaho, Montana, and Utah. Fewer than half voted in 13 states and the District of Columbia. Most low-turnout states are in the South. But the South is the only region in which voter turnout has been growing. (It was 45 percent in 1972, 48 percent in 1976, and 50 percent in 1980.)

Voter turnout varies across presidential elections and among states for any one election. There are also large turnout differences for presidential and congressional races. Figure 5–2 shows the pattern of these differences. Voter

FIGURE 5–2

Voter Turnout in Presidential and Congressional Elections

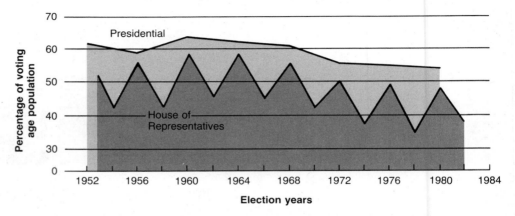

Source: *Statistical Abstract of the United States* (Washington, D.C.: U.S. Government Printing Office, 1980), pp. 500–01; *Congressional Quarterly Weekly Report,* various issues.

TABLE 5–2

Presidential Election Turnout in the States

Region and state	Percent of voting-age population	
	1976	1980
East:		
Connecticut	64	61
Delaware	57	55
District of Columbia	33	36
Maine	64	65
Maryland	49	50
Massachusetts	63	59
New Hampshire	61	57
New Jersey	58	55
New York	52	48
Pennsylvania	54	52
Rhode Island	60	59
Vermont	58	58
West Virginia	57	53
South:		
Alabama	46	49
Arkansas	51	51
Florida	49	49
Georgia	42	41
Kentucky	48	50
Louisiana	49	53
Mississippi	48	52
North Carolina	43	44
Oklahoma	56	52
South Carolina	40	41
Tennessee	49	49
Texas	46	45
Virginia	48	48
Midwest:		
Illinois	61	58
Indiana	62	58
Iowa	63	63
Kansas	59	57
Michigan	60	60
Minnesota	73	70
Missouri	57	59
Nebraska	58	57
North Dakota	70	65
Ohio	56	55
South Dakota	64	68
Wisconsin	67	67
West:		
Alaska	50	58
Arizona	48	45
California	52	49
Colorado	59	56
Hawaii	50	44
Idaho	63	68
Montana	65	65
Nevada	45	41
New Mexico	54	51
Oregon	63	62
Utah	69	65
Washington	61	58
Wyoming	60	53
Nation	54	53

Source: *Statistical Abstract of the United States, 1982–83* (Washington, D.C.: U.S. Government Printing Office, 1982), p. 491.

turnout in congressional elections is usually lower than in presidential elections. From 1952 to 1980, the average turnout for presidential contests was 59 percent; for congressional races, it was 48 percent. But, as Figure 5–2 shows, congressional turnout has a "sawtooth" pattern. The midterm turnout is much lower than when congressional choices are made at the same time as presidential choices. This cannot occur just because of the impact of state voter registration laws. Rather, it results from lower voter interest in midterm elections. There are no presidential candidates to attract national attention through wide media coverage. The high visibility of the presidential contest greatly increases voter turnout.

Presidential election turnout has declined since 1960 among almost all groups. But there are two important exceptions. The voting rate has increased among southern blacks and southern white women. Voting by blacks in the South shot up strikingly from 1952 to 1968. Their voting rate more than doubled between 1960 and 1968, spurred by the Voting Rights Act of 1965. And the traditionally large gap in voting rates of southern men and women was, by 1976, nearly closed (Cassel, 1979).

On occasion, issues or candidates in state or local elections spur voter turnout. When in February 1983, black Congressman Harold Washington ran in Chicago's Democratic mayoral primary, nearly 78 percent of Chicago's eligible voters went to the polls. Turnout exceeded 80 percent only in the white ethnic wards on Chicago's northwest and southwest sides. But Washington captured the nomination because of huge increases in black registration and the solid support of black wards (Green, 1983).

Many commentators on American politics bemoan the low levels of turnout in our elections. Causes and remedies are controversial. If all people of voting age had to be registered, turnout would rise. But American policy makers hesitate to remove the voluntarism in elections. Vigorous competition between Republicans and Democrats and efforts by parties to "get out the vote" effectively increase turnout levels. This suggests that strengthening party organizations might be useful (Patterson and Caldeira, 1983).

The voting situation

The voting situation itself may affect elections. Voter turnout may be influenced by the number of polling places avilable per 1,000 voters. The polling station may be distant, hard to find, or otherwise inadequate. If so, people can be discouraged from voting.

Bad weather on election day affects voter turnout. There is the story about one-time Denver mayor Ben Stapleton. He knew how to turn bad weather to his benefit on election day. When heavy snowstorms threatened to keep voters away, he made sure that friendly precincts were well plowed, but was slow about cleaning the streets in opposing precincts.

In addition if there is no contest, if candidates are unopposed, or if races are very one-sided, interest in voting is apt to be low.

The ballot   The nature of the ballot voters use may influence how they vote. The position of names on the paper ballot or the voting machine affects the number of votes candidates receive. Those whose names are first on a vertical ballot list or on the top row of a voting machine are preferred (Bain and Hecock, 1957). This is especially true for less important public offices for which

Harold Washington's campaign for mayor of Chicago drew an enormous turnout of blacks to the polls. During the campiagn, Mayor Washington's supporters carried a large "8," referring to the number of the Democratic lever on Chicago voting machines.

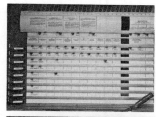

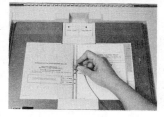

Methods of voting differ. Since the administration of elections is mostly a matter of state laws, different voting systems are in use in the United States. Many Americans make their voting choices on voting machines [top]. Voters make their choices by pressing levers next to candidates' names. Where paper ballots are used [middle], voters mark an "X" in the appropriate spaces following candidates' names. Many new voting systems are now available, including those where the voter makes punches in the ballot corresponding to the chosen candidates' name. [bottom].

candidates are not well known. If names are entered alphabetically, the winners tend to have names like Ayres, Allen, Alston, or Albert. (Aadvark would be a good political name under these circumstances!) People named Zanes, Zielbrecht, or Zwingli never seem to win. Because of this **position effect,** many jurisdictions rotate candidates' names by precinct on the ballot or the voting machine. That way, every candidate gets the advantage of being listed first in some precincts.

Two general ballot forms are used in U.S. elections, the **party-column** and the **office-bloc ballots.** The party-column ballot, used in most states, is set up so that all the candidates of one party are listed in one column (or row on the voting machines); all those of another party are listed in another column, and so on. At the top of the column is a spot in which the voter may vote for all the candidates of one party. In the office-bloc ballot, candidates are listed according to the offices for which they are running. For instance, all the candidates for president appear together, then all the candidates for governor, and so on. The party-column ballot encourages straight-ticket voting; the office-bloc ballot aids split-ticket voting (Rusk, 1976: 503; Campbell et al., 1960: 275–76).

Split-ticket voting   Of course, split-ticket voting occurs for reasons other than the form of the ballot. Most Southerners, for instance, identify themselves as Democrats. Yet in recent presidential elections, Republican candidates have won victories in southern states. In particular, many southerners voted for Republican candidates Richard Nixon in 1972 and Ronald Reagan in 1980, but voted Democratic for congressional or state and local offices. Figure 5–3 shows the trend in split-ticket voting with the proportions of voters who (1) voted for the candidate of one party for president and the other party for representative, and

FIGURE 5–3

Split-Ticket Voting, 1952–1980

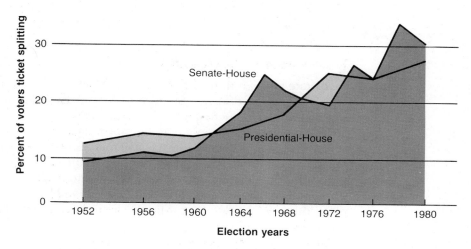

Source: David B. Hill and Norman R. Luttbeg, *Trends in American Electoral Behavior,* 2d ed. (Itasca, Ill.: F. E. Peacock, 1983), p. 35. Reprinted by permission of Professor Stephen D. Shaffer, Mississippi State University, who analyzed SRC/CPS Election Study data in his paper, "A Multivariate Explanation of Rising Ticket Splitting," presented at the 1982 annual meeting of the Southern Political Science Association.

(2) voted for the candidates of different parties for the House and Senate. In 1980, about 28 percent of voters chose the candidates of different parties for president and House, compared to only about 12 percent who were ticket splitters in 1952. House-Senate ticket splitting shows a similar trend. Although the party-column ballot, which makes straight-ticket voting easy, is used in more states than the office-column ballot, "the electorate since 1950 has displayed a willingness to engage in ticket splitting on an unprecedentedly massive scale" (Burnham, 1982: 112).

THE ELECTORAL SYSTEM

On January 6, 1981, members of the House and Senate met in a joint session. Vice President Walter Mondale presided. Four "tellers," two for the House and two for the Senate, publicly counted the electoral votes for president and vice president. Of the 538 votes, Ronald Reagan and running mate George Bush got 489 votes. Jimmy Carter and Walter Mondale received only 49 votes. As presiding officer, Mondale had to announce that Ronald Reagan had been elected president and George Bush had been elected vice president. That was the official election. The 538 electors had been chosen by the voters in the election of November 4, 1980. They had gone to their respective state capitals on December 15 to cast their electoral votes. Then their votes had been sent to the President of the Senate. But the president and vice president were not *constitutionally* elected until January 6, 1981. The same process took place between November 1984 and January 1985. How does this system work?

The Constitution does not provide for the *popular* election of the president. Though many of us do not realize it, we do not vote directly for the president. Rather, we choose electors who later officially elect the president. The Constitution provides that these electors be chosen in each state "in such manner as the legislature thereof may direct." Every state legislature now provides that electors are chosen by popular vote. But in the 1800s, electors were often chosen by the legislatures themselves. Today, the electoral college system is a central feature of "the strategic environment within which the drama of a presidential election is played" (Polsby and Wildavsky, 1984: 50).

The selection of electors

Each state gets a number of presidential electors equal to the number of its senators and representatives. So each state gets two electors for its two senators and an added number equal to its House members. A state's representation in the House is based on population, so the largest states get the most electoral votes. Thus, California, with two senators and 45 House members, now has 47 electoral votes; the other states' electoral votes are figured in the same way. There are 435 House members and 100 senators. Therefore the states' electoral votes add up to 535. In 1961, the 23rd Amendment to the Constitution provided three electoral votes for the District of Columbia. Thus, the total number comes to 538.

There is variety in choosing presidential electors. But most are elected on the **general ticket system.** This means that in each state all the electors for each party run together as a slate. Thus, when a voter votes for president, he or she is really voting for a number of electors equal to the state's congressional del-

Presidential electors cast their votes. In December following the November presidential elections, electors in each state cast their ballots for president and vice president. These 1980 Delaware electors, meeting in the state capitol in Dover, cast their votes for Ronald Reagan under the supervision of Delaware's secretary of state [second from right].

egation. The one exception is Maine. It adopted a district system in 1969. Two of the state's four electors are chosen statewide; two are picked in each congressional district. In the presidential elections of 1972, 1976, and 1980, the Republican candidate carried both districts. So, in these elections the Maine electoral vote was not divided.

Where do the electors come from? This is determined by state law. In 1980, electors were nominated by state political party conventions in 38 states. In most other states, electors are picked by state party committees or in primary elections. In Pennsylvania, state law requires each presidential candidate to choose the electors for his party. So, most of the individuals who serve as candidates for presidential elector are chosen by political parties. Usually, they are chosen to confer a minor honor recognizing loyal service.

In the November election, voters choose among slates of presidential electors. But in most states the electors' names do not appear on the ballot. Only the names of the presidential and vice presidential candidates appear. In 1980, only the candidates' names were listed on the ballot in 38 states and the District of Columbia; in 12 states, both the candidates' and the electors' names appeared. But whether the electors' names are on the ballot or not, the voter is choosing electors. In each state, the slate of electors with the most votes wins. Stated differently, the presidential candidate who polls a plurality (more votes than anyone else, but not necessarily a majority) of a state's popular vote wins *all* the state's electoral votes.

Casting the electoral vote

Presidential electors are for the most part loyal party people. They are not expected to use independent judgment in voting. Rather, they are expected to vote for the nominees of their party's national nominating convention. Most of the time that is what they do. Their voting is so automatic that, as we have seen, only the candidates' names, not the electors', are on the ballot in most states.

In 21 states, presidential electors must by law vote for the nominees of their national party convention or the presidential candidate receiving a plurality of their state's popular votes. Or they are pledged to support the party nominees because this is required by the party organizations. But in the other states, electors only need to vote following the duties prescribed by the Constitution and the laws of the country or their state.

These conditions have brought about the so-called **faithless elector** problem; an elector can vote for a candidate other than the winner of the popular vote in his or her state. From 1820 to 1944, this never occurred; but this changed in each of six subsequent elections (1948, 1956, 1960, 1968, 1972, and 1976). Electors voted for a person other than the one entitled to the vote. Most recently, when the 1976 electoral votes were counted, a Republican elector from Spokane voted for Ronald Reagan instead of Gerald R. Ford. Ford was entitled to the vote; he had won the popular vote of Washington. In none of these elections did the defection change the election outcome. The faithless elector problem is more hypothetical than real.

Counting the electoral votes

The electoral votes are officially counted before a joint session of Congress in the January after the popular election. To win the electoral count, a candidate must receive an **absolute majority**—270 of the 538 electoral votes. If no candidate gets a majority, the House proceeds to elect a president; the Senate elects a vice president. In such a case, 50 votes are cast for president in the House, each state delegation casting one vote. Thomas Jefferson was elected president by the House of Representatives in 1801 because he and Aaron Burr each got 73 electoral votes. No candidate had a majority of the electoral vote in 1825; the House then elected John Quincy Adams. For more than 150 years, this backup election procedure has not been required.

In the electoral college system, a candidate with a popular vote plurality can lose the electoral vote. In 1876, Democrat Samuel J. Tilden got 254,000 more popular votes than Republican Rutherford B. Hayes. But Hayes became president because he got 185 electoral votes to Tilden's 184. There was widespread fraud in the election, though. No one can be sure the popular votes were correctly counted.

A purer case occurred in 1888. Democrat Grover Cleveland got 91,000 more popular votes than Republican Benjamin Harrison. But Harrison got 233 of the 401 electoral votes. Harrison had won several key states by thin margins but lost other states by large margins. President Cleveland accepted his defeat; Harrison became president. But Cleveland got his revenge in 1892 by clearly defeating Harrison.

No such peculiarity of the system has occurred for nearly a century. It is possible though, by figuring different patterns of popular votes, to show that recent close presidential elections might have resulted in an electoral victory for the minority candidate. (This can be done easily for 1960 and 1968.)

Many presidents have not received a popular majority. But they got more popular votes than their opponents and a majority of the electoral votes. In nearly two fifths of the presidential elections since 1824, the winner has won less than half the popular vote. Lincoln was elected in 1860 with less than 40 percent of the popular vote; his closest opponent, Stephen A. Douglas, got 30 percent of the popular vote. More recently, Nixon was elected with 43.4 percent of the popular vote, versus 42.7 percent for Hubert Humphrey. Because Nixon resigned, Gerald R. Ford became president in 1974 without having been elected at all!

The impact of the electoral college system

The electoral college system has one major impact in electing the president. It greatly magnifies in electoral votes the popular vote of the winner and greatly lessens that of the loser. The winner gets a manufactured majority in electoral votes. For instance, Nixon beat Humphrey in 1968 by less than 1 percent of the popular vote. But Nixon received 56 percent of the electoral vote. In 1972, George McGovern got 38 percent of the popular vote (compared to Nixon's 61 percent). But he won only 3 percent of the electoral vote. And Ronald Reagan received just a bare majority of the popular votes in 1980 (50.7%). Yet he got 91 percent of the electoral vote.

The magnification of electoral majorities occurs because of the winner-take-all rule. The candidate who wins a mere plurality of a state's popular vote wins *all* of that state's electoral votes. This is called the **Matthew effect.** In Matthew 13:12 it is written: "For whosoever hath, to him shall be given, and he shall have more abundance; but whosoever hath not, from him shall be taken away even that he hath." That is the way the electoral college system works. Presidential candidates who have many popular votes are given electoral votes in even greater proportion; candidates who have few popular votes are given electoral votes in much smaller proportion.

The relationship between popular and electoral vote percentages for Democratic presidential candidates from 1880 to 1980 is given in Figure 5–4. It shows that candidates who only get about 40 percent of the popular vote tend to get less than a fifth of the electoral votes; those who get about half the popular vote tend to get about half of the electoral votes; and those who get roughly 60 percent of the popular vote are apt to get more than 80 percent of the electoral votes. Though a president may win a small victory in the popular election, he will get a decisive majority in the electoral vote.

Officially counting electoral votes. The president is officially elected when the electoral votes are counted before a joint session of Congress. Here we see the official tally being taken in the House chamber in January 1961, showing that John F. Kennedy had won 303 electoral votes. Ironically, Vice President Richard Nixon [seated below the flag], Kennedy's 1960 election opponent, was required to announce the result to the assembled members of Congress.

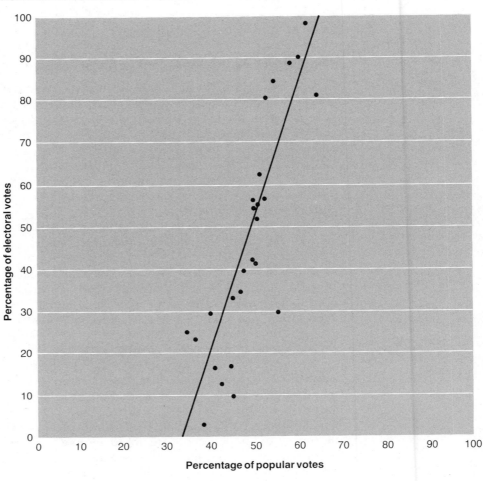

FIGURE 5—4

Democratic Candidates' Popular Votes and Electoral Votes, 1880—1980

The electoral college system also gives small but measurable advantages to people in some states and hurts those in others. This happens because, despite population, each state gets two electoral votes for its two senators and because

RULES OF THE ELECTORAL COLLEGE GAME

Getting elected president and vice president of the United States involves the following rules of the electoral college game.

1. Each state gets the same number of presidential electors as it has members of the U.S. Congress the District of Columbia gets three electors. Altogether there are 538 electoral votes to be cast.

2. Presidential electors run in each state (and the District of Columbia) on a statewide basis. The electors of each party run as a slate. The slate of elec-

tors getting the most popular votes is elected in each state. This is the winner-take-all rule.

3. To be elected president or vice president, candidates must win an absolute majority, 50 percent plus one, of the electoral vote. With a total of 538 presidential electors, this means that to win, a candidate must get at least 270 electoral votes.

4. If no candidate wins a majority of the electoral vote, the House of Representatives proceeds to elect a president. The Senate elects a vice president.

of the winner-take-all rule. Alaska, with a 1980 census population of 400,481, got three electoral votes in the 1984 election; Delaware, with a 1980 population of 594,338, also got three electoral votes. The "voting power" of the people of Delaware was not as great as that of Alaskans. But the winner-take-all rule gives the greatest influence in presidential elections to the largest states—California, New York, Pennsylvania, Texas, Ohio, Illinois, and Michigan. These states are the focal points in presidential elections since their large blocs of electoral votes are cast as units. Thus, the urbanites of the populous states of the East and West gain the biggest advantage from the electoral college system (Yunker and Longley, 1976).

Electoral college reforms

For many years, there have been proposals to change the method of electing the president (Sayre and Parris, 1970: 69–134). Proposals include casting the electoral vote automatically, dispensing with presidential electors. This would get rid of the problem of the faithless elector. It has also been proposed that the electoral vote in each state be proportioned accordingly to the popular vote for each candidate. This would abolish the winner-take-all rule. It has been suggested that electors be chosen by districts rather than on a statewide basis. This would make the electoral vote more proportional to the popular vote (Peirce and Longley, 1981: 131–80).

By far the most popular proposed reform of the electoral college has been the so-called direct vote plan. This would abolish the electoral college system completely. Under this proposal, the president and vice president would be elected by a direct popular vote. This reform was identified with former Senator Birch Bayh (D-Ind.). His plan involved a direct popular vote if the winning ticket gets at least 40 percent of the popular vote. If not, a runoff election would be held between the two leading tickets. Such a reform passed the House of Representatives in 1969; it was killed in the Senate in 1970. In 1977, President Carter included the direct vote proposal in his package of election system reforms. Nothing came of it. Because such a change requires a constitutional amendment, its adoption is difficult.

The direct vote plan would eliminate what many see as the main problems of the present system; these are the faithless elector, the winner-take-all rule, the two electoral votes given each state regardless of population, and the possibility that the popular-vote winner will not get a majority of electoral votes. But critics of this plan worry about possible undesirable effects. They fear that the two-party system, fragile enough under the present system, might be further weakened. A candidate could be elected who had great support in some parts of the country, but little support in others. This would thus make it difficult to represent the whole country. The outcome of the election would be more affected by differences in voter turnout among the states. And critics of the direct vote plan question the desirability of the runoff election, which would be expensive. Also, critics question whether enough Americans would take part in a runoff election (Longley and Braun, 1975: 66–69; Best, 1975). They are not very prone to vote in national elections as it is.

The electoral college, though not well understood by most of us, is a controversial institution. It has a subtle yet potent impact on presidential politics. The founders wanted presidents to be chosen, not by the people at large, but by a group of people who would use their own knowledge and judgment. This hope waned with the emergence of popular candidates, nationwide campaigns, and political parties. Yet the college itself remains as a reminder of the founders' experiment. It is a potential vehicle for distorting the popular will in choosing our chief executive.

The congressional election system

Presidential elections are dramatic, and the presidential election system is controversial. But the congressional election system is equally important. The most salient features are the apportionment of members, the creation of districts, and the decision rules for election.

Seats in Congress are apportioned among the states according to the requirements of Article I of the Constitution. The Constitution prescribes equal representation of the *states* in the U. S. Senate; each elects two senators. Moreover, the Constitution awards each state at least one member of the U. S. House regardless of population. The additional House members—from the 51st to the 435th—are apportioned among the states by population.

Apportionment takes place every 10 years, after the federal census. As population shifts, states gain or lose congressional seats. Today's shifts pit the older industrial Northeast against the growing South and West—the Frostbelt against the Sunbelt. After the 1980 census, 17 seats shifted. The big winners were Florida, California, and Texas; the big losers were New York, Illinois, Ohio, and Pennsylvania. Census results are so important to states and regions that census taking itself has become highly political. The 1980 census, for instance, was plagued by lawsuits charging that certain areas or racial groups were undercounted.

Once the census is complete and states are awarded their congressional seats, congressional district boundary lines must be drawn. Here, several observations can be made. First, the so-called **single-member** district system is used; states are divided into a number of districts equal to the number of congressional seats to which they are entitled. This is in contrast to **multiple-member** districts where each constituency chooses several representatives. The latter system is used in some European democracies and, in fact, in the election of some American state legislators.

Second, congressional districts are formed by the state legislatures. Following a change in the number of congressional seats awarded to a state, or in the state's population, the legislature must redistrict. In 1964, the U. S. Supreme Court held, in the famous case of *Wesberry* v. *Sanders*, that congressional districting must be done according to the "one person, one vote" principle—in other words, on the basis of equal population. Later Supreme Court decisions required congressional districts to be equal in population within each state. If the state legislature fails to meet this standard, a federal court is likely to order elections to be conducted in court-drawn equal-population districts.

Third, because districts must be equal in population, the time-honored practice of **gerrymandering** has new life. This is the art of drawing district boundary lines to gain the most partisan advantage. In the early 19th century, during the governorship of Elbridge Gerry, a Massachusetts legislative district was oddly shaped for partisan purposes. When it was suggested that the district wiggled across the landscape like a salamander, someone suggested that the district should be called a "gerrymander." We show the original gerrymander, and a

Blamed on Governor Elbridge Gerry, an 1812 northeastern Massachusetts district [left] was the first in a long line of creatively drawn districts, mapped so as to give the prevailing political party an electoral advantage. The most celebrated recent gerrymandering has been in California, where U.S. Democratic Representative Phillip Burton served as the architect for drawing new congressional district boundary lines in 1981 and again in 1983. The Los Angeles area districts [right] provide good examples of Burton's gerrymandering. Notice the "squiggly" 32d district [shaded dark], which connects San Pedro and parts of Long Beach to Downey through the so-called "Bellflower corridor"; the district was made 2–1 Democratic. The 27th district [shaded light] is especially notable; it wiggles along the shore from Santa Monica to Torrance, and then sails around Republican Palos Verdes Peninsula to land again at San Pedro. The 27th was created to provide a safe Democratic seat, replacing an entrenched Republican.

FIGURE 5–5

Gerrymandering—Old and New

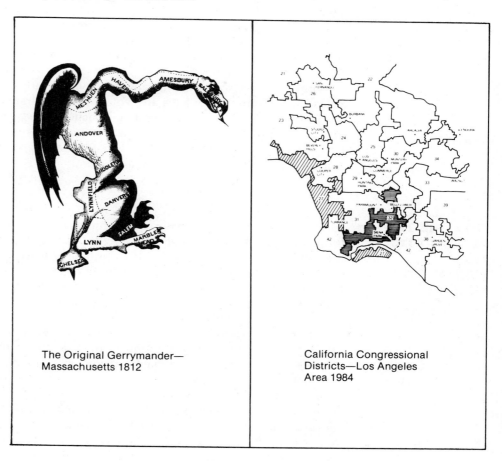

The Original Gerrymander— Massachusetts 1812

California Congressional Districts—Los Angeles Area 1984

modern illustration, in Figure 5–5. There are two gerrymandering techniques, jokingly called packing and cracking. **Packing** a district is drawing the lines to include as many of one party's voters as possible. This limits that party's seats or makes the district safe for an incumbent. In **cracking,** an area of one party's strength is split between two or more districts to minimize that party's voting leverage.

Finally, legislators are chosen by **plurality vote.** The candidate who gets the most votes wins. It need not be by a majority. Thus, congressional elections have a winner-take-all feature. There is only one seat to win in each congressional district, the candidate with the most votes wins "all" of the seats. Consequently, there is a Matthew effect in congressional elections. Though not as sharply defined as in the presidential system, the multiplier in congressional elections rewards the majority party quite handsomely. For instance, in the 1982 congressional election, the Democrats won 56 percent of the popular votes for members of the House, but they won 62 percent of House seats. The Republicans captured 43 percent of the popular votes across the country, but garnered only 38 percent of House seats. The electoral system persistently gives the

Democrats some advantage nationally. This is partly because they tend to win in smaller congressional districts and in those with low voter turnouts. But in several states the electoral system favors in Republicans electing state legislators (Tufte, 1973: 543–44); the system also favored Republicans in congressional elections prior to the New Deal. At this point, the GOP was dominant. Of course, the partisan advantages of the Matthew effect are magnified if there has been widespread gerrymandering.

Within the electoral system, candidates vie for offices and citizens cast their votes. In so doing, candidates and voters provide drama in important national events—presidential and congressional elections. Because our elections are significant events involving partisan choices by voters, we should examine patterns of voting behavior. Doing so will set the stage for summarizing the results of the most recent major electoral event—the 1984 presidential election.

WHO ARE THE DEMOCRATIC AND REPUBLICAN VOTERS?

It is probably easier to explain why Americans do not vote than to say why they do. After the November 1980 election, the Gallup poll asked people why they did not vote. More than half were unable to vote. They were not registered; they were not citizens; they were ill or traveling; or they did not get an absentee ballot. Another 15 to 20 percent indicated they just were not interested (see Table 5–3).

Like political participation generally, voting varies with socioeconomic factors more than anything else (Wolfinger and Rosenstone, 1980). Educated affluent people vote in greater numbers than do the poorly educated with low incomes. Age, too, has a marked bearing on voter turnout. More voters are between the ages of 35 and 64 than from the young groups. Beyond these factors, voters in general have attitudes that differ from those of nonvoters. They are more interested in politics; they are more concerned about the outcome of elections; they have a stronger sense of civic duty; and they are stronger in their party ties. But Republican and Democratic voters are different in their socioeconomic, personal, and other characteristics (see Table 5–4).

TABLE 5–3

Reasons for Not Voting in Presidential Elections

Reason	Percentage in			
	1980	1976	1972	1968
Not registered	42	38	28	34
Didn't like candidates	17	14	10	12
No particular reason	10	10	13	8
Not interested in politics	5	10	4	7
Illness	8	7	11	15
Not an American citizen	5	4	*	*
New resident	4	4	8	10
Traveling, out of town	3	3	5	6
Working	3	2	7	3
No way to get to polls	1	2	*	*
Didn't get absentee ballot	*	1	1	2
Miscellaneous	2	5	13	3

*Less than 1 percent.
Source: *Gallup Opinion Index*, 183 (December 1980), p. 29.

TABLE 5—4

Democratic and Republican Voters in 1976 and 1980

	Percentage voting for			
	1976		1980	
Group	Democrat (Carter)	Republican (Ford)	Democrat (Carter)	Republican (Reagan)
National	50	48	42	52
Sex				
Male	50	48	37	54
Female	50	48	45	46
Race				
White	47	52	36	55
Nonwhite	82	16	82	14
Education				
College	48	52	35	53
High school	54	46	43	51
Grade school	58	41	50	45
Occupation				
Professional and				
business	41	57	33	56
White collar	46	53	42	48
Manual	57	41	46	47
Age				
Under 30 years	50	48	44	42
30—44 years	49	49	37	54
45—59	47	52	39	55
60 and older	47	52	40	54
Religion				
Protestant	44	55	37	56
Catholic	54	44	40	51
Politics				
Republican	9	90	11	84
Democrat	77	22	66	26
Independent	43	54	30	54
Region				
East	51	47	42	47
Midwest	48	50	40	51
South	54	45	44	51
West	46	51	35	53
Union membership				
Members of labor				
union families	59	39	47	44

*Less than 1 percent.

Source: CBS News/*New York Times* surveys reported in Gerald M. Pomper, *The Election of 1980* (Chatham, N.J.: Chatham House Publishers, 1981), pp. 72–73.

Socioeconomic status

Business people and professionals tend to support Republican candidates for president. More than two thirds of them voted for Nixon in 1972; well over half voted for Ford in 1976 and for Reagan in 1980. The poor have been a declining element in Democratic voter support. This is largely because the proportion of poor people has declined overall. Working-class people usually vote Democratic by big margins. Nixon's landslide victory in 1972 came because more than half of the Republican votes were cast by manual laborers. Job differences were reflected in the 1976 election. More than half of the business and professional people voted for Ford; more than half of the manual workers voted for Carter. But in 1980, blue-collar workers voted equally for Reagan (the winner) and Carter.

There are similar differences among the college educated, those who only went to high school, and those who did not go beyond grade school. A majority of the college educated voted for the Republican presidential candidate in all recent elections. An exception was the Democratic landslide victory of 1964; Lyndon Johnson got a majority of the votes of almost all classes. In contrast, most of the grade-school educated vote for Democrats. The exception was 1972 when Republican Richard Nixon won a majority of votes of most demographic groups, except blacks.

Race, religion, ethnics

Voters of Irish, Polish, or Italian descent usually have been Democratic presidential supporters. But blacks form the most heavily Democratic voting group. Blacks have voted increasingly Democratic since 1952. They now comprise nearly a fifth of that vote. In 1976 and 1980, more than 80 percent voted for Carter.

Catholics and Jews have normally voted heavily for Democratic candidates. Only in 1972 and 1980 did a majority of Catholics vote for a Republican for president. Even "born again" Protestant Jimmy Carter got a large proportion of the Catholic vote in 1976. The most notable presidential year for the Catholic vote was 1960. John F. Kennedy, a Catholic, was the Democratic candidate. Nearly half his votes came from Catholics (Axelrod, 1972:16). In contrast, Republican voters have been mostly white and Protestant.

Sex and age

On the whole, sex differences in voting behavior have not been very important. They emerge mainly because of sex difference in socioeconomic status and age. In 1972 and 1976, both sexes supported Democratic and Republican presidential candidates in about the same proportions. But in 1980 a large majority of men voted for Reagan; women were about evenly divided. There was much speculation that a "gender gap" might affect Reagan's reelection, and in fact, he suffered some loss of support among women in 1984.

Younger voters usually vote more Democratic than do older voters. Voters who are middle-aged or older tend to vote Republican. This is mainly because the older generation has, over time, always been more Republican. It is not because people become more Republican as they get older. But in 1980, voters under 30 about equally supported Reagan and Carter. And there were more votes for John Anderson, the independent candidate (11 percent) among those under 30 than among other age groups.

Trade union membership

Voting is affected by the social groups to which people belong. One very compelling membership is in labor unions. For many years, labor-union families have been heavily Democratic. Since 1952, union members and their families have supplied about a third of the Democratic vote for president. In 1972 there was a huge defection of union members to Nixon. But a large union majority supported Carter in 1976. In 1980, Carter won more support among union members than Reagan. But his support was much smaller than it had been in 1976. However, about three fourths of all adults are living in families that do

Hispanic Americans express their support for former Vice President Walter Mondale in his bid for the 1984 Democratic presidential nomination.

Democrats count on trade union support. At this political convention United Mine Workers showed their support for the candidacy of Franklin D. Roosevelt, the Democratic Party standard bearer in 1932.

not include union members. These nonunion families contribute heavily to the support of Republican presidential hopefuls.

Place of residence

Democratic presidential candidates draw more support from the central cities than do Republicans. About 10 percent of the population lives in the central cities of 12 major urban centers. They provide about 15 percent of the Democratic presidential vote. Voters outside the central cities are more Republican. More striking, though, are regional differences in Republican and Democratic voting.

The southern and border states have generally been Democratic. They provide about one fourth of the votes for Democratic presidential candidates. But in recent presidential elections, Republicans—Goldwater in 1964, Nixon in 1972, and Reagan in 1980—won the electoral votes of southern states. In 1972, only 29 percent of southerners voted for McGovern. Over 40 percent voted for him in other regions. In 1976, Carter got his strongest support in the South. But Reagan won more southern support in 1980 than Carter. Though regional differences are on the downswing (politics has become more nationalized), they are still noticeable.

EXPLAINING THE VOTE

Accounting for why people vote as they do became much more effective with sample survey data. Adequate national election surveys only date back to the 1940s. Before then, election analysis depended on studying overall official returns. It was not possible to tell how individuals voted. Sample surveys, or public opinion polls, give data on voters' attitudes and traits. They also report on how each voted. Many things influence voting behavior. Three factors have proved to be very important. These are (1) party identification, (2) candidate

TABLE 5–5

Party Identification in the United States

Percentage who are	October 1952	October 1956	October 1960	November 1964	November 1968	November 1972	November 1976	November 1980	November 1982
Strong Democrats	22	21	20	27	20	15	15	18	20
Weak Democrats	25	23	25	25	25	26	25	23	24
Leaning Democratic	10	6	6	9	10	11	12	11	11
Independent	5	9	10	8	11	13	15	13	11
Leaning Republican	7	8	7	6	9	11	10	10	8
Weak Republicans	14	14	14	14	15	13	14	14	14
Strong Republicans	14	15	16	11	10	10	9	9	10
Apolitical	3	4	3	1	1	1	1	2	2
Total	100	100	100	100	100	100	100	100	100

Sources: Warren E. Miller, Authur Miller, and Edward J. Schneider, *American National Election Studies Data Sourcebook, 1952–1978* (Cambridge, Mass.: Harvard University Press, 1980)), p. 81; Codebooks of the 1980 and 1982 University of Michigan Center for Political Studies National Election Surveys.

appeal, and (3) the impact of issues. The influence of these three factors may change from election to election.

Party identification

One of the most persistent traits in political behavior is the distribution of party identification (Niemi and Weisberg, 1976: 160–438). As Table 5–5 shows, party loyalties have been very consistent since 1952.

We may assume that election outcomes are influenced by short-term and long-term forces. Short-term forces include candidate appeal and the strength of the issues. Long-term forces are those voting habits that recur and endure. Party loyalty is the most important of these. It is like an elastic cord that ties voters to one party. The cord is fairly inelastic for strong partisans. Even very strong short-term forces will move the average strong party members only a little way. Few will vote for the opposition party candidate. For the less strongly attached, the cord stretches more easily; short-term forces often cause defections in their voting. Independents who have no sense of party tie at all are "unanchored." They are highly susceptible to short-term forces in any one election (Miller and Levitin, 1976: 34). Party identifiers are more apt to vote than independents. For instance, in 1980 more than two thirds of the strong Democrats and Republicans voted; only 43 percent of the independents voted (Abramson, Aldrich, and Rohde, 1982:90).

Most party members vote for the presidential candidate of their party. But in some elections, short-term forces are so strong that defections skyrocket. Defections to Nixon and American Independent party candidate George Wallace were great among weak Democrats and those with Democratic leanings in 1968 and 1972. In 1964, there were marked defections from Barry Goldwater among weak Republicans. The 1976 election was more "normal" than the three previous ones. Partisan loyalists gave party candidates consistent support. But defections were again prominent in 1980.

Growth of "independence"

Independents have been the most volatile voters both in election turnout and in support for presidential candidates. Except for the 1964 election, most in-

George Wallace's American Independent Party won nearly 14 percent of the popular vote in the 1968 presidential election. Wallace, though strongest in his native South, took his third party campaign to California, speaking to the state convention of the American Independent Party in Sacramento.

dependents have voted for the Republican presidential candidate since 1952 (Asher, 1984:77). But "leaners" and independents are especially prone to split-ticket voting. Since 1952 there has been a long-run trend toward erosion of partisan loyalties and a pointed increase in the number of independents.

The growing proportion of independents in the electorate has not come mainly from conversions of party members. More important has been the dramatic infusion of young people into the electorate. These new voters are less apt than any other group to be regular party members (Converse, 1972). In 1952, before 18-year-old voting and the effect of the World War II baby boom, only about 7 percent of voters were under 25; by 1978 this rose to 19 percent. The increase in independent voters was largely due to this huge influx of younger people, most of whom had not developed firm party loyalty (Miller and Levitin, 1976: 192–99).

Also, in the 1960s there were major shifts away from the Democratic party in the South, especially among young southerners. A large part of the rise in the national proportion of independents came because of these shifts. Republicans gained few adherents. Many southerners identified themselves as independents. They supported George Wallace's third-party movement (Glenn, 1972).

Candidate appeal

Candidates and campaigns do have an effect on how and why people vote. At the presidential level, the major party candidates are highly visible. Their personalities, family backgrounds, physical features, and personal and political styles receive much attention during campaigns. But the impact of candidate appeal

---

HOW TO TELL DEMOCRATS FROM REPUBLICANS

A few years ago, an anonymous wit drew up a list of the main differences between Democrats and Republicans. A Republican congressman from California, Craig Hosmer, included this anonymous author's formulation in the *Congressional Record*. It reads as follows:

Democrats buy most of the books that have been banned somewhere. Republicans form censorship committees and read them as a group.

Republicans consume three fourths of all the rutabaga produced in this country. The remainder is thrown out.

Republicans usually wear hats and almost always clean their paint brushes.

Democrats give their worn-out clothes to those less fortunate. Republicans wear theirs.

Republicans employ exterminators. Democrats step on the bugs.

Democrats name their children after currently popular sports figures, politicians, and entertainers. Republican children are named after their parents or grandparents, according to where the most money is.

Democrats keep trying to cut down on smoking but are not successful. Neither are Republicans.

Republicans tend to keep their shades drawn, although there is seldom any reason why they should. Democrats ought to, but don't.

Republicans study the financial pages of the newspaper. Democrats put them in the bottom of the bird cage.

Most of the stuff you see alongside the road has been thrown out of car windows by Democrats.

Republicans raise dahlias, Dalmations, and eyebrows. Democrats raise Airedales, kids, and taxes.

Democrats eat the fish they catch. Republicans hang them on the wall.

Republican boys date Democratic girls. They plan to marry Republican girls but feel they're entitled to a little fun first.

Democrats make up plans and then do something else. Republicans follow the plans their grandfathers made.

Republicans sleep in twin beds—some even in separate rooms. That is why there are more Democrats.

The appeal of candidates. President Dwight D. Eisenhower [top] appeals to the crowd. "Ike" was a very popular president in the 1950s. President Ronald Reagan [middle] wades into a crowd of "hardhats" during the 1980 campaign. President John F. Kennedy [bottom] had the appeal of youth; he was the youngest president the country has ever had.

FIGURE 5—6

The Electoral Impact of Candidate Appeal

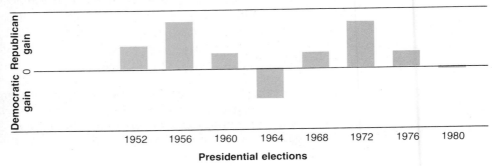

Source: Herbert Asher, *Presidential Elections and American Politics*, 3d ed. (Homewood, Ill.: Dorsey Press, 1984), pp. 113, 156, 164.

on elections varies. Eisenhower had exceptional candidate appeal in the two elections of the 1950s. He entered the White House as the nonpartisan hero of World War II in Europe. But the outcomes of the 1964, 1972 and 1980 elections were more rejections of candidates than positive appeal. Republican Goldwater in 1964 and Democrat McGovern in 1972 drew negative reactions even from their own parties. In 1980, Americans rejected President Carter for his poor performance. Figure 5–6 shows the net effect of the candidates on the vote from 1952 to 1980. Note that except for the 1964 election, Republicans have been helped substantially more by the appeal of their candidates than have Democrats. Sometimes, as in 1972, this appeal has made a decisive difference; in that election, the net advantage to the Republican candidate was about 8.5 percent. In other elections, the net effect of candidate appeal has been relatively small. The net effect of Carter and Reagan was negligible in 1980, reflecting "the overall lack of enthusiasm for both nominees" (Asher, 1984: 163).

The impact of issues

The nature of issues has changed in presidential elections. So, too, has the relative importance of "the issues" in election outcomes. In the 1940s, our main concerns had to do with winning World War II. Then came labor problems and inflation. In the 1950s, the Korean War became a major political issue. In the early 60s, the major problems were race relations and civil rights. By the mid-60s, the Vietnam War had become our chief concern. After Vietnam, economic problems were the chief political issues; in the 1980s, our main concerns were unemployment and inflation.

At the same time, we have become more aware of national issues and problems. This is partly because education levels have climbed. We have become more sophisticated politically. This is suggested by unmistakable growth in the

FIGURE 5—7

The Effects of Party, Issues, and Candidates on Voting

Source: Frederick Hartwig, William R. Jenkins, and Earl M. Temchin, "Variability in Electoral Behavior: The 1960, 1968, and 1976 Elections," *American Journal of Political Science* 24 (August 1980), p. 554.

consistency of our political attitudes. Also, there is more ideological polarization, though the electorate is still not highly ideological. We now have "a more educated and cognitively competent public" than before the 1960s (Nie, Verba, and Petrocik, 1979:148).

As a result of the greater impact of "the issues" in presidential politics, so-called **issue voting** has been growing. Issue voting involves how voters feel about issues and whether they vote for candidates who have the same positions on issues as themselves. Figure 5–7 shows the changes in issue voting between 1956 and 1976. It indicates the correlations between voters' attitudes

A show of unity. President Jimmy Carter and Massachusetts Senator Ted Kennedy were rival contenders for the 1980 Democratic presidential nomination. At the last minute, Kennedy withdrew from the race, but he made a rousing speech at the Democratic national convention in New York. Here, President Carter applauds as Senator Kennedy waves to cheering delegates.

and their vote. Issue voting was fairly low in 1956 and 1960; it spurted upward in 1964, declined in 1968, shot back up in 1972, and declined some again in 1976.

In contrast, **party voting** (the relation between party membership and voting), the best guide to voting behavior, declined irregularly over the 1960s. Party voting did get something of a shot in the arm in the 1968 contest between Richard M. Nixon and Hubert Humphrey; and the 1976 race between Jimmy Carter and Gerald Ford heightened party voting somewhat. But party and issue voting are not incompatible. Evidence shows that partisans have become more issue oriented than in the '50s. This was most true in 1964 and 1968 (Pomper, 1975: 166–85). Party loyalty and issues worked together for about 26 percent of voters in the 1976 election; 17 percent were voting by issue position rather than by party; 30 percent were voting by party despite their feelings on issues (Nie, Verba, and Petrocik, 1979: 377).

The electorate is not made up of numskulls who cannot make rational choices based on important national issues. But the voter depends on the choices offered. Research shows a great potential for issue voting. Candidates can make it possible to choose on the basis of issues. They can show they are clearly distinct from one another on issues. Then many voters will choose on that basis. If, though, the choice is among those who differ little on issues, then voting will be more along party lines.

Social class voting

A striking difference between the voting behavior of Americans and Europeans is the lack of class voting here. **Class voting** means that for instance, most working-class people vote for one party (in Europe, usually a socialist, labor, or communist party). Most middle-class people vote for another party (usually conservative, center, or Christian Democratic). In our country, working-class people tend to vote Democratic; middle-class people tend to vote Republican. But class voting has never been strong, and it has declined since the '40s. This is because we have weak social class identification and lack class consciousness. We also lack a major socialist or labor party. (This may itself be due to the fluid character of our class structure.)

The extent of class voting can be shown from data for each presidential election. Subtract the percentage of nonmanual (white-collar, business, and professional) workers who vote Democratic from that of manual workers (skilled and unskilled workers) who vote Democratic. This "index of class voting" is shown for recent presidential elections in Figure 5–8.

FIGURE 5–8

Class Voting in Presidential Elections

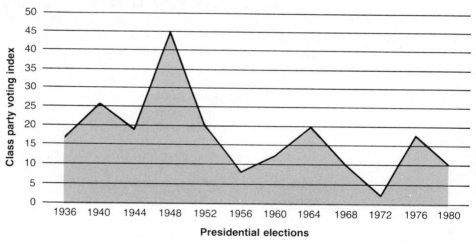

Sources: Paul R. Abramson, *Generational Change in American Politics* (Lexington, Mass.: D. C. Heath, 1975), pp. 7, 15–17; "Class Voting in the 1976 Presidential Election," *Journal of Politics*, 40 (November 1978), p. 1070; 1980 class-voting score from Paul R. Abramson, John H. Aldrich, and David W. Rohde, *The 1980 Election* (Washington, D.C.: Congressional Quarterly Press, 1982), p. 110.

Class voting was strongest in the 1948 Truman-Dewey contest. A huge majority of working-class people voted for Democrat Truman; a large majority of middle-class voters chose Republican Dewey. But class voting has generally, though unevenly, declined since then. Solid working-class support for Democrats has eroded. They have more and more won middle-class votes. More than half of Truman's support in 1948 came from the working class. But working-class support for Democrats steadily declined in later elections. By 1972, only a little over a third of Democratic voters were working class. By the same token, in 1948 only a fourth of those who voted Democratic were middle class. But by 1956, four out of five Democratic votes came from the middle class. By 1968, middle-class, Democratic votes equaled or exceeded those of working-class voters (Abramson, 1975: 23–25).

THE ELECTORAL DECISION

The nature and causes of personal voting choices are of great interest. But elections are collective decisions affecting the whole nation. These decisions give analysts a basis for finding patterns of electoral behavior for parties as a whole. At a more mundane level, they provide the personnel to run the government.

The classification of elections

Elections can be classified using two criteria: Did the party with the largest number of members win or lose? Did the vote totals follow former elections or show much change? By using these criteria, four distinct types of elections have been analyzed (see Figure 5–9). An election may be classed as *maintaining*. Party loyalties are stable and the candidate of the majority party wins. The 1976 election of Carter is an example.

If the majority party candidate loses, the election is classed as *deviating*. This occurred in 1952 and 1956. A Republican, Eisenhower, was elected president despite the fact that a majority of Americans identified themselves as Democrats. In a deviating election, short-term forces overpower the long-term effects of party loyalty. When basic changes take place in the distribution of party membership but the majority party candidate wins, this is a *converting* election. Finally, the normal majority party candidate may lose due to changing party loyalties. Then the election is called *realigning*. The distribution of party membership has been stable since World War II. But deviating elections have been commonplace. Eisenhower's election in the 1950s, Nixon's elections in 1968 and 1972, and Reagan's election in 1980 showed this.

The first party realignment took place in the early 1830s. It ended with the election of Martin Van Buren in 1836. The Democrats were then dominant until the Civil War. The election of Abraham Lincoln for the second time in 1864 was a realigning election. It ushered in a Republican dominance that lasted for 75 years. The election of 1896 showed the changing shape of the Republican coalition. That election was followed by Republican presidential victories in all but one election up to the New Deal. The exception was the deviating elections of Woodrow Wilson, a Democrat, in 1912 and 1916. Finally, the election of 1928, though won by Republican Herbert Hoover, showed a basic shift to the Dem-

FIGURE 5–9

A Classification of Presidential Elections

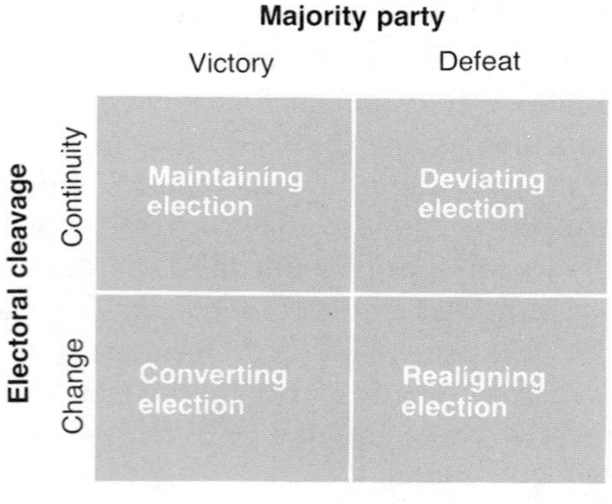

Source: Gerald M. Pomper, *Elections in America*, 2d ed. (New York: Dodd, Mead, 1980), p. 86.

A new style of campaigning. In 1916, the campaign of Woodrow Wilson for president and Thomas Marshall for vice president initiated the use of the campaign van.

ocratic party. It was fed by a growing economic depression, climaxing with the stock market collapse in 1929. Democrat Franklin D. Roosevelt's first victory in 1932 showed the rise of the so-called New Deal coalition of the Democratic party. This lasted intact until the early 1960s. It still holds shape in many ways.

The 1964 election showed changes. The cause was the increasing numbers who said they were political independents. Political scientists have argued the meaning of these changes. Some believe that major and lasting shifts in electoral splits were under way. Some see the increase of independents as meaning that voters are not aligned. This portends basic future political changes (Burnham, 1970). The long-term forces affecting elections may change at a glacial pace. It is hard to see realignments while they are occurring. Thus, it is hard to interpret the long-run meaning of current developments. So analysts disagree in their interpretation of changes since 1964. Each new election brings changed forecasts for future developments. The interpretation of past changes is also altered. Here, as with other kinds of analysis on a large, national scale, hindsight is the most scientific of methods!

Presidential elections of the 1980s

One persistent theme in commentaries on post–World War II presidential elections is that the New Deal coalition is surely crumbling. A major electoral realignment is forecast. The electoral fortunes of Republican and Democratic can-

Trade unions take part in politics. Former Vice President Mondale's campaign for the Democratic presidential nomintion drew wide support from labor unions like the ILGWU.

didates have waxed and waned in the last 40 years. But no lasting voter realignment on a major scale has taken place. The presidential elections of the 1980s confirm the volatile nature of electoral politics. Republican presidential election success could stimulate a pro-Republican realignment. It is just as likely to encourage a Democratic resurgence. Even a new political party may develop. But "since 1952, neither major party has been able to win more than two presidential elections in a row and support for the major parties has swung widely from election to election" (Abramson, Aldrich, and Rohde, 1982: 239). This volatility will probably continue.

The 1980 election Jimmy Carter was unknown to most Americans when he began to campaign for the 1976 Democratic nomination. Early in the race, the press referred to him as "Jimmy Who?" But his marathon campaign paid off. Carter was the overwhelming choice of the Democratic convention. In the general election against incumbent Gerald Ford, Carter won by a small margin. But Carter's term in office was not very happy or successful. It was plagued by growing inflation and continuing unemployment. At the end, the Iranian hostage crisis arose. He came to be viewed by many as an ineffective president.

The Republican nomination in 1976 had been a close call for Gerald Ford. He was nominated by a narrow margin over Ronald Reagan, former Governor of California. Many Republicans felt that Reagan was the best candidate and could have won. But he would have to wait for another time. The 1980 presidential campaign began in August 1979. At that time, Republican Congressman Philip M. Crane of Illinois announced his candidacy. Six other Republicans followed: former Governor John Connally of Texas, former Ambassador George Bush of Texas, Senator Robert Dole of Kansas, Congressman John Anderson of Illinois, Senate Minority Leader Howard Baker of Tennessee, and former Governor Ronald Reagan of California. They faced more primaries than ever before in election history. The race finally narrowed to Reagan versus Bush after Anderson lost to Reagan in Illinois. But Reagan's edge over Bush grew steadily. At the Republican convention in Detroit, Reagan won the nomination by a large margin. He chose his principal opponent, Bush, as his running mate.

President Carter relied heavily on his incumbency to win the Democratic nomination. But his renomination was disputed. He was challenged by Governor Jerry Brown of California and, more seriously, by Senator Edward Kennedy of Massachusetts. Kennedy became the president's greatest threat. But Kennedy's effort was ill fated. In the midst of the primary, Islamic revolutionaries seized the American Embassy in Teheran, the capital of Iran, and held the Americans there captive. The hostage crisis in Iran temporarily improved Carter's popularity, and his campaign efforts paid off. He easily won the early caucuses and primaries. His wide victory in the Illinois primary in March virtually sealed his nomination. But Kennedy did not withdraw from the race until the convention met. There, Carter was renominated by a 2 to 1 majority. Vice President Mondale was again chosen as his running mate.

After the Illinois primary, it became clear to Anderson that he could not win the Republican nomination. So, on April 24 at Washington's National Press Club, he declared as an independent candidate. Later he named as his running mate Democrat Patrick J. Lucey, former governor of Wisconsin and Ambassador to Mexico.

The candidates differed on economic issues. But the campaign focused mainly on style. Carter charged that Reagan might lead the country into war. Reagan

BC

in·cum·bent n.

AN IN PERSON THAT GOES OUT
WHEN AN OUT PERSON COMES IN.

WILEY'S DICTIONARY

WILEY'S DICTIONARY

retorted to Carter's "scare" tactics. Much campaign energy was invested in the question of who would debate whom on television. The League of Women Voters wanted to sponsor three-way debates (Carter, Reagan, and Anderson). Carter refused. A Reagan versus Anderson debate was televised in September; some polls (notably the Harris survey) declared Anderson the winner. In October, a 90-minute Carter-Reagan debate was televised. It got a Nielsen audience rating of nearly 60 percent, well above the first Carter-Ford debate in 1976. Of those who watched, the CBS News/*New York Times* poll showed that 44 percent believed Reagan had won; 36 percent thought Carter had won. The value of the two 1980 debates is debatable. Comedian Johnny Carson was moved to comment on the Carter-Reagan debate: "The debate was wonderful—it kind of took our minds off the issues for a while!"

The polls showed the on-and-off appeal of the candidates. Anderson support generally declined. The Gallup polls suggested voter indecision between Carter and Reagan. The polls showed that the lead changed hands five times between April and the end of October. The precise results of various polls differed. All agreed on the eve of the election, though, that the outcome was "too close to call."

The verdict on November 4 was not close. Although Reagan received just over half the popular votes, Carter won only 41 percent. Just short of 7 percent voted for Anderson. But Reagan's bare majority of the popular vote won him a large electoral vote majority. He captured the electoral votes of 44 states, a total of 489 votes. Because the "winner take all" rule of the electoral college system was at work, Reagan won a landslide in the electoral vote, even though only slightly over half of the popular votes had gone to him.

The following brief observations may be made about that election:

1. The 53 percent turnout was about the same as the turnout in 1976. Both elections had the lowest turnouts since 1948. But the decline in election participation had ended.
2. A total of 21 candidates vied for president. But the major party candidates won over 90 percent of the votes. The independent candidacy of John Anderson was not much of a threat to two-party politics.
3. Carter had won a sharply partisan contest in 1976. But he could not hold the support of his own party in 1980. More than three fourths of Democrats backed him in his first race; only two thirds voted for him in 1980. Reagan, in contrast, was overwhelmingly supported by Republicans; one fourth of Democrats supported him, too.
4. In 1976, Carter won his native South. He also did well in the Northeast and

Midwest. But he did poorly west of the Mississippi. The 1980 election in the West was a heyday for the Republicans. Reagan swept the plains states, the West Coast, and the Southwest by large margins. He also won the Deep South except Carter's home state of Georgia. In fact, Carter did not win a majority of the votes in any region. He did best in the South and worst in the far West.

5. Reagan's victory was widespread. He won majorities among traditional Democratic voters, including Catholics, Jews, and southern whites. The only large bloc of voters that stayed loyal to Carter was blacks. He won 82 percent of their votes in 1980; this was the same percentage as in 1976. But black voters were not able in 1980, as in 1976, to win the electoral votes of the South for Carter. This was due to huge Reagan support among southern whites.

6. Republicans won striking victories in congressional races. They gained House seats and captured control of the Senate. The Reagan White House would have greater Republican congressional support than any since the first Eisenhower administration.

The 1976 election was a maintaining election. But Carter won traditional Democratic votes only by narrow margins, except among blacks. The 1980 election was a deviating election. The Democratic party remained dominant (though not firmly so). But Republican Reagan won a majority of the popular vote. Partisan voting was somewhat restored in 1976; but voters widely abandoned party loyalty in 1980. Republican gains were impressive in the growing South and Sunbelt states.

The 1984 election   If the 1980 election was, to some extent, a repudiation of the incumbent president, voters gave incumbent President Reagan a sweeping personal political victory in 1984. He garnered 59 percent of the popular vote on November 6, won a majority in every state except Minnesota and the District of Columbia, and enjoyed a landslide win in the electoral college with 525 votes.

Former Vice President Walter F. Mondale won the presidential nomination of the Democratic national convention, meeting in San Francisco in July, but only after a briskly contested preconvention fight. Seven other contenders vied

Winner and loser. Winning an election is exhilarating; losing one comes hard. Winner Ronald Reagan [left] gives the "thumbs-up" sign of victory at a rally on election eve in Los Angeles. Loser Walter F. Mondale [right], with his wife Joan, solemnly waves to supporters after conceding to President Reagan in the St. Paul, Minnesota Civic Center.

On the campaign trail. Geraldine A. Ferraro, Democratic vice-presidential candidate, speaks in Sacramento, California.

Presidential candidates welcomed to Kansas City. Cartoonist Ken Westphal drew this caricature of the 1984 presidential candidates, Ronald Reagan and Walter F. Mondale, engaged in a debate over American foreign policy. This large drawing, showing the two candidates vying for the "presidential cup," was hung in the hall in Kansas City where the debate was held.

for the Democratic nomination (discussed in more detail in Chapter 6). Initially, Senator John Glenn of Ohio seemed the most viable alternative to front-runner Walter Mondale. But Senator Gary Hart of Colorado turned out to be Mondale's principal nemesis after Hart's stunning win in the New Hampshire primary late in February. Throughout the weeks before the party convention Mondale managed to maintain a lead in delegates chosen in caucuses or elected in primaries, but Hart won in a number of states, including California. When the convention assembled, Mondale won the nomination by a divided vote. Nearly 2,200 delegates voted for Mondale, and 1,200 voted for Hart. About 485 voted for Rev. Jesse Jackson, the Chicago-based civil rights activist who attracted widespread support among blacks.

Divisiveness among Democrats in their presidential choice was partly al-layed by their unprecedented nomination of Representative Geraldine A. Ferraro of New York for vice-president. She became the first woman vice-presidential nominee of a major American political party.

The Democrats' contentiousness was starkly contrasted by the serene Republican conclave in Dallas in August. Free of any controversy over its ticket for 1984, the Republicans enthusiastically nominated President Ronald Reagan and Vice President George Bush. In his acceptance speech, Reagan said the American voters were about to be offered "the most clear-cut political choice in half a century." In accepting the Democratic party's nomination, Mondale had been more specific. Most notably, he promised to reduce the federal deficit by two thirds in his first term; more importantly, he pledged to raise federal taxes. In his acceptance speech, Mondale said "Let's tell the truth. Mr. Reagan will raise taxes and so will I. He won't tell you. I just did."

Although the campaign ranged across various domestic and foreign policy issues, Mondale devoted much more attention to these issues than Reagan did. Reagan's campaign stressed general economic well-being ("Are you better off than you were four years ago?"), and condemned Mondale's promise to raise taxes in order to reduce the federal budget deficit. Mondale's pledge to raise taxes, though an accurate assessment of revenue needs, played into the hands of his opponent. Many voters resonated to Reagan's counterpromise not to raise taxes. And, many Democratic candidates found the tax pledge to be an uncomfortable burden on their own campaigns. For instance, former Mississippi Governor William Winter, challenging the reelection of incumbent U.S. Senator Thad Cochran, said, "With that tax program, Mondale is like an 800-pound gorilla. You have to carry him around on your back because there's no place to put him down."

Three televised "debates" were held, two featuring the presidential candidates and one, the vice presidential contenders. As in the past (see Chapter 8), the meetings were rigidly structured so they were more like parallel press conferences than true debates. And while none of the candidates made major errors, Reagan's lackluster performance in the first clash briefly raised the hopes of Mondale supporters. The president rebounded in the second meeting, so the debates did little to alter the election's course overall. As usual, the press and the pundits focused on style more than substance.

The polls played a highly visible role in charting the course of the campaign. Many opinion polls were in the field, and their estimates of the people's choices often varied wildly. While polling seemed to indicate a close race just after the Mondale-Ferraro nomination in July, in retrospect this proximity proved

Dan Rather and CBS news team provide election night reporting of the 1984 presidential election.

ephemeral. Figure 5–10 shows the trends in presidential choice over the full campaign year, drawn from Gallup polls. Less volatile than other polls, Gallup showed Reagan in the lead from the beginning of the year and, in its final preelection survey, predicted the final result of the popular vote exactly.

On election day a record number of voters turned out to give Ronald Reagan an overwhelming victory. He got 59 percent of the popular vote, a boost from the 51 percent he had won in 1980. In contrast, Mondale got only 41 percent of the vote, the same proportion Jimmy Carter had won four years earlier. Reagan won lopsided majorities in every state but one. Mondale won his home state, Minnesota, by only about 15,000 votes out of more than 2 million cast in

FIGURE 5–10

The 1984 Gallup Polls

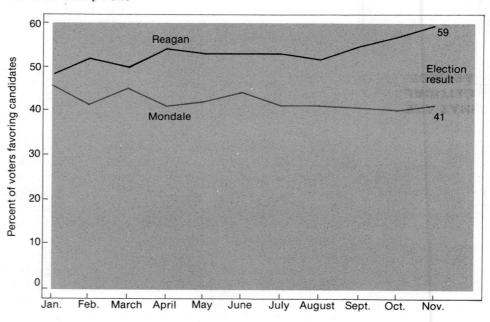

FIGURE 5–11

The Electoral Map for 1984*

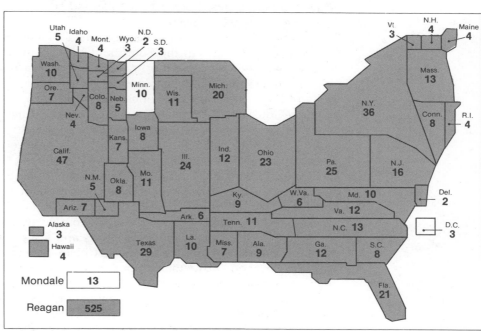

*States sized according to their populations.

Voting in 1984. In the voting booths voters in Dallas, Texas, make their choices for president and for many other offices.

that state. Mondale did win 86 percent of the vote in the District of Columbia, so he gained its three electoral votes in addition to Minnesota's 10. With 59 percent of the popular vote, Reagan captured 98 percent of the electoral vote (see Figure 5–11).

We can offer the following observations about the 1984 election:

1. Presidential election turnout increased about 1 percent over what it had been in the two previous elections, the first increase in turnout since 1960. The number of registered voters reached a historic high, but a somewhat smaller proportion of registered voters actually went to the polls than in 1980. About 72 percent of registered voters cast presidential ballots.

2. In addition to the candidates fielded by the Republicans and the Democrats, 15 other political parties presented candidates in at least one state. Although none achieved much visibility, one minor party—the Libertarians—ran candidates for Congress in a large number of districts, in addition to running candidates for president and vice president.

3. Reagan won overwhelming support from Republicans, but Mondale could garner the support of only about three fourths of Democrats. As in 1980, about a fourth of those voters claiming to be Democrats voted for Reagan. In addition, more than 60 percent of Independents voted for Reagan.

4. Spurred by the primary campaign efforts of Rev. Jesse Jackson and by widespread organizational effort among blacks, 89 percent of black voters chose

Mondale over Reagan. Although there were significant increases in black voter turnout, blacks made up only about 11 percent of the 1984 electorate. And in some southern states, black activism spurred successful voter registration drives by conservative white groups.

5. Reagan's victory was pervasive, spread widely across the country, but his showing was stronger in the South and West than in the Midwest or Northeast. Reagan won 60 percent or more of the two-party vote in 32 states.

6. Demographically, Reagan's victory was sweeping in scope. He won a majority of those in all age categories, including voters from the ages of 18 to 24 who previously had been inclined to support Democratic presidential candidates. He won majority support from both men and women, but about 66 percent of men voted for him compared to only 54 percent of women. Some analysts attributed this "gender gap" to the presence of Geraldine Ferraro on the Democratic ticket, thus attracting women voters (and perhaps pushing some men toward Reagan-Bush). Two thirds of Protestants voted for Reagan, but so did a majority of Catholics. Nearly 70 percent of Jewish voters chose Mondale. Blacks voted overwhelmingly for Mondale, but nearly two thirds of whites voted for Reagan. Although Hispanics in Texas and California remained fairly loyal to the Democratic candidate, most Cuban-Americans supported Reagan. And Reagan won substantial support from "white ethnics," such as German-, Irish-, or Polish-Americans.

7. Although the election was a tremendous personal victory for President Reagan, it was not a Republican landslide. The Democrats gained two seats in the U.S. Senate, leaving the margin at 53 to 47 in the GOP's favor. The Republicans gained 14 seats in the House of Representatives, leaving the Democrats with a 253 to 182 majority. The Democrat's control of the House, coupled with the strength of moderates in the Senate, foreshadowed powerful constraints on major policy shifts.

Watching the victory announcement. President Ronald Reagan and his wife, Nancy, watch CBS commentator Roger Mudd report the 1984 election results.

CONCLUSIONS

Elections are the centerpiece of democratic government. In many countries they are a sham. They mask authoritarian regimes forbidding elections that could shift government control. Only a few countries have elections which give voters real choices and strong voices in deciding who will govern.

American presidential elections do not occur under ideal conditions. Too many people do not take part; many who vote are not well informed about the choices or the consequences of their choice; too often candidates avoid making their policy positions clear; opportunities for political malpractice—corruption, improper use of money, unfair campaign practices—are too often taken. The electoral system is not perfect; various improvements are possible.

At the same time, presidential politics have, on the whole, been quite competitive. Voters have been offered clear choices. They have increasingly shown ability to make choices on the basis of issues rather than mindlessly, irrationally, or crassly. Most adults can be eligible to vote if they want to; the corrupting influences of money in politics have come under some control; and the electoral system has worked fairly well both to ensure victory for the most popular candidate and to weaken divisive tendencies in our politics.

By discouraging minor parties, the rules of the electoral system foster two-party politics. This encourages political coalitions before elections rather than afterward. No one knows how to create an ideal electoral system. The present system helps maintain political patterns seen as desirable. So the American election system performs reasonably well.

In this chapter, we tried to underscore the following major features of elections and voting in the United States:

1 Turnout of voters varies in presidential elections. But it has generally declined since the 1950s. It is lower in America than in many European countries. Voter turnout also varies among the states. Traditionally it has been rather low in the South. Turnout is higher in presidential election years than in midterm congressional elections.

2 Voting is affected by context. Ready availability of polling places, weather conditions, and the nature of the ballot can stimulate or depress turnout.

3 The electoral college system is used to choose the president and vice president. The single-member district, plurality-vote system is used for electing members of Congress. These systems produce magnified majorities. By discriminating against minor parties, they help to maintain two-party politics. Because of the uncertainties and biases of these electoral practices, efforts have been made to change them.

4 Socioeconomic status and age have powerful effects of voting. Voters tend to be older, better educated, higher paid, and hold of higher-status jobs than nonvoters. The Democratic vote comes mostly from the working-class, blacks and other ethnic minorities, Catholics and Jews, young voters, union members, southerners, and central city residents. Republicans tend to be in businesses and professions. They are white, Protestant, older, in non-union families, and live in the northern and western states. But these are gross characterizations. There is a lot of overlapping.

5 Party identification is the most persistent single influence on American voting. The distribution of party identification has stayed highly stable for at least 25 years. But some changes have been occurring. This is shown in the higher number of independents and in the increased Democratic party identification among blacks.

6 Candidates and issues variously influence presidential elections. But political issues have become more important in affecting voters' choices among candidates.

7 Social class is a weaker feature of voting behavior here than in most other democratic countries. Some presidential elections have caused more class voting than others. But in general, class voting has been declining over the last 25 years.

8 Although voters make individual choices for president and among candidates for other offices, elections are collective decisions. Their overall features vary. Maintaining and deviating elections have been most common in the post-New Deal era. But converting and realigning elections have clearly occurred at important points in our electoral history.

FURTHER READING

ASHER, HERBERT (1984) Presidential Elections and American Politics. 3d ed. Homewood, Ill.: Dorsey Press. An analysis of presidential elections since 1952 which draws on national election surveys of voters to focus on party identification, political issues, and campaigning by candidates.

NIE, NORMAN H., SIDNEY VERBA, and JOHN R. PETROCIK (1979) The Changing American Voter. Enl. ed. Cambridge, Mass.: Harvard University Press. This book uses survey data to show how voters have changed since the 1950s as they have become increasingly dissatisfied and disillusioned.

PEARCE, NEAL R., and LAWRENCE D. LONGLEY (1981) The People's President. Rev. ed. New Haven, Conn.: Yale University Press. A historical analysis of the electoral college system, along with discussion of reforms.

POLSBY, NELSON W., and AARON WILDAVSKY (1984) Presidential Elections. 6th ed. New York: Charles Scribner's Sons. A masterful analysis of presidential elections which underscores the strategies political leaders and parties use to seek nomination and election.

WOLFINGER, RAYMOND E., and STEVEN J. ROSENSTONE (1980) Who Votes? New Haven, Conn.: Yale University Press. An insightful analysis of the effects of sociodemographic variables and registration laws on voter turnout.

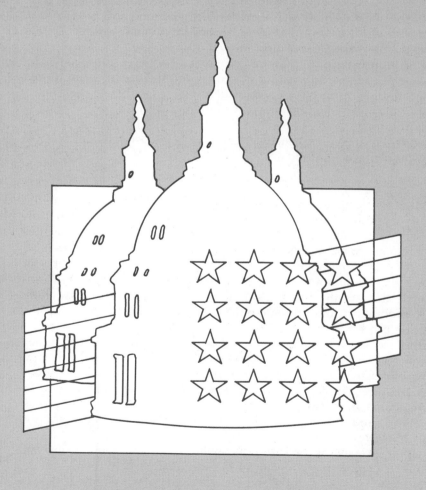

6
Political Parties

The scene was the ornate caucus room of the Cannon House Office Building on Capitol Hill. Crystal chandeliers gleamed on a sight unknown in modern American politics. A full 16 months before the 1984 elections, Democratic hopefuls were courting members of the House—164 of whom would be delegates to the Democratic nominating convention.

Outside the closed doors, listeners discerned that the highest applause levels were for former Vice President Walter F. Mondale. Mondale won his audience with the clear message that he was not anti-Washington and proud to call himself a politician. The dig was at President Reagan and former President Carter, both of whom ran as Washington outsiders.

Ohio Senator John Glenn, then Mondale's chief adversary, got a cooler reception from the 175 House Democrats who attended the caucus. The former astronaut appeared confused by queries about key votes in 1981, when many congressional Democrats, Glenn included, went along with Reagan's domestic spending cuts (Lardner, 1983). Other contenders appeared before the caucus on other days. When the House caucus got around to choosing its delegates, a lion's share were pledged to Mondale.

* * * * *

In prospecting for delegate support on Capitol Hill, the Democratic hopefuls attested to the continuing strength of political parties. Despite the increasing independence of American voters, and the power of media appeals in reaching them, parties remain potent forces in screening and promoting candidates.

Political parties have many guises. Traditional, broad-scale parties, like the Democrats and the Republicans, are the most obvious. They began with the start of mass elections in the 1800s. They have developed complex structures for recruiting, promoting, and unifying officeholders. For a time, they monopolized the voting process in this country.

These parties are not, however, the only groups deserving the label "political." Most Americans call themselves Democrats or Republicans. But their loyalties are rarely intense. Candidates have to recruit followers—or hire firms—to run campaigns, raise funds, and contact voters. Advertising, media, and direct mail consultants help mobilize voters. Interest groups—unions, professional associations, and industry groups, to name a few—play important and growing roles in electoral politics.

In this chapter, we define and describe political parties, their forms and functions. First we explore party loyalties—the so-called party in the electorate. Then we show how parties organize and choose candidates, mainly at the na-

Starting gate. Eight Democratic hopefuls before Dartmouth College debate in January 1984, marking start of televised presidential race.

tional level. Finally, we consider partisan ties among officeholders. This is the so-called party in the government.

WHAT ARE POLITICAL PARTIES?

Political parties are defined many ways; no definition is universally accepted. Edmund Burke, the 18th-century English conservative, defined party as a body of people "united for promoting by their joint endeavors the national interest upon some particular principle in which they are all agreed." This is quite idealistic, especially if applied to our diverse parties. Other definitions stress organization mobilizing large groups of candidates, party workers, and voters. Still others begin, as we shall, with the various ways parties show themselves in real political life.

The hub of the parties' functions is the effort to capture the reins of government. Thus, a political party can be defined as "any group, however loosely organized, seeking to elect governmental officeholders under a given label" (Epstein, 1967: 9). Parties therefore reflect enduring partisan loyalties in the electorate. They are formal organizations engaged in a variety of activities. And in the government they are networks of officeholders.

How are parties different from other types of political groups? This is not always easy to define. As we will see in Chapter 7, interest groups nowadays invest heavily in electoral politics. However, political parties are the primary entities that contest elections. Moreover, the issues and concerns of parties are typically broader than interest groups, which voice the needs of an industry or a cause or a special class of people. If they are to elect their slates of candidates, parties cannot afford to be parochial; they must appeal to voters on a wide range of issues.

Two parties—with variations

The most obvious fact about our parties is that there are normally two, and only two, of them. For most of our history, elections have been dominated by two broad coalition parties: Federalists versus Anti-Federalists; Democrats versus Whigs; Republicans versus Democrats.

Yet there is nothing sacred about two-party politics. Many countries have multiparty systems. Elsewhere, one-party governments (military juntas or ideological or nationalist movements) control political life. Why, then, is the two-party system seemingly a fixture in the United States?

"Two-partyism" is not easy to explain. Some people think there is a basic dualism in politics based on personality, character, or ideology: optimists versus pessimists, extroverts versus introverts, progressives versus traditionalists. If this is so, why aren't there two-party systems in all countries? So people have tried to identify a peculiar American dualism. The battle over the Constitution, some think, reflected tension between eastern financial and commercial interests and western frontiersmen. This later shifted to a North-South conflict, then to urban-rural or rich-poor conflicts (Key, 1964: 229 ff.).

The best explanation for two-partyism lies in the electoral rules of the game. Ours are *winner-take-all* contests. Few, if any, rewards await those who come in second. *Unitary executives* and *single-member legislative districts* ensure that there will be only one victor for each office. Countries with more than two major parties usually have multiple-member districts. In these countries, minority parties can hope to gain offices somewhat in proportion to their overall electoral strength (Duverger, 1954). But in the United States there are only winners and losers. There is nothing in between. To wield influence, a splinter party must force a major party to adopt its objectives. Or it must replace one of the existing major parties.

Once a two-party pattern is established, powerful forces keep it going. Politicians have a vested stake in the system that put them in power. They pass election laws designed to entrench the major parties and erect barriers against third-party intrusion. Laws discourage minor parties from getting on the ballot. Voting machines and ballots are often designed to encourage straight-ticket voting. But two-partyism is not simply a matter of legal manipulation. As we will see, many voters have long-standing party preferences that are notably firm and stable over time.

However widespread the two-party system, it is by no means a monopoly. Two-partyism is a broad concept that ignores many variations. Truly balanced competition between the parties is fairly rare. Try to think of two-partyism as an ideal or norm which describes the overall picture but not specific elections or constituencies.

Presidential competition between the two parties has been close over the past 100 years. In the 25 presidential elections from 1888 through 1984, Republicans won 14; Democrats won 11. Since World War II, several elections have been very close, especially 1948, 1960, 1968, and 1976. There have been long stretches of "one-and-a-half parties" rather than strict two-party competition (see Table 6–1). Party realignments in the "critical elections" of 1860 and 1896 threw the Democrats into temporary eclipse; Franklin Roosevelt's coalition did the same thing to the GOP in the 1930s.

Below the national level, strict two-party competition is even less the norm.

TABLE 6—1

Shifting National Party Fortunes (partisan control of the White House and Congress)

	Presidential elections		House of Representatives		Senate	
	Democrats	Republicans	Democrats	Republicans	Democrats	Republicans
1861–1931 (37th–71st Congress)	4	14	12	23	5	30
1931–1986 (72d–99th Congress)	8	6	26	2	22	5

Many congressional districts are nearly always "safe" for one party or the other. Indeed, the number of truly competitive, "marginal" districts has dwindled in our era (Jones, 1964; Mayhew, 1974). At the state level, Austin Ranney (1976) has developed an "index of competitiveness." This is drawn from election results and serves as a "snapshot" of shifting party balances. Applying this index to the 1974 to 1980 period, a team of political scientists (Gibson et al., 1983: 66) classed 8 states (most southern) as one-party Democratic; 20 states were either modified one-party Democratic or modified one-party Republican; 22 states, or fewer than half, were two-party competitive (see Figure 6–1). In the 1970s, the Democratic party strengthened its position in 12 states.

The smaller the electoral unit, the less competitive it is likely to be. Local

FIGURE 6—1

State Party Systems

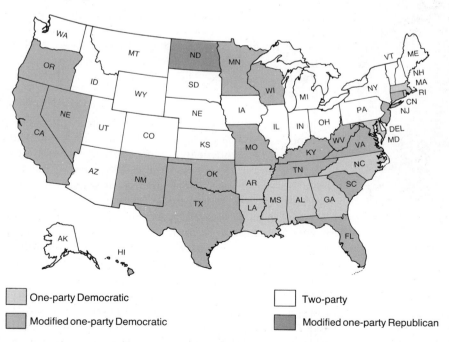

One-party Democratic · Two-party · Modified one-party Democratic · Modified one-party Republican

Source: John F. Bibby, Cornelius P. Cotter, James L. Gibson, and Robert L. Huckshorn, "Parties in State Politics," in *Politics in the American States: A Comparative Analysis*, 4th ed., ed. V. Gray, H. Jacob, and K. N. Vines (Boston: Little, Brown, 1983), p. 66.

constituencies may be too small to have a balanced mix of social, economic, and population ingredients. Thus, those features that strongly favor one party may prevail. A "typical" Democratic district tends to have mostly working-class voters, Catholics, blacks, Hispanics, Jews, or other ethnic groups. A "typical" Republican district has executives and professionals, higher-income groups, Protestants, and older ethnic stocks.

Another barrier to local competition can be poor media coverage of local elections. National and statewide elections draw press coverage. Thus, all contenders have a chance at public attention and support. In local races, however, coverage may be scanty or confusing. Traditional patterns then prevail. Many states are listed as one party in Figure 6–1 because of local elections. But these states do swing back and forth in presidential, senatorial, and gubernatorial contests.

Finally, one-party dominance may be encouraged by gerrymandering— drawing district lines to maximize the dominant party's reelection chances. In short, even though we consider ours a two-party system, the parties do not always compete on equal footing.

Minor parties

Two-party dominance is also challenged by minor-party factions or movements. Since the 1830s, some 100 minor parties have contested presidential races. Sometimes they have affected the outcome. Historically, the average vote for all minor-party candidates has been a little more than 5 percent of the total. There are two types of minor parties, which differ sharply in their aims and impacts.

One type is the **sectarian party.** It is formed around a single issue or ideology. Such parties may be fleeting or durable. Without exception, they are small and have no chance of winning office or even wielding much influence over the major parties. They enter the election mainly to air their goals. Examples are the Socialist Labor, Socialist Worker, Prohibition, Libertarian, and Communist parties.

Splinter parties, in contrast, are broad-based third parties that form around a charismatic candidate or a burning issue the major parties have put aside. Such movements can be powerful. They can throw the election one way or the other. They also reflect major unresolved issues that could form the basis for party realignment (Rosenstone et al, 1984). (See Table 6–2.) In the 1860s a splinter party, the Republicans, merged the antislavery movement with long-standing regional concerns (tariff protection and cheap western land). It became a dominant major party. In 1912, the GOP was split by Theodore Roosevelt's progressive Bull Moose faction. This helped send Democrat Woodrow Wilson to the White House. Former Illinois Representative John Anderson pulled 7 percent of the 1980 vote because of widespread discontent with the two major candidates, Carter and Reagan.

Minor parties are constant reminders of our diverse politics. They are germinators of new ideas: abolition of slavery, women's suffrage, direct election of senators, the 14th amendment, regulation of monopolies, farm price supports, Social Security, and the progressive income tax were all first proposed by third parties. And such groups convey a warning to major parties: ignore emerging public concerns and you risk defeat or obsolescence.

Sectarian. Eugene V. Debs (1855–1926) ran four times for president on the Socialist ticket, once receiving 1 million votes. Though no serious threat to the major parties, Debs drew followers among intellectuals. (Poet Carl Sandburg is at Debs' left.)

Splinter and sectarian partisans, John Anderson (left) won 7 percent of the 1980 presidential vote with his Independent party, a "splinter" movement. More "sectarian" are Sonia Johnson, 1984 Citizens Party candidate for president, and Ed Clark, Libertarian Party banner carrier in 1980.

TABLE 6—2

Third-Party Ventures*

Candidate (Party)	Year	Percent of popular vote	Electoral votes
William Wirt (Anti-Masonic)	1832	8	7
Martin Van Buren (Free Soil)	1848	10	0
Millard Fillmore (Whig-American)	1856	22	8
John Bell (Constitutional Union)	1860	13	39
John C. Breckinridge (Southern Democrat)	1860	18	72
James B. Weaver (Populist)	1892	9	22
Theodore Roosevelt (Progressive)	1912	27	88
Eugene V. Debs (Socialist)	1912	6	0
Robert M. La Follette (Progressive)	1924	17	13
George C. Wallace (American Independent)	1968	14	46
John B. Anderson (Independent)	1980	7	0

*Based on third-party candidates receiving 5 percent or more of the popular vote.

**PARTIES
IN THE
ELECTORATE**

Political parties are regarded by social scientists as *reference groups*—groups that give cues or reference points to people. Thus, party membership may be seen as a psychological attraction to one or another party.

Party identification

Party identification is a measure gathered from surveys. "Generally speaking," the interviewer asks, "do you usually think of yourself as a Republican, Democrat, Independent, or what?" Respondents who name a party are probed on the strength of their ties; those who claim to be independents are asked whether they lean toward one party or the other. The result is a scale of party ties. It

FIGURE 6–2

Political Party Identification, 1952–1984

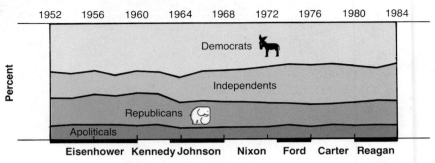

Source: American National Election Studies, Center for Political Studies, University of Michigan.

Landslide loser. Arizona Senator Barry Goldwater, here "whistlestopping" with his wife, carried only five states in 1964 but built conservative forces within the GOP.

indicates the strength as well as the direction of partisanship. Devised in the 1940s, the measure has since been used in major opinion surveys.

Distribution of party loyalties is one of the most persistent traits of our political life. This has been true at least since the 1940s (Niemi and Weisberg, 1984). Party balance has not changed radically in more than a generation (see Figure 6–2). The major long-term trend has been the growth of independents, at the expense of both the major parties. The GOP suffered a setback in 1964 with the presidential candidacy of Senator Barry Goldwater (R-Ariz.). Its base narrowed still further in the mid-1970s in the aftermath of President Nixon's resignation. However, the basic three-to-two Democratic edge among partisans remained virtually unchanged throughout the period.

Party loyalties are not everything. Elections—at least national and state-wide—are often closer than the overall party balance would indicate. During the period covered by Figure 6–2, Republican presidential candidates won six times, four of them by wide margins; Democrats won three times, only once by a landslide (1964, against the hapless Goldwater). Democratic congressional candidates captured from 53 percent to 55 percent of the two-party vote nationwide in 1980 and 1982.

The social groups associated with each party help explain the difference between party loyalty and election results. The Democrats tend to attract lower socioeconomic groupings, who as a rule vote less often than the average. The GOP, on the other hand, owns the allegiance of higher socioeconomic groupings, who are more faithful in going to the polls. Moreover, Republicans today hold a commanding advantage in organization and funding. This means they are better able to mobilize their supporters. This leads to the notion of a *normal vote*—party identification balance, with the additional factor of voting participation. Here, the Democrats' edge is trimmed to 53 to 55 percent nationally. This figure is pretty close to the two-party margin of votes in House and Senate contests nationwide.

Still, the normal vote concept fails to account for swings in presidential elections. Since 1952 these have been captured by the "minority" GOP twice as many times as by the "majority" Democrats. The long-term party loyalty factor can be temporarily deflected by such short-term forces as candidates or issues. This may explain the disparity. Many Democrats, for example, voted for Eisenhower in the 1950s without altering their basic party allegiance.

Many analysts go further and contend that party identification is a misleading indicator of voting preferences. This is true especially in highly visible national and even statewide contests. They prefer actual voting records (which may depart from underlying party loyalties) or views about which party can best cope with the leading problems of the day. This yields an even more fluid picture of partisan attachments.

Average people today wear their party mantles lightly. More than 8 of 10 people in one study (Dennis, 1966) thought that "the best rule in voting is to pick the candidate regardless of party label." A majority think parties confuse issues more than clarify them. They feel government would work better without party conflict, and that parties cause needless conflicts.

Nonpartisan party. Nuclear Freeze movement exemplifies plethora of party-like groups.

Voters' loyalties are weakening. "Perhaps the most dramatic political change in the American public over the past two decades," a team of voting analysts writes, "has been the decline of partisanship" (Nie, Verba, and Petrocik, 1976: 47–48). They summarize the decline as follows:

1. Fewer people have steady, strong ties with a party.
2. Party affiliations are less a guide to voting.
3. Parties are less often used as standards of evaluation.
4. Parties are less often objects of positive feelings of citizens.
5. Partisanship is less likely to be passed from one generation to the other.

By the late 1970s, it was apparent that voters no longer held clear views of what the parties stood for or exactly how they differed. One survey late in 1983— a time of party warfare over Reagan programs—asked which party was best able to handle the country's problems. For 8 of the 12 problems listed, voters either saw no difference between the parties or had no opinion. Today's elections are not interim battles in a long-running struggle of party loyalties. Instead, they look more like isolated skirmishes. "Candidate images have become so paramount . . . that each election breaks the mold of the one that preceded it" (White and Morris, 1984: 48). The political party becomes, as one politician put it, "a Hertz car we all rent around election time."

In short, partisanship in America is not rigid or unchangeable. And yet it remains surprisingly tenacious; it controls or limits party activities in many different ways. Parties draw their strength from somewhat different social and economic groupings; their activists diverge even more sharply in characteristics and political views.

Democrats versus Republicans

People have fairly clear mental pictures of the two parties because the social composition of Democrats and Republicans has differed. This has been true since the advent of modern party divisions in the 1930s (see Table 6–3). For example, business and professional people tend to support the Republican party. More than two thirds of them voted for Nixon in 1972; well over half voted for Ford in 1976 and Reagan in 1980 and 1984. Working-class people usually vote Democratic by big margins. Nixon's landslide victory in 1972 came because more than half the GOP votes were cast by people in manual occupations. Similar differences occur on the educational spectrum. People with less than a high school education lean toward the Democratic party. High school graduates and those with some college (though not graduate work) tend to be Republican.

TABLE 6–3
Democrats versus Republicans: Group Leanings

Respondent's demographic identification	Percentage of subgroup belonging to Democratic and Republican parties		Democrats' margin over Republicans
	Democrats	Republicans	
Sex:			
Male	37%	23%	+14
Female	42	24	+18
Race:			
White	36	26	+10
Black	71	3	+68
Religion:			
Protestant	39	28	+11
Catholic	45	19	+26
Jewish	54	11	+43
None	27	9	+18
Education:			
Less than high school graduate	49	18	+29
High school graduate	38	23	+15
Some college	34	27	+7
College graduate	31	34	– 3
Postgraduate	34	27	+ 7
Age:			
Under 30	34	21	+13
30–39	39	18	+21
40–49	41	23	+18
50–59	43	27	+16
60 and over	45	29	+16
Occupation:			
Professional/technical	34	28	+ 6
Managerial/administrative/			
sales	31	33	– 2
Clerical/kindred	38	25	+13
Skilled	38	21	+17
Unskilled	49	16	+33
Farmers	38	43	– 5
Household union membership:			
Union household	48	16	+32
Nonunion household	37	27	+10
Family income:			
Less than $10,000	47	17	+30

Respondent's demographic identification	Percentage of subgroup belonging to Democratic and Republican parties		Democrats' margin over Republicans
	Democrats	Republicans	
$10,000–19,999	41	24	+17
$20,000–24,999	40	26	+14
$25,000–34,999	42	22	+20
$35,000–49,999	36	28	+ 8
$50,000 and over	24	44	–20
Region:			
Northeast	37	24	+13
New England	35	19	+16
Middle Atlantic	38	26	+12
North Central	37	24	+13
East North Central	37	22	+15
West North Central	38	29	+ 9
South	46	20	+26
South Atlantic	46	21	+25
East South Central	45	21	+24
West South Central	46	18	+28
West	37	28	+ 9
Mountain	30	31	– 1
Pacific	39	27	+12
Self-described class:			
Lower class	47	14	+33
Working class	43	18	+25
Middle class	37	28	+ 9
Upper class	34	29	+ 5
Religion and ethnicity:			
Black	71	3	+68
Protestant German/Austrian	27	38	–11
Catholic German/Austrian	44	20	+24
Protestant Irish	41	28	+13
Catholic Irish	41	25	+16
English/Scottish/Welsh	33	33	0
Italian	44	18	+26
Polish	44	17	+27
Scandinavian	36	28	+ 8
Other ethnic groups	37	20	+17
No ethnicity stated	36	24	+12

Note: The proportions of Independents within each subgroup are not shown here but can be computed by subtracting the total percentages of Democrats and Republicans from 100.

Source: National Opinion Research Center surveys (1980, 1982, 1983). Reprinted in *Public Opinion* 9 (October–November 1983), p. 24.

Religious and group affiliation also affect party leanings. Protestants constitute a somewhat higher proportion of the Republican party. These differences are less than in the past. Union households are more prominent in the Democratic party. However, crossover voting is quite frequent, as in voting for Reagan. The most dramatic difference in party composition is racial: blacks are roughly one fifth of the Democratic party, but are practically nonexistent among Republicans.

The parties score differently among different age groupings. Social scientists agree that people are profoundly affected by decisive events that take place when they first enter political adulthood. Thus, those who gained political consciousness during the New Deal and its aftermath were more Democratically inclined than those who came of age earlier. Recent surveys show that the GOP does best at extremes of the age population: those who are just entering political adulthood, and those in the very oldest categories (who came of age before the depression). Conversely, Democrats do best among the generations that came of age during the Franklin Roosevelt years, or in the 1960s and early 1970s.

Recently, much has been made of the so-called "gender gap": the alleged tendency of women to tilt toward the Democratic party and men toward the Republican. The situation is a bit confused. The differences observed in the 1980s are indicated in Table 6–4. As can be seen, women are more Democratic than men by about a 5 percent margin. The overall trends seem to suggest an increasing party polarization of men and women as women comprise an ever-larger portion of the electorate. About three fifths of all Democrats and almost half of all Republicans are now women. However, sex differences in partisan identification are less pronounced than differences in attitudes toward the president, opinions on specific issues, or actual voting behavior.

In more subtle social attitudes, partisans are not very far apart, and indeed have gradually grown more similar. As one scholar observes (Ladd, 1983: 41), "In the early 1980s . . . Democrats and Republicans differ not at all in family size. . . . A century ago a Republican presidential campaign could decry the Democrats as the party of 'rum' (as well as 'Romanism' and 'rebellion')—but no more. The GOP is as 'wet' as its opposition."

In recent years, surveys show that the Democrats have emerged as a kind of "everyone party." That is, Democrats have more adherents than the GOP in virtually every social grouping. That by no means leaves the Democrats secure from challenge. The number of independents and the high incidence of crossover voting must be considered. But it does give the Democrats a broad, disparate quality not matched by the GOP. A recent assessment (Ladd, 1983: 41) is that

> The Republicans have just a few bailiwicks in partisan identification—and only one of these seems secure, among those with family incomes of $50,000 a year and higher. The GOP also has a slight edge among those with bachelors' degrees (although not among persons with post-graduate education), among people in business and managerial jobs, among (perhaps) residents of the mountain states, and, outside the South, among Protestants of British and German ancestry. But that is about it.

This gives the two parties very different strategic challenges. The Democrats must coordinate their scattered ranks without watering down their appeal. "We're in favor of a lot of things, and we're against mighty few," Lyndon Johnson once boasted of his party. The Republicans' challenge is quite differ-

TABLE 6–4

Party Identification by Sex (1983)

Party	Percent	
---	Men	Women
Republican	26%	24%
Democratic	42	47
Independent	32	30

Source: The Gallup Poll (7,669 interviews, July–August 1983)

ent: breaking out of their minority status to appeal to wider circles of voters. "The Republican Party is a Fred Astaire movie in the age of *Flashdance*," quipped activist Representative Newt Gingrich (R-Ga.). "Either we change, or we remain doomed to spend our lifetimes as a minority" (Farney, 1984).

Activists versus followers

Adherents of the two parties are by no means carbon copies of each other. Differences in ideology and issues may not be striking among party followers, but they are sharp among leaders and activists. Party activists tend to be better informed and more committed to issues and ideologies than ordinary voters. Democratic convention delegates, for example, are to the left and GOP delegates to the right of their parties' rank-and-file voters (McClosky, Hoffman, and O'Hara, 1960; Plissner and Mitofsky, 1981). This is shown strikingly in Figure 6–3 which compares the leanings of 1980 convention delegates with party voters and adults in general. (The 1984 figures were virtually the same.)

Basic issues of priorities and the government's role in national life divide Republicans and Democrats at all levels in the 1980s. Democrats are more ready to use government to achieve social goals. Republicans would limit government's welfare role but are more apt to condone "big government" in defense, security, law enforcement, and intelligence.

These differences, added to the fact that activists tend to hold stronger views than the average voter, lend additional weight to the parties' efforts to achieve harmony on issues and in candidate selection. Activists often want party endorsement for their policy viewpoints, sometimes even at the risk of alienating voters without strong party loyalties. On the other hand, party strategists realize that they must moderate or compromise for broad appeal.

As we will see, opening up the presidential nominating process in the 1970s brought in waves of issue- and candidate-oriented activists. These new "political elites" are described as "amateurs" or "purists." Among Democrats these included "new politics" advocates—antiwar activists, some minority groups, and

FIGURE 6–3

Convention Delegates and Their Constituencies (how delegates to 1980 conventions characterized their political leanings, compared with rank-and-file members of their parties and the public)

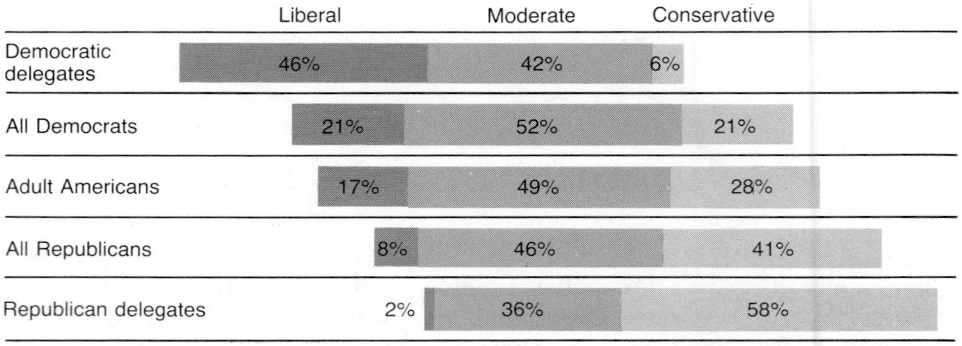

	Liberal	Moderate	Conservative
Democratic delegates	46%	42%	6%
All Democrats	21%	52%	21%
Adult Americans	17%	49%	28%
All Republicans	8%	46%	41%
Republican delegates	2%	36%	58%

Source: *New York Times*/CBS Poll (August 1980), *New York Times*, August 13, 1980, p. B–2.

proponents of various social causes. In the GOP there is the so-called "new right," which views the party as a channel for a variety of right-wing social, moral, and economic causes. They sometimes clashed with the older generation of party leaders, who emphasized compromise to achieve victory at the ballot box. These clashes between ideology and electability may have been exaggerated (Stone and Abramowitz, 1983). But balancing the two goals is something all activists must weigh.

Thus, the two parties are at odds with themselves on many issues. To consolidate disparate interests and appeal to independents, they must fuzz over many divisive issues. This leads to the "something-for-everyone" character of party appeals (Downs, 1957). Watering down their appeals, however, may create crises among the parties' most dedicated and loyal adherents. It is a tension that plagues both major parties, especially the "majority" Democrats.

PARTIES AS ORGANIZATIONS

American political parties are a paradox. Virtually all observers describe them as weak and elusive; many claim they are dying if not already dead. Yet, the parties are strongly organized, and they have become more so over the last generation. In formal structure, in the reach of their rules and services, and in their legal underpinnings, the political parties are stronger than ever.

Membership

Few people in this country are "card-carrying members" of a political party. (However, some party organizations do in fact issue cards to contributors.) Far more people are "registered" party members. In the 38 closed-primary states, voters must declare party membership before voting in the primary election. In open-primary states, voters just ask for the ballot of the party in whose primary they wish to vote. Most people are casual about party registration. They do not have to support the party, add to its coffers, or even vote for its candidates. In one-party areas, many people register with the leading party just to vote in its all-important primaries, even when their sympathies lie elsewhere. Many people register as independents. They think it a privilege to be loyal to no party and to renounce all of them.

State and local organizations

State and local parties, their organizations and leaders, are the building blocks of electoral politics. Structurally, the parties are creatures of state laws. These laws specify how parties and their candidates get on the ballot; who are party members through registration procedures; what the parties do; how they finance their activities; and what procedures they should follow. As creatures of state law, "the parties have increasingly become adjuncts of state government" (Bibby et al., 1983: 75). Thus, grass-roots party structures vary from state to state.

Local party structures parallel elective offices and voting districts. Sorauf (1984: 66) says that these structures "form great step pyramids of the myriad, overlapping constituencies of a democracy committed to the election of vast num-

County convention. Democrats in Johnson County, Iowa, convene in a local gymnasium.

bers of officeholders.'' At the bottom are ward and precinct committees and their members. Then there are committees for city, county, state legislative, and congressional offices. These often overlap and are independent because the district lines are not parallel.

At the state level, each party is headed by a state chair and central committee. The latter may vary from 20 members to nearly a thousand. Members are elected by county committees, state conventions, or party primaries. Typically the party is directed by an executive committee drawn from the central committee. Day-to-day leadership is in the hands of a state chair elected by the central committee or state convention.

County, city, ward, district, and precinct units parallel the state structure. That is, they are usually controlled by an elected committee headed by a chairperson. Each party level is responsible for calling caucuses or conventions, conducting campaigns, raising campaign funds, and mobilizing voters.

Most state party organizations have headquarters located in the state capital or other major city. These are staffed by at least a handful of full-time salaried employees. A survey conducted in 1979–80 found that the average state party had about 7 staff members, with a quarter of the states having 10 or more people (Bibby et al., 1983: 77). Party finances ranged from the $14,000 expended by Vermont Democrats in 1979 to in excess of a million dollars a year. (The latter figure was for several state GOP organizations.) In terms of budgets and staffs, state party organizations have grown over the past generation. The increase was dramatic for Republicans, slower for Democrats. This trend belies the widespread notion that party organizations are withering on the vine.

What functions are performed by these party organizations? A recent canvass of 54 state party organizations by Gibson and colleagues (1983: 201–205) identified two kinds of tasks: **institutional support** and **candidate support.** Five types of party activities fall into the first category: (1) raising funds, (2) conducting registration and get-out-the-vote programs, (3) sponsoring public opinion surveys, (4) developing and promoting issue positions, and (5) publishing newsletters.

State parties also focus on candidates by: (1) contributing money, (2) providing services, (3) helping to recruit candidates, (4) influencing the selection of national convention delegates, and (5) making preprimary endorsements. Activity levels range widely from state to state; the average state party apparatus today enters most of these areas. Most state parties, for example, offer candidate support services like advertising and media help, research, public opinion polling, seminars, fund raising, and advice on organization and bookkeeping. Stress on primaries to select candidates may blunt parties' direct influence; but half the state party leaders make some kind of preprimary endorsement. In most of these areas, state parties are substantially more active today than they were two decades ago.

Needless to say, state parties differ widely in size, strength, and effectiveness. As a rule, Republicans throughout the country have stronger organizations than Democrats—a pattern reflected in the national parties as well. Equally important, state party structures are surprisingly strong and active. One team of scholars concluded (Gibson et al., 1983: 206) that "it is quite difficult to find . . . much support for the thesis that party organizations have weakened. Indeed, most indicators warrant the contrary conclusion."

Local parties   Less is known about local party structure. Moreover, it is hard to generalize about local parties, beyond saying that they usually boast officers but little staff or financial support.

Still, many local organizations are quite active, especially during campaigns. Leaders in a majority of the local parties surveyed recently reported the following campaign activities: distributing literature, arranging fund-raising and campaign events (like rallies), contributing money, mounting telephone campaigns, buying newspaper ads, distributing posters or lawn signs, coordinating countywide efforts, and preparing press releases. About 7 out of 10 local parties took part in recruiting candidates; only about half of them worked with candidate organizations in mapping strategy (Gibson et al., 1982). Overall, local parties do not seem to have withered as organizations. Yet, some of the most spectacular cases of party decline are at the local level.

The urban machines   In our major cities, there once flourished a peculiar type of organization—the urban political machine. These entrenched and disciplined organizations were usually led by a citywide "boss" and a group of ward or precinct "bosses." They did many things to win support from rank-and-file voters. Machine-controlled patronage jobs—in police, fire, transit, and other city departments—were given to the faithful. Precinct and ward officials helped their people find jobs; they aided those in trouble with the law; they assisted merchants in getting city contracts, licenses, and police protection; and they dispensed a variety of personal and social services. Machines like New York's Tammany Society also sponsored social activities—from baseball teams and singing groups to clambakes and picnics. For waves of unschooled immigrants who flooded the cities at the turn of the century, the machines offered protection, help, participation, and a sense of identity. In exchange for their votes, confused and often illiterate immigrants could get a job, a helping hand in case of trouble, and even a sense of belonging.

Strong party organizations linger in a few large cities. But few, if any, could be called "machines" in the old sense. And some, like Chicago's once-proud Democratic organization, are torn by ethnic and racial factionalism.

The machines broke down because the things that fueled them—votes, jobs, services—slipped from their grasp. Civil service reforms insulate most jobs from party control. Even when patronage is available—as in federally subsidized jobs

Machine politics Chicago style. Mayor Richard Daley of Chicago (1902–76), last of the old-time city political bosses.

Grass roots. Yard signs promote local candidates in Virginia.

for the hard-core unemployed—it does not build strong local parties (Johnston, 1979). Welfare services, once dispensed by party ward heelers, now flow from state and federal agencies. Most of today's voters do not want party bosses telling them how to vote. And they are less tolerant of the corruption that pervaded the machines.

The old-style urban machines were the peak in party organization. Today's state and local party organizations, as we have seen, are far more genteel and muted. Yet they are far from breathing their last; indeed, the formal trappings of the parties seem to be enjoying a significant revival.

National parties

The emergence of national party images and appeals is now a major trend (Longley, 1980). President Eisenhower once remarked that national parties did not really exist in America. Today, his name graces the Republican Party's stately headquarters on Capitol Hill. Nearby, the Democrats are building their first permanent national headquarters. Like the state parties, the national party organizations are active and growing.

The permanent apparatus   The parties' ongoing business is in the hands of national committees, chairpersons, and headquarters staffs. Their functions are quite diverse; they do not focus only on presidential contests.

The Republican and Democratic national committees consist of people from each state and territory who meet at intervals. State committee representatives may be chosen at state conventions, by the state's delegation to the national convention, by the state's central committee, or in a primary election.

The national committees are very large (Republicans, 176 members; Democrats, 371) and varied. They reflect geographic, factional, and candidate groupings. According to Cotter and Hennessy (1964: 39), "The national committee members have very little collective identity, little patterned interaction, and only rudimentary common values and goals." Their occasional meetings are "largely for show and news-making purposes."

Day-to-day direction of the national parties is in the hands of the national chairpersons. They direct the headquarters staff, make public statements on the party's behalf, and try to fuse intraparty factions into an effective force. If the party controls the White House, the president will pick the chairperson. In 1983,

Democratic National headquarters (left), under construction near Capitol Hill, and Republican National Headquarters (right), named for Dwight D. Eisenhower, on Capitol Hill.

Party chairs. Charles Manatt, Democratic national chair (top); Senator Paul Laxalt, GOP general chair (center); Frank J. Fahrenkopf, Jr. (bottom), GOP operating head.

Reagan named his close friend Senator Paul Laxalt (R-Nev.) to the newly created post of GOP "general chairman." Laxalt, in turn, designated Frank J. Fahrenkopf, Jr., former Nevada party chairman, to assume operating leadership as Republican National Committee chairman. The arrangement underscored the president's stake in the party's organization while leaving detailed direction in the hands of a professional. Few presidents have lent as much support, even symbolic, to the party apparatus. The strongest party chairpersons are those who grasp the reins of a divided party and work to pull its factions into a winning coalition. The most notable have been Democrats Paul Butler (1955–60) and Robert Strauss (1972–76) and Republicans Ray Bliss (1965–69) and William Brock (1977–80).

These days, the parties offer a full range of services to federal candidates. They maintain libraries of information on national issues, conduct seminars for candidates, sponsor public opinion surveys, mount national media campaigns, and help raise funds. In some cases, they move into local areas to persuade attractive would-be candidates to throw their hats in the ring. This must be done with great care to avoid stepping on the toes of local leaders and factions. Still, GOP congressional victories in 1978 and 1980 were credited in part to successful national efforts in recruiting strong candidates.

The two parties face different challenges at the national level. The Democrats have tried to bring together their scattered racial, ethnic, and regional groupings and to create loyalty in the national party. As we shall see, this struggle has been played out largely through presidential nomination rules.

The GOP challenge, on the other hand, was to break out of its minority status and the stigma of Watergate (Cotter and Bibby, 1980). Funding was no barrier; in recent years Republican committees have taken in four or more times what Democratic groups have gained. With their backs to the wall in the mid-1970s, Republicans poured money and talent into developing a truly sophisticated national campaign support. They provided computer services, extensive polling, television studios, speech outlines, candidate recruitment and training, analyses of issues, fund-raising staff, and a host of other services not matched by the Democrats. They encouraged local candidates and gave them financial and technical help. The GOP even ran a series of ads on nationwide TV urging people to "Vote Republican. For a change." They did so well that seasoned political analysts credit a number of GOP victories to the party's organizational superiority. Since losing the White House in 1980, the Democrats have concentrated on building a comparable structure; but they have a long way to go to achieve parity.

Other groups and people are part of the national parties. Some, such as women's and youth groups, are more or less under the national committee's control. Others are groups of officeholders—for example, congressional party caucuses and mayors' and governors' conferences.

There are also loose groups that represent the parties' factional wings. In the GOP, the Ripon Society speaks for the party's small liberal faction. It is named for the Wisconsin town that claims to be the party's birthplace. Citizens for America (CFA) was launched in 1983 as a grass-roots organization to lobby for President Reagan's policies outside the regular GOP organization. The New Democratic Coalition advanced the cause of liberal Democrats in the late 1960s; recently, the Coalition for a Democratic Majority has rallied conservative Democrats.

Platform writers. Rep. Geraldine A. Ferraro (N.Y.) opens sessions of the Democratic Platform Committee, which she chaired in 1984. With her (left) is Democratic National Chairman Charles Manatt.

National conventions The presidential side of the national party is mainly seen every four years, during the nominating convention. Here, state, local, candidate, and issue factions come together briefly under one roof. Important party business is conducted at these conventions. Floor deliberations are usually formal; the key decisions are to ratify (and sometimes change or reject) decisions of various party committees.

The *Platform Committee* hears the views of party leaders and interest groups and figures out how the party stands on issues. Platforms may be controlled by the party's dominant faction or candidate (or the incumbent president). If the factions are divided, platform writers have to compromise. In 1984, for example, the GOP platform was written largely to White House specifications; the Democrats' document was drafted mainly by Walter Mondale's allies, with key concessions to Gary Hart and occasional bows to Jesse Jackson.

The *Rules Committee* recommends procedures for conducting convention business. Many rules are already set and are just readopted by each convention. Others may be changed to give one candidate an advantage. (For example, the number of nondelegate demonstrators allowed on the floor may be changed.) Or a change may be convenient for the TV networks (for example, the number and length of speeches).

The *Credentials Committee* compiles an official list of delegates and checks the credentials of delegates and alternates. Sometimes disputes break out between rival delegates or slates. Delegates' qualifications may be challenged. Often such contests are fought on the floor. The results give an early hint of the relative strength of rival candidate factions.

Finally, the *Committee on Permanent Organization* recommends people for permanent convention posts, including chairperson. Its work is normally not disputed.

In view of their large size and short duration, conventions are hardly deliberating bodies. They tend to ratify rather than debate; their rally aura makes for colorful TV coverage. Most bargaining is done off the convention floor.

Convention sessions used to be marathon affairs. But pressure from the TV networks, not to mention the momentum from primary contests, led to streamlined conventions.

CHOOSING CANDIDATES

The nominating process shapes the parties more than any other factor, except perhaps the traits and constituencies of elected offices themselves. Lately, more and more people are taking part in the nominating process. This, of course, dilutes the power of party leaders.

Caucuses and conventions

Caucuses are the oldest nominating device. These are simply meetings of partisans to discuss and decide on candidates, policies, or strategies. Parties used caucuses to conduct business when they were small, elite groups. Caucuses flourished even before the Constitution was adopted. Through 1824 congressional caucuses named presidential candidates. In that year the Republicans (Jeffersonians) chose John Quincy Adams over the more popular Andrew Jackson. The choice was condemned as a "corrupt bargain." Thus discredited, the congressional caucus for choosing presidential candidates was soon abandoned.

Caucuses are still widely employed for conducting party business, though not often for actual nominating. Elected officials meet in *legislative caucuses* to choose leaders and debate issues and strategies. Local caucuses often debate issues or pick delegates (or delegate candidates) to state and national conventions. In the 1984 presidential nominations, for example, precinct, town, or county caucuses were used by one or both parties in 26 states as part of two-

Caucus voting. Democrats in a Des Moines, Iowa, precinct vote their presidential choices.

or three-tiered processes leading to statewide conventions for selecting delegates.

Caucuses are more party-centered than primaries; they entail more old-fashioned face-to-face campaigning with party activists. This places a premium on organization and loyalists who (as was said of George McGovern's 1972 supporters) are "the kind of people who stay until the end of the meeting."

Most members of the vast party in the electorate are merely spectators to such proceedings. Participation in politics tends to be lower in states choosing delegates through caucuses and conventions then in states using primary elections. In a highly touted caucus system like Iowa's, no more than 15 percent of the party's voters take part.

Nominating conventions are a true American invention. Conventions were adopted in the 1830s to replace congressional caucuses for choosing presidential candidates and spread to the states and localities. Depending on how the delegates are chosen, conventions can broadly represent all party factions. And they are public spectacles, drawing attention to party activities and arousing excitement among the party in the electorate.

Yet conventions soon displayed the same drawback as caucuses: they could be manipulated by party bosses who controlled the selection of delegates. So state legislatures began to regulate convention procedures. And the parties themselves set up detailed rules for delegate selection.

Local party workers prefer large numbers of delegates and alternates. That way they have a better chance of being picked. The 1984 presidential conventions were the largest in history: Democrats had 3,933 delegates and Republicans 2,235, not counting alternates. The parties use complex formulas to allocate delegates among states. Parties want to stress broad geographic representation; but they also have to reward their most loyal supporters.

To understand the pressures within the parties, consider the Democrats' rules for allocating delegates in 1984. (These were the most complicated rules in the party's history.) Most convention delegates (3,001) were what party officials called "plain old delegates," or PODs. All pledged to candidates, PODs were allocated to the states using a formula based on the state's population and past Democratic vote. Another 305 delegates, also pledged to candidates, were a 10 percent add-on of party and elected officials. On top of these were three kinds of unpledged delegates ("superdelegates"), free to back any candidate they chose. First were 114 chairs and vice chairs from the states and other jurisdictions. Second were 400 unpledged party and elected officials, including about three fifths of the Democratic members of Congress. Finally there were nearly 60 "Hawaii bonus" seats—for states having Democratic officeholders in excess of the seats otherwise provided (Perry, 1984).

While most debate over allocating delegates has centered among Democrats, the Republicans have not escaped controversy. Their formula favors small states over large ones, including most of the Northeast corridor. Thus a Republican delegate from Illinois or New Jersey represents five times as many GOP voters as one from Alaska or Wyoming. This results from a uniform bonus system, under which each state voting Republican gets the same number of bonus delegates regardless of its size.

There have been clashes in both parties between *amateurs* stressing issues or ideologies, and *professionals,* mainly interested in winning elections and upholding the party system. In the old days most delegates were chosen by caucuses not primaries. Then, professionals controlled the delegates. Now, many states have primaries. Since the late 1960s, the selection process has opened up. Delegates are more apt to represent candidate or issue factions (Kirkpatrick, 1976). That is, the professionals have lost ground to the amateurs (Soule and McGrath, 1975).

Convention delegates are still not a cross section of the voting public. Whites, males, and upper-income groups are overrepresented. So are the parties' cores of support: Catholics, Jews, and trade unionists for the Democrats; Protestants and business people for the Republicans (Mitofsky and Plissner, 1980). In recent years, both parties have tried to broaden delegations by recruiting women, blacks, and minorities.

Direct primaries

Primary elections were pushed by turn-of-the-century reformers. They thought primaries would stop bossism and broaden popular control over nominations. First used in Wisconsin in 1903, the primary idea spread like wildfire; in 1955, Connecticut became the last state to adopt it. Though all states have primary laws, some let parties choose whether to nominate by primary, convention, or some combination. Thus, primaries are not universal. Primaries have loosened party leaders' grip on the nominating process, transferring it to state control.

Primaries are creatures of state law. Thus, elections are supervised by state officials. States have differing rules about who can take part in primaries. Party leaders, of course, prefer strict rules that reward party loyalty and help leaders shape the outcomes.

In **closed primaries,** voters must affirm their party preference to vote. This system is found in 38 states. In some states, voters must register their party affiliation before the primary. In others, voters only have to declare themselves at the polls to establish party registration. Thus, some primaries are more "closed" than others. In certain states, voters can be challenged if they have not supported the party in the past; but such challenges are rare and almost impossible to prove. What sets closed-primary states apart is that party affiliation, however established, is considered permanent until the voter goes through the process of changing it. Rules vary from state to state, but they clearly discourage casual crossing of party lines.

Nine states conduct a so-called **open primary.** Rather than register by party, a voter can vote in either party's primary (but not both). This does not involve registration and is not permanent. The most open of all are the *blanket* primary (Alaska, Washington) and the *nonpartisan* primary (Louisiana). In the former, voters can take part in more than one party's primary by moving back and forth from office to office. In the latter, all candidates for the same office are grouped together with no party affiliation listed.

Primaries are used to select candidates for some offices in all 50 states. In most states, only primaries are used; some use party conventions to select candidates in certain races. Four southern states (Alabama, Georgia, South Carolina, and Virginia) let the parties decide whether to hold conventions or primaries. The dominant Democrats usually opt for primaries because their nominations are more often contested. The GOP usually holds conventions.

Several states combine conventions and primaries. Utah and Colorado, for example, hold *preprimary conventions* to endorse candidates. Typically the convention's choice wins the primary; candidates carrying the convention overwhelmingly (70 to 80 percent of the votes) are deemed nominated. In other states (for example, Connecticut, Delaware, and New York), primaries are held only if candidates receive a specified share of the convention's delegate vote (from 20 to 35 percent, depending on the state). Conventions tend to bolster party organizations and inhibit "outsider" candidates. As Bibby et al. write (1983: 73), "The principal effect of the convention system, even if it is only one step in the overall nominating process, is that it permits a greater party influence on candidate selection."

Preprimary endorsement of candidates is widespread. Five states provide for preprimary endorsements by law; in 13 others parties are permitted optional or extralegal endorsements (Morehouse, 1980). Even more often, state party figures make endorsements to indicate party approval of candidates.

Most southern states require a second, or *runoff*, primary between the top two candidates if no one gets a majority the first time. Historically runoffs were aimed at giving coherence to Democratic selections. Because of the party's regional dominance, selection was (in the common phrase) "tantamount to election." Therefore, the value of the nomination, combined with the party's own factionalism, draws a horde of candidates lacking broad support. The two-tiered primary gives candidates a chance to build that support.

In his 1984 campaign, Jesse Jackson declared war on the runoff primary. He argued that it gave white voters a chance to cluster around a white candidate and shut out black contenders. No doubt the runoff primary has at times worked to block the nomination of blacks. In other cases, it has been the means of forging coalitions of blacks and moderate whites against strong Republican contenders.

The effects of primaries   Direct primaries have been something of a disappointment to reformers. Primaries open the door to wider participation in nominations. But they normally attract fewer voters than general elections. (The exception is some one-party areas where primaries are more important than general elections.) Primaries are less publicized than general elections. Therefore, they tend to attract voters who are older, richer, better educated, and more politically aware. Primary voters are also more committed to issues and more loyal to the party (Ranney, 1976).

State registration laws or other election rules do not seem to affect the extent of primary voting. Neither does how competitive the contests are. But some factors do seem to have influence: (1) campaign spending by the candidates (for publicity draws attention to the contest), and (2) the general level of education. Turnout is much higher in states with well-educated populations (Ranney, 1977: 26–35).

Even in highly touted presidential contests, voting in direct primaries is not remarkable. Only 36 percent of the eligible voters in primary states voted in 1980, when there were lively contests in both parties. Four years later, some 26 million people took part in primaries or caucuses to nominate presidential candidates. This was about one of every seven Americans of voting age, and less than one fourth of those who voted in the geveral elections.

On the whole, primary voting mirrors candidate and media attention. Thus Democratic figures for 1984 were generally higher—because of the close contest, and because of Jackson's efforts to mobilize black voters. With Reagan unopposed, GOP voting was down. Overall, primary voting is disappointing. The

Votes versus Delegates, 1984
In Democratic caucuses

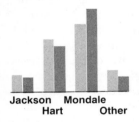

Jackson   Mondale
   Hart   Other

Key:
Percent of caucus vote
Percent of delegates

In Democratic primaries

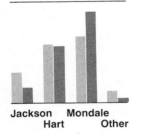

Jackson   Mondale
   Hart   Other

Key:
Percent of popular vote
Percent of delegates

Source: Rhodes Cook, "Mondale's Primary Weakness Bodes Ill for November Hopes," *Congressional Quarterly Weekly Report* 42 (June 16, 1984), pp. 1441–44.

highly-touted New Hampshire primary, which has become a media event, brought all of 101,000 Democrats to the polls in 1984—14 percent of the state's voting-age population. The same proportion voted in the massive California primary, where Democrats had to wade through long ballot lists of district delegates pledged to each candidate in order to cast their vote.

Most politicians and many political scientists blame direct primaries for speeding the decline of political parties. Certainly primaries have weakened party control over nominees. Party leaders can influence the results of primaries by endorsing certain candidates; but it is harder to control an election than a caucus or convention. With the rise of mass media, would-be nominees can appeal to the public over the heads of party leaders. Indeed, candidates must build their own networks of support separate from those of other party officeholders.

For this reason, primaries are also costly. Unless they start with commanding advantages, candidates must mount almost the same kind of campaign in the primary as in the general election. The scale and thrust are different. But the same techniques—personal appearances, direct mailing, canvassing, and media advertising—are normally required. Thus, the spread of primaries has helped boost the costs of running for office.

Nonpartisanship   Sometimes reformers have tried to do away with party labels altogether. Nebraska elects its legislators on a nonpartisan basis. In many states, local officials (mayors, school boards, judges, councils, and the like) are picked the same way. There are no party labels on the primary ballot. The top two candidates in the primary face each other in the general election. (If the winner has an absolute majority in the primary, he or she may be declared elected.)

Some say that getting rid of party labels can protect local elections from divisive national issues. In fact, however, parties often help to recruit and promote candidates. When the parties keep their hands off, other factors—newspaper endorsements, or civic group sponsorship—may serve as party substitutes helping voters sort out competing claims. Still, without party labels, voters often find it impossible to figure out what, or who, the candidates stand for. They may grasp at trivial things. (If all else fails, the candidates' last names will do.) Or they may throw up their hands in despair and not vote. No doubt this helps explain why turnout is lower in local elections than in national ones.

A special case: presidential nominations

The presidential nominating process is unique in many ways. It is the nation's longest-running road show. It attracts nonstop attention from politicians and the press. It is also unbelievably complex. As one commentator says (Ranney, 1974: 72): "In America the presidential nominating game is played under by far the most elaborate, variegated, and complex set of rules in the world. They include national party rules, state and local party rules, state statutes (especially those governing presidential primaries), and a wide variety of rulings by national and state courts." Every presidential nomination is a mixture of candidates, strategies, tactics, interest-group support, and rules of the game. Winners are those who are best able to exploit these ingredients.

The "insider strategy"   Before the 1970s, would-be candidates treated the convention as a large-scale caucus. They tried to win support by gaining favor

"Insiders." Hubert Humphrey and Edmund Muskie, 1968 running mates, appealed to traditional Democratic groups.

with various leaders—bosses who controlled blocs of delegates. With this strategy the party was viewed as a bunch of blocs or factions that had to be appeased. Candidates lacking broad first-ballot support resorted to an insider strategy known as the **dark horse:** combining with other forces to knock off the front-runners while trying to stay in everyone's good graces. When the front-runners faded, the dark horse's name was put forward, maybe in some "smoke-filled room" of party leaders. The insider strategy assumed that candidates did not control the choice of delegates. Rather, they had to win favor with the delegates (and their leaders) once the delegates had been picked.

The insider strategy, modern style, is a springboard for candidates with a lot of support from party leaders and interest groups allied with the party. Incumbent presidents or candidates who are hands-down front-runners are most likely to be in this fortunate situation. They woo the party faithful and line up endorsements from leaders. Recent "insider" campaigns have been run by Hubert Humphrey (1968), Gerald Ford (1976), Jimmy Carter (1980), and Walter Mondale (1984), among others.

With so many delegates chosen in open contests, and with such a diffuse party in the electorate, no candidate can rely solely on support from party influentials to sweep to victory. All the candidates named above, for example, faced stiff challenges from "outsiders" who claimed broad popular appeal and denounced "back-room" politics. Though favored by traditional Democrats and boosted by rules designed for front-runners, Walter Mondale had to prove himself in the 1984 race against more independent voters (who rallied behind Gary Hart, although John Glenn was earlier thought to appeal to them) and much of the black community (which was stirred by Jesse Jackson's candidacy).

Although the insider strategy is not enough by itself, candidates and their managers still have to use it. Through personal appeals, direct mailings, social events, and hospitality suites, candidates woo delegates and leaders. This includes those who are unpledged or pledged to other candidates. Once they are chosen, all nominees must employ insider tactics. They must rally activists from the party's factional blocs for the general election effort. Barry Goldwater failed to appease GOP moderates in 1964; George McGovern was estranged from middle-of-the-road Democrats in 1972. This doomed their campaigns.

The "outsider strategy"   The public nature of presidential nominations is, for better or worse, a fact of our times. In 1968, less than half the national convention delegates were chosen by primaries. In 1984, about 55 percent were picked by primaries in 33 states and territories; this was down from 1976, when three quarters of the delegates were picked that way in 36 states and territories.

Presidential primaries have been around since the early 1900s. But politicians long scoffed at them. (Harry Truman, no political novice, called them "eyewash.") After 1968, however, there was an upheaval among Democrats and, to a lesser degree, among Republicans. Backers of Democratic Senator Eugene McCarthy that year attempted to challenge President Lyndon Johnson and found to their dismay that many avenues of influence were closed to them. Although the convention was months away and not all the candidates were identified, delegates had already been chosen. Rules and procedures were chaotic, irregular, and often secret. Candidates with minority support got few delegates if any; certain groups (blacks, women, and youth, in particular) were underrepresented. A Commission on Party Structure and Delegate Selection (the McGovern-Fraser Commission) was named by the 1968 convention to suggest reforms. According to the commission, "Meaningful participation of Democratic voters in the choice of the presidential nominee was often difficult or costly, sometimes completely illusory, and, in not a few instances, impossible."

MEDIA THEMES AND MESSAGES: DEMOCRATIC CONTENDERS, 1984

The campaigns of major Democratic presidential contenders in 1984 illustrate how media appeals flow from the candidates' campaign themes. Campaign advisers study the candidates' strengths and weaknesses, and assess their standing with the public. They then fashion media messages—often embodied in slogans—designed to improve their candidates' share of the voter "market." Consider the following:

Walter F. Mondale, former vice president and Minnesota Senator. As front-runner in the Democratic race, Mondale's TV ads ignored name recognition, stressing character definition to protect the candidate's lead. ("He dares to be cautious," an adviser explained.) The theme: Mondale speaks softly but talks tough. Sample slogans: "Walter Mondale's presidency will start from strength." "He's been tested. This president will know what he's doing." The most famous Mondale ad was the "red phone," referring to the White House-Kremlin hot line. It showed only a red phone, with a red light that flashed ominously as the announcer spoke: "The most awesome, powerful responsibility in the world lies in the hand that picks up this phone. The idea of an unsure, unsteady, untested hand is something to really think about. . . . Mondale—this president will know what he is doing."

Gary Hart, Colorado Senator. Earliest ads had a futuristic, high-tech format which conveyed a fresh image. Hart himself was shown, without script, uttering Kennedy-like platitudes: "I think the American people want leadership. They want purpose. They want directions. They want problems solved. They want answers. They want proposals. They want ideas." Later, responding to his pollsters' advice on how to capture voters unimpressed with Mondale, the Hart ads honed in on the "new ideas" theme. In each ad, the tag line repeated the theme and recalled problems of the Carter-Mondale years: "New leadership. We can't afford to go back."

John Glenn, Ohio Senator and former astronaut. Glenn was a national hero turned presidential challenger. He had name recognition but needed to prove himself a worthy contender. (Another candidate sarcastically called him "Sky King.") There were two stages in Glenn's media campaign. First, establish Glenn as a political leader ("You know him as an astronaut, an American hero. But how much more do you know?") The ads moved from film clips of his space triumphs to his military experience and Senate career. Second, stake out issue differences with Mondale. This second wave of ads attacked Mondale (and the "Carter-Mondale administration") on economics, defense, and foreign policy.

Reubin Askew, former Florida governor. Name recognition was paramount for someone with a distinguished public service record but little national exposure. Sample slogan: "Reubin Askew. If you get to know him, you'll probably vote for him." In one ad, Askew introduced himself in the style of the famous American Express ads. ("You know me," he began. "In just 30 seconds I could never tell you all that I've been a part of or all that I hope to do for America in the future." He then offered to send information to viewers who called or wrote.) Insofar as Askew's ads dealt with politics, they tried to separate him from the herd by portraying him as "The Different Democrat."

Alan Cranston, California Senator and Senate Democratic Whip. Cranston's ads took another approach to the name recognition problem. They hammered at the two issues to which Cranston hitched his campaign: full employment and ending the arms race. ("There will be no question about the purpose of the Cranston presidency," the candidate declared in one 30-second spot. "I will be the first president totally committed to stopping the arms race. I will be the only president since Franklin Roosevelt to put the full weight of his office behind getting people back to work.") Other ads criticized President Reagan for committing U.S. troops in Lebanon, and attacked Mondale's and Glenn's timidity on the issues.

Source: From Martin Schram, "Four Democrats Launch Media Blitz in New Hampshire and Iowa," *Washington Post*, January 13, 1984, p. A 3.

FIGURE 6—4

Changing Democratic Nominating Rules*

Rule	1972	1976	1980	1984
Timing:				
Restrict delegate selection events to a 3-month period (the "window")			✓	✓
Conditions of participation:				
Restrict participation in delegate selection events to Democrats		✓	✓	✓
Proportional representation:				
Ban all types of winner-take-all contests			✓	
Delegate loyalty:				
Give candidates the right to approve delegates identifying with their candidacy		✓	✓	✓
Bind delegates to vote for their original presidential preference at convention on first ballot			✓	
Party and elected officials:				
Expand each delegation by 10 percent to include pledged party and elected officials			✓	✓
Further expand each delegation to include uncommitted party and elected officials ("superdelegates")				✓
Demographic representation:				
Encourage participation and representation of minorities and traditionally underrepresented groups (affirmative action)	✓	✓	✓	✓
Require delegations to be equally divided between men and women			✓	✓

*The check mark indicates years that major rule changes were in effect.
Source: *Congressional Quarterly Weekly Report* 41 (August 6, 1983), p. 1612.

Since 1968, The Democrats have tinkered with their nominating rules every four years (see Figure 6–4). The McGovern-Fraser guidelines, adopted for 1972 and revised through 1980, opened up the delegate selection process. Delegates were to be chosen in a "timely manner," with certain safeguards. Each state was urged to include blacks, women, youth, and ethnic minorities in its delegation. Within the states, delegates had to be fairly apportioned. Later, statewide winner-take-all primaries were banned. Also prohibited were "loophole primaries," in which candidates could capture all delegates from individual congressional districts by winning only a plurality of the vote.

The post-1968 reforms transformed the nominating process, especially in the Democratic party. "From a system in which primaries played a supporting rather than a leading role," Polsby (1983: 63) concluded, "the United States rapidly moved toward a nominating system in which primaries dominated the process."

The GOP has undergone similar but far less spectacular changes. The party has tried to open up its nominations and broaden the groups represented. But it starts from a narrower base than the Democrats; its internal rifts are less deep. Thus, the party has held back from nationalizing its selection rules. It retains a confederational structure; states take the first step toward changes (Bibby, 1980). For example, the GOP never banned winner-take-all primaries. Still, where state electoral laws were changed in response to Democratic party turmoil, the GOP often had to shift its practices.

Open delegate selection is a long, tedious, and scattered ordeal. The formal process starts no less than 14 months before the election itself, when in two states the GOP elects committees which will choose their convention delegates. The Iowa caucuses are in late February, the New Hampshire primary in early March. Even before this, the candidates are in full cry; the media are busy pronouncing winners and losers. Across the country trek the candidates, advance crews, and reporters. The climax is the giant California primary in early June.

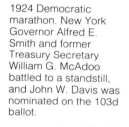

1924 Democratic marathon. New York Governor Alfred E. Smith and former Treasury Secretary William G. McAdoo battled to a standstill, and John W. Davis was nominated on the 103d ballot.

Many delegates are chosen in open primaries or caucuses. Thus, the leading candidate typically comes to the fore long before the convention convenes. The delegates ratify a popular choice already made in full public view; since 1956, *all* nominees have been named on the first ballot. (Past conventions were often marathon affairs. This was especially true for Democrats, who had a two thirds rule for nominations. In 1924, 103 ballots were needed to pick the nominee, John W. Davis.)

Highly publicized primary and caucus victories not only produce delegates. They also give some candidates momentum—"Big Mo," as George Bush put

it. With prodding by candidates' promoters and the press, results are often distorted by a game of expectations to establish "front-runners" and "also-rans." A candidate might win 40 percent of a state's vote. Is this an impressive victory or a fatal setback? It all depends. It is a victory if the candidate is a long shot whose bid has been dismissed by the pros. It is a setback if the candidate is a front-runner who was expected to do much better. Victories or defeats, especially very early or near the climax of the campaign, exert a powerful pull.

Even when no delegates are at stake, the nomination race runs full tilt in the media. Frequent opinion surveys and straw polls—of doubtful significance early in the game—provide fodder for stories touting this candidate or that as "the one to beat."

Reporters and pundits are eager to declare big winners and big losers, even if the results fall somewhere in between (Weaver, 1976). Such publicity can spotlight obscure candidates or tarnish the image of well-known ones. In turn, the results affect the candidate's name recognition among the public, the zeal of the workers, and the generosity of financial backers. In 1972, Senator George McGovern was the clear front-runner when the convention convened. Yet he got only about 30 percent of the primary votes and caucus-convention support. Jimmy Carter, with about 39 percent of voter support in the various states, blew away his rivals and dominated the 1976 convention.

All candidates today must in some sense mount "outsider" campaigns. They must look beyond the party leaders to demonstrate their popular appeal through media exposure and favorable poll standings. Candidates who lack special ties with party inner circles must take the outside route. They thus force party leaders to take notice. John F. Kennedy in 1960 used his public appeal as leverage to gain the support of party bosses. In 1984 contenders as diverse as John Glenn and Jesse Jackson bid for public support to bolster their assault on the party nomination.

Revolt of the partisans The "reformed," primary-oriented nominating process may have defects. The clearest losers were the party organizations, including their leaders and elected officials. The debate on this point raged mainly among Democrats. The party's Commission on Presidential Nomination (the Hunt Commission), authorized by the 1980 convention, eventually summarized the predicament (Democratic National Committee, 1982: 3):

> Primaries have proliferated, removing decision-making power from party caucuses and conventions. Our national convention has been in danger of what one critic has called a "rubber stamp electoral college." To an alarming extent our party's public officials have not participated in and thus have felt only a limited responsibility for our recent national conventions.

This indictment of the post-1968 reforms reflected growing impatience of party leaders and scholarly commentators with what the reforms had produced in the way of candidates and campaigns. Of course, some of the party's preoccupation with rules tinkering stemmed from its electoral dilemma; in the three elections since the reforms, Democrats won the White House once and lost twice by wide margins. Still, complaints about the process were not without substance.

Elected delegates may be so tied to causes or candidates that they stray far from average voters' views. A leading student of conventions (Kirkpatrick, 1976: 330) pointed out,

> Participatory politics poses a special pitfall for political parties: the danger of mistaking those who turn out to participate in party governance for "the people," for the voters to whom the party is answerable on election day. The Democratic experience of 1972 not only demonstrates the persistence of class characteristics of political elites, it illustrates the errors of concluding that "open" processes and thousands of meetings will produce a convention in which "the people" are represented. Herein lies the reason that conventions based on "open" participatory politics may turn out (as in 1972) to be less representative of party rank and file (and other voters) than conventions peopled by labor leaders, political "bosses," and public officials.

The author of this quote, political scientist and conservative Democrat Jeane J. Kirkpatrick, found a home in the Reagan administration as U.S. Ambassador to the United Nations. She was not alone in questioning the choice of anti-Vietnam War candidate McGovern in 1972; he lost to President Nixon in a landslide.

The post-1968 nominating methods were also faulted because they bypassed party leaders and elected officials. In 1972–1980, few party influentials—committeemen and women, council members, elected officials—appeared among the national convention delegates. (An average of 48 Senators and Representatives were seated at these conventions, compared with 117 in 1968.) This meant that the convention's choice carried little weight with the party regulars. In 1972 and 1980, surveys reported that up to a third of Democratic voters abandoned their party's presidential ticket. This defection rate was unmatched by either party in any election since 1950.

The estrangement of party leaders also hinders successful candidates in forging effective governing coalitions with other Democratic officeholders. Candidates are led to mobilize factions at the expense of building broad coalitions that will enable them to govern (Polsby, 1983: 65). Jimmy Carter ran for president apart from party leaders; once elected, he lacked the contacts needed for party support of his programs.

In 1980, the Democrats authorized a commission—the fourth since 1968—to reassess their nomination rules. The Hunt Commission, named for its chairman, North Carolina Governor James B. Hunt, Jr., studied the situation and in 1982 presented a series of recommendations. They were accepted with few alterations. Taken as a whole, the Hunt Commission's changes represented a major departure from the post-1968 reforms. Major 1984 revisions flowing from the commission's recommendations were:

1. About 22 percent of the delegate seats would be reserved for party and elected officials. Most of them would be "superdelegates," unpledged to any candidate. Included would be 164 Representatives and 27 Senators (three fifths of all Democrats in Congress), plus a variety of governors, mayors, and other officials. (However, the pressures to back candidates were powerful; three quarters of the members of Congress chosen as "unpledged" delegates had actually announced for one of the candidates.)

2. Proportional representation—allocating delegates to candidates strictly according to their share of the primary or caucus vote—was relaxed somewhat. States could adopt a winner-take-more system; top vote getters in each district would get one extra delegate. Or they could return to the "loophole" primary (formerly prohibited) allowing winners to take all the delegates in a given district.

"NOW, ABOUT THE RULES..."

3. The nominating process was shortened by five weeks—early March through early June. This was not wholly successful in deterring states from holding early contests. Nor did it altogether curb "front-loading" (that is, producing "winners" and "losers" early in the game).

4. A controversial 1980 rule requiring all delegates to vote for their original presidential preference on the first ballot (a rule pushed by Carter to prevent defections to Massachusetts Senator Edward M. Kennedy) was weakened.

5. The commission reaffirmed the party's commitment to proportional representation of women and minorities, and to ban crossover voting (that is, open primaries).

The new system took a big step in the direction of restoring party leaders' influence. It also boosted the chances of an "insider" candidate like Walter F. Mondale, who had close ties with party officials and key interest groups allied with the party. Yet it was not immune from attack. Black activist Jesse Jackson, entering the contest in December 1983, charged that the rules were rigged against outside or late-entering challengers. He argued especially against the rule denying delegates to candidates with less than 20 percent of a primary's votes. While Jackson's complaints were dismissed by most Democratic regulars, they were a potent threat.

Meanwhile, other groups of Democratic regulars—especially organized labor—decided that they, too had been pushed out of the "reformed" process and should reassert their interests. Labor leaders were especially vexed by the "New Politics" coalition of Vietnam War opponents, minorities, feminists, and other challengers of the status quo. Meeting with key Democrats, AFL-CIO head Lane Kirkland won a bigger labor voice in party affairs. Of the Democratic National Committee's 25 members at large, 15 are union representatives, 5 of whom serve on the executive committee.

Spurred by Kirkland, the AFL-CIO decided to take an even bolder step: endorse a candidate a year before the election itself. This maximized labor's leverage in choosing the candidate and increased its share of convention delegates committed to a candidate. In October 1983, Walter Mondale was given labor's nod. He was endorsed not only by the AFL-CIO, but also by the National Education Association and other groups. This confirmed Mondale's front-runner status, as labor's extensive staff and resources were grafted onto the candidate's own organization. The AFL-CIO's political action committee, COPE (Committee on Political Education), was enlarged to provide better labor support for favored candidates.

The endorsement plan underscored labor's place at the party's bargaining table. It also carried potential hazards (Raskin, 1984). Choosing between two or more candidates loyal to labor's interests could prove a distinct embarrassment for the labor movement. (Fortunately for the unions, Mondale was the only credible prolabor contender, Senator Edward M. Kennedy having bowed out of the race. Even so, California's Senator Alan Cranston was also a faithful labor supporter and held up the endorsement by arguing forcefully that he deserved labor's favor.)

More important, union leaders risked being written off as paper tigers if rank-and-file union members failed to back up their choice. Thus, in 1983, union chiefs conducted elaborate polls of their members before giving the nod to

Fritz and friend. AFL-CIO president Lane Kirkland, whose organization endorsed Walter Mondale and aided his campaign, has a word with his candidate during the New York primary battle.

Mondale. And when Mondale's candidacy flagged, the unions threw their campaign machinery into high gear and pumped money and workers into the effort. (In the Iowa caucuses, which Mondale won, about half the participants came from union families, and 70 percent reported having been contacted by the AFL-CIO.)

Labor endorsement has its drawbacks for the candidate. It could invite charges of being beholden to "special interests." This is especially dangerous in view of organized labor leaders' low standing among the general public. (Labor's dilemmas are detailed in Chapter 7.) As labor's choice in 1984, Mondale was accused by his opponents of having "promised everything to everyone."

An assessment   How successful was the 1984 "revolt of the partisans"? The picture is mixed. The rules were supposed to tilt the game somewhat back toward the party's "insiders." They were designed to yield a clear winner who could forge a consensus among the party's factions.

Certainly the rules did favor the insider strategy. The party's elected officials and other leaders played a bigger role than they had in years. So did key constituent groups like the major unions. (The AFL-CIO boasted some 600 delegates at the San Francisco convention.) And, of course, the choice of most of these core partisans, Mondale, became the nominee.

The circumstances of Mondale's nomination, however, cast doubt on the reformers' other goals. His victory was neither easy nor clearcut. Though he remained the choice of the core party faithful, his rivals held claim to more volatile elements of the party that would be needed to win the presidency. These included younger and more independent-minded voters (Hart) and newly activated black voters (Jackson). Moreover, the delegate "bonuses" Mondale gained from the new rules gave his rivals the chance to attack the whole process as unfair. (In the end they won concessions for 1988.)

If anything, the process underscored the Democrats' diversity and dispersion. Perhaps the party merely lacked in 1984 a candidate who could successfully bridge all of its factions (though it is hard to imagine who such a candidate might be). Perhaps, too, it illustrates a deeper truth: rules changes cannot by themselves produce a unified party.

Pitfalls of popular choice?   Today's nominating politics are more open than the old smoke-filled rooms. But they are prolonged and costly. They favor candidates who are unemployed (unless they are incumbent presidents): that is, those who have the time and the single-minded passion to devote to running for office.

Should potential presidents be put through such ordeals? Some people think the grueling process exposes candidates to realistic pressures. It puts them in contact with the public and the press; it also exposes misjudgments made under pressure. Others think the process is a joke. They feel it shows little about ability to serve in the White House. As a veteran political reporter wrote (Ehrenhalt, 1984: 167): "Virtually every aspect of this year's Democratic marathon—the 'cattle show' public appearances, the pledges to special interest groups, the thousands of fund-raising phone calls, the courtship of the press—has brought out the worst in the good candidates as well as the bad ones."

Some reformers would rather have a series of multistate regional primaries or even one national primary. This would shorten the nomination campaign and reduce wear and tear on candidates. Defenders of the current system say it provides a variety of settings for candidates to prove themselves. "As long as there are many things we demand of a president—intelligence as well as popularity, integrity as well as speaking ability, private virtue as well as public presentability," argue Polsby and Wildavsky (1984: 226), "we ought to foster a selection process that provides a mixture of devices for screening according to different criteria." Some contend that candidates like McGovern or Carter could only have emerged from individualized contests. Others counter that the success of such candidates proves the system is defective.

For the time being, Republicans are "staying the course," as Democrats still tinker with their rules. And there is no consensus on how to alter the parties' jerry-built nominating systems. Conflicts between party leaders and the broader electoral party will continue to make wholesale solutions difficult, if not impossible. Democratic party leaders were able to recapture some of their lost control for the 1984 race. But the inevitable cost was exposure to attacks from "outsider" candidates, like Gary Hart and Jesse Jackson, who charge the system is rigged to exclude certain segments.

Democrats are committed to further rules changes for 1988 that will meet some of the Hart-Jackson demands and modify the 1984 arrangements. A package of changes, accepted as a "unity deal" by the Mondale forces, and mandated to a new rules commission, would somewhat dilute the role of party and elected officials. Specifically, the proposed changes would: (1) reduce the number of unpledged party and elected officials ("superdelegates") from 14 percent to a maximum of 7.5 percent; (2) change the threshold for winning a delegate from the mandatory 20 percent of the vote in a caucus or primary to 15 percent—a step toward the proportional representation urged by Jackson; and (3) open up delegate-selection caucuses in states like Texas and Michigan, where Hart contended that restrictive rules paved the way for Mondale victories in 1984.

Factors more fundamental than rules changes, moreover, affect nominating politics. They will make it difficult to go back to the smoke-filled rooms. Among these are the role of the mass media, the profound shifts in campaign funding patterns, and the prevalence of popular norms of participation. All these features point in the direction of somewhat weaker party control of nominations. None of them suggests that modern nominating trends can easily be reversed.

Jimmy Carter, president of the flesh, attempting to win support for his election in 1980.

CAMPAIGNING FOR OFFICE

Once nominated, the candidate's battle is only half won. Now comes the general election campaign, with its noisy mix of personal appearances, speech making, advertising, and symbolic appeals. For candidates fresh from wresting the nomination in primaries, the general election may seem like more of the same. For those who gained nomination by an easier path, the election campaign brings them before the public for the first time. All candidates, though, here face the entire electorate, not just their own partisans.

Strategies, themes, and slogans

The key decision faced by candidates and their managers is choosing a *campaign strategy*. This is the campaign's overall tone or thrust. It will determine how to deploy such resources as time, money, and personnel to produce a favorable voter response. To design a winning strategy, the candidate must first ponder these questions. What type of office am I seeking? Am I the incumbent or the challenger? Am I the candidate of the majority or the minority party? Are my face and career familiar to the voters, or am I unknown? What images do the voters already have of me? What issues or problems are uppermost in the voters' minds? What resources—money, support, volunteer effort—will I command during the campaign?

What is the office?   Level of office affects the campaign. Candidates for president, for instance, can be sure that their name and face will reach the voters. The mass media's relentless coverage assures that. But many electoral contests attract little media attention. This leaves the task of communication more or less to the candidates themselves.

The incumbency factor   Incumbency normally, though not always, works in the officeholder's favor. Every incumbent, from city council members to the president, has resources and privileges that can be used to draw public attention and build support. Incumbents are better known than challengers. They have built-in ways of reaching voters—speeches, press coverage, newsletters, staff help, ability to help constituents, and sheer familiarity with the issues.

Even presidential challengers, though by no means ignored, find it hard to match the pomp and circumstance the president commands in performing official duties. Running for reelection in 1972, President Nixon visited mainland China during the New Hampshire primary and Moscow during the California primary. These were publicity coups that robbed Democratic contenders of valuable exposure during two critical periods. In 1980, Carter stopped campaigning altogether under the pretext that the Iranian hostage crisis demanded his full attention. This approach is sometimes known as "campaigning from the White House rose garden." It has the advantage of showing the candidate in a presidential role rather than as just another politician.

Incumbency can be a liability, though. Popular unrest, policy fiascos, or scandals can turn the table against officeholders. Faced with inflation at home and national humiliation abroad, President Carter was the target of discontent in 1980. Challenger Ronald Reagan's strategy, devised by his survey analyst Richard Wirthlin, was twofold: first establish Reagan's credibility as a reliable leader, not an extremist; then spotlight Carter's record. In the TV debate when Reagan asked people whether they were better off than they were four years before, his strategy hit home.

Majority or minority   Majority-minority party status is often difficult to assess; states or districts vary widely and split-ticket voting is common. In one-party areas, majority-party candidates have little need to campaign; their nomination is tantamount to election. Opponents may drop campaigning for the same reason. Or they may take desperate measures to catch the voters' attention.

Democrats have been the majority choice for party identifiers since the Roosevelt realignment of the 1930s. So a typical Democratic campaign stresses party loyalty, past party achievements, and voter registration. The theory is that the higher the turnout, the better for the majority party. GOP campaigns, in contrast, aim at blurring party differences: the party has conducted "me-too" campaigns (1940–48); run a popular hero (Eisenhower in 1952, 1956); or exploited splits in the majority party (Nixon in 1968 and 1972). The 1980–84 Reagan strategy was a combination of all these: the candidate was a movie actor who quoted Franklin Roosevelt and wooed dissident Democrats.

What are the voters thinking?   Other questions affecting strategy can be answered by public opinion surveys. Skilled analysts can pinpoint popular views and suggest ways of dealing with them. Already well-known candidates try to cash in on "name recognition"; lesser-known candidates have their names repeated over and over again in advertising. Candidates known for openness or friendliness highlight these qualities; those who are less glib may stress experience and competence. Candidates who have made tough, unpopular decisions are billed as persons of courage. And so on.

Popular moods change; so do desired candidate images. In crises, voters prefer experience, competence, and reassurance. After the Watergate scandals, voters seemed to value honesty and openness above all other virtues.

Slogans   Campaign strategy is often distilled into a single theme or slogan. John F. Kennedy in 1960 was a model of a fresh young generation. He used the theme, "Get America Moving Again." In 1972, President Nixon's advisers saw that voters respected the presidency but were lukewarm toward Nixon. Hence their theme, "Reelect the President." The Republicans' 1980 slogan, "Vote Republican. For a change!" stressed that the GOP was not to blame for the country's ills.

Slogans are employed also to simplify campaign arguments and pierce through public and media indifference. In 1984, for instance, Gary Hart used a "new ideas" theme to tap voters' uneasiness about the past Democratic record. To cast doubt on Hart's theme, Walter Mondale grabbed a slogan from America's fast-food wars ("Where's the beef?"). It may not have been edifying; but it was not ignored, either.

Campaign techniques

Implementing strategy is the grueling job of the candidate's organizers. Contenders used to rely on party leaders to wage their battles; in certain places, this is still done. But typically, party organizations are incomplete and fragmented; they command neither the workers nor the money to mount effective campaigns. The old party pros have been replaced by new professionals, available for sizable fees.

Many campaign management firms offer a complete range of services. They can draw up strategies and use them according to the candidate's desires or pocketbook. Other firms offer special services: survey research, direct mail appeals, coordinating volunteers, advertising, and financial management and accounting (Sabato, 1981).

Helped by modern technology, these firms take on projects that dwarf the efforts of even the best-oiled old-style machines. Richard Vigurie—whose company specializes in direct mail appeals—estimated that his computers spewed out 50 million letters on behalf of conservative groups and candidates during 1977. And what was a political off year. The mailings yielded between $15 and $20 million. That about equaled the combined take of the Republican and Democratic national committees (Shogan, 1977: 10).

Contacting voters   A key phase of campaigns is direct voter appeal, sometimes through door-to-door canvassing. In strong party areas this was a basic duty of ward, precinct, and block captains. The political machine leaders' abil-

Local party action. Precinct captain on the job at polling place on election day.

ity to "deliver the vote" was the ultimate test of success. In certain places, the candidates still give out "walking-around money" to urge local captains to get out the vote and provide small financial inducements for voting.

Today, few areas boast tight organization. So candidates must recruit workers, usually volunteers. They are brought in to campaign door-to-door, make sure voters are registered, supply campaign literature, and turn out the vote. Such workers may run telephone banks in central headquarters or walk the precincts. Not only are they expected to get out the vote; they have to produce large crowds for candidate appearances and party rallies as well.

Using the media   With TV, candidates can partially bypass face-to-face voter appeals by using ads and news programs. Ad agencies prepare radio and television "spots" that display the candidate's themes and messages.

Because TV is an expensive, broad medium, its appeal is general. The ads embody the candidate's basic strategy. In the 1984 race for the Democratic nomination, front-runner Walter Mondale's ads ignored name recognition but stressed his experience and toughness. His most notable ad featured a red "hotline" telephone with the message that Mondale was the most seasoned candidate for handling international crises. In contrast, Gary Hart's TV ads stressed his new generation of leadership, offering "new ideas." Radio stations reach more specialized groups of listeners. Thus candidates can tailor their appeals to a station's audiences.

The mix of appeals   The population of an electoral district dictates which techniques will be most effective. Heavy media campaigns are most economical if only a few newspapers or radio-TV outlets cover the entire area, with a small spillover into neighboring areas. For a congressional candidate in a huge city like New York or Los Angeles, TV ads would be too expensive and would reach millions outside the district.

Local voter traditions also affect campaigns. Appearances at plant gates or union halls may suffice for some areas. But shopping center rallies and coffee hours are more the style elsewhere. The delicate job of the planner is to mesh the candidate's message with the voters' special traits.

A matter of resources   Techniques must suit the candidate's resources. They must fit not only with finances but also with volunteer support, party backing, and personal skills.

Finances. Money buckets at political rally.

Money is a must for nearly everything in a campaign. Just about any technique can be used if there is enough money to pay for it. To be sure, money is not everything in politics. But many campaigns fail for lack of it; many others spend much of their energy trying to get it. What politicans call *early money*—money available at the start for planning and purchasing ads and radio-TV time—is most useful. With such seed money, the candidate can gain visibility and credibility that will mobilize workers and attract more money. Candidates who face stiff contests in both the primary and the general election have a really tough decision to make. Should they ration their funds and risk losing the primary? Or should they spend a lot on the primary and risk running out of funds later?

Nonmonetary resources are often just as valuable. They give a candidate exposure that would otherwise have to be paid for. Support from a strong party machine or a powerful union may attract free publicity and volunteers. Large numbers of excited volunteers or skilled operatives are also valuable.

MONEY AND ELECTIONS

Our campaigns are very costly. In 1984, some $700 million was spent on campaigns for federal office. Half went into the presidential race, half to congressional races. There is no mystery surrounding booming campaign costs. Inflation accounts for some of it. So does population growth and a growing electorate. And many candidates use new, high-cost methods to reach the voters. This involves mainly TV, but computer mailings and other appeals are also used. Opening up the process and using nonparty campaigners are other factors that have boosted costs. An old-style campaign involved a caucus or convention nomination and scores of workers for canvassing. It was obviously cheaper than a modern campaign with large-scale primaries and media appeals. In short, reaching voters is a costly business.

Haves and have-nots

A more important issue is how money is spread among candidates. Fiscally speaking, some candidates are more equal than others. The most expensive campaign in the history of the U.S. Senate was the 1984 Senate contest in North Carolina between right-wing Senator Jesse Helms (R) and moderate Governor James B. Hunt (D). Around $20 million was spent, much of it pouring in from out of state. Two years earlier, department store heir Mark Dayton spent $7 million—nearly all his own money—in a losing bid to unseat Minnesota GOP incumbent Dave Durenberger. The average Senate campaign in a competitive state may cost millions; House races often involve $200,000 or more.

Incumbents have a double-barreled advantage over challengers: although they need less, they receive more. They are better known and have government-subsidized ways of reaching voters. So incumbents presumably need less money to get their message across. A few, like Wisconsin's veteran Senator William Proxmire (D), report no contributions and no spending.

Incumbents attract more money than challengers do. Perhaps this is because they are deemed better "investments"; contributors want a return for their dollars in access or favors. In the 1982 elections, House and Senate incumbents drew almost 3.5 times as much political action committee (PAC) money as did challengers. (PACs will be discussed later in this chapter.) This ratio is consistent with recent elections. In fact, incumbents often end up with a surplus. That money is saved for future campaigns or given to needier party candidates.

Incumbents' edge. Through visibility, personal wealth, or campaign contributions, incumbents like senators John Heinz (R–Pa.) or Robert Dole (R–Kan.) begin far ahead of challengers.

Controlling campaign funding

Financial inequalities exist between incumbents and challengers, and between wealthy and poor donors. And this has led to demands for legal controls. Reforms are urged not just to clean up campaign financing. There is also a wish to shift political influence from those who rely on donations to those who depend on other resources. Several methods control the role of money in campaigns. Primary among these are (1) disclosure of contributions and expenses, (2) limits on contributions, (3) free radio and TV time for candidates, and (4) public financing of campaigns.

In the wake of the Watergate scandal, the federal government and many states passed broad laws using some or all of the above methods. The Federal Election Campaign Amendments were signed by President Ford in October 1974.

A Supreme Court Ruling in January 1976 upheld certain parts of the law and voided others (*Buckley* v. *Valeo*, 424 US 1). In the midst of the confusion, Congress passed a revised act that reconciled the rulings with the original intent. The 1976 act was amended three years later to ease the paperwork for candidates and committees. Major parts of the law are as follows:

Limits on individual contributions   People can give no more than $1,000 per candidate for presidential and congressional primaries and $1,000 more per candidate in the general elections. This can total no more than $5,000 in any one year. Primary, runoff, and general contests are considered separate elections; but all presidential primaries are lumped together as one election. Individuals may give up to $20,000 per year to a political party. And they may spend an unlimited amount independently to promote a party or a candidate. Independent spending of more than $250 must be reported. The person must declare, under penalty of law, that these expenditures were not made in secret agreement with the candidate. (Up to $1,000 for a candidate or $2,000 for a party in individual volunteer expenses—housing, food, personal travel—are not reportable donations.)

Limits on party contributions   National party committees may give directly to candidates for the House ($10,000 each) and Senate ($17,500). They may also spend a certain amount on behalf of their presidential tickets, even if their candidates have chosen public financing. And they may spend unlimited amounts on *independent* efforts not tied to specific candidates.

In addition to direct donations, there are *coordinated* expenditures. These are funds the party pays out for services that candidates request— including polling or TV ad production. Candidates have a say in how the funds are spent. For the Senate, party committees may spend two cents for every voting-age person in a state. In 1982, these figures ranged from about $37,000 to about $666,000. For House candidates, committees may spend no more than $18,440 in coordinated funds. Coordinated funds are used in general elections but not in primaries.

Contributions by nonparty groups   Labor unions, corporations, and membership groups may advocate to their stockholders, personnel, or members the election or defeat of a clearly named candidate. Expenses for this purpose are not limited. However, amounts over $2,000 must be reported. The groups must declare, under penalty of law, that the funds were not spent in secret agreement with the candidate. Such groups do not have to report expenses used to influence voters on issues or ballot propositions. Unions and corporations may spend an unlimited amount for "nonpartisan" registration and voter drives.

Corporations and labor unions may not give corporate or union funds directly to candidates. Under the 1976 campaign finance amendments, however, they may use their own funds to pay for administrative or fund-raising costs of separate, voluntary funds of political action committees (PACs). For some time, PACs have been a common way to channel corporate or union energies into campaign war chests. Corporations typically have PACs with names like "Good Government Club," to which executives donate. And almost all unions have PACs. The best known of these is the AFL-CIO's Committee on Political Education (COPE). On the surface, such groups are wholly voluntary; but it does not take a cynic to suspect that subtle social pressures help keep the money flowing.

Other types of groups are covered by the finance law. Multicandidate committees may give no more than $5,000 per election to a candidate. These committees must have more than 50 members and must support five or more candidates. Such committees may also give up to $15,000 per year to a political party.

Controls on candidates' spending   There are no restrictions on how much candidates or their supporters may spend. (The exception is presidential candidates who accept public financing.) Nor are there restrictions on how much candidates may contribute to their own cause. But strict accounting is required. All donations of $50 or more must be recorded; donors of more than $200 must be named. Accounting of funds must be made by a single committee for each candidate, with regular reports of receipts and expenses.

Optional public financing for presidential candidates

The law provides public financing for presidential contenders. Money comes from income tax checkoffs. Matching public funds are available to each primary candidate who meets the eligibility requirement. Candidates must raise at least $100,000—at least $5,000 in 20 or more states. Only the first $250 of private donations is matched by the government. No more than 45 percent of the funds available can go to candidates of a single party. In the general election, candidates may opt for full public campaign funding. Minor-party or independent candidates may receive a portion of full funding, based on past or current votes received. Candidates who accept public funding must agree to overall spending limits.

A number of groups, most notably the citizens' lobby Common Cause, have lobbied for public funding of Senate and House campaigns. Congress refused to include such a provision in the 1974 act covering public funding. No doubt this was to preserve the financial edge of incumbents. However, spending limits were set for House and Senate candidates. (Incidentally, these are way below the level normally needed for challengers to unseat incumbents.) The Supreme Court held that these overall spending limits were unconstitutional. The main effect is to limit publicly funded presidential campaign spending but leave congressional contests open to unlimited spending.

The Federal Election Commission   To administer its complex features, the act set up a six-member Federal Election Commission (FEC). Its members are appointed by the president and confirmed by the Senate. The commission may issue regulations and advisory opinions, conduct investigations, and prosecute violations. Beset by political pressures from all sides, the commission has had a stormy history.

Postreform trends

Since modern reporting methods started in the early 1970s, three leading trends have been noted: the growth of PACs, the rise of independent spending, and shifts in the funding mix.

No lack of PACs   Political action committees (PACs) are thriving, partly because the law favors them. In 1974, there were 608 PACs; 10 years later, there were 3,700. All types of PACs have grown in numbers, but corporate PACs have grown most of all.

PACs have grown in financial clout as well as numbers (see Figure 6–5). PAC

FIGURE 6—5

Growth of PAC Contributions to Federal Candidates

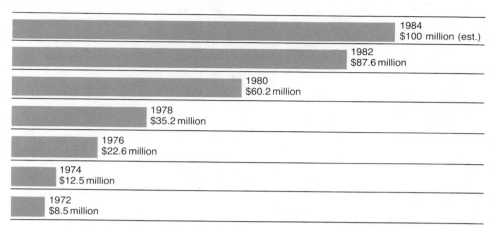

1984
$100 million (est.)

1982
$87.6 million

1980
$60.2 million

1978
$35.2 million

1976
$22.6 million

1974
$12.5 million

1972
$8.5 million

Source: Federal Election Commission.

donations to federal candidates in 1984 hovered around $100 million; the figure was $8.5 million in 1972. PAC money forms an ever-larger portion of House candidates' election budgets; its proportional role in Senate races seems not to have changed (Malbin, 1979).

In direct giving to candidates, the most generous PACs are those of important unions or trade associations. The biggest givers to federal candidates in 1982 were the Realtors' PAC ($2.1 million), the American Medical Association PAC ($1.7 million), the United Auto Workers ($1.6 million), the Machinists' Nonpartisan Political League ($1.45 million), and the National Education Association PAC ($1.2 million).

The rise of "independent" spending   Also growing is *independent spending*—made without the cooperation or consent of candidates. According to FEC figures, $5.7 million was spent this way for or against 81 candidates in 1982.

PACs that launch independent campaigns are usually formed to advance a philosophy or issue. In 1982, the biggest such campaign was the Congressional Club, a conservative group that spent nearly $10.5 million. Other independent groups that year were the Fund for a Conservative Majority and National Conservative PAC (NCPAC), and the liberal National Committee for an Effective Congress.

The majority of independent efforts go to *negative* campaigns. These are aimed at discrediting a candidate and boosting the opponent. NCPAC in 1980 targeted six liberal Senators; four of them were defeated. How well such tactics work is not clear. The defeated liberals all faced uphill battles with or without NCPAC; some may even have rallied their forces by fighting "vicious out-of-state campaigns."

Changing funding patterns   The level and mixture of campaign funding has shifted since the early 1970s. Gary C. Jacobson (1984: 40–41) has pinpointed the following trends: (1) money available for federal campaigns has grown steadily; (2) private individuals continue as the most important source of funds; (3) non-party PAC contributions have grown both in dollars and in proportion to total campaign spending; and (4) though parties' direct contributions have lagged somewhat, their total contributions (including indirect and coordinated spending) are higher than ever before, mainly because of GOP spending.

PAC funds seem to be more important to candidates than ever before. This is certainly true for House contenders; the picture for Senate contenders is less clear. One source that has grown in importance is the candidates' own pocketbooks. They can spend any amount of funds of their own. As a result, a number of rich contenders have given generously in their own behalf. Donations from other individuals, in contrast, do not seem to have changed in importance.

Parties may also give direct or coordinated aid to candidates. Republicans outspent their Democratic counterparts by wide margins in recent elections. This includes efforts of the Republican House and Senate campaign committees, as well as the National Committee itself. Democratic party committees traditionally lag in spending, and they have far to go to catch up to the GOP levels.

Unresolved issues in campaign finance

"IN THE BAD OLD DAYS, THERE USED TO BE POLITICAL MACHINES"

Campaign funding changes in the 1970s did not clear up the most vexing problems. Most important, they have failed in their main goal of limiting the impact of big money in politics. Big money is alive and well. But now it flows through a somewhat wider range of issue and candidate groups. Many of the best-funded PACs are built on large numbers of mail-solicited donations, not a few "fat cats."

Campaign finance laws are so riddled with loopholes that money freely flows into federal elections. One problem surfaced in 1984 when more than 130 supposedly independent Mondale "delegate committees" raised and spent funds separate from the nationwide Mondale effort—which operated under legal ceilings. If the state groups were truly separate from the Mondale effort, their actions would have been legal; but mounting criticisms, plus allegations that funds were being transferred between the delegate groups and the national campaign, forced Mondale to halt the separate fund raising.

The flap over the Mondale delegate committees was only the tip of the iceberg. Special-purpose accounts are used by national parties to accept donations that would be illegal if given directly to campaigns. Tax-exempt foundations are used by parties and PACs to take donations in excess of legal limits. Creative accounting and "independent spending" on behalf of candidates are used to skirt the $5,000 limit on what PACs can give directly to candidates. Bankers and other monied people can lend money or extend credit to candidates under loose rules. And money is moving underground, thwarting federal enforcement and disclosure efforts.

All in all, the financing system bears an increasing resemblence to pre-Watergate days. "You can do just about anything, as long as you take care," said one party official (Jackson, 1984).

Second, the reforms did little to reduce inequalities between incumbents and challengers. In fact, the changes may really help keep incumbents in office; they also make it harder for challengers to raise the money they need (Jacobson, 1980).

Third, the reforms have not resolved the question of what aid should be regulated. A backer who gives time or services to a candidate makes an in-kind donation; this may be every bit as valuable as cash. For example, members of unions (or other groups) donate a lot to campaigns. They use telephones, get out the vote, and do other valuable but free chores. Likewise, a public figure, such as an entertainer, can donate talents to a candidate through a concert or public appearance. How are these donations counted? The laws emphasize money. They have not dealt with how to weigh other forms of donations.

Finally, reforms may have sped the decline of old-style parties. There are several reasons: (1) candidates may pour unlimited funds of their own into a campaign; (2) interest groups may do the same through independent spending, thereby airing their views about candidates without regard to limits on giving or spending; (3) under present law, PACs spread funds among many candidates of both parties.

The campaign finance changes of the 1970s have had a deep impact on the election process, as did the primaries and ballot reforms earlier in the century. For reformers, the new rules were justified by their intended goal: reduce the power of big money. Yet political scientists tend to see such reforms as shifts of influence from one set of groups to another. "Don't kid yourself that you back public financing to prevent Watergates and corruption," said a leader of Common Cause, a citizens' lobby. "You do it to change the system."

Complaints against the power of money abound; several efforts have been launched to promote changes. Common Cause has mounted a large campaign against PAC contributions. So has a blue-ribbon group called Citizens against PACs. Party leaders are not against PACs per se. But they do want to lift restrictions on party spending for candidates. Short of a major scandal, little change seems likely; incumbent legislators who would approve any changes are major beneficiaries of the present system.

PARTIES IN GOVERNMENT

Parties are not only voter loyalties or electoral coalitions, though that is their main reason for being. Their job does not stop once votes are counted and the winning candidates take office. Officeholders retain their partisan goals and foster ties with like-minded people to develop, pass, and implement the policies and programs they favor. Moreover, they cultivate and strengthen grass-roots links with partisan supporters.

Parties and policymaking

It is trendy to belittle party rhetoric. Many contend that those running for office cannot be believed, and that parties are no different from each other—"Tweedledee and Tweedledum." Of course, it would be risky to stake your life on party promises. But if you are willing to listen to politicians, you will gain insight into current issues. Patterson and McClure (1976) showed that voters are more apt to learn about the issues from campaign advertising than from TV network news.

Parties differ significantly over policies; they also strive to implement their preferences. In a revealing study, a political scientist examined major party platforms between 1944 and 1964 and determined what they had done to make good their promises (Pomper, 1968: 149–92). He found that the platforms were quite different. They either stressed different issues or made opposing promises. And at least 7 of every 10 promises were eventually kept by parties in power.

What do partisans do once they are elected? Often they seem more dedicated to career advancement than to policies or principles. But they do use party ties to fulfill their duties. Party platforms can be blueprints for executives and legislators. Party caucuses and meetings help officeholders exchange information and support. They can then form coalitions to enact and carry out policies.

In legislative chambers party loyalties are the most notable feature of day-to-day life. (Nebraska's nonpartisan legislature is the one exception.) Democrats are on one side of the hall, Republicans on the other. Party caucuses pick presiding officers, chairpersons, and members of committees. Majority-party leaders preside over sessions, control the agenda, and use parliamentary rules to their advantage. Party leaders help teach new members the traditions. They whip up support from partisans for bills and resolutions backed by the party. And in spite of party weaknesses, membership still is the best way to predict how legislators will vote (Mayhew, 1966).

Partisanship also runs through executive agencies. Presidents, governors, and other chief executives often claim to rise above party strife; they become "president (or governor or mayor) of all the people." But they cannot escape the fact that they are leaders of their parties as well as public agents.

Chief executives name key aides and department heads and give out patronage. In doing so, they draw mostly on their party base and the interest groups that support their party. Naming too many members of the opposing party to key jobs draws criticism from the party faithful.

Groups with the best access to decision makers are typically more prominent in the party ranks. For the GOP this means business people and conservative activists; for the Democrats it means union officials, ethnic and racial group leaders, and intellectuals. As we have seen, there are marked and lasting differences in the groups the parties draw on for electoral support; the same groups provide personnel and policy advice for the winning party.

Party government

Many scholars and politicians advocate **party government.** This means parties should put forth united programs and have the clout, if elected, to carry them out. "At their best, American political parties are a great deal more than mechanisms for filling offices," asserted an American Assembly study group (1982: 4):

> They can be—and frequently have been in the past—robust institutions which both facilitate social change and preserve public consensus. . . . [They] provide a means of attracting, nourishing, testing, and assessing new public leadership from and for oncoming generations. . . . At their fullest potential, political parties are mediating institutions that provide some measure of continuity, stability, and orderliness in politics.

People who back stronger parties favor some or all of the following reforms: less emphasis on primary elections to choose national convention delegates, better convention representation for party officials and officeholders; use of state caucuses or conventions to endorse candidates in party primaries; channeling of funds, public or private, through the parties; and strengthened party organizations that actively cultivate issues and support candidates. In some of these respects—mainly in national organizations and rule-making efforts—the parties are stronger than ever before (Cotter and Bibby, 1980).

THE STATE OF THE PARTIES

The last generation has not comforted advocates of stronger, more responsible parties. The parties no longer entirely control nominations. The campaign help they offer is no better, and often less reliable, than what can be coaxed from friendly interest groups or bought from consultants. Jobs and welfare services were once provided by party machines; now they are in government hands.

The parties once fulfilled social roles: entertainment, fellowship, and a sense of belonging. These are no longer needed in an era of TV, pro sports, movies, and other escapes. Old-fashioned party clambakes or torchlight parades were once a highlight of local life. Now they are tame stuff indeed. In short, the parties' social functions, so important in the 1800s and at the turn of the century, today have a hazy future.

Today, the parties present a puzzling paradox. Party organizations seem to be vigorous and active, perhaps more so than in earlier days. Yet party loyalties are thinner than ever; voters seem to view parties as irrelevant to most of their pressing concerns. In government, officeholders often forsake partisan loyalties for other channels of action. This leads to a serious question: how long can party organizations remain robust if there is no solid support from either the electorate or officeholders?

Some observers think future party alignments may depart from past patterns. Long-standing party ties and groups are withering away. There is evidence, moreover, that virtual party monopoly over the electoral process is crumbling. The predicament is personified by Jeane J. Kirkpatrick, the political scientist and longtime Democrat who served in the Reagan administration and starred at the 1984 GOP convention. Kirkpatrick hadn't bothered to change her party registration, she said, because "I no longer regard party as relevant to the major problems of our times" (The New York Times, 1984).

Other observers think political parties will revive. They argue that the antiparty spirit of the 1960s and 1970s was a passing phenomenon. It was fueled by cynicism and alienation that came with social unrest, the Vietnam War, and the Watergate scandal. The nonpartisan surge was mainly among younger people who entered the system during this unrest and disillusionment. Will these people develop more traditional party ties as they grow older? Will the parties regain their control over leadership recruitment? No one knows for sure.

Political parties were a strikingly successful response to the quick expansion of the electorate in the 1800s. They enabled politicians to consolidate their appeals to the new mass electorate which could be shaped into faithful followings. Parties helped new voters choose sides and make some sense of the changing and often baffling world of politics. Whether parties as special forms of electoral coalitions will survive, or whether they will yield to other types of electoral groups, only time will tell. In the next chapter we will consider an equally important type of political coalition: the interest group.

CONCLUSIONS

In this chapter, we have described the workings of political parties and how they evolved. The following points are especially important:

1 The major goal of parties is to elect candidates or slates of candidates to public office. They do this by choosing candidates and mobilizing voters. Political parties emerged and thrived in the 1800s and early 1900s. At that time, liberalized voting laws created a mass electorate.

2 Americans think of a two-party system dominated by Democrats and Republicans. In fact, party coalitions have shifted repeatedly during our history. Many areas are dominated by one party, and splinter parties are not unknown.

3 Party loyalties are part of citizens' basic political attitudes and still are the strongest predictor of voting. However, party loyalties are fading as candidates and issues grow in importance.

3 Party organizations are surprisingly vigorous at all levels. State and federal laws increasingly regulate party operations; the parties themselves have spawned many rules and regulations.

4 Candidate selection has evolved from caucuses to conventions to primary elections. A series of reforms has widened the circle of potential participants and loosened the grip of traditional party leaders.

5 Party coalitions often bind officeholders. The average citizen seems not to take the parties too seriously, but many commentators remain impressed with their potential for promoting responsible policymaking.

FURTHER READING

CROTTY, WILLIAM J. (1984) American Parties in Decline. 2d ed. Boston: Little, Brown. A thoughtful analysis of American political parties' declining influence among the voters, in campaigns, and in Congress.

SORAUF, FRANK J. (1984) Party Politics in America. 5th ed. Boston: Little, Brown. A basic textbook on political parties that examines their organization, their relationship to voters, their role in contesting elections, and their impact on government.

SUNDQUIST, JAMES L. (1983) Dynamics of the Party System. Rev. ed. Washington, D.C.: Brookings Institution. A penetrating historical analysis of shifting party coalitions in America.

7

Political
Interest
Groups

Across Lafayette Park from the White House stands a stately building with classical lines and fluted pillars: 1615 H Street, the home of the United States Chamber of Commerce. The building exudes importance and power. The chamber is the largest business lobbying group in the country; its more than 200,000 members, all but 5,000 of them businesses, include virtually all of the nation's major companies. However, more than 90 percent of the membership is from companies with 100 employees or less.

The chamber's influence extends far beyond the nation's capital. A word from 1615 H Street can deluge Capitol Hill with thousands of letters. It can tie up legislators' phones with incoming calls or shake free thousands of dollars for a candidate's war chest. The chamber's magazine, *Nation's Business*, has 850,000 paid subscribers, more than any other business journal. Its weekly television program reaches 90 percent of the country; its $3.5 million satellite American Business Network (BizNet) beams three to five hours of business and economics programming each day to members and the general public (Crittenden, 1982).

A block to the east, just beyond historic St. John's Church, stands another imposing building. It is more massive but lacks the chamber's classical lines. This is headquarters for the AFL-CIO, the nation's major labor body. The AFL-CIO is made up of 96 affiliated unions with a membership of about 14 million, roughly one fifth of the total U.S. labor force.

The AFL-CIO represents a declining portion of American workers and has not had a real friend in the White House since the 1960s; but its influence should not be dismissed. Its annual income exceeds $30 million; its political arm, the Committee on Political Education (COPE), mounts impressive voter registration and mobilization drives and helps bankroll liberal candidates. Its network of affiliated unions and their locals gives AFL-CIO a foothold in widely scattered communities.

* * * * *

Washington is filled with groups like the Chamber of Commerce and the AFL-CIO. Few have the size or visibility of these two; but all aim to bend the instruments of government in their direction. Taken as a whole, these groups have a great deal to say about what our government does and how it does it.

In this chapter we explore what some have called "the group basis of politics." First, we define interest groups and distinguish them from political par-

The U.S. Chamber of Commerce, Washington, D.C.

ties. These days this is no easy task. Then we outline the major types of groups. We try to analyze their resources and liabilities in political arenas. Next, groups' techniques for influencing policy are explained. Finally, we ponder the effects of groups on our politics: Do they represent the public interest, or do they thwart public will?

GROUPS, POLITICAL AND OTHERWISE

People join together for many reasons. Some want to make friends; some want to share ideas or promote common interests; others seek intellectual or spiritual betterment; still others organize to spread their ideas and press their demands on government.

The groups that concern us here are involved in politics. Our focus will be on such groups as labor unions or trade associations, not sewing circles or motorcycle clubs. However, the line between political and nonpolitical groups is often crossed. A motorcycle club, for example, exists because like-minded people want to get together, socialize, and engage in joint activities, including recreation. Such a club may seek to persuade public officials to permit off-road riding facilities. Or it may lobby against laws requiring cyclists to wear helmets. Then it has entered politics. Similarly, churches and religious sects, though not basically political, are repeatedly drawn into politics. They may mobilize their

The AFL-CIO headquarters building in Washington, D.C.

Sociability and clout. AFL-CIO get-together on the White House Lawn.

members on such issues as world peace, criminal justice, pornography, or abortion. And they lobby for tax-exempt status or tax deductions for charitable giving.

By the same token, political groups can fulfill personal, nonpolitical needs. Labor unions and retirees' associations, for example, sponsor social events, sell group insurance, and arrange group vacation tours. Fulfilling such individual needs cements members' ties; it helps mobilize members for broader political goals.

It is virtually impossible, therefore, to say a group is always political or always nonpolitical. So we will call a group political when it functions politically. In other words, it becomes a political interest group when it seeks to press its claims on other parts of society through political action and influence (Truman, 1971: 33).

How do political parties differ from other types of political groups? As we have seen, the parties' main aim is to win elections. An interest group (Schattschneider, 1942: 187) is "an association that tries to bring about the adoption and execution of certain policies without nominating candidates for the great offices, without fighting election campaigns, and without attempting to get complete control of government." This distinction has blurred in recent years, as we shall see; but it provides a rough working definition.

HOW WIDESPREAD ARE GROUPS?

Everyone who has glimpsed our society has been impressed by its number and variety of organized activities. In the 1830s, Alexis de Tocqueville, the French traveler and social critic, wrote that "in no country in the world has the principle of association been more successfully used or applied to a greater multitude of objects than in America."

Few would dispute his view. Associations of all kinds are everywhere. A few are large national groups whose names are known to everyone; but these are merely the tip of the iceberg. Regional, state, and local groups are beyond counting. This is not just because they are so numerous, but because they come and go so rapidly.

Why so many groups?

The large number of organized activities flows from the profusion of modern life. Like other industrialized nations, ours is a developed society. It is economically, socially, and culturally diverse. Activities and relationships are highly specialized; they demand specialized organizations to represent and link them.

Legal guarantees If diversity is the seed of group formation, legal protection of freedom is the soil in which it flourishes. James Madison (*The Federalist*, No. 10) put it directly: "Liberty is to faction what air is to fire, an element without which it instantly expires." Essential to group formation and function are such Bill of Rights guarantees as freedom of speech, freedom of association, and freedom to petition the government. Nonprofit groups enjoy also a range of statutory aids—for example, tax exemptions and low-cost postal rates.

Diversity and decentralization Reflecting this diversity, our government is highly decentralized. Authority and responsibility are spread among 50 states and thousands of counties, cities, and special districts, about a half million government bodies in all. Decentralization causes people to organize on a great many levels, to wage battles over public policy on a variety of fronts (Truman, 1971: 519). A narrow, specialized interest may have little chance of affecting the national government; but it may influence or even control a local community. Conversely, small, local minorities may join other like-minded groups to wield great power.

Decentralized government, as we have seen, leads to a decentralized party system—"more *pluribus* than *unum*," as one scholar put it. The lack of unified, disciplined parties gives interest groups more leeway to influence government action. The parties are exposed to pressures from outside groups; party hold upon those in office—executives and legislators—is so loose as to give lobbyists license to try and shape government policies.

The "participation revolution" Groups have pervaded American life from the earliest times; yet students of politics are startled by the explosion of groups in recent decades. No one really knows how many groups there are; one recent study found a majority of the sampled groups had been formed since World War II, especially since the early 1960s (Walker, 1983). As of 1980, there were nearly 15,000 national nonprofit associations of some kind—40 percent more than in 1968 (Salisbury, 1983: 357). Two political scientists (Cigler and Loomis, 1983: 11) recently declared that "a 'participation revolution' is occurring in the country as large numbers of citizens are becoming active in an ever-increasing number of protest groups, citizens' organizations, and special interest groups. These groups often are composed of issue-oriented activists or individuals who seek collective material benefits." Growth has been especially notable among groups that are not primarily economic—those with social, ethical, or ideological goals.

Why has this group explosion occurred? While no one cause can be isolated, a combination of the following can explain the trend:

1. Ours is an increasingly educated populace, linked by ever-more sophisticated and specialized communications media. We have moved beyond bread-and-butter issues to a wide variety of "quality-of-life" concerns. Some of these issues have spawned broad-scale movements. Civil rights, environmental protection, consumerism, and opposition to the Vietnam War are a few that have achieved notable successes.

2. Few of the issues listed above sharply divide Democrats from Republicans (as we noted in Chapter 6). Thus, activists have to move outside the parties to push causes most effectively.

3. Today's interest groups are assisted by new techniques and technologies

Goal or aspiration? A group demonstrates against South Africa's policies of racial separation.

that enhance traditional group functions. Examples include grass-roots organizing, computerized mailings, fund-raising appeals, and specialized communications.

4. Partly in response to citizen activism, our political and government structures have become more open and accessible. Recent trends include declining political party strength; campaign financing laws; decentralization in Congress and the executive branch; open-door decision making; and laws encouraging or even sponsoring interest-group input.

Joiners and nonjoiners

The multiplicity of groups has led some writers to assume that, as a whole, all citizens are equally represented. Some even feel there is a kind of natural balance because of the open marketplace in which interests can be organized into groups.

However widespread, groups are not universal. Not all parts of our society are equally prone to join groups. Thus, the sheer number of groups does not mean that they fairly represent people's interests. Some people are "joiners"; they belong to many clubs and associations. Others belong to none.

What proportion of us take part? In a nationwide survey (Verba and Nie, 1972: 41–3), 62 percent of those polled belonged to at least 1 of 16 types of voluntary groups. These ranged from labor unions to recreational groups to religious organizations. About two thirds of these members said they were active in some way. Thus, about 4 of every 10 adults are active members of at least one group. As for groups that are mainly political—partisan groups, political action groups, and voters' leagues—only about 8 percent of the adult population takes part.

Group membership does not faithfully mirror the total population. As with other forms of participation, those who join and take part tend to be richer and better educated (Milbrath and Goel, 1977: 110–13). More men take part in groups than women; more middle-aged than young or old people join groups; and those with strong community ties take part more than newcomers or transients. Thus, the same characteristics of people who take part generally are also true of membership in voluntary groups.

Group involvement also sparks political activity. The more groups you belong to, the more apt you are to take part. This is because groups themselves publicize and stimulate action. They spread information on issues affecting their members, begging, cajoling, or shaming them to take part.

In politics as in the rest of life, the squeaky wheels get the grease. Those who join groups are more apt to make themselves heard. In general, the educated and wealthy are better represented by groups than are the uneducated and poor. That is what some commentators mean when they refer to "the biases of the pressure-group system" of politics (Schattschneider, 1960).

ECONOMIC GROUPS

Interest groups are not new to America. The Founders knew well the causes and effects of group activities; they were themselves skilled organizers. James Madison, in No. 10 of *The Federalist*, defined **faction** (not yet something different from parties or other types of groups) as "a number of citizens, whether amounting to a majority or minority of the whole, who are united and actuated by some common impulse of passion, or of interest." The most common and lasting sources of faction, Madison said, are economic interests caused by unequal distribution of property.

Today, as in Madison's time, most groups form for economic objectives. These are mainly producers or those in a given occupation, profession, or job category. (Not all are in the private sector. Public-sector unions and professional

---

JAMES MADISON ON THE CAUSES OF "FACTION"

The latent causes of faction are . . . sown in the nature of man; and we see them everywhere brought into different degrees of activity, according to the different circumstances of civil society. A zeal for different opinions concerning religion, concerning government, and many other points . . . ; an attachment to different leaders ambitiously contending for preeminence and power; or to persons . . . whose fortunes have been interesting to the human passions, have, in turn, divided mankind into parties, inflamed them with mutual animosity, and rendered them much more disposed to vex and oppress each other than to cooperate for their common good. . . . But the most common and durable source of factions has been the various and unequal distribution of property. Those who hold and those who are without property have ever formed distinct interests in society. . . . A landed interest, a manufacturing interest, a mercantile interest, a moneyed interest, with many lesser interests, grow up of necessity in civilized nations, and divide them into different classes, actuated by different sentiments and views. The regulation of these various and interfering interests forms the principal task of modern legislation.

The Federalist, No. 10 (1787)

Bosses of the Senate. In the late 19th century, trusts dominated economic life and wielded great power. This form of corruption fueled support for direct election of senators.

groups must be reckoned with in many policy fields.) However, the fastest-growing category of groups seems to be noneconomic.

The business community

Corporations   The most common business organizations, corporations, have rarely been shy in dealing with government. A corporation's "interest" is profit and its "members" are managers, workers, and stockholders. A number of firms encourage members of their "corporate family" to speak out on issues affecting the firm's well-being.

Business firms inevitably affect the politics of local communities where they have facilities. At the federal level, many large firms use Washington offices to keep contact with officials. Smaller firms call on lobbying consultants, law firms, or trade associations to speak for them. Today's giants are the *multinational corporations.* Their affairs cross national boundaries; their agents deal with officials in many countries.

Trade associations   Trade associations are made up of business firms in the same field. They are business's chief way of influencing government. As early as 1741, a New York City bakers' guild was embroiled in a dispute over an ordinance fixing the price of bread. Today's trade associations are among the most visible lobbying groups in Washington. There are probably 40,000 trade associations in the United States, counting local chapters and independent or regional groups. The size of trade associations varies widely. The Motor Vehicle Manufacturers Association, for example, has only 12 members—mostly huge enterprises. But the National Automobile Dealers Association includes 22,000 companies. Thousands of other trade groups, embracing almost every type of business or industry, deal with legislators and bureaucrats (Bauer, Pool, and Dexter, 1963). They dispense information and other services for their members. They wage public relations campaigns to win praise and support for their in-

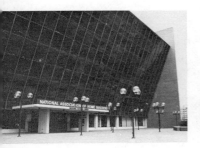

National Housing Center, D.C., home of the home builders.

dustry. And, of course, they lobby for legislation to protect and enhance the industry.

Umbrella groups   The business community has many general-purpose voices. The U.S. Chamber of Commerce and the National Association of Manufacturers (NAM) stand out. The former is a federation of local chambers of commerce, firms, individuals, and trade and professional groups. NAM, with 13,000 corporate members, speaks mainly for big business. Although the two discussed merging, differences in outlook have kept them apart.

Small business   Big business tends to define the business viewpoint in Washington. Small, local firms also have vocal lobbies; more important, they get a warm reception on Capitol Hill. The largest group is the National Federation of Independent Business (NFIB). It claims half a million members. There is even a National Association of Small Business Investment Companies to represent firms that issue loans guaranteed by the Small Business Administration. Small-business representatives are conspicuous and wield influence in small- and medium-sized towns. They are courted by legislators who covet seats on congressional small-business committees.

Organized labor

Local trade unions date from the nation's beginnings. Indeed, the first strike in this country is thought to have been in 1786, when a group of printers in Philadelphia sought a minimum weekly wage of six dollars. But large-scale unions were disorganized, short-lived, and fiercely opposed by employers. Then in 1886, the **American Federation of Labor** was formed. It focused on the skilled crafts; AFL-affiliated **craft unions** grew to more than one million members by the turn of the century. As its leader, Samuel Gompers (1850–1924), said, the AFL stressed economic bargaining with employers. It also favored *voluntarism*—the right of skilled workers to control their own internal concerns. It avoided political action to achieve higher wages and better working conditions.

After a while, the AFL stepped up its political activity. But it remained a group for skilled laborers. Semiskilled or unskilled workers in mass-production industries could not protect their jobs. They did not have the control wielded by the craft unions. Therefore, these workers formed more militant, political groups, the **industrial unions.** In 1935, these fused into what became the **Congress of Industrial Organizations** (CIO). Its most eloquent spokesman was the head of the United Mine Workers, John L. Lewis (1880–1969).

The two labor groups merged in 1955. The resulting AFL-CIO now embraces nearly 100 unions. Members range from teachers to plumbers, meat cutters to government workers. With 14 million dues-paying members speaking for some 50 million people, it is labor's loudest voice. Yet several strong unions are outside the federation. One, the International Brotherhood of Teamsters, is the largest union.

Bargaining over wages and work conditions is left largely to individual unions. But political action is directed by the AFL-CIO and the large international unions. Political arms like COPE are financed by union contributions; they carry out registration and campaign drives.

Labor's voice is firmest on economic issues that directly touch its members. These include labor-management relations, job safety, minimum wages, and

House of labor. Lane Kirkland (left), former merchant seaman and long-time labor executive, takes over in 1979 as AFL–CIO president from George Meany (1894–1980), the federation's first president and dominant figure for 24 years.

social security. Unions often lobby on such issues as welfare, antipoverty, federal aid to education, and even foreign policy.

Politically, organized labor is badly divided. It was long aligned with the Democrats. But labor's leanings have flagged as New Deal issues fade and union members blend into the nation's middle class. In 1980, AFL-CIO leaders stood firmly with President Carter; yet some groups, such as the Teamsters and the building trades unions, made no secret of their GOP leanings. About 44 percent of all votes from labor families went to Reagan. He responded by touring Teamster headquarters during his first postelection visit to Washington.

Reagan's presidency, however, galvanized most labor leaders' opposition and strengthened their determination to remain allied with the Democrats. But labor resolved to have a place at the party's table, rather than watch from the sidelines while nonlabor candidates like McGovern or Carter were nominated. Thus, the unions endorsed a candidate for the 1984 nomination (see Chapter 6).

Organized labor's share of the work force is dwindling. Today less than a fifth of the nation's workers are members. Union strength is highest in older industries, such as steel and automotive, that are declining in importance. Indeed, competitive pressures in such industries have led unions to accept modest settlements to limit labor costs and keep the industries alive. Labor's future rests in part in organizing new generations of service and public-sector workers; but these people are less wedded to the union ideal than were their parents or grandparents.

Organized labor's strengths and weaknesses were reflected in the 1981 walkout of 13,000 members of the Professional Air Traffic Controllers Organization (PATCO). The tight-knit union had a string of grievances against the Federal Aviation Administration (FAA). But strikes by federal workers are forbidden by law, and President Reagan's economic austerity program left him little leeway to meet the controllers' demands. The administration declared that the striking workers had quit. It improvised a scaled-down air schedule with supervisors and military controllers, and set about rebuilding the air traffic system. The public tended to support the president, while labor leaders themselves were divided. The incident heralded harder times for labor, both at the bargaining table and in the court of public opinion.

Professional groups

Professional associations are related to unions but tend to represent higher-status occupations. Membership is limited to persons formally trained for specific careers (Ziegler and Peak, 1972).

Professional associations control standards of admission to their professions. Thus, they keep close ties with professional schools. They often help in licensing practitioners. Having locked up the profession's exclusive status, they defend members against outsiders (nonprofessionals or paraprofessionals) and look after members' economic well-being (McConnell, 1967; Lowi, 1969).

Strategic position, not numbers, gives professional groups their clout. The nation has 650,000 lawyers, for instance, more per capita than any other industrialized society. They have a bewildering procedural system that enhances the profession but serves questionable social purposes. Japan trains more engineers to design better products, asserts Derek Bok, president of Harvard University and former dean of its Law School. But the United States trains lawyers whose activities contribute to "a stifling burden of regulations, delays and legal uncertainties that can inhibit progress and allow unscrupulous parties to misuse the law to harass and manipulate their victims" (Taylor, 1983: A17). Bar association panels screen candidates for judgeships—a practice that, while informal, often determines who sits on the bench. The upshot is that citizens must approach the legal system largely on the legal profession's own terms.

Physicians use their unique prestige in our culture; their major organization, the American Medical Association (AMA), speaks loudly and often decisively on their behalf. For many years, the AMA led the fight against federal health insurance. The hated "socialized medicine" was portrayed as violating the intimate doctor-patient relationship. When medicare was started in 1965, the AMA lost its battle; but it made sure members profited handsomely from medicare-medicaid business. And the AMA has lobbied to keep the government from cutting costs or regulating doctors' fees. The AMA has been pressed by rival health groups; but it remains active on many fronts involving fees, drug legis-

Health industry association headquarters in the nation's capital.

First, Our House; Then the White House

Teamster clout. In a first postelection visit to the nation's capitol, Reagan and Bush pay respects at headquarters of the Teamsters, who supported them. (Cover of Teamster magazine.)

Environmentalism. Cover of recent *Friends of the Earth* magazine.

lation, medical research, and federal health support. Using the doctors' financial resources, the AMA's Political Action Committee (AMPAC) ranks high among lobby groups in spending.

Many other professions have associations. There are groups of real estate agents, contractors, veterinarians, barbers, and beauticians. In many states, professions are regulated by state licensing boards. The boards are loaded with association members. They work under state laws that regulate entrance to and exit from the profession, and dispensing of professional services.

In the last decade or so the rights of professionals to define services and set conditions for dispensing them have met increasing challenges. But most professions are well organized and lobby vigorously with legislative and administrative bodies to preserve their monopoly positions.

Agriculture

Farm interests recur in our politics. Until the Civil War, farmers equaled or outnumbered all other workers. Early farm groups, like the **Grange** (founded in 1867), fought the railroads' tyranny over producers. The **American Farm Bureau Federation** arose with government help as a clientele organization for local farm bureaus set up under the Smith-Lever Act of 1914. Other groups developed to fight for family farms and against low farm prices. These include the **National Farmers Organization** (1955), and the **American Agriculture Movement** (1977), middle-class revolts against declining farm revenues.

Farmers' protest. "Tractorcade" sponsored by the American Agriculture Movement publicizes low farm incomes.

Another group fostered by government action is the **National Rural Electric Cooperatives Association.** This is a federation of local rural electric associations (REAs). Through government loans, these agencies provide cheap power for rural areas.

The influence of farm groups has waned, as has the farm work force. Agriculture is essential and is the country's largest export; but fewer people live on farms than ever before. According to the 1980 census, only 2.5 percent of the nation's people (5.6 million persons) lived on farms, barely a sixth of the number 30 years ago. Moreover, farm groups are sharply split over the level and form of government aid.

Specific commodity groups, however, continue to wield much power. For example, dairy associations contributed more than $1.8 million to House campaigns in the early 1980s. Thus, the dairy industry has succeeded in maintaining high price-support programs. Other producers—tobacco and sugar come to mind—maintained prices and warded off competition through legislative means. They do this through strong regional ties, shrewd contributions to legislators' campaigns, friendly congressional committees, and a clientele agency—the U.S. Department of Agriculture.

NONECONOMIC GROUPS

Groups not directly linked to economic interests or production have flourished since the 1960s. These are often called citizens' or "public-interest" groups. Indeed, they are the fastest growing type of group; according to one survey, more than half of them have formed since 1960 (Walker, 1983).

Such a group, says Berry (1977: 7), is "one that seeks a collective good, the achievement of which will not selectively and materially benefit the membership or activists of the organization." These groups do not represent people's interests as producers or wage earners but as consumers, taxpayers, users of goods, services, and the nation's resources, and pursuers of ideals.

Such groups flourish. This defies Olson's (1965) assumption that those pursuing "collective" benefits—received by everyone in a class or segment of society regardless of group membership—will have great difficulty forming and surviving. The problem is *free riders*. That is, "rational" individuals in such broad groupings—consumers, for example—should not choose to bear the costs (time, dues, membership) of participating because they can reap the benefits of the group (favorable legislation, for instance) whether or not they join. The free-rider problem especially plagues large groups; the larger the group, the less likely an individual will see his or her contribution as affecting success.

Yet explainable or not, citizens' groups flourish and grow in numbers. As Walker (1983: 397) observed, "the political system is beset by a swarm of organizational bumblebees that are busily flying about in spite of the fact that prevailing theories cannot explain how they manage it." Commentators agree that this is the fastest growing class of groups, representing perhaps a fifth or more of all active political associations.

Citizens' groups can overcome the free-rider problem in several ways. First, they may find sponsors—wealthy individuals or foundations—to bankroll the organization and reduce dependence on member contributions. An educated, affluent class of people provides a huge pool of potential group organizers and supporters—people seeking symbolic rather than material benefits. Contemporary technology—media appeals and targeted mailing, for example—makes it easier than ever before for groups to seek out their constituencies. Finally, government itself can initiate or sponsor group activity. For example, government services inevitably create "clienteles" for those services, and also often spawn groups dedicated to continuing or expanding the services. In other cases, government sets up a policymaking procedure that encourages people to organize to participate effectively.

Still, representing large and scattered constituencies has good and bad points. Broad, spread-out groupings are hard to mobilize, especially when their goals are broad and diffuse. On the other hand, they don't have overt economic motives; thus, such groups can shape a favorable public image as fair and impartial. Yet noneconomic groups are not the only ones that wrap their demands in the "public interest." In most respects, the techniques of these groups are similar to others.

Environmentalists

The first environmental groups were the Sierra Club, the National Wildlife Federation, and the Audubon Society. They were formed by people who wanted to preserve the country's natural beauty. The post–World War II economic boom brought smog alerts, nuclear fallout, and pesticides. It also produced a new wave of groups. They include Friends of the Earth, Environmental Action, and the League of Conservation Voters. There are also many local action groups; some sport colorful names like Get Oil Out (GOO), Group Against Smokers' Pollution (GASP), and Group for Organic Alternatives to Toxic Sprays (GOATS).

Environmentalism's high-water mark came in the early 1970s. Two new government bodies, the Environmental Protection Agency (EPA) and the Council on Environmental Quality (CEQ), were created during the Nixon years. Congress passed 13 major environmental laws in seven years; these included the National Environmental Policy Act of 1969 and the 1970 Clean Air Act (Ornstein and Elder, 1978). Environmentalists saved the brown pelican and the bald eagle from pesticides; they got sweeping changes in waste disposal; and they pushed through auto pollution limits that added perhaps $800 to the price of the average car.

Most environmental groups are small and have little member funding. Their best resource is publicity. They can shape and mobilize public opinion by dramatizing threats to natural resources. The high point was Earth Day, April 22, 1970—a massive demonstration, patterned on anti-Vietnam War marches, to defend the environment. Environmental Action targeted the "Dirty Dozen" antienvironmental legislators; it also named its "filthy five" allegedly polluting companies. As one legislator said, "You can't build a highway now without some group telling you that it will be harmful to a ladybug colony or an ant heap."

In the 1980s, the environmental movement suffered reverses and resurgence. Reaction to cost and red tape resulted in a stalemate over renewing many environmental laws (Cook and Davidson, 1984). The Reagan administration's antienvironmental thrusts were typified by the stormy careers of Interior Secretary James G. Watt and EPA Administrator Ann Gorsuch Burford. Yet this helped revitalize the groups and agitate their members. Environmental regulations are complex and beg for simplification; but surveys show the public wants

Groups in conflict. Everyone knows the auto industry, but who speaks for clean air? Herblock sees this as an unequal contest. Do you agree?

continued environmental protection, even though it may hike consumer costs and reduce productivity.

Civil rights

Since World War II, the civil rights bloc has been a potent political force. Civil rights groups sway public attitudes and mobilize constituencies at the grass-roots level; they also exert direct pressure on government.

The earliest groups led the fight for black rights. The National Association for the Advancement of Colored People (NAACP), founded in 1909, sponsored actions leading to the Supreme Court's 1954 school desegregation decision (*Brown* v. *Board of Education*, 347 U.S. 483). Another group, the National Urban League, stands behind more than 100 local groups and runs a large national program.

Today's civil rights organizations represent a wide range of concerns. There are those speaking for Hispanics, Chinese-Americans, children, the handicapped, and women as well as blacks. In addition, there are allied church, union, and civil liberties associations. About 165 groups are included in the Leadership Conference on Civil Rights; this umbrella organization, founded in 1950, coordinates groups in the civil rights movement. In recent years, the conference battled the Reagan administration over renewing the Voting Rights Act, controlling the U.S. Commission on Civil Rights, and creating a holiday honoring the birthday of martyred civil rights leader Martin Luther King, Jr. In all cases, they mustered broad bipartisan support.

During the 1960s, civil rights activists gained results through petitions and mass protests. The March on Washington for Jobs and Freedom brought 200,000 to the Lincoln Memorial in 1963. It featured a stirring speech by King. This protest pushed demands for tougher enforcement of antibias laws and helped pass historic civil rights laws in 1964 and 1965.

"I have a dream." The civil rights movement, one of history's great group efforts, was voiced in 1963 by the Rev. Martin Luther King, Jr. As 200,000 people cheer, the countenance of Lincoln broods over the scene.

Dream deferred? 20 years after King's "I have a dream" speech, Martin Luther King III and D.C. Delegate Walter Fauntroy celebrate a law creating a national holiday honoring the slain leader.

Today's civil rights community is more broad and scattered than it was in the 1960s. Impressive support can still be rallied for basic civil rights enactments. But interests today run the whole gamut of government policy—from insurance and pension guarantees to the rights of children and families. As with environmentalists, these groups have been revitalized by the Reagan administration's alleged departure from civil rights goals.

Public interest groups

A bewildering variety of groups has emerged to voice other citizen concerns. One of the most notable is Common Cause. Founded in 1970, it has two major goals: "change political structures so they will be more responsive to social needs and . . . produce a major reordering of national priorities."

Common Cause is bipartisan but is often seen as left of center. It is unabashedly a lobbying group, with a large Washington staff. Its campaigns have aimed at ending the Vietnam War, granting the vote to 18-year-olds, changing the congressional seniority system, reducing restrictions on voter registration, strengthening legal controls over lobbying and campaign spending, and streamlining government structure. Common Cause takes major credit for passage of post–Watergate campaign finance reforms; it has recently declared war on the financial clout of PACs.

Common Cause is not mainly a grass-roots group; but it publicizes its membership (more than 200,000), its referenda on issues, and its active state affiliates. It voices many concerns of upper-middle-class professionals. In this, it resembles the League of Women Voters, with which it is often allied in lobbying campaigns.

The best-known citizens' lobbyist is Ralph Nader, the consumer advocate and lawyer. He burst on the scene in 1965. At that time a Senate inquiry found that he had been harassed by a giant automobile firm after he wrote a book critical of auto safety standards.

Nader built on this publicity and on single-minded absorption in his work. He turned his advocacy into a lobbying industry. He employed swarms of young, idealistic, low-paid workers to research and write reports on public issues. These reports, publicized by Nader, form the basis for lobbying efforts by his groups, Congress Watch and Public Citizen. Nader and his aides have looked at a wide variety of questions, mainly consumer protection and opposition to nuclear power. Again, the Reagan administration has been a Nader target.

Among the numerous citizens' organizations are two ideological groups, Americans for Democratic Action (ADA) and Americans for Constitutional Action (ACA). ADA is "an organization of progressives, dedicated to the achievement of freedom and economic security for all people everywhere, through education and democratic political action." ACA supports "constitutional conservatism." It was founded to counter ADA. Each year, both groups rate members of Congress, based on selected lists of key votes. Naturally, scores on the two indexes are virtual opposites.

Churches and religious groups have long had agents in Washington. They join with other groups to lobby on such matters as civil rights, church-state relationships, and disarmament. Recently a bevy of evangelical groups, such as the Moral Majority, Christian Voice, and the National Christian Action Coalition, have appeared. They favor prayers in schools and heavier military spending; they are against abortion, homosexual rights, and the Equal Rights Amendment.

In recent years the National Conference of Catholic Bishops has launched several efforts to influence national policy. Their issues include opposition to abortion (a goal shared by some Protestants), control of nuclear weapons, and economic justice. Some prelates have even implied that voters should judge candidates solely on such issues. Needless to say, church involvement in volatile issues can be potent—antislavery, prohibition, and civil rights come to mind. Yet each foray into politics risks dividing church members and exposes church leaders to rough-and-tumble political clashes.

Government lobbyists

Not only private groups lobby. Some represent elected and appointed officials of other governments — mainly states, counties, and municipalities. Crucial portions of their budgets hinge on decisions made in Washington. Thus, their representatives have become more vocal; many of them have offices in the "Hall of the States" near Capitol Hill. They have natural affinities with state delegations and regional caucuses in Congress.

The **National Governors Conference** provides state governors with a national platform. The conference, originally an extension of periodic governors' meetings, expanded its activities in the 1960s. It remains a loose group because members are highly visible, partisan figures. "It consists of an alliance of 50 prima donnas, the highest elected officials within the states, leaders and rarely followers" (Haider, 1974: 24).

Governors. Indiana's Robert Orr confers with Kentucky's Martha Layne Collins at the National Governors' Conference.

Lobbying is only a sideline for the **National Conference of State Legislatures.** Its main aims are research and serving as a clearinghouse for information on state problems. Its headquarters are in Denver, but 40 percent of its staff is in Washington.

Cities are represented by two groups, the **National League of Cities** and the **U.S. Conference of Mayors.** Their missions intertwine; for four years (1970 to 1974), their staffs were merged. But differing views and styles have kept them apart. The USCM represents the largest cities. It tends toward liberal views on civil rights, housing, transportation, and federal programs. The League represents smaller towns, has a more complicated structure, and tends toward a moderate course.

The **National Association of Counties** (NACO) has more than 2,000 county governments as members. Its annual conferences attract thousands of elected and appointed officials. The group reflects disparate interests, because counties vary widely in population and organization. NACO stands behind both large and small units. It tends to avoid controversial issues. Members have had access to the Reagan White House. They supported early administration efforts to cut federal domestic spending; when local grants were threatened, however, county officials followed city officials in opposing further cutbacks.

Federal money is the prime target of government lobbyists. Thus they have fought to continue such popular programs as revenue sharing, model cities, mass transit, and Urban Development Action Grants (UDAG). Also, local lobbyists have labored to keep tax exemption for private-purpose municipal bonds, which now comprise a majority of all municipal bonds. Typically issued by special entities (like housing authorities or economic development groups), the bonds are funneled to private borrowers for things such as plants, shopping malls, stores, home mortgages, and student loans. Finally, state and local governments argue for more freedom in using federal funds and making policies. For example, they want to decentralize and decategorize program grants and they want fewer strings on federal monies.

These government representatives comprise a kind of "third house" of elected officials at the national level. They "provide another form of political representation at the national level, one founded not on functional lines or shifting congressional boundaries but on representation of interests based essentially on geopolitical units—states, counties, and municipalities" (Haider, 1974: 306).

Single-interest groups

Many citizens' groups organize around a single cause or issue. Their efforts are bent toward realizing their goal, against which they measure all politicians. Single-interest groups are not new. The antislavery crusade of the mid-19th century was a very successful single-interest drive. The Anti-Saloon League's move to prohibit alcohol was another. For a while, its policies became the law of the land.

Seal of the National Rifle Association.

What is novel about today's groups is not their character or techniques. ("At the start of the century, without so much as a microchip to aid it, the Anti-Saloon League had a mailing list of more than half a million people" Schlozman and Tierney, 1983: 363.) It is their number and variety that impress contemporary observers. They range from antivivisectionists to anti-nuclear-power activitists, from gun control to antiabortion proponents. Many urge members to vote on their issue without regard to other considerations. More than one politician has been defeated because group members—gun owners or antiabortionists, for instance—cast their votes solely on that issue.

Needless to say, politicians tend to frown on such tactics. They argue that public stewardship mixes many ingredients and should not be reduced to simplistic formulas, no matter how persuasive. But to adherents, goals take on paramount importance.

And many other groups

The number and scope of political groups are truly staggering. Nearly every association can turn into a political group if its interests are at stake. This includes women, Hispanics, senior citizens, professors, consumers, foreign governments, federal employees, judges, and all kinds of ideological or social groups.

It is tempting to condemn such groups as "special interests" when they enter the political arena. Yet all of us are sooner or later affected by lobbying or "pressure." After all, most of us try to put pressure on the government at some time.

This does not imply that everyone is equally represented by interest groups. As noted, organized interest groups have a definite class bias. Middle- and upper-income groups are better organized than lower-income groups. Surveys consistently show that group membership varies with income, occupation, and education.

To some, such as the late political scientist E. E. Schattschneider (1960: 30), this means that "large areas of the population appear to be wholly outside of the system of private organization." There is considerable truth to this view; many categories of people—nonunion workers, consumers, mental patients, and the poor—are politically underorganized. Yet the proliferation of groups has aided such people. Even those who belong to no groups at all may actually be represented by groups with related interests or causes. People may also make up for lack of schooling, money, or status by joining groups. To see how this can work, we must examine how a group's characteristics affect its political style and influence.

GROUP RESOURCES

Let us consider two contrasting organizations: the Carlton Group and the National Education Association (NEA). These are two of the thousands of groups that try to shape public policy; they illustrate the wide range of resources and techniques open to interest groups.

The so-called Carlton Group is small and informal. It consists of a dozen or so men and two women who meet every other Tuesday for breakfast in a private salon of Washington's Sheraton-Carlton Hotel, three blocks from the White House (Cowan, 1982). The group's objective is to shape America's tax code to business's advantage. Its great triumph was the so-called Economic Recovery Tax Act of 1981. This act, in addition to President Reagan's three-year, across-the-board tax cut, adopted an accelerated depreciation scheme for which business had been lobbying for several years. Business firms stood to save $158 billion in taxes in the act's first five years; labor charged it virtually repealed corporate income taxes. Since then, the Carlton Group has pointed its efforts at fighting new business taxes while urging other steps to cut federal deficits. On specifics, though, the group's constituent organizations often part company.

In structure Carlton is a **catalytic group** (Riggs, 1950); it exchanges information and coordinates other groups. Members are top lobbyists, lawyers, and economists from major business groups: for example, the U.S. Chamber of Commerce (200,000 members), the American Business Conference (100 mid-sized companies), the National Federation of Independent Business (500,000 small firms), and the Business Roundtable (chief executives of some 200 major companies). A few key law firms and corporations with large Washington offices regularly send representatives. Over the breakfast table, members discuss why constituent groups should support or oppose certain policies. By tapping their organizational bases, they can mobilize almost every major segment of the business community, ranging from top board rooms to small, unincorporated firms to local chambers of commerce.

The Carlton Group has few organizational trappings and few resources of its own. Its members avoid the limelight and were distressed at stories written about the group following the 1981 tax cut. "Getting the Carlton Group out of the headlines" was how the group's organizer described his role.

The National Education Association could not escape headlines even if it wanted to. The NEA is an organization of nearly 2 million teachers. Its annual budget approaches $50 million. Its Washington staff exceeds 500 (Ornstein and Elder, 1978: 43).

Like the Carlton Group, the NEA has had its political triumphs. The most notable was the 1979 creation of the Department of Education, a long-held goal.

More recently, NEA was embroiled in controversy over Reagan's proposed "merit pay" for teachers to improve the nation's schools. Its major concern is the welfare of America's teachers; however it also speaks on a variety of social and economic policies.

The NEA is a large and varied organization; thus, it commands a variety of resources for affecting public policies. Its lobbyists are familiar in the corridors and offices of Capitol Hill and in agencies downtown. Ads and bumper stickers ask citizens to "support your schools." The NEA's huge membership attracts attention from candidates and officeholders; indeed, it was widely assumed that Carter pushed the Department of Education to gain NEA support in 1980. The group makes the most of its numbers and wealth by rating legislators' votes and rewarding its friends with PAC funds.

Both business leaders and teachers are forces to be reckoned with. But each group has different characteristics affecting resources, techniques, and effectiveness. These differences focus our attention on group attributes.

Group size

The most obvious attribute of a group is its size. Some, like the Carlton Group, have only a handful of members. Others, like the NEA, have millions. Some enroll members directly; others operate indirectly, as federations of local groups; still others have a few members but gain money and support through direct-mail soliciting.

Mass groups can, of course, be impressive. Leaders of such groups can assert, sometimes rightly, that they speak for millions of people. Yet large groups are hard to organize and maintain. Individuals who support the group's goals may reason that they can save themselves the costs of joining yet still reap benefits (Olson, 1965). Because of diversity of views, large groups are hard to mobilize to achieve concrete political objectives.

Large groups can overcome such barriers through shrewd strategies. Many offer members basic services, turning to politics incidentally to further members' interests. Union locals, for example, attract members by representing them in negotiations with employers; the American Automobile Association draws members for its accident insurance and travel aids. Both types of groups use member services as a springboard for political action. Others hold members by monopolizing a valuable resource—access to a government board or commission, for example. Still other groups—most notably ideological and single-issue groups—gain members by compiling huge mailing lists and soliciting funds by targeted mailings.

Motorists' lobby. American Automobile Association in suburban Virginia.

Status and money

Another attribute of groups is the *socioeconomic status* of their members. Some groups, like those of doctors or judges, have a flattering public image; others, like truck drivers or stevedores, do not have that advantage. Nowadays the public trusts social and political groups less than it once did. Yet opinion surveys still show that medicine is a highly regarded profession. The AMA uses this image, along with generous funding, to shape the nation's health-care system.

The group's strategic position is related to status. Does it command indispensable information or services? The legal profession's sway does not rest

Air Line Pilots
Association,
Washington
headquarters.

mainly on status. (Actually, lawyers are widely distrusted.) It comes from proximity to legal and government information needed in policymaking. Another example is the Air Line Pilots Association. Their views on safety and flight-crew size are heeded not just because of pilot prestige, but also because of fear of work stoppages.

Some groups seem to command endless funds for political action; others have little to spend. If a group is large, it can pool members' resources through dues or gifts—as do labor unions. They are well financed by masses of middle-income members.

Lack of funds is by no means fatal to a group. Any group with a credible cause or candidate and a little seed money can mount an extensive direct-mail campaign. A direct-mail firm will do this for part of the proceeds. Low-status groups may also substitute for funds by gaining public attention and sympathy for their cause. Lacking virtually all political resources, groups can stage protest demonstrations to make their point (Lipsky, 1968).

Political skills

A group's **political resources** or **skills** affect its political actions. The legal profession, for instance, has a "special relationship" with the political world. Lawyers' skills—advocacy and negotiation—easily convert into the coin of political influence. Lawyers, with their flexible work schedules, can engage in politics. It also helps explain why so many legislators and key government managers have legal training.

In contrast, look at doctors or engineers. They are higher than lawyers in status. But their work skills are not closely linked to politics. And their heavy daily schedules discourage the socializing that marks politically active people.

Low-status groups have similar differences in resources and skills. Printers, air controllers, or maritime workers are easily organized. They work together on the job for long stretches of time and form easy and sometimes garrulous relationships. Tuna fishermen or farm laborers, in contrast, tend to work alone. They are hard to bring together, much less organize; political skills are remote from their daily routines. If they lack middle-class leaders or sponsors with technical and organizational know-how, they are unlikely to be heard. Any group of people has a unique mix of skills and resources that may help push it into the political realm or keep it apart. This mix may enhance or hamper effectiveness.

Distribution of group members

The way a group's members are scattered throughout the population affects its makeup and approach to government. Several questions are vital. Is the group spread throughout the nation? Or is it concentrated in certain places? Is the group more likely to have leverage at the local or national level?

The geographic base   Legislators are picked geographically. Thus, concentrated groups will influence them. Politically active college students, for instance, can sway legislators; large blocs of students are in certain districts and can affect elections. Likewise, the maritime industry is highly concentrated in seaport towns and cities. There, its impact on the local economy magnifies its importance to area legislators. Other groups, like professional societies, have less impact because they are more evenly scattered throughout the nation.

Local or nationwide?   Membership patterns also dictate whether groups seek access at the local, state, or national level. Early in the civil rights movement, for instance, blacks and other minorities were often thwarted in the very areas of their greatest concentration, especially in the South. Yet northern urban ethnic areas have a key place in their states (and in turn, the electoral college). This made civil rights issues a strong factor in presidential politics. Civil rights groups naturally turned to the national government. They went especially to the president to redress local discrimination.

By the same token, groups disadvantaged on the national stage may seek to guard their interests at local or state levels. This is the meaning of "states' rights" versus "federal intervention": groups with divergent bases for access to government always turn to the level most friendly to them (McConnell, 1967: 91–118).

The organizational equation

Whatever the outward form, organization is part of the life of all groups. It may be as simple as informal habits or norms in a small face-to-face group. Or it may be actual "private government," a structure with officers, legislative councils, referenda (sometimes formally monitored), constitutions, and bylaws. Such groups are not very different from public governments. They have leaders and followers, networks of communication, norms, and traditions.

Oligarchy   Leaders and followers emerge in all groups. The noted sociologist Robert Michels (1915) termed this the **iron law of oligarchy:** in all associations power tends to gravitate to a few strong members. Not all groups are equally made up. Some are lively, with many freely taking part; others are dictatorships of the few.

What affects how centralized a group is? A host of factors. But a few general statements can be made. Oligarchy is probably seen more in large groups with low-status members who are geographically diffuse. Democracy is more feasible in small groups with high-status members (or members of relatively equal status) who have frequent face-to-face relationships (Lipset et al., 1956). A group may seem oligarchic, yet internal dynamics may give followers subtle control over its leaders (Moe, 1980).

Whose business is it?   Degree of popular control concerns people outside as well as inside the group. A group may make political demands, for example, in a labor contract, an import quota agreement, or a law conferring benefits. Such demands may well cost citizens, taxpayers, or consumers who had no part in the bargaining.

Whether a group's demands really reflect members' views internally is sometimes open to question. Even so-called public interest groups may not be democratic. As one student (Berry, 1977: 187) concluded, "In examining the organization of public interest groups, what is most interesting is not that they are oligarchic in practice, but that there are not even formal concessions to a democratic structure in a majority of membership groups."

Few groups regularly poll their members. (Common Cause is a conspicuous exception.) Some have only the most haphazard ways of finding out members' views. Many groups are guided by tiny cliques of activists; inactive members may not care or may not know what their leaders are doing. Active dissent is sometimes bullied into silence.

People should question claims of those who speak in the name of their group. Politicians learn to look critically at statements of group spokespersons. Alert public officials learn which groups can be trusted to reflect members' real concerns.

TECHNIQUES OF INFLUENCE

All political groups try to influence government policymaking. Truman (1971) pointed out that one prerequisite for influence is *access*; that is, reaching one or more key decision points in the government. Cultivating access is common to most collective political activity. It occupies much time and energy of group leaders.

Group leaders value access for a personal reason. It helps prove their usefulness. Members must constantly be reminded of leaders' efforts on their behalf. Thus, group leaders often seem as interested in having their day in court as in actually getting good results.

The type of access and how it is achieved depend on the group attributes we just discussed: size, socioeconomic status, political resources and skills, distribution of membership, and organization. Not all groups have equal resources for gaining access. And different groups choose different tactics to gain access.

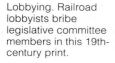

Lobbying. Railroad lobbyists bribe legislative committee members in this 19th-century print.

Lobbying

Lobbying has been a staple group technique ever since the rise of legislative assemblies. In the early 1800s, **lobby agents** swarmed in anterooms and cloakrooms of legislative chambers seeking personal favors; the term, shortened to **lobbyists,** has stuck ever since.

Although the term had not been coined, the right to lobby was set forth in the Bill of Rights. The First Amendment provides that "Congress shall make no law . . . abridging the freedom of speech or of the press; or the right of the people peaceably to assemble and to petition the government for redress of grievances." Thus, lobbying is constitutionally protected. Steps to regulate or limit it must take this into account.

Lobbying is linked to the cherished right of free speech. Yet it has a bad connotation to the public, and it has sometimes deserved that reputation. Until the turn of the century, pressure groups often bribed or bullied officials. In the 1830s, when Congress fought with President Andrew Jackson over the Bank of the United States, it was found that Daniel Webster, a Massachusetts senator, was retained by the bank. During the Grant administration, 12 members of Congress allegedly received stock in the Crédit Mobilier, a joint-stock company. In return, they gave sizable grants for building the Union Pacific Railroad, which controlled the Crédit Mobilier.

Today, vote buying is usually subtle. It involves tacit agreements on financial or other support for reelection campaigns. Occasionally, bribes are taken or offered, though. In the "Abscam" probe of the late 1970s, FBI agents posed as representatives of an Arab sheik. They proved that some legislators would trade votes for cash.

Who are the lobbyists?   Several thousand individuals and groups register each year as lobbyists with the clerk of the House and the secretary of the Senate. A current directory counts more than 10,000 "Washington representatives" (Close, 1983). This under the broad definition of "persons working to influence government policies and actions to advance their own or their client's interests." The largest component (about 4,000) consists of officers of 1500 unions and trade and professional associations with Washington offices. Some are familiar names; others are such groups as the International Banana Association, the International Teleconferencing Association, and the National Institute of American Doll Artists. Another 1,250 representatives handle government relations for individual corporations. An equal number are advocates of noneconomic causes, ranging from handgun control to school prayers, from saving whales to saving the unborn. Finally, there are 2,500 or so lawyers and consultants representing clients (including foreign governments) on Capitol Hill or before administrative agencies.

There are more lobbyists than ever before. First, as noted, there has been an explosion in the number of political groups, especially noneconomic advocacy groups. Second, groups have migrated to Washington to be near the seat of government. One survey found that since the 1970s an average of 2.7 associations moved to Washington *every week;* by 1975, Washington replaced New York as the most popular headquarters for such groups (Pika, 1983: 304), and more than 1,700 of them now make their home in the nation's capital.

Many organizations recruit lobbyists from within. Others, though, turn to "hired guns," people with inside knowledge of government processes like for-

Lobbying. Representative James R. Jones (D–Okla.) is lobbied outside the Capitol by several lobbyists opposed to the MX missile, including (r) Fred Wertheimer, Common Cause president.

mer legislators, Capitol Hill staffers, or executive managers. Such insiders can earn far more than they could working for the government.

Remember, though, lobbyists are not always "other people." Often they are just average folks disturbed enough over an issue to express concern by writing or contacting elected officials. According to a 1976 House survey, 8 percent of those polled had seen or talked with their representative about some matter. And 29 percent had written a letter, sent a telegram, or signed a petition about some problem or issue (U.S. House of Representatives, 1977: 835). In short, lobbying is not a remote activity of a few shady people; it is constitutionally guarded free speech and petition. Everyone can do it, and many of us actually do.

Direct lobbying   Not only are there more groups and individual lobbyists active in the nation's capital, they are also more active in more ways. "More of everything" is how two political scientists summed up their survey of lobbying activities of a sample of 174 organizations (Schlozman and Tierney, 1983: 362). The techniques used by interest groups are summarized in Table 7–1.

"Classic" lobbying involves directly contacting legislators (or bureau chiefs, cabinet members, or White House aides). In Washington and state capitals, lobbyists are judged for their skill in giving information and persuading others. This means buttonholing legislators, giving testimony, supplying technical information, or making informal social contacts.

How do lobbyists approach legislators or other officials? Contrary to folklore, contacts are usually open, even routine. The lobbyist's chief job is giving information to a decision maker. In a legislature, lobbyists start with members of key committees or subcommittees. Or they go to those who already support the lobby group's aims. Such members, in turn, relay the group's point of view to their colleagues (Bauer, Pool, and Dexter, 1972).

Lobbyists thus play an *informational* role; they spread information among legislators and aides too busy to find it on their own. Lobbyists become known for the quality of their information; those who are ill informed, or whose facts prove unreliable, are not likely to be effective.

Contacting decision makers is not as simple as it once was. Power is now widely dispersed on Capitol Hill and throughout executive agencies. Thus, in Congress, members who are not on the specific committees can still shape the policy in question. As one executive-branch lobbyist said, "It used to be that all one had to do was to contact the chairman and a few ranking members of a committee; now all 435 members and 100 senators have to be contacted."

A favorable hearing   Many techniques are open to the lobbyist seeking a favorable hearing from a committee or subcommittee. Some legislative panels owe their existence to group pressures; veterans' affairs, small business, and aging are examples. A lobbyist's group may try to stack a committee's membership in its favor. In fact, committees attract members with constituents who gain from what the committee does. Farm-belt legislators are on agriculture committees; bankers are on banking committees; westerners are on natural resource committees. This self-selection process helps interests that dominate a particular field. Lobbyists for weaker interests have a tougher task; they must persuade their friends to accept what may be an unrewarding, frustrating assignment. Thwarted by one committee, a group may turn to another that promises to be more compliant.

Group representatives influence committee proposals and reports. They often

TABLE 7—1

Techniques Used by 174 Sampled Interest Groups (1982)

Technique	Percent of groups using it
Testifying at hearings	99%
Contacting government officials directly to present your point of view	98
Engaging in informal contacts with officials at conventions, over lunch, etc.	95
Presenting research results or technical information	92
Sending letters to members of your organization to inform them about your activities	92
Entering into coalitions with other organizations	90
Attempting to shape the implementation of policies	89
Talking with people from the press and the media	86
Consulting with government officials to plan legislative strategy	85
Helping to draft legislation	85
Inspiring letter-writing or telegram campaigns	84
Shaping the government's agenda by raising new issues and calling attention to previously ignored problems	84
Mounting grass-roots lobbying efforts	80
Having influential constituents contact their congressman's office	80
Helping to draft regulations, rules, or guidelines	78
Serving on advisory commissions and boards	76
Alerting congressmen to the effects of a bill on their districts	75
Filing suit or otherwise engaging in litigation	72
Making financial contributions to electoral campaigns	58
Doing favors for officials who need assistance	56
Attempting to influence appointments to public office	53
Publicizing candidates' voting records	44
Engaging in direct-mail fund raising for your organization	44
Running advertisements in the media about your position on issues	31
Contributing work or personnel to electoral campaigns	24
Making public endorsements of candidates for office	22
Engaging in protests or demonstrations	20

Average number of techniques = 19

Source: Kay Lehman Schlozman and John T. Tierney, "More of the Same; Washington Pressure Group Activity in a Decade of Change," *Journal of Politics* 45 (May 1983), p. 377.

appear as witnesses at hearings to air their views and "get them on the record." They may sit in on committee meetings called to work on the details of a bill. Information generated by a group may form a key part of the committee report that comes with the bill. Such reports often frame the issues for debate and present the case for what the committee recommends.

A new technique for gaining a favorable hearing is to sponsor or support an informal caucus of senators or representatives. More than 80 such caucuses now exist in the two chambers (Hammond, Stevens, and Mulhollan, 1983: 278–79). Many are inspired by lobbyists and work closely with private-sector groups. The Textile Caucus, the Steel Caucus, and the Tourism Caucus work closely with respective industry groups. Regional caucuses like the Northeast-Midwest Coalition (the so-called Frostbelt Coalition) cooperate with city and state officials.

Lining up the votes   When a bill is being argued in the parent chamber, lobbyists buttonhole members. They shore up support, gain last-minute commitments, and find out how the voting will turn out. They are often relied on to help take an accurate "whip count" of the members. This in turn helps decide parliamentary strategy. If there are enough votes for passage, legislators can press for a quick vote; if it is in doubt, they can stall to bring around the undecided.

Last-minute campaigns to pass or defeat bills on the chamber floor can be spectacular. This phase of the legislative process is most visible to the public. Thus, at this stage, direct lobbying can be best supplemented. A flood of mail, telegrams, phone calls, or delegations can persuade legislators. Such last-minute efforts often bring results. But they may be too late to change the basic thrust of the measure.

Effective lobbyists are in on the act from the start. They help shape a bill as it comes from a committee or subcommittee. Once the shape has been fixed, an opposing group has a vexing choice. It can try to amend the bill on the floor or go all-out to kill it.

Grass-roots lobbying   Most lobbying on major issues includes broad efforts to spark positive public feelings. Grass-roots lobbying assumes that constituents will sway politicians more than will well-paid lobbyists.

Large groups, like labor unions, have the built-in advantage of numbers; this helps them create huge floods of sentiment. A group may have few members but a big bank account; then it can stir grass-roots support through costly ads or public relations campaigns. Groups that are neither large nor well financed may get free publicity through media events.

One milestone in grass-roots lobbying occurred in 1983. That year the American Bankers Association (ABA) scuttled a plan to withhold taxes directly on interest and dividends from bank and saving accounts. Economists had urged that the government recover billions of dollars that annually go unpaid; thus, interest withholding was proposed by Presidents Kennedy (1962) and Carter (1979) and each time soundly defeated. The idea was revived in 1982 by Senate Finance Chairman Robert Dole (R-Kan.) to help counter skyrocketing deficits; it was included in the "revenue enhancement" act of that year.

But Dole reckoned without the ABA, which represents nearly all of the nation's 14,000 banks. The largest banks saw little difficulty in implementation; but smaller banks feared the added costs of the plan. For the ABA, "withholding loomed as a good opportunity to prove the ABA still cared about the little guy" (Keller, 1983: 35).

By late 1982, the ABA rolled into high gear. Fourteen thousand member banks received free kits for raising public fears. Posters for bank lobbies proclaimed: "Congress wants a piece of your savings. What they need is a piece of your mind." Senate offices received from 150,000 to 300,000 pieces of mail; Dole himself added 13 employees to send out responses. Many denounced the bankers' tactics (President Reagan condemned them as a "selfish interest group"). But both houses dutifully repealed the withholding provision. (Consumers were hardly better off, however, because Congress authorized the IRS to implement a confusing "backup withholding" scheme.)

Used at the right moment, grass-roots campaigns—sometimes called "hot-button" tactics—can be strikingly effective. But they must be used sparingly.

Not even large and wealthy groups can charge up their troops simply by passing orders down the line. Members must be directly touched by an issue. If not, they are apt to ignore leaders' efforts. Grass-roots mobilization demands large-scale organization, effective communication, and precise timing.

Also, legislators are accustomed to mass letter-writing campaigns. They suspect "inspired mail," for example, floods of letters or telegrams. Thus, seasoned lobbyists use the technique sparingly. They reserve it for large, basic issues. Like a deadly weapon, it should not be used when smaller tactical weapons will do.

Coalitions   Most political issues touch more than one interest group. Lobbyists can profit by cooperating with like-minded groups. Pooling information and contacts works to the advantage of all. Not surprisingly, lobbyists closely watch the actions of other groups and look for chances to cooperate.

Sometimes a number of groups create a new organization. This catalytic group (Riggs, 1950) coordinates work in one cause. Catalytic groups coordinate lobby efforts in many fields. Their work helps primary groups exchange information and focus efforts. The Carlton Group was described; another example is the Leadership Conference on Civil Rights. This coalition of labor, religious, and ethnic groups lobbies on civil rights bills.

Regulating the lobbies   Congress and most states have lobbying laws. Most require some form of registration and disclosure. This throws "the antiseptic light of publicity on the lobby." The 1946 Federal Regulation of Lobbying Act (P.L. 79-601) is the basic statute. It requires paid lobbyists to register with the clerk of the House and the secretary of the Senate. They must also file quarterly financial reports.

The act defines a **lobbyist** as any person "who by himself, or through any agent or employee or other persons in any manner . . . solicits, collects, or receives money or any other thing of value to be used principally to aid . . . the passage or defeat of any legislation by the Congress."

The act does not seriously hamper lobbying activities. Large loopholes exempt many interest groups from even registering. The act applies only to those whose principal purpose is to influence legislation. Some large groups decline to register. They claim lobbying is not their main purpose, but incidental to other activities. Also, lobbying is defined by the act as direct dealings with members of Congress. That excludes such techniques as grass-roots lobbying or electronic communications.

Further rules on lobbying are set by House and Senate codes of ethics. They ban members from taking gifts above a certain value; they also limit outside income to 15 percent of salary, and restrict lecture fees. (One interest-group technique is having key legislators speak at meetings for large fees.)

Groups that receive government funds face certain lobbying restrictions not shared by other groups. Lobbying expenses may not be paid for with public funds. Also, organizations receiving federal contracts or grants must say how much private money they spend on lobbying and report lobbying costs separately. The restrictions, embodied in OMB regulations that took effect in 1984, resulted from Reagan Administration efforts to "de-fund the left," or stop government-funded lobbying by nonprofit groups, mainly liberal, that received federal grants. Two earlier drafts of rules were dropped because of heavy criticism, and the final regulations were adopted only when defense contractors were included. Still, restrictions on nonprofit groups are stricter than on defense contractors; and the idea of restricting lobbying, even when federal money is involved, is highly controversial.

Loopholes in the laws are sometimes revealed by exposés of lobbying abuses. This sparks periodic demands for tougher rules. Mainly a broader definition of lobbying and more detailed reporting rules are asked for. Such laws must not interfere with the flow of information from specialized interests to lawmaking bodies. They must not infringe on free speech, press, assembly, and petition. At some point, such rules could have a "chilling effect" on legitimate group activities; not going past this point is a delicate issue for lawmakers and judges.

There are periodic efforts to plug loopholes in lobby laws. None has succeeded. In 1978, Congress debated a bill for stronger registration and reporting rules. One version would have required reporting not only direct contacts with members of Congress but also indirect grass-roots efforts. Like most attempts to control lobbying, such proposals raise the issue of balancing the public's right to know about lobbying with the lobbyists' right to free speech and petition.

Entering the electoral arena

Interest groups can step onto the electoral stage to help or hinder elected officials. Legislators and lobbyists are quite aware of the importance of the next election. They may avoid speaking of it outright during dealings; but both know that lobbyists can use funds or grass-roots influence to affect the vote.

Funding candidates   Many groups give money directly to friendly candidates; others launch registration or get-out-the-vote drives; still others tell members to reward friends or punish enemies at the polls. As might be expected, groups with money or large memberships are most apt to use these techniques.

Campaign funding is limited by complex rules. Corporations and unions, for instance, cannot, under federal law, contribute directly to campaigns for federal office. Yet they can give indirectly; they may set up PACs like the AFL-CIO's Committee on Political Education (COPE) or Tenneco's Employees' Good Government Fund. Such PACs may give directly to candidates (up to $5,000 per candidate per election). Corporations and unions may also spend any amount to inform their own members, personnnel, or stockholders on issues of interest. And they may use their own funds to pay administrative and fund-raising costs.

Union members and corporate employees are often pressured into PAC giving. "I know it isn't mandatory to give," said a corporation executive. "But the word around the water cooler is that if you don't give or if you give less than the amount expected based on your salary, you're liable to be called in for a pep talk from the divisional president" (Sansweet, 1980: 1).

With such boosts, PACs are flourishing. Though all types of PACs increased, corporate PACs grew the most. They went from 89 in 1974 to more than 1,500 in 1984. Labor PACs nearly doubled over the same period (see Figure 7–1).

PAC funds flow straight to favored candidates. Or they flow indirectly to educating the public, turning out the vote, or providing volunteer campaign help. These so-called independent expenditures must be independent of the candidates' own efforts; but the restrictions are hard to enforce. It is often hard

FIGURE 7–1

Growth of Political Action Committees, 1974–1984

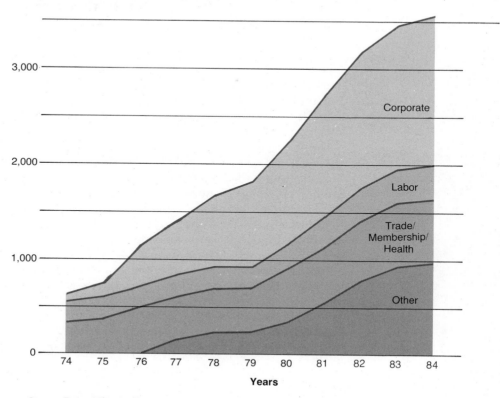

Source: Federal Election Commission.

to distinguish labor's efforts from those of the Democratic National Committee during presidential campaigns; by the same token, many groups work hand in glove with the Republican cause.

Many PACs, however, are strictly nonpartisan; they spread donations where the funds will do the most good. For most PACs, that means making sure that incumbent legislators are taken care of. Incumbent Senators and Representatives received more than three times as much PAC money as did challengers during the 1981–1982 congressional election cycle, according to figures compiled by the Federal Election Commission. Given the high reelection rates of members of Congress, such donations are smart politics. As an official of a business PAC remarked in explaining a large contribution to one liberal Democrat, "It's more fun to back a winner than a loser."

PAC funding lets interest groups take part directly in campaigns. Both incumbents and challengers know they must appeal to various PACs to finance their political careers. Interest groups may not nominate or elect candidates. But they sponsor and sustain candidates' campaigns in important ways.

Generating publicity   Groups that lack size and wealth can still have clout through publicity that may affect elections. Disclosing scandals and making candidates' views public are methods.

A common technique is compiling voting records and scoring legislators by the group's standards. Members of Congress are rated by nearly 100 groups. These range from the American Bakers Association to the National Taxpayers Union.

There are great differences in the group ratings. Figure 7–2 gives 1983 ratings of Senators gathered by a leading labor group (AFL-CIO), a leading business association (U.S. Chamber of Commerce), and two ideological groups, one liberal (Americans for Democratic Action) and one conservative (Americans for Constitutional Action). The two parties split fairly neatly on these scales: Democrats lean toward labor and liberalism, while the GOP tilts to business and conservatism. Not all such indexes reveal such clear party lines.

These voting indexes help lobby groups inform their members. They show whether legislators vote "right" or "wrong" on issues affecting the group. They also set grounds for independent campaigns for or against certain legislators. Thus, people have a shorthand way of judging how incumbents perform.

Such ratings are not always correct, though. Voters should beware of taking them literally. For one thing, votes used in the indexes may be carelessly chosen. Procedural votes may be confused with substantive stands. Complex factors that cause members to vote in a given way may be ignored. Many angry legislators have spoken on the House or Senate floor denouncing groups for distorting their records. (In 1984 a religious group awarded a 100-percent "re-

FIGURE 7–2

How Lobbyists Rate Senate Democrats and Republicans, 1983

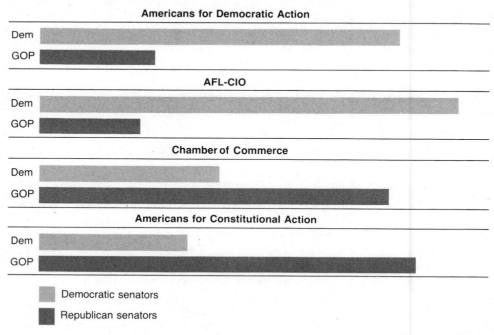

The groups and numbers of floor votes used for their indexes are: Americans for Democratic Action (20 selected votes); AFL–CIO (17 votes); U.S. Chamber of Commerce (19 votes); and Americans for Constitutional Action Research Institute (20 votes). All figures are for Senators in 1983.
Source: *Congressional Quarterly Weekly Report* 42 (July 14, 1984), 1695.

port card" to a legislator who admitted sexual misconduct with a 17-year-old female page. Other legislators with unblemished records received zero ratings.)

Groups are also sometimes accused of targeting legislators already in trouble at the polls. If the election is lost, the group claims credit for hitting its target.

The lesson to be learned is: let the voter beware! Ratings may simplify one's choice at the polls, but they can also distort an elected official's total record.

Executive lobbying

Among the most conspicuous lobbyists on Capitol Hill are from the White House and executive agencies. "Merely placing a program before Congress is not enough," declared President Lyndon Johnson—probably the shrewdest legislator ever to serve in the White House. "Without constant attention from the administration, most legislation moves through the congressional process at the speed of a glacier" (Johnson, 1971: 448). Ever since Washington dispatched Treasury Secretary Alexander Hamilton to consult with members, chief executives have been trying to influence legislative activity.

These days, all executive agencies have congressional liaison offices. Their function is to meet requests for information and assistance; they also to try to see that the administration's viewpoint is conveyed to congressional committees and legislators. Especially in final negotiation, administration lobbyists can play a critical role.

The judicial arena

Interest groups also take part in the judicial process. They do this less obviously than in legislative chambers or electoral campaigns. Groups sometimes lobby to have certain types of persons picked as judges. Recently women and minorities have pressed for broader standards in judicial selection. They criticize the vast number of white males on the bench.

Groups often sponsor court fights. Courts are active makers of public policy; but they are not equally accessible to all. Litigation takes time and is very costly. This aids large organizations, business firms, and groups that can hire legal talent. Many policies have been refined in the courts with interest groups and the government as the chief litigants. Civil rights, environmental protection, and workplace safety are examples.

The legal trail blazed in the 1940s and 50s for black civil rights was largely subsidized by the NAACP. Using its funds for court fights, the NAACP carefully chose test cases. It brought those cases to court at the best moment and under the best conditions. After a long line of rulings against discrimination in education, the NAACP challenged the concept of "separate but equal" schools. That concept was struck down by the landmark 1954 Supreme Court decision, *Brown* v. *Board of Education*. The NAACP's chief counsel, Thurgood Marshall, argued the case before the Supreme Court and later became a justice himself.

Another way groups can enter court fights is by filing *amicus curiae* ("friend of the court") briefs. In this way, groups that are not litigants can still submit briefs giving their views and showing their concern. The 1978 *Bakke* case challenging special admissions programs for racial minorities was an example. Scores of groups filed briefs. Most favored special admission programs and opposed Bakke's stand.

Court politics. Federal troops escort black students to Little Rock High School to implement 1954 *Brown* v. *Topeka* decision (1957).

INTEREST-GROUP INFLUENCE

Everyone concedes that interest groups have an important part in politics. But just how important are they? Newspaper accounts sometimes give the idea that a legion of all-powerful groups buys legislative votes. It may seem policymakers are controlled in a shadowy underground of influence peddling.

The limits of influence

Sometimes the picture of vast interest-group power is true. The American Medical Association succeeded in stalling national health insurance for a generation; the civil rights movement produced victories in the 1960s; environmentalists won many new statutes in the 1970s.

Yet none of these groups could have reached its goals without a social and historical setting that supplied the raw materials for influence. The AMA used physicians' prestige and popular fears about "socialized medicine." Civil rights activists gained publicity from years of outrages in the segregated South; they gained political clout from concerned blacks in the urban North. Environmentalists were helped by widespread alarm over pollution. Also, these groups succeeded within a narrow range of issues. None tried to alter major foreign policy, tariffs, or tax laws.

Finally, the strength of these groups ebbed as conditions changed. After a while, exploding medical costs and public discontent with medicine overrode the AMA's pressure against health insurance. Widespread resistance to such things as busing and affirmative action slowed the civil rights movement. Worries over productivity, red tape, and energy supplies have halted extension of environmental protection. The groups do not lack resources or influence; but they, like other strong groups, are limited by issues, circumstances, and time.

Segmented power

Interest-group power is limited by our complex, multilevel, multistage political system. Not all organized interests at all levels, local to national, get involved. More often, decision making is *segmented* into thousands of distinct but overlapping networks of power. It makes little sense to talk about political power in sweeping terms. It is more correct to talk about such political arenas as military contracting, employment and training programs, resource conservation, cotton subsidies, housing, banking regulations, Detroit school business, Sacramento planning and zoning, and thousands of similar segments. Some arenas are highly competitive; most have a few key actors (Hayes, 1981).

Subgovernments   At the national level, subgovernments strive to dominate policy in a given field. Bureaucratic agencies, congressional subcommittees, and interest groups are linked. This is shown schematically in Figure 7–3. They work in numerous policy fields: milk pricing, sugar quotas, oil production, and weapons system contracting are a few. If the actors in such subsystems agree, they can control the outcomes that affect policy. This is not necessarily a conspiracy. It just shows that very few policies gain broad public attention over any length of time.

Sometimes, events break open these "cozy triangles" of power. A scandal over the drug thalidomide pressured legislators to set strict drug-testing standards. Ralph Nader, an outsider, forced adoption of stiff auto safety standards. But the public's attention span is brief. After such upheavals, the subgovernments may slip back into a stable pattern. At best, a new balance of power is imposed by the brief crisis. Not all public policy can be explained in terms of such segmented arenas. But much of it conforms to this picture.

FIGURE 7–3

Subgovernments: "The Cozy Triangles"

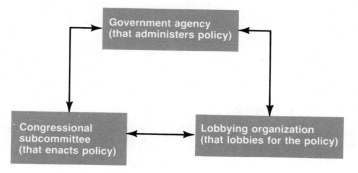

Government agency (that administers policy)

Congressional subcommittee (that enacts policy)

Lobbying organization (that lobbies for the policy)

"I DON'T THINK I CAN KEEP UP WITH YOU"

Some writers stress the complexity and fluidity of the links between interest groups and government. The cozy triangles notion is too simple and rigid, they claim; a broader term like ''issue networks'' might be more accurate (Heclo, 1978). There is much truth to this observation. With the rise of citizen groups, not to mention the popularity of investigative journalism, these relationships can be exposed to public criticism. Moreover, the multiplicity of groups makes it harder for a few to monopolize policymaking.

Groups often seem effective in pressing their demands. But the fact is that such groups do not usually have to win over the whole political system. America has many specialized policy arenas. Thus, groups generally gain their goals by capturing a relevant body of decision makers. This is why people must organize to influence policies. It also shows the vastness of our politics and the difficulty of watching all that is going on.

Today, interest groups seem to have supplanted political parties as the chief channel for conveying citizen opinion to the government. In fact, groups represent people's views with a variety and richness that parties cannot match. And while groups cannot produce broad governing coalitions, they can, and do, reflect the factionalism inherent in modern America.

CONCLUSIONS

Several conclusions can be drawn from our discussion of interest groups:

1 Our society contains a vast number of groups. Few are wholly political. Most, though, can and do enter the political arena under certain circumstances. Group activity is protected by the Constitution and has marked our whole history.

2 Americans are not equally represented by interest groups. The educated and rich are better represented than the uneducated and poor. Segments of the population are politically underorganized.

3 To influence political decisions, groups draw upon many resources. They include size, status, money, relevant political skills, geographic distribution of members, and organization. Groups short on some resources (such as money) can substitute other resources (such as numbers or publicity) to make an impact.

4 Lobbying is a leading technique of group influence. Groups seek more than just access to officials. They seek public acceptance through grassroots techniques and legal victories through group-sponsored court cases.

5 Interest groups are more and more active in the electoral arena. The tools include contributing to political action committees (PACs), independent spending, and publicizing officials' voting records.

6 Group influence varies with the issue, arena, and time. ''Subgovernments'' are one example of the segmented nature of political influence in this country.

FURTHER READING

BERRY, JEFFREY M. (1984) The Interest Group Society. Boston: Little, Brown. A readable introduction to the topic that surveys recent trends.

CIGLER, ALLAN J., and BURDETT A. LOOMIS (1983) Interest Group Politics. Washington, D.C.: Congressional Quarterly Press. A collection of up-to-date studies by leading students of interest groups.

HAYES, MICHAEL T. (1981) Lobbyists and Legislators. New Brunswick, N.J.: Rutgers University Press. An intriguing and stimulating analytical study, summarizing the literature and proposing new approaches.

LOWI, THEODORE J. (1969) The End of Liberalism. New York: W. W. Norton. A critical treatment of the theory and practice of interest-group politics since the New Deal.

TRUMAN, DAVID B. (1971) The Governmental Process. 2d ed. New York: Alfred A. Knopf. A landmark study of interest groups that develops a general theory of group action and applies it to various political arenas.

8
Media in American Politics

Navy Lieutenant Robert O. Goodman, Jr., was reunited with his family via satellite on the network morning news programs. It was a total marriage of political event and media theater.

Goodman was an American flyer captured by the Syrians after raids over Lebanon. In a political gamble, Democratic presidential candidate Jesse Jackson traveled to the Middle East, consulted with Syrian President Hafez Assad, and persuaded him to release Goodman. The news was relayed by satellite to millions of early-morning TV viewers. The first live pictures of Goodman and Jackson were carried by "The CBS Morning News." Then, also through live transmissions, the young flyer was united with his father on ABC's "Good Morning, America," and with his mother and brother on NBC's "Today" show. One of Goodman's first questions on learning of his release was, "Does that mean I get to talk to Bryant Gumbel [cohost of the "Today" show]?"

The Goodman rescue was a perfect union of political and media reality (Shales, 1984). And it turned out to be one of those "instant" media events: within four months, only 1 percent of the public listed it as a memorable public event (Robinson and Clancy, 1984: 15).

* * * * *

Communication is vital to politics. Some have called it the nervous system of the body politic, transmitting messages between the various parts (Fagan, 1966). The modes we know best are the so-called mass media: newspapers and magazines, radio, TV, and movies. Special communications are used within political elite groups. Nor should we forget the most common communication of all: face-to-face contact.

The media are something of a puzzle to students of politics. Their impact on our lives is immediate and pervasive. But their political impact is still not well understood. In this chapter we examine communication as a social process. We also discuss media forms, organization, and the types of messages spread through the media. Then we try to assess the media's effects on our political system.

WHAT IS COMMUNICA-TION?

A straightforward framework for looking at communication is offered by political scientist Harold D. Lasswell (1948: 37–51): "Who Says What, in Which Channel, to Whom, with What Effect?" Communication thus includes a source, a message, a medium (or channel), an audience, and an effect.

The source and the audience

Many levels of communication can be categorized in terms of *who* (source) is speaking to *whom* (audience).

Politicians, for instance, communicate with masses of people. Presidents, party leaders, and interest-group spokespersons spend much time spreading ideas and mobilizing the masses. Conversely, people send messages to leaders in many ways: letters and phone calls, audience reactions, and votes are a few. One way to classify governments is to look at the two-way communication between elites and masses. In dictatorships, messages flow mostly from the top down; in democracies, the flow is two-way.

TV diplomacy. Robert Goodman, Sr., looks on as his son, freed from captivity in Syria, appears with the Rev. Jesse Jackson, who negotiated the release.

Leaders transmit their ideas to concerned **attentive publics.** Members of politically active groups like trade unions are swamped with newsletters and pamphlets outlining issues that affect working people. The same is true of corporation executives, gun owners, civil libertarians, and other special groups. Such information can influence policy in specialized fields, even though little of it reaches the mass media.

In complex societies, sources and audiences often interlock. Parts of a news briefing may directly reach the general public on the network news; the rest may be seen only by the press or TV producers. They sift and shape the material before passing it on to the next audience: their editors and producers. It is like the game of gossip-chain; a news event passes through many hands before we see it in a paper or newscast.

Certain people play a key role in passing information to friends and neighbors. These **opinion leaders** are alert to media accounts. They relay information to friends and co-workers who watch the media less. This "two-step flow of communication" is a crucial link in spreading political information (Katz, 1957: 61–78).

The medium and the message

The academic view tends to stress politicians' formal messages. Speeches, press releases, government reports, and party platforms fall into this category. Just as important are informal messages, such as off-the-cuff remarks, "leaks," or private communications. The "informed source" is a staple for reporters. Clues from an unnamed informer, "Deep Throat," helped reporters Robert Woodward and Carl Bernstein unravel the Watergate scandal in the mid-1970s. Politicians as diverse as Ronald Reagan and Jesse Jackson have been embarrassed when private or personal remarks became public.

Communication channels include the mass media. These are *print* (newspapers, magazines, special journals) or *electronic* (radio, TV, and telegraph). We have a vast number of media organizations. Table 8–1 shows the major categories and the number of outlets in each.

An outlet's character and limitations affect how messages are sent. This means some messages are more easily sent by one medium than another. Complex arguments are best said in print, through books and articles. The emotional parts of an event are most powerfully conveyed by TV, the fastest and most intimate medium. Before TV, the horrors of war were reported by many talented people. Two notable ones were Stephen Crane's fictional account of a Civil War battle (*Red Badge of Courage*) and Edward R. Murrow's radio broadcasts from World War II London. Yet TV news clips from the Vietnam War in the late 1960s did more than any nonvisual account to cause revulsion against the war. "The medium is the message" was Marshall McLuhan's thesis (1964). This may be an overstatement, but contains a kernel of truth.

The effects

The impact of communication is in one sense total and pervasive. We need communication to persuade, influence, and even conduct social life. But it is hard to isolate its effects on politics. Social philosophers and commentators are aware that the media have an irresistible pull on politics. But what is the direc-

TABLE 8–1

Major Media Outlets in the United States

Newspapers:	
Daily	1,687
Semiweekly	600
Weekly	6,798
Less frequent	66
Total	9,151
Periodicals:	
Daily	182
Semiweekly	94
Weekly	1,376
Semi-monthly	658
Monthly	4,096
Bimonthly	1,348
Quarterly	1,711
Other	1,344
Total	10,809
Radio stations:	
Commercial AM	4,726
Commercial FM	3,490
Noncommercial FM	1,104
Total	9,320
Television stations:	
Commercial VHF	536
Commercial UHF	334
Noncommercial VHF	107
Noncommercial UHF	172
Total	1,149
Cable television systems	5,800

Sources: *IMS Ayer Directory of Publications* (Fort Washington, Pa.: IMS Press, 1984) p. viii; *Broadcasting-Cablecasting Yearbook* (Washington, D.C.: Broadcasting Publishing, Inc., 1984), pp. A-2, D-3.

tion of the pull? Studies are far from conclusive. We shall have more to say about this after we discuss the communications process in detail.

ORGANIZATION OF THE MASS MEDIA

Every communication medium springs from technological and social advances. First, language (spoken, then written) was invented. Printing presses and cheap paper made mass culture possible. Then came the telegraph, telephone, and in this century, radio, TV, and advanced forms of data transmission. Each advance affected social organization. Organized communication has many results: knowledge becomes more organized; institutions are formed just for communicating; and the body politic gains a collective memory (De Fleur and Ball-Rokeach, 1975: 1–14).

The print media

Newspapers   More than 9,000 newspapers are printed in the United States. This is by far the largest number in any nation; but it is one fourth fewer than our all-time high around World War I. Most newspapers are weeklies, but the 1,700 dailies boast the most readers and the most political clout.

Decline of newspapers? Modern newspapers are often vast enterprises. They can involve thousands of employees and equipment worth millions. Competition for readers and ad revenues is keen; many weaker papers cannot compete. Other media have shattered print's monopoly over mass dispersion of information.

Newspapers are constantly being forced to shut down or merge with other papers. New York City had 14 general newspapers in 1920; today it has 3. Philadelphia once had 13 papers; now it has 1. Only about 50 cities have rival newspapers. Fierce competition and rising costs squeeze smaller papers especially hard. Many rivals share printing plants to cut costs; a federal law—the Newspaper Protection Act of 1970—allows such cooperative efforts through an unusual exemption from antitrust rules.

Large chains—Gannett, Newhouse, Knight-Ridder, Cox, and others—account for two thirds of all daily papers and three fourths of the circulation. Almost all papers rely on syndicated features and wire services—especially Associated Press (AP) and United Press International (UPI)—for all but local news and ads.

Newspaper formation has not kept pace with population growth. There are about 25 percent fewer daily papers today than at the outbreak of World War I. Nine out of ten "urban places" (towns of 2,500 or more) had their own dailies in 1880; by 1961, this figure had fallen to less than one in three.

Localism Central ownership is growing; but U.S. newspapers are still local and dispersed (Bagdikian, 1971). Only recently have national papers been readily available in the whole country when they are published. These include *USA Today*, *The Wall Street Journal*, and *The Christian Science Monitor*. Otherwise, newspapers are local.

The reasons for localism are political and economic. There are half a million local government units of some sort in the United States; most have an immediate impact on citizens. Schools, police and fire protection, land use and zoning, local highway routes, and property tax rates are all decided by local bodies. No national paper could ever cover such things, so some papers specialize in home-town news. They often boost revenues by running legally required announcements of local government actions.

Advertising is vital for survival of local publications. Ads are the lifeblood of mass media. Most personal income is spent at some 1.7 million local retail stores. Suburban papers, the "underground press," and shoppers' weeklies are successful because of local advertising.

Diversification in print The number of daily papers is declining, but other publications are growing. There are news magazines, such as *Time*, *Newsweek*, and *U.S. News and World Report*. There are journals of opinion, such as the conservative *National Review*, the neoconservative *Public Interest*, the neoliberal *Washington Monthly*, and the liberal *Nation* and *New Republic*. Thousands of magazines and newsletters cater to every conceivable work or recreational interest. Trade and professional groups rely on periodicals to define and mobilize membership. Many large businesses have "house organs" for employees, stockholders, and customers.

Few of these are political; but nearly all convey political information at times. *Rolling Stone*, which began as a rock musicians' biweekly, branched out to the

Labor press. A few of the hundreds of union newspapers.

rock culture, drugs, protest, and politics. Its political correspondents have turned in widely praised, if offbeat, looks at presidential campaigns. *Playboy* is surely no political organ; but it pushes more liberal laws concerning sexual conduct and sometimes runs stories about political figures. Diverse journals—*Oil and Gas Weekly*, *Air and Space Digest*, *Today's Health*—air issues that affect, respectively, the petroleum industry, the aerospace industry, and the medical profession.

A good example of specialized journalism is the labor press. Some 800 union journals have a combined local, national, and international circulation of more than 30 million. The two largest are *The International Teamster News*, a monthly magazine, and the United Auto Workers' *Solidarity*, a monthly paper. Each has a circulation of nearly 2 million. Most labor papers are bland; they print staid pieces on legislation affecting workers, consumer news, and tons of routine union reports, mainly local. As one labor editor explained, "Most union newspapers are long on flattery for the incumbent officers and short on comment for the rank and file" (Nader, 1977). A small but growing number of labor papers, though, give lively coverage to union elections and other controversies.

Electronic media

Radio   U.S. commercial broadcasting was born in 1920. That same year, KDKA in Pittsburgh aired the Harding-Cox presidential election returns, the first major news event covered electronically.

Radio quickly became mainly an entertainment medium. Yet it is a powerful political instrument. Politicians in the 1930s and 1940s (from FDR to Hitler) grasped its importance and used it to mobilize support. Radio reporting, especially during World War II, brought home the drama of world events. Modern politicians as diverse as Richard Nixon and Jimmy Carter used radio to deliver their messages; Ronald Reagan scheduled brief weekly radio talks on his policies.

Despite the rise of TV and other media, radio is a growing business. Today there are more than 4,700 commercial AM stations; 3,500 commercial and 1,100 noncommercial FM outlets. Recent growth is largely in the FM sector because of superior sound quality. (Better AM sound is on the way.) Americans own some 470 million radios, more than ever before. Almost every home is reached by radio; the average family has more than five sets. About 123 million are in cars, trucks, and boats.

Radio, like print, must specialize to compete with other media. Today's stations stress a given format to appeal to certain audience segments. Major formats include all news, country-and-western music, popular music (including top 40, middle of the road, rhythm and blues, and album-oriented rock), classical music, and ethnic and educational programming. Within each category, programming tends to be identical; a "top-40" station in Duluth sounds just like one in Miami. Specialized programming allows advertisers, commercial or political, to pinpoint the audiences they want to reach. Campaigners therefore buy ads to reach intended audiences at the best times.

Television   Developed in the 1930s, TV burst on the scene after World War II and spread far faster than earlier media. Today, 98 percent of all households have at least one TV; about half have more than one. About 74 million are color sets. There are more than 1,100 TV stations, three fourths of them commercial.

So far, TV has been wildly profitable. In 1981, the industry reaped a $1.5 billion profit from $9.8 billion in revenues; these are far higher than comparable figures for radio. National TV ads are expensive (the average is $100,000 for 30 seconds of prime time). And TV depends on ad revenues even more than do radio or papers. Indeed, most aspects of the industry are costly.

Because of its cost, television has thus far been quite centralized. Three fourths of all commercial stations have tied to one of the three national networks. In the top 50 markets, where 75 percent of the people live, three commercial networks (NBC, CBS, ABC) and one noncommercial network (PBS) capture most of the audience, especially in prime evening hours.

Most TV programs are national. Local live programming is a little more than 10 percent of all TV content. As for all the rest, one former FCC chairman said that local stations "throw the network switch, or open a syndicated film package as they would a can of beans." During prime evening hours, about 95 percent of the material comes from the networks.

Recently, localism has crept in even among network affiliates. Cheaper technologies like video recording and microwave transmission have enhanced local newscasts. In 1984, presidential candidates geared their schedules to appear on local news programs—a free and noncommercial forum.

In the United States, the audience is vast and diverse. Thus, TV content, political and nonpolitical, tends to be bland and inoffensive. Newscasts stress fast-breaking stories, not interpretation or commentary. Crusading journalism is rare.

For sheer impact, though, TV has no equal. From 1952 through 1980, TV offered gavel-to-gavel coverage of presidential conventions. As a result, the parties had to streamline procedures and format. Television covered the 1954 Army-McCarthy hearings; this sidetracked Senator Joseph McCarthy's red-

TV ad. Family watches Mondale appeal.

FIGURE 8–1

The Independents' Growing TV Audience Share

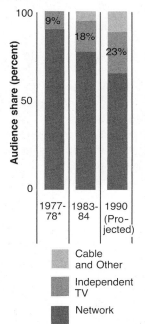

Source: Laura Landro, "Independent TV Stations Assume Bigger Role in Broadcast Industry." *The Wall Street Journal* (May 11, 1984), p. 33. Reprinted by permission of *The Wall Street Journal*, © Dow Jones & Company, Inc. May 11, 1984. All Rights Reserved.

hunting career by exposing his personality and tactics to the public. Senate hearings on organized crime (1951) and Watergate (1973) mixed high drama, humor, and entertainment. The events following President Kennedy's 1963 assassination were watched in 96 percent of all homes. During that time, TV sets were on an average of more than 31.5 hours. At such moments, TV saturates an audience as no other medium can.

With its huge audiences and high production costs, commercial TV is a homogenized, middle-of-the-road medium. Even with a safe format of sports, adventures, sitcoms, variety, and talk shows, TV eats up talent and program ideas as fast as they appear. Recently, viewers have been increasingly restive over the quality and selection of network programs; the networks' share of the audience has declined more than 10 percent in the last five years (Schwartz, 1984). (See Figure 8–1.)

So TV is ripe for the diversification that has already transformed radio and print. One technology for such a change is the 6,000 or so operating cable systems linked by satellite transmission. Cable TV began in the 1950s to extend TV reception to remote areas and help big-city reception. Now about 4 of every 10 TV homes are served by cable; the number is growing. The largest cable system (in San Diego) boasts 210,000 subscribers; some systems have fewer than 100.

Cable itself may be overtaken by newer technologies that offer the same benefits without costly wiring: multipoint distribution services (MDS) transmit programming by microwaves; direct broadcast satellites (DBS) beam programming directly to homes, bypassing local TV stations and cable systems.

New programming patterns are emerging. Whatever the technology, the systems feature wide variety (up to 108 channels). This includes the three commercial networks, PBS, other commercial outlets, and specialized channels for sports, movies, the arts, news, public affairs, and the like. There are channels for local government, do-your-own-thing public access channels, and the prospect of leasing channels to community groups—business, labor, religious, ethnic.

Already the effects of this diversified "narrowcasting" can be seen. The Cable News Network (CNN) built a respectable audience with an all-news format;

Cable News Network. Combining cable technology with all-news format, CNN is a venture of Ted Turner, flamboyant owner of the Atlanta Braves.

C-SPAN (Cable-Satellite Public Affairs Network) has an audience of some 3 million for broadcasts of House sessions, committee hearings, speeches, and public affairs discussions. Other public affairs ventures are likely at the local and state levels. Private-sector groups like the U.S. Chamber of Commerce, the AFL-CIO, and others have already launched extensive cable-TV efforts.

The new technologies may end the commercial TV networks' monopoly and promote cultural pluralism; but their impact on political information is less clear. While electronic media can create powerful political images, they are geared mainly to entertainment. In the future as in the past, politics and government will be a relatively minor part of the TV picture. With more variety, however, the new TV era offers more to the politically motivated part of the audience. If a variety of politically active groups use new TV technology to inform and mobilize their constituencies, this will underscore the fragmented nature of the political system.

Government regulation

Democracies give wide berth to communications media. Free speech and press were central political and philosophical issues in the Old World; in the Colonies, papers and journals thrived because they could publish without royal licenses or taxes. Their privileged role was acknowledged in the First Amendment, which enjoins Congress to "make no law . . . abridging the freedom . . . of the press."

This does not mean that media are free from government influence or control. Like all businesses, they are subject to many regulations, large and small. The news business, too, is sensitive to government pressures. And electronic media, unlike print media, operate in the publicly owned electromagnetic spectrum; therefore, they are subject to federal regulation.

Print media The First Amendment makes the press the only private industry expressly protected by the Constitution. Most newspeople think this gives them almost complete freedom to gather and print news and opinions as they see fit. If a story clashes with other constitutionally protected values, the remedy is not prior restraint but after-the-fact court action.

Editors have complete freedom to decide what goes in or stays out of their journals, even if the result is unfair. In a unanimous decision (*Miami Herald Publishing Co.* v. *Tornillo,* 1974), the Supreme Court struck down a Florida law requiring papers to give candidates free space to reply to newspaper criticisms. A paper involves a "crucial process" of editorial judgment that lies beyond government regulation, Chief Justice Warren Burger wrote for the Court. "A responsible press is an undoubtedly desirable goal," he noted. "But press responsibility is not mandated by the Constitution and like many other virtues, it cannot be legislated." Hence, editorial judgments are covered by the First Amendment.

On the other hand, people have weapons to fend off the press. Private citizens can shield themselves from publicity's glare. When a person becomes the subject of public interest, though, the courts usually allow media coverage—even when the coverage is harmful or obnoxious. A person may lose rights of privacy by becoming a public figure, by being charged with (or the victim of) a crime, or even by granting interviews. Press restraint protects most rape victims. And reporters respected a family's request to withhold the last name of their son, born with a severe immune deficiency and placed in a germ-free "bubble." This restraint lasted until the boy died of the ailment.

People whose reputations or careers have been damaged by a published story may sue for libel. To win such a suit, plaintiffs must prove the material both false and damaging. Public officials suing for libel must also show that the story was published "with knowledge that it was false or with reckless disregard of whether it was false or not" (*New York Times* v. *Sullivan,* 1964). In practice it is hard to prove willful and reckless libel. For example, suits have been brought against such media heavies as the *Washington Post* and CBS News "60 Minutes." The suits uncovered questionable practices but did not win judgments because they could not show "reckless" falsehood. Nor is this the only reason public officials rarely sue for libel. A court case guarantees that the charges receive publicity and makes the official seem to bully the press.

Faced with harassment or career threats, however, public figures are increasingly turning to suits against the press. According to surveys, people feel that society's institutions, including the press, intrude too much on private lives. News executives worry about the public image of TV crews climbing trees outside a presidential aide's home, or newspaper reporters rummaging through an official's garbage can. No doubt this had something to do with CBS's 1982 decision to settle out of court in two multimillion-dollar libel suits brought by public officials against its outlets in Philadelphia and Chicago.

Recently, the courts have eased procedural barriers to libel suits against the media. They may also be edging toward relaxing the *Sullivan* rule. Some cases suggest, for example, a narrower definition of a "public figure." (Those who, like the hero who saves airplane crash victims, are inadvertently thrust into the limelight may be excluded; so might those in the public eye solely from press exposure.) Whether courts will also relax the *Sullivan* test of "reckless falsehood" is unclear.

Libel trial. Comedienne Carol Burnett testifies in her successful libel suit against *National Enquirer*, which accused her of boisterous behavior in a Washington restaurant.

Reporters can also be limited if coverage of criminal trials could affect the outcome. Some convictions have been reversed because of sensational press coverage. To protect such cases, judges have sometimes barred the press from some or all of a court case, even when court sessions were open to the public. Such "gag orders" are fiercely resented by the press; many dispute their constitutionality. The founders were well aware of the evils of private trials; thus, the Sixth Amendment guarantees the right to "a speedy and public trial." A 1976 Supreme Court ruling struck down a gag order on a famous murder trial and suggested other remedies. These included moving the trial to avoid local publicity and filing after-the-fact suits against unfair reporting (*Nebraska Press Association* v. *Stuart*).

Some government dealings are privileged and beyond press freedom. Much government information is given security classification. This ranges from law enforcement investigations and military secrets to certain financial decisions that could cause economic chaos if released early. In the 1982 fiscal year, the federal government created 17.5 million secret documents—98 percent of them originating in the Defense Department and Central Intelligence Agency. Of these documents, a half million were "top secret," 5.5 million "secret," and 11.5 million merely "confidential."

Reporters and editors typically respect classified information, either from a sense of civic duty or a desire to cultivate the goodwill of government news sources. In 1961, for instance, the *New York Times* withheld information about a planned invasion of Cuba (the Bay of Pigs invasion) for fear that advance word would doom the operation. (As it turned out, the invasion failed anyway.)

Certain secrecy rules have been challenged as excessive or inconsistent with a free society. In 1971, the *New York Times* published the so-called "Pentagon Papers," no doubt recalling their part in the Bay of Pigs fiasco a decade earlier. The 7,000-page secret Defense Department study, describing how the U.S. became enmeshed in the Vietnam War, was "leaked" by former security aide Daniel Ellsberg. The Supreme Court ruled (*New York Times Co.* v. *U.S.*, 1971) that the government had been overly cautious in restricting the information and that publication did not harm the nation's security.

Most government records, however, are open to citizens; no reason need be given to request the records. This is the nub of the Freedom of Information Act (FOIA). Enacted in 1966 and strengthened in 1974, it places on government agencies the burden of proving they are entitled to withhold information. Needless to say, agencies protest the cost of FOIA compliance and are ingenious in developing reasons for not complying; these reasons have recently been more sympathetically treated by the Justice Department. Although press groups originate only 5 percent of all FOIA requests, they have staunchly resisted efforts to limit the act.

The scope of press liberty inevitably breeds controversy. The Constitution gives what seems to be a total right to report and publish. But there are competing rights, both for individuals and for national security.

Electronic media　Unlike printed publications, radio and TV have been regulated by the government nearly since their inception. The present law, the Communications Act of 1934 (as amended), firmly sets the electromagnetic spectrum as a national resource to be given out and regulated.

The **Federal Communications Commission** is a seven-person board appointed by the president and approved by the Senate; it grants temporary monopolies (to-five- to-seven-year licenses) to companies likely to run their stations "in the public interest, convenience or necessity." The FCC also regulates interstate and foreign transmissions by wire, cable, and satellite.

The FCC's power over electronic outlets flows from its licensing authority. Licenses are renewed every five (TV) or seven (radio) years. Although bought from the FCC for a small fee, licenses in major markets are, in truth, worth millions of dollars. Licenses are supposed to be granted only to firms that operate in the public interest and meet standards of community service. The FCC has tried, for instance, to curb monopolies in news outlets. This was done by banning papers from owning radio and TV outlets in their communities and by limiting the number of radio and TV outlets owned by a single firm. No one entity may own more than seven stations in each service—AM, FM, or TV. No owner may have two stations of the same service in the same community, nor may owners buy outlets in other media in the same community. TV stations may not buy cable TV franchises. And networks are not allowed to own cable systems. The FCC in 1984 unveiled a liberalized ownership rule (12 stations in each service rather than 7) and planned to lift nearly all ownership limits by 1990. Because of fears voiced over owner concentration, however, the new rule was held in abeyance.

The FCC cannot censor broadcast material, but it does use licensing power to enforce certain standards. But when the FCC moves into program content, it is on controversial ground. It has adopted the so-called **fairness doctrine,** which means licensees must make reasonable efforts to discuss varied views on controversial issues of community importance. A chance for reply must be given—free of charge if no paid sponsor can be found. In the case of elections, equal time must be offered to all candidates.

Many broadcasters believe the fairness doctrine is so ambiguous that it causes stations to avoid controversy. Thus the doctrine's very goal is defeated. But the doctrine has been upheld by the Supreme Court (*Red Lion Broadcasting Co.* v. *FCC,* 1969). "It is the rights of the viewers and the listeners, not the rights of the broadcasters, which are paramount," wrote Justice Byron White for the Court. "It is the purpose of the First Amendment to preserve an uninhibited marketplace of ideas in which truth will ultimately prevail, rather than to countenance monopolization of that market, whether it be by the government itself or a private licensee."

The FCC has recently moved to deregulate broadcasting. While it has by no means quit the licensing business, the FCC has eased program standards and simplified reporting rules. Stations are no longer required to present a minimum amount of news or public affairs programs, or to limit the number of commercials they air each hour. Broadcasters can arrange political debates that exclude minor-party candidates. Abandoning the fairness doctrine altogether has been weighed.

Industry complaints about paperwork and red tape helped bring these changes. More to the point, detailed program standards were designed when there were a few general-purpose outlets. The rules make less sense when there are many stations—six times the number of daily newspapers—and other media catering to the public's specialized needs.

Those who would like to see the FCC upgrade program quality oppose deregulation. One FCC chairman called TV a "vast wasteland" and tried to pressure the industry into higher standards. Citizens' groups voice complaints: programs are filled with sex and violence; children's programs are unhealthy; minorities are portrayed unfairly; and so forth. Given conflicts over the scope of government power over electronic media, it is unclear how far the deregulation drive will go.

The federal government affects the electronic media in yet another way. It helps fund noncommercial radio and TV as an alternative to commercial outlets. The Public Broadcasting Act of 1967 formed the **Corporation for Public Broadcasting** (CPB) to parcel out federal money for noncommercial radio and TV. In 1969, CPB in turn set up the **Public Broadcasting Service (PBS),** an "interconnection service" that schedules, promotes, and distributes shows to local stations. In 1971, CPB set up **National Public Radio** as a programming and interlinking service for that medium. PBS works with stations and agencies to get ideas and find funding for shows or series. Federal funds for public radio and TV have declined in recent years.

THE NEWS GATHERERS

The press corps

The image of the crusading reporter lends journalists a glamor usually reserved for surgeons or trial lawyers. But journalism is at best an unformed profession. There are, for instance, no universal standards for becoming a journalist. Although there are more than 100 accredited journalism schools, many news executives prefer to hire liberal arts graduates or those with a flair for writing and dealing with people.

Who are they? Journalists tend to come from the middle class. They are also well educated. One study found that 98 percent of the Washington press corps had attended college (Hess, 1981). Some assume that journalists are left-wingers; others charge they are unwitting lackeys for business interests that own media outlets. In a recent survey, 59 percent of the journalists questioned said they were middle-of-the-road and so were the organizations they worked for (Friendly, 1983). Most journalists consider themselves independent progressives—open-minded, nonpartisan, and suspicious of all authority.

Where are they?   The vast majority of journalists cover local news for one of the nation's 9,100 newspapers. A medium-sized paper (40,000 circulation) will boast a news staff of 35 or 40 people; it will spend more than $1 million a year on its news operation. Full-time reporters usually cover specialized beats. They might handle city hall, the courts and the police, business, society, sports, or outlying communities.

The average paper rarely covers national politics directly. National news may be covered if it comes through a local official, or through a national figure making a local appearance. A Ralph Nader study found that 72 percent of all daily papers have no Washington reporter or even a *stringer* (someone who contracts to write for a "string" of papers). The same is true for 96 percent of all TV stations and 99 percent of all radio stations. For all but the largest newspapers or chains, national and world news are covered by wire-service or syndicated copy.

Fewer journalists are found in radio and TV than in the print media. Networks hire specialists on the White House, Congress, diplomacy, and the courts;

beyond that, there is little specialized reporting. The average radio or TV station draws at least four fifths of its news from AP or UPI, which present shortened versions of stories sent to the print media. The rest of the news is local, often borrowed from local newspaper leads. News staffs are small. There may be one or two people for a smaller radio or TV station; a handful may work for larger outlets. Almost all are on general assignment; that is, they handle any news story that comes along.

The Washington press corps   Much of the nation's political news and analysis comes from the Washington press corps. This is a diverse group of 4,000 or so journalists. At the top are those whom Timothy Crouse (1973) called "the heavies." These are the correspondents, columnists, and bureau chiefs with so much clout that they have personal access to public officials. Many names are familiar—David S. Broder and Benjamin Bradlee of the *Washington Post*, Tom Wicker and Hedrick Smith of the *New York Times,* Jack Nelson of the *Los Angeles Times*, and columnists Joseph Kraft, George Will, and James J. Kilpatrick.

The largest group is reporters for the nation's papers. Then there are members of the Washington bureaus of major chains. Smaller papers sometimes have one- or two-person bureaus or contract with one of the 200 or so stringers.

The Associated Press and United Press International bureaus are the largest news organizations. These huge news services telegraph stories to thousands of clients throughout the world. Thus, wire-service reporters must be able to write quick leads, summarize detailed events simply, and write in a bland, down-the-middle style.

Though wire-service reporters have beats, they must be ready to fulfill requests from local clients. A Portland editor may call for a story on the Oregon delegation's meeting with the Forest Service over the Mt. St. Helens disaster. Some reporter must then drop what he or she is doing and dig out the story.

"Media heavies." Top row, from left: David Broder, national political reporter; Georgie Anne Geyer, syndicated columnist; James J. Kilpatrick, conservative columnist; Joseph Kraft, foreign affairs columnist. *Bottom row:* Mary McGrory, liberal columnist; Jack Nelson, *Los Angeles Times* Washington bureau chief; Carl Rowan, liberal columnist; George Will, conservative columnist.

Writing for a wire service, one harassed UPI reporter complained, "is like having a thousand mothers-in-law."

The specialized press is also amply represented in Washington. It channels news to business people, trade associations, and other special groups. *Women's Wear Daily* has an alert Washington bureau. So have the *Journal of Commerce*, the *Army Times,* and a host of newsletters and reports. Such reporters rarely show up at White House press conferences or in congressional press galleries. But they busily follow bills or policy statements in committee rooms or the halls of agencies.

The gatekeepers

If reporters are the front lines of the news system, editors and producers are the traffic cops. The term **gatekeeper** is used to describe these obscure but key people who decide what appears in print or on the air. Their function is the same, whether the title is "news editor," "city editor," "wire editor," "film editor," or "executive producer."

Every news operation gets a flood of potential items—from reporters, wire services, news syndicates, and press releases. Only a small part can be presented as news. The available space for stories—the **news hole**—varies with the medium. For newspapers it is about one fourth of the total space; the rest is used for ads. Radio and TV outlets use less than 10 percent of their air time for news or news-related matters. (The one exception is the all-news station.) A half-hour network news show boils down to about 22 minutes of news—10 or 15 stories.

The gatekeeper has a vexing task: fit news items into the tight space, or time, supplied by the medium. One study (Bagdikian, 1971) found that the average gatekeeper scanned five times as many stories as could be used. For listeners or readers, it is as if 80 percent of the world's reported events never happened.

Counting costs What makes gatekeepers decide as they do? Some choices are made when the stories are assigned. Once a reporter has used time and energy to research and write a story, an editor does not want to "kill" it—even if it is dull. In electronic media, coverage costs are even higher. So producers send film crews only to the most promising news events and are apt to use the film once it has been shot. (In small cities, TV reporters may double as camera operators; in large cities, union contracts usually require two-, three-, or four-person crews for every story.)

Cost-conscious gatekeepers do not like to send well-paid reporters or camera crews to wait for something to happen. They prefer to cover scheduled events, such as speeches or press conferences. These events are in turn planned to attract just such notice.

The medium shapes the message Gatekeepers must balance the important with the interesting. They must appeal to a wide range of readers or viewers. In print, editors favor unusual stories with color, conflict, and personalities. Radio news must be brief and fast moving; to build interest, short taped statements or interviews, often procured by phone, add to news stories.

Television producers look for stories with visual interest. Pageants, crowd scenes, and natural disasters are ready-made for TV cameras. An in-depth story may take twice as much air time as a news piece (say, two minutes rather than one). Thus, the simple and direct tends to drive out the complex or abstract.

Critics often fault radio and TV for surface news coverage. The average paper, of course, has far more news. The transcript of a 22-minute nightly network TV news show would not fill half the front page of the *New York Times*. Electronic news also shies away from complex background stories and focuses on colorful, fast-breaking events. Studying TV coverage of the 1972 campaign, Patterson and McClure (1976:21–22) found that TV reports spent far more time on campaign hoopla than on issues or candidates' records. "Watching the evening network news leads to a rather trivial perspective of what elections are all about," they commented. "It trivializes politics, turns it into a game."

What the electronic media lack in depth they make up for in speed and emotional impact. When people want the latest bulletins, they turn to radio or TV. A page of print cannot have the unique impact of, say, 30 seconds of film showing Senator Joseph McCarthy bullying a witness or retreating Vietnamese soldiers clinging to helicopters. Each medium, in short, is best suited for certain types of stories. Each tends to emphasize those stories at the expense of others. In this sense, the medium shapes the message.

Corporate perspectives   How much power do owners or advertisers wield in gatekeeping decisions? No doubt the values of the large corporations that own most media filter into the editorial rooms. Editorial policy, of course, is more tightly controlled than news coverage. Editors are often given a free rein until the front office sends an editorial on a key issue—say, a candidate endorsement. Advertisers, too, sometimes sway editorial decisions. This is especially so in small-city outlets which place a premium on being cordial with Main Street merchants. Larger enterprises can, and often do, assert their independence when news coverage jeopardizes advertisers' goodwill.

Most media outlets are themselves big, costly enterprises. It would be naive to expect them to forsake all big-business interests. Let's say a TV network is part of a conglomerate that also makes books, bowling balls, and bombers. Who would deny that subtle tactics can be used to bring those interests to the public? Also, the heads of news organizations tend to be business managers, not newspeople. Their judgments often clash with journalistic rules revered by reporters and editors.

WHAT IS NEWS?

News is, to put it bluntly, what the news media report. People disagree sharply over what is newsworthy—that is, what news media should report. Newspeople themselves differ over just what and how they should report.

News deals with current events that we need or want to learn about. To be classed as news, events must be *recent* (or at least recently disclosed), *quickly conveyed*, and *relevant* to the audience. Timeliness and immediacy are qualities of newsworthiness. When everyone knows about an event, it ceases to be news. Even though an event may be momentous, it is not newsworthy if it is remote from the public's interests and lives.

Surface versus significance

The debate over the nature of news turns on whether *surface events* or *underlying conditions* should be stressed (Roscho, 1975). This reflects the ancient debate over what reality is. Is it things that can be seen or heard or touched? Or is it basic concepts that can be understood but not directly sensed? If news is the former, it need only be described as correctly as possible. If the latter, it must be explained and interpreted. The former notion dominates, as the following rules of thumb suggest:

1. News media tend to focus on surface events. They describe concrete matters—wars, summit meetings, speeches, and press conferences.
2. One theory says that "names make news." Using this rule, reporters focus on highly visible people who, they assume, fascinate the public. Hence, much attention is paid to celebrities.
3. Surprise or strangeness heightens newsworthiness. There is an old journalistic cliche: "When a dog bites a man, that is not news; when a man bites a dog, *that's* news." The unexpected event stands out more than the expected.
4. Bad news tends to be more intriguing than good news. Danger creates suspense and rivets our attention. Thus, the oft-heard complaint that "you never print any good news" may have merit. When bad news is the norm, though, a sudden flow of good tidings will be newsworthy.
5. Finally, conflict is newsworthy. It makes summing up the event easier; it creates suspense over the outcome. Thus, all kinds of contests—from football games to election campaigns—are news staples.

What is reported therefore simplifies reality. The true complexity of things is distorted. Reported facts are the tip of the iceberg of reality. To be reported, that reality must assume an easily recognizable form: a fire, a wreck, an arrest, a speech, a vote, a price change, a proposal to build a road. Subtle events—a shift in social values, or the decline of a world power—are harder to report. Thus, they are usually left for historians or social analysts. As the distinguished journalist Walter Lippmann once said about the Russian Revolution, "The hardest thing to report is chaos, even if it is evolving chaos."

Is objectivity possible?

With the rise of the mass-audience press in the 19th century, journalists developed the standard of *objectivity*. To appeal to many readers, newspeople found they had to vouch for the truth of their work. Hence, reporters were told to observe accurately and tap reliable sources. "You can't write that unless you can quote somebody!" was a common editor's warning. This rule of thumb survives: during the Watergate inquiry, *Washington Post* editors told reporters Woodward and Bernstein that two sources were needed to back up any statement before it could be printed.

Investigative journalists. Carl Bernstein (left) and Bob Woodward, then metro reporters for the *Washington Post*, dug out the story of a lifetime: the Watergate burglary coverup by the Nixon White House.

If people are given facts as raw material, the argument runs, they can make up their own minds about what the facts mean. The American Society of Newspaper Editors' Canons of Journalism, written in 1923, express the norms of objective and impartial reporting: "Sound practice makes a clear distinction between news reports and expressions of opinion. News reports should be free from opinion or bias of any kind. This rule does not apply to so-called special articles unmistakably devoted to advocating or characterized by a signature authorizing the writer's own conclusions and interpretations." The 1947 report of the Commission on Freedom of the Press, the Hutchins Commission, emphasized this concept: news should be truthful, complete, and intelligent accounts of the day's events in a context that gives them meaning.

More recently, the norm of objectivity has come under fire. Radio and TV have broken the print journalists' hold on fast-breaking news. Thus, the print media have sought new roles. News magazines such as *Time* and *Newsweek* show that how stories are presented can be as important as the facts themselves; opinions are inserted in the guise of adroit phrases and witty lines. Columnists such as Jack Anderson blend investigation and comment.

Thoughtful reporters admit that biases are inherent in picking and editing stories. Some reporters slant stories one way or another in response to their editors' preferences. Also, the muckraking, or crusading, tradition remains alive among journalists. It is especially fashionable in times of trouble or discontent. Thus, in the 1960s there arose a "new journalism" in which reporters told readers their biases, often recording in detail their personal reactions to what they were covering.

The press is often charged with ideological bias. Studies have detected little, if any, ideological slanting of the news. What has been found, however, is the more subtle kind of "bias" we have noted: biases for the concrete over the abstract, for the anecdotal over the analytical, and for tried-and-true formulas over the unconventional.

The debate over how factual reporting can be embraces two issues. First, as we have seen, how much space should be given to *interpretation* as opposed to concrete events? Most reporters and editors think that readers need some interpretation to put the facts into context. The amount varies with the occasion: wire-service stories on breaking news events have little interpretation; news magazines and many papers often run background stories or opinion pieces.

The second issue is *objectivity* versus *bias*. Reporters' norms stress objectivity, and most stories in print or on the air reflect this objectivity. But there is a place for crusading journalism; and the highest rewards, like Pulitzer prizes, often go to those who move outside the everyday canons.

Reporters and sources

Most news doesn't just happen: it is arranged. Some people know more than others or can express themselves better. These people are the *sources* reporters rely on for their stories.

Occasionally the reporter's sources are anonymous. However, the reporter's editor should be privy to the sources. When reporters and editors are casual about their sources, the results can be disastrous. A sensational *Washington Post* story, "Jimmy's World," about an 8-year-old drug addict, proved to be a fabrication. The hoax was uncovered only after the story won a Pulitzer prize; the prize was withdrawn and the reporter fired.

Relationships with sources are usually formal—an interview, press conference, or press release. Hess (1981: 17–18) found that Washington reporters conducted about five interviews for every story, but that they rarely used documents or other written sources.

Reporters and sources are locked in a love-hate relationship. Each has what the other wants: sources have information; reporters have the power to create publicity, the lifeblood of political careers. Whatever their private feelings, re-

"You might wonder why I called a press conference and you might also wonder who I am."

Press contacts. Lawmakers being interviewed in the Capitol by radio reporters after a key vote.

porters sense that they cannot disclose certain things if they want future interviews. Sources, for their part, know that getting friendly with key press corps members can pay off in good publicity.

Scheduled events, such as press conferences and news releases, are the bread and butter of day-to-day news gathering. For sources, such devices control the timing and format of the information they give out. Reporters find them a great convenience. They can avoid the time-consuming task of tracking down stories. In a news-conscious place like Washington, reporters' daily schedules are easily filled up by going to press conferences and reading documents and press releases. Though such practices are scorned as spoon-feeding, nearly all reporters rely on them.

Press conferences Presidential press conferences are the most visible public exchanges between a news source and reporters. Started by Herbert Hoover, they have become an institution. The press expects them to be held periodically. Franklin Roosevelt, who had a warm relationship with reporters, held them twice a week. Harry Truman had one every 10 days; Dwight Eisenhower and John Kennedy held press briefings about every two weeks. So did Lyndon Johnson, until his ratings in the polls began to dive. Nixon, who hated journalists as a class, held few. He preferred off-the-cuff interviews with friendly journalists.

Articulate presidents use press conferences to capture public attention and build support. Presidents prepare for them thoroughly; press aides compile

Informal press conference. Franklin Roosevelt, who liked reporters and had close ties with them, held twice-a-week press conferences around his desk in the Oval Office.

briefing books and sometimes plant questions with friendly reporters. For their part, reporters (according to one White House correspondent) "go in there memorizing our own little question and barely pay attention to the other questions." *Washington Post* veteran Haynes Johnson (Washington Post Writers Group, 1976) explained some of the drawbacks of the press conference:

> Questions are often self-serving, or occasionally obsequious. There are all too few sharp exchanges, or pointed follow-ups or relentless pursuits of the sort that provide fresh insights into the president's thinking, or help to explain his actions. Important topics are often ignored or glossed over. Under the eye of the television camera, the conferences have been transformed into nationwide theater. Style, not substance, wins acclaim and builds reputations. Some of the questions are, in reality, speeches or personal points of view. The press, like other professions, is not without its prima donnas.

The result is not only unenlightening, it also plays into the president's hands. "The press conference had become a form of political theater," Broder (1981) observes, "played by the president to the TV audience, in the presence of an obstreperous and distracting mob of reporters."

To quell the clamor of post-Watergate press conferences, President Reagan's advisers instituted several reforms. Most important, reporters must stay seated and raise their hands for recognition; they no longer leap and shout to gain the president's attention. Reporters have assigned seats, to help the president call them by name and segregate the tough questioners from those who can be counted on for softer queries. Amplifiers hidden in the president's bulletproof podium help him hear the questions. "Reagan's press conferences are not nearly

Media event. Reporters clamor for attention but White House press conferences are structured events.

the spontaneous encounters the average television viewer might suspect," one White House reporter (DeFrank, 1982: 27) comments. "On the contrary, they have evolved into elaborately choreographed exercises in damage control."

Radio and TV networks typically grant White House requests for free air time for announcements or major speeches. Government-licensed outlets, stations do this in the public interest. This "free use of an expensive commodity" allows presidents to choose when they appear (Minow et al., 1973). Occasionally, however, White House requests are turned down because the purpose is deemed too partisan. Opposition leaders sometimes ask for equal time to reply to the president; some of these requests—for example, to counter the State of the Union address—are granted.

Off the record   A step removed from formal press briefings are off-the-record comments made to help journalists prepare their stories. They flatter reporters because of their air of confidentiality; also, they provide the makings of a "scoop" without legwork. They are just as useful for officials who can shape coverage without being quoted.

Informal rules of the game set three categories of off-the-record remarks: the *not-for-attribution* quote ("a senior White House official said . . ."); the *back-grounder* ("the administration is worried that . . ."); and the *deep backgrounder*, used only on the reporter's own authority. Much off-the-record information is deliberately "leaked" to the press. A leak tests the political waters. Or it airs a controversial view that cannot be expressed officially. Most frequently, it tells the source's side of a story—as often as not after the source has lost some bureaucratic struggle. "If you quote me, I'll deny I said it," many off-the-record sources say.

Backgrounders are controversial. The Associated Press code is not clear-cut: "News sources should be disclosed unless there is a clear reason not to do so. When it is necessary to protect the confidentiality of a source, the reason should be given." Reporters publicly deplore the use of backgrounders, but most use confidential sources. A Washington correspondent once started a group called the Frontgrounders, which held only on-the-record interviews. It was soon abandoned because few officials would grant such interviews.

Off-the-record remarks also cause friction between sources and reporters. When the remarks are tantalizing, however, the media are apt to use them. The 1984 presidential campaign featured an anti-Jewish reference by candidate Jesse Jackson, made informally but eventually reported. Then, President Reagan was quoted in an off-hand jest made while testing his microphone before a radio broadcast. "My fellow Americans," he said, "I am pleased to tell you I have just signed legislation which outlaws Russia forever. The bombing begins in five minutes." The networks had agreed that informal remarks prior to the president's radio talks would be off the record; and, although the remark was recorded, the networks hesitated to use it. When written reports filtered out, however, they caused an uproar abroad. So the networks aired the tapes and announced they would henceforth be free to use remarks that in fact left the studio. ("If it's piped out, it's fair game.") Meanwhile, the media announced they would no longer protect off-the-record comments made on candidates' campaign planes.

The editorial tradition

The news media cherish their right to comment on events—normally in editorials. Early papers in this nation were savagely partisan, usually allied with a political party or faction. Today's print media are more restrained (most call themselves "independent"). But they still devote a good deal of thought and craftsmanship to their editorials. Most editorial pages include letters to the editor and syndicated columns by such writers as David S. Broder, Joseph Kraft, George Will, and James J. Kilpatrick.

"STONE WALLS DO NOT A PRISON MAKE"
A Prophecy from Harper's Weekly of January 8, 1872.

Thomas Nast. Boss Tweed shown as jailbird in famous 19th-century cartoon.

Editorial cartoons are a special form of commentary. Dating from the earliest days of newspapers, cartoons make a special contribution to politics. Artist Thomas Nast (1840–1902) invented the Democratic donkey and the Republican elephant. His vicious cartoons ruined the career of one of the strongest political bosses, New York Tammany Hall chief William Marcy Tweed. Nast's tradition flourishes in the work of such modern cartoonists as Herbert Block and Pat Oliphant of the *Washington Post,* Tony Auth of the *Philadelphia Inquirer,* and Paul Szep of the *Boston Globe* (Hess and Kaplan, 1975).

Electronic media have a hazier editorial tradition. As users of publicly owned air waves, radio and TV stations must give access to varying points of view. They also risk offending segments of their broad audience. Still, editorials do appear on the air. The high point of electronic commentary, most critics agree, was in the 1950s and 1960s, when "CBS Reports" and "NBC White Papers" brought distinguished commentary on many topics. Edward R. Murrow produced notable exposes of McCarthyism and the plight of migrant workers. Stricter application of the fairness doctrine later dampened network enthusiasm for this sort of program. But local stations often air editorials, opposing viewpoints. Commentators such as Bill Moyers, Roger Mudd, and David Brinkley enliven regular newscasts.

The news magazine concept came to TV in CBS's highly successful "60 Minutes" and its imitators. Strictly speaking, it is more interpretive journalism than commentary. PBS pioneered with several successful shows—among them

"Washington Week in Review," "Wall Street Week," and "The Lawmakers." As major networks decline and cable TV airs more varied programs, we can expect more specialized news and commentary shows.

THE MEDIA'S POLITICAL IMPACT

The media intrude on every phase of public life. Yet their precise impact is a matter of keen debate. Many theories and research studies center on media effects, but no one is quite certain what they all add up to.

To round out our survey of political communications, we will focus on three areas of media influence: (1) political socialization and learning, (2) campaigns and elections, and (3) the conduct and performance of government.

Political learning

By providing information about politics and government, the media help to socialize people into politics. Media images of politicians are among the first political things children are exposed to. Such exposure is reinforced through a lifetime of viewing or reading.

Children are exposed to media in large doses. Grade-school children spend about 27 hours a week watching TV—nearly as much time as they spend in school. Recent studies show that mass media rival parents and teachers as sources of political information (Kraus and Davis, 1976). Also, those who teach children—mainly parents and teachers—lean a great deal on media-based information.

What children learn and how they evaluate it depend on their stage of mental development. Very young children respond to concrete objects and events; by their teens, young people can cope with abstract concepts and complex reasoning. At first, images of authority figures (parents, presidents, or law officers) are highly positive. But these images fade as children grow up, learn more, and lose some of their idealism (Comstock et al., 1978).

Adults are also heavy users of the media. The average American spends nearly three hours a day watching TV; but "watching" may be casual and offhand. He or she also spends two hours listening to radio, 20 minutes reading a paper, and 10 minutes reading a magazine. Time spent with the mass media has risen by 40 percent since the advent of TV. It comes mostly at the expense of other leisure activities (Robinson, 1977). Figure 8–2 shows the upward trend in TV use. College-educated people conform to the trend, but at a lower level.

Television is the broadest source of information. Since the early 1960s, TV has been the chief source of news; today about 65 percent of all people rely chiefly on TV for their news (see Figure 8–3). More than half rate TV as the most believable news source.

More than 4 out of every 10 people report that they get all their news from TV. Those who get their news from a mixture of sources are not only better informed, they are also more interested and active in politics. Those who lean wholly on TV are apt to be passive spectators in other ways as well. They are an "inadvertent audience"; they just happen to be in front of the set when political news is broadcast, and don't take the trouble to tune it out. Few people seek out political news on TV. "No matter how much some critics may deplore

FIGURE 8–2

Trends in Hours of Television Viewing

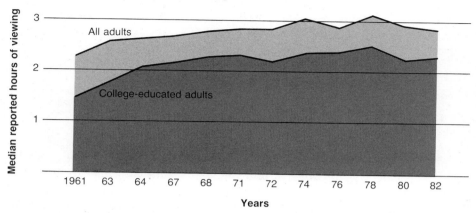

Source: The Roper Organization. Used with permission of the Television Information Office.

the sketchiness of television's political coverage," Ranney (1983: 11) observes, "the fact is that television gives considerably more attention to politics than most viewers feel they need or want."

Subtle values—transmitted through entertainment, comic strips, and sports—affect our approach to politics. Old films portray Knute Rockne inspiring his team to "win one for the Gipper"; modern coaches declare that "nice guys finish last." Through these, citizens absorb values that apply as much to waging campaigns or fighting wars as to playing football. Many such values are conveyed by the media even though they are not labeled political.

What exactly do people learn from the media? How does this knowledge shape their behavior? The conclusions are tentative. The media's strongest role is in giving visibility or importance to a problem or personality, the so-called **agenda-setting function.** People may or may not learn facts from the media. But they

FIGURE 8–3

Major Sources of News

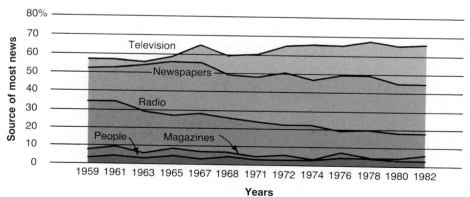

Note: Totals add up to more than 100 percent because multiple responses were allowed.
Source: The Roper Organization. Used with permission of the Television Information Office.

take cues about what and who should be taken seriously (Shaw and McCombs, 1977).

As for specific information, the picture is less clear. It seems that people gain only limited facts from the media; they remember little but can recall details mentioned to them (Graber, 1980: 138–41). Factual learning is greatest if people have little prior knowledge. The most important things people gain from the media are general feelings about events: apathy, cynicism, fear, trust, acquiescence, or support.

The media in elections

Campaigns and elections cannot help but be media events. After all, they are efforts to communicate and persuade. Some campaign communications—ads, brochures, and billboards—are controlled by campaigners themselves. Other communications, like mass media coverage, lie outside the campaigner's control. Campaigners want to turn media coverage to their advantage: not only is it free, but it is more believable than paid advertising.

Campaign communication has passed through at least five distinct stages (Heard, 1966). At first, candidates engaged in little public campaigning, leaving things in the hands of supporters and the partisan press. Andrew Jackson's election ushered in the "torchlight era" of stump speeches, parades, and costly entertainment. An era of campaign literature—ads and mass mailings—came after 1880. This was displaced in 1928 by radio campaigning; in turn, this was displaced by TV in the 1950s. At each stage, politicians aimed their messages past the immediate audience and at the press who held the key to the larger audience.

Media campaigning   Political contests are ready-made for the mass media, and they draw extensive coverage. Media attention shapes today's electoral politics in several key ways.

First, it has diluted party influence, especially in presidential elections. Candidates no longer win their party's approval, then appeal to the public through the media. Today they go over party leaders' heads through the media to win popular acceptance and gain nominations. Paid consultants can usually give more assistance in media campaigns than party officials.

Second, the media help screen potential candidates at the nominating stage, when party labels do not separate the candidates. Reporters describe candidate behavior and personalities, try to name winners and losers in primary caucuses and elections, and pinpoint candidates' errors.

Third, the media shape alternatives. Certain types of candidates are likely to do better than others in making media appeals. Franklin Roosevelt was a master at radio communication. The fact that he was confined to a wheelchair might have impaired his impact on television. Ronald Reagan, a long-time actor, took to TV as if he had invented it. A host of lesser TV-age candidates have come on the scene sporting good looks and informal speaking styles.

Fourth, the media have altered the selection process itself. They have encouraged the spread of "open" procedures like primaries; they have made public less formal events like caucuses and straw polls. These contests have rendered anticlimactic the nominating conventions, which themselves have been streamlined to accommodate the media.

Covering the horse race   Campaigns are closely covered by the media. The

TABLE 8–2

Content of Presidential Election News, 1976

Subject of coverage	Network evening newscasts	Erie Times/ News	L.A. Herald Examiner	L.A. Times	Time/ Newsweek
Game					
Winning and losing	24	26	25	20	23
Strategy, logistics	17	19	18	19	22
Appearances, hoopla	17	14	14	12	9
Subtotal	58	59	57	51	54
Substance					
Issues, policies	18	19	18	21	17
Traits, records	7	6	5	8	11
Endorsements	4	4	5	6	4
Subtotal	29	29	28	35	32
Other	13	12	15	14	14
Total	100	100	100	100	100

Note: Table based on a random sample of the election news coverage provided by each news source. The network figures are the combined average for the ABC, NBC, and CBS evening news programs. The figures for the *Erie Times* and *Erie News* and those in *Time* and *Newsweek* also have been combined because the separate figures were substantially the same.

Source: Thomas E. Patterson, *The Mass Media Election* (New York: Praeger Publishers, 1980), p. 24.

clash of personalities, the campaign appearances, and the uncertainty of results attract reporters like moths to a flame. As Peters (1976: 56) remarked, reporters know "much about the process of being elected and little about what the government does or how it could be improved." So, campaign stories stress the "game" or "horse race" rather than issues or policy positions (see Table 8–2).

What is more, today's journalists stress the game more than their predecessors did. In the 1948 presidential election, candidates' official speeches and statements dominated the news (Berelson, Lazarsfeld, and McPhee, 1954: 236). Today, reporters balk at being vehicles for candidates' statements; they prefer conveying the contest in their own way. Voter interest in the substance of elections seems to be losing ground. Two thirds of voter conversations recorded in 1948 concerned candidate positions and qualifications; in 1976, only a third focused on substance (Patterson, 1980: 105).

THE GAME OF POLITICS, ACCORDING TO TELEVISION NEWS

[According to television news] politics is essentially a game played by individual politicians for personal advancement, gain, or power. The game is a competitive one, and the players' principal activities are those of calculating and pursuing strategies designed to defeat competitors and to achieve their goals (usually election to public office). Of course, the game takes place against a backdrop of governmental institutions, public problems, policy debates, and the like, but these are noteworthy only insofar as they affect, or are used by, players in pursuit of the game's rewards. The game is played before an audience—the electorate—which controls most of the prizes, and players therefore constantly attempt to make a favorable impression. In consequence, there is an endemic tendency for players to exaggerate their good qualities and to minimize their bad ones, to be deceitful, to engage in hypocrisies, to manipulate appearances; though inevitable, these tendencies are bad tendencies . . . and should be exposed. They reduce the electorate's ability to make its own discriminating choices, and they may hide players' infractions of the game's rules, such as those against corruption and lying.

Source: Paul H. Weaver, "Is Television News Biased?" *Public Interest,* Winter 1972, p. 69.

On the spot. Gary Hart pressed by media in an appearance.

Reporters try to heighten the sense of competition. The media are eager to name winners and losers in primaries, caucuses, or straw polls; if there are no clear winners, the press tries to declare them. Before the caucuses and primaries begin, this means relying on candidate-preference surveys—notoriously unreliable at this early stage.

Once the balloting begins, the press starts calling the race. Carter's 1976 campaign took off when he won the Iowa caucus votes. (Actually "uncommitted" won with 37 percent of the vote to Carter's 28 percent.) Four years later, George Bush gained credibility in Iowa. As Bush's press secretary confessed (Bonafede, 1980a: 1134), "The ride we got out of Iowa gave us an enormous boost—probably undeserved. It projected us into a front-running status we did not deserve. It seemed to indicate that we were in a two-man race. Our expectations became too high. . . . But there is no doubt about it: a ride by the press makes a lot of converts." The Iowa caucuses proved pivotal for Gary Hart's 1984 drive. Although Mondale won impressively, Hart came in second with 15 percent (12,600 votes). The press announced that Hart had bumped John Glenn as the leading alternative to Mondale, and seven days later that prophecy was fulfilled in New Hampshire's primary.

Early nominating contests, or those competing with few other news events, get extra attention from reporters. The Iowa caucuses and the New Hampshire primary are especially hyped as bellwethers. (For Democrats this is ironic: neither state is found in the party's presidential column very often.) One study of the 1976 primaries found that the New Hampshire results received 170 times as much network news time per Democratic vote as the outcome in New York (Robinson, 1977: 80–81). The result is front-loading of the selection process: Candidates who surge ahead in the early contests are "front-runners" who hold "commanding leads"; they may be pressed by "leading challengers" who emerge from the pack to be taken seriously by the press.

Another focus of press attention is candidates' mistakes; misstatements, slips of the tongue, or other errors are given undue attention. In 1972, Democratic front-runner Edmund Muskie was sidetracked by the "crying incident"; he allegedly broke down while answering vicious personal attacks by the right-wing *Manchester* (N.H.) *Union-Leader.* Jesse Jackson's alleged anti-Jewish slur was taken

" QUICK... WHAT'S THE CAPITAL OF WYOMING?"

up by reporters in 1984. In both cases, reporters seized on the event to dramatize traits they had seen in the candidates—temperament in Muskie's case, arrogance in Jackson's.

Candidates and their managers, by the same token, try to mold the view of reality conveyed by the media. They try to foster the picture of victory against great odds, no matter what the real situation. As Elizabeth Drew noted (1976: 89), "A classic problem for candidates is how to inflate their prospects in order to attract allies and followers without creating a standard against which they can be measured unfavorably."

When reporters are unsure how to interpret events, they sometimes follow the lead of influential reporters. In the *New York Times*, R. W. (Johnny) Apple wrote that Senator McGovern had made a surprisingly strong showing in the 1972 Iowa caucuses. That prompted other reporters to take up the same theme. The same happened in 1976, when Apple reported that Carter was doing well in Iowa; the story itself became a political event. Crouse (1973) called this "pack journalism."

In reporting on conventions, reporters are eager to exploit conflict and division. They often blow it out of proportion. The TV networks, committed to extended convention coverage, may seize on minor stories during a dull convention. The trial balloon of Gerald Ford's vice presidential candidacy in 1980 was such a case. It was pushed by some TV reporters to heighten interest in the Reagan-controlled convention (Bonafede, 1980b). Because conventions now tend to ratify earlier choices, the networks have backed away from giving gavel-to-gavel coverage.

The media are more potent during the nominating campaign than during the general election. In the campaign's early phases, candidate visibility is a key variable; after that, it is assured, at least in presidential races. Also at the nominating stage, voters don't have party labels to guide them; hence, they are more susceptible to impressions conveyed by the media.

Studies of media influence in general election campaigns yield mixed results. Most show little effect on vote preferences (Patterson and McClure, 1976). But there is some evidence that newspaper accounts and endorsements especially can influence voters (Erickson, 1976). As in nominations, general election contests are usually reported as horse races, with little attention paid to candidate stands or qualifications.

Televised debates   Candidate debates are the most notable use of TV to bring campaigns to the people. Though the direct effect of debates on election results is mixed, their impact on campaign strategy and activists' opinion is considerable.

Modern debates began in 1960 with four TV appearances of John Kennedy and Richard Nixon. Most observers (including the candidates) thought the crucial first debate turned the tide in Kennedy's favor. It showed him as vigorous, well spoken, and capable; he seemed fully the equal of Vice President Nixon (who was tired, ill, and badly made up for the cameras). Actually, opinion polls showed little overall opinion shift as a result of the debates (Katz and Feldman, 1962). But Kennedy's impressive showing sparked many Democrats worried about the candidate's youth and inexperience.

The next debates were in 1976. President Ford and contender Jimmy Carter appeared three times; the vice presidential nominees appeared once. As before, the debates seemed to have little impact on voter intentions. But again,

Presidential debates. The 1960 debate between Democratic presidential candidate John F. Kennedy and Republican candidate Richard M. Nixon [upper left] was the first of the modern presidential debates. It helped Kennedy establish himself as a credible candidate. Jimmy Carter was the challenger in the 1976 debates [upper right] against incumbent President Gerald Ford. The debates may have helped popularize Carter, who only a few months before had been referred to in the press as "Jimmy Who?" In 1980, the Carter-Reagan debate [lower left] pitted a defensive incumbent Jimmy Carter against Ronald Reagan, an experienced movie actor. In 1984, the Reagan–Mondale debates [lower right] again helped the challenger, but did not change the electoral result.

an incident received much commentary in the press. President Ford made a mistake about Eastern Europe in the second debate which fostered the view that Carter had won the debate.

In 1980 President Carter and Ronald Reagan debated only once. (Carter refused to take part in an earlier debate featuring Reagan and Independent John Anderson.) The event, only a week before the balloting, probably helped fuel a last-minute Reagan surge. Carter tried to paint Reagan as a dangerous extremist by harping on the need for international disarmament. Reagan parried these thrusts and portrayed himself as an average guy. Toward the end of the debate, he moved in with the clincher; voters should ask themselves, he said, whether they were better off than they had been four years before. For most voters, the answer was obvious.

Several aspects of debates should be mentioned. First, reporters tend to cover debates as they do other aspects of campaigns—as personal contests rather than as forums for issues. The press is eager to declare who won or lost and is on the lookout for mistakes or misstatements.

Second, fearing missteps in such confrontations, candidates and their managers try to limit the elements of confrontation. The debates are often genteel affairs. There is little real clash of personalities or views, little or no dialogue between the candidates, and little real follow-up by the questioners. (Debates among contenders for the 1984 Democratic nomination were loosely structured, allowing candidates to question each other and respond to audience queries; but the Reagan-Mondale debates followed the traditional format.)

Third, debates seem to have scant direct impact on how we vote. Indeed, candidate performances tend to reinforce earlier views rather than make converts (Sears, 1977). This is important, though: a candidate's performance may, as in 1960 (Nixon versus Kennedy), fire up (or dampen) enthusiasm of partisan activists.

Finally, debates are tactically more desirable for candidates who are "behind." Those who are not incumbents, who are less known or respected, or who trail in the polls need to prove themselves and are thus likely to push for debates. Candidates who already have an advantage do not want to give exposure to their challengers.

Presidential debates show challengers on an equal footing with incumbents or front-runners. Kennedy's youth and inexperience were not an issue after he proved himself a match for Nixon, vice president for eight years. Carter, relatively unknown, looked presidential by meeting toe-to-toe with President Ford. Fears about Reagan's hawkishness faded as he turned aside Carter's attacks and showed himself a reasonable, reliable man.

Candidates and their managers understand the equalizing effect of debates. Smarting from 1960, Nixon refused to debate in 1968 or 1972 when he was front-runner. Lyndon Johnson took the same stand in 1964. In 1976 and 1980, challengers pressed for debates; incumbents resisted until sagging polls convinced them to gamble. Challenger Mondale wanted six debates in 1984 but got only two.

Presidential debates are now a key part of campaign strategy. Whether they are actually held depends on "whether in the future both candidates will calculate that they stand to gain more than they will lose by debating" (Ranney, 1983: 28).

Media effects on results Many believe the mass media shape election outcomes. But research findings are mixed. One of the earliest scientific studies of voting behavior was the so-called Erie County (Ohio) study. The authors concluded that the media had little impact on voting behavior (Lazarsfeld, Berelson, and Gaudet, 1944). Other studies bear this out. One, of the 1972 presidential elections, concluded that TV network newscasts had little impact on voters (Patterson and McClure, 1976).

Most experts think media sharpen or reinforce existing opinions rather than change them. Most people hold basic attitudes that color their assessment of anything they read or see. This is why two people can draw opposite conclusions from the same material. Also, many suffer from what one writer calls "videomalaise"; they are cynical and distrust the press.

But the media have a unique ability to lend visibility to candidates or ideas. The media may not affect *how* something is viewed, but they do determine *whether* it is viewed at all.

This is why politicians say: "I don't care what you print about me—just spell my name right!" It accounts for politicians' constant struggle to get their names and faces before the public, to achieve name recognition. And it may help explain why the most visible politicians—longtime incumbents or candidates with famous names—seem to have success, other things being equal.

There is one controversial issue: whether media announcements of results before the polls close affect the outcome. Survey procedures are sophisticated and include "exit polls," in which samples of voters are interviewed as they leave voting places. Thus, TV can sometimes project winners well before voting is over. Politicans believe this discourages people from going to the polls. The evidence is mixed. However, Carter's early defeat and concession in 1980

Fair or unfair? Exit polls allow media to "call" elections even before the polls close—a controversial practice.

is credited with discouraging Democratic voters on the West Coast, probably causing the defeat of some representatives in close races. Media executives dispute the results and assert their right to announce projections as soon as they are available. Moves to limit projections are likely to founder on the First Amendment. So for now the matter is left to voluntary restraints by the media themselves.

The media and governing

The media greatly affect day-to-day conduct of government. As already seen, government officials and reporters are locked in a relationship of mutual need and conflict.

Media and the branches of government   Presidents and other chief executives are prime targets of media coverage because they are easily described, understood, and reported. Presidents are almost always in the spotlight. From Theodore Roosevelt to Ronald Reagan, presidents have used their unique media coverage to focus public attention and spark support. As we will see in Chapter 9, presidents and their staffs spend much of their time planning and scheduling activities for greatest media exposure.

In contrast, Congress is harder to cover. Not that Congress is ignored; it gets coverage equal to the president's, even in presidential election years (Graber, 1980: 66). Yet Congress is at a disadvantage. With more than 500 politicians, it has no single focus of attention. Its work is scattered and often dull—not the stuff of TV drama.

In 1979, the House cautiously brought in closed-circuit TV coverage of floor proceedings. Fearing bad publicity, the House kept control over the cameras. Normally, only speakers are shown (so that no empty seats would appear). The proceedings are beamed to Capitol Hill offices and, via C-SPAN (Cable-Satellite

Public Affairs Network), to cable subscribers throughout the country. The Senate has considered but rejected TV coverage of its sessions.

Congressional committee hearings are sometimes televised, and a few provide high drama. The Senate inquiry into organized crime (1950), the Army-McCarthy hearings (1954), the Watergate hearings (1973), and the Nixon impeachment deliberations (1974) were all windows into the legislative process.

Many journalists cover the legislative output of Congress, but few cover individual members—their voting records or roles in committee or floor deliberations (Davidson and Oleszek, 1985). So local newspapers, radio, and TV outlets—most without Washington reporters—rely on legislators themselves for information. Most legislators organize their offices and their schedules to provide such information. Virtually all senators and most representatives have one or more press aides. Both chambers have recording studios, where members can tape radio or TV messages at costs far below commercial rates. Most legislators make use of such services. Such activities help inform constituents and aid reelection as well.

The judiciary gets the least media exposure of the three branches of government. The nature of court proceedings is partly at fault. Decisions are complex and must be interpreted by skilled communicators; few news operations can afford to assign experienced and skilled reporters. Thus, reporting of the courts seems more sketchy and less accurate than that of other government branches (Grey, 1968).

Government officials know they need sympathetic press coverage to promote their programs and protect their jobs. Some (for example, former Secretary of State Henry Kissinger and former Special Trade Representative Robert Strauss) cultivate the press corps and are rewarded with generous publicity and friendly treatment. Agencies, too, realize they must tend their public image to win the funding and programs they want. All have public affairs offices; highly visible agencies—the military services, the FBI, and NASA—work hard to polish their media images.

Yet officials are also wary of the press's watchful eye. The media cannot cover all government activities; but officials know that reports of "waste, fraud and abuse" invite negative publicity. Many agencies lack glamor and are prone to bad publicity. Their PR goal is damage control, in which "no news is good news."

Media effects on governing Communications media are politically important not just because politicians and officials spend so much time catering to their needs. The media actually shape government processes and institutions, and even the content of policies. Ranney's (1983: 124–55) arguments about TV's effects apply to other media as well. Though certainly debatable, his ideas deserve serious thought:

1. The media may compress the time decision makers have to initiate programs and achieve results. Television and print media are eager for stories and action; the media world moves fast and favors neat solutions.
2. Media coverage may reduce options by spotlighting proposed solutions prematurely, inviting criticism, and eliminating alternatives from consideration.
3. By highlighting leaders who simplify policies, take extreme stands, and fight courageously, the media may weaken the less glamorous processes of compromising and building coalitions.

4. By spotlighting elected officials and ignoring bureaucratic politics, the media may have "helped the unelected officials in both the legislative and executive branches to fill the policy making vacuums left by the declining power of the elected officials" (Ranney, 1983: 155).

Finally, the communications media tend to reinforce traditional American distaste for government and politicians. Journalists are cynical about politics; they belittle politicians' motives, words, and actions. This may lower public confidence in government institutions. Of course, many people—including journalists—expect the press to act as a sort of fourth estate, watching over officials and keeping them responsible. How faithfully the media play this role is open to question.

"Were it left to me to decide whether we should have a government without newspapers, or newspapers without government," Thomas Jefferson observed, "I should not hesitate a moment to prefer the latter." Yet, when he was president and received barbed criticisms from the press, Jefferson lamented that "the man who never looks into a newspaper is better informed than he who reads them; inasmuch as he who knows nothing is nearer to truth than he whose mind is filled with falsehoods and errors." Such is the ambivalence between the press and government.

CONCLUSIONS

Several major points emerge from our study of the media's role in politics.

1 For political events to have any impact, they must be communicated. Communication is a complex process involving sources, messages, media (or channels), audiences, and effects.

2 News gatherers work for many news outlets, more often for print media than for electronic media. News outlets in the United States are usually local, but broadcast networks and wire services are national. All media forms are becoming diversified.

3 News sources and reporters are locked in a mutually dependent relationship. For mutual convenience, formal contacts—such as press conferences and press releases—are favored. But there is also a hierarchy of off-the-record contacts. This includes "leaks" which serve the needs of both reporters and sources but may hamper decision making.

4 Gatekeepers determine what news will be passed on to the public. Each medium has certain advantages and disadvantages for handling different types of news.

5 Newsworthiness involves timeliness and immediacy. Two basic issues surround the concept of news: Should it interpret or should it just report concrete events? Should (or can) news be truly objective, or must it necessarily be biased?

6 Everyone agrees that the media shape our politics in key ways; but commentators disagree on the exact effects. The media are especially important in political learning, both for children and adults; political campaigning; and the relationships between government agencies and the public.

FURTHER READING

GRABER, DORIS (1980) Mass Media and American Politics. 2d ed. Washington, D.C.: Congressional Quarterly Press. A collection of essays on how media affect the political agenda, office holders, and foreign and domestic policy making.

HALBERSTAM, DAVID (1981) The Powers that Be. New York: Alfred A. Knopf. A fascinating anecdotal history of the rise of current media giants: CBS, Time Inc., *The New York Times, The Washington Post,* and *The Los Angeles Times.*

HESS, STEPHEN (1981) The Washington Reporters. Washington, D.C.: Brookings Institution. A survey of members of the Washington press corps—their backgrounds, views, jobs, and work habits.

RANNEY, AUSTIN (1983) Channels of Power. New York: Basic Books. A sensible survey and evaluation of literature bearing on the role TV has played in shaping our current politics and government.

PART 4

Government Policymakers

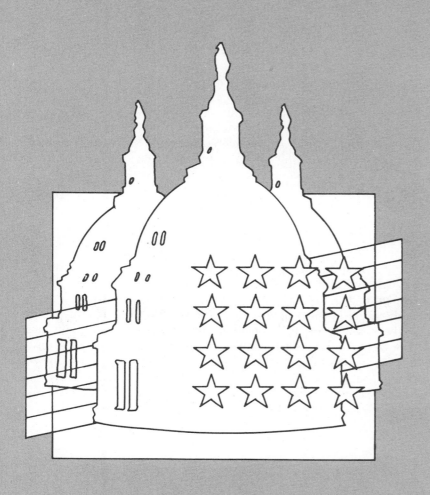

9
The Presidency: Promise and Reality

In his first year in the White House, Ronald Reagan dominated Congress as few presidents have. His spending and tax proposals framed the debate. When Democratically-controlled House committees came up with spending cuts that Reagan and his Budget Director, David Stockman, considered inadequate, a Republican substitute was hastily drafted the day before the floor vote. The GOP package (called Gramm-Latta II, after its authors, Representatives Phil Gramm and Delbert Latta) was so quickly put together that it was filled with penciled-in additions, crossed-out items, misnumbered pages, and even the name and phone number of a budget staff aide. Errors and all, it passed the House.

The president's success infuriated Democrats, who held a majority in the House. "A popular president is attempting to tyrannize a whole Congress," declared Rules Committee Chairman Richard Bolling (D-Mo.) "I don't know what it will take to satisfy them," huffed Majority Leader Jim Wright (D-Tex.), "I guess for the Congress to resign and give them our voting proxy cards" (Davidson and Oleszek, 1981: 334).

When the dust had settled, Congress recovered its composure soon enough. Needless to say, the legislators didn't resign or turn in their voting cards. In a year's time, the initiative in budget and tax proposals had moved back to Capitol Hill. And in the November 1982 elections, Democrats campaigning against "Reaganomics" gained 26 seats in the House. Reagan's initial momentum had been stalled if not halted.

* * * * *

Reagan was not the first president to feel both glory and defeat in the office. This paradox has affected other modern presidents. Some—including Wilson, Hoover, Truman, Johnson, Nixon, and Carter—suffered deeply from it. The promise and harsh reality of this unique office provide the focus for this chapter. We outline the constitutional dimensions of the presidency and discuss precedents and powers used by activist presidents. Then we outline the day-to-day duties of the office—administration, politics, ceremony. The structure of the White House—who works there and how they are organized—will also concern us. Knowing how the office really works helps explain why some think the presidency, despite its trappings, is little more than a glorified clerkship.

Master communicator. Ronald Reagan uses dollar bill to explain his budget policies to the TV audience.

THE CONSTITU-TIONAL POWERS

In creating the presidency, the Constitution's drafters were forced to improvise. On the one hand, as advocates of parliamentary power, they had no intention of installing an all-powerful executive. No monarchy—not even a constitutionally limited one—would suffice. Strong, legitimate legislative bodies were deeply implanted in the soil of the New World—through the colonial (later state) legislatures, the Continental Congresses, and finally the Articles of Confederation.

Yet this very tradition of strong legislatures and weak executives was causing trouble. The Articles did not provide a stable political and economic system. Congress could not provide for the common defense, conduct relations with foreign powers, or regulate commerce and coinage. James Madison noted that executives in the new nation had become "ciphers," while legislatures were "omnipotent." He charged that constitutional limits were "readily overleaped by the legislature on the spur of an occasion." James Wilson, often called the father of the presidency, wanted an executive with "energy, dispatch, and responsibility." Alexander Hamilton, a champion of strong government, wrote that "energetic government" was the most prized goal of the convention (*The Federalist*, No. 70). Gouverneur Morris, head of the constitutional convention's drafting committee, also favored a strong, independent executive.

James Wilson of Pennsylvania, father of the presidency.

The constitutional formula

These men—Madison, Wilson, Hamilton, and Morris—were among the brightest at the constitutional convention. They guided their colleagues to a series of fateful decisions that outlined the modern presidency (Pritchett, 1982: 118–121).

An elected individual The president is one person. Some feared that a one-person executive too closely resembled a king. They proposed a collegial executive or council to check executive power, but these notions were rejected.

Even more important, the president is elected independently, and is not picked by the legislature. Most who favored a strong executive preferred popular election. (Hamilton was an exception. He was as close to a monarchist as a colonial patriot could be.) But the small-state delegates objected. Thus evolved an awkward compromise, the electoral college. But it proved to be a victory for popular government. Within a few years, most states had laws providing that electors be picked by popular vote.

A vague mandate The president has broad, vaguely described powers. Article II of the Constitution begins with the so-called vesting clause. It states that "Executive power shall be vested in a president." Is this just a description of the office? Or is it a way to expand vastly the Constitution's listed powers? No one knows for sure.

There is also the "take care clause." This provides that the president "take care that the laws be faithfully executed." This is probably a simple injunction

289

to enforce laws passed by Congress, but presidents have sometimes used it to justify broad exercise of powers.

Blended powers The president exercises key powers along with Congress. These are legislating, administering laws, and conducting foreign affairs. Although this is called "separation of powers," the overall effect is quite different. In practice, *separate* institutions *jointly* exercise powers. As Madison observed, the Constitution creates not a system of separate institutions doing separate functions, but one of separate institutions sharing functions, so that "these departments be so far connected and blended as to give to each a constitutional control over the others" (*The Federalist*, No. 48).

In lawmaking, for instance, the president plays a crucial part. He can convene one or both houses of Congress in special session. Though he cannot introduce legislation directly, he "shall from time to time give to the Congress information on the state of the Union, and recommend to their consideration such measures as he shall judge necessary and expedient." The president also signs or vetoes legislation within 10 days after it has passed Congress. To overrule a veto, a two-thirds vote is needed in each house. (Unlike some state governors, the president lacks the "item veto," but He must accept or reject a bill *in toto.*) In the so-called pocket veto, the president can veto a bill without sending it back to Congress. But this occurs only if Congress adjourns and prevents the president from returning the legislation within the prescribed 10-day period.

The president must see that laws are faithfully carried out. The writers of the Constitution surely meant him to be the chief officer of the executive branch. They gave him power to appoint "officers of the United States," with Senate advice and consent. He selects judges, ambassadors, consuls, and other federal officers; congressional assent is not needed for lower-level appointees. He can demand written reports from department heads. (The Constitution nowhere speaks of a cabinet. It only mentions principal officers of the executive departments.) The president can also grant pardons and reprieves.

On the precise structure of executive agencies, the Constitution is silent. Cabinet-level departments and many other agencies are formed by statutes. These often specify the programs and policies of these agencies. In short, while the president is the chief administrative officer, Congress takes the lead in designing the executive branch's structure and detailing its tasks.

Even in diplomacy and national defense, the Constitution divides powers between the president and Congress. Because these were traditionally royal matters, they resist legislative involvement. Even champions of legislative rights and balanced constitutions, like the philosophers Locke and Montesquieu, held that executives should have unchallenged authority to deal with foreign powers and cope with crises. The Constitution thus grants the president wide discretion in such matters. He appoints ambassadors and other envoys; he negotiates treaties; he is commander-in-chief of the armed forces.

Yet even here, the Founders preferred to blend functions. The Senate must approve ambassadors, envoys, and other major presidential appointees. Treaties must be ratified by the Senate. Only Congress, which most directly represents the people, can declare war. (An early draft of the Constitution gave Congress the power to "make war." On second thought, the Founders changed this to "declare war.") Through its cherished power of the purse, Congress can direct the flow of funds and equip the armed forces.

Copilot. Congress strives to share "war powers" with a questioning President Reagan.

The presidency is the most innovative and daring invention in our political framework. It has been copied, but never duplicated, by nations that have adopted constitutions like ours.

Presidential succession   The constitution wisely provides that the vice president shall serve as president in case the president dies, resigns, is removed, or is unable to discharge the duties of office. This has provided a smooth transition when presidents have died or (in four instances) have been assassinated in office.

A more vexing problem, presidential disability, is addressed by the 25th Amendment (ratified in 1967). The vice president becomes *acting* president in two situations: (a) the president informs Congress in writing that he cannot perform the duties; or (b) the vice president and a majority of the cabinet, or of some "other body" created by Congress, decide the president cannot perform the duties. The president can reclaim the office at any time unless the vice president and a majority of the cabinet or other body contend that he has not recovered. In this event, Congress would decide the issue. The president would resume office *unless* a two-thirds vote of both houses backed the vice president. This procedure is yet to be tested. It arose from concern over the impact of serious presidential disabilities: Woodrow Wilson's stroke in 1919 disabled him for the rest of his term; Dwight Eisenhower's 1955 heart attack caused temporary disability.

When President Reagan was hospitalized with a gunshot wound after an assassination attempt in March 1981, the nation came close to using the disability procedure. Vice President Bush, on a speaking tour when the incident occurred, rushed back to take charge informally. Meanwhile, senior White House staffers and a few cabinet members monitored events from the White House. But Reagan recovered quickly from surgery and the Amendment's formal procedures were not invoked.

If the vice presidential office becomes vacant, the president nominates someone to fill it, subject to confirmation by a majority vote of both houses of Congress. This procedure, also contained in the 25th amendment, has already been used twice. Vice President Spiro Agnew, indicted for taking bribes, resigned his post in October 1973. House Minority Leader Gerald R. Ford was picked by President Nixon to take Agnew's place and was confirmed by the Senate and House. Nearly a year later, Nixon himself resigned as a result of the Watergate scandal. As Nixon's successor, Ford in August 1974 picked former New York Governor Nelson A. Rockefeller as Vice President. He was confirmed after long hearings in both chambers.

"Invitation to struggle"

The Constitution provides an independent and potentially strong chief executive. The powers were not clearly defined, undoubtedly because the drafters were treading on new ground. As students of Locke, Montesquieu, and other 18th-century thinkers, the drafters reserved Article I for the powers of Congress; it details the basic powers of government as 18th-century intellectuals saw them.

There were few precedents to guide the drafting of Article II. This article deals with executive powers. It is perhaps the most loosely drawn of all the

Fateful moment. Leaving the Washington Hilton Hotel on March 30, 1981, President Reagan is shot and wounded by a gunman.

provisions. It includes breathtaking powers expressed in vague words. What is the "executive power" vested in the president? What is the meaning of the "take care" clause? Just what are the president's powers as commander-in-chief?

At the same time, presidential powers are blended with those of Congress and the courts. As constitutional scholar Edward S. Corwin once observed, the Constitution is an "invitation to struggle" among the arms of government. This has been most evident in the relations between the president and Congress in spending, treaty, and war powers.

The precise nature of this struggle cannot be drawn from the Constitution. Rather it is left to history. To understand the makeup of today's presidency, we must study the office's history. The Constitution provided the springboard for today's strong presidency. But it only hints at the struggles.

A PRESIDENTIAL JOB DESCRIPTION

Writing a modern job description for the President of the United States is not easy. One scholar, Thomas E. Cronin (1980: 154–84), approaches the challenge in an interesting way. He groups the president's tasks into three broad, related policy areas, or *subpresidencies:* foreign affairs and national security, aggregate economics, and domestic policy.

Within each of these three subpresidencies, at least seven types of roles are performed. The result is the matrix of tasks shown in Figure 9–1. The president cannot do these jobs separately, but must weave them all into a daily schedule. This forces crucial and often uncomfortable choices to save time, energy, and influence.

The subpresidencies

Foreign affairs and national security   The president is the nation's chief agent in dealing with foreign powers. He is responsible for drafting foreign policy; as commander-in-chief, he is charged with ensuring the nation's security. These are life-and-death matters that are hard to delegate, so they generally take precedence. A study of State of the Union addresses found that national security matters occupy more presidential attention than any other topic (Kessel, 1974). Also, a president's emphasis in this field tends to grow over time in a pattern related to the voting cycle. His focus on national security mounts during his first term; then it drops in the reelection year, only to rise even higher during his second term.

This focus on foreign and national security affairs is tied to several factors. Presidents are assumed to have more leeway and better information in these areas than they do for domestic problems. Thus, Congress and pressure groups are weaker in foreign than in domestic policy.

Presidents like to be known as "peacemakers," to strive for "a generation of peace" as their legacy. "Running for the Nobel Peace prize," Cronin calls this. Meeting with other heads of state to grapple with foreign policy seems more presidential than bargaining with local politicians or haggling over federal reclamation projects. So, modern presidents place the highest priority on foreign policy and national security objectives that need their personal involvement.

Aggregate economics   The facts of economic boom and bust are brought home again and again to average people through their paychecks and weekly

Commander in chief. President Reagan views North Korean positions from DMZ.

FIGURE 9–1

A Presidential Job Description

		The "subpresidencies"		
	Types of activity	Foreign policy and national security	Aggregate economics	Domestic policies and programs
Higher priority	Crisis management	Military crises; Cuban missiles, 1962; Iranian hostages, 1979–81; Grenada invasion, 1983	Coping with recessions (e.g., 1981)	Confronting air controller's strike, 1981
	Symbolic leadership	Presidential state visit to Middle East or to China	Boosting confidence in the economy	Visiting disaster victims; greeting military or civilian heroes
	Priority setting and program design	Balancing pro-Israel policies with need for Arab oil	Devising economic "game plan"; shaping budget proposals	Designing a new welfare program
	Recruitment leadership	Selection of secretaries of state, defense; U.N. ambassador; arms negotiator	Selection of Secretary of Treasury, Office of Management and Budget director	Nomination of federal judges, members of regulatory commissions
	Legislative and political coalition building	Selling Panama Canal Treaty, arms sales to two chambers	Lobbying for energy or anti-inflation legislative packages	Winning public support for deregulation, educational reforms
	Program implementation and evaluation	Encouraging negotiations between Israel and Egypt	Implementing tax cut or fuel rationing	Improving quality of health care, welfare, retraining programs
Lower priority	Oversight of government routines	Overseeing U.S. bases abroad; maintaining foreign aid	Overseeing the Federal Reserve or the IRS	Overseeing National Science Foundation or Environmental Protection Agency

Higher priority ←——————————————————→ Lower priority

Source: Adapted from Thomas E. Cronin, *The State of the Presidency*, 2d ed. Copyright © 1980 by Thomas E. Cronin. Reprinted by permission of the publisher, Little, Brown and Company, Inc.

bills for groceries, housing, and other products. If this were not enough, quantitative economic indicators exist; we can follow unemployment rates, consumer price indexes, gross national product, interest and mortgage rates, stock market averages, and personal income figures. Such figures are widely aired. Public officials eagerly await and follow them. Politicians and interest-group leaders debating a president's successes or failures often cite them.

Presidents are seen as managers of the nation's overall economy—even when their actions can do little. They are expected to have "game plans" (like "Reaganomics") aimed at fostering a healthy economy and keeping inflation and unemployment in check. Presidents are blamed for economic downturns, though not always given credit when the economy rallies.

Presidents have many broad and narrow cures for economic ills. A key element in the economy is the federal budget. It not only sets priorities in its economic activities, but also affects what resources are available in the private sector. Tax proposals have a similar influence by encouraging some kinds of economic activity and discouraging others. The supply of money is regulated by the Federal Reserve Board. Members of "the Fed" are supposed to be independent of the administration; but forceful presidents try to reach agreements with the board about its policy goals. Many other federal policies (for example, credit or securities controls) can be adjusted to change the economy.

Domestic policies   Carrying out domestic policies takes a large chunk of the federal government's personnel and budget. No one knows how many policies or programs the government really runs. One study stopped at about 1,300—by no means the full number. Programs range from law enforcement and health care to maritime subsidies, farming research, and aid for the fine arts.

As chief executive, the president is responsible for overall management of the federal establishment—structure, top personnel, priorities, and day-to-day activities. On the whole, federal agencies and programs are well entrenched and resist bold restructuring. Once in a while, presidents turn their attention to revamping the federal establishment: Johnson's "war on poverty," Nixon's brief flings with welfare reform and government decentralization, Carter's vow to streamline the federal structure, and Reagan's drive to halt government growth are examples (Nathan, 1983). Yet domestic issues are often pushed out of the president's schedule by pressing security or economic matters.

Whenever presidents take a stand, they risk stepping on the toes of the groups affected. No doubt this explains why every president since Franklin Roosevelt has despaired at the state of federal organization; they have all found it easier to start new programs than stop old ones. A White House aide was referring to domestic policy tangles when he said: "Everybody believes in democracy until he gets to the White House, and then you begin to believe in dictatorship because it's so hard to get things done. Every time you turn around, people just resist you, and even resist their own job" (Cronin, 1980: 223).

In addressing one policy area, a president must weigh its impact on other areas. Almost everything the federal government does, for example, affects foreign relations in some way; and foreign relations, in turn, affect the nation's overall economic health. Likewise, government programs, no matter how small when viewed apart, together set the government's fiscal role and ability to deal with foreign powers. In handling the three subpresidencies, a president has a set of roles, or types of involvement, from which to choose.

Types of involvement

Crisis management   In times of danger, presidents have to direct the government's response and rally the public. Examples are the bombing of Pearl Harbor in 1941, the invasion of South Korea in 1951, the Soviet launch of Sputnik in 1957, Soviet placement of missiles in Cuba in 1962, the ghetto riots of 1968, the fuel shortage in late 1973, Iranian seizure of U.S. hostages in 1979, and the Lebanon and Grenada interventions in 1983.

A president has little control over the timing of crises. Yet when they happen, the president must thrust aside other duties to manage the government's response.

Public support for the president peaks during crises, when people are dismayed and fearful over unfolding events. So, presidents and their advisers sometimes try to stimulate a crisis atmosphere over what are really long-range

Crisis management. The Oval Office is focal point for monitoring Iranian crisis during its final days in January 1981. President Carter sits on his desk, center, back to camera. Big crises engage top advisors: clockwise, from left, CIA Director Stansfield Turner; two unidentified staff aides; White House advisors Hamilton Jordan and Jody Powell; Counsel Lloyd Cutler; Carter; Secretary of State Edmund Muskie; Treasury Secretary G. William Miller; National Security Advisor Zbigniew Brzezinski; Vice President Walter F. Mondale; and Attorney General Benjamin Civiletti.

problems. Dwindling support for President Johnson showed his failure to keep up a crisis atmosphere over the Vietnam War. Despite short-lived crises such as the Gulf of Tonkin incident and the 1968 Tet offensive, the war dragged on. Expected victories did not occur; the nation at last tired of the whole thing.

Carter also was undone when he could not keep up a crisis atmosphere for the energy situation—which he called "the moral equivalent of war" (promptly dubbed MEOW). The crisis was real enough. But it was gradual, not sudden; in the future, not immediate. Though Carter started several new energy programs, the public never quite accepted his call for conservation and self-denial. The Iranian hostage seizure, from November 1979 to January 1981, was another crisis that dogged Carter. At first, Carter's stock rose as people rallied against the Iranian terrorists. But as the months dragged on, the anger mixed with embarrassment over Carter's weakness.

Symbolic leadership   Presidents are supposed to honor the nation's traditions, stir hope and confidence, and foster a sense of national unity and purpose. "The presidency is a bully pulpit," said Theodore Roosevelt—who relished this role. Or, as Franklin Roosevelt put it, "the presidency is not merely an administrative office. That is the least of it. It is preeminently a place of moral leadership. . . . That is what the office is—a superb opportunity for reapplying, applying to new conditions, the simple rules of human conduct to which we always go back" (Corwin, 1957: 273).

Symbolic tasks transcend partisanship and stress unity over divisiveness. Therefore, they are prominently featured in presidential schedules. The symbolic role is displayed in patriotic festivals, ground-breaking or dedication ceremonies, funerals of famous people, and other ceremonies.

Presidents also use symbolism to focus public thinking on their goals and programs. Johnson turned off lights in the White House in 1964 to dramatize his austerity budget; Jimmy Carter marched in his own inaugural parade to stress his plain-folks style.

Priority setting   Since the New Deal, presidents have been expected to present a small number of broad priorities, revealing the direction they wish the nation to take.

Each year, the president has chances to give such priorities concrete form. On November 15, the president submits the current services budget. This projects the cost of keeping up current federal programs and spending levels through the next fiscal year. On the 15th day after Congress convenes in January, the president submits a budget message, with complete spending and revenue projections for the next five years. Through the rest of the budget process, until the new fiscal year begins on October 1, the president and his advisers help shape budget decisions. They testify and lobby with congressional budget and appropriations committees. The president even threatens to veto bills that depart from his goals. Once the money is appropriated, the president can still affect priorities by deferring or stretching out spending (Fisher, 1975).

Another opportunity for priority setting is the annual State of the Union message. In this message, the president proposes new programs or revisions of present ones. Yearly reports on the economy and employment are also platforms for priority setting. So are periodic speeches or reports on special subjects. Speaking engagements are often used to air the president's priorities.

Reagan's early months were a classic example of priority setting. Elected on a platform of spending cuts, Reagan and his advisers quickly acted on that promise. They began to rewrite the fiscal 1982 budget, which had already been given to Congress by Jimmy Carter. The hectic process featured complex bargaining centered in the Office of Management and Budget (OMB), between budget officers and various interests represented in the new administration. The result was unveiled six weeks later. It slashed $40.4 billion from Carter's requests and reflected quite different priorities. Defense spending was boosted; there were cutbacks in some basic entitlement programs (such as food stamps), and cuts in social programs funded annually. Presidential messages were used to outline the new priorities; appearances by the president and top aides carried the message to grass-roots groups.

Often presidents put their priorities in program packages—FDR's New Deal, Truman's Fair Deal, Kennedy's New Frontier, Johnson's Great Society, and Nixon's New American Revolution.

Recruitment leadership   One of the best ways presidents can put their mark on the government is by people they appoint to key federal posts. Priorities and programs will not go forward without competent, like-thinking people in cabinet and subcabinet spots. Through appointments to long-term judgeships or regulatory commissions, presidents can affect policymaking well after they leave office.

Recruitment peaks at the outset of a new presidency. Many jobs—about 3,000—must be filled in a brief time. As Cronin (1980: 164) points out: "Ironically, at the time when a president has the largest number of jobs to fill and enjoys the greatest drawing power, he has less time and information available to take advantage of this major prerogative than at any other point in his administration." Recruiting is normally frustrating and time-consuming for all concerned. Reagan's initial recruitment effort was typical. It sputtered along for months while other activities, particularly budget redrafting, were in high gear.

Recruiting able people is no easy task. No president can know more than a small fraction of those who should be considered. Some of the president's friends—such as campaign aides and financial backers—may be unsuitable. Others may fall victim to bargaining among interested individuals and groups. To be successful, aspirants must have backers on Capitol Hill and within the president's electoral coalition; they must also surmount FBI investigation and scrutiny of their careers and financial dealings.

Appointees, for their part, are not always eager to work for the government. Some just do not want to move to Washington. They may face salary cuts if they join the federal payroll. Many, too, do not like revealing their financial assets, forfeiting their privacy, and having their outside activities restricted.

Many, therefore, decline to serve; those who serve usually do so for a short time. An appointee in the executive branch stays for an average of 18 months. Most of these people arrive and leave almost unnoticed by the White House. Heclo (1977) calls presidential appointees "a government of strangers." Their varied paths to government and their brief service greatly reduce their impact on the departments and agencies they direct on the president's behalf.

Of equal or greater impact are a president's appointments to the bench, both the Supreme Court and lower courts. Some presidents, such as FDR and Nixon, shaped the Supreme Court for a whole generation. Others, like Carter, make no Supreme Court appointments but influence the judicial system through lower-court selections. Not all judges conform to expectations; one fourth of all Supreme Court justices consistently rule against the philosophy of the president who chose them (Scigliano, 1971).

The president's appointment power is not exercised alone, but with "advice and consent" of the Senate. Wide berth is traditionally given presidents in picking cabinet and subcabinet aides. Not since Eisenhower has an appointment been withdrawn because the Senate was opposed; but two of Reagan's subcabinet designees were in effect rejected. One withdrew his name in the face of opposition; the other was turned down by the Senate committee considering the nomination. More often, appointees are confirmed even when there are reservations about their expertise or integrity.

With appointees to regulatory commissions or judgeships, Congress takes a livelier role. The Senate has rejected one fifth of all presidential Supreme Court nominees. Most recently it turned down two southern conservatives whom Nixon nominated. District court judges are normally subject to "senatorial courtesy." This tradition ensures Senate consultation, if not approval, before names are formally submitted.

For their advisers, presidents have a freer hand. Few White House aides (one exception is the OMB director) require Senate confirmation. Presidents tend to prefer working with trusted, long-time associates. Kennedy had his "Irish mafia," skilled politicians (not all Irish) who had run his Massachusetts and national campaigns. For Nixon, it was "the Prussians," a group of hard-bitten types who supervised the president's program and controlled access to him. Carter's Georgia advisers held positions close to their chief and were blamed by many for the White House's clumsiness in dealing with Washington power centers. Reagan's White House was run by a few key advisers: Chief of Staff James A. Baker, Deputy Chief of Staff Michael K. Deaver, and earlier staff members like Edwin Meese and William Clark.

Conformity versus diversity among advisers is a question all presidents must resolve. Many, however, fail to face it squarely. Some, such as Johnson and Nixon, demand so much loyalty and conformity that dissenting ideas rarely reach them. Others, such as Roosevelt and Kennedy, welcome clashes of opinion and effectively meld diverse aides into a working team.

Recruiting leaders, then, is an important duty of a president. The type of people presidents can attract, the kind of loyalty and *esprit de corps* they can spark, say as much about their effectiveness as their programs or causes.

Coalition building   Another task for the president is building political and legislative coalitions to push his aims. Coalition building involves working with the legislative branch and party and interest-group leaders. Some presidents prefer to think of themselves as "above politics." They shy away from coalition building, which is so political. Yet coalition building is essential. Without it, the lofty phrases of the president's speeches would not bear fruit in legislation, programs, or policies.

Though as necessary as priority setting, coalition building is far more difficult and frustrating. It takes patience, compromise, and diplomacy. Of all modern presidents, FDR was probably the best at it. He used the whole range of presidential resources to swing Congress, the Democratic party, the press, and the public behind his New Deal programs. Lyndon Johnson was probably the most adroit legislative tactician in the White House. Ronald Reagan combines effective one-on-one persuasion with masterful use of the media to put pressures on lawmakers.

By contrast, Nixon often lagged in following through on his proposals: complex reform plans for welfare policy and government reorganization were announced but soon dropped; staff follow-through on his New Federalism package was uneven. Carter was also faulted for inept follow-through and failure to court congressional leaders in selling his programs.

Implementation   Presidents sometimes act as if their duties end once a legislative proposal is accepted. But that is just the start. The law or program must be carried out by an agency willing and able to do the job; staff must be found to supervise the new program; procedures and regulations must be set; and once the wheels are turning, it should be (but often is not) monitored to see whether it is working as planned.

Implementation is a weak link in our government. Often laws have such vague or contradictory goals that it is hard to know just what they are supposed to do. Federal agencies often have firm ideas about their missions and battle to protect their roles. Lobby groups and congressional subcommittees are always watching administrators, striving to bend programs to their purposes rather than to the president's. Most domestic programs give out funds or services to state, local, or private groups. This makes it physically impossible or politically unfeasible for the president to keep up supervision. Evaluation—seeing whether programs really work—is a bureaucratic stepchild. It is rarely done and even more rarely heeded.

Following through on programs is unglamorous and politically risky. Presidents are rarely inclined or have the time to pursue it. That is why political history usually focuses on how presidents influence the passage of legislation; it rarely mentions whether the legislation made any difference.

Oversight of government routines   The federal government is a machine of awesome size. It has hundreds of agencies and almost 3 million civilian employees. In theory, the president manages this apparatus; in practice, there is little time to do this.

Beyond picking key staff members and his cabinet (who usually choose *their* staff aides), the president has little personal contact with staffing. Also, as an administration grows older, key personnel, even in cabinet posts, tend to be promoted from within, not selected from outside. Only a few thousand government employees work under the president's direct supervision. The others have civil service rules to insulate them. If presidents want to coax more diligent or responsive work from these employees, they must do so through symbolic acts—a combination of inspiration and reproach from his "bully pulpit."

For the most part, presidents are not inclined to supervise government routines. It is unglamorous work, low in priority. The benefits are scattered and all but invisible. Every now and then, scandals involving federal employees demand presidential attention; but even here, a president will strive to steer clear of the impact of such scandals. This is another reason, no doubt, that presidents keep their hands off government routines.

Here, then, is one description of the presidency: three subpresidencies and seven forms of presidential involvement. They are listed roughly in order of importance, as seen by presidents themselves. Presidents tend to veer from domestic policies to macroeconomic and national security matters. They tend to neglect low-payoff implementation and routine management in favor of more glamorous and pressing activities in crisis management, symbolic leadership, or priority setting.

Some assignments, such as international crises, are thrust on presidents. Like it or not, they must respond because the public expects it. Other roles are left to their choosing. They can emphasize, delegate, or even ignore certain roles. Shrewd presidents allocate their limited time and influence to stress the priorities and programs they wish to leave as legacies.

In allocating their energies, presidents show their own styles, interests, and political skills. Sometimes their choices are highly personal: FDR, a stamp collector, personally approved postage stamp designs; Kennedy, a former naval officer, worried about naming new naval vessels. But most of the time, purposeful presidents and their aides carefully determine how, or whether, to become personally involved. Too many demands are made—too many people clamor for attention—for presidents to do otherwise.

"Bully pulpit." Theodore Roosevelt was a vigorous stump speaker and adroit phrasemaker.

THE ELECTIVE KINGSHIP

At the heart of the President's powers is visibility. He can capture public attention and mobilize approval and support. "In the presidential office as it has been constituted since Jackson's time," wrote the political commentator Henry Jones Ford (1898: 293), "American democracy has revived the oldest political institution of the race, the elective kingship. It is all there: the recognition of the notables, and the tumultuous choice of the freeman, only conformed to modern conditions."

Far more important than any constitutional powers is the president's ability to focus public attention on his initiatives and programs. As the only nationally elected figure (except the vice president), he is the constant object of media attention. He embodies the government as no one else does. In skillful hands, this is a unique resource for getting popular pressure behind his programs.

The best-known American

The president is the prime psychological symbol in politics. He is by far the "best-known American" (Greenstein, 1974). Almost everyone at least knows his name—something that can be said of no other politician. Not even the best-known celebrities, entertainers, and athletes (who may be known by as much as 90 percent of the people) can claim this.

As the best-known political actor, a president plays key roles in the political learning of children and young people. The president is the first political person they become aware of. By age nine, most children can name the current president. This reflects the importance of the presidency. Also, first-learned objects tend to condition perceptions of later-learned objects. In contrast to the president, other politicians may seem vague and mysterious, hard to understand. Many children, for instance, think members of Congress are "the president's helpers." Such ideas are not confined to the very young. A recent survey among 13- and 17-year-olds found that half at both ages thought the president could appoint members of Congress.

Researchers during the Eisenhower and Kennedy eras were impressed by the president's image as a benevolent leader. Children held a rosy view of presidents; adults more often than not gave incumbent presidents high marks for performance. Ratings of presidential performance always ran higher than did those of Congress and other government bodies.

Popular images of the president eroded after the upheavals of the late 1960s and early '70s. For many, the Watergate scandal ended the myth of the presidency. Trust in the office—indeed, in all politics—slid. Throughout these adversities, however, citizens retained a glowing image of strong, successful presidents—like FDR, Truman, Kennedy, and Eisenhower (who top all-time popularity polls).

Public expectations for presidents therefore remain high. Despite a brief lapse following Vietnam and Watergate, the public expects above all that presidents appear strong and decisive; wider presidential authority is supported. As Wayne (1982: 34) summarizes: "The presidency continues to be viewed as a large, multifaceted office, and the president as the wearer of many hats. . . . The ability to be forceful and decisive, to make good policy, and to inspire confidence are remembered as the qualities of previous presidents that would be most useful today."

A widespread belief that Ronald Reagan had these qualities probably contributed to his victory. Some feel his decisiveness in office fueled a modest yet unmistakable revival of confidence in the political system.

Public expectations can be a resource for presidents; they are also a club to be wielded against presidents who fail to live up to them. Probably the public expects too much and blames too quickly. As Edwards (1983: 196–98) notes, citizens expect contradictory things of their chief executives: leadership and responsiveness, flexibility and firmness, statesmanship and political savvy, openness and control, empathy and distinctiveness. No doubt this is why a number of presidents have left office in various levels of disfavor. Johnson, Nixon, Ford, and Carter are examples. Whenever a president is in tune with popular desires, people are eager to give allegiance. When a president betrays that trust or fails to fulfill expectations, frustration swiftly sets in. High expectations are not erased by disappointments.

Underdog. Harry Truman, whose popularity sank lower than Nixon's after Watergate, came from behind to defeat New York's Governor Thomas E. Dewey in 1948.

Presidential popularity fever chart

Whatever the public's view of the presidency, assessment of individual presidents varies widely. Since the 1930s, analysts have asked what sort of job people think the president is doing. Because major surveys ask this about once every two weeks, we now have an accurate "fever chart" of presidential performance from the Roosevelt era to the present. (See Figure 9–2 and Table 9–1.)

Three presidents—FDR, Eisenhower, and Kennedy—throughout their terms had approval of the majority holding opinions. Other presidents have had rollercoaster rides of highs and lows.

FIGURE 9–2

A Fever Chart of Presidential Popularity

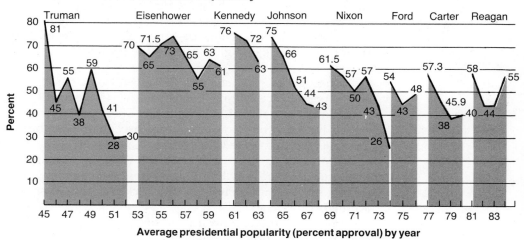

The questions are: "How would you rate the job the (incumbent president) is doing—excellent, pretty good, only fair, or poor?" Favorable responses are "excellent" and "pretty good."
Source: American Institute of Public Opinion (Gallup poll).

TABLE 9–1

Popularity Ratings of Presidents

President	Percent "favorable" ratings*		
	High	**Low**	**Average**
Roosevelt (1933–1945)	84	54	68
Truman (1945–1953)	87	23	46
Eisenhower (1953–1961)	79	49	66
Kennedy (1961–1963)	83	57	70
Johnson (1963–1969)	80	35	54
Nixon (1969–1974)	68	24	48
Ford (1974–1977)	71	37	46
Carter (1977–1981)	75	21	47
Reagan (1981–)	68	35	50

*The percentages are of respondents who answered this question favorably: "Do you approve or disapprove of the way (name of incumbent) is handling his job as president?"
Source: American Institute of Public Opinion (Gallup poll).

Honeymoon and morning after Every modern president, no matter how popular, has started with a honeymoon period; public expectation and approval are high. It is followed by slipping support. As seen in Figure 9–2, this decline is sometimes slight, sometimes steep.

Recent presidents have suffered noticeable declines in support. Truman, upon FDR's death, was approved by 87 percent of the people. That was the highest approval score ever recorded. But at one point he was approved by only 23 percent—about the lowest score yet. Johnson had highly favorable ratings in his first two years in office. Later he sank below 50 percent. Nixon was praised by 62 percent in January 1973—after the Vietnam peace was concluded. But he steadily declined over the next 18 months as Watergate findings took their toll. Shortly before he resigned, his rating fell to 24 percent.

What affects public appraisal of a president's performance? In looking at the ebb and flow over the past 40 years, at least five factors seem to have an impact.

Current events and conditions Because presidents are the most visible and understandable part of the government, they are praised or blamed for whatever happens in the public arena. "When the economy goes sour, or war drags on, or domestic violence erupts, the president is available to take the blame. Then when things go right, it seems the president must have had a hand in it" (Barber, 1977: 5).

Current events and changes do indeed make short-term waves in a president's popularity. During Carter's term, for instance, brief but measurable downturns were recorded by pollsters after several events. In his first energy speech he called on us to cut energy use. (Many by then doubted the energy shortage.) Many resented the Panama Canal treaty as a "giveaway." Bert Lance, Carter's friend and choice to head the Office of Management and Budget, resigned under fire. Whether the president is personally to blame or not, public opinion *makes* him responsible. "The buck does indeed stop at the White House" (Kernell, 1978: 521).

Some think the downward pull on presidents' popularity is caused by the **coalition of minorities** (Mueller, 1973). As presidents decide and act, they alienate staunch opponents of the actions. These people may be a minority, but if their views are strong enough, they will turn from the president's leadership.

With more and more decisions, the number of such groups grows. In Carter's case, issues such as energy and the Panama Canal pushed his ratings down.

Others hold that shifts in support are caused by a "fickle" segment of the public—the less partisan, less knowledgeable, and less involved in politics. They uncritically add to a new president's support at first. But they quickly turn away when things go wrong. "Unrealistic expectations are followed by an inexorable disillusionment" (Stimson, 1976: 9).

Probably no one reason lies behind these shifts. Some seem to stem from the coalition of minorities; others surely flow from the quirks of the least informed people. Whatever the precise causes, presidents clearly cannot help but be linked in the public mind with social and political events and trends. Whatever the circumstances, people think the president is closely involved.

Rally-round-the-flag   Another factor affecting presidential popularity is the rally-round-the-flag phenomenon, a crisis event that boosts the president's popularity. The crisis should be international, must involve the United States and especially the president, and must be dramatic and sharply focused. Numerous rallying points have occurred in the past 30 years. These include major crises (the Cuban missile crisis of 1962, the Iranian hostage crisis of 1979), military intervention (Grenada in 1983), major diplomatic developments (the Vietnam peace treaty of 1973, the Camp David accords of 1978), and dramatic technical breakthroughs (the Soviet launching of Sputnik in 1959).

A classic rallying of public opinion took place late in 1979, when militants captured 52 U.S. hostages at our embassy in Iran. In one month, Carter enjoyed the largest surge in a president's popularity in the four decades of the survey. But the crisis dragged on, the anger and humiliation grew, popular support dwindled, and the president became the object of our frustrations.

Economic cycles   Another factor in public support is the *domestic economy*. The higher the unemployment or inflation rate, the lower a president's popularity is apt to be. On the other hand, recovery does not seem to add to popularity as much as a slump hurts it.

War   A *war* involving the United States also affects presidential ratings. But the effect varies with how the public views the war. A popular conflict such as World War II brings rally-round-the-flag support. By contrast, an unpopular contest, such as the Korean War (called "Truman's war") or the Vietnam War in its latter days, lowers ratings.

Scandal   Finally, a major scandal can speed decline in presidential popularity. This is most true if the president himself is involved. The gradual but constant fall in Nixon's support in the months before he resigned is a recent example.

The president as symbol

The symbolism of the presidency is a constant feature of our life, despite the ebbs and flows of presidential popularity. Given their unique visibility, it is not surprising that presidents are often—perhaps too often—the object of adulation, hopes, fears, and frustrations. Beyond partisan or program support, they have a central place in public emotions.

This symbolic role is seen dramatically when a president dies or is very ill. News of Eisenhower's 1955 heart attack caused the stock market to drop to its lowest point since the 1929 crash. When Kennedy was killed in 1963, four of every five people reacted as they would to the death of a loved one. Half of all citizens, in a national survey, said they wept; 43 percent said they lost their appetite; 48 percent could not sleep; and 68 percent said they were nervous and tense.

Kennedy was a young, vigorous man; but there was similar mass sorrow at the deaths of Warren Harding and Franklin Roosevelt. Such displays do not occur when an ex-president dies; few people are affected the same way by the death of a favorite celebrity or athlete. So mourning seems to be a response to the loss of a leader, not just the loss of a revered figure.

As national leaders, presidents stand for unity and security. They are at the helm of the ship of state. When they are suddenly gone, the ship seems adrift and the helm untended.

ENLISTING PUBLIC SUPPORT

With public approval such a potent resource, presidents and their advisers spend much time trying to fathom the public mind. In the words of a Nixon aide, "Will it play in Peoria?"

Taking the public's pulse

All presidents rely on scouts, trusted friends, or aides. These people travel the country and read the public's pulse. Franklin Roosevelt, paralyzed by polio, used his wife Eleanor and his alter ego, Harry Hopkins. They met with local leaders to find out their views. Mrs. Roosevelt was a familiar sight around the country in the 1930s and 40s, acting as her husband's emissary. She developed a style and skill that later brought her fame as "the first lady of the world." Some presidents do it themselves. Promising to bring fresh breezes of populism to the nation's capital, Jimmy Carter set out on an ambitious program to meet with the people. He had White House phone-ins and visits with average people.

People rarely hold back in telling the president their views. A large staff keeps busy handling the flood of mail and phone calls received at the White House—as many as 50,000 letters and an average of 1,000 calls a day. Since 1960, mail has risen by 600 percent, largely because of expanded television coverage of the president.

Public opinion polls give modern presidents precise measures of attitudes. Most Presidents are avid poll watchers—at least when the polls are good. Lyndon Johnson used to carry flattering survey clippings in his wallet and whip them out to show White House visitors. As the Vietnam War dragged on and his ratings soured, his interest in the polls lagged. The last three presidents have had their own survey specialists to interpret findings and recommend steps to enhance presidential popularity with given groupings.

Presidential appeals

"A president must understand that he is expected to be the great national explainer," advise Grossman and Kumar (1981: 314–315). Thus, presidents and their advisers spend much time arousing public opinion for White House pro-

"Going to Talk to the Boss." Woodrow Wilson appeals to public opinion, 1919.

grams. How much presidents resort to direct public appeals and how effective they are, depend on personal style and communication skills.

All presidents use speeches, personal appearances, and symbolic events to publicize themselves and their programs. "Presidents can make the most of media coverage when they present their messages through activities that are likely to receive favorable coverage" (Grossman and Kumar, 1981: 314). Because they get more invitations than they can accept, they choose appearances for the most exposure and impact. (Even if they are not invited, they can simply show up and steal the spotlight.) Or they can simply schedule their speech in the White House's East Room and invite their own appointees and friendly legislators as the audience. Tours are planned to spotlight a president's objectives. Woodrow Wilson was haunted by Senate opposition to his Treaty of Versailles in 1919. So he launched his desperate western tour to "lay my case before the people." After a tiring series of 40 speeches and many impromptu appearances, in an era without microphones, he collapsed. The victim of a crippling stroke, he never fully recovered.

Presidents must effectively use mass media if they are to prevail over others competing for the public's ear. In the preelectronic era, this meant a healthy set of vocal cords and a flair for colorful phrasemaking. Theodore Roosevelt's lively turns of speech, Woodrow Wilson's graceful and learned speeches, and Ronald Reagan's easy-going directness show the successful use of oratory.

Nowadays, presidents must adapt to the requirements of radio and TV. Franklin Roosevelt mastered radio; his 20 fireside chats and countless live radio speeches helped sell his New Deal domestic programs and rally the nation during World War II. Kennedy and Reagan were to TV what FDR was to radio. Their good looks and casual speaking styles ideally suited the medium.

Radio mastery. A master of radio communication, Franklin D. Roosevelt inspires citizens in one of his 1930s "fireside chats." Handicapped by polio and unable to stand or walk unaided, FDR had a good speaking voice, a sharp wit, and a flare for phrasemaking.

The White House employs speech writers, directors, and consultants to help presidents polish their media style. It is hard to imagine a president today facing the public without practice and coaching. Carter, for example, developed a casual style. He revived the fireside chat to draw attention to his plainfolks appeals. Reagan uses simple props to dramatize his economic messages. The president has a unique advantage in electronic communications. Not only does he get more automatic publicity than anyone else, but he can usually have free radio and TV time for the asking. Franklin Roosevelt started the practice of asking the networks for free air time; his successors have continued it. Such requests are rarely turned down. But opposition-party members often ask for, and sometimes get, time to reply. Consider the huge cost of radio and TV time; it costs a quarter of a million dollars or more for a half hour of prime TV time. This use by presidents amounts to "a free use of an expensive commodity" (Minow, Martin, and Mitchell, 1973).

A presidential address carried at the same time by the three major TV networks blankets a vast audience. A prime-time speech usually reaches 70 million or more people. To reach an audience of that size in person, one would have to go before capacity crowds 48 times in each of the 26 mammoth stadiums used by pro football teams from Boston to San Diego—1,248 speeches (Minow, Martin, and Mitchell, 1973: 19).

One of the most dramatic presidential appeals of modern times was President Reagan's speech before a joint congressional session in April 1981. His sweeping budget plan was being considered by Congress. He had just recovered from an assassin's bullet. Public attention was riveted on him as he

WOODROW WILSON ON THE PRESIDENT'S CONSTITUENCY

His is the only national voice in affairs. Let him once win the admiration and confidence of the country, and no other single force can withstand him, no combination of forces will easily overpower him. His position takes the imagination of the country. He is the representative of no constituency, but of the whole people. When he speaks in his true character, he speaks for no special interest. If he rightly interprets the national thought and boldly insists upon it, he is irresistible; and the country never feels the zest for action so much as when its president is of such insight and caliber.

Woodrow Wilson, *Constitutional Government in the United States* (New York: Columbia University Press, 1908), p. 68.

Television star. John F. Kennedy launched live televised press conferences, which proved a good platform for his mental agility and wit.

challenged Congress to approve his program. It was a performance that harked back to Franklin Roosevelt's "100 days" of 1933 or Lyndon Johnson's Great Society of the mid-1960s.

"The national voice"

Presidents' unique visibility, the wide publicity given their words and deeds, lie at the heart of the office's power. This popular link was glimpsed briefly in Andrew Jackson's time; it marked the presidencies of the two Roosevelts, Wilson and Kennedy. "His is the only national voice in affairs," wrote Wilson (1908: 68) five years before entering the White House. "Let him once win the admiration and confidence of the country, and no other single force can withstand him, no combination of forces will easily overpower him." Overstated perhaps, but still a fair idea of what the modern presidency can do.

THE PRESIDENT AND CONGRESS

It is often said that "the president is the chief legislator." This is not strictly true. Only House and Senate members may introduce legislation. Both chambers have committees that gather information, hold hearings, and bargain over the details of bills and resolutions—this comes even before the entire membership votes on them. If the president is a legislator, he has powerful rivals.

Like other government powers, legislating is a blended power in which the president is a key party. If presidents cannot actually introduce bills, they can propose them; if they cannot physically take part in the legislative process, their agents and allies can make their presence felt; if they cannot cast a vote on the House or Senate floor, they can affect the vote by using, or threatening to use, veto power.

The president's legislative powers

The president's legislative role is formally based on the opening clause of Article II, Section 3: "He [the President] shall from time to time give to the Congress information on the state of the Union, and recommend to their consideration such measures as he shall judge necessary and expedient."

Early presidents saw this as a routine, even odious, duty. Modern presidents see it as "*the* statement of legislative priorities" (Light, 1982: 160)—to fo-

State of the Union. Modern presidents lay out agendas in annual prime time speeches to Congress. Here are (clockwise from top left) Dwight Eisenhower, John F. Kennedy, Richard M. Nixon, Jimmy Carter, Gerald R. Ford, and Lyndon B. Johnson. Politics buffs will note the vice presidents (Johnson, Walter Mondale, Nelson Rockefeller, and Hubert Humphrey) and House speakers (John W. McCormack, Thomas P. O'Neill) sitting behind the presidents.

cus the attention of Congress and the public on high-priority legislation. It was Woodrow Wilson who first went to Capitol Hill to deliver his State of the Union messages in person; ever since, his successors have done likewise (now in prime TV time) to push their programs. After his first year in office, with its hectic passage of New Deal legislation, FDR praised the cooperative spirit that had prevailed. "Out of these friendly contacts," he said in his annual address, "we are, fortunately, building a strong and permanent tie between the legislative and executive branches of the government. The letter of the Constitution wisely declared a separation, but the impulse of common purpose declares a union." Not all presidents view their relations with Congress in such benign terms; after 1937, FDR himself faced constant war over domestic policies. Yet the close ties of the legislative and executive branches are a main feature of national policy-making.

Presidents cannot dictate what Congress will or will not consider. But, by pointing out legislative priorities, they help shape the congressional agenda. They can focus attention, publicize priorities, and mobilize public opinion. By doing this, they indicate what they see as the leading issues of the moment and what legislation the public is likely to expect. Thus, they supply Congress with something that its scattered and decentralized structure prevents it from providing for itself—an agenda. And though legislators often decry White House pressure, they complain just as loudly when presidents fail to convey their priorities.

Budget making and clearance

How do presidents reach their legislative priorities? These may arise from personal beliefs, campaign promises, or demands of influential backers (Table 9–2.). In fact, there are always far more claimants for White House support than can be satisfied at any one time.

The formal mechanisms for sifting and choosing among the thousands of legislative proposals are *budgeting* and *central clearance*. These functions are performed by the president's management arm, the Office of Management and Budget (OMB). Along with budget requests, federal departments and agencies submit to OMB their proposals for new laws or revisions of old laws. OMB's analysts then comment on the proposals. Consulting with White House staff members, OMB selects those that fit the president's goals. The final say remains with the president. He accepts or rejects initiatives urged by the cabinet, staff aides, legislators, or lobbyists.

Selling the president's program

Except when giving certain speeches, presidents are not normally seen on Capitol Hill pushing their legislative program. They do not, for instance, testify before committees. (In 1977, though, congressional energy committees went to the White House to receive President Carter's "testimony" on his energy package.)

The brunt of the selling job rests with cabinet and agency officials. Usually flanked by aides, they sit again and again before Hill committees to argue for the president's stands, even those with which they differ in private. Almost every day, several top administration officials are on Capitol Hill meeting with

TABLE 9—2

Sources of Ideas for the President's Agenda

Source	Percentage of respondents mentioning
External sources	
Congress	52%
Events and crisis	51
Executive branch	46
Public opinion	27
Party	11
Interest groups	7
Media	4
Internal sources	
Campaign and platform	20
President	17
Staff	16
Task forces	6

Note: Respondents (past and present White House aides) were asked the following question: Generally speaking, what would you say were the most important sources of ideas for the domestic agenda?

The number of respondents was 118.

Source: Paul C. Light, *The President's Agenda* (Baltimore, Md.: Johns Hopkins University Press, 1982), p. 86.

some committee or subcommittee. Key officials are in special demand as witnesses. Their statements and responses are watched closely for clues as to what the president will accept or reject in legislation.

At a later stage, when bills are being worked over ("marked up") in committee sessions, administration experts are usually consulted. Sometimes they sit in the meeting room to advise and guide. The relationship between congressional committees and administration experts varies markedly; it depends on how close the president's objectives are to those of the committee leaders. If a committee sympathizes with the president's proposal, the ties are likely to be close and cordial. If the committee's goals are at odds with the president's, the relationship will be cool or combative; the president's spokespersons will keep at a safe distance from committee deliberations.

To push their aims, presidents command the largest corps of lobbyists in the

Linking the branches. Conference between President Reagan and congressional leaders. From left, House GOP Leader Robert H. Michel, Senate GOP Leader Howard H. Baker, Jr., Reagan, House Speaker Thomas P. O'Neill, Senate Democratic Leader Robert C. Byrd, and House Democratic Leader Jim Wright.

nation's capital; they are legislative liaison officers from the White House and various agencies. The White House Congressional Liaison Office manages the president's day-to-day relations with senators and representatives. It follows the progress of bills in which the president is interested. All departments and agencies, too, boast legislative liaison staffs that follow legislation dealing with their organization and answer congressional requests. These staffs are expected to adhere to the White House viewpoint; their prime loyalty, though, is to their organization, not to the president.

White House liaison staffers keep in touch with Capitol Hill developments. They deal especially with congressional leaders. They coordinate the activities of administration spokespersons and alert the president when personal intervention is needed.

Conversely, liaison staffers should impress on the president and his aides the importance of getting along with Congress. They must warn of the political repercussions of certain actions. A president may need to close a military base in a key congressional leader's district; the liaison officer must tell the president what will happen if he does so. Presidents and their advisers easily become restless over the balky ways of Congress. Its failure to give quick allegiance to the president's proposals is often vexing. This restlessness must be tempered by political realism. One of President Nixon's liaison chiefs started wearing a button with the slogan "I Like Congress" to remind other staffers of congressional sensibilities. From all accounts, the gimmick was not very successful.

Dispensing favors

Presidents can give out countless favors, big and little, to woo congressional support. The most effective ones raise the standing or ambitions of a senator or representative. A presidential appearance in the home base of the legislator is usually a plus. Alert administrators allow legislators, especially those of the president's party, to announce new federal projects in their state or district. The idea is to help legislators foster the view that they have the president's ear.

Patronage is less important than it once was. But it can still cement relations with influential legislators. Staff jobs or seats on government advisory committees can be used to reward a legislator's protégés or key backers.

Lesser perquisites can also be used. The pens the president uses to sign bills into law are passed out to the bill's supporters, along with signed pictures of the ceremony. These mementos have prized places on congressional office walls. So do autographed pictures of the president and his family. (When Carter sent out unsigned pictures, there was grumbling in congressional cloakrooms—after all, didn't every post office have such a photo?) Access to the White House, for serious policy talks or for a gala dinner, is always flattering. When Senator J. William Fulbright's (D-Ark.) Senate Foreign Relations Committee became a forum for anti-Vietnam War views in the 1960s, Fulbright was left off White House guest lists, even when by protocol he should have been invited.

The veto power

The president's final weapon in lawmaking is the veto. The president must sign or veto a bill within 10 days after it is sent to him. (Bills and joint resolutions go to the president for signature; simple resolutions, as statements of congres-

Bill signing. Climaxing the lawmaking process, President Lyndon Johnson signs bill launching the $1 billion War on Poverty. Note the handful of pens, each used for part of the signing, which will be given to the bill's sponsors.

sional views, do not.) A two-thirds vote in both houses is needed to override a veto—a formidable majority for congressional leaders to muster.

Veto threats   The veto is the nuclear deterrent in the president's arsenal. If Congress does not override the veto, it must drop the matter or draft a new bill more in line with the president's views.

Like the atom bomb, the veto has been more useful as a threat than in practice. Most of the time, legislators would rather have a bill passed than not, even if they must yield certain points.

When the White House and Congress are controlled by opposing parties, and when an election is just around the corner, things can change. Congressional leaders are not above sending the president a bill that they know he will reject. If it is vetoed, they can take the issue to the country, picturing the president as heartless or unresponsive. Presidents can, of course, also take their case to the people, saying that they are holding the line against an irresponsible Congress. (Modern presidential vetoes are presented in Table 9–3.)

Pocket vetoes   If the president fails either to sign or return the bill within 10 days, it becomes law anyway—*unless* Congress by adjourning has kept him from returning the bill for further action. This is the so-called pocket veto, a tempting device because it lets the president kill a bill without an obvious veto. The pocket veto means that Congress must start the bill all over again; it forecloses an early vote to override the veto.

Presidents sometimes try to use pocket vetoes when Congress has recessed for only a brief time. Nixon's frequent use of pocket vetoes was one part of his war against Democrat-controlled Congresses. In December 1970, he pocket vetoed the Family Practice of Medicine Act (P.L. 91–696), which had passed the House, 412–3, and the Senate, 64–1. Thus, he was seeking to evade an almost certain override of his veto. The bill's chief sponsor, Senator Edward Kennedy (D-Mass.), took the case to court. The court struck down the president's interpretation of the pocket veto. The case did not reach the Supreme Court. The lower-court decision (buttressed by a later memorandum from the attorney general) seemed to establish the pocket veto as limited to the final adjournment of Congress, when further action is precluded. However, the issue was raised again when President Reagan pocket vetoed an El Salvador aid bill during the 1983 congressional session. Challenged by a bipartisan group of leaders in both chambers, the president's broad reading of the pocket veto provision was again rejected by a U.S. Court of Appeals panel.

President Andrew Johnson vetoes radical reconstruction legislation pushed by Congress.

TABLE 9–3

Modern Presidential Vetoes

President	Regular vetoes	Pocket vetoes	Total vetoes	Vetoes overridden
Roosevelt	372	263	635	9
Truman	180	70	250	12
Eisenhower	73	108	181	2
Kennedy	12	9	21	—
Johnson	16	14	30	—
Nixon	24	19	43	5
Ford	48	18	66	12
Carter	13	18	31	2
Reagan (through 1984)	16	7	23	3

Source: Gary L. Galemore, Congressional Research Service (1984).

Applying grass-roots pressure

In the end, the president's most potent legislative weapon is his standing in the country. If he is riding high in the polls, his natural competitors—senators, representatives, bureaucrats, and lobbyists—will think twice before crossing him. But if he is being knocked about by public criticism, others sense they can openly defy him.

When the popular Eisenhower was in the White House, Democratic leaders (who controlled Congress all but two of those years) hesitated to attack him directly. They preferred a posture of "responsible" opposition. In contrast, the Democratic 93d Congress (1973–74) mustered the courage to fight Nixon on various fronts, once it saw that he was undermined by the Watergate scandal. Legislators who had been shy about opposing Nixon suddenly found the voice to speak out.

The popular Eisenhower and the post-1973 Nixon are extreme examples; but people in Washington read the president's popularity all the time. They take his public rating into account when deciding whether, and how often, to bow to his wishes.

The president versus Congress?

Which is more powerful, Congress or the president? Has power shifted toward Congress or toward the president? Journalists forever chalk up the president's "wins" and "defeats" on this or that measure; some publications print "box scores" showing the president's success in coaxing bills through Congress.

An overview of president's success on Capitol Hill is given in Figure 9–3. The figure shows congressional approval of issues on which presidents have taken a clear-cut stand. All modern presidents have gained congressional approval of at least half the measures on which they took a stand. The most successful were Eisenhower, Johnson, Kennedy, and Reagan. But presidents have

FIGURE 9–3

Presidential Success on Capitol Hill (1953–1983)

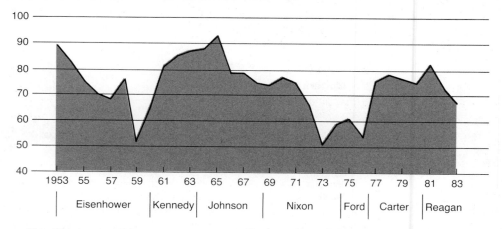

Note: Figures are annual percentages of presidential "victories" when presidents took clear-cut positions.
Source: *Congressional Quarterly Weekly Report* 41 (December 31, 1983), pp. 2782–83.

to struggle for Capitol Hill support. In turn, this support tends to decline in the later years of a president's tenure. Partisan swings affect presidents' success rates. So does the temper of the times; the 1970s in particular brought low support from Capitol Hill.

The relative power of the president and Congress is an elusive question. For one thing, influence itself is hard to measure, especially in the complex, multifaceted series of events that go along with most policy enactments. Second, what is most "influential" in the legislative process? Is it the initiation of an idea, the final passage, or some other phase of the process? Third, whoever reaps credit for legislation depends heavily on the media. Here, presidents have a marked advantage over Congress.

Presidents automatically command public attention when they propose legislation. Yet their proposals may be no more than hasty borrowings from ideas that have been floating around Capitol Hill for years.

Still, several conclusions can be drawn concerning the power of the two branches. First, the *absolute* power of *both* branches has risen historically. The reason is that federal government itself has grown. In the 1700s, government was small and remote from the daily lives of most Americans. Today, government intrudes into almost all aspects of our lives. You can see this in the growing congressional and presidential workload. Both the president and Congress, then, have shared in the fact that government has been a "growth industry."

Second, most commentators agree that the president has gained power in relation to Congress over the long haul. For most of the 1800s, and even into this century, presidents were outshone by leaders on Capitol Hill; in the post–Civil War years, the presidency was very weak. Woodrow Wilson referred to our system at that time as "congressional government." Today the president has more resources than ever to affect legislation and mobilize public opinion.

Finally, the president and Congress have varying degrees of influence in different policy fields. In some subjects, the president has almost free rein; in others, he is well advised to defer to legislative coalitions. Foreign policy and national security have been traditional sectors of presidential leadership. In contrast, Congress has kept a tight grip on measures that aid geographic and interest-based segments of the public; examples are tax code, tariffs and trade restrictions, grant-in-aid programs, and all types of public works projects (including the placement of military bases).

THE PRESIDENT AS CHIEF ADMINISTRATOR

The president heads the world's largest organization—the U.S. government. It has almost 3 million civilian employees and 2 million in the military. As we have seen, most presidents have little time or desire to intrude in day-to-day administrative affairs. But they recognize that this vast federal setup must implement their goals and carry their programs and services to average citizens.

There is a very long road between a program idea and the end result. An alert, responsive federal structure can react quickly to changing events and enhance the effect of programs. A sluggish or uncoordinated follow-up can blunt the impact of programs.

As chief executive, the president is formally responsible for government conduct and effectiveness. He appoints secretaries of the various departments (cabinet members) and heads of key agencies, members of regulatory commissions, and ambassadors—about 4,000 appointments in all.

These officials are supposed to act as the president's emissaries. They are expected to carry the idea of political control throughout the government. But in practice, presidential appointees are pulled in opposite directions, their loyalty to the White House challenged by their agency and its constituencies.

The White House versus agency loyalties

Agencies cherish their own traditions and rights. More important, they have their own allies on Capitol Hill and among interest groups. These forces shape agency viewpoints and goals as much as or more than the president does. The president and his aides are certain to be gone in four or eight years, but these people will stay. Who, then, is the agency going to listen to?

Thus, cabinet officers and other key officials are sometimes harassed men and women. They are appointed by the president and serve at his pleasure. At the same time, they cannot last long without support or at least assent from the civil servants in their agency, the congressional leaders who support and fund the agency, and the lobby groups affected by its activities. Secretaries of labor, for instance, must keep effective lines open to key labor leaders, especially in the AFL-CIO and major independent unions. That is why nearly every secretary of labor has been either a labor leader or someone close to the labor movement.

Once in a while, an agency's constituents may force an appointee to resign. Reagan's first Interior Secretary, James G. Watt, spurned the traditional role of mediating between his department's battling clienteles—environmentalists and public-lands users (cattle, timber, mineral, and energy interests). Support from these groups eroded; and after a string of public indiscretions, Watt was left with few allies and had to resign in October 1983.

Conversely, strong support may keep agency heads in office even after they have lost the president's confidence. Several presidents thought about removing FBI chief J. Edgar Hoover. But his popularity and unassailable public image kept him on the job for 48 years, until his death in 1972 at age 77.

J. Edgar Hoover, FBI director 1924–72, ran an independent agency but was reappointed by successive presidents because of his public popularity.

The president and the subgovernments

Despite constitutional authority and the power to appoint, presidents confront networks of entrenched interests that neither they nor their deputies can untangle.

For one thing, not one but many federal agencies have a stake in the outcome of most policies. Thus, time and effort are needed to lay the metes and bounds of each agency's duties. This is usually done by convening interagency task forces.

Committees on Capitol Hill are also touchy about changes that might lessen their influence. Shifting the Forest Service from the Agriculture Department to the Interior Department would no doubt please the House Interior and the Senate Energy and Natural Resources committees, which handle interior matters. But it would meet with strong opposition from the two agriculture committees.

Behind both executive agencies and congressional committees are lobby groups with a direct stake in keeping or changing policies. Faced with the veto power of these subgovernments, many presidents have despaired of achieving major shifts in program content or priorities.

Therefore, it is no surprise that every president since FDR, liberal and conservative alike, has railed against the complex, confused, uncontrollable federal setup. "To change anything in the Na-a-a-vy," said Roosevelt, an old Navy man himself, "is like trying to punch a feather bed. You punch it at one end, and then you punch it at the other, and the whole thing's back where you started. You punch it with your right and you punch it with your left until you are finally exhausted, and then you find the damn bed just as it was before you started punching" (Neustadt, 1976: 110).

The reorganizational imperative

Almost all modern presidents have struggled to remold the federal structure. They have had varying degrees of success. Harry Truman went so far as to call on the Democrats' arch foe, Herbert Hoover, to head a major reorganization effort; Dwight Eisenhower did the same thing a few years later. Lyndon Johnson proposed merging the Commerce and Labor departments, but quickly dropped the plan when business and labor groups spoke up.

In 1971, Richard Nixon unveiled a sweeping reorganization scheme. It would have formed four superdepartments, with all other agencies relegated to a lower status. Two years later, Nixon devised a cunning plan to tighten the reins on departments and agencies. He infiltrated their staffs with loyal White House staffers, forcing the agencies to report through four supercabinet members who were loyal Nixon advisers. This plan was dropped when the Nixon administration was crippled by Watergate (Nathan, 1983).

Nixon's successors have had no more success. Candidate Jimmy Carter promised sweeping reforms in government organization; President Carter moved more cautiously. His reorganization effort stalled; he ended up creating two new departments—Energy and Education. Reagan vowed to downgrade those new departments; he soon gave up the effort.

Understandably, presidents tend to see themselves as powerless Gullivers in the land of Lilliput. They feel hemmed in by government stubbornness and alliances of interest groups and congressional committees. But they have at least one tactic to bypass the subgovernments and assure responsive, loyal help. They can enlarge the White House staff and expand its duties. It is a technique that modern presidents have not been able to resist.

THE WHITE HOUSE BUREAUCRACY

The White House bureaucracy is the most striking feature of the modern institutionalized presidency. As mentioned, it has grown by leaps and bounds since the 1930s. Today the presidential bureaucracy has some 1,500 employees. (The figures are very unreliable, because employees are often detailed to the White House from other agencies.) The president's key advisers are in the Executive Office of the President, of which the White House Office is a part. Included in the EOP are several agencies that generally manage and coordinate functions for the executive branch.

The size of the president's staff invites criticism. Cronin (1980: 244) argues that the presidency has become a large complex bureaucracy itself, rapidly acquiring the many dubious characteristics of large bureaucracies in the process: layering, overspecialization, communication gaps, interoffice rivalries, inadequate coordination, and an impulse to become consumed with short-term, urgent operational concerns at the expense of thinking systematically about the consequences of varying sets of policies and priorities and about important long-range problems.

Various presidents have promised to pare down the White House payroll but have utilized the staff, whether members were credited to the White House or borrowed from other agencies.

The White House office

The White House Office itself has some 350 people who report directly or indirectly to the president. Most job titles tell little of their functions. There are counsel to the president, counsellor to the president, assistant to the president, and special assistant to the president, as well as directors of various offices. It is not easy to generalize about the duties of these people, which reflect the personal style and political priorities of the president. There are several distinct categories of staff functions, though.

Personal advisers   Chief aides on substantive and political matters coordinate and funnel information and advice flowing into the White House from many sources. Some are true experts, such as Henry Kissinger, Nixon's foreign policy specialist, or James Schlesinger, Carter's energy czar. Others are generalists, such as Kennedy's Theodore Sorensen, Johnson's Bill Moyers, Carter's Hamilton Jordan, and Reagan's Edwin Meese.

A few presidents have appointed chiefs of staff to exercise broad directorship over the White House and sometimes act as the president's alter ego. Sherman Adams, an efficient but crusty former New Hampshire governor, played this role for Eisenhower until scandal forced him to resign. Using the Eisenhower model, President Nixon chose H. R. (Bob) Haldeman as his first chief of staff. Haldeman was the leader of the so-alled "Prussians" who surrounded the president. They screened him from access by all but a select handful of trusted advisers. When Haldeman was fired for involvement in the Watergate cover-up, he was replaced by General Alexander Haig, who had the task of mapping out Nixon's retreat from office.

Ford and Carter resisted the chief-of-staff system; but it has since been reinstated as a way of managing the white House apparatus. Recent presidents, however, have tried to give access to a range of staff aides and outside advisers.

National security aides   The National Security Council (NSC) dates from 1947. It is made up of the president, vice president, secretary of state, and secretary of defense. Its advises the president on the national security implications of foreign, military, and domestic policies. Its small staff of professionals gives the president a counterweight to advice coming from the Defense and State Departments and the CIA. Henry Kissinger was NSC chief for Nixon; Zbigniew Brzezinski for Carter; Robert McFarlane now serves for Reagan.

The NSC gained power because presidents distrusted what they were being told by such old-line agencies as the departments of State and Defense. But these agencies questioned whether their rights should be usurped by presiden-

Multifaceted expert. James Schlesinger, who served four Cabinet level posts in three administrations.

"WELL, STAFF, ANY BRIGHT IDEAS ON HOW TO CLOSE THE RACE AND GENDER GAPS?"

Who has the chief's ear? In this version, ideologues and pragmatists contest over White House policy.

tial staff. Under Reagan, the secretaries of state insisted on a predominant role over national security advisers.

Domestic advice   During the Nixon years, a domestic counterpart to the NSC, the Domestic Council (now the Office of Policy Development), was set up by executive order (Kessel, 1975). Its membership comprises the "domestic cabinet" (heads of such departments as Treasury, Justice, Interior, Labor, Commerce, and Energy, plus administrators of such agencies as the Veterans Administration and the Environmental Protection Agency); it has a professional staff like that of the NSC. Stuart Eizenstat was domestic adviser to President Carter. He gained wide respect for his role in putting together presidential alternatives in domestic policies. The office has been downgraded under Reagan, who gives lower priority to domestic policy formulation.

The National Security Council and the Office of Policy Development show the cabinet's tendency to fall into distinct components that cover foreign and domestic affairs. These councils are mainly coordinating agencies. They bring agency heads together to give and receive advice. If presidents distrust the advice they receive from agency heads, they can get alternate information and plans from White House staff aides to these councils.

Legal advice   The White House counsel's office has existed since FDR's time. Some counsels wielded great influence with their bosses, not only rendering legal advice but policy formation, speechwriting, and political strategy. Since 1974 and the post-Watergate ethics laws, the office has come to the forefront in protecting the president and the official family from scandals or improprieties. Reagan's counsel, Fred W. Fielding, who heads what he terms his "great little law firm" of seven lawyers, handles a wide range of assignments for his client. The office reviews every speech the president delivers, every bill that is signed or vetoed, every official announcement, and every matter that might have legal bearing on the president (Kamen, 1984). Its duties have apparently become institutionalized, although its influence rests in part on the counsel's personal rapport with the president.

Press aides   Other White House staff fall into categories. The press staff manages the president's relationships with the White House press corps. It conducts press conferences, supervises press arrangements during presidential trips, and keeps in touch with the media. The press secretary, who heads this office, is one of the president's main advisers. The secretary expects to be consulted on the consequences of major decisions and himself gives daily press briefings. A small staff within the press section monitors press coverage of the White House. They then write up a daily condensed version of major news stories and editorial comment for the president's morning reading.

Lobbying　The congressional liaison staff manages day-to-day White House relations with Capitol Hill. The chief liaison officer (assistant to the president for legislative affairs) advises the president about possible Hill reactions to White House actions. This liaison aide is apt to hear first, and most strongly, about criticisms of White House actions. The staff is usually no more than 8 to 10 professionals. (Typically they have prior Hill experience.) They make day-to-day contacts with senators, representatives, and Hill staffers.

Liaison aides　Other presidential aides keep in touch with various specialized "publics." Many groups plead to be represented on the White House staff; they look for an adviser who "has the ear of the president." The pleas are most insistent from groups that, unlike business, labor, or agriculture, lack a regular cabinet agency to look after their interests.

Some presidents have given in and designated staff people to link the White House to certain groups—governors and mayors, blacks, Hispanics, ethnics, women, scientists, and so forth. Carter and Reagan, however, opted for an omnibus approach: a White House office to conduct liaison with a variety of groups and orchestrate campaigns for key presidential programs. (Ann Wexler built this office for Carter; Elizabeth Dole and Faith Whittlesey continued under Reagan.)

Housekeeping functions　Housekeeping of various sorts must be done to keep the White House working. People are needed to arrange schedules for the president and chief aides, to handle trips or visits, to answer mail, to plan White House dinners and social affairs. There is a French-trained chef, and even skilled calligraphers to hand-print invitations to state events. The First Lady has a social secretary and a press secretary as well as others who help answer mail and arrange her travel.

Our president is head of state as well as head of government. Therefore, the White House is more than a residence or a place of business; it is the closest thing we have to a royal palace or a national shrine. Thus, it is the setting for official visits and a glittering social life. State visitors stay in historic Blair House, across the street. A White House invitation is a prized possession for almost everyone, and a White House tour is a highlight of a trip to Washington. (Some guests go so far as to take "souvenirs," such as silverware.)

White House pomp and circumstance have been criticized, especially when President Nixon dressed White House guards in operetta-style uniforms and used trumpet fanfares and formal entrances and exits for noted visitors. Ford and Carter trimmed the pomposity; but Reagan restored some of the former glitter. Whatever the style, the White House remains a symbolic place and a setting for momentous meetings and conferences.

Protocol. President and Mrs. Kennedy greet the late Shah of Iran and his Empress (center), 1962.

The executive office of the president

The advisers already discussed are the front line of advisory and staff support for the president. They make up the White House Office. But a number of other agencies are a part of the Executive Office of the President. Though all such agencies report to the president, their value as advice givers or agents depends solely on how the president chooses to use them.

The Office of Management and Budget   Of these agencies, the OMB is surely the most important. It is the president's right hand in managing and monitoring the bureaucracy. OMB is an elite corps of professionals who analyze and screen budget requests from the departments and agencies; they work out procedures that promote economy, efficiency, and coordination; and they coordinate and clear agency advice on proposed bills. Though civil servants, OMB staff adopt a posture of loyalty to the president. They are the president's agents, expected to reflect and voice his priorities.

OMB's leverage is the yearly budgetary process. The office makes all executive agencies prepare budget requests, justify them under OMB scrutiny, and accede to OMB suggestions for shifts and cuts. OMB's suggestions are passed on to the president. He makes final decisions and resolves major issues, then submits the budget to Congress. (Congress has its own budget making process, described in Chapter 10.) If an agency wants to challenge an OMB recommendation, it may. But its chief officers must be willing to go straight to the president or one of his chief advisers to raise the issue. Needless to say, OMB is admired and feared by executive agencies and their managers.

In the Reagan administration, with its commitment to slowing growth in domestic spending, OMB became the cockpit for shaping the president's program. Its director, former Michigan Representative David A. Stockman, led the fight for budget cutbacks.

From its role with the budget, OMB has evolved other powers. It screens agency legislative requests—the so-called **central clearance function** (Neustadt, 1954, 1955). Thus, OMB puts the president's stamp on the legislative agendas of executive agencies. OMB has experts in program management, agency structure, personnel management, and evaluation of federal programs. It also coordinates federal regulations, information programs, and statistical indicators.

The Council of Economic Advisers   Another key agency is the Council of Economic Advisers (CEA), formed by the Employment Act of 1946. It is supposed to watch the national economy, advise the president on economic developments, and suggest policies for promoting economic growth, stability, and employment. The council's three members are appointed by the president with the advice and consent of the Senate. They are normally senior academic or business economists. The council's staff of economic analysts prepares studies and reports.

Council chairmen sometimes have a close relationship with the president, working as key advisers. Walter Heller, Kennedy's CEA chairman, spread the gospel of Keynesian economics, pushed a 1964 tax cut to spark the economy, and was widely credited as an architect of the mid-1960s economic expansion. Nixon's chairman, Paul McCracken, also served as a close presidential adviser. His influence was shared by such other powerful figures as George Shultz and John Connally, both Secretaries of the Treasury. One of Reagan's CEA chairmen, Martin Feldstein, gained notoriety by warning against huge deficits when other counselors were trying to downplay them. Today's CEA chairmen are relegated to a secondary rank, though they enjoy special status because of expertise and command of technical data.

The Secret Service   While not technically a part of the president's official family, the Secret Service (under the Treasury Department) is a constant companion to everything the president or White House advisers do. Time was when presidents mingled freely with common people; that age ended with the assassination of President Kennedy in 1963. Subsequent "incidents" or threats have led to ever tighter security procedures.

Security is a major consideration in scheduling the president's travel or appearances outside the White House. Locations are carefully inspected; attendees at speeches or meetings are screened and searched. Sometimes, it is claimed, security checks become a device to rid the president's entourage of protesters. But in most respects, presidents and their advisers consider security a constraint: it limits the president's mobility, and it entails cumbersome and costly planning whenever the official family ventures beyond the White House confines.

The vice president

Historically, the vice presidency has been a frustrating, ill-defined job. Its first occupant, John Adams, complained that "my country has in its wisdom contrived for me the most insignificant office that ever the invention of man contrived or his imagination conceived." Throttlebottom, the vice president in George Gershwin's 1931 musical, *Of Thee I Sing,* had to join a White House tour to see the inside of the building. From all accounts, vice presidents like Richard Nixon, Lyndon Johnson, and Hubert Humphrey found the experience frustrating and humiliating.

Vice President. George Bush plays active role in Reagan administration.

Recent vice presidents—Walter Mondale and George Bush—have shown, however, that the job can have broader dimensions. Underpinning their success was a decision to pursue utmost loyalty to the president, and to express dissent only in private, if at all.

Today's vice presidents play the following roles: (1) the constitutional duty of presiding over the Senate, voting in case of ties, and even (rarely) trying to sell the president's program to senators; (2) assisting the president in administrative duties, sitting in on cabinet sessions, presiding in the president's absence, and coordinating interagency projects for the president; (3) serving as the president's emissary to foreign countries; and (4) being the president's "troubleshooter" in appearing before domestic audiences, and especially in attacking the administration's political opponents.

The cabinet

The cabinet, composed of department heads (and others of cabinet rank, like the UN ambassador), is a creature of history unknown to the Constitution. Most presidents convene their cabinets periodically, but few have used them to make decisions. Selected for varying reasons, cabinet members come to view themselves as champions of departmental interests rather than as collective decision makers.

Recent presidents, however, have entered office vowing to use the cabinet more effectively. Some have convened the cabinet regularly. Reagan formed six cabinet councils, each composed of several secretaries: commerce and trade; economic affairs; energy and natural resources; food and agriculture; human resources; and legal policy. These councils met frequently, sometimes with the

Cabinet. White House session of the Reagan Cabinet.

president but always with White House staff support. They discussed working papers and tried to relate the president's overall policies to their respective domains.

Coordinating agencies   Other White House agencies encourage concerted action on policies involving many departments and other agencies. As we have noted, it is often hard to persuade agencies to cooperate. Interagency committees and task forces abound. They often function like summit meetings of sovereign powers, with each agency's representative striving to guard its own turf. For this reason, presidents set up coordinating staffs. The theory is that a White House agency can exploit the president's prestige to "knock heads" and impel agencies to work together.

Certain policies have thus been coordinated through White House staff agencies at one time or another. These include environmental protection (Council on Environmental Quality), inflation (Council on Wage and Price Stability), international economics (Council on International Economic Policy), and trade negotiations (Office of the Special Representative for Trade Negotiations).

Needless to say, a position on a White House organization chart does not always ensure the clout to get the job done. The president's personal intervention is often needed to persuade administrators that some agency autonomy must be given up in the interests of coherent policymaking.

THE SWELLING OF THE PRESIDENCY

During the last four decades, the presidency has turned into a large establishment. The reasons for this "swelling of the presidency" are not far beneath the surface.

Gravitation to the White House

After FDR, presidents began to gather new functions, especially in crisis settings. They needed staff assistants who were instantly available and personally loyal. Many came to believe that the president and his aides were best equipped to solve knotty problems and initiate urgent government efforts. Congress, too, tends to hold the president personally responsible for such matters. Therefore, they have authorized such White House agencies as the National Security Council, the Council of Economic Advisers, and the Council on Environmental Quality.

Successive presidents, Democrat or Republican, have grown restless with how established bureaucratic agencies perform. These agencies have become more and more cumbersome in resolving today's public problems. Many problems, such as international trade, inflation, and energy shortages, defy delegation to any one department. Writes Cronin (1980: 245):

> Occupants of the White House frequently distrust members of the permanent government. . . . Departmental bureaucracies are often viewed from the White House as independent, unresponsive, unfamiliar, and inaccessible. They are suspected again and again of placing their own, congressional, or special-interest priorities ahead of those communicated to them from the White House.

It is no surprise, then, that presidents surround themselves with their own people, whose loyalty and dedication keep the president's causes alive in the hostile world of special interests.

Flaws in the presidential bureaucracy

The swelling of the presidency is a mixed blessing. For one thing, presidential advisers tend to lack constituencies outside the White House. Unless their single-minded loyalty to their boss is counterbalanced by wide experience in politics and government, they may give ill-informed advice.

Also, the advisory system is only as good as those the president chooses. Some presidents, such as Roosevelt and Kennedy, relished the presence of first-class intellects bold enough to challenge the president's own ideas. Others, such as Nixon and Johnson, had fragile egos and were more comfortable surrounded by flatterers.

Finally, there are many chances for abuse in a swollen White House establishment. Much of its work is broad and only vaguely defined. Lines of power are rarely clear. This means that aides waste time jockeying for position and access to the president. It is too easy for such people to embark on their own projects to win their boss's attention and approval. They may trade on White House prestige and those magic words, "The president wants. . . ." The White House "plumbers' " group, of Watergate fame, was one such scheme. This mix of irresponsibility, lack of a constituency, and vague authority has led some (Hess, 1976) to urge that presidents downplay their own staff and give more duties to cabinet appointees.

Despite these drawbacks, the White House establishment is here to stay. It is another reflection of the modern, institutionalized presidency. It provides presidents with staff support to strive to do what citizens expect. It helps them communicate with the public, stay in touch with varied interest groups, and provide legislative leadership.

As we have seen, presidents prefer to surround themselves with loyal underlings. Presidential appointees in departments and agencies—even cabinet members—can be captured by agencies, their clienteles on Capitol Hill, and lobbyists. White House aides lack this base of operation. They are the president's own people; and their loyalty is both their strength and their weakness.

PRESIDENTIAL POWER: TOO MUCH OR TOO LITTLE?

After Vietnam and Watergate, it became popular to put down the "imperial presidency." Checks on presidential power from Congress, the courts, and public opinion were emphasized. As Arthur M. Schlesinger, Jr., wrote in 1973, "The pivotal institution of the American government, the presidency, has got out of control and badly needs new definition and restraint." George Reedy, former press secretary for Lyndon Johnson, pointed to the pomp and pageantry that had come to surround the institution. "By the 20th century," he wrote (1970: 22), "the presidency had taken on all the regalia of monarchy except robes, a scepter, and a crown."

If the trappings of power are impressive, the reality of that power is elusive. Presidents themselves are impressed not by their power, but by the strong forces that work to limit and negate it. In his last months in office, Harry Truman spoke wryly of his successor, Eisenhower. "He'll sit here," he would say, tapping the desk for emphasis, "and he'll say, 'Do this! Do that!'—*and nothing will happen!* Poor Ike—it won't be a bit like the army. He'll find it very frustrating" (Neustadt, 1976: 77). In a TV interview in December 1962, Kennedy confessed that Congress looked much stronger from the White House than from a senator's office.

Presidents of both parties and varied persuasions have been dismayed and frustrated at the limits of their influence. Nixon was obsessed with this. He thought he had received a mandate from the people, yet he saw himself thwarted on every hand by hostile forces. To subvert those forces, Nixon devised a variety of strategies. These included taking apart federal programs, drafting reorganization plans, White House infiltration of agencies, and spying to ensure a landslide victory in 1972. We might say that Watergate grew out of a weak, frustrated presidency, not an imperial one. At the least, we can say that both the people and the president expect far more than the presidency can ever fulfill.

The mood since Vietnam and Watergate has fluctuated wildly. At first, there was massive reaction against presidential leadership, accompanied by widespread cynicism about government. Other political actors—including Congress and the media—rediscovered their will to resist presidential moves. Ford and Carter thus conducted their presidencies on weak strategic ground. Yet their incapacity to cope with such challenges as inflation or foreign crises brought counter-demands for strengthened leadership. Commentators lamented presidential inability to "form a government"; some even resurrected old proposals to bind Congress to presidential initiatives through changes borrowed from parliamentary systems. Despite Nixon's successors' promises to rid the presidency of royalty and myth, public and press attention remained riveted on the office.

Reagan's stunning success in selling his program on Capitol Hill in 1981 showed that strong leadership rested more on circumstances and skills than on institutional arrangements. Reagan continued to be seen as a strong leader, even when his policies and programs were resisted or thwarted. These events are only the latest in the recurrent ebb and flow of executive powers. They mirror again Edward S. Corwin's description of the Constitution as an "invitation to struggle" over power.

For their part, presidents have every reason to foster the cult of the presidency. They rightly sense that public attention and support are their strongest resources for putting their imprint on public policy. Other institutions—Congress, the press, the bureaucracy, and the courts—have vital roles to play; but they lack the president's capacity to gain the public imagination. And they are ill equipped to provide coherent or coordinated leadership.

The American public, for its part, wants to believe in presidential leadership. Its high hopes as each new administration begins are continuing evidence. And with the right person in the White House, the public may fulfill its hopes.

CONCLUSIONS

In this chapter, we have explored the paradoxes of the presidency—a job which, as Thomas Cronin says, "is always too powerful and yet it is always inadequate" (1980: 22). We have underscored the contrasts between the image and reality of the office—between its possibilities and its limitations.

1 Although champions of the rights of legislative bodies, the founders wrote a potentially powerful presidency into the Constitution. Having little to guide them, they sketched Article II of the Constitution in vague terms and left history to work out the details.

2 The president's substantive duties may be classed in three "subpresidencies": foreign affairs and national security, aggregate economics, and domestic policies.

3 In addressing these concerns, presidents engage in various types of involvement: crisis management, symbolic leadership, priority setting, recruitment of aides, coalition building, implementation, and oversight of government routines.

4 The crux of the president's power lies in the office's unique visibility and ability to focus public attention and mobilize public support.

5 In shaping national policy, presidents must cope with Congress—a large body of leaders elected from constituencies that are not national. Presidents have a number of tools for leading Congress. These include agenda setting, central clearance, legislative liaison, dispensing of favors, and veto powers. In the end, the most potent weapon is grass-roots support.

6 The federal bureaucracy is the other great institutional challenge. In theory, presidents head the bureaucracy. In fact, they struggle simply to avoid being controlled by it.

7 Organizationally, presidents are aided by their own bureaucracy—the White House Office and the larger Executive Office of the President. This bureaucracy is shaped by the president's personality and style. It is a useful but potentially dangerous instrument.

FURTHER READING

CRONIN, THOMAS E. (1980) The State of the Presidency. 2d ed. Boston: Little, Brown. An ingenious interpretation of the promise and limits of the presidency, based in part on interviews with White House staff members, cabinet officials, and department advisers.

FISHER, LOUIS (1985) Constitutional Conflicts between Congress and the President. Princeton, N.J.: Princeton University Press. A provocative examination of legislative-executive relationships based on historical and political factors.

HESS, STEPHEN (1976) Organizing the Presidency. Washington, D.C.: Brookings Institution. A critical examination of White House organizational arrangements from FDR through Ford.

NEUSTADT, RICHARD E. (1979) Presidential Power: The Politics of Leadership from FDR to Carter. New York: John Wiley & Sons. An influential exploration of the dilemmas faced by modern presidents in seeking to maximize their influence.

10
Congress: Politicians and Policymaking

The House of Representatives put on a running daytime TV drama in 1984. For months, a small group of militant Republicans had been giving speeches on the House floor, lambasting Democratic leaders for bottling up conservative measures. House floor proceedings are broadcast by a cable-satellite system to millions of homes, and so the militants were beginning to be noticed.

Speaker Thomas P. O'Neill (D–Mass.) countered by ordering House TV cameras (previously fixed only on members who were speaking) to pan through the chamber, showing that the GOP militants were declaiming to empty seats. One of them, Newt Gingrich of Georgia, then took the floor to denounce O'Neill. As members streamed into the chamber to see the fray, O'Neill himself lumbered down the aisle.

"Will the gentleman yield?" O'Neill growled. Gingrich yielded.

"My personal opinion is that you deliberately stood in that well before an empty House and challenged these [Democrats] and you challenged their Americanism," O'Neill shouted, waving his finger at Gingrich, "and it is the lowest thing that I have ever seen in my 32 years in Congress" (*Congressional Record*, 1984: H3843).

At that, Deputy GOP Leader Trent Lott of Mississippi leaped to his feet and demanded that the Speaker's words be "taken down" as violating House rules. The parliamentarian advised the presiding officer that O'Neill was out of order, and he so ruled.

The clash on the House floor was without modern precedent. Beyond the personal drama, it reflected deep clashes over policy, ideology, and politics. It underscored the era of divided government, in which Republicans held the White House and Senate, while Democrats controlled the House.

* * * * *

Presidents may propose, but it is Congress that disposes. The Founders, staunch believers in legislative power, gave Congress broad policy authority, including making all laws "necessary and proper" to implement the enumerated powers. Presidents and their advisers without exception chafe at congressional limitations; none has been able to overcome them for long. Even a strong and popular chief executive like Ronald Reagan, who seemed unstoppable during his first year in office, later found himself stalemated by rival leaders on Capitol Hill.

Upper left: Representative Robert S. Walker (R–Pa.), addresses House. *Upper right:* Camera pans empty House chamber as Rep. Walker speaks. *Lower left:* Representative Newt Gingrich (R–Ga.) denounces Democratic leaders. *Lower right:* Speaker Thomas P. O'Neill (D–Mass.) responds to critics.

MEMBERS AS REPRESENT-ATIVES

According to democratic theory, the legislative branch is uniquely the people's voice. "Here, sir, the people govern," observed Alexander Hamilton—himself no friend of popular institutions. "This body," said a former member of Congress, "is a mirror in which America can see herself." Executive agencies are anonymous and even secret; the courts work in magisterial isolation. But our traditions dictate that Congress remain open and accessible.

Who are the legislators?

The constitutional requirements of office are fairly broad: age (25 years of age for the House of Representatives, 30 for the Senate); citizenship (seven years for the House, nine for the Senate); and residency in the state.

The residency requirement is sometimes hard to apply, given Americans' mobility. Voters seem to prefer candidates with long-standing ties to the state or district. But well-known people sometimes are elected from places where they reside only in the loosest sense.

How representative?   In practice, the gateways to election are much narrower than the constitutional requirements. So not all Americans have an equal chance of serving.

As a whole, the members of Congress are an elite group. The average representative is in his or her late 40s; the average senator, mid-50s. That is a decade or so older than the average voter. The educational level of members is high. The professions dominate—especially law (about half the members), business, agriculture, education, and journalism.

The "log cabin to Capitol Hill" myth does not apply to today's legislators. One study (Matthews, 1960) showed senators tend to come from middle- and upper-class families. Only a handful of blacks and Hispanics serve, though their number is growing. Congress has also been a mostly male institution; in the 98th Congress, there were only 22 women, 2 of whom were in the Senate. Indeed, only a hundred or so women have ever served in Congress since the first, Jeannette Rankin (R-Mont.), was elected in 1916. At first many were elected on the so-called "widow's mandate"—when their husbands died in office (Gertzog, 1984). Now, however, most pursue their own political careers; their growing influence on Capitol Hill was underscored in 1984 when Geraldine Ferraro (D-N.Y.) was chosen vice presidential candidate.

This means that Congress is made up of people who do not strictly represent the population in terms of age, education, wealth, color, or sex. (The same, of course, applies to the courts and the executive branch.)

Virtual representation   Must Congress be demographically representative? Not necessarily. Legislators can speak effectively for voters of different social rank or lifestyle. Legislators from farming districts, for instance, can voice farmers' concerns even though they themselves have never plowed a field or milked a cow. This is called virtual representation.

Speaking for constituents is natural for legislators. They are in the business of cultivating public support. Before coming to Congress, most senators and representatives apprentice in state and local politics, especially in state legislatures. As transplanted locals, legislators reflect the values and attitudes of their home districts. If they lose touch with constituents' demands, they risk losing office.

Yet there is no real substitute for having a grouping's own member serve in Congress. The presence of women and minority lawmakers, for example, has heightened Congress's sensitivity to the needs of those groups. And for voters of those groupings, having one of their own in office symbolizes a "coming of age." Such legislators become rallying points for group members throughout the nation.

The public looks at Congress

Americans are of two minds about Congress. As an institution, it is an enigma to most people. Its large size, puzzling procedures, and measured pace all blur its image. Individual legislators, in contrast, are more understood and approved.

Congress as policymaker   Most people think of Congress in public-policy terms. They expect Congress, like the president, to solve problems and keep

FIGURE 10–1

A Fever Chart of Congressional Popularity

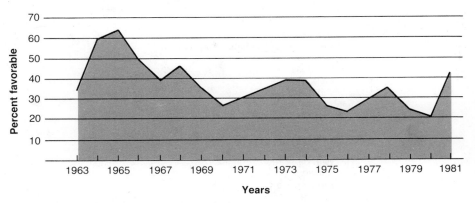

Question: "How would you rate the job done this past year by Congress—excellent, pretty good, only fair, or poor?" Favorable responses are "excellent" or "pretty good."
Source: The Harris Survey.

the ship of state on an even keel; they also expect Congress to respond to the president's initiatives (Parker, 1974).

Public approval of Congress rises and falls with economic conditions, wars and crises, and feelings of cynicism; these are the same factors that affect views of presidential performance (see Chapter 9). If people feel pleased about the state of the nation, they tend to approve the work of Congress; if they are unhappy, fearful, or cynical—as they were in the 1970s—they hold Congress in low esteem (see Figure 10–1).

Legislators as representatives   As for individual legislators, people have far more detailed expectations. If Congress is mysterious and distant, incumbent legislators are fairly well known in their states or districts. They are judged less on policy contributions than on their service to their districts: How accessible are they? How well do they communicate with voters? Do they help in solving voters' problems? And do they have the ability to "bring home the bacon" in the form of federal contracts and grants? (Parker and Davidson, 1979)

Legislators and their staffs spend much time and effort fulfilling these expectations. It usually pays off. Voters repeatedly proclaim their representative to be "the best congressman in the whole country." At the same time, they express disgust with Congress in general (Fenno, 1975). A recent Harris survey found that nearly twice as many people rated their own representatives positively as gave similar marks to Congress as a whole.

The public's final verdict on its legislators is at the polls; here, the picture is just as inconsistent. Incumbent representatives usually win; senators lose somewhat more often.

Legislators' roles

Lawmaking or errand running?   Legislators differ widely in how they represent the people. (See Table 10–1.) Some are errand runners. They spend most of their time keeping contact with their home bases and answering constituents' requests for help. Errand runners include freshmen legislators unsure of

328

TABLE 10–1

A Representative's "Average Day"

Activity		Average time
In the House chamber		2:53 hours
In committee/subcommittee work		1:24 hours
Hearings	26 minutes	
Business	9 minutes	
Markups	42 minutes	
Other	5 minutes	
In his/her office		3:19 hours
With constituents	17 minutes	
With organized groups	9 minutes	
With others	20 minutes	
With staff aides	53 minutes	
With other representatives	5 minutes	
Answering mail	46 minutes	
Preparing legislation, speeches	12 minutes	
Reading	11 minutes	
On telephone	26 minutes	
In other Washington locations		2:02 hours
With constituents at Capitol	9 minutes	
At events	33 minutes	
With leadership	3 minutes	
With other representatives	11 minutes	
With informal groups	8 minutes	
In party meetings	5 minutes	
Personal time	28 minutes	
Other	25 minutes	
Other		1:40 hours
Total average representative's day		11:18 hours

Source: U.S. House of Representatives, Commission on Administrative Review, *Administrative Reorganization and Legislative Management* (95th Congress, 1st session, 1977, H. Doc. 95–232), pp. 18–19.

reelection; those from competitive or marginal districts; those whose districts are so close to the nation's capital that voters expect them to be back home each weekend; and senators near the end of their term who face a close reelection fight.

Other legislators channel their energies into legislative tasks. They let their staff aides handle back-home relations. Such legislators are mostly from safe districts. Or they have high seniority or leadership posts; or they are so firmly entrenched that they have few reelection fears.

The pivotal factor seems to be whether a member is electorally vulnerable or safe. The vulnerable member is closely tethered; the safe member is freer to be a statesman (Davidson, 1969). When push comes to shove, most legislators will slight their legislative duties to go back home and mend fences to keep their jobs. As one representative put it, "All members of Congress have a primary interest in being reelected. But some members have no other interest."

Whom to listen to? Legislators also differ widely in their approach to law-making tasks. Their workload is so heavy that they cannot be fully informed on every matter. So they seek cues on how to vote from many sources. Some rely on their own knowledge or conscience; others follow instructions, either actual or implied, from their voters.

Skillful legislators anticipate voter reactions. They learn to spot those issues that most concern their constituents. Legislators have freedom of action because most people are uninformed or unconcerned about most issues (Miller

and Stokes, 1963). Elected officials tend to agree with the legislator who said that although everything he did had a relationship to the district, the district was not his only basis for choice.

Legislators are attuned to different constituencies. Some say they use the whole nation's welfare as a guide; others speak for purely local interests. Usually, legislators find it impossible to relate to the whole voting public. Rather, they rely on their own views of their district and on aides who pass on cues about voter needs or desires (Miller and Stokes, 1963).

Home style

As important as legislators' stands on issues is how they project themselves in their home states or districts. Richard F. Fenno, Jr. (1978) calls this the legislators' **home styles.**

Home styles are made up of several factors. One is how legislators allocate resources. How do they use staff, office, or financial resources? How do they use their greatest resource—their own time? One study of 419 representatives found that the average member made 35 trips home (not counting recesses) and spent 138 days there (counting recesses). Nearly one third of these members returned to their districts every weekend.

A second factor in home style is the legislators' "presentation of self" in face-to-face contacts with voters and in voicing issues and informing voters.

Finally, legislators form certain themes to explain their work in Washington to the voters. They know far more about issues than the average person, so they can usually explain their behavior well enough to please all but the most demanding listeners. A few legislators bolster their home image by "running against Congress." They defend their own record while faulting their House or Senate colleagues.

Constituency outreach   An important point of contact between legislators and the electorate is constituency service. This includes answering mail, solving constituents' problems, making speeches in the state or district, putting out newsletters or press releases, and meeting with voters.

Many of these are **casework** tasks—helping people cope with an ever-more complex government bureaucracy. (The leading types of casework are listed in Table 10–2.) Besides handling constituents' problems (for instance, investigating errors in social security or veterans' payments), legislators use casework to build support for reelection. In a 1976 study, 15 percent of all adults reported that they or a member of their family had asked for help from their representative. Seven out of ten of those said they were satisfied with the way their request was handled.

Legislators' workloads are now staggering. "It was a pretty nice job that a member of Congress had in those days," recalled former Representative Robert Ramspeck (D-Ga.), who came to Washington in 1911 as a staff aide. At that time, letters to legislators were confined mainly to the problems of rural mail routes, pensions for veterans of the Spanish-American War, free seed, and once in a while a legislative matter. One clerk was enough to handle the mail. Now constituencies are larger and more sophisticated, and the government has a bigger role in peoples' lives. Expert staffs, in Washington and in district offices, are needed to cope. So legislators now head large and growing bureaucracies, and staff members play a big role in policymaking.

TABLE 10—2

What Is "Constituency Casework"?

Category of cases	Percent*
Inquiries about legislation	16
Requests for a government job	8
Help with Social Security	8
Hardship discharges from the military	7
Requests for government publications	7
Seeking appointments to military academies	4
Help with unemployment assistance benefits	4
Tax problems	2
Legal problems	1
Miscellaneous problems	49

*Figures total more than 100 percent because some respondents are included in more than one category.

Source: U.S. House of Representatives, Commission on Administrative Review, *Final Report* (95th Congress, 1st session, 1977, H. Doc. 95–272): II, p. 830.

Perquisites   The government subsidizes senators' and representatives' offices to help them keep in touch with their people. But this is often derided as fringe benefits or perquisites. The House has an array of benefits; Senate subsidies vary with the size of the state. The average House member is allowed a payroll of nearly $400,000 a year; Senate payrolls range from nearly $700,000 (for Delaware and Alaska) to more than $1.3 million (for New York and California). House members are limited to 22 aides, but senators can hire as many people as they can get for the money.

The average representative receives perquisites valued at over $1.2 million for each two-year term; the average senator's office operation requires more than that in a single year. Such resources are needed; but they also help to stimulate support and firm up the legislator's reelection chances. In the hands of a skillful incumbent with an able staff, these resources give an edge that few challengers can beat. It is surely a factor in how often incumbents are returned to office.

Legislators and their careers are one aspect of Congress. Some say this is the main aspect (Mayhew, 1974). Legislators are ambassadors from their states or districts. Their careers depend very little on what Congress accomplishes as a whole. But they depend a great deal on the legislators' relationships with local voters. From all accounts, this side of Congress is prospering. Despite public cynicism about politics and Congress, most individual legislators get high ratings and are reelected in overwhelming numbers.

Yet an elected politician's life is mentally demanding and physically wearing—a situation not likely to abate. Many retire voluntarily to escape the pressures. Others think that the attention members pay to their own careers affects their lawmaking performance. It is to the lawmaking tasks that we now turn.

COMMITTEE AND SUBCOMMITTEE GOVERNMENT

Committees and subcommittees are the key policymaking bodies in Congress. As Woodrow Wilson (1885: 79) observed long ago, congressional government is committee government: "Congress in session is Congress on display, but Congress in committee is Congress at work."

A ROUGH IDEA OF CONGRESSIONAL ALLOWANCES, 1984

There are two conclusions about allowances: (1) they have risen greatly in recent years; and (2) the exact figures are hard to obtain.

Following is a list of available figures for House and Senate allowances in 1984. In some cases, no dollar value is given because it is hard to determine the range of reimbursed costs—for example, in travel or telephone reimbursements. Most of the 1984 allowances can be transferred from one account to another.

	House	Senate
Salary	$72,600*	$72,600*
Washington office		$668,504–1,343,218†
Staff	$379,480	
Committee legislative assistants	‡	$207,342
Interns	$1,840	—
General office expenses	$47,300	$36,000–156,000†
Telephone/telegraph	15,000 long-distance minutes to district	§
Stationery	§	1.4–25 million pieces
Office space	2–3-room suites	5–8-room suites
Furnishings	§	§
Equipment	Provided	Provided
District/state offices		
Rental	2,500 sq. ft.	4,800–8,000 sq. ft.
Furnishings/equipment	$35,000	$22,500–31,350
Mobile office	—	One
Communications		Provided by Senate Computer Center
Automated correspondence	§	
Audio/video recordings; photography	§	§
Travel	Formula (min. $6,200; max. approx. $67,200)	§

*Salary established January 1, 1984; leaders' salaries are higher.
†Senators are allowed expenses based on a sliding scale linked to the state's population.
‡Provided for members of Appropriations, Budget, and Rules committees.
§Expenses are covered through the general office expenses line item. In most cases supplies and equipment are charged at rates well below retail levels.
Source: Committee on House Administration; Senate Committee on Rules and Administration.

The urge to specialize

Almost all legislation comes from, or is refined by, committee work. By any set of standards, the House and Senate are complex: the Senate has 20 committees and 107 subcommittees; the House has 27 committees and 148 subcommittees. There are also four joint committees (with five subcommittees)—not to mention many temporary panels, boards, and commissions. The various House and Senate committees are listed in Table 10–3.

Despite attempts to streamline, committee and even subcommittee autonomy is formidable. One scholar (Polsby, 1968: 556) concluded: "Committees nowadays have developed an independent sovereignty of their own, subject only to very infrequent reversals and modifications of their powers by House party leaders backed by large and insistent majorities."

Types of committees

Standing committees   Committees are pivotal in the legislative process. Therefore, they have evolved into specialized types and have specified roles.

TABLE 10–3

The Committees of Congress

Senate	House of Representatives
Agriculture, Nutrition, and Forestry (18)	Agriculture (41)
Appropriations (29)	Appropriations (57)
Armed Services (18)	Armed Services (44)
Banking, Housing, and Urban Affairs (18)	Banking, Finance, and Urban Affairs (46)
Budget (22)	Budget (31)
	⎧ Energy and Commerce (42)
Commerce, Science, and Transportation (17)	⎨ Science and Technology (41)
	⎩ Merchant Marine and Fisheries (39)
Energy and Natural Resources (20)	Interior and Insular Affairs (39)
Environment and Public Works (16)	Public Works and Transportation (48)
Finance (20)	Ways and Means (35)
Foreign Relations (17)	Foreign Affairs (37)
	⎧ Government Operations (39)
Governmental Affairs (6)	⎨ District of Columbia (11)
	⎩ Post Office and Civil Service (24)
Labor and Human Resources (18)	Education and Labor (31)
Judiciary (18)	Judiciary (31)
Rules and Administration (12)	⎧ House Administration (19)
	⎩ Rules (13)
Small Business (9)	Small Business (41)
	Standards of Official Conduct (12)
Veterans' Affairs (12)	Veterans' Affairs (33)
Select committees:	Select committees:
Ethics (6)	Aging (60)
Indian Affairs (7)	Intelligence (14)
Intelligence (15)	Narcotics Abuse and Control (25)
Special committee:	Children, Youth and Families (25)
Aging (15)	Hunger (17)

Note: Number of members is indicated in parenthesis.

The most common is the standing committee, which has a fixed jurisdiction and is regarded as permanent. It lasts beyond any given two-year Congress. (Of course, each house may change or abolish a committee at any time, though this rarely occurs.) Standing committees handle major policy categories. These include foreign policy, banking, finance, public works, law enforcement, general government affairs, and the like. In the 98th Congress, the Senate had 16 standing committees; the House had 22.

Most standing committees have subcommittees. In the House, committees of 20 or more members must set up subcommittees.

Several key distinctions are made among committees, including whether it is *legislative* or *nonlegislative*. Legislative committees can report bills to the full chamber; nonlegislative committees just investigate and prepare reports. All standing committees are legislative; so, too, are some select and special panels. Joint committees are mostly nonlegislative.

There is another distinction, between *authorizing* and *fiscal* committees. Most standing committees are the former. They authorize, or draft, the substance of government policies, subject of course to the vote of the full chamber. The legislation they write empowers the government to do certain things, such as running training programs or prisons or diplomatic missions. But this does not allow the government to spend money for programs or to raise money for the

Select panel. The Senate's Select Committee on Intelligence meets to review CIA activities. Panel Chairman Barry Goldwater (R–Ariz.), right front, confers with Vice Chairman Daniel Patrick Moynihan (D–N.Y.). Both have clashed with CIA Director William Casey (left rear), talking with Senator Alphonse M. D'Amato (R–N.Y.).

Treasury. This is done through appropriations (spending) or revenue (taxing) bills.

To coordinate taxing and spending legislation, Congress has set up a complex budget process. This both coordinates revenues and expenditures and sets guidelines. We will explain this at a later point. In brief, the three types of fiscal committees are *taxing* (Senate Finance; House Ways and Means), *spending* (Senate and House Appropriations), and *budgetary* (Senate and House Budget).

Temporary committees   In addition to standing committees, at any given time there are also temporary committees, formed to undertake a particular task, such as a study or an investigation. Sometimes temporary committees can report legislation on a certain topic; sometimes they just make recommendations.

Temporary committees take several forms. **Select committees** are normally appointed by the presiding officer. **Special committees** are appointed through each party's normal committee assignment process. The House speaker also can appoint **ad hoc committees.** These are made up of members of the two or more standing committees that have jurisdiction over parts of a question. In recent years, such committees have been appointed to deal with matters of energy and the offshore outer continental shelf.

Joint committees   Formed by concurrent resolution or legislation, joint committees draw members from both the House and the Senate. This is one way to coordinate a bicameral legislature. But legislators are jealous of the prerogatives of their own chambers and tend to be suspicious of joint committees. Today, there are just four joint committees, two of which—Printing and Library—handle housekeeping matters. A third, the Joint Committee on Taxation, is a holding company for a small but valued staff that advises taxing committees in the two chambers. The fourth, the Joint Economic Committee, is a forum for macroeconomic discussions and periodic reports. None of the joint committees has the power to report legislation directly to the two chambers.

Conference committees   A more common joint body is the conference committee. This is actually an ad hoc panel formed to work out differences when a bill passes the two houses in different forms. Conferees (called managers) are picked by the presiding officer of each house, on the suggestion of the chairmen of committees that handled the bill.

The conferees deal with the points of disagreement between House and Senate versions. They are then expected to back the positions of their own chambers. However, conferees from each house vote as a bloc. To avoid deadlock, then, they must either compromise or "recede" from the position of their chamber. Sometimes conferees are blamed for yielding too much to the other chamber or for adding new provisions to the legislation.

Committees owe their power to the volume and complexity of the legislation brought before Congress. Only by dividing its workload can a legislative body hope to keep abreast of the demands of modern government. Also, committee power is aided by three features of the modern Congress: *careerism, seniority,* and *decentralization.*

Committee assignments and careerism

New senators and representatives must set up a beachhead in the nation's capital. The committees they are assigned to are crucial to their political fates.

All four congressional parties (that is, the House and Senate Democrats and Republicans) have bodies that make committee assignments: the Senate Democratic Steering Committee, the House Democratic Steering and Policy Committee, and the Republican committees on committees. All assignments are then ratified by the full party contingent. Democrats call this their caucus; Republicans call it their conference.

Legislators do not just wait for assignments to come their way. They submit their preferences and, if they are alert, they lobby party leaders and influential senior colleagues. There is constant pressure to raise the number of committee seats by adding committees or subcommittees and by increasing their size. Today the average senator serves on 12 committees and subcommittees; the average representative serves on 6.

Career goals   Legislators view committee assignments in terms of career goals and hopes. Fenno (1973) lists at least three goals that can be furthered by committee service. First, some committees boost their members' reelection prospects. These include panels that deal with local or regional interests, or with industries noted for heavy PAC campaign contributions. Such topics are, most notably, agriculture, banking, commerce and energy, merchant marine, transportation, interior, and public works.

Second, committee membership helps legislators contribute to policymaking. Some committees satisfy this need yet lack direct election payoffs. Included are those dealing with the judiciary, education and human resources, foreign affairs, and similar broad policy topics.

Finally, some committees are valued because of their influence within the House or Senate. Members of these decide on critical matters. In this category are some of the most prestigious committees: taxing (Senate Finance, House Ways and Means), spending (Appropriations), budget, and internal scheduling (House Rules).

The pecking order   Some committees are more coveted than others. This leads to an informal pecking order. The House designates its committees as

Senate Foreign Relations Committee. *Front (from left)*: Alan Cranston (D–Calif.); ranking Democrat Claiborne Pell (R.I.); chairman Charles H. Percy (R–Ill.); Nancy Landon Kassebaum (R–Kan.); Charles McC. Mathias, Jr. (R–Md.). *Second row:* Joseph R. Biden, Jr. (D–Del.); John Glenn (D–Ohio); Paul E. Tsongas (D–Mass.); Paul S. Sarbanes (D–Md.); Rudy Boschwitz (R–Minn.); Richard G. Lugar (R–Ind.); Howard H. Baker, Jr. (R–Tenn.); Edward Zorinsky (D–Neb.); Larry Pressler (R–S.D.); and Jesse Helms (R–N.C.).

exclusive, semiexclusive, or *nonexclusive.* Members assigned to an exclusive committee do not normally serve on any other standing committee. (They may, however, serve on special or joint bodies.) The exclusive committees are Appropriations, Rules, and Ways and Means. Semiexclusive committees include most of the major authorizing panels. Members are usually limited to one such assignment, though they may also hold seats on nonexclusive committees. The nonexclusive committees include the housekeeping committees and those with narrow or less attractive jurisdictions.

When legislators transfer among committees, they drift toward the more prestigious ones (Bullock, 1973). In the House, the most attractive committees are the three exclusive committees plus Armed Services and Foreign Affairs. The Senate's most attractive committees are Foreign Relations, Finance, Appropriations, and Armed Services.

A number of legislators, however, seek seats on minor committees for the publicity value or because they realize the close link between these committees and their constituents' concerns. The committees on Aging, Small Business, Veterans' Affairs, and Merchant Marine and Fisheries (House) are in this category. Some legislators value these assignments more than any others.

Criteria for assignments   As far as possible, party leaders try to make assignments following members' wishes. Special attention is given to new members and to members from marginal districts, who need a boost to be reelected. In filling seats on top committees, party leaders are also pressured to reflect regional or ideological factions within the party. On the taxing and spending committees, certain states or economic interests feel they have a right to be represented; if "their seat" is vacated, they press for a proper replacement.

Some committees, in contrast, are not very attractive; members must be persuaded to serve. One example is the House District of Columbia Committee. It

has little to offer legislators from outside the Washington D.C. region. The Senate, which had trouble staffing its District of Columbia Committee, transferred its work to the Governmental Affairs Committee in 1977.

Biased memberships   Many committees do not represent Congress as a whole. In general, committees attract legislators who are keenly interested in the subject matter with which they deal (Shepsle, 1978). This simple fact has vast consequences. Among other things, it helps lubricate the committee system. Highly motivated legislators are likely to take their committee work seriously; members who have been dragooned into service are not.

Self-selection also tilts the committees in certain policy directions. Liberals move toward committees dealing with education and human resources. Farm-belt legislators are most likely to want seats on the agriculture committees. The "resources" panels—House Interior, Senate Energy and Natural Resources— overrepresent western states, where most public lands and national parks are found. In short, committees are often biased in favor of their major programs or clienteles.

The specialization norm   New senators and (especially) representatives are told to focus on committee work and do their homework so they will gain expertise. Members cannot possibly know the details of each piece of legislation. So they often rely on "cues" from colleagues who serve on the committee involved and understand the issue. Legislators considered experts on a given issue are listened to because in Congress, as elsewhere, knowledge is a basis for influence.

As we shall see, nonmembers have many ways to influence measures that come out of a given committee. But the committee's judgment must be trusted on most measures.

The rule of seniority

No feature of Capitol Hill life has drawn as much criticism as the seniority system. A Ralph Nader study (Green, Fallows, and Zwick, 1972) once derided seniority as "survival of the survivors."

Seniority is neither a formal rule nor a requirement. The rule can be stated simply: once assigned to a committee, members have a right to reappointment and to advance by seniority (defined as continuous terms of service). The senior majority-party member is normally named chairman.

Pros and cons   Defenders of seniority point out that it helps reduce conflict in Congress. It provides for the automatic selection of committee leaders; it also enhances the independence of Congress, because it forces presidents to deal with committee leaders whose posts are almost untouchable. Last, seniority fosters professionalism; it discourages hopping from one committee to another.

Critics of seniority argue that it wastes the talents and energies of younger legislators; it puts leadership in the hands of old and sometimes feeble members; and it helps scatter power within the two houses, making concerted party government almost impossible.

Top to bottom: Senate Democratic leader Robert C. Byrd (D–W.Va.); Representative (1953–59); senator since 1959. Alan Cranston (D–Calif.); Senate Democratic whip; senator since 1969. Ronald V. Dellums (D–Calif.), who chairs the House District of Columbia Committee. Dante B. Fascell (D–Fla.), House Foreign Affairs chairman; representative since 1955. Henry B. Gonzales (D–Tex.) has represented San Antonio since 1961.

Top to bottom:

Mark O. Hatfield (R–Ore.); Senate Appropriations chairman; senator since 1967. Nancy Landon Kassebaum (R–Kan.), who chairs subcommittees on the Senate Commerce and Foreign Relations panels. Claude Pepper (D–Fla.); House Rules Committee chairman and champion of the elderly; former senator (1936–51); representative since 1963. Dan Rostenkowski (D–Ill.); chairman of the House Ways and Means Committee. In the House since 1959.

The gravest charge against seniority, especially from 1937 to 1971, was that it fostered biased policymaking. By rewarding long service, seniority awards chairmanships (and ranking minority-party posts) to legislators from the safest seats—the regions under the parties' firmest control. When the Democrats were the majority, this meant an overbalance of southern conservatives.

Combating seniority   Reform politics in the 1960s and 1970s were mainly efforts to give more legislators a chance to exert power in the committees. Little by little, the prerogatives of seniority were chipped away.

The attack on seniority came on three fronts. First, revolts against ineffective chairmen in several committees resulted in new committee rules limiting the chair's power. Second, party caucuses pressed their right to approve all committee assignments, including chairmanships. Several committee chairmen were actually rejected by the House Democratic Caucus and replaced. Third, subcommittees grew in number and autonomy. This multiplied leadership posts and further limited the chairmen's power. By the 1970s, in fact, many committees were little more than holding companies for their subcommittees. Subcommittee government is now common in both houses—though the degree of decentralization varies from committee to committee (Smith and Deering, 1984: 125 ff.).

Seniority today   Now the seniority system is less important than it once was. Assignments, including chairmanships (and ranking minority posts), are proposed by each party's steering group or committee on committees; these choices are then ratified by the full party membership in each house. Once committee membership is settled, the committee's Democrats and Republicans decide on subcommittee setup, members, and leaders.

Within committees, seniority now counts for little. Chairmanships, according to one observer (Ehrenhalt, 1981: 535), are "a title, awarded by seniority, that allows the bearer to parcel out committee funds and not much else." A strong chairman, such as John Dingell (D-Mich.) of House Energy and Commerce, dominates colleagues by force of personality or skill, not by age or tenure.

Subcommittees are often where the action is. Those chairmanships are worth fighting for, and contests often break out over them. (In contrast, since 1975 no senior claimant has been denied a full-committee chairmanship.) Younger members in both chambers often control the subcommittees—a sort of "juniority system" (Ehrenhalt, 1981).

Committee leadership posts are spread more broadly than ever before. In the 98th Congress (1983–84), Republican senators held an average of more than two committee or subcommittee chairmanships; in the House, about half of all Democrats (who controlled that chamber) were committee or subcommittee chairmen. Committee leadership posts are well balanced among the parties' various regions and factions. Within committees, it is hard for chairmen to juggle subcommittee assignments, jurisdictions, or chairmanships to hoard power or influence legislation.

Committee democratization underscores the dispersion of authority in Congress. There are more leaders than ever and more centers of power. This puts added pressure on party leaders. It poses the problem of how, or whether, Congress is going to get its members and committees to work together to produce timely, coherent policies.

Committee politics

No two committees work in exactly the same way. Each has a unique external environment; internally, each is a unique mix of members, ideologies, and styles.

Outside forces   Committees must respond to the procedures and moods of the larger chambers. Some committees, though, are more independent than others. Those dealing with technical subjects have great leeway. Their expertise is respected. Committees that handle hot issues can expect aggressive intervention from noncommittee colleagues.

Some committees are arenas for intense interest-group struggles; others are almost ignored by lobbyists. The human resources committees (Senate Labor and Human Resources, House Education and Labor) and the judiciary committees are real battlegrounds for contending groups—mainly business, labor, educational, and civil rights groups. In contrast, few groups pay much attention to the housekeeping committees (Senate Rules and Administration, House Administration).

Some committees deal with aggressive executive-branch agencies; others face weak or divided agencies, or none at all. For instance, foreign policy committees (Senate Foreign Relations, House Foreign Affairs) hear from few lobbyists but feel strong executive pressure. In a sense, the prime constituent of these committees is the State Department. The human resources committees face several departments (mainly Labor, Education, and Health and Human Services), which vie for program dollars. Sometimes committees foster alliances with executive agencies and relevant pressure groups; such **subgovernments** are a pervasive yet varied phenomenon.

Internal patterns   In responding to these outside factors, committees adopt their own patterns of behavior. Some have vigorous chairmen; others have

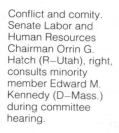

Conflict and comity. Senate Labor and Human Resources Chairman Orrin G. Hatch (R–Utah), right, consults minority member Edward M. Kennedy (D–Mass.) during committee hearing.

fragmented leadership or hardly any at all. Some are highly partisan (for instance, the human resources committees) because they deal with bread-and-butter partisan issues. Others (such as appropriations committees) have a consensus view of their mission that pulls in most if not all members.

Committees have distinct ways of fulfilling their missions. Fenno (1973) terms them **strategic premises.** These premises help the committee respond to their own members' goals, other House and Senate members' demands, and outside pressures.

Jurisdictional rivalries

Once a bill is introduced in each house, it is referred to the appropriate committee, based on the chamber's rules and precedents. Likewise, committee rules or precedents govern intracommittee assignment of bills to subcommittees.

Once a measure is referred to a committee or subcommittee, it cannot normally be reassigned. But more and more, bills are jointly referred to two or more committees. President Carter's 1977 energy package was split among six Senate committees, six House committees, and a House ad hoc energy committee charged with reviewing the whole package. During a two-year Congress, about 1,500 House bills and several hundred Senate bills are referred to two or more committees.

Legislators and their staffs often draft bills so that they will find their way to a favorable committee. A legislator can also word a bill to enlarge the scope of his own committee. For instance, a law already handled by the committee may be amended, adding new responsibilities or subjects.

Such flexibility has two results. On the one hand, it provides multiple points of access to the legislative process. If one committee is hostile, another may be friendly. In recent clashes over prayer in public schools, for instance, the House Judiciary Committee—dominated by opponents of school prayer—had no intention of reporting a proposed constitutional amendment on the subject. But the Education and Labor panel, with jurisdiction over education, quickly processed and brought to the floor a bill giving religious groups "equal access" to school facilities. (The bill finally passed.) Some rival chairmen work out informal agreements setting up the limits of each committee's duties. More often, committees strike out on their own. They focus on a narrow segment of policy and ignore the work of other committees.

Given the scattered power in Congress, the committee system totters on the verge of chaos (Davidson and Oleszek, 1977). Despite realignments in 1946, 1974 (House), and 1977 (Senate), jurisdictional entanglements among committees are everyday occurrences.

PARTY LEADERSHIP IN CONGRESS

With the pervasive diffusion of power on Capitol Hill, it may seem odd to talk about leadership in Congress. Yet some legislators are more equal than others. Congressional power may not be as centralized as in a bureaucratic agency, but inequalities of influence are very real. The main centralizers of congressional power are the political parties and their leaders.

Leadership in the House

The House has an uneven history of strong leadership. In the 1800s, speakers sometimes centralized power and whipped the House into line. Today's speakers, by contrast, rely mainly on persuasive skills, shrewd advisers, and a precise sense of timing to exert influence. Some, like the legendary Sam Rayburn (1940–46, 1949–52, 1955–61), parlayed these powers into forceful control of the chamber.

The leader's powers   Speakers manage House business. They control an array of formal powers that help regulate the flow of legislation—including the power to recognize members on the floor (grant them the right to speak). Speakers can vote to break ties. They can refer bills to committees. And they can appoint members of select and conference committees. Now speakers have the power to refer bills jointly or sequentially to two or more committees. And they can name ad hoc committees to consider broad proposals. If they are Democrats, Speakers pick their party's members of the Rules Committee, subject to caucus approval.

Speakers also have unwritten powers, depending on their charisma or bargaining skills. They influence committee assignments. They coordinate the activities of the various committee and subcommittee chairmen. And they take the lead in scheduling bills for floor consideration.

The speaker is helped by the majority leader, who by tradition succeeds him when he retires or dies. The majority leader is the chief floor spokesman for the party. He schedules bills and maximizes his party's voting strength. He in turn, is assisted by the chief majority whip and deputy whips. The latter notify members of pending business, poll them on their intentions; and try to bring members to the floor at the right moment to vote on key issues. The minority leader (the opposition party's candidate for speaker) and the minority whip perform similar tasks. But they have fewer rewards to dispense to their colleagues. Party leaders are judged on how they "count the House" (predict the outcome of votes), schedule key debates and votes for best effect, and gather majorities for key measures.

The caucus   The basic unit of party governance is the **caucus** (or conference, as the Republicans call it). It comprises all of a party's members in the chamber. At the start of each new Congress, the caucuses convene to ratify committee assignments and chairmanships; after that, they meet from time to time to discuss issues or party procedures. They rarely endorse policies. The Republican positions are voiced by the GOP Policy Committee, usually after the issues have been aired in full conference.

Both parties have bodies that propose committee assignments for ratification. They are the Democratic Steering and Policy Committee and the Republican Committee on Committees. The two parties also have campaign committees to prepare materials and dispense funds to candidates.

Leadership in the Senate

In the smaller Senate, strong leadership has been the exception rather than the rule. Not until the end of the 1800s did visible leaders appear. And they were no match for the powerful speakers then in the House. (Rothman, 1966).

The presiding officer of the Senate is quite insignificant. The vice president,

Henry Clay (Ky.), first of the strong House Speakers (1811–14; 1815–20; 1823–24).

Thomas B. ("Czar") Reed (R–Me.), House Speaker (1889–90; 1895–99), strong parliamentarian and author of the "Reed rules."

Joseph G. ("Uncle Joe") Cannon (R–Ill.), last of the "strong" Speakers (1903–11), whose power was curbed by 1910 revolt.

Modern Speakers. Thomas P. ("Tip") O'Neill (D–Mass.), House Speaker since 1977, speaks under portrait of legendary Sam Rayburn (D–Tex.), Speaker 1940–46, 1949–52, 1955–61.

though the formal presiding officer, is not a member of the body. President pro tem is an honorary title given to the senior majority-party senator. But most of the time, freshman senators take turns presiding.

Floor leaders and whips in the Senate operate much as they do in the House. They have much looser reins on their troops. Senate floor leaders have different leadership styles. Lyndon Johnson's unique success as majority leader (1955–61) stemmed partly from his persuasive skills. He fostered a consensus atmosphere that encouraged senatorial courtesy, specialization of activities, and deference to senior members (Matthews, 1960). The unique character of the 1950s also aided Johnson; party and seniority leaders were mostly conservative, and President Eisenhower did not press for much new legislation. Liberals were angered at control by a tight ruling clique. They tried to appeal to public opinion over the heads of conservative Senate elders (Huitt, 1961).

The Senate changed radically in the post-Johnson years. Membership turnover democratized the body. The power of the so-called inner club was destroyed. Many of the earlier folkways, such as specialization and deference to seniority, were weakened or erased (Ornstein, Peabody, and Rohde, 1981). Committee assignments and staff resources were widely distributed. "We've had a dispersion of responsibility," explained Mike Mansfield (D-Mont.), who followed Johnson (1961–76).

Majority leaders continue to shape the Senate in subtle though powerful ways. Mansfield's successor was Robert C. Byrd (D-W. Va.) (1977–80). He wielded power through procedural mastery and unanimous agreements to control floor schedules and debate. When the Republicans took over the Senate, Howard Baker (R-Tenn.) became majority leader (1981–84). He capitalized on his party's consensus on economic matters and close work with committee leaders.

Party leaders at work

Congressional leadership hinges on party status in the House and Senate. The majority party organizes the two houses. Its size and unity determine how effective this control will be. In addition to determining congressional leadership, parties play a crucial organizational role.

Duties and powers   Party leaders strive to bind together the scattered individuals and work groups of Congress. They orchestrate efforts to produce coherent legislative results. Randall Ripley (1967) specifies six major functions of party leaders, (known simply as "the leadership"): (1) organizing the party, (2) scheduling business, (3) promoting attendance of members for important floor votes, (4) distributing and collecting information, (5) maintaining liaison with the president and his top advisers, and (6) persuading members to act in accordance with party policies.

In attempting to shape legislative events, party leaders draw on four types of resources (Ripley, 1967). First, they are in a pivotal spot to use the chamber's rules for partisan ends. The leaders of the majority party, for instance, can hold off scheduling a controversial bill until enough votes are garnered for passage. Second, they can influence many of the tangible rewards for individual members—the most important are committee assignments. Third, they control many psychological rewards. Party leaders can often shape the attitudes of House colleagues toward a member; isolation is the possible fate of the maverick. Finally, party leaders can dominate internal communication. Thus, they can monopolize vital information: knowledge of the upcoming schedule, the substance of bills, and the leanings of other congressmen or of the president.

Party voting Parties are the most stable, significant groupings in Congress. Party discipline is low. But party loyalty is firm and is the leading determinant of voting in the two houses.

Republicans tend to vote together because they represent similar constituents; the same is true for Democrats, though to a lesser degree. Congressional mavericks have voting records that diverge from those of other party members. They tend to come from districts with traits resembling those of the opposition party. Figure 10–2 shows the differences in voting between the two parties' Senators, as reflected in ratings by business and labor groups.

FIGURE 10–2

U.S. Senators' Voting as Ranked by Business and Labor, 1983

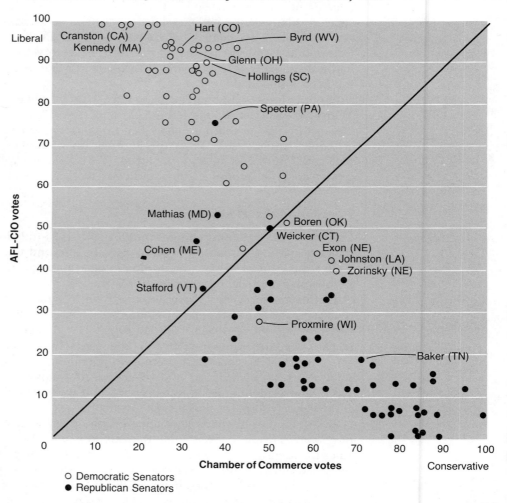

○ Democratic Senators
● Republican Senators

Senators whose scores deviate from those of the majority in their party, or who are especially prominent (as, e.g., presidential candidates or Senate leaders) are indicated by name.
Source: *Congressional Quarterly Weekly Report* 42 (July 14, 1984), 1695.

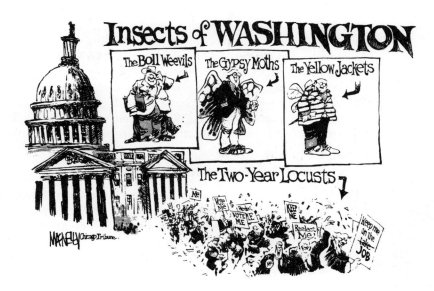

Capitol Hill species. Boll Weevils (southern conservative Democrats), Gypsy Moths (liberal Republicans), Yellow Jackets (conservative militants), and others.

In the past generation, the parties split most consistently on foreign trade (tariffs), degree of government activism, fiscal and monetary policy, conservation, and health and welfare. "Only on issues which failed to ignite significant ideological controversies, which promised little reward to the party faithful, or which did not mobilize significant economic interest groups did the parties fail to present clearly differentiated records to the voter" (Turner and Schneier, 1971).

According to one study (Froman and Ripley, 1965), six factors affect the success of party leadership. Victories are more likely when: (1) leadership activity is high; (2) the issue is more procedural than substantive; (3) the visibility of the issue is low, thereby reducing pressures that could counteract party loyalty; (4) the visibility of the action is low (for instance, party unity is usually easier to achieve in an unrecorded vote than on a roll call); (5) there is little pressure from constituencies; and (6) state delegations are not bargaining with leaders over specific demands.

Party fragmentation Many forces chip away at party lines. Regional differences are especially potent. Traditionally, southern Democrats are less loyal to their party than are nonsoutherners. Southern Democrats and Republican conservatives often merge into a so-called **conservative coalition.** In the early 1980s, the Conservative Democratic Forum, a group of 44 House Democrats sometimes called "boll weevils," voted with the GOP on many issues and helped pass Reagan's budget and tax bills. Less often, moderate northeastern Republicans deviate from the conservative mainstream of their party. Some intraparty factions have shifted in recent years. North-South differences over race have lessened within the Democratic party. In the GOP's ranks, conservatives dominate, but moderate "gypsy moths" are a sometimes potent minority.

There are other powerful influences on legislators. They include interest groups, state and regional delegations, committees and their clienteles, and informal voting blocs. In sum, party loyalty, though stubborn, is challenged on every side, and its overall impact is puzzling.

Like our political parties in general, congressional parties are the despair of friends and critics alike. To serve as unifying forces, they must counter the pull of constituency and group interests as well as the autonomy of the committee structure. Many observers have looked with horror at the seeming chaos of congressional parties. They have urged steps to achieve a modicum of party government, or party solidarity, within the halls of Congress.

The rise of informal caucus groups

On Capitol Hill the number of voting blocs or informal caucus groups with varying influence is growing. Nearly 100 such groups have appeared. They are mainly bipartisan House groups, though some are strictly partisan and others draw members from both chambers.

Such groups are not exactly newcomers. During the 1800s, regional and issue-based factions were rife. In part this was because members from the same state or region often gathered at the same boarding houses during the brief legislative sessions (Young, 1966).

The modern-day model is the Democratic Study Group (DSG). This group formed in 1959 to promote the interests of liberal members. At first, it was a minority bloc. By the mid-1970s, the DSG had some 250 members, a majority of House Democrats. It led many House "reforms" in the 1970s, such as assaults on the seniority system. The DSG aided members with campaign funds and weekly newsletters highlighting controversies to be fought on the House floor.

Since the 1970s, the number of informal caucus groups has soared (Mulhollan and Hammond, 1983). There is a Black Caucus, a Women's Caucus, and a Hispanic Caucus. There are industry groups such as the Textile Caucus, the Steel Caucus, and the Tourism Caucus. And there are regional groups such as the Western State Coalition, the Rural Caucus, and the Northeast-Midwest Coalition (the so-called Frostbelt caucus). Informal congressional groups are listed in Table 10–4.

Some groups are partisan. Both parties have "class clubs." These are groups of members who enter the House in a given year. The 75 freshmen Democrats elected in 1974 formed such a group. They hired a small staff, interviewed seniority candidates for committee chairmanships, and helped to topple three chairmen.

Other party groups follow the example of DSG in promoting ideological causes. Republicans have an array of groups, ranging from the right-wing Republican Study Group to the small, liberal Wednesday Group. Several GOP groups, such as the Marching and Chowder Society, the Acorns, and the SOS, combine business with fellowship.

State and regional delegations, not to mention state party caucuses, also meet. Their purpose is twofold. They focus attention on matters of mutual concern. And they help in the exchange of information among members of various committees.

Informal caucus groups are as varied as Congress itself. Some are highly organized and well financed. They have staffs, whip systems, and newsletters. Others are mainly paper organizations—designed to let the folks back home

Black, Hispanic caucuses. Jesse Jackson at Capitol Hill meeting with caucus members (*from left*) Robert Garcia (N.Y.), Baltasar Corrada (P.R.), Ronald V. Dellums (Calif.), and Walter E. Fauntroy (D.C.).

TABLE 10—4

Informal Congressional Groups, 1984 *

House

Democratic
Calif. Democratic Congressional Delegation (28)
Congressional Populist Caucus (15)
Conservative Democratic Forum ("Boll Weevils") (38)
Democratic Study Group (228)
House Democratic Research Organization (100)
Ninety-Fifth Democratic Caucus (35)
Ninety-Sixth Democratic Caucus (20)
Ninety-Seventh New Members Caucus (24)
Ninety-Eighth New Members Caucus (52)
United Democrats of Congress (125)

Republican
House Republican Study Committee (130)
House Wednesday Group (32)
Ninety-Fifth Republican Club (14)
Northeast-Midwest Republican Coalition ("Gypsy Moths")
Republican Freshman Class of the 96th Congress
Republican Freshman Class of the 97th Congress
Republican Freshman Class of the 98th Congress
Conservative Opportunity Society

Bipartisan
Ad Hoc Congressional Committee on Irish Affairs (110)
Budget Study Group (60)
Congressional Agricultural Forum
Congressional Automotive Caucus (53)
Congressional Border Caucus (12)
Congressional Coal Group (55)
Congressional Emergency Housing Caucus
Congressional Human Rights Caucus (150)
Congressional Mushroom Caucus (60)
Congressional Rural Caucus (100)
Congressional Steel Caucus (120)
Congressional Territorial Caucus (4)
Congressional Travel and Tourism Caucus (154)
Federal Government Service Task Force (38)
House Fair Employment Practices Committee
Local Government Caucus (22)
Northeast-Midwest Congressional Coalition (196)
Task Force on Devaluation of the Peso

Task Force on Industrial Innovation and Productivity
Conference of Great Lakes Congressmen (100)
Congressional Arts Caucus (186)
Congressional Black Caucus (21)
Congressional Caucus for Science and Technology (15)
Congressional Hispanic Caucus (11)
Congressional Metropolitan Area Caucus (8)
Congressional Port Caucus (150)
Congressional Space Caucus (161)
Congressional Sunbelt Council
Congressional Textile Caucus (42)
Export Task Force (102)
House Caucus on North American Trade
House Footwear Caucus
New England Congressional Caucus (24)
Pennsylvania Congressional Delegation Steering Committee (5)
Tennessee Valley Authority Caucus (23)

Senate

Democratic
Moderate/Conservative Senate Democrats (15)

Republican
Senate Steering Committee

Bipartisan
Border Caucus
Northeast-Midwest Senate Coalition (40)
Senate Caucus on the Family (31)
Senate Coal Caucus (39)
Senate Drug Enforcement Caucus (44)
Senate Footwear Caucus
Senate Steel Caucus (46)
Senate Wine Caucus

Concerned Senators for the Arts (35)
Senate Caucus on North American Trade
Senate Children's Caucus (18)
Senate Copper Caucus (18)
Senate Export Caucus
Senate Rail Caucus
Senate Tourism Caucus (60)
Western State Coalition (30)

Bicameral

Ad Hoc Congressional Committee on the Baltic States and the Ukraine (75)
Congressional Alcohol Fuels Caucus (90)
Congressional Clearinghouse on the Future (84)
Congressional Senior Citizens Caucus
Environmental and Energy Study Conference (37)
Long Island Congressional Caucus
New York State Congressional Delegation (36)
Pennsylvania Congressional Delegation (27)
Renewable Energy Congressional Staff Group (50)

Arms Control and Foreign Policy Caucus (129)
Coalition for Peace through Strength (232)
Congressional Caucus for Women's Issues (129)
Congressional Jewelry Manufacturing Coalition
Congressional Wood Energy Caucus
Friends of Ireland (80)
Military Reform Caucus
Pacific Northwest Trade Task Force
Pro-Life Caucus (60)
Senate/House Ad Hoc Monitoring Group on Southern Africa (53)
Vietnam Veterans in Congress (38)

*Numbers of members, where available, in parenthesis.
Source: Sula P. Richardson, Congressional Research Service

know their legislators are alert to a given issue. Whatever their status, such groups reflect the profusion of today's politics and are an alternative to party groups.

HOW SOMEBODY'S BRIGHT IDEA BECOMES A LAW

The House and Senate have each evolved distinct rules to govern their activities. This follows the constitutional provision that "each House may determine the rules of its proceedings" (Article I, Section 5).

Legislative rules and procedures are closely tied to ongoing political conflicts over policy. Rules are far from neutral. They promote certain types of strategies and discourage others. Rules are resources, and mastery of them is a form of power in Congress.

There is very little that the houses cannot do under the rules, so long as the action is backed by votes and support. If members are of one mind on an issue, for instance, they can suspend the rules or invoke unanimous consent (assuming nobody objects). In a few minutes they do what might otherwise take months. Yet such consensus is not easily obtained. The rules persistently challenge backers of legislation to prove that they have votes and support. At the same time, little prevents roadblocks at every turn, except the tacit agreement that congressional business must go on.

Bill introduction

Less than 3 percent of all bills introduced in Congress become laws. In the 97th Congress (1981–82), some 11,000 bills were introduced, but only 529 passed.

Proposals for bills must be introduced (put in the "hopper") by a House or Senate member. The proposal may actually be drafted by anyone—legislators or their staffs, lawyers from a committee or a subcommittee or the House or Senate Counsel's Office, a congressional support agency (such as the Congressional Research Service), a presidential staff member or an executive agency staff, even a private lobbying group. Such proposals cover all subjects for which someone thinks "there oughta be a law."

Legislation comes in several forms. Bills are either *public* or *private*. A public law applies to whole classes of persons; a private bill is to help or relieve specific people. Bills of either type must be passed by both houses and signed by the president to become law. Joint resolutions are handled in the same way and have the force of law. Concurrent resolutions, though passed by both houses, merely express the opinion of Congress and are not signed by the president. Simple resolutions, introduced in either house, apply to that house only.

When proposals are introduced, they are printed and assigned a number. Examples are S. 1 or H.R. 1; S. Res. 1 or H. Res. 1; S.J. Res. 1 or H.J. Res. 1; S. Con. Res. 1 or H. Con. Res. 1.

Committee deliberation

The critical stage comes when a measure is referred to a committee. Just a small portion of proposals can be favorably reported or even processed by commit-

HOW A BILL BECOMES LAW

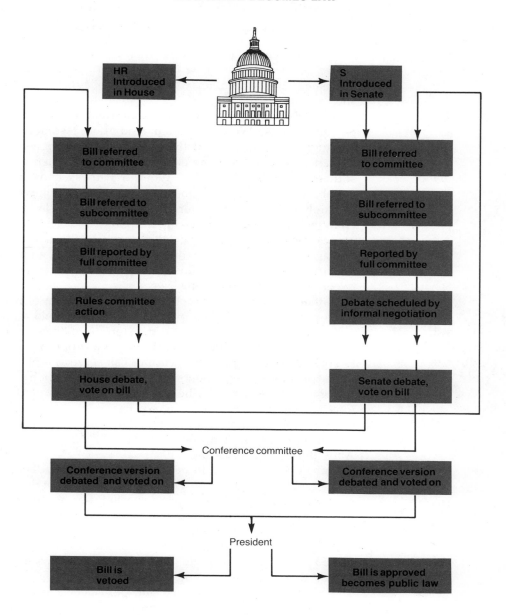

tees. Committees report about 5 percent of the measures referred to them. Committee chairmen may or may not refer a bill to a subcommittee. (In the House they are supposed to.) And a committee may or may not actually consider a bill.

A committee or subcommittee may decide to act on a bill. If so, it usually does so in three stages: staff research, committee hearings, and *markup sessions*.

Research Committees and subcommittees have staffs which gather materials on the subject at hand and prepare briefs. At some point, the staff will draft a document that forms the basis for a report on the subject. Good staff members become experts in their subject. They familiarize themselves with existing legislation, major unresolved issues, and current thinking in the field.

Hearings   Formal hearings are the most common way committees gather information on a bill or a problem area. These may last an hour or drag on for months. They may gain national attention or (more likely) play themselves out before small audiences in a hearing room. Committee hearings are normally published, and form a key part of the public record on a given proposal or issue.

As a procedure designed to elicit information, congressional hearings would get low marks. Witnesses often read their testimony from prepared texts. Meanwhile, legislators leaf through the texts or sign mail or review files. Attendance is haphazard; members come and go, often taking time to greet constituents or talk with aides. When a witness ends a statement, committee members comment or ask questions in turn, starting with the senior members.

Rarely is there a true interchange between legislators and the witness; generally, while a member is asking questions, his colleagues do not intrude. Witnesses have few defenses if legislators use the questioning for a speech or demagoguery. Usually only one witness appears at a time. (Witnesses are often buttressed by assistants.) This affords few opportunities for a clash of ideas between witnesses of opposing views.

Gathering information is, however, but one aim of hearings. Hearings also focus public attention on a problem. They may build a record of support for a given viewpoint, give interest-group representatives a chance to express their views, or test the political acceptability of a proposal.

For individual legislators, hearings can serve as a platform to promote themselves or remind constituents that they are on the job.

For society as a whole, hearings are sometimes exciting dramas where evil forces are ferreted out and purged. Examples include periodic crime or lobby investigations or inquiries into scandals. They may even be national confrontations, such as the Army-McCarthy (1954), Nixon impeachment (1974), or the Anne Burford-EPA hearings (1983).

Once views are aired in hearings, committee leaders must decide to report, change, or drop legislation. The hearings may affect their decision. Widespread support for the measure may be revealed; serious controversies and problems may surface; or the hearings may show that the measure's time has not yet come. On the other hand, hearings are not open, neutral searches for information. Committee leaders often map out hearings. They invite witnesses to make specific points, lay the groundwork for what they intend to recommend, or lead their committee to the desired action.

Markups   Bills are adjusted and perfected in **markup sessions.** These are meetings in which committee members debate the bills' provisions. Most markup sessions are open to the public. But they are typically preceded by private bargaining. Discussion is usually limited to committee and staff members. From time to time, though, outside experts—executive-branch lawyers, for instance—are called on for advice. Votes are taken on controversial matters.

At last, when all issues have been resolved, committee members vote on whether to report a measure. If a subcommittee handles the bill, it reports it to the full committee, which in turn votes to report to the chamber.

Bypassing the committee

What happens if a subcommittee or a committee fails to act on a measure? (This is what usually happens.) Almost always, this spells death for the measure, at least for that Congress. The committee is said to have "pigeonholed" the bill. Because few measures enjoy majority support, committees that pigeonhole bills usually reflect the parent chamber's will. Even the bill's sponsors may be relieved when it dies in committee. Many bills are introduced to placate constituents or lobbies, but do not express a legislator's own views. Often committees take the heat for burying measures that their colleagues would rather not vote on.

Backers of a pigeonholed bill have few options. Bypassing a committee is cumbersome and controversial. The measure can be taken up on the House or Senate floor by **unanimous consent** or by **suspending the rules.** (This latter requires a two-thirds vote.) But these procedures are not likely to succeed if the committee is adamant. Also any committee that refuses to report a bill may be discharged of its duty. This requires a motion signed by a simple majority of the chamber's members. The discharge is then voted upon, according to different procedures in each house.

These options are rarely invoked for two reasons. First, committee specialization is strong in both chambers. Members who challenge prerogatives can expect retaliation from the committee. Second, committees learn to predict the moods of the larger body. Committee leaders like to respond to their colleagues' demands; they pride themselves on reporting bills that command broad support in the House or Senate.

From committee to the floor

Once a bill or a resolution is reported by a committee, it must get onto the House or Senate agenda.

The House   In the House, a bill reported from committee is placed on one of five *calendars,* or lists of pending business. These calendars, in rough order of importance, are *House* (authorization bills); *union* (revenue or spending bills); *private* (dealing with private matters and affecting individuals); *consent* (uncontroversial bills that, however, may be stopped by a member's objection); and *discharge* (motions to discharge a committee from considering a measure).

In the House, certain bills are privileged. This means they may be taken up without passing through the Rules Committee. These include appropriations and revenue bills and a few other specific groups of measures. On specified days, bills on the consent or private calendar may be called up directly for House action. If two thirds of the members present agree, a bill may then be debated under suspension of the rules.

With these exceptions, bills go to the Rules Committee. It writes a "rule" governing floor debate on the measure. When a rule is requested by a legislative committee, the Rules Committee must first decide whether to hold hearings; if it decides to do so, it may vote on whether to grant a rule. The rule specifies a time for debate and whether amendments are in order (*open* versus *closed*). It also tells whether points of order (procedural challenges) will be waived for certain parts of the bill.

The House has granted extensive scheduling powers to its Rules Committee. It thus stands as the gatekeeper between the legislative committees and the House floor. But it can also withhold bills from floor action and bargain to include or delete given provisions. Therefore, the Rules Committee often moves beyond its traffic cop role to that of final arbiter over the content of bills.

Control of the Rules Committee is crucial in the House. Strong 19th-century speakers, such as "Czar" Reed and "Uncle Joe" Cannon, chaired the Rules Committee, using it as a lever for controlling schedules and committee assignments. In 1910, there was a revolt against Cannon's arbitrary powers. The speaker was ousted from the Rules Committee; committee assignments were delegated to the party caucuses. Between 1937 and 1967, conservatives dominated the Rules Committee. They sometimes delayed or killed legislation desired by party leaders.

Today's Rules Committee tends to be an arm of the majority-party leadership (Matsunaga and Chen, 1976). If the speaker is a Democrat, he may nominate all Rules Committee Democrats, subject to caucus ratification.

The Senate   The Senate is more informal and relaxed than the House with its Rules Committee and five calendars. Senate bills are usually called up by unanimous consent. Because one senator can object to this procedure, the majority and minority leaders consult to gain consent. Unanimous consent, of course, can be used to bring about any procedure; and recent floor leaders have used it to control the pace and length of debate. It takes the form of complex **unanimous consent agreements** (often called "time agreements") which may specify the amendments to be considered, set times for votes, and waive points of order. Getting interested senators to make such agreements is a leading task of floor leaders. Through such agreements, the Senate can sometimes control its debate as tightly as the House can.

Floor debate

Floor debate is the most visible part of lawmaking. A bill's supporters and opponents marshal their forces and contest the pros and cons. Amendments are introduced, debated, and voted on. For most legislation, the floor debate and votes on final passage are the only events the media report. The floor debate can involve eloquence and high drama: momentous issues are joined and votes weighed in the balance.

Yet, as any visitor to Capitol Hill can tell you, routine House and Senate floor debates are a far cry from this colorful image. Attendance is often sparse. Members may not listen intently to the proceedings; they may wander about the chamber, consult with colleagues, or even read newspapers. The speaker may drone on about his subject, probably reading from a prepared text.

The reason is that floor debate covers ground already well plowed in committee hearings or markup sessions. Few people are startled by the arguments; they have heard them before. Thus, floor debate is designed to air key issues and provide a chance for members to vote on them.

Floor debate is controlled by a bill's managers—senior committee or subcommittee supporters. Opposition time is controlled by senior opponents; they are also from the relevant committee or subcommittee. Other members are allowed to speak or "revise and extend" their remarks to air their views. (That is, they may submit a written statement for the record.) Exchanges, called **colloquies,**

Filibusters. Louisiana's Democratic Senator Huey Long (1913–1935), "the Kingfish," was a fiery orator. His filibusters— "extended debate," the Senate calls it— included reading the phone directory and repeating recipes for "potlikker," a southern dish. *Below*, Senator William V. Roth, Jr. (R–Del.) carries pillows and blankets after 1982 gas-tax filibuster.

are often staged among supporters of a position or between supporters and opponents—again to put their views on public record. If legislators or their staff are unhappy with the wording of a specific argument, they can spruce it up before the *Congressional Record* goes to press. As in committee sessions, staff aides are on hand to help the bill's main sponsors and opponents.

Quorums, a majority of members, are required in each house to conduct business. Quorums are not always physically present on the floor. But they are supposed to be available for votes. Members may ask for *quorum calls* if they want to delay the proceedings or merely draw more members to the floor. When the House is considering a bill sent by the Rules Committee, it sits as a Committee of the Whole. This requires a quorum of only 100 members and allows more informal procedures.

In the smaller and more leisurely Senate, the rules of debate are simpler and more lenient. The Senate cherishes its privilege of free, unrestricted debate. When a small number of senators are unalterably opposed to a course of action, they may engage in an extended debate, called a **filibuster.** Its object is to make a last-minute appeal to the public or merely to stall other business and wear out the opposition. A **cloture** rule is available to shut off debate. It needs a vote of three fifths of the senators and is sometimes invoked.

Senatorial courtesy demands that members be given ample time to pursue the subject at hand; repeated efforts to tighten the cloture rule have met with mixed success. At present, even if cloture is invoked, every senator in theory has up to an hour to speak on the measure being considered. In the past, filibusters were used to bring the Senate to a complete halt; however, under Senator Byrd, a "track" system, engineered by unanimous consent, was followed. It allowed a filibuster to proceed during one time period while other business was disposed of in other periods.

Congressional voting

The most visible outcome of congressional deliberation is a law or resolution that the two chambers vote on. Every legislator has the right and duty to cast a vote.

Members of Congress cast votes on a staggering number of issues, both large and small. About 800 votes are recorded in the House in two years; almost 1,000 are recorded in the Senate. Since the 1950s, the number has risen tenfold in the House, fourfold in the Senate.

Despite the large number of floor votes, the average senator or representative is recorded on 9 of every 10 votes on the floor. This is in part because absenteeism may be raised as a campaign issue. If a member is not present to vote, he or she may be announced as "paired" with another member holding the opposite position.

Voting may be by voice, by division (standing), or by recorded vote. During Committee of the Whole deliberations, the House also uses teller votes. Traditionally, these obliged members to file down the aisle to be counted by tellers, members chosen for the task. Until 1970, members' names were not recorded in teller votes—unless reporters in the gallery could quickly take down the names of members voting one way or the other. In that year, the House allowed recorded teller votes on the request of one fifth of a quorum, either in the House or in a Committee of the Whole. Not only has this put members' votes on public view; it has also sparked far more votes on the House floor.

The House now records its votes electronically. Members insert ID cards into machines scattered throughout the chamber. Then they push a button: yes, no, or present (abstain). The results are displayed on a giant illuminated tote board on the chamber's front wall. Voting in the House is thus simple and fast (about 15 minutes.)

When votes are called, bells ring throughout rooms and hallways on either the House or Senate side of Capitol Hill. Members pour from their offices, committee chambers, or other haunts—including the gym, the swimming pool, and one of several bars—and make their way to the floor. After their votes are recorded, they wait long enough to find out the results, then drift away. For a brief moment, the chamber exudes the drama of the legislative process.

Interpreting votes Legislators' votes on the House or Senate floor are not always easy to interpret. Often votes are taken on procedural matters that are somewhat independent of the issue at hand. Members may be unhappy with the way issues are posed. For example, an amendment is badly drafted or a good bill is loaded down with objectionable features. Sometimes legislators straddle both sides of an issue to appeal to constituents. For instance, they may vote *against* final passage but *for* a substitute version of a bill.

One must be cautious, then, in interpreting a legislator's vote on the floor. Nonetheless, nearly 100 lobbies—ranging from Common Cause to the American Bakers Association—figure out voting indexes to rate "friendly" and "unfriendly" legislators. These indexes are not always balanced. The National Education Association, with 1.8 million members, is the nation's largest teachers' union. In 1980, it pegged its campaign support almost totally to the teachers' top legislative priority—creation of a federal Department of Education (Hunt, 1980). One liberal who lost NEA support complained that "on every other issue, I've been on NEA's side, but they went nuts on this one."

Determinants of voting Taken as a whole, legislators' votes are remarkably consistent. Political scientists studying the patterns have identified a number of factors associated with members' floor votes. They include party, constituency, ideology, and presidential support or opposition.

Party affiliation is the strongest factor linked with votes. In a typical year, a third to a half of all floor votes could be called party votes. (So-called party unity votes occur when a majority of voting Democrats oppose a majority of voting Republicans.) The number of party votes is declining in the long run; the minority party wins about a third of such votes in a typical year.

Each legislator votes his or her party line about two thirds of the time. Republicans tend to be more cohesive than Democrats, who at times are badly split. Partisan voting, as we have seen, is rooted in constituency differences: Democrats tend to reflect urban, ethnic, and racial interests; the GOP is more upper-class, white, and from small towns. These natural tendencies are strengthened by shared policy goals and membership in partisan groups.

Party loyalties are reinforced by partisan groups on Capitol Hill. New members turn to their parties for committee assignments. They meet with fellow partisans to exchange information and tips about issues to be voted on. Still, legislators realize that their votes must be explained to their voters; no party leader is as persuasive as the folks back home. "I'm going to dance with them that brung me," Representative Phil Gramm (Tex.) announced in bolting the Democratic ranks to support President Reagan's budget plans. (Later, Gramm switched parties, became a Republican, and was returned to office by his conservative constituents.)

Switcher. Texas Republican Phil Gramm, who resigned his House seat as Democrat in 1983, was later elected as a Republican, and went on to run for the Senate.

Constituency pressures dominate certain votes. It is natural for legislators to reflect their constituents' views when they cast votes. For one thing, elected representatives usually share the opinions of "the folks back home." For another, the threat of defeat hangs over the heads of legislators who defy constituents' wishes on key issues. Not many legislators are turned out of office for defying local sentiments. But there is a handful of such cases in every election. That example is more than enough to keep other legislators in line.

Members also hold ideological commitments that surface in their voting (Schneider, 1979). One ideological grouping is the so-called conservative coalition. This collection of Republicans and conservative Democrats emerged in the late 1930s in reaction to the New Deal. It enjoyed its greatest successes between 1939 and the 1950s and staged a comeback in the early 1980s (Manley, 1973).

Presidents also affect legislators' votes; political commentators are always keeping score of a president's wins and losses on Capitol Hill. The following conclusions can be drawn from examining presidents' success rates:

1. All modern presidents have gained approval for a majority of the measures on which they took a position.
2. Partisan swings have an impact; when their party also controls Congress, presidents win three fourths or more of the votes on which they take a position.
3. Support for presidential positions is by no means assured and, in fact, tends to drop as the administration "ages."
4. Congressional support for presidents' positions was extremely low in the 1970s but seemed to have rebounded in the early 1980s.
5. Presidents are taking clear-cut positions on a rising *number* of issues, but these represent a declining *percentage* of congressional votes.

Cue giving and cue taking   There is a baffling number of votes on a wide range of issues. No wonder legislators rely heavily on the advice of others in deciding how to vote. Members seek out a wide variety of cue givers, including party leaders, presidential stands, committee experts, lobby representatives, and informal caucus groups.

Kingdon (1981) talked with representatives right after they cast votes. Based on these interviews, he devised a model of cue taking that predicted legislators' votes about 9 times out of 10. Much of the time, of course, legislators have no trouble making up their minds. They often have firm convictions or public stands on a given issue. This also happens when all the influencing factors—for example, party leaders, interest groups, staffs, the White House, and constituency interests—point in the same direction.

If members get conflicting signals on an issue, Kingdon found that they turn first to trusted fellow members; constituency pressures rank second. Party leaders and interest groups are far less important. When members break from the stance indicated by a consensus of their cue givers, it is usually to follow their own conscience.

No model can capture every twist or turn in a senator's or representative's voting record. However, most legislators behave predictably on most votes. Not only does such consistency simplify their decisions, it also helps explain their votes to other people.

From bill to law

After it passes one house, a measure is sent to the other house. Passage by one house does not ensure passage or even consideration by the other. The measure must even be introduced separately, in identical or different form. Measures may begin in either chamber. However, the Constitution specifies that the House originates revenue bills; by convention, it also originates appropriations bills. In such fiscal matters, the Senate often plays the role of an appellate body. It adjusts and sometimes liberalizes House-passed provisions.

The second chamber to approve a measure may request a conference committee to resolve differences between the House and Senate versions. If the originating chamber consents, conferees are picked to represent the views of the two houses. The conference report is resubmitted to the two chambers to be ratified.

Once duly passed by both houses, a bill or a joint resolution is conveyed to the president. He must sign or veto the measure within 10 days. If he fails to sign it, it still becomes law—unless Congress adjourns and prevents the president from returning it.

The legislative process is long and mazelike, filled with hazards for a measure's sponsors. Many measures are proposed; few make their way to final passage. Measures can be halted at many points in the process. Therefore, the legislative process can be said to have a conservative impact on policymaking. Groups opposed to all or part of a measure have *defensive advantages*. They can amend or kill the measure at dozens of points throughout the process. This is perhaps as it should be. Our national government would be vastly overloaded if everyone's "bright idea" were suddenly transformed into law.

THE POWER OF THE PURSE

Raising and spending money for the government's aims lie at the heart of the prerogatives of Congress. The "power of the purse" was the lever by which parliaments for centuries gained bargaining advantages over kings. The Constitution's authors were well aware of this. Thus, they gave Congress full power of the purse. There are two components of this power: *taxing* and *spending*.

Taxing power

The House of Representatives is the most representative chamber. It is thus awarded the constitutional privilege of originating tax legislation (Article I, Section 7). This lends special significance to the House Committee on Ways and Means. It has jurisdiction over more than just taxes. It also controls a host of related matters—debt, customs, trade, social security, and welfare laws. It is no surprise that the committee is a prized assignment. Vacant seats are hotly contested by would-be members and by competing regions and special interests.

The Senate's counterpart is the Committee on Finance. Although the House originates revenue bills, "the Senate may propose . . . amendments" (Article I, Section 7). Historically, the Senate has tinkered with House-passed bills, playing a review or appellate role for interests unhappy with the House's work. Thus, the Senate earned a reputation for adding special-interest ("Christmas tree") tax provisions.

Occasionally the Senate actually takes the lead in tax measures. The GOP-controlled Senate twice grasped the tax initiative in the 97th Congress (1981–82). In 1981, the Senate Finance Committee was eager to push the president's tax-reduction plans, but waited until the Democratic-led House sent a tax bill for amendment. The next year, however, when new taxes were needed, the Senate panel under its chairman, Robert Dole (R-Kan.), actually processed a bill and took it to conference with the House, which had no bill of its own. This unusual procedure occurred because House Democrats did not want to take the lead in enacting new taxes in an election year.

Much attention is paid revenue matters. Yet revenue policies are badly meshed and only sporadically coordinated with overall economic conditions. Partially to remedy this state of affairs, revenue issues were integrated into a new congressional budget process enacted in 1974. House and Senate budget committees, using Congressional Budget Office reports, now introduce resolutions covering the overall size and shape of both revenue and spending laws. Needless to say, the taxing committees do not take kindly to such challenges to their powers. War has often broken out between the two sets of committees—especially in the Senate. It remains to be seen whether tax policies can be drawn into a coherent package.

Spending power

The power of Congress over government spending is no less sweeping than its power to raise revenue. According to Article I, Section 9: "No money shall be drawn from the Treasury, but in consequence of appropriations made by law." Though ambiguous, this spending power is the legislature's best weapon in overseeing the executive branch (see Figure 10–3).

The funding process The Constitutional mandate is carried out through yearly appropriations bills voted by the House and the Senate. By tradition, the House acts first. Executive budgets are considered in detail by the House and Senate appropriations committees or, more properly, their subcommittees. Each committee has 13 subcommittees with parallel jurisdictions; each year they examine agency requests. Agency heads justify their budget requests during hearings, answering questions about operations and programs. Based on these hearings, the subcommittees report appropriations bills which are usually ac-

FIGURE 10—3

Major Steps in the Budget Process

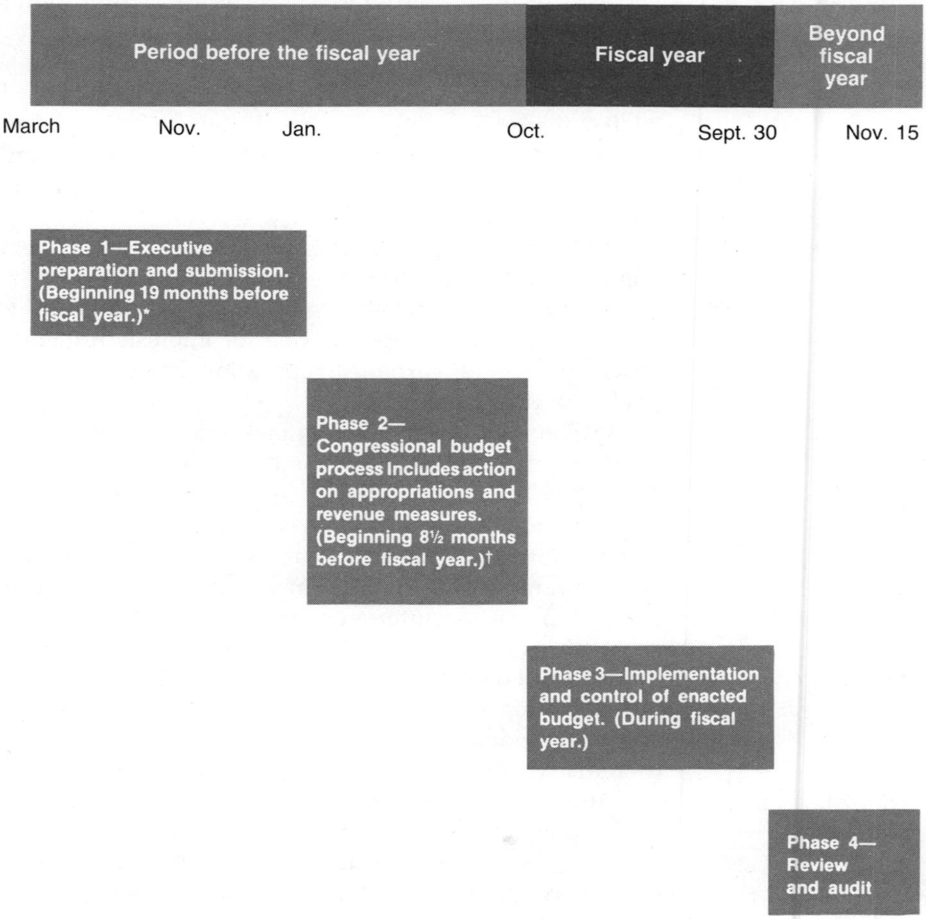

Period before the fiscal year	Fiscal year	Beyond fiscal year

March	Nov.	Jan.	Oct.	Sept. 30	Nov. 15

Phase 1—Executive preparation and submission. (Beginning 19 months before fiscal year.)*

Phase 2—Congressional budget process includes action on appropriations and revenue measures. (Beginning 8½ months before fiscal year.)†

Phase 3—Implementation and control of enacted budget. (During fiscal year.)

Phase 4—Review and audit

*The president's budget is transmitted to Congress within 15 days after Congress convenes.

†If appropriation action is not completed by September 30, Congress enacts temporary appropriation (i.e., continuing resolution).

Source: General Accounting Office, *A Glossary of Terms Used in the Federal Budget Process*, 3d ed. (Washington, D.C.: U.S. Government Printing Office, March 1981), p. 7.

cepted by the House or Senate. (The full appropriations committees rarely reverse subcommittee decisions.)

Appropriations subcommittees play somewhat differing roles in the two bodies. House subcommittees, with ingrained habits of budget trimming, are the cutting edge of congressional funding powers. Their budget figures are almost always accepted by the full House. Senate subcommittees play the role of appeals courts. They hear agency complaints about House figures and often grant more generous funding. Normally, final funding figures are somewhere between House and Senate levels.

Funding as oversight The yearly appropriations process is an effective way of overseeing executive agencies. Because the process is repeated year after year, legislators become familiar with agencies and programs. And because funding is the lifeblood of any executive agency, appropriations committees find bureaucrats very attentive to criticisms or suggestions.

Appropriations panels tend to focus on details, leaving larger problems and priorities somewhat blurred. Subcommittees work on agencies and programs within their jurisdictions, with last year's spending level as a starting point. There is little chance to weigh priorities and choose among competing funding options. The congressional budget process, involving the House and Senate budget committees, was set up partly to fix this defect.

Congress appropriates funds only for programs already authorized by law. Historically, authorizations were open-ended. They were renewed only when Congress got around to rethinking or changing the programs. In the past two decades, Congress has written more and more limited authorizations—for five years, three years, even one year. Thus, agencies must return to Congress not only for funding, but for the basic legislation as well. In grasping for control of executive activities, Congress thus makes administrators ask for renewal of authority more often. This multiplies the opportunities for oversight. It also increases the number of votes that must be taken on identical or similar questions year after year, or even within the same year.

Moreover, a number of authorizations have pushed growing portions of federal spending outside the yearly appropriations process. These so-called "uncontrollable" funds are expended not through appropriations, but automatically in accord with eligibility requirements (entitlements), trust funds, or long-term contracts.

Such programs, now three fourths of annual federal outlays, are not really uncontrollable; but they can be modified only by rewriting the basic laws that established them. In 1983, for example, Congress and the president forged an agreement to trim social security benefits and raise taxes to rescue this popular "uncontrollable" from financial crisis.

Congressional budget making

The Budget and Impoundment Control Act of 1974 (P.L. 93–344) was a landmark innovation. It sprang from two roots: tensions between Capitol Hill and the White House, and internal conflict between congressional committees.

Background of the 1974 act   External pressures on Congress were the chief impetus for the new congressional budget process. President Nixon impounded unprecedented amounts of funds in his first term, about $30 billion. Nixon in early 1973 was mounting an intensive "battle of the budget," threatening more impoundments if the Democratic Congress did not budge. He charged that Congress was fiscally irresponsible. Senators and representatives were hard pressed to defend their prerogatives. A more responsible budgetary process was one answer to such presidential challenges.

Another impetus for change lay in fights between authorizing and fiscal committees. Because of biased memberships and clientele favoritism, authorizing committees generated intense pressure for funding programs under their purview. To make sure that their pet programs continued, these committees sometimes advocated *backdoor spending*—direct Treasury borrowing, contract authority, entitlements, and trust funds. This removed such programs from the yearly appropriations processes. Short of these measures, committees turned

Budgetmakers. House and Senate budget panel chairmen, Representative James R. Jones (D–Okla.) and Senator Pete V. Domenici (R–N.M.), before budget conference.

to authorizations (often annual) with dollar amounts attached; this kept up pressure for "full funding" of the programs they sponsored.

What resulted was frequent warfare between authorizing and fiscal committees. As champions of their programs, the authorizing committees accused the appropriating committees of ignoring expert judgment and providing meager funding. The appropriating committees, for their part, built the image of the Dutch boy with his finger in the dike, holding back the greed of authorizing committees. Appropriating bodies felt more and more helpless in halting runaway spending. "Backdoor spending" was growing. Therefore, appropriating bodies handled less than 30 percent of annual federal outlays; the rest fell into various categories of uncontrollables. And for programs subject to yearly appropriations, the pressure for full funding was strong and unremitting.

How the process works The Budget Act set up procedures for Congress to determine national budget priorities and review presidential impoundments. It created House and Senate budget committees; the Congressional Budget Office, a full-time professional staff for analysis; a complex set of new budgetary procedures; a timetable for budgetary actions; a change in the fiscal year; requirements for standardized budget terminology and information in the president's budget; and new provisions for controlling presidential impoundments.

All standing committees are supposed to submit reports to the House and Senate Budget committees by March 15 (see Table 10–5). These reports are used to form the first concurrent budget resolution for the fiscal year beginning October 1. They include the committees' views and estimates on matters within their jurisdiction. This is meant to force authorizing committees to take a hard

TABLE 10—5

Congressional Budget Timetable

Deadline	Action to be completed
15th day after Congress convenes	President submits his budget, along with current services estimates.*
March 15	Committees submit views and estimates to Budget Committees.
April 1	Congressional Budget Office submits report to Budget Committees†
April 15	Budget Committees report first concurrent resolution on the budget to their houses.
May 15	Committees report bills authorizing new budget authority.
May 15	Congress adopts first concurrent resolution on the budget.
7th day after Labor Day	Congress completes action on bills providing budget authority and spending authority.
September 15	Congress completes actions on second required concurrent resolution on the budget.
September 25	Congress completes action on reconciliation process implementing second concurrent resolution.
October 1	Fiscal year begins.

*Current service estimates are estimates of the dollar levels that would be required next year to support the same level of services in each program as in this year's budget.

†The Budget Committees and the Congressional Budget Office (CBO) have found April 1 too late in the budget process to be useful; hence CBO submits its report(s) in February, although April 1 remains the date required by law.

view of spending for programs for which they are responsible. The committees must also assign priorities to present or potential programs within their jurisdiction.

From the authorizing committees' reports, the House and Senate Budget committees prepare their first concurrent resolution. This is reported by April 15. It states spending targets for each major budget category. (There are now 17.) Adopting such targets has forced the House and Senate to make tough choices. They limit the leeway of authorizing and appropriating panels. Budget targets and ceilings impinge upon committee policymaking authority by setting outer spending limits. They force committees to specify priorities and choose among programs. Funds are not simply authorized for all programs that have well-organized support.

Meanwhile, the appropriations subcommittees work their way through the president's budget, which is presented in late January. By summer, Congress is supposed to act on appropriations bills. This phase is supposed to be completed a week after Labor Day. Then the budget committees draw up a second concurrent resolution. It sets ceilings and reconciles the earlier targets with the later appropriations actions of Congress. The government fiscal year begins on October 1; soon after that the process begins again for the following year.

Congress's budget process is not self-enforcing; delays and loose ends mark the process; because of inflation, budget estimates made one week may be outdated the next. (Budget resolutions are not public laws; they are joint resolutions Congress adopts to discipline itself.) By the 1980s, the timetable that was actually followed strayed from that in Table 10–5. The *reconciliation* procedure came to the forefront.

Under the original act, reconciliation occurred at the end of the budget process to bring spending in line with the binding targets of the second budget resolution. After 1980, this was pushed forward several months. The resulting two-stage process works this way. During stage one, Congress adopts a first budget resolution giving each authorizing committee a dollar figure and a deadline to report legislation for achieving the savings. During stage two, the budget panels combine committee recommendations into an omnibus reconciliation measure. The 1981 reconciliation package, embracing some $140 billion in savings over a three-year period, overshadowed other budget steps and even the entire appropriations process.

In an era that stresses the limits of government activity, the congressional budget process is a powerful tool. In 1981, President Reagan selected the budget process, not a package of new legislation, as the forum for his initial program. Aided by Budget Director David A. Stockman and key allies on Capitol Hill, the president used the budget mechanism as a lever to change government policy.

Since these procedures started, the House and Senate budget committees have played a key role in organizing decisions on spending and revenue (Schick, 1980). Generally, the budget committees have avoided setting line-item (specific) funding limits. But the committees or their leaders sometimes oppose bills reported by other committees to hold the line on spending targets. The budget committees also have the power to recommend revenue levels, including *tax expenditures* or loopholes. These are revenues forgone by the federal government to achieve certain policy goals.

Budget strongman. David A. Stockman, director of the Office of Management and Budget, used knowledge of Congress's budget process to push President Reagan's economic program and win key Capitol Hill victories.

Behind the senators and representatives stands a large bureaucracy. Legislators rely on staffs to handle the growing workload. Staffs communicate with local voters, help run committee and floor sessions, even frame issues and clarify choices.

There are four main types of congressional staffs: personal staffs (some 10,000 workers); committee staffs (about 3,000 people); housekeeping staffs on Capitol Hill; and supporting agencies, such as the Congressional Research Service and the General Accounting Office. The supporting agencies employ about 18,000 workers. They serve many public and private needs in addition to those of Congress.

The first two categories—personal and committee staffs—have more than doubled in size since the early 1960s (see Figure 10–4). Before World War I, senators outnumbered their paid personal staff members; by 1976, there were almost 3,300 such aides. At first, legislators were leery of voting for enough staff assistance. They feared charges of wasteful spending. But these objections were overruled as legislators tried vainly to cope with the workload and compete with executive expertise.

FIGURE 10–4

Member and Committee Staffs (1891–1981)

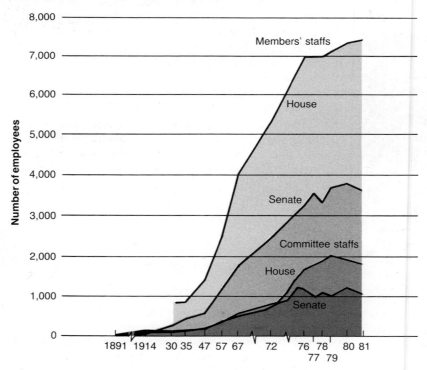

Source: Norman J. Ornstein, Thomas E. Mann, Michael J. Malbin, and John F. Bibby, *Vital Statistics on Congress, 1982* (Washington, D.C.: American Enterprise Institute, 1982), p. 111.

Personal staffs

Hill intern. College students flock to congressional offices, like the House Republican Conference (shown here).

Personal staffers. Legislative director (left) and administrative assistant confer with their boss, Representative Dan Glickman (D–Kan.).

The 10,000 or so staff aides who work in legislators' offices support and foster their bosses' careers. Senators' personal staffs range in size from 13 to 71; they average about 36. Representatives' staffs average about 17.

Personal aides do many things. Constituent relations are their most time-consuming job. This includes casework and projects, handling requests for information, correspondence, and meeting with local voters and lobbyists. Press relations also get high priority. Other staff aides handle a broad range of tasks that embrace information gathering, lawmaking, policy formation, and office management.

Job types　A legislator's good right arm is the administrative assistant (AA). He or she supervises the legislator's office and gives political and legislative advice. At best, an AA functions as the legislator's alter ego, bargaining with colleagues, voters, and lobbyists.

The legislative and research functions of a legislator's office are usually handled by one or more legislative assistants (LAs) and researchers. Their tasks include working with and representing the legislator's interests. Often they follow committee sessions the legislator cannot attend. LAs research, draft, read, and analyze bills and other materials. They also write speeches, floor remarks, and articles.

Legislators who are chairmen or ranking minority members of committees are entitled to committee-based aides. (All senators are entitled to staff attached to their major committees.) The functions of these aides sometimes mingle with those of the personal staff.

Caseworkers handle questions on certain types of constituents' problems. For instance, they deal with social security or veterans' benefits. They are valued for their knowledge of federal programs and their lists of phone numbers. They know which bureaucrats to call for quick answers.

Most personal staff aides work in crowded Capitol Hill offices. But more than a third of representatives' personal staffs and a fourth of senators' staffs are based in their home districts or states. Members of Congress have from one to six local offices in key locations at home. More and more voter contacts and casework are handled there.

Private domains　Personal staffs are guided by the legislators' ideologies, interests, personalities, institutional positions, and personal roles or styles in performing the duties of office. Legislators are masters of these little kingdoms. They (or their office managers) personally hire (and fire) every staff member. Although most staff members are well paid, they have no job rights and can be removed at any time.

Legislators insist that this system is dictated by the political nature of their office tasks and the need for loyal aides. But abuses occur; there have been frequent charges of discrimination and irregular assignments. In 1976, a Capitol Hill secretary, Elizabeth Ray, charged that she lacked clerical skills but had been hired to give sexual favors to Representative Wayne Hays (D-Ohio). The resulting uproar ended Hays's career in Congress and forced a wide-ranging study of House ethics and office procedures. But no major changes were made in congressional staffing practices.

Committee staffs

Committee staffs are largely a product of the post–World War II era. The Legislative Reorganization Act of 1946 gave each congressional committee a permanent source of funds for professional and clerical help. Since then, committee staffs have grown by leaps and bounds.

Staff functions Committee staffs draft bills, investigate, gather information, and negotiate with lobbyists and bureaucrats. They maintain the pace of the legislative process—planning hearings, writing committee briefing papers, and preparing reports. According to Fox and Hammond (1977: 119–20), "Committee aides report that they work with congressmen in hearings, on the average, about once a week, and in markup, conference, and executive sessions about once a month. They work on legislation more frequently, 'at least once a day,' and write remarks once a week."

It is no exaggeration to say that committee staffs are responsible for the bulk of lawmaking, even key policy choices. The final decision lies in the legislators' hands. But the choices they consider are framed by the committee staff.

Resource or crutch? Legislators are quick to admit they depend on staffs. Staff assistance is a prime power resource on the Hill. Indeed, the desire for staff help explains much of the pressure toward spreading out committee and subcommittee leadership posts. Today, separate staffs serve majority and minority members on almost every committee.

There are fewer senators than representatives; so senators must be generalists rather than specialists. Thus, the Senate more readily delegates legislative functions to its committee staffs than does the House.

Historically, representatives have prided themselves on "doing their own homework." They have resented bargaining with Senate staff members in conferences with "the other body." Yet House ways are changing. Constituency demands, multiple committee and subcommittee assignments, and the growth of public-policy issues all have an effect. These pressures have forced House members to reassess their schedules and delegate legislative tasks.

When Republicans assumed Senate control in 1981, they made a point of trimming committee staffs and budgets by around 10 percent. They could afford to do this; they stood to gain staffs in their shift from minority to majority status. In the House, cuts were made in the budget but not in staff. Whatever future adjustments are made, large staffs are firmly established.

Like the president, legislators face a dilemma; they cannot function without staff help, but they risk becoming captives of their staffs. Committee staffs are essential for complex lawmaking. Yet by delegating responsibilities to their staffs, senators and representatives take risks. They could lose touch with information and policy details.

Housekeeping staffs

Congress long ago outgrew the Capitol Building. On the Senate side of Capitol Hill are three major office buildings and several converted hotels and apartments. The House side has three major buildings and two annexes. Maintenance and construction are supervised by the Office of the Architect of the Capitol.

Other housekeeping functions are done separately by the two houses. The

Capitol Hill bureaucracy. The growing staff resources of Congress are reflected in Capitol Hill architecture. On the Senate side (left) are the Russell (1), Dirksen (2), and Hart (3) Senate office buildings. More Senate annexes are to the left (4). In front of the Capitol (rear of photo) stand the Supreme Court (5) and two Library of Congress buildings, the domed Jefferson Building and, behind it, the Adams Building (6 and 7). On the House side of the Hill (right) are four huge buildings: from rear, the Library of Congress's Madison Building (8) (housing the Congressional Research Service) and the Cannon (9), Longworth (10), and Rayburn (11) office buildings. All these congressional buildings are linked by underground passageways. To the right of Cannon is a House office annex (12). Other buildings of interest are the Republican party's national headquarters (13) (right of the Library's Madison building) and the headquarters of the United Brotherhood of Carpenters and Joiners (14) (lower left corner).

TABLE 10—6

Congressional Support Agencies, 1984

Agency	Staff size
General Accounting Office	5,100
Congressional Research Service	858
Congressional Budget Office	222
Office of Technology Assessment	139
Total support agencies	6,319

Source: *Appendix of the Budget of the United States, Fiscal 1982* (Washington, D.C.: U.S. Government Printing Office), pp. I–A4ff.

Senate and House each have clerks' offices. They handle documents, stationery, public records, and disbursing. Sergeants at arms in the two bodies handle a wide range of functions. They deal with the press galleries, broadcasting studios, telephones, post offices, and police forces.

Supporting agencies

Various congressional support agencies play important roles on Capitol Hill (see Table 10–6). Though all are congressional agencies, some also offer services to other agencies and to private citizens. Among these agencies are the following.

Congressional Research Service   Housed in the Library of Congress is the Congressional Research Service (CRS). It dates from 1914 and now has more than 800 employees. In one year, CRS receives more than 400,000 requests from legislators and committees. CRS helps members of Congress meet constituents' requests for information. But CRS also employs experienced professionals who provide substantial research services, including issue analyses, legal research, and reports on the status of bills. CRS staff members are often loaned to committees to help them prepare reports and stage hearings.

General Accounting Office (GAO)   The GAO was set up by the Budget and Accounting Act of 1921. It audits federal agencies, reviews agencies' financial management, settles claims, collects debts, and provides legal services. GAO is headed by the comptroller general, appointed for a 15-year term by the president, with Senate confirmation. GAO audits are done by a professional staff of some 5,000 people scattered throughout the world.

Recently GAO has tried to mesh its activities more closely with the needs of Congress. About a third of GAO's work now stems from congressional requests, mainly for oversight and program evaluation (Mosher, 1979). GAO staffers respond to committee and member requests and testify before congressional panels. They brief members on federal programs and work with committees. They develop questions for use in hearings and give legal opinions and comments on pending bills.

Office of Technology Assessment (OTA)   Created in 1972, OTA helps Congress anticipate and plan for the results of technology. OTA is governed by a 10-member Technology Assessment Board composed of senators and representatives. A director runs the agency. During its early years, OTA stressed the study of major technological innovations. These involved critical materials, the oceans, transportation, energy, food, health, and research and development. OTA's staff alerts Congress to developments that may need new legislation. Technology assessment is a vague concept, and OTA at first had a hard time defining its mission and building support on Capitol Hill.

Congressional Budget Office (CBO)   The newest support agency is CBO, set up in 1974 by the Congressional Budget and Impoundment Control Act. As an adjunct to the congressional budget process, CBO provides basic data and analyses of alternative fiscal, budgetary, and program options. The 200 or so people who staff CBO give Congress macroeconomic analysis. This resembles what the president gets from the Office of Management and Budget and the Council of Economic Advisers.

The CBO staff forecasts economic trends. It keeps score on whether congressional committees are conforming to budget targets and makes cost projections of proposed new programs. By April of each year, it prepares a report on budget alternatives. By statute, CBO deals solely with committees, especially the House and Senate Budget committees and other fiscal panels.

Legislation by staff?

Senators and representatives must have staff support to keep pace with the demands made on them. Even at its present level, the congressional establishment is but a tiny fraction of the 2.8 million people who hold civilian posts in the executive branch. At their best, congressional staffs provide alternative premises to guide legislators' decisions.

The question is whether staffs exert excessive power, like the tail that wags the dog (Malbin, 1980). "This country is basically run by the legislative staffs of the members of the Senate and the House of Representatives," complained one senator. Another offers a more balanced view: "Dependency on staff is great. Domination, no. Dependency, definitely. There is no question of our enormous dependency and their influence. In all legislation, they're the ones that lay out the options."

Congressional staffs are necessary. They have changed the face of the legislative branch by inserting bureaucracy into what was originally a personal function.

CHANGE IN CONGRESS

Belittling Congress is an American pastime. A 19th-century observer, Lord Bryce, remarked that "Americans are especially fond of running down their congressmen." The executive and judicial branches have nothing to compare with the

public image of cartoon character Senator Snort, the florid but incompetent windbag. Political wit, from Mark Twain and Will Rogers to Herblock and Johnny Carson, always singles out Congress for special attention. Legislators themselves often contribute to this shabby public image. They portray themselves as gallant warriors against the evils of Congress: they "run *for* Congress by running *against* Congress" (Fenno, 1975: 280).

Serious critics, mainly scholars and journalists, fault Congress on a number of grounds. The prevalent textbook image of Congress combines disorder, corruption, and inertia. Average people, in opinion polls, seem to agree that these are defects of the legislative branch.

Despite Congress's reputation for inertia, it has changed dramatically during the past decade. Our era is hard on legislatures the world over; Congress has been subject to severe challenges. Some pressures come from the external environment. There have been changing public expectations, fast-moving events, and competing institutions. Such pressures challenge Congress to adapt by changing its practices or work habits. Other pressures come from internal stresses, mainly membership turnover, factional shifts, and changing norms. For Congress to survive, it must relieve these stresses by adjusting its procedures and power structures. Congress has responded to both sets of pressures; how successfully remains to be seen.

CONGRESSIONAL DECLINE AND RESURGENCE

Historically, Congress has been an equal partner in policymaking. The founders viewed the legislative branch as the keystone of democracy. They spelled out the powers of Congress in Article I of the Constitution. Except in times of crisis, Congress has aired and refined the great issues of the day. After periods of strong presidents, such as Jackson, Lincoln, or Wilson, it has regained the initiative. Sometimes, it has all but eclipsed the presidency. In the late 1800s, Woodrow Wilson (1885: 31) saw Congress as "the predominant and controlling force, the center and source of all motive and of all regulatory power."

Few observers today would describe Congress in such expansive terms. "The decline of Congress" has been universally cited. Friends as well as foes have done so, liberals as well as conservatives, members of Congress as well as outsiders. Journalists have enjoyed taking members of Congress to task for their perquisites, their junkets, their occasional corruption, even their sexual exploits.

Yet, to paraphrase Mark Twain, the reports of the demise of Congress have been greatly exaggerated. True, the shaping experiences of this century—two world wars, the depression, and the extended Cold War—expanded the policymaking role of the president. Especially in foreign policy, Congress has yielded much of its constitutional power to "advise and consent." It has done so by deferring to the president's ability to respond to fast-moving world events. But the disillusionment that followed the Vietnam War and Watergate led to a basic debate: How desirable is concentrated executive power? Since Nixon's resignation, Congress has shown renewed vigor in defending its prerogatives in foreign and domestic policymaking (Sundquist, 1981).

Such congressional folkways and traditions as seniority have inspired generations of editorial writers and cartoonists. But the traditions have changed so

The pendulum swings. Senate Watergate investigators helped uncover evidence which eventually drove President Nixon from office. From left to right, Senator Howard H. Baker, Jr. (R-Tenn.), Chairman Sam Ervin (D–N.C.), Committee Counsel Sam Dash, Senators Herman Talmadge (D–Ga.) and Daniel K. Inouye (D–Hawaii).

much that they are almost unrecognizable. New organizations have brought a new generation of problems to Capitol Hill.

Congress will always be controversial. Unlike the president or the courts, it conducts its business largely in public. Its faults are out in the open for all to see. A presidential message may patch over quarrels among White House advisers or rivalries among agencies; a judicial ruling may cloak the uncertainties or biases of judges. People are therefore apt to conclude that the president speaks with one voice; they might conclude that the courts embody magisterial wisdom. No such illusions surround the actions of the legislative branch. Congress speaks with 540 voices. It reflects the variety and contradiction embodied in American society itself.

Congress mirrors the people. The president may embody people's hopes and aspirations; the houses of Congress reflect their interests. Public expectations may place impossible demands on the chief executive; the babel of interests places equally impossible burdens on the legislative branch. No body of politicians can satisfy the demands of all major groups or interests, especially in an age of scarce resources. Nor can such a body represent those demands without making incoherent or even contradictory decisions. That is the dilemma of Congress as a representative institution.

CONCLUSIONS

In this chapter, we considered the members of Congress and their legislative tasks. We have tried to cast light on the intricacies of the lawmaking process—not only the enactment of bills and resolutions, but also budget making, oversight, and the congressional staff apparatus.

1 The legislative duties of Congress embrace the whole range of the government's activities. The elaborate rules of the two houses not only promote orderly deliberation, but also allow political preferences to be registered at many stages in the lawmaking process.

2 Congressional government is committee government. Committee deliberation falls roughly into three stages: staff research, committee hearings, and markup sessions. Bypassing a committee is hazardous and not often done.

3 Party coalitions, though seemingly fragile, are persistent and powerful. Alongside party and committee structures, a network of informal caucuses has grown linking legislators with common regional, industry, ethnic, or philosophic goals.

4 Procedure in the House is relatively rigid. But the Senate is a more informal body. It makes many procedural arrangements by unanimous consent.

5 A key lever for controlling the executive branch is the legislature's historic power of the purse. The rise of so-called "uncontrollables," though, weakens this leverage.

6 Under congressional budget-making rules, House and Senate Budget committees prepare target spending and revenue figures. They also monitor how closely various committees follow those targets.

7 In response to workload demands, there are sizable congressional staffs—personal, committee, housekeeping, and supporting agencies.

8 A great deal is said about the "decline of Congress." But post-Vietnam and post-Watergate Congresses have displayed renewed independence and vigor.

FURTHER READING

DAVIDSON, ROGER H., and WALTER J. OLESZEK (1985) Congress and Its Members. 2d ed. Washington, D.C.: Congressional Quarterly Press. An interpretive textbook on the "two Congresses" notion: the institution that makes policy versus the members who seek reelection.

DODD, LAWRENCE, and BRUCE OPPENHEIMER, eds. (1985) Congress Reconsidered. 3d ed. Washington, D.C.: Congressional Quarterly Press. A useful collection of original articles outlining aspects of recent congressional developments.

FENNO, RICHARD F., JR. (1978) Home Style. Boston: Little, Brown. A path-breaking exploration of House members' relationships with constituents in their home districts.

RIPLEY, RANDALL B. (1983) Congress: Process and Policy. 3d ed. New York: W. W. Norton. A basic textbook on Congress covering all aspects of congressional behavior, with particular emphasis on Congress as a policymaking institution.

11

The Bureaucracy

Betty Jones, a mother of four young children, has received public aid for seven years. She is now in the county welfare office in Los Angeles proving for the 14th time in those seven years that she is eligible to continue getting help. She has been in the office for five hours waiting for her turn. The office does not take appointments. The surroundings are dingy. She had no one to care for her two preschool children, and so they are with her. The children are cross, hungry, and tired. They had to catch the bus at 7 A.M., transfer twice, and ride for an hour to get to the office at 8 A.M. when it opened.

Now it is 1 P.M. The pace has slowed for the last two hours as those in charge went to lunch. Those dealing with the clients are notably on edge today; they have many cases to review and are shorthanded. Two of their usual staff of ten are ill; a ruling of a distant Washington, D.C. agency called the Office of Management and Budget has "frozen" two slots. Betty doesn't know whom she will see; whoever it is won't know her or remember her anyway. Most of the workers seem to dislike her, though she doesn't know why.

Betty is worried about getting home in time to greet her first- and second-grade children when they return from school. She has to leave in an hour to make it. But will she miss her chance to be interviewed? Will she have to waste another day on a pointless trip to answer the same questions and fill out the same form?

Bill Smith is a cattleman in Wyoming. He has 10,000 head of cattle and needs access to federal land for some of them. It is time to renew his grazing permit. He also must ask for a change in his permit that will allow him to add 500 head to the 2,000 already grazing on public land.

A few months ago the advisory committee, of which he is a member, made a suggestion to the Department of the Interior, which controls the land: allow one owner to graze up to 2,500 cattle on public land. So Bill should have no trouble getting the change. The fees charged by the government have not changed for six years and are quite low.

This afternoon Bill has to go to the bank and the hardware store at the county seat. He also expects to drop by the office of the Interior Department. In 15 minutes he can complete the simple form that will both grant him the added herd and extend his permits for another year. He and Al Greene, the government agent who has run the office for 10 years, are old friends; Bill is looking forward to chatting with Al while taking care of his business.

* * * * *

Which is the real bureaucracy: Betty's or Bill's? In fact, they both are. Bureaucracy can provide services efficiently and smoothly; it can also complicate people's lives for no apparent reason.

Public employees. 2d Lt. Marilyn Koon, Air National Guard pilot, is a federal employee. The schoolteacher is a local employee.

Governments exist in part to provide services. They also exist to keep order. Both of these broad public purposes require organizations that are generally called **agencies** of the government. These agencies make up the government **bureaucracy.** (Private groups such as unions, churches, businesses, and colleges, also have bureaucracies.)

Bureaucracies have a number of traits. Each part of a bureaucracy (the single bureau or agency) has a clear identity. The Bureau of Land Management is distinct from the Bureau of Reclamation, even though both are in the Department of the Interior. Each agency has an exact list of its employees and rules for replacing those who leave. Each has certain things to do (often called *programs*) that are, at least in theory, related to achieving broad goals and missions. Each agency works by dividing the labor among employees and groups of employees. These workers are set up in some sort of hierarchy. Different grades or ranks tell who reports to whom and who is equal to whom.

Normally, agencies also set up procedures that should be automatic and help make contacts with clients impersonal. They stress written communication, building files, and set up rules to govern employee behavior.

In this chapter we will focus on the federal bureaucracy in recent years. It has become more difficult to tell federal bureaucrats from state and local ones. Many of the latter administer federal funds and get salaries from these funds but are formally employed by a state, city, or county. State and local bureaucrats outnumber those formally called federal bureaucrats. About one in every five people in the American labor force works for some government organization, including the public schools. Many of you will no doubt become government employees.

This chapter begins with a review of the nature of today's federal bureaucracy. Next it looks at the major aspects of the political setting of bureaucracy.

Then it takes up the question of whether bureaucracy is autonomous or effectively controlled. Finally, it assesses the impact of bureaucracy on public policy.

MODERN BUREAUCRACY: AN OVERVIEW

Large problems require large organizations to solve them. In this century, the various governments in our system have responded to problems believed to be both large and within the government's proper scope of activities. Typically they have responded by creating many bureaucracies. These bureaucracies have, for the most part, survived for a long time and have become larger, more complex, and more important in terms of the services they provide.

The pervasiveness of bureaucracies

Bureaucracies abound in our life—and in the life of any other modern country. Some are governmental; many are private. Government bureaucracies, unlike private ones, make rules that people normally obey without thinking since they have the force of law behind them. There are ways to appeal or evade these rules, but most of the time they are accepted and obeyed.

Life in the United States is subject to many rules, decisions, and activities of bureaucracies—both public and private. For example, your life as a college student might be affected by these programs and activities of federal bureaucracies:

The dorms, classrooms, and labs you use were almost surely built in large part with federal money.

You may help finance your education with one of several kinds of loans or grants from federal agencies (for example, basic opportunity grants or educational aid for veterans).

You may earn money through the federal work-study program.

You may work on research projects funded with federal money.

Some of the subject matter of your courses might come from federally funded research.

The ethnic and racial makeup of your student body might result from affirmative action rulings and programs.

If you are a woman, you might have available new athletic facilities and programs because of antidiscrimination laws.

You may be taking an ROTC program.

All citizens interact with bureaucracies. You pay federal income tax and social security tax. You are affected by regulations requiring air pollution devices on cars, or control of food additives and medicines.

You must also interact directly and indirectly with state and local bureaucracies as a citizen and as a college student. There may be state aid to colleges in your state. There may be loans for students. There may be a special state law on civil disruptions on campus. And you pay state and local taxes, such as a sales tax, state income tax, and local income tax. If you register or drive a car, vote, or collect unemployment compensation, you must deal with state or local bureaucracies. And, of course, you must also deal with college bureaucracies: the registrar, bursar, academic departments, campus police, and student aid offices.

Contact with the bureaucracy. New Yorkers line up for unemployment insurance. An elderly woman gets personal attention from a volunteer worker in a public program in South Carolina.

Bureaucracies in the federal executive branch administer programs set up by statute. They are responsible to Congress for carrying out the specific provisions of the laws creating such programs. Presumably they will do this in an efficient and rational way. But once a bureaucracy is formed, its workers spend some of their time making sure it keeps going. Its mission as stated in the statute takes up only part of the bureaucracy's time.

Some degree of bureaucracy is inevitable in modern society if a government offers any services at all. But the size of bureaucracies can vary, depending on how the services are offered. For instance, income redistribution to the poor could be achieved through an income tax that combines negative taxes (payments to the poorest people) with tax payment by more affluent people. Some bureaucrats would be needed in such a scheme, but their number could be small. Income redistribution may also be sought through a whole range of specialized programs such as welfare, medical care, aid to education, housing programs, day-care programs, training programs, and food stamps. Each program then will be administered its own bureaucracy. More bureaucrats and even more agencies will no doubt be formed to keep track of efforts aimed mostly at the same group of people.

Bureaucracies have both strengths and weaknesses. An agency that is working well can:

> Proceed in an orderly and predictable way to process its work, including work resulting from contacts with citizens.
>
> Work impartially and fairly, treating all people alike.
>
> Keep a staff of qualified professionals.
>
> Keep a staff whose hiring and advancement depend on merit (if a civil service system is in place and working).
>
> Keep good records and files that can be used to track down the facts in any specific dealings with a client.

Many problems can plague bureaucracies and the people they are supposed to serve. Bureaucracy can:

> Be rigid in applying rules so that they "go by the book" and cannot cope with exceptional cases.
>
> Treat clients impersonally, rudely, and without respect.
>
> Be slow in processing their work.
>
> Create meaningless paperwork.
>
> Be subject to hidden political forces so they cater to some clients at the expense of others.
>
> Be unresponsive to central leadership of high-ranking officials, including the president.
>
> Be staffed by workers who are so worried about job security that they cannot produce adequate services.

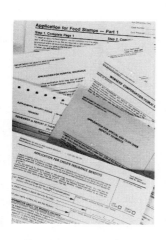

Paperwork. Forms allow the bureaucracy to keep necessary records and process benefits. They can also frustrate citizens required to fill them out.

The constitutional context of federal bureaucracy

Bureaucracy is provided for indirectly in the Constitution and discussed briefly in *The Federalist* papers. The framers surely knew that government needed organizations, but they had no idea how large they would grow. Articles I and II mention executive departments and department heads. They create areas of government action that clearly need agencies for implementation. And they empower Congress to give the president, department heads, or the courts power to appoint various officials.

In short, the Constitution gives Congress the power to create agencies and programs, and to delegate powers to those agencies. Sometimes the president is barely involved, if at all, in those delegations. Because of the scope of bureaucratic activities, judicial and presidential restraints on those activities can be used only selectively. Congress has more potential for controlling bureaucracy, but it lacks the incentive to do so because members of Congress and bureaucrats usually both gain from pursuing the same ends.

In Chapter 2 we sketched the growth of bureaucracy during the two-hundred-year history of the independent United States. Bureaucracy has proliferated, as have programs. But there is no reason to portray the United States as peculiarly dominated by bureaucracy. All modern, industrial societies have lots of bureaucrats. However, there is one unique feature in the United States: Our bureaucrats are very active in building and participating in their own coalitions and networks of allies dedicated to specific policy goals. Bureaucracy in the other developed Western nations tends to be more neutral in terms of policy. (See Aberbach, Putnam, and Rockman, 1981.)

The organization of the federal bureaucracy

The federal bureaucracy is both vast and complex. Its size is suggested in Table 11–1, which summarizes civilian government employment in 1981 by function. A column is also included for state and local employees. This column shows that state employees are over four times more numerous than federal employees. The federal column reveals that most federal civilian employees work either in national defense and international relations or in the postal service. About half of all state and local employees work in education, most of them as teachers.

TABLE 11–1

Civilian Government Employment by Function (1981)

	Distribution of employees (percent)	
Function	Federal government	State and local governments
National defense and international relations	35%	0%
Postal service	23	0
Education	1	52
Highways	*	4
Health and hospitals	9	11
Public welfare, police, fire, sanitation, parks and recreation	2	14
Natural resources	10	2
Financial administration	4	2
All other	17	16
Total	101†	101†
Total number of employees	2,865,000	13,103,000

*Less than 1 percent.
†Does not add to 100 because of rounding.
Source: *Statistical Abstracts of the United States* (Washington, D.C.: U.S. Government Printing Office, 1982), p. 303.

TABLE 11–2

Civilian Employment in Selected Agencies of the Federal Government (1982)

Agency	Number of employees (000s)	Percent of all federal civilian employees
Departments:		
Agriculture	114	4%
Commerce	34	1
Defense	1,018	36
Education	6	*
Energy	19	1
Health and Human Services	148	5
Housing and Urban Development	15	1
Interior	74	3
Justice	55	2
Labor	19	1
State	24	1
Transportation	61	2
Treasury	126	5
Independent agencies:		
U.S. Postal Service	664	23
Veterans Administration	223	8
All others	200	7
Total	2,801	100%

*Less than 1 percent.

Source: *Statistical Abstracts of the United States* (Washington, D.C.: U.S. Government Printing Office, 1982), pp. 266–67.

The size of various federal agencies and departments, of course, reflects the functional distribution of employees. Thus, in 1982, 36 of every 100 federal civilian employees worked in the Department of Defense and 23 of every 100 worked in the Postal Service. Table 11–2 summarizes both the number and percentage of employment in selected federal agencies in 1982.

One way of portraying the complexity of the federal bureaucracy is through organizational charts. Figure 11–1 shows the organization of the entire federal executive branch in simple form, while Figure 11–2 is a simplified version of the major organizations within a single federal department, the Department of Health and Human Services.

The decisions that led to the complex organization portrayed in the two figures built up over time. Both charts represent the outcome of many debates and struggles. Organization charts may seem dry to the reader, but they are the end product of often fierce political struggles. One long-time inside observer of such debates summarized the situation well (Seidman, 1980: 15):

> Organizational arrangements are not neutral. We do not organize in a vacuum. Organization is one way of expressing national commitment, influencing program direction, and ordering priorities. Organizational arrangements tend to give some interests and perspectives more effective access to those with decision-making authority, whether they be in the Congress or in the executive branch.

There has been nothing inevitable or natural about the particular development patterns of the executive branch. Conscious decisions were made to create new agencies, to transfer duties or units between agencies, and—sometimes, at least—to end them. Decisions about arranging units and functions within agencies are made all the time.

FIGURE 11–1

Organization of the Federal Executive Branch

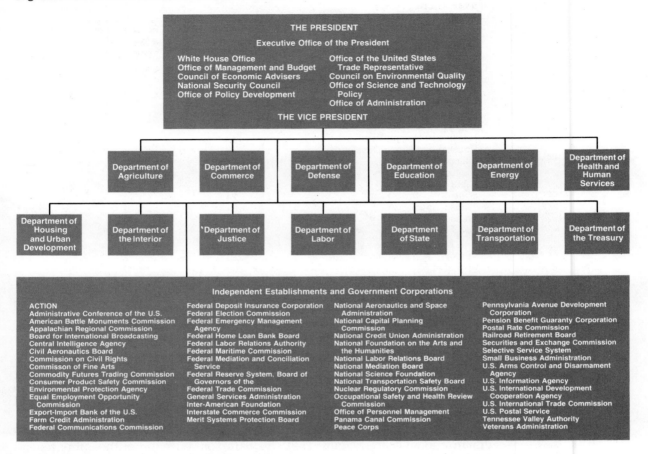

Source: *The United States Government Manual* (Washington, D.C.: U.S. Government Printing Office, 1983), p. 810.

Some decisions create a home for a new or largely new activity. The National Aeronautics and Space Administration (NASA) began in 1958 to respond to the launching of Sputnik by the Soviet Union. This marked the start of our serious space effort. The Office of Economic Opportunity, formed in 1964, marked the start of the War on Poverty, and housed many programs, both new and existing, in the social welfare field.

Some decisions are made to spotlight programs that are already under way. The federal government's part in controlling air pollution involved changing the responsible agencies a few times. This occurred as pollution drew more attention and effort from the different people involved (Jones, 1975). The moves started when backers of stronger federal action realized that the Public Health Service in the Department of Health, Education, and Welfare opposed aggressive action. Several arrangements were tried before the Environmental Protection Agency was at last created and assigned air pollution matters.

Federal departments are often formed to cluster activities and give them more prominence. The Departments of Agriculture (1862); Labor (1913); Commerce

FIGURE 11–2

Organization of the Department of Health and Human Services

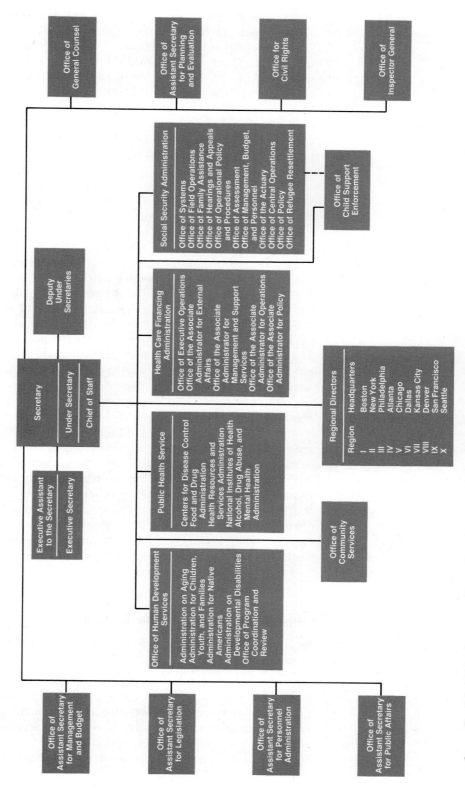

Source: *The United States Government Manual* (Washington, D.C.: U.S. Government Printing Office, 1983), p. 824.

(1913); Defense (1949); Health, Education, and Welfare (1953); Housing and Urban Development (1965); Transportation (1966); Energy (1977); and Education (1979) were set up for these reasons. Ronald Reagan, in his 1980 campaign, pledged to scrap both Energy and Education as symbols of different policy emphases. As president, however, Reagan was unable to deliver on either promise and, by 1984, had suspended these proposals.

Some organizational decisions play down an activity. Presidents Nixon and Ford, who opposed the war on poverty idea, successfully eliminated the Office of Economic Opportunity. Most of the office's programs were eliminated but, a small residue was moved to a new, minor agency—the Community Services Administration. That agency went out of business in 1981.

Some organizational shuffles are also undertaken to promote efficiency, improve the quality of services, and save money. These are the usual public justifications offered when reorganization is proposed.

What is the president's role in reorganizing? In theory, the president is responsible for the executive branch. In practice, he tries to have an impact in the areas most important to him. In many areas he must just go along with the present way of doing things. Between 1939 and 1973, under an often-renewed statute, the president was given wide powers to make changes, but Congress kept the power to veto those changes. Between 1949 and 1973, presidents proposed 74 changes; Congress vetoed 9 of them.

In 1973, Congress did not renew this statute mainly because of its war with Nixon over many programs andd political questions. In 1977, Carter asked Congress to renew the authority. After some debate, he was given the power almost unanimously. However, the status of this procedure is in doubt since the Supreme Court declared the legislative veto unconstitutional in 1983.

Presidents often start their terms with grand hopes of rearranging the bureaucracy. In the 1976 campaign, Jimmy Carter pledged to cut the federal bureaucracy from an alleged 1,900 agencies to 200. He was only successful in cutting some advisory committees. Carter shelved major reorganization plans in early 1979 when his aides told him he had no chance of getting them through Congress. Ronald Reagan came to office pledging a smaller bureaucracy in general. As he entered his fourth year in office in 1984, total federal civilian employment remained at about the same levels as when he became president in January 1981. The numbers fell in some agencies but rose in others. Internal reorganization in some agencies, however, did help reduce federal activity in areas of little or no interest to the Reagan administration.

The social purposes of federal agencies

Throughout our history agencies have been formed for one of four broad social purposes:

1. To provide services that are necessary and desirable, and that cannot be provided by those outside the government. These include national defense, diplomacy, mail, and housekeeping for the government itself.
2. To promote and help fund specific economic sectors, such as farmers, labor unions, or parts of private business.
3. To regulate the conditions under which different kinds of private activity can or cannot take place.

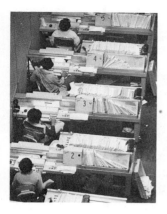

Mail sorting. Bureaucracies provide vital services we take for granted.

Two instances of regulation. A federal inspector grades beef. President John Kennedy honors Dr. Frances Kelsey, who led the effort to ban thalidomide, a drug that deformed babies before birth. Senator Hubert Humphrey observes.

4. To redistribute part of society's income and other benefits to the less fortunate.

In 1789, there were small bureaucracies only in general services. They were defense (the War Department), diplomacy (the State Department), and the government's financial and legal business (the Treasury and Justice Departments). The first bureaucracies to be added (the Post Office and Navy Departments) were still in the services area.

In the mid-1800s, several new agencies were created (primarily the Departments of the Interior and Agriculture). They administered subsidies for private activities, such as building railroads and settling the West; internal improvements like roads; and protecting growing domestic industry with tariffs on foreign imports. (The latter was done by the Treasury Department.) New units were formed to administer policies aimed at providing incentives for private activity.

Beginning in the late 1800s, some agencies were formed mainly to regulate. They controlled the conditions under which different private activities could and could not take place. There have been at least four major waves of regulatory activity, and each left bureaucracies that became permanent (Wilson, 1975).

The first wave came between 1887 and 1890. It produced the Interstate Commerce Act (to regulate railroads) and the Sherman Antitrust Act (to regulate trusts formed to achieve monopolies). The second wave came between 1906 and 1915. It produced the Pure Food and Drug Act, the Meat Inspection Act, the Federal Trade Commission Act (to prevent unfair business practices such as deceptive advertising), and the Clayton Act (to strengthen antitrust law).

The third wave came in the 1930s. It produced the Food, Drug, and Cosmetic Act; the Public Utility Holding Company Act (to prevent the concentration of economic power in public utilities); the Securities Exchange Act (to regulate the stock market); the Natural Gas Act; and the National Labor Relations Act (to prevent unfair labor practices by business). The fourth wave began in the late 1960s and was aimed at protecting consumers and the environment. It produced the Water Quality Act, the Clean Air Act, the Truth in Lending Act, the National Traffic and Motor Vehicle Safety Act, amendments to drug control laws, and the Motor Vehicle Pollution Control Act. However, rhetoric about and some attempts at deregulation became prominent in the late 1970s and into the 1980s.

In addition, the 1930s saw a response to the vast social problems caused and revealed by the depression. The federal government created programs and agencies concerned with redistribution to the less fortunate. Thus, over the years, agencies were formed that are now housed in the Departments of Health and Human Services, Education, Housing and Urban Development, Labor, and Justice. Independent agencies were also formed. They included the Office of Economic Opportunity (now defunct), the Commission on Civil Rights (the scene of a major political struggle between the Reagan administration and civil rights groups in 1983 and 1984), and the Equal Employment Opportunity Commission (also subject to a major change in philosophy under the Reagan administration).

Throughout the 1800s Congress watched over agencies with great care, and so they did not develop much independent political weight. But, as agencies grew in size and number, they began to develop that power. At the same time,

Congress gave them more power and paid less attention to their use of it. The foundations were laid for "the bureaucratic state" (Wilson, 1975). When government increased its scope in the 1930s, Congress increased the leeway it gave bureaucracy. Power was delegated in a vague way, and this increased the basis for almost independent bureaucratic influence (Lowi, 1979).

ADMINISTRA-TION AND POLITICS: AN INSEPARABLE PAIR

Administrators and their agencies are political actors. They are heavily involved in politics because they can bargain about program goals and how to give out power and funds. Forming and carrying out policy both fall in large part within the province of the bureaucracy. Both are highly political processes. Bureaucracies do not passively administer the laws entrusted to them. They also help shape those laws, and they have leeway in what they do with the laws. Policy matters decided by Congress and the president, and administrative matters decided by bureaucrats involve the same political choices and issues (Meier, 1979). The bureaucracy is far more involved in politics in our country than in the countries of Western Europe (Rourke, 1976; Aberbach, Putnam, and Rockman, 1981). In Europe, the bureaucracy was important long before political systems became democratic. Here, democracy came before large bureaucracy formed. Thus, it was natural for our bureaucracies to proceed as political actors.

Our top civil servants—and the agencies they shape—compete directly with other people and agencies for scarce resources (Neustadt, 1973). So the only way civil servants can have the impact they want is by developing the political skills to compete successfully for those resources.

Bureaucracies have many constituents. They include individuals, interest groups, Congress as a whole and in parts (subcommittees), and parts of the executive branch (such as the president, the White House, and the Office of Management and Budget). In a general sense, constituencies for bureaucracies are all those who see themselves as affected—in any way—by the policies and acts of bureaus. The bureaucrat wants to build supportive constituencies. Activists in these constituencies want to create bureaucracies that favor their interests.

Relations with clients

Clients are people who deal with bureaucracy and benefit from its activities. Organized groups that may benefit can also be thought of as clients.

Clients as individuals Americans are apt to be skeptical about government bureaucracy. They rate the actions of private business much higher. A 1977 Gallup poll found that two thirds of us think federal employees do not work as hard as those outside government. But people are much more positive about their own experiences with bureaucracy (Katz et al., 1975). They are pleased with the treatment they get from agencies that provide services, such as those giving help in finding a job, job training, workers' compensation, unemployment compensation, public assistance, hospital and medical care, and retirement benefits. They are less pleased with the treatment they get from agencies that regulate them or limit their behavior, including agencies dealing with taxes and police matters.

Attention to clients. A volunteer attorney in a federal program consults her client, a restaurant owner.

TABLE 11–3

Opinion of Fairness and Efficiency of Government Agencies

	Percent rating fairness positively	Percent rating efficiency positively
Own experience with service agency	80	72
Own experience with constraint agency	51	41
Government agencies in general	42	29

Source: Based on Daniel Katz, Barbara A. Gutek, Robert L. Kahn, and Eugenia Barton, *Bureaucratic Encounters* (Ann Arbor: Institute for Social Research, University of Michigan, 1975), pp. 120–24.

People are prone to feel that service agencies give equal treatment to all clients. But they think regulatory agencies are more apt to treat the wealthy and those with influence better.

People rate their own contact with service agencies very positively; their contacts with regulatory or constraint agencies are less positive. And government agencies in general are rated lowest. Table 11–3 shows public opinion of the fairness and efficiency of bureaucracies.

People use government services less than they could. About one third of those who could be helped by certain services do not search them out. The main reason is that people do not know about the programs.

Clients as groups   Client groups and bureaus try to reach an accord so they can live more easily with each other. In some ways the ideal relationship for both bureaucrats and those groups in society with whom they interact is one of mutual support based on common interests. It may be, of course, that the general public does not view such mutual support as desirable. Hostility figures into some relationships. The public may be well served by some distance between bureaus and their client groups.

A number of factors foster cooperation and policy accord between an agency and client groups. First, an agency and its clients may exchange personnel. In that case, policy agreement will likely be high simply because the same people alternate in important positions inside and outside of government. Such exchange is common. In the late 1970s, a Common Cause report showed that about half of those appointed to regulatory commissions came from regulated companies or the law firms that work for such companies. On leaving office, about half went to work for these companies or law firms. The report also showed a high rate of personnel exchange between federal energy, nuclear power, defense, and food and drug regulation agencies and private companies in those sectors.

"THE NOVEL THING ABOUT TURNING OVER THE WEATHER SERVICE IS THAT IT WOULD BE DONE OFFICIALLY"

Second, an agency can help create external groups to support it. This usually results in long-run basic policy agreements. Sometimes it is hard to tell which body is more important—the agency or the spin-off group. For instance, the Department of Agriculture fostered the American Farm Bureau Federation. The Department of Labor aided growth of labor unions, which often have special access to parts of the department. The Department of Labor also helped finance an interest group—the Interstate Conference of Employment Security Agencies. This group lobbied the department to create policies, opposed by some top department officials, for state employment agencies. The officials were almost helpless when they faced the united opposition of the bureaucrats in their own department and the group whose staff they funded.

Third, most agencies create and use advisory committees that draw impor-

Listening to the interested public. Representatives of the Army Corps of Engineers hold a hearing on a proposal to fill in some of Lake Michigan.

tant members from client groups. These committees help to make sure that agency policy does not vary from what the clients want (Brown, 1972).

Fourth, programs and agencies that subsidize rather than regulate are much more apt to agree with their clients. Both want the greatest flow of benefits. This provides jobs and influence for the agencies and benefits for their clients. The Army Corps of Engineers has close relationships with groups that benefit from its water projects (Drew, 1970). Members of Congress would like to bolster this relationship. In early 1977, when President Carter tried to cut out or postpone some water projects, he quickly learned that the agency was stronger than he was.

Fifth, groups that have positive access to Congress—mainly to subcommittees—have an extra lever to use with agencies.

Relations with Congress

Congress and the bureaucracy interact all the time. Both have ideas that require legislation to be implemented. They have to react to each other to work out the details. The ideas that become law need a bureaucracy to implement them. Congress oversees some parts of this process.

The normal relationship: mutual support   Bureaucrats need to build support in Congress, mostly with the subcommittees responsible for their bureaus. This does not mean that the bureaucrats will not do their job. But it may mean that many decisions are shaped at least in part by their desire to please their congressional allies. Statements by bureaucrats such as the following (Fenno, 1966: 308–9) show the strength of that desire:

> Sometimes you wonder just who you are working for. . . . Sometimes I'll go over to the committee and talk about something with them. The first time I went, they told me it was confidential. And I said, "When I came through that door, I started working for the committee. Whatever goes on in here just didn't happen as far as I'm concerned when I leave here." And I tell them that everytime. Sometimes, I'm over here and the secretary or someone will try to worm it out of me what's going on. But they know I won't tell them. . . . I've gone out and tried to develop contacts with congressmen, because that's the way the game is played. . . . Some people higher up in the department object to our having any informal contacts with congressmen, but we'll just have to get around that, I guess.

The instincts of subcommittee members regarding bureaus in their realm run in two directions at once. First, they seek to develop mutual support that might enhance the gains of members and constituents. Second, they seek to keep up congressional prerogatives and a "congressional presence" so that the bureau, other members of Congress, and constituents know they are "doing their job."

Many circumstances require interaction: budgeting; agency organization and reorganization; the forming, changing, and ending of agencies; personnel matters; evaluation of program performance; and decisions about where projects should be. On all of these decisions the members of Congress (usually in a subcommittee) and the bureau (represented by a few top officials) have a stake in reaching agreements that benefit both.

Budget decisions are most vital from the agency point of view. Agencies need good relations both with subcommittees that provide funds and with outside support groups to ensure budgetary success (Fenno, 1966). Agency budget growth is a function of external support. An agency with strong support from outside interest groups gets large increases in its budget. The rapport the agency builds with the subcommittee is critical in determining how much of any year's request the committee will get. Agencies in good standing with their subcommittee will get most of their requests. Those on shakier ground will risk heavier cuts in their requests.

In pursuing their relationship, members of Congress and bureaucrats use many specific techniques (Ripley and Franklin, 1984). The techniques are used by both sides in attempts to maintain institutional prerogatives, keep policy and program preferences, and maximize personal standing. Each party has strong incentives to reach agreements that help both.

A budget hearing. Secretary of Defense Caspar Weinberger testifies on the 1985 defense budget before a congressional committee.

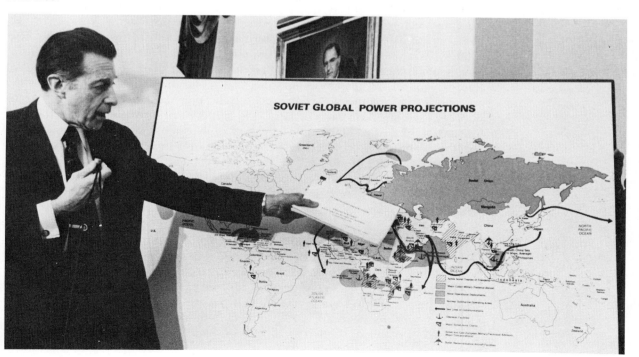

SOVIET GLOBAL POWER PROJECTIONS

The unusual relationship: continued hostility An agency can get crossways with the wishes of Congress. A good example of what can happen in such a situation is provided by the Federal Trade Commission (FTC). Before 1977, the FTC kept a low profile in choosing cases to prosecute. (Katzmann, 1980). But in 1977 a new and aggressive chairman was appointed. The FTC's new line seemed more proconsumer and antibusiness (especially big business). As a result, business people helped get Congress to restrain the FTC.

Congress began to signal the FTC to slow down. The peak of the congressional attack came in the spring of 1980. For four years the agency had not had its authorizing legislation renewed, and so it could not get regular funding through appropriations. Congress passed a new authorization law in the spring of 1980 giving the legislature a formal role in overseeing the agency. Most important, Congress could veto any FTC rules that did not need presidential agreement. The restrictions would have been even more severe but President Carter intervened and got some anti-FTC forces in Congress to back down. In the turmoil, the FTC actually closed down for lack of money for three days in May and June 1980. This was another symbolic reprimand from Congress.

Problems continued into the Reagan years. In 1982, Congress by legislative veto disapproved an FTC rule which had been 10 years in the making; it required used-car dealers to disclose defects in the vehicles they sold. The Supreme Court declared the legislative veto unconstitutional. Congress immediately began seeking alternatives for keeping a tight rein on the FTC. The saga of hostility seems likely to continue.

Congressional oversight of bureaucracy Bureaucrats are given great latitude in administering programs that affect the lives of many citizens. Congress retains an interest in seeing how the bureaucracy carries out its responsibilities under the law. **Oversight** is the term applied to multiple activities by Congress designed to yield information about bureaucratic behavior. Such information is supposed to lead to congressional decisions about how to make programs better and bureaus more efficient and responsive.

Congress has often affirmed its formal commitment to oversight. The Legislative Reorganization Act of 1946 enjoined all committees to exercise "continuous watchfulness" over administrative units within their jurisdiction. The 1970 Reorganization Act was more specific: "Each standing committee shall review and study, on a continuing basis, the application, administration, and execution of those laws, or parts of laws, the subject matter of which is within the jurisdiction of that committee." The power of oversight was underscored in 1974 by House committee reforms and the Budget and Impoundment Control Act. Senate committee reforms in 1977 added the concept of "comprehensive policy oversight." This gave committees a mandate to look at broad questions even if they extended into other committees' jurisdictions. Congressional committees wield strong weapons, statutory and informal, in carrying out oversight mandates.

Many different congressional activities can be designated as oversight. These include legislative vetoes and other statutory requirements, congressional investigations, and congressional power over executive-branch appointments.

Legislative vetoes Beginning in the Hoover administration, Congress started writing provisions in laws giving them a chance to veto administrative action. (These provisions have appeared in 15 different forms.) Congress could stop proposed bureaucratic action by a vote of some kind (sometimes by only one house or even one committee), without presidential approval. In close to 300 provisions in almost 200 laws the power was invoked. In mid-1983 the Supreme Court apparently declared all of these provisions unconstitutional as a violation of the separation of powers. As with many Supreme Court decisions, however, the exact meaning of the ruling is not totally clear. At this point, we should simply note that one formal tool found useful in overseeing has been removed from the congressional arsenal.

Other statutory requirements   If Congress objects to an administrative action it can, in effect, overturn or prevent carrying out of the action. Congress may do this in one of several ways: (1) through a single-purpose provision that overturns a specific rule; (2) by changing program authority to remove an agency's jurisdiction over the matter in question; (3) by placing limits on the agency through authorization or appropriation measures; (4) by requiring interagency consultation; and (5) by requiring congressional notification before an action is taken (Kaiser, 1980).

Congress stays alert to trends by requiring departments and agencies, and even the president, to submit information or reports on many matters. The Constitution, of course, authorizes the president to report periodically on the state of the union. Other presidential reports are mandated by law. For example, a yearly economic report is required under the 1946 Employment Act.

Department and agency heads traditionally file annual reports. These are now supplemented by special reports. Many laws require administrators to look at a specific problem and report back to Congress, usually within a set period. Recommendations, too, are often mandated.

Congressional investigations   Congress has the power to gather information that will help it discharge its duties. "A legislative body," wrote Telford Taylor (1955: 21–22) during the stormy McCarthy era, "is endowed with the investigative power *in order to obtain information,* so that its legislative functions may be discharged on an enlightened rather than a benighted basis."

Executive activities are examined during Capitol Hill appearances by department or agency heads. Hardly a day passes when key administration officials do not appear before House and Senate committees. The question-and-answer format used lets legislators follow up inquiries and is a flexible type of oversight.

Climactic hearings. Senator Joseph McCarthy (R–Wis.) lectures about communist conspirators during the 1954 Army-McCarthy hearings. McCarthy's adversary, Joseph Welch, the Army's special counsel, looks skeptical.

World War II investigation. Senator Harry Truman of Missouri chairs a special committee to oversee defense spending in 1943.

The first congressional inquiry was in 1792. It concerned General St. Clair's disastrous expedition against the Wabash Indians. During the Civil War, Lincoln's actions were scrutinized by the Joint Committee on the Conduct of the War. After Lincoln's death, another joint committee led Congress's takeover of reconstruction plans. In World War II, the Senate's Special Committee to Investigate the National Defense Program was chaired by a little-known Missouri senator named Harry Truman. It served as a model for legislative oversight. The committee provided responsible watchfulness; it aired charges of graft and corruption, and it saved the government billions of dollars. In 1954, there were the dramatic Army-McCarthy hearings. They were ostensibly convened to probe Senator Joseph McCarthy's (R-Wis.) farfetched charge that the U.S. Army was "soft on communism." The basis was that the Army had promoted a New Jersey dentist who allegedly refused to answer questions about "Red" connections. The televised hearings helped to expose McCarthy's shallowness and cut short his stormy career.

Congress is a political body, a fact reflected in its inquiries. Members of Congress are quick to seize the benefits from inquiries about executive wrongdoing or inefficiency: public acclaim for uncovering scandals, partisan advantage for exposing malfeasance by the opposition party, political advantages for voicing the unhappiness of interest groups over how certain programs are run, even the personal self-advertisement from being in the spotlight. Congressional investigations are political as well as informational tools.

Another trait of congressional investigations is that they tend to focus on *specific* charges or events. They rarely look at questions of philosophy or grand design. Critics sometimes complain that Congress should be like a corporate board of directors. It ought to restrict itself to broad policy questions. Detailed questions of program operation should be left to administrators.

Yet legislators rarely adhere to administrative theory. Again, the explanation is political: specific instances of wrongdoing or inefficiency are likely to attract the media; broader questions are not. Criticizing an administrator whose limousine and chauffeur cost the taxpayers a few thousand dollars a year is a sure headline getter; criticism of an ill-designed program costing billions may well be ignored.

Overseeing through publicity is exemplified by Senator William Proxmire's (D-Wis.) "Golden Fleece awards." Proxmire presents the award each month to an agency that he thinks has spent money carelessly. One month he castigated the Law Enforcement Assistance Administration (LEAA) for a study of why prisoners escape; another month he criticized the National Park Service for studying misbehavior on public tennis courts. The agencies' anguished explanations always receive less attention than Senator Proxmire's charges.

Congressional power over appointments Another oversight tool is Congress's influence in approving and removing executive-branch officers. The Senate has constitutional power to advise on and consent to many presidential appointments. Usually, the Senate approves appointees. Though few are rejected, others are simply left unconfirmed. Some are eventually withdrawn by the president, who then submits new names. A nomination that faces defeat is normally withdrawn to spare the nominee and the president embarrassment.

There is more involved in screening appointees than just checking qualifications. The Senate has a political stake in confirming executive nominees (Moe, 1975). Confirmation is an adjunct to legislative oversight of executive agencies.

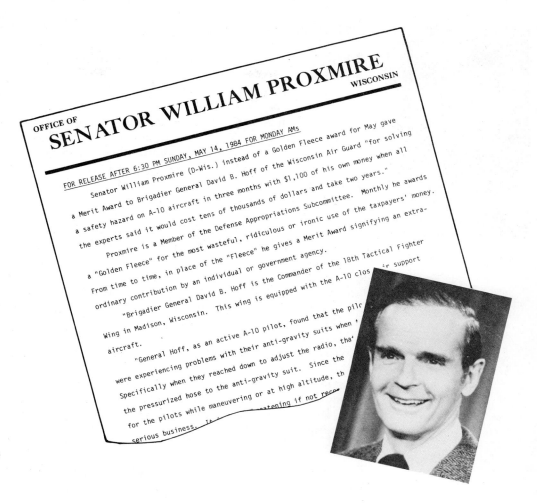

OFFICE OF

SENATOR WILLIAM PROXMIRE
WISCONSIN

FOR RELEASE AFTER 6:30 PM SUNDAY, MAY 14, 1984 FOR MONDAY AMs

Senator William Proxmire (D-Wis.) instead of a Golden Fleece award for May gave a Merit Award to Brigadier General David B. Hoff of the Wisconsin Air Guard "for solving a safety hazard on A-10 aircraft in three months with $1,100 of his own money when all the experts said it would cost tens of thousands of dollars and take two years."

Proxmire is a Member of the Defense Appropriations Subcommittee. Monthly he awards a "Golden Fleece" for the most wasteful, ridiculous or ironic use of the taxpayers' money. From time to time, in place of the "Fleece" he gives a Merit Award signifying an extraordinary contribution by an individual or government agency.

"Brigadier General David B. Hoff is the Commander of the 18th Tactical Fighter Wing in Madison, Wisconsin. This wing is equipped with the A-10 clos___ ir support aircraft.

"General Hoff, as an active A-10 pilot, found that the pil__ were experiencing problems with their anti-gravity suits when ___ Specifically when they reached down to adjust the radio, tha' the pressurized hose to the anti-gravity suit. Since the for the pilots while maneuvering or at high altitude, th serious business. I___ ___tening if not reco___

Senator Proxmire and the bureaucracy. In a monthly press release the senator usually lambasts an agency with a Golden Fleece award. Occasionally he gives a Merit Award to a frugal bureaucrat.

An official who has gone through the confirmation ordeal presumably becomes more sensitive to future legislative requests.

Senators also tend to take a proprietary interest in agencies and programs handled by their committees. They prefer administrators who are easy to deal with. They look for people mindful of the committee's prerogatives and sympathetic to the political support groups with which both the agency and the committee must bargain.

The extent of Senate aggressiveness depends on the office for which a nominee is considered. Normally, the Senate allows the president wide discretion in picking cabinet members; the theory is that he is entitled to his own advisers. Heads of independent agencies and commissions are scrutinized more closely. The theory here is that they serve not only the president, but Congress and the public, as well.

In extreme cases, Congress can remove officials by *impeachment*. The president, vice president, and all civil officers of the United States can be impeached for "treason, bribery, or other high crimes and misdemeanors." Under Article I of the Constitution, the House "shall have the sole power of impeachment"; the Senate "shall have the sole power to try all impeachments." If the House

Congress and executive appointments. Edwin Meese is sworn in before the Senate Judiciary Committee in 1984 for confirmation hearings on his nomination by President Reagan to be attorney general.

votes to impeach an official, it tries the case before the Senate; a two-thirds vote is needed to convict.

The potent weapon of impeachment has been used only 12 times in our history. Only two of these cases involved the executive branch; Presidents Andrew Johnson and Richard Nixon. The other cases involved judges.

How effective is oversight   The record of Congress in overseeing the executive branch is generally conceded to be spotty at best, abysmal at worst. Certainly, few congressional committees fulfill the 1946 Reorganization Act's injunction; they rarely exercise "continuous watchfulness" over federal agencies under their purview. A leading student of the subject (Ogul, 1976: 5) concludes, "There is a large gap between the oversight the law calls for and the oversight actually performed."

Most critics speak as if overseeing must be continuous and comprehensive. They speak as if the unblinking eye of Congress should watch all government activities at all times. But the government's vast size and scattered activities make such a goal impossible to achieve. The best we can hope for is frequent spot checks of executive activities. They should be conducted often and without warning so that fear of congressional review is always there.

Oversight does not often get the attention of legislators. Like most people, members of Congress tend to see legislating mainly as passing laws. They view the process as closed when the president signs a bill. Exposing defects in the legislation might yield some publicity. But it also carries the risk of making legislators unpopular with the bill's sponsors, administrators, and beneficiaries. Oversight is most likely when legislators are willing to incur these political risks. It may take place, for example, when they strongly oppose the bill that has been enacted, or when they support the bill but feel that administrators are thwarting its purposes.

Relations with the president and the office of management and budget

The president   The president, of course, only one person. The thought of one person controlling close to 3 million civilians and many military bureaucrats boggles the mind. In fact, presidents can only use their control selectively and sporadically. They do not intervene in most routine matters.

Even in important matters, a president may find that the bureaucracy is not following his policies. In 1962, our country and the Soviet Union were negotiating about Soviet missiles in Cuba. The Soviet Union alleged our missiles in Turkey were just as close to Soviet borders. President Kennedy said he had ordered removal of the U.S. missiles in Turkey some time before. But the military bureaucrats had not carried out his order, apparently because they disagreed with the president. This case is especially dramatic because the president is commander-in-chief and this was a military matter. Bureaucrats in less visible and sensitive areas have even more leeway to interpret presidential orders.

Presidents may make statements about the impact they are going to have on the whole bureaucracy. But they really have to pick a few policy areas they think are most important and try to make sure the bureaucracy follows their will in those areas. President Nixon felt the bureaucracy was sabotaging his policies, and had an elaborate plan for gaining more effective control. But the plan failed (Nathan, 1983). Nixon had a four-part strategy to achieve an "ad-

End of the Cuban missile crisis. The military ignored a presidential directive to remove U.S. missiles in Turkey and made the president's position more difficult as he tried to get the Soviet Union to remove its missiles from Cuba. They did: here a Soviet ship departs Cuba with missiles in November 1962.

ministrative presidency''; it would reduce his dependence on Congress and increase his control over the bureaucracy. Nixon tried to name his own trusted loyalists to positions. He tried to make significant use of budget impoundments and reductions. He tried to shuffle parts of the bureaucracy. And he gave careful attention to the writing of regulations by agencies as a way of gaining policy control.

President Reagan made a more focused assault on the bureaucracy than had his predecessors. He was determined to make at least some key agencies—such as those dealing with environmental matters, civil rights, consumer protection, and social programs—responsive to his policy preferences. He used all of his powers and those of his appointees to effect the changes he wanted. Those powers involved appointments, the latitude given the administration under the 1978 civil service law to assign senior civil servants, reductions in the number of employees, and internal reorganizations of individual agencies (Nathan, 1983; Newland, 1983).

Morale plummeted at many agencies. In April of 1982 the *Washington Post* printed the results of a survey of over 500 federal workers in six agencies. Only 25 percent of those surveyed rated morale in their agency as excellent or good. 74 percent rated it as not so good or poor. Seventy percent found their work somewhat less satisfying or much less satisfying than two years before. Fifty-five percent were very concerned or somewhat concerned that they would lose their job.

Controversy broke out over the policies and appointments in the agencies targeted for the most change. Names such as James Watt, Secretary of the Interior, or Anne Gorsuch Burford, head of the Environmental Protection Agency, became literal household words. In the end, Reagan was able to attain at least part of his goals.

The president has some personal leverage over the bureaucracy. His staff in the White House Office gives extra leverage. Much of his own impact comes

"LEAVE THE FACADES — IT'LL BE JUST LIKE HOLLYWOOD"

Controversial administrators. James Watt, as Secretary of the Interior, and Anne Gorsuch Burford, as head of the Environmental Protection Agency, were both aggressive in pushing Reagan administration policies. Both had strong supporters and opponents and both left government after a few years.

through appointments to major positions in the bureaucracy. But there are not many such positions. Just before Carter's election, a count made by the House Post Office and Civil Service Committee showed that in the whole bureaucracy, the president could make only 916 appointments. In another 792 positions at the policymaking level, incumbents (Schedule C appointments) did not have civil service protection. This meant a presidential appointee (a secretary, undersecretary, or assistant secretary of a department) could make personnel changes. There were also 969 jobs defined as in support of top policymakers. But these jobs included secretaries, chauffeurs, and administrative assistants. The president must rely on himself and his closest advisers in filling these positions. He must rely on the good judgment of some of those 916 in making changes in the 792 other positions to form a network of trusted leaders throughout the bureaucracy. This total of about 1,700 positions was the same when Ronald Reagan took office. (A "plum book" listing jobs open to presidential appointment came up with the same total.)

Through the Civil Service Reform Act of 1978, Reagan had an extra lever his predecessors lacked. That act created a new Senior Executive Service (SES) of about 8,500 of the highest civil servants in government. By joining it, people got a chance for higher pay and cash bonuses. But the president also got new authority to transfer these people. Reagan used this authority to promote his policies. The president previously had some impact on senior civil servants, especially political independents, (Cole and Caputo, 1979), but the SES increased the impact.

The direct appointments open to the president are a tiny number in a huge bureaucracy. Even that number shrinks further when one notes that 188 of those jobs are U.S. attorneys and marshals (basically the field staff of the Justice Department); 135 are in the foreign service (ambassadors); 69 are members of the U.S. delegation to the UN; and 63 are on boards and commissions of the State Department. The number remaining may be small compared to the total bureaucracy. But even so, the president cannot possibly appoint only people he knows and trusts. Thus, many appointments will be suggested by those he either trusts or owes some political debt. In fact, the president will never meet many appointees.

Presidents also have problems counting on their own appointees to carry out administration policies faithfully. These appointees often are, in many ways, "strangers" in Washington (Heclo, 1977). They are new to the city and do not stay very long. And they are, of necessity, put in situations where lack of experience and high turnover stand out. This is in contrast to the experience and low turnover of other people in key policy roles: career bureaucrats, congressional staff, and members of Congress (Ripley and Franklin, 1984).

In addition even direct presidential appointees have their own policy preferences. They often respond to the policy networks of those with whom they deal daily. Thus, they may strongly disagree with presidential wishes. Under Jimmy Carter, for instance, the HEW Secretary Joseph Califano developed a national health insurance plan (never enacted) which was quite different from the president's preference. Even some Reagan appointees began defending programs and agencies not supported by the president. Terrel Bell, Secretary of the Department of Education, although appointed to a supposedly doomed agency, became a reasonably effective supporter of its continued existence.

Congress often drafts statutes that logically require White House coordination of agency heads. But members of Congress often frown on such coordination if it is attempted.

The Office of Management and Budget   For the last four decades the greatest help presidents received in trying to affect the bureaucracy came from the Office of Management and Budget (OMB). This agency has been in the Executive Office of the President since 1939. Until 1970 it was called the Bureau of the Budget.

OMB performs four major functions in dealing with federal agencies. It clears the legislative proposals agencies want to make to Congress. It prepares budget requests for future years. It manages spending in the current year. And it oversees agency management. Also, OMB personnel work with agency personnel to gather and exchange information.

The two functions involving money have been a key OMB role no matter who has been president. Legislative clearance and management functions have had their ups and downs in terms of bureau influence. At the end of the Ford Administration the impact of OMB on these two areas had waned, while Carter again relied heavily on it in these areas (Berman, 1979). Reagan also relied heavily on OMB in all areas in which it is involved.

OMB as an institution has changed many times. During the Nixon-Ford years, it became more hierarchical and politicized. The norm of "neutral competence" declined (Heclo, 1975). This caused some loss of overall legislative planning ability in OMB. Also it made OMB more politically visible and vulnerable as it was more closely linked to specific political goals.

Carter also had a politically visible OMB. He both involved it in volatile issues and made more political appointments to its top positions. His first appointee to the directorship, Bert Lance, became controversial because of his former banking practices. Lance was forced to resign in mid-1977. Reagan also made a highly visible appointment as his first OMB director—a young Republican congressman named David Stockman, who brought an aggressive style to OMB. Stockman was both a powerful and controversial figure in the years following Reagan's inauguration.

OMB is a professional organization, but it also has room for much presidential input. Since the Bureau of the Budget was created in 1921, each president has used it differently in dealing with agencies, Congress, and the public. This is most true since it was transferred to the Executive Office in 1939.

The agencies responsible for individual programs and OMB often disagree. But there have also been instances of close and cooperative relations. When there are arguments and bad feelings, agencies may have enough political support to compromise with OMB or completely avoid a negative OMB decision. Agencies may, for instance, appeal to the White House. (That was less possible during the Nixon-Ford years than previously.) Or they may appeal to Congress for changes in laws. In general, the potential for OMB control of agencies diminished with the Budget and Impoundment Control Act in 1974. This act reduced the president's power to refuse to spend money assigned by Congress for specific purposes. It also made the director and the deputy director of OMB subject to Senate confirmation.

Some agencies develop close ties with OMB. In some cases it is charged that such closeness results in OMB laxness with regard to an agency. For example, in 1975 four of the six OMB officials (called "examiners") assigned to oversee the budgets and activities of the CIA, National Security Agency, and other in-

OMB. Director David Stockman is an important figure in the Reagan administration. Here he even gets jelly beans from the president.

telligence agencies had worked for the very agencies they were to oversee; length of service was between 3 and 20 years.

OMB officials are loyal to several sources of support: the president and the presidency in both a personal and an institutional sense; OMB as an agency; and the agencies overseen. Any OMB employee is apt to show some loyalty to all three sources of support, but the mix can differ for each person.

Relations between bureaucratic units

Temporary bureaucratic cooperation. The Federal Emergency Management Agency coordinates the efforts of many agencies after disasters such as floods or tornadoes. Here a family enters a Disaster Assistance Center, which can handle temporary housing, food stamps, loans, and counseling.

Bureaucratic units must work with each other from time to time. Their jurisdictions may overlap and their programs may reach the same clients. Thus, at some points their work should be coordinated. Members of different units may be put on interagency committees to promote cooperation. In general, the units are wary of each other and real cooperation is rare. Normally, the behavior of such units ranges between uneasy truce and open hostility. Each unit is mainly concerned with its own budget, personnel, programs, clients, aims, rules, space—in short, its own "turf." No coordination or forced cooperation works well.

The following instance of lack of cooperation between units is typical. In 1975, the State Department was working with Canada on a water diversion project in North Dakota that would affect a drainage basin extending into Canada. The Canadians opposed the project as a pollution threat in violation of a 1909 treaty between the two countries. State Department bargainers were told by the Interior Department, which would handle the project, that there were no alternatives that would lessen the pollution problem. Therefore, State had to bargain on the basis of a plan that was opposed by the Canadians.

In fact, the Interior Department did have alternatives that would have met some of the objections. But an assistant secretary of the Interior had written a memo ordering withholding them from the State Department, the Canadians, or "local interests" in North Dakota and Minnesota. This deliberate withholding of information made the task of one agency (State) harder and helped another agency (Interior) to build a project its own way.

The sources of bureaucratic power

Bureaucracies have two major sources of power: technical skill and political standing (Rourke, 1976; Meier, 1979). Agencies, especially federal agencies, usually have more experts than any other actors in the policy process. This expertise lets bureaucrats advise political officials on what policies to adopt. It also helps give great leeway to bureaucrats in starting up programs.

Also, government bureaus and their key employees can rally political support for their jurisdiction, policy, agency size, and budget claims. Someone who disagrees with the policies of an agency faces a tough job if that agency is well run and entrenched. Not only is the weight of knowledge likely to lie with the agency, the agency may also be in a strong political position. People and groups pushing an alternative view almost always have to rely on building counter coalitions. They seek support from people and groups in the legislative branch, the private sector, and other parts of the bureaucracy. They may look to the White House or dissidents in the agency itself. But the design of the federal bureaucracy works against overturning bureaucratic positions. Opponents do not have as much knowledge of the facts.

The situation is somewhat different with many state and local bureaucracies. A number are very weak in terms of staff size and expertise. They may be outclassed by other actors, especially large groups in the private sector. Often, for instance, a state body is charged with overseeing insurance or utility rates. But it depends almost exclusively on those companies for information and thus for its positions on rates. Such complete domination of a federal bureaucracy is rare.

AUTONOMY AND CONTROL

American bureaucracy can be described by two sets of conflicting adjectives. On the one hand, it often behaves as if it were *autonomous*. But it can also seem to be *controlled*; it is highly influenced by outside forces. It can also often be described as *conservative*. In that sense, it promotes only existing policies. Yet at other times, its policies can be quite *progressive*.

The autonomy of bureaucracy stems from its size and fragmented nature and from the civil service system. Size and fragmentation make the physical aspects of control—whether by the president, OMB, Congress, or the public—very difficult. The civil service system has grown since 1883. It protects most government employees from being fired for political reasons. It also gives them a regular career ladder.

But bureaucratic autonomy is not used to reach a single set of goals. Bureaucratic workers differ on what is right in any given instance. They can and do argue. These arguments, when added to those between units, create a lively ongoing debate over points of policy inside and outside the bureaucracy. This debate can be so lively as to lead to open rebellion, despite the formal rules of hierarchical decision making. During the Nixon years, for instance, staff members in both HEW and the Justice Department made effective protests against foot dragging on civil rights. There were protests against new policy directions in several agencies during the Reagan administration, but with little apparent effect.

Bureaucrats tend to be relatively liberal on policy matters. Disagreement with very conservative policies is most likely. However, there is no evidence that bureaucratic attitudes differ from predominant attitudes of the general population about basic institutional structures or the form of the national economy (Rothman and Lichter, 1983). And only some bureaucrats are most strongly interested in policy matters, others focus mostly on professional questions, still others simply on their own careers (Downs, 1967; Wilensky, 1967).

The bureaucracy also admits outside influence into its inner workings, partly because of movements of personnel. Some people from outside the career service enter policy-level jobs. Others who stay outside the career service may serve as influential part-time consultants. A few come and go as appointees. Clients and legislators and their staffs also work closely with bureaucracies.

Much of the time bureaucracy has a conservative impact on policy. Bureaucrats tend to set up routines that make supporting what exists easier than making strikingly new policies. Some of what exists, though, may not have a conservative effect. Congress may legislate innovative programs for the bureaucracy to run, and our bureaucracy itself sometimes creates programs that are seen as quite innovative and progressive (Rourke, 1976: 154):

Farmers in the last century and more recently trade unionists and the urban poor have looked to executive agencies for the redress of their grievances against more powerful segments of society, and the services of these organizations have provided the means by which the welfare and status of these disadvantaged groups have been greatly improved. In Europe . . . such groups more commonly have identified bureaucracy as part of the political system that must be overcome if public policy is to be changed in ways that are advantageous for them.

Is bureaucracy controlled, or does it just work its will with few checks? The least effective controls come from the public, which has little leverage. Some controls can be exercised by Congress, the president and the organs of the presidency, and the courts.

In some ways, Congress can best effect coordinated control. But, in fact, the political interests of members tend to prevent this (Fiorina, 1977 and 1979). When there is no effective control of this sort, members can increase their impact on single agencies and programs. Often this effort can help them with the electorate back in their states or districts.

Within the executive branch we noted limits on the president and the OMB in coordinating control. Some such control is possible by the top ranks of the bureaucracy. But people in these ranks may be ignored by the civil servants with whom they must work (Heclo, 1977).

In short, there are no reliable sources of coordinated and central control within the government itself. But each of them can have some effect.

The public has only blunt weapons to control bureaucracy. And it usually has little interest in doing so. Bureaucrats themselves are wary of citizen participation in policy matters. But they are not wholly against it. Middle-level bureaucrats are not completely reliable supporters of democratic norms and ideals. They are, however, more democratically inclined than is the general public (Wynia, 1974).

Inside an agency, the chief and top-level staff have many ways to gain control over the bureaucracy. But these can be overcome by the resistance of subordinates. In many cases, Congress has deliberately kept the top leadership of federal departments weak in terms of staff and authority, preserving a special, direct relationship with the smaller units of these departments.

Determined heads of agencies can push their organizations, but only with unrelenting work. The Department of the Interior is a good example of an agency that went in two very different directions under back-to-back secretaries. But neither of them was entirely able to get all he wanted. The first was Cecil Andrus, Secretary of the Interior during the Carter administration (1977–1981). He endorsed a variety of proconservation policies and got some movement from the department. But, near the end of his tenure as secretary, he made the limits of his power over his own bureaucracy clear (*Washington Post,* October 9, 1980; *New York Times,* November 18, 1980):

> When I was governor, I could implement a decision quickly. I could even implement a poor decision. . . . Here you can't even implement a good decision in timely fashion.
>
> It's like playing 100 games of chess, and you're one person playing against the other hundred, and you have to run around to make all your moves. It's competitive and fascinating, but tiring.
>
> There are so many competing interests on every issue. You end up compromising with Congress to get bills passed and compromising with your own bu-

Secretary of the Interior
Cecil D. Andrus and
some of his
department's clients.

reaucrats and those in the other government agencies to make them work. By the time you get a good idea implemented, it doesn't really resemble its parents.

His successor, Reagan's appointee James Watt, was secretary from 1981 until his resignation in late 1983. Watt pursued very different policies. He tried very hard to move the department to a prodevelopment stance. He soft-pedaled conservation and environmental concerns. Like Andrus, he had some success. One of his assistant secretaries testified that Watt also faced limits, however (Mosher, 1983: 1230): "Everyone assumes that Watt wakes up every morning, scratches his bald head and says, 'Let's go out and rape the coast of California today.' But it just doesn't happen that way. There are rules and laws we have to live with."

Even aggressive secretaries face problems. Laws are set up giving the details of programs; they cannot be changed, no matter what the secretary wants. Some of these laws also give final authority not to the secretary, but to a lower-ranking bureaucrat who may not even be a presidential appointee.

BUREAUCRACY AS A POLICY ACTOR

Bureaucratic survival

If we compared federal organizations created in 1923 with those that survived until 1973, we would find a very high survival rate (Kaufman, 1976). Great social changes took place during these 50 years, caused by the depression, World War II, and the social unrest of the 1960s. Yet 148 of the 175 federal agencies existing in 1923 had survived (about 85 percent). And 109 (about 62 percent) had barely changed their status. They were still in the same federal department; they were at about the same spot in the hierarchy. Twenty-seven agencies were abolished during the period. But their activities did not end—they were moved to other units.

Even agencies with small functions develop backers. Members of Congress and interest groups make them very hard to kill. The chairman of the American Battlefields Monuments Commission said, seemingly with a straight face, after Congress once again gave blessing to his funding, "You see, the people who criticize us don't really know us. And all we have to do to get them to understand is to give them the facts" (*Washington Post,* February 4, 1977).

Even units charged by presidents with cleaning up the bureaucracy have a hard time finding targets they think can be sunk. In mid-1979, for instance, OMB only came up with three after more than a year of looking: the Annual Assay Commission set up in 1792 and still performing functions which had been obsolete for more than 10 years; the U.S. Marine Corps Memorial Commission, which had not done anything for more than 20 years; and the Low Emission Vehicle Certification Board, which had done nothing for 3 years—there were no vehicles (presumably electric) to certify for government purchase.

But agencies do change. Their missions charge, their budgets change, and their personnel change. Some survive even after their original tasks are finished because they get involved in new ones. NASA had a severe funding and personnel decline after reaching its first goal—putting a man on the moon. But it succeeded in getting new tasks. Its current task—the space shuttle—is so costly that its fortunes in terms of budget and employees have revived strongly.

Changes in administration can also have some impact, although agencies are

An agency achieves its goals. *Left:* the safe landing of the first flight of the space shuttle in April 1981. *Right:* the successful climax of a decade of activity by the National Aeronautics and Space Administration as the first man walks on the moon in 1969.

skilled at fending off presidents. At a gross level, Ronald Reagan has been unsuccessful at eliminating the Department of Education, the Department of Energy, and the Economic Development Administration in the Department of Commerce. However, he has been successful in making sizable personnel cuts in agencies such as the departments of Education, Housing and Urban Development, and Labor, and in the Environmental Protection Agency.

Bureaucratic performance

How well does the federal bureaucracy perform? The question is simply put; the answer is hard because, in fact, the question is not at all simple.

One aspect of performance deals with honesty. Corruption—bribes, theft, and using official positions to make money—does occur. This happened on a large scale in the General Services Administration in the 1970s. But it is rare. There are more subtle forms of corruption, of course. An official may favor a private interest even though he or she does not stand to gain in a direct sense.

But the more important questions about performance are even harder to answer. There are at least three major sets of such questions (Fried, 1976). First, whose values and what values are pursued? Does an agency seek the goals of the people and groups to whom it is responsible? Is it responsive to those people and groups? Second, with what success are the values pursued? Is the agency effective in reaching its goals? Third, what procedures does the agency use in seeking its goals? Does it respect individual and group rights as it seeks its goals?

All of these questions bear on the vital issue of government legitimacy. Public attitudes toward any one agency or the whole bureaucracy are shaped by how these questions are answered. If most people think that most agencies are pursuing proper values fairly and with some success, then those agencies will be considered legitimate. On the other hand, there may be a widespread view that agencies are seriously deficient on one or more standards. Then the legitimacy of the agencies (and of government in general, since bureaucracy is such a large part of it) is in some danger.

An agency with legitimacy problems. The Occupational Safety and Health Administration (OSHA) got little support from anyone. An inspector is pictured here.

One example involves the Occupational Safety and Health Administration (OSHA), created in 1970. It had alienated almost everyone by 1980. Most viewed it, in effect, as an illegitimate agency. It put off employers with its many detailed regulations. It put off organized labor by not focusing on general aspects of occupational diseases and injuries. (Instead, it looked at single violations.) Therefore it had not reduced the rates of such diseases and injuries. Members of Congress were also displeased with the agency because of the large number of complaints they were getting and the work that those complaints caused. Early in the Carter term, the agency set out to change course and recoup its fortunes, but it did not succeed. Reagan has pledged to clip OSHA's wings.

There is, of course, no definitive answer to the question of how any one bureau performs, let alone how the whole bureaucracy is performing. The answer depends on the mix of values held by any one observer. But if an observer uses the broad standards suggested here, fair answers based on more than emotion can emerge.

CONCLUSIONS

Our main concern has been to introduce you to the complexities of bureaucracy in the United States, especially at the national level. Bureaucracy is at the heart of day-to-day government activities. It deserves serious attention from every student of government and, in fact, from every citizen. Our discussion leads us to a few general conclusions:

1 Bureaucracy is inevitable in a modern nation. But its size and organization are not ordained. They represent many choices: How many services will the federal government provide? What is the nature of the delivery system used to transfer these services to clients? And what is the relative political weight of client groups?

2 Federal agencies do not just carry out policies made by elected officials. They help shape the policies that they ultimately carry out. And in the implementation process, agencies have further leeway to give their own meanings to the policies.

3 The federal bureaucracy is vast. It is best understood if viewed as a collection of separate fiefdoms, not as an integrated whole. Each agency is involved in a different network of political contacts. Agency leaders try to cultivate support with a large number of these contacts.

4 Skillful bureaucrats can help their agencies toward their most important goals. But they must also take account of the goals of Congress, the president and his appointees, and client groups.

5 Bureaucratic agencies rarely die. Therefore, people and groups that need good performance from such agencies should try to push them in desired directions. They should not nurse the unrealistic hope that they can eliminate the agencies. This advice applies equally to presidents and average citizens.

FURTHER READING

FRIED, ROBERT C. (1976) Performance in American Bureaucracy. Boston: Little, Brown. A thoughtful examination of how well the U.S. bureaucracy does its job.

HECLO, HUGH (1977) A Government of Strangers. Washington, D.C.: Brookings Institution. An examination of the relationships between political appointees and career bureaucrats.

KAUFMAN, HERBERT (1981) The Administrative Behavior of Federal Bureau Chiefs. Washington, D.C.: Brookings Institution. A close analysis of what these key bureaucrats can and cannot do.

MEIER, KENNETH J. (1979) Politics and the Bureaucracy: Policymaking in the Fourth Branch of Government. North Scituate, Mass.: Duxbury. A short, basic text that analyzes U.S. bureaucratic behavior.

SEIDMAN, HAROLD (1980) Politics, Position, and Power: The Dynamics of Federal Organization. 3d ed. New York: Oxford University Press. A discussion by a long-time "insider" of what is at stake when questions of government organization are decided.

12
The Courts

By the end of the term, Stevens was accustomed to watching his colleagues make programmatic rather than principled decisions—shading the facts, twisting the law, warping logic to reconcile the unreconcilable. Though it was not at all what he had anticipated, it was the reality.

Description by Woodward and Armstrong of the reaction of
Justice John Paul Stevens to his first year on the U.S. Supreme Court in
The Brethren *(1979: 442), a book on Supreme Court decision making based*
largely on interviews with the justices' law clerks.

It has taken this long-ago Supreme Court law clerk a good while to reach this point, but it seems to me . . . that Bob Woodward and Scott Armstrong rendered a very real public service in *The Brethren* by detailing an unmistakable picture of the Supreme Court as a political rather than a legal institution. . . . Precisely because the important issues that come before the court are broad matters of public morality and political statesmanship rather than narrow questions of law, it was inevitable that the justices and their law clerks would turn out as activists fighting for their own views on public questions, just as do their legislative counterparts.

Joseph L. Rauh, Jr., Supreme Court law clerk in the 1930s, in the
Washington Post, *March 5, 1980.*

The Brethren . . . proposes a . . . thesis: The Supreme Court operates not only by principled persuasion but also by negotiation, even bargaining. That statement is undoubtedly true now, as it was in the beginning and perhaps ever shall be. Justice William Johnson explained it to Thomas Jefferson, and in his judicial opinions wrote about negotiations with the 19th-century Marshall court.

Walter F. Murphy, political science professor, Princeton University, in a
review of The Brethren *in the* Washington Post, *December 16, 1979.*

* * * * *

Surely these people—two journalists, a Supreme Court justice (if the journalists' description of him is accurate), a former clerk to two justices, and a political science professor who has studied the Supreme Court for years—cannot be talking about the U.S. Supreme Court. Is that Court not composed of nine old men in modified choir robes who behave gravely, intellectually, and in accord with the logic of the law? Do not U.S. courts, especially the Supreme Court, simply make "just" decisions? Do they not avoid political disputes that occupy lesser people such as presidents, members of Congress, and bureaucrats?

The U.S. Supreme Court in 1984. *Seated, from left:* Thurgood Marshall, William J. Brennan, Jr., Warren E. Burger, Byron R. White, and Harry A. Blackmun. *Standing, from left:* John Paul Stevens, Lewis F. Powell, Jr., William H. Rehnquist, and Sandra Day O'Connor.

In fact, the people quoted are right on target: our courts are part of the government. They are also political. They make decisions about matters that are vital to people, groups, social classes, and other parts of the government. Like legislatures, executives, and bureaucracies, courts make policy. "Justice" is not a mystery. Neither is it the sole province of courts. There are degrees of justice in the acts of all parts of government, including courts. And the policies made by courts, like those made by other organs of government, result from complex interactions among a number of individuals who often have different views of what makes good public policy. Though there are some unique aspects to court functions and processes, courts are deeply involved in politics as they help shape and carry out public policy.

In this chapter we will first look at the general nature of courts and the law. Then we will examine the relation of courts and the law to justice and public policy. This will suggest the ways in which courts differ from and are similar to other governing institutions. Second, we will give an overview of the whole U.S. court system. Third, we will discuss the work of the federal courts, stressing the importance of the Supreme Court. But we will also show that much work gets done in other federal courts. Fourth, we will focus on a number of political aspects of the federal courts. Fifth, we will probe some aspects of the policy impact of courts. (We reserve a major set of policy areas in which the courts have a major impact—liberties and rights—for separate treatment in Chapter 13.) Sixth, we will explore the question of how active courts should be. Finally, we will offer a short assessment of the federal courts as institutions that influence American public policy.

COURTS, LAW, AND PUBLIC POLICY

A court employee. Although less visible and important than Supreme Court Justices, this court stenographer, who produces accurate transcripts of proceedings, is also essential to keeping judicial machinery working.

Many people work in the judicial branch at all levels, including judges, clerks, and secretaries. Others work in government jobs that deal with courts: prosecutors, such as district attorneys at the local level and U.S. attorneys at the federal level; legal staffs that help government units make decisions about legal actions, such as city attorneys or the legal staffs of various parts of the Justice Department, the Department of Education, the Patent and Trademark Office, and almost every bureaucratic agency at the federal level; corrections officials, such as wardens and guards; and police, such as local and state police and the Federal Bureau of Investigation. In addition, most of the more than 500,000 lawyers in the country deal with courts at least part of the time. Lawyers are "officers" of courts. These people and bodies work at tasks that collectively spell out the reality of law enforcement and define part of what *justice* means in practice.

The nature of law and judicial policies

In many ways, all law is public policy. Both *public law* (cases involving a government) and *private law* (cases not involving a government) have great bearing on the public. Laws affecting property (which have emerged through a long history of private suits) define much public policy in the area of property. Law, in whatever form, is a central means for allocating values. When these values—the tangible and symbolic rewards people strive for—are allocated, public policy is formed. At the same time, there is competition for these allocations. This competition places law, and the interpreting and making of law by courts, firmly in the middle of politics.

Courts interpret law constantly, adding new dimensions and details. Courts, in effect, make law through their powers of interpretation. In our nation, they have varied in their attitude toward how much change in existing law they should make through interpretation. They have never been completely passive. Often they have been very aggressive. Even in passive times, judges consciously made public policy by what they did not do and say and by restricting broad principles that had been pushed in more aggressive times.

When judicial and nonjudicial policies are compared, one can see that the subject matter—what is at stake—is broadly the same. Courts, legislatures, executives, and bureaucracies are concerned with distributing the benefits and protections of government. They all are concerned with regulating private activity and with adjusting social conflict. But there are important differences between judicial and nonjudicial policies (Jacob, 1984). The first and most obvious lies in who is responsible for making decisions. For judicial policies, these people are judges and special groups of lawyers. For nonjudicial policies, the most important decision makers are in Congress, the executive branch, the bureaucracy, and the private sector.

The range of issues addressed by nonjudicial policies is almost unlimited. Courts rarely address some issues, especially broad economic policy and foreign relations. Many judicial policies are not very visible except to those directly involved and to the legal community. Nonjudicial policies are likely to be visible to more people more quickly because they are more likely to affect large numbers of people immediately. A smaller number of people are thus affected by most judicial policies. Those who decide nonjudicial policies usually direct these policies at all or much of society. Judges restrict their policies (decisions) to persons directly involved in a specific case. These policies, though, may indirectly touch larger segments of the population. Much of the time, judicial decisions involve judges telling government agencies what they can and cannot do. These decisions affect broader segments of society indirectly, though often very importantly.

Courts and conflict resolution

Courts hear and decide disputes between a variety of parties on many issues. A large number of public and private bodies other than courts also use both formal and informal processes to help resolve disputes (Sarat and Grossman, 1975). Administrative agencies conduct hearings to resolve disputes; police intervene in family quarrels; civil rights commissions hold hearings; college disciplinary boards decide on student behavior; arbitrators help settle labor-management disputes; insurance companies negotiate claims; and marriage counselors

Conflict resolution. This scene from a TV show, "People's Court," is a familiar one in real life, too.

try to help couples work out problems. But courts are the major public institutions using formal processes to help resolve conflict. Thus, they are the most visible and, in some ways, the most important.

American courts, like all courts, help resolve some of society's disputes. But court procedures can vary. The range of disputes over which they have jurisdiction, the number of people affected by their decisions, and their impact on our basic constitutional structure can vary. In general, U.S. courts have a much more important part in the government than the courts in other industrialized nations. The scope of U.S. courts' jurisdiction and areas of action is limited. Yet it is much less limited than that of courts in other nations. Many people are affected by U.S. court decisions because of the widespread use of case precedent by many courts and by legislatures and executive branches at all levels. In some instances, there is a short lag between a judicial decision in a case and widespread social application of the principles of that case. But in other instances, there may be little effect or it may take a long time to be felt. And our courts, especially the Supreme Court, have long been assumed to be constitutional courts. That is, they are courts that have the power to affect the basic structure of the nation's government at all territorial levels. They can affect how that apparatus conducts itself, including its treatment of individual rights.

Some claim that the U.S courts are so important because our nation tries to assure individual rights and because of the nation's federal structure. Countries such as Great Britain also have democratic political systems with a broad range of protected rights for individuals. Yet their court systems are not nearly as important. Other countries, such as Canada or Switzerland, have federal structures that involve complex questions about distributing powers among territorial levels. They also place a high value on individual rights. Yet their court systems are not as important as ours (Goldman and Jahnige, 1976).

Two features of U.S. courts set them apart from other bodies that resolve conflict. First, U.S. courts deal only with cases in which two parties have a difference of opinion. There must be a concrete question involving an injury that one party is alleged to have committed against the other. The parties may be people, classes of people, groups, corporations, or governments. The alleged injury may involve a crime or a civil matter, such as property or domestic relations. Either party may bring the grievance (suit) against the other party according to established procedures, laws, and jurisdictions of specific courts. The focus of the court is on the actual conflict or disagreement in the specific case or suit.

Second, U.S. courts mostly hear cases in which an injury is already alleged to have occurred. U.S. courts will intervene in some cases to prevent future or continuing injury by issuing injunctions and restraining orders. But they will not consider cases in which two friendly parties create a legal controversy to get a court ruling on some matter of mutual concern. Except for a few state courts in limited classes of cases, U.S. courts will not issue advisory opinions requested by public officials on the constitutionality of statues.

In recent years, Americans have increasingly brought matters to court. We are characterized as a "litigious society," one in which individuals are very quick to file lawsuits. Why is this so? Several factors are involved. First, laws have become more complicated in recent years and have created more opportunities for lawsuits. Second, Americans tend to think in terms of "rights" and the logical place to get enforcement of these rights is in courts. Third, Americans have

a special reverence for courts in general and look at them as a natural location for pursuing their personal, corporate, and class interests. Fourth, we are a society in which lawyers are numerous, increasing in number, and underworked. They have incentives to seek clients and get those clients to bring suit. We have well over half a million lawyers in the United States. By comparison, Japan has 20 times fewer, even when the relative size of the two populations is taken into account.

AN OVERVIEW OF THE AMERICAN COURT SYSTEM

The United States has a large and complex court system. The federal courts are only a part of that system; and the Supreme Court is only a part of the federal courts. The 50 state court systems differ, but all systems have a variety of **trial courts** and one or more levels of **appellate courts,** where the losers in the trial courts can try again.

The federal court structure is portrayed in Figure 12–1. It has a three-level central structure (the Supreme Court, courts of appeals, district courts) and a number of special courts, the most important of which are shown.

Some special courts deal with geographic areas: the District of Columbia and the few U.S. territories as Guam and the Virgin Islands. These courts function in much the same way as state courts. Other special courts have functions and jurisdictions related to specific subject matter.

The central court structure at the federal level contains one Supreme Court, 12 courts of appeal, and 90 district courts in the 50 states and the District of Columbia. The Supreme Court is in Washington. Courts in the two lower levels are spread throughout the country and have fixed geographic jurisdictions. The Supreme Court has nine justices. The 12 Courts of Appeal have 144 permanent judgeships. Each circuit has between 4 and 23 judges, depending on the workload.

Every state has at least one district court, and the most populous states have up to four. Each district court has between 1 and 27 judgeships, depending on the workload, with a total of 500 district judgeships in the 50 states and the District of Columbia. Some senior judges—those over retirement age—carry partial workloads to help keep the business of the courts moving. One Supreme Court justice is assigned to supervise certain activities in each of the 12 circuits of the system.

The federal courts face a large and growing workload. The Supreme Court *docket* (list of cases awaiting attention) grew fourfold from the late 1930s until

---

TRIAL AND APPELLATE COURTS

Trial courts are courts in which cases are first heard. The trial of the issues between two parties may take place before a judge and a jury or before a judge alone.

Appellate courts are courts in which appeals from the losing party in a trial court are heard.

In the federal court system, district courts are the primary trial courts. Courts of appeals are strictly appellate courts. Except in cases involving states or foreign diplomats—both quite rare—the U.S. Supreme Court is an appellate court.

In states, there are two types of trial court: general jurisdiction, which hear all kinds of cases (district or circuit courts) and limited jurisdiction, usually county or municipal courts. Most states have two levels of appellate courts, including a state supreme court.

FIGURE 12–1

Major Federal Courts

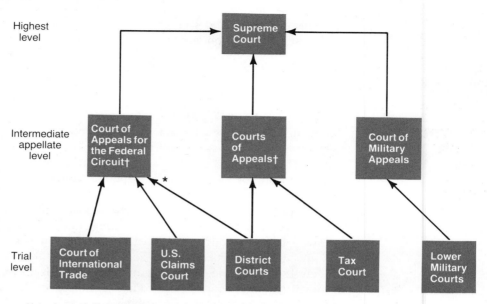

Note: Arrows indicate most common routes for appeals.
*For patent cases and some civil cases in which the U.S. government is a defendant.
†Also hear appeals concerning administrative agency decisions.
Source: Adapted from Lawrence Baum, *The Supreme Court* (Washington, D.C.: Congressional Quarterly Press, 1981), p. 10.

the 1970s. It remained about stable during the 1970s and then began to grow again, more slowly, in the 1980s. In the 1981 term (1981–82 in calendar terms) a total of 5,311 cases were on the docket. The court granted review to just over 4 percent of the cases in which review was sought. Virtually all of the rest were denied, dismissed, or withdrawn. A few were summarily decided, and some received no action.

In that same term, the Court heard oral argument on 184 cases. The justices decided 170 cases with signed opinions that stated the reasoning behind the decisions and also allowed for written concurring opinions and written dissents with reasons. They decided another 10 cases without providing signed opinions. The Supreme Court has almost total discretion over what cases it accepts. This authority, granted in 1925, allows the Court to keep its case load manageable.

District courts and courts of appeal must hear all cases brought to them that are properly within their jurisdictions. Their workload has increased dramatically. Between 1960 and 1982, the number of cases in courts of appeal went from fewer than 4,000 a year to almost 28,000. In that period the number of civil cases filed in district courts grew from fewer than 60,000 a year to over 200,000. The criminal case workload of the district courts grew from 27,000 in 1960 to over 41,000 by 1975, but had shrunk to under 33,000 by 1982.

Much of the increase in civil cases comes from congressional acts in the social welfare and civil rights fields that create what are called "federal questions" (Ball, 1980). Legislation such as the Civil Rights Acts of 1960 and 1964, the Freedom of Information Act of 1966, the Federal Coal Mine Health and Safety

Act of 1969, the Occupational Safety and Health Act of 1970, the National Environmental Policy Act of 1970, the Truth-in-Lending Act of 1970, the Equal Employment Opportunity Act of 1972, and the Consumer Products Safety Act of 1972 all resulted in more work for the federal courts. The ever-growing number of lawyers also helps increase the courts' work. Lawyers find reasons to file suits so as to keep themselves in work.

In 1982, more than 16,000 people worked in the federal court system. In addition to judges, there were staff members for the judges (clerks, secretaries), probation officers, bankruptcy referees, U.S. magistrates, court criers, court reporters, nurses, interpreters, custodians, and others. The most important staff members are law clerks who help judges deal with the mound of business before them. (There were 33 for the nine Supreme Court justices in 1980.) They are temporary workers, the best graduates of good law schools who serve for a year or two before starting their own careers. They have some influence on some cases, but tend to exaggerate their own importance (see Woodward and Armstrong, 1979).

THE WORK OF THE FEDERAL COURTS

The constitutional setting

The Constitution sets up the federal judiciary in very few words. With two short paragraphs in Article III, the framers created a Supreme Court, left the creation of other federal courts to Congress, and defined the jurisdiction of federal courts. In the first year of the new government, 1789, Congress quickly fleshed out the federal courts through the Judiciary Act.

The system of checks and balances created in Philadelphia left the courts in an ambiguous position, particularly with regard to interpreting acts of Congress. The courts were also in the middle of the debate between federal and state power. This resulted in the compromises leading to the American brand of federalism.

Many framers felt that the courts should naturally have some power in interpreting acts of Congress. Courts should be able to declare acts unconstitutional because the Constitution was supreme over all statutes and the courts would surely be interpreting its meaning in specific cases. In *the Federalist*, Alexander Hamilton argued that the Supreme Court would have the power of judicial review of congressional acts. That is, the Court could declare them unconstitutional and therefore null and void. But not everyone agreed.

In the famous case of *Marbury* v. *Madison* (1803), the Supreme Court itself addressed this issue. The Court declared that it did, indeed, have the power to review acts of Congress. This declaration applied to a congressional law that had increased the kinds of cases the Supreme Court could hear in the first place. The Court ruled that Congress had erred in giving it jurisdiction that properly belonged with the district courts.

The early Court was shy about using its now explicit power. It did not again declare a congressional act unconstitutional until 1857. In that year, in the *Dred Scott* case, the Court proclaimed the Missouri Compromise, which distinguished between slave and free states, unconstitutional. Only after the Civil War did the Supreme Court increase its use of judicial review.

The Court also moved early in the 1800s to support the national side in the debate over whether national laws automatically took precedence over conflict-

Judicial review. In the second use of its judicial review power, in 1857, the Supreme Court stirred up considerable antagonism, as evidenced by this poster from the time.

ing state laws. In *McCulloch* v. *Maryland* (1819), the Court made two vital rulings. It upheld a broad interpretation of the power of the national government to legislate; then it held that state laws infringing on that power were unconstitutional.

Even within the framework of these two broad rulings, the Supreme Court has moved cautiously. It can be independently aggressive, but it is also dependent on Congress, the president, and the bureaucracy. Therefore, it cannot risk head-to-head conflicts very often. Its dependence on Congress lies in such areas as the structure of the whole court system, the Supreme Court's jurisdiction (which cases it can hear on appeal from other courts), the number of judges, and the salaries of judges. It depends on the president and the bureaucracy to enforce many decisions. Without executive branch action, many decisions would be mere bits of rhetoric.

The federal courts also depend in the end on the goodwill or at least the sufferance of the people. In this they are basically the same as Congress or the executive branch, even though federal judges have lifetime tenure and are not subject to election.

Formal jurisdiction

The formally defined jurisdiction of the federal courts is broad, although the Supreme Court has been seeking to limit access to the federal court system in recent years. All cases involving the Constitution, statutes passed by Congress, treaties involving the United States, and admiralty or maritime matters can automatically be brought before federal courts. It does not matter who the parties are. Also, a case can be brought before the federal courts if it involves any of the following parties: (1) the United States, (2) two or more states, (3) a state and one or more citizens of another state, (4) citizens of different states in disputes involving more than $10,000 (a figure set by statute), (5) a state or citizens of a state and foreign nations or citizens, and (6) foreign diplomats.

Basically, the federal courts may address a very wide variety of subjects. Congress has passed laws in a vast array of areas; this opens those areas to federal court action if cases concerning them are brought before courts. Congress can remove appellate jurisdiction from the Supreme Court (it has done so only once). It cannot, though, remove jurisdiction from the federal court system as a whole. The Constitution specifies this. Nor can Congress alter the kinds of cases that can be originally brought before the Supreme Court. This is also specified in the Constitution.

Scope of action

Federal judges have some leeway in setting the substantive areas in which they will intervene. Thus, for instance, early in this century the federal courts were aggressive in economic regulation, usually to limit federal or state action. Since the late 1930s, this has mostly washed away. In the 1950s and particularly in the '60s, the federal courts became more and more aggressive in civil liberties. They especially looked at rights of racial minorities and accused criminals. In the 1970s, the federal courts seemed intent on being more aggressive in a number of social policy areas. This was more widespread in the lower federal courts

Air disaster in Chicago. A federal judge ordered all DC–10 aircraft in the United States grounded as a result of this crash in May 1979.

than in the more conservative Supreme Court of the late 1970s, and was also seen in many state courts (Horowitz, 1977).

Today the courts are involved in an immense range of social policies. They often respond to aggressive litigants as well as acts of Congress that create new occasions for lawsuits. Instances are easy to find in the daily newspapers. For example:

Concorde supersonic jets are landing in New York City because a federal judge decided that the New York Port Authority had no power to ban them.

A federal judge ordered the grounding of DC-10 aircraft after a fatal crash in Chicago in May 1979.

A federal judge stopped the cancellation of three Amtrak passenger trains by administrative action.

A federal judge held up the implementation of many strip-mining regulations developed by the Interior Department's Office of Surface Mining after the passage of the federal strip-mining law in 1977.

Federal judges can, through the work of court-appointed officials, make or review all important decisions in school systems under court order to desegregate. For example, a federal judge issued more than 400 rulings between 1974 and 1983 in overseeing the details of school desegregation in Boston. Federal judges can oversee, in detail, districting for state legislatures or seats in the U.S. House of Representatives.

Courts have expanded their area of impact partly because some judges have thought such expansion proper. This is often done in response to a public that has become more willing to file suits; often to deal with new and complicated areas of government action such as environmental policy; and often to cope

COURTS AND SOCIAL POLICY: A SAMPLER

In just the past few years, courts have struck down laws requiring a period of in-state residence as a condition of eligibility for welfare. They have invalidated presumptions of child support arising from the presence in the home of a "substitute father." Federal district courts have laid down elaborate standards for food handling, hospital operations, recreation facilities, inmate employment and education, sanitation, and laundry, painting, lighting, plumbing, and renovation in some prisons; they have ordered other prisons closed. Courts have established equally comprehensive programs of care and treatment for the mentally ill confined in hospitals. They have ordered the equalization of school expenditures on teachers' salaries, established hearing procedures for public school discipline cases, decided that bilingual education must be pro-

vided for Mexican-American children, and suspended the use by school boards of the National Teacher Examination and of comparable tests for school supervisors. They have eliminated a high school diploma as a requirement for a fireman's job. They have enjoined the construction of roads and bridges on environmental grounds and suspended performance requirements for automobile tires and air bags. They have told the Farmers Home Administration to restore a disaster loan program, the Forest Service to stop the clearcutting of timber, and the Corps of Engineers to maintain the nation's nonnavigable waterways. They have been, to put it mildly, very busy, laboring in unfamiliar territory.

From Donald L. Horowitz, *The Courts and Social Policy* (Washington, D.C.: Brookings Institution, 1977), pp. 4–5.

Separate but equal? Before the U.S. Supreme Court decreed in the case of *Brown v. Board of Education* (1954) that racial segregation of the schools could not be required by state laws, children in a number of states were required to go to all-black or all-white schools. Two schools from the 1940s are pictured.

with the greatly increased use of class action suits—action brought in the name of an entire class of individuals, such as welfare recipients, criminals in prison, or owners of an allegedly defective model of automobile. There are also some important areas in which there has been little judicial action. These include almost all foreign policy and some domestic policy involving such questions as raising revenue.

In certain areas, the courts may become the major policymakers for a time, though Congress and the executive branch usually get involved before long. For instance, courts played a very big role in desegregation, integration, and affirmative action. But even in these areas the executive branch and Congress were active, if only in a negative way, before the Supreme Court's 1954 *Brown v. Board of Education* decision declared unconstitutional state laws requiring segregated public schools. There had been a great deal of judicial activity in the area before that time, but after the 1954 decision all three branches of government had to be involved for progress to be made in line with the decision.

Subsequent decisions by federal judges, especially in the South, were essential in pushing equality and desegregation of education as well as voting, jury selection, and other matters (Bass, 1981). Actions by Congress and the president and executive branch were also essential. The 1954 decision by the Supreme Court by itself could not have done much to eliminate racial discrimination and segregation.

Hierarchy and the flow of judicial business

Each state has a court system that comes into only occasional contact with the federal courts. Each state also has its own judicial hierarchy and rules. Only when cases involving federal laws or the Constitution come up in state courts can those cases be ultimately reviewed by the U.S. Supreme Court.

Federal district courts are basically courts of first instance—that is, the first courts to hear cases. (Only some matters from the Interstate Commerce Commission come to the federal district courts as appeals from previous decisions.) These cases are usually heard by a single district judge. (Some are heard by three judges.) Some jury trials are held in district courts. The 12 U.S. Courts of Appeal get their cases from three sources: the district courts, the Tax Court, and the independent regulatory commissions. The majority come from district courts. There, the losing party has a right of appeal to the court of appeals in all instances. Most courts of appeal cases are decided by three judges. In a few cases, all the judges decide.

Part of the total American court structure. The Illinois Supreme Court in Springfield is pictured.

The Supreme Court gets its appellate business from four sources: state supreme courts in the instances mentioned earlier, the Court of Appeals for the Federal Circuit, directly from the district courts in some cases, and the courts of appeal. Most cases come from state supreme courts and federal courts of appeal. The Supreme Court has a number of procedures for deciding what it will hear. Thus the most visible and most influential judicial pronouncements on public policy—those from the Supreme Court—are made on subjects chosen at the Court's discretion.

Lawyers also have some room to decide what questions are taken up by the Supreme Court. They may elect not to appeal certain cases if they think they will get a negative result. For instance, in the mid-1970s, lawyers saw that the Supreme Court was becoming more hostile to broadening the scope of individual rights. Therefore, they chose to keep certain issues away from the Court. Given our diverse court system, the chances of getting positive rulings from state, federal district, and federal appeals judges are enhanced if there is no clear-cut Supreme Court pronouncement.

The losers in court suits—even if they lose in the Supreme Court—have other avenues of appeal, mostly to Congress and the state legislatures. For example, a number of Supreme Court decisions limited the impact of the federal Freedom of Information Act. The act was supposed to make more information on the internal workings of the federal government available to the public. Those pushing for maximum availability induced Congress to make the law more explicit. In effect, a successful appeal to Congress overthrew the Supreme Court decisions.

The Supreme Court makes the broadest and most significant decisions over time. But all our courts can significantly affect public policy. In the end, many questions of largest significance to society wend their way to the Supreme Court and receive judgment. But a number of years may pass between the time an issue enters the courts and the time the Supreme Court gives a definitive ruling. And what appears to be definitive may, in fact, be far less than that for several reasons. It may be unclear. It may only cover a small range of the conditions to which it presumably refers. The Supreme Court may change its mind in whole or in part in later decisions. Or interpretations of lower courts may vary from what the Supreme Court was saying.

State courts in particular have a lot of room in dealing with areas the Supreme Court handles. In the area of constitutional rights, for instance, state courts may conclude that state constitutions set stricter standards than the Supreme Court. This happened in 1975, when the Supreme Court of California required stricter limits on police searches and seizures than those set in 1973 by the U.S. Supreme Court.

COURTS AND POLITICS

Courts are important instruments of public policy. Therefore, it follows that they are enmeshed in the politics of the nation. Courts differ from legislatures, bureaucracies, and chief executives (just as those bodies and individuals differ from one another). But those differences *do not* include isolation from political life. As individuals, many judges and justices are active in public life even as they sit on various courts. Justices such as Warren Burger, William Rehnquist, and William Douglas, in recent years, were particularly active in making public speeches. When Justice Louis Brandeis was on the Supreme Court (1916–1939), he financed the activities of Felix Frankfurter, then a law professor at Harvard and later a Supreme Court justice himself, in pursuing public policy goals important to Brandeis (Murphy, 1982). A number of Supreme Court justices have advised presidents privately.

Courts are involved in politics in many ways. The structure of the federal courts is, in part, political. Picking federal judges is a highly political process. Both the party identification and geographic origins of judges affect their decisions. The Supreme Court displays a special kind of politics related to small-group decision making. Finally, courts are involved in highly political relations with Congress, the executive branch, and interest groups.

The structure of courts

The structure of courts is not fixed. The Constitution gives Congress power to create the federal judiciary. According to the Constitution, there must be a Supreme Court. But other than that, Congress has had a free hand in shaping the federal judiciary. Even the number of members on the Supreme Court is up to Congress. But after an abortive attempt in 1937 to increase the Court's size from 9 to 15, it seems likely that its size will not change.

Several features of court structure are subject to statutory change: the number of judges, the number and jurisdiction of courts, the location of courts, and the geographic makeup of appellate circuits. All of these features have sparked

The pursuit of policy goals. Supreme Court Justice Louis Brandeis (*above*) helped finance the policy activities of Harvard Law School professor Felix Frankfurter (*below*) in the 1920s and 1930s. Frankfurter later also became a Supreme Court justice.

political debate at one time or another. A recent instance in which court structure became a live political issue occurred in the 1960s. Southern conservatives in Congress tried to redraw appellate court boundaries to put a greater number of southern states into a more conservative (that is, segregationist) circuit. Integrationists in Congress blocked this move (Richardson and Vines, 1970: 17–18). Dividing the circuit covering the Deep South was·again considered in the late 1970s. There was similar controversy, but the issue was resolved with relative ease and Congress made the division.

The selection of federal judges

Presidential appointment to the Supreme Court. Lyndon Johnson and Thurgood Marshall, the first black justice, at the time of appointment in 1967.

Supreme Court justices   Supreme Court appointments always attract attention. On some occasions, nominees get very special attention. This is particularly true when there is a departure in the nature of the appointee. The appointment of Louis Brandeis by President Wilson in 1916 attracted much interest because he was the first Jewish justice appointed. Justice Thurgood Marshall's appointment by President Johnson in 1967 received wide acclaim, since he was the first black justice. By the same token, the nomination of Sandra Day O'Connor by President Reagan in 1981 attracted unusual notoriety because she was the first woman nominated to the Court.

Sandra O'Connor was serving on the Arizona Court of Appeals at the time of her nomination. She had been an active and conservative Republican politican before becoming a state court judge. She served five years in the Arizona Senate, becoming the first woman majority leader. Although her candidacy was espoused enthusiastically by conservative Republican U.S. Senator Barry Goldwater of Arizona, some ultraright groups felt O'Connor might not be conservative enough on sensitive issues like abortion. But the Senate confirmed Justice O'Connor without a single dissenting vote in late September 1981.

Between 1789 and mid-1984 101 men and one woman sat on the Supreme Court. Most presidents, especially in recent years, have seen Supreme Court appointments as uniquely theirs, though a few presidents in the past paid only slight attention to these vacancies. The Senate must confirm the president's choices for the Supreme Court by a majority vote. (In fact, it must do so for all judicial nominations.) Presidents sometimes consult (with leading members of Congress, party leaders, trusted friends, and even sitting justices) in deciding whom to pick for Supreme Court vacancies. But they usually take a very personal interest in their choices. This is both because the Supreme Court has a significant policy impact and because the symbolic value of the choice means so much.

A woman justice. President Reagan ended exclusively male membership on the Supreme Court with his appointment of Sandra Day O'Connor in 1981.

The Senate does not confirm Supreme Court nominations routinely and automatically. Nixon's nominations of Clement Haynsworth in 1969 and G. Harrold Carswell in 1970 were rejected. During our history, the Senate has turned down 11 Supreme Court nominees. Another 15 nominations were killed because either the president withdrew the nomination or the Senate postponed action or failed to act on it.

The Senate's successful opposition to 26 appointments suggests that it has not been a rubber stamp for the president. Rejections have occurred for various reasons (Abraham, 1975; Scigliano, 1971). Sometimes the Senate opposed not the nominee but the president making the nomination. In other cases, a nominee has been involved with a highly debatable public issue and has thus been

Two losers. The Senate rejected two Nixon appointees to the Supreme Court: Harrold Carswell (*top*) and Clement Haynsworth (*bottom*).

controversial. Sometimes the Senate has used opposition to a nominee to express its dislike of Court decisions. At times, the opposition of a few strong senators has defeated a nominee. Sometimes a majority of the Senate thought a nominee had unacceptable political beliefs. Some nominees have been turned down because their qualifications or ability appeared to be too low. In most successful Senate rejections, several of these reasons pertained.

The American Bar Association's Standing Committee on the Federal Judiciary (set up in 1945–46) has sought a role in Supreme Court choices akin to its strong role in other federal court nominations. It has not, as yet, achieved such influence. President Nixon tried giving it more influence. But he was embarrassed by its hesitancy to support several potential nominees in whom he was interested, and so its influence waned.

Presidents seek people for the Supreme Court who agree with them ideologically and are usually of the same political party. Ideological agreement is, of course, hard to define. There is a broad range of public issues and great differences between the agenda of the president and that of the Supreme Court. Also, when persons join the Supreme Court, they are bound by legal precedent, Court traditions, and the views of eight senior colleagues. So they do not have the exact policy impact that presidents hope for or expect. Most presidents have been embarrassed or angered by the behavior of their appointees on at least some occasions.

Over time a president who pays careful attention to his Court appointments can change the general tenor of Court decisions. After Franklin Roosevelt appointed a number of justices, the general shape of Court decisions on such matters as the power of the government to regulate the economy and civil liberties changed. The Court sanctioned government regulation that it had opposed before. It began to be more active in protecting individual liberties such as free speech. The Burger Court, largely shaped by President Nixon, differs in some important respects from previous courts. This is most true in its reluctance to define constitutionally protected liberties broadly.

In addition to competence, party affiliation, and ideology, the president also gives some attention to regional balance on the Court and perhaps to ethnic and religious representation. Thus far, all but two of those who have served on the Court have been male and white; most have been Protestant; most have come from upper social strata; and most had much prior experience in politics or public office (Schmidhauser, 1959).

Other federal judges   The appointment of federal judges for district courts and court of appeal is more complex than the appointment of Supreme Court justices because these judges are both more numerous and less visible. Again, the Senate must confirm presidential nominees. Senators often play a leading part in urging candidates for such judgeships on the president. A number of people become involved in negotiating the choice with the president's representative, usually the Attorney General. Senators are quite important in picking district judges, since each district lies completely within a single state. Incumbent federal judges (including Supreme Court members) have particular influence. Various political party leaders in addition to senators often speak up. The Standing Committee on the Federal Judiciary of the American Bar Association (ABA) makes suggestions, and the candidates themselves usually take part.

President Eisenhower told his Attorney General to give the ABA committee veto power over candidates. Yet he chose a few whom the ABA rated "not

THE INGENIOUS QUARTERBACK!

qualified." The ABA has at times pressed for automatic veto power. But the political realities of the appointment traditions and the importance of the jobs have worked against that.

Most often, if a senator of the president's party opposes a nominee for a judgeship in his or her state, the Senate will reject that choice. This is called **senatorial courtesy.** Senatorial courtesy does not mean senators can name the winning candidate for an opening, but they can usually prevent an appointment.

The most reliable predictor of who will get appointed to openings on the federal bench is party affiliation. Presidents give few of these prized openings to members of the other party. With the exception of Gerald Ford, all presidents in the last five decades (beginning with Franklin Roosevelt in 1933) made more than 90 percent of their appointments to district courts and courts of appeals from their own party. Ford appointed just over 80 percent from his own party. In his first two years in office, Ronald Reagan was, by a narrow margin, the most partisan of all. Of his first 87 appointments to these important judgeships, 85 were Republicans (98 percent).

As they do with Supreme Court nominations, presidents and their advisers try to pick people for federal judgeships whose views are like their own. But presidents must also pay a variety of debts and make a number of calculations in making appointments. For example, Kennedy appointed a number of southern segregationists to federal judgeships to build southern support in Congress for legislative initiatives outside of the civil rights area.

Until very recently, there were few women, blacks, or Hispanics serving as judges in the federal judiciary. President Carter had a number of new judgeships to fill and made a determined effort to increase the representation of these groups. Table 12–1 contains information on the number and percentage of appointments to courts of appeals and district courts that went to women, blacks, and Hispanics under the last five presidents. Carter was the most active in appointing individuals from all three categories. Reagan seemed least concerned with finding black nominees, and also appointed very few women and Hispanics.

What kinds of people become federal judges? They often come from lower social strata than do Supreme Court justices. But they are still from the more privileged classes. Like Supreme Court justices, they tend to have had a lot of political experience and visibility. They are almost all natives of the state in which they will sit. Most are natives of the region served by the court of appeals to which they are appointed. Except for the obvious difference of party, recent presidents, including Reagan, have all appointed people from the same general background to federal judgeships (Goldman, 1983). Most have been judges, prosecutors, or both. Most have also been activists in their political party.

The impact of party and public opinion

The party affiliation of federal judges is related to the kinds of decisions they make (Goldman, 1975; Nagel, 1961; Richardson and Vines, 1970; Carp and Rowland, 1983). Democratic appeals judges are generally more liberal than Republicans. The party split is strongest on economic issues. In the late 1950s and early '60s, for instance, Democratic district judges made decisions more favorable to organized labor than Republican district judges did.

After 1968, the split on civil liberties questions also became pronounced (Rowland and Carp, 1980). Democratic judges were more likely to favor the defendant in criminal cases; minorities, aliens, or women in class action suits on discrimination; and people instead of governments in cases involving free speech or freedom of religion.

Public opinion also affects the decisions of federal courts. Consider race relations cases brought before southern judicial districts in the late 1950s and early '60s. Blacks would more likely gain a favorable ruling in a case if it was tried in a district with a low black population; they would more likely lose in a district that had a high black population (Richardson and Vines, 1970: 95–100). This is not surprising. Most judges were native to the districts, and all of them white. In southern politics, the most segregationist or racist stands have generally come from those areas with the most black people because white public

TABLE 12–1

Appointments of Women, Blacks, and Hispanics to Courts of Appeal and District Courts, 1963–1982, by President

President	Total number of appointments	Women		Blacks		Hispanics	
		Number	Percent	Number	Percent	Number	Percent
Johnson, 1963–69	162	3	2%	7	4%	3	2%
Nixon, 1969–1974	224	1	*	6	3	2	1
Ford, 1974–77	64	1	2	3	5	1	2
Carter, 1977–81	258	40	16	37	14	16	6
Reagan, 1981–82	87	3	3	1	1	2	2

*Less than 0.5 percent.

Source: Calculated from data in Sheldon Goldman, "Reagan's Judicial Appointments at Mid-Term: Shaping the Bench in His Own Image," *Judicature* 66 (March 1983), pp. 339, 345.

opinion in those areas has been most hostile to blacks. Those from areas with fewer black people have tended to be more moderate. But a new breed of southern federal judge has recently appeared. The relationship noted above has become much weaker (Giles and Walker, 1975).

Changing public opinion about the Vietnam War paralleled changing behavior of federal district judges in sentencing convicted draft evaders (Cook, 1977, 1979; Kritzer, 1979). As public opposition to the war grew, judges became more and more likely to give lighter sentences, as mild as probation.

The internal politics of decision making in federal courts

On certain occasions, a court decision is made by more than one judge. In those cases, the internal politics of decision making helps explain the decisions. Most federal district court decisions are made by a single judge, though a few require three judges. Appeals court decisions and Supreme Court decisions are generally shared, except for some procedural matters. Supreme Court justices pay close attention to each other. They closely watch the adjustments they need to make to retain goodwill, even though they have different opinions. The chief justice can be especially influential in shaping Court decisions (Rohde and Spaeth, 1976).

The Supreme Court must perform three major decision-making tasks: decide what cases will be heard; decide the case itself in the simple sense of determining who wins and who loses (the decision as such); and decide what reason to give for the decision (the opinion). Each task is governed by a number of formal and informal rules and procedures. Each is affected by the general norm that precedent (the content of previous decisions) is important and should not be changed lightly. The Supreme Court does, though, sometimes directly overrule a previous decision. The Court adheres to precedent less firmly on constitutional than on statutory questions.

On some matters, the chief justice may think it especially important that the Court speak with one voice. Therefore, he may stall and maneuver until he can get a unanimous opinion on a critical case. Chief Justice Warren clearly felt that the decision ruling state-enforced school segregation unconstitutional needed such unanimity, and he worked long and hard to achieve it. Chief justices have long used their power to assign the writing of decisions to get statements relatively close to their own policy preferences (Slotnick, 1979). Chief Justice Burger has tried to assign the writing of majority opinions when he was in the minority on a case. This represents a change in the traditional practice. Usually the senior justice in the majority assigns the opinion if the chief justice is in the minority.

Access to the federal courts: Congress, the executive branch, and interest groups

Federal judges can afford to be independent in many important ways. Except in rare cases of personal misbehavior, they have lifetime tenure. But they are not completely isolated from society and the other institutions with which they must interact. Social trends will eventually be reflected in their views. The evidence on sentencing draft evaders already noted supports this view.

A number of people and groups have some influence over the appointment process that determines who sits on the federal bench. Congress, the executive branch, and interest groups all have additional points of access and ways of affecting the courts. Congress controls the number of federal judges, courts, and circuits, and the structure of appellate jurisdiction in the federal system. It has often added judgeships to create added coveted jobs for party loyalists as well as to increase the efficiency of the court system.

Congress has changed the Supreme Court's appellate jurisdiction only once, but the threat is always present. After the Civil War, Congress prevented the Supreme Court from considering some Reconstruction laws by removing those laws from appellate jurisdiction. In the 1960s, some conservatives in Congress were upset by a series of Warren Court decisions extending the constitutional rights of criminal defendants. They tried without success to limit the Supreme Court's jurisdiction in some criminal matters coming from state courts. More recently, efforts have been made to limit federal court authority over school desegregation, school prayer, and other controversial issues.

Congress has several other ways of changing Court decisions. First, members can try to reverse decisions by statute. Sometimes the Court drops broad hints that it would welcome a new statute in an area; but sometimes Congress just enacts legislation engendering preferences that differ from those of the Court. Second, Congress can try to amend the Constitution. Three fourths of the state legislatures must approve such a measure. A number of amendments have been threatened because of Court decisions, but only a few have been adopted. The 11th Amendment (adopted in 1795) clarified federal jurisdiction over suits against states. This came after a Court ruling on a matter disturbing to the states. The 13th, 14th, and 15th Amendments were adopted after the Civil War. They were needed to deal with the Court's statements in the *Dred Scott* case (1857) about blacks' lack of citizenship. The 16th Amendment (adopted in 1913) allowed a federal income tax. This came after the Court had ruled such a tax unconstitutional. The 26th Amendment (adopted in 1971) lowered the voting age to 18 for all elections. This followed a Court ruling that Congress could lower the age for federal elections but not for state and local elections. Finally, Congress can show its displeasure with federal court decisions by refusing to increase the pay or benefits of judges. Congress cannot, though, decrease judges' compensation while they are in office.

The executive branch has one major access route to the federal courts other than appointment power. This involves the relationship between the federal courts and government lawyers. U.S. attorneys—the government prosecutors in each federal judicial district—and their aides deal closely with the lower federal courts. This closeness can vary a lot, though, from judge to judge. Some judges identify with the office of the U.S. attorney to the extent that they want it to succeed in its prosecutions. They offer advice on cases to prosecute, strategies to adopt, and other details of the prosecutors' role. Such identification is aided by the fact that both attorneys and judges are usually party activists; many of the attorneys also aspire to a judgeship later in their career (Goldman and Jahnige, 1976: 80–84; Eisenstein, 1978).

The solicitor general (the chief advocate for the Justice Department) deals closely with the Supreme Court. For example, he uses restraint in petitioning the Court for hearings. He thereby helps increase the chances of favorable treatment when he does petition.

The techniques interest groups use to influence federal court decisions are different from those used in approaching Congress and bureaucratic agencies. Interest groups help sponsor test cases by telling their legal staffs to work on them. The cases in which the Supreme Court outlawed racial segregation in public schools were sponsored by lawyers for the National Association for the Advancement of Colored People (NAACP).

Interest groups give judges information and arguments in two other ways. First, in pending cases, an interest group may file an *amicus curiae* brief. This is a written argument on some or all of the points in the case. Even though the group filing such a brief is not a direct party to the case, judges do read and absorb some of the information. In the Bakke case (1978), which dealt with reverse discrimination, about 60 *amicus curiae* briefs were filed. Conservative interest groups have increasingly used this technique in recent years (O'Connor and Epstein, 1983). Second, interest groups generate and help place articles favorable to their points of view in periodicals, such as law reviews, that are read by judges.

THE POLICY IMPACT OF COURTS

Federal courts are active in many policy areas. The Supreme Court is the most important policymaking court. We start with an overview of its agenda. Then we address the question of compliance with court decisions. Finally, we ask what sort of public reaction court pronouncements receive.

The Supreme Court agenda

Most of the time, the Court chooses to hear cases involving a government as one of the parties. Even in cases where both parties are private, they are contending over matters stemming from government policy. These might include labor-management relations, patent policy, or bans on discrimination.

The Court deals with public law most of the time, though it can and does venture into private law. Within the domain of public law, the Court deals with a broad range of issues. By far the largest—and most important—involves liberties, rights, and the meaning of equality (see Chapter 13).

Another major area of Court activity is economic issues—often stemming from government regulation. These might include labor-management relations, antitrust cases, environmental cases, and regulation of stocks, bonds, and other securities.

Before 1937, the Court spent much time on questions of what the federal government could do in the economic realm and what was reserved to state and local governments. Since 1937, the Court has taken the position that whatever the national government wants to do in domestic economic policy cannot be stopped solely because it involves powers reserved to state and local governments.

The Court also becomes involved in defining federalism: What units of government can act on what matters? Cases in this area were vital in the early years of the nation as the various governments defined their roles. In recent years there have been fewer cases but some of them have some practical importance. Some also deal with civil liberties.

The Court sometimes gets involved in interpreting the president's powers.

SELECTED SUPREME COURT DECISIONS, 1981 AND 1982 TERMS

Ruled that the National Association of Colored People (NAACP) is not liable for economic damages suffered by merchants who lost business as a result of a local boycott led by an NAACP official.

Held that voters may limit the use of busing to achieve school desegregation, but only if the action does not limit constitutional rights or put special burdens on blacks.

Determined that school districts must provide specialized services for handicapped students that allow them to benefit educationally, but those services need not guarantee that handicapped students can maximize their potential.

Declared unconstitutional the women-only admissions policy of the School of Nursing at the Mississippi University for Women.

Found unconstitutional a New York law requiring landlords to permit installation of cable television equipment for a nominal fee.

Upheld a method for state taxation of U.S.-based multinational corporations that greatly increased the potential for state revenues.

Permitted searches without warrants in certain situations involving customs officials and boats and police and automobiles.

Prohibited employers from discriminating between male and female employees in the type of medical insurance coverage given their spouses.

Approved Minnesota's plan for giving tax deductions for tuition and other expenses to parents of students in both public and private schools.

Required New Jersey to draw new lines for its congressional districts because that state had failed to justify population differences of less than one percent in districts created after the 1980 census.

In 1952, it declared the seizure of the steel mills by President Truman unconstitutional, even though Truman made this decision because the mills were closed by a strike during the Korean War. Truman acquiesced and returned the mills to company management. In 1974, the Court ruled unanimously that President Nixon could not withhold the Watergate tapes from the courts. Nixon also acquiesced.

In mid-1983 the Court made what appeared to be a sweeping decision that rendered "legislative veto" provisions of about 200 laws, passed since the early 1930s, unconstitutional because they violated the separation of powers requirements of the Constitution. The decision required a reaction from Congress but whether the decision fundamentally alters power relationships between Congress and the executive branch is not clear. There is also some evidence that the legislative veto was not a particularly effective form of congressional control (Craig 1983).

In relations that seem to be wholly private, the justices have been willing to rule some kind of agreements unconstitutional. They do so on the ground that the power of government, usually state or local, is needed to enforce these agreements. For example, in 1948, the Court ruled that provisions in real estate deeds that prevented the owner of a house or lot from selling the property to nonwhites could not be enforced in courts.

There are other examples of cases involving private parties that become tinged with a public character: a labor union certified by the government as an official bargaining agent; a nominally private library that receives some public funding; and a restaurant owner who leases government property. None of these private parties can engage in discriminatory practices, especially those based on race.

Compliance with court decisions

When a defendant is sentenced to prison by a court and all appeals have been lost, he or she complies most of the time (barring escape). But the degree of compliance with many important court decisions varies. In such cases, courts are speaking to other institutions. They are either banning or requiring some activity. Different people in those different institutions—such as the lower federal courts, state and local courts, and federal, state, and local bureaucracies—may hear a court saying different things. And in some cases, they may choose not to hear what the court is saying at all. There is, in short, nothing self-enforcing about most court decisions. This is obviously true for very broad rulings, such as the 1954 Supreme Court decision on public school segregation. Other examples involve the decision in 1973 that women have a right to abortion (Bond and Johnson 1982), the ruling that prayers in public schools are unconstitutional (Muir, 1968), and details of police procedures in handling accused criminals (Milner, 1971). In dealing with accused criminals different police departments used different procedures under the same Supreme Court decision. Even transmitting Court decisions to those expected to carry them out can be a problem (Wasby, 1976).

Compliance with court decisions is likely to vary. Court decisions may be unclear; there may be differing interpretations of these decisions; or those called on to comply may wish to evade the decisions. This does not mean that courts do not have an impact, but the impact may be murky. Court decisions may seem, at first glance, to be clearer and more precise than other statements of policy, such as statutes or presidential speeches. In fact, that is not the case.

Public opinion and the Supreme Court. Court decisions, and individual members of the Supreme Court, may arouse highly-charged public opinion. Warren Court decisions in the 1950s and 1960s sparked unsuccessful efforts to impeach the chief justice. This billboard appeared in many parts of the country.

Public attitudes toward courts

The federal court system has a number of publics or constituencies. *Constituency* is most often used in connection with elected officials. Federal judges are, of course, not elected. Yet over time the opinions of both mass and elite publics indirectly place some constraints on court decisions and directly affect the degree of compliance with those decisions.

Courts may not respond to day-to-day changes in opinion. But over time, strong trends may develop that alter both the views and people in the White House and Congress. Then the views of the Supreme Court and other federal courts will surely also alter through the choice of new judges with views more responsive to current opinions. Such change takes time. It depends on vacancies, though new judgeships can be created and filled quickly.

In the late 1960s, there was growing public displeasure with the liberal decisions of the Court under Chief Justice Earl Warren. In the 1968 presidential campaign, Richard Nixon played on this feeling. After he became president, he appointed more conservative justices to the Supreme Court. Thereafter, Court decisions began to take a more conservative direction. Later, public approval of the Court began to increase.

The public is selective about what it likes and does not like about the Supreme Court's policy performance. Most people know little about court activities and do not notice them most of the time. This gives the courts much leeway to move without offending public opinion. General support for the courts as institutions also tends to remain strong in spite of temporary policy disagreements. People become annoyed with specific decisions, but do not conclude that the structure or powers of the courts should be altered.

PUBLIC REACTION TO LEADING DECISIONS OF THE WARREN AND BURGER COURTS

Rulings favored by a clear majority of the public

1954 decision outlawing public school segregation

1964 decision that both houses of state legislatures must be apportioned on "one-person, one-vote" basis.

1965 decision preventing states from stopping the use and passing out of information on contraceptive devices.

1970 decision that the voting age could be lowered to 18.

1973 decisions allowing presumably tougher standards by states and localities in banning obscene materials.

Rulings on which the public was evenly divided

1967 decision outlawing a state statute prohibiting interracial marriages.

1973 decision declaring that abortions in the first three months of pregnancy were legal.

Rulings opposed by a clear majority of the public

1963 decision outlawing religious practices in public schools.

1965 decision that banned the mandatory registration of members of the Communist party with the federal government.

1966 decision that the police must immediately advise a criminal suspect of his or her right to remain silent and have a lawyer.

1972 decision striking down the death penalty.

1973 decision that tuition reimbursements or tax relief for the parents of parochial school students were unconstitutional.

1972 decision that journalists could not protect the identity of their news sources from grand juries.

Source: *Gallup Opinion Index*, August 1973, pp. 11–13.

HOW ACTIVE SHOULD COURTS BE?

Where do the policy activities of unelected courts belong in a representative democracy? Should the courts be strong or weak? Should they be active in making policy statements? Or should they defer to decisions of elected officials?

The question of judicial *activism* versus *restraint* has been continuously debated throughout our history. Those who believe in judicial self-restraint have two main reasons for their view. They may feel that the courts are elitist, nondemocratic parts of the governing system and so should always defer to the more democratic bodies: elected legislatures and executives. They may also dislike some of the courts' current decisions.

Those who favor activism also have two basic reasons. They may feel that an elitist, nondemocratic check on what might be the follies of elected agents is necessary and legitimate. This is especially so in guarding individual rights against what might be unwise decisions supported by the majority. They may also like some current court decisions that probably would not be approved through regular legislative and executive means.

The debate over the place of appointive courts in a democracy is really more complex than it seems. Three facts make unrealistic a simple rejection or acceptance of the view that courts are undemocratic elites. First, as discussed, courts

---

THE CASE FOR JUDICIAL ACTIVISM

Democracy is not simple. Our government is not based on the principle that today's majority forthwith gets all it wants. Our Constitution on its face disaffirms that theory, by providing expressly that Congress may not do certain things, whether or not its majority think them wise. Our government works through many officials at varying distances from the electorate; our Senate is "undemocratic," on any simplistic assumption; second-term Presidents can never answer to the voters; many other officials are by design isolated from elections.

To the judicial process as to other processes in government, are committed the conservation and furtherance of democratic values. The judge's task is to identify those values in the constitutional plan, and to work them into life in the cases that reach him. Tact and wise restraint ought to temper any power, but courage and the acceptance of responsibility have their place too.

Deference to other branches of government is called for in measure. But a mere reflex of deference may fail to make reasonable differentiations. Deference to the judgment of Congress, as expressed in formal law, is not the same as deference to the judgment of a subcommittee of the House of Representatives, or to that of a New York policeman. Deference even to Congress must have its degrees, and seems least justified when the congressional determination is as to the extent of

an express prohibition (like those in the Bill of Rights) placed by the Constitution on Congress itself.

As for the greater practical wisdom of political officials, that too is a mixed bag. Controversy today mainly concerns three clusters of problems: racial discrimination, freedom of expression, and fair criminal procedure. As to the third, judges are the best experts we have. As to racial discrimination, it is hard to see how the question of "expertness" enters. . . . As to freedom of expression, some weight may be given to the legislative determination of danger attending certain utterances, but often this judgment must perforce be made in the judicial process, if it is to be based, as fairly it must, on the facts of each case. . . .

The judicial power is one of the accredited means by which our nation seeks its goals, including the prime goal, indispensable to political as to personal health, of self-limitation. Intellectual freedom, freedom from irrational discrimination, immunity from unfair administration of law—these (and others similar) are constitutional interests which the Court can protect on ample doctrinal grounds. They often cannot win protection in rough-and-tumble politics. The Supreme Court is more and more finding that its highest institutional role is the guarding of such interests.

Source: Charles L. Black Jr., *Perspectives in Constitutional Law,* rev. ed. (Englewood Cliffs, N.J.: Prentice-Hall, 1970), pp. 4–5. (Charles Black is a well-known professor of law at Yale University.)

are subject to potential restraints from the elected parts of the government. Even activist judges often restrain themselves. They may feel they are risking a loss of jurisdiction through congressional action. Or they may think they are provoking a president to instruct his agencies not to enforce unpopular decisions.

Second, controversial political issues (and that includes almost every issue of much importance in the nation) are never finally settled by the courts. Nor are they settled by any other branch of government. There is constant debate through which decisions are shaped, amended, reshaped, and adjusted. The solutions reached are almost never final, whether arrived at by courts, legislatures, or the executive branch.

Third, much policy dispute takes place between the courts and bureaucracies, not between the courts and Congress or the president. Both the courts and bureaucracies are unelected and staffed by lifetime appointees.

In short, the debate over judicial activism should not be oversimplified. It cannot reasonably be reduced to simplistic statements about the difference between elected and unelected organs of government.

In recent years there has been a distinction between what can be called a negative form of judicial review and a positive form of judicial activism. Judi-

THE CASE FOR JUDICIAL RESTRAINT

Under the familiar principle of judicial review, the courts in construing the Constitution are, of course, authorized to invalidate laws that have been enacted by Congress or by a state legislature but that those courts find to violate some provision of the Constitution. Nevertheless, those who have pondered the matter have always recognized that the ideal of judicial review has basically antidemocratic and antimajoritarian facets that require some justification in this Nation, which prides itself on being a self-governing representative democracy. . . .

Once we have abandoned the idea that the authority of the courts to declare laws unconstutitonal is somehow tied to the language of the Constitution that the people adopted, a judiciary exercising the power of judicial review appears in a quite different light. Judges then are no longer the keepers of the covenant; instead they are a small group of fortunately situated people with a roving commission to second-guess Congress, state legislatures, and state and federal administrative officers concerning what is best for the country. Surely there is no justification for a third legislative branch in the federal government, and there is even less justification for a federal legislative branch's reviewing on a policy basis the laws enacted by the legislatures of the 50 states. Even if one were to disagree with me on this point, the members of a third branch of the federal legislature at least ought to be elected by and responsible to constituencies, just as in the case of the other two

branches of Congress. If there is going to be a council of revision, it ought to have at least some connection with popular feeling. Its members either ought to stand for reelection on occasion, or their terms should expire and they should be allowed to continue serving only if reappointed by a popularly elected Chief Executive and confirmed by a popularly elected Senate.

I know of no other method compatible with political theory basic to democratic society by which one's own conscientious belief may be translated into positive law and thereby obtain the only general moral imprimatur permissible in a pluralistic, democratic society. It is always time consuming, frequently difficult, and not infrequently impossible to run successfully the legislative gauntlet and have enacted some facet of one's own deeply felt value judgments. It is even more difficult for either a single individual or indeed for a large group of individuals to succeed in having such a value judgment embodied in the Constitution. All of these burdens and difficulties are entirely consistent with the notion of a democratic society. It should not be easy for any one individual or group of individuals to impose by law their value judgments upon fellow citizens who may disagree with those judgments. Indeed, it should not be easier just because the individual in question is a judge.

Source: William H. Rehnquist, "The Notion of a Living Constitution," *Texas Law Review* 54 (May 1976):695–96, 698, 705–6. (William Rehnquist became a justice of the Supreme Court in 1972.)

cial review in the classic, negative sense means that the Supreme Court (and other courts as well) can review laws and the acts of officials at all levels of government (national, state, and local). It can then declare those laws or acts unconstitutional—the courts can say that they go beyond the limits set by the federal Constitution. Judicial review in this sense is negative; the courts say that certain activities may *not* be legislated or take place. Positive activism means that the courts tell other organs of government (federal, state, and local) what they *must do* (keep schools open, increase welfare benefits, redistrict legislative districts).

The Supreme Court declared 122 federal statutes unconstitutional between 1789 and September 1979 (Abraham, 1980: 304–10). A few of these declarations were about major statutes. Examples are the Missouri Compromise, federal child labor laws, and statutes that contained the economic heart of the first New Deal in the early 1930s. But most of the statutes were relatively minor, and the Court decisions did not bring harsh congressional reaction. In the 1983 decision ruling on the legislative veto, the Court presumably declared some 200 legislative provisions unconstitutional at once.

The declarations between 1789 and 1979 were not evenly spaced. Before 1864, only two congressional acts were declared unconstitutional. Between 1864 and 1936, the Court was very active in making such declarations (a total of 71). It was most active in the 1920s and early '30s. Then a very quiet period set in until the 1960s, and only a few acts were declared unconstitutional. Three such decisions were made between 1936 and 1953. The Court had become almost as shy as it had been in the nation's early years. Gradually it became more aggressive. Four declarations were made from 1954 through 1958. And from 1960 through mid-1979 it declared 42 acts unconstitutional. It should be noted that the Court headed by Chief Justice Warren Burger was as aggressive in this regard as that of Earl Warren. From 1953 through 1969 the Warren Court made 25 declarations, and from 1969 through mid-1979 the Burger Court made 21.

The Court held over 1,000 state laws and local ordinances unconstitutional during the same period (Baum, 1981). Before the Civil War, the Court was shy about such actions—35 were taken before 1860. Since then, there have been variations roughly paralleling the pattern in declaring national statutes invalid. But, of course, the numbers are much higher.

These numbers suggest that the Supreme Court has been consistently active since 1953 and that the Warren and Burger courts should not be regarded as polar opposites. The Burger Court has continued to look closely at free speech issues. It has, though, been much less concerned with constitutional rights for accused criminals than was the Warren Court. Yet the Burger Court has not seemed ready to reduce its activity in reviewing federal statutes. In fact, since 1864, the inactive years from 1936 to 1953 stand out as the exception, not the norm. During those years, the Court moved away from an emphasis on economic cases toward a greater concern with civil liberties. The Court was then groping and rethinking its priorities. It also did not wish to act decisively because of the fierce criticism it had received over its role in the 1930s. Those debates climaxed with a nearly successful attempt to increase the size of the Court in 1937. Now, though, Court Justices, regardless of their broad political and judicial differences, seem confident about placing the Court in the political life of the nation. Both the Warren and Burger Courts used their policy discretion quite openly (Shapiro, 1978). Their opinions often invented language and concepts to justify their views. On many important issues there was no compelling legal reason to rule as they did. They were engaged in a policy debate and could have come down in several ways. Their policy preferences helped lead them to the final result.

During the past several decades, hardly a controversial social issue has escaped the attention of the Court. Among this wide range of issues have been abortion, race relations, criminal justice, busing to achieve racial balance in schools, presidential rights of confidentiality of conversations and documents, obscenity, and drawing the lines of legislative districts.

As already noted, the Court's aggressiveness toward state laws and local ordinances, like its stance toward federal laws, has varied over the years. Overall, though, far more state and local laws than federal laws have been declared unconstitutional. Likewise, the Court's areas of concern with regard to state laws and local ordinances have varied. The largest difference between the Warren Court and the Burger Court has involved criminal justice procedures. In this area, the Warren Court was very aggressive. It found state and local laws and practices unconstitutional and ordered remedies. The Burger Court has been much less willing to declare practices in this area unconstitutional, and it has moderated some Warren Court rulings.

In recent years, many courts have ordered positive action by other government agencies more frequently (Horowitz, 1977; Glazer, 1975).

THE FEDERAL COURTS AS POLICY ACTORS: A SUMMARY ASSESSMENT

The federal courts, including the Supreme Court, are important parts of our government. But their policy importance and visibility have varied. In the 1960s and 70s, the courts became more and more visible and important. In part this was because aggressive judges moved into a vast number of policy areas. In part it was because all sorts of people were more inclined to seek legal or judicial solutions to problems.

The federal courts, especially the Supreme Court, provide broad policy guidance for the nation. They provide relatively little justice for individuals (simply because they reach so few individuals). But they may provide some justice for classes of individuals, such as minorities and criminal defendants.

Courts sit squarely in the middle of our political life. There is bargaining between people inside and outside the judicial system. Courts, like all U.S. government institutions, are limited in their power. The constraints on courts are more severe than those on Congress, the president, and the bureaucracy. But these constraints still leave the courts with a good deal of power. For good or for ill, courts help govern the United States and its people.

Do the courts—especially the Supreme Court—lead or follow other institutions and public opinion in the kinds of policies they make? As with most important questions about our government, the answer is not clear. Some claim that the Supreme Court is just part of a ruling national policy alliance. It is never far behind or far ahead of the general drift of both public and policymakers' opinion (Dahl, 1957; McCloskey, 1960). Others (Casper, 1976) claim the courts have added a more independent and innovative input into public policy. For the 1960s and '70s, the latter view seems reasonable. But this does not mean that the former view is inaccurate for our history as a whole. Perhaps a middle-of-the-road judgment is most accurate (if not very exciting). The courts can sometimes push national policy and opinion in a few substantive areas. But in most areas they are pushed and limited by the same forces and context that push and limit the government and society as a whole.

Some forces, such as the weight of precedent and long tenure for justices, favor slow change in the content of decisions. Yet the Supreme Court does make major changes in its policy stances. Thus, the Warren Court of the 1950s and 60s became known as a pioneer in both racial integration and constitutional rights for criminal suspects. But, typically, it was replaced by the more conservative Burger Court. The new Court was likely to make relatively small changes in existing decisions. But small changes can, of course, add up to significant change overall. In the 1980s, the Supreme Court began making selected changes in the liberal doctrines of the past but did not move as quickly and uniformly to the right as some had predicted, hoped, or feared.

CONCLUSIONS

In this chapter we focused on the federal courts, particularly the Supreme Court, as both governing and political institutions. They are also legal institutions. That, however, does not set them apart from the other organs of government. These other organs also deal with making and interpreting law on a daily basis. This overview of the courts leads to several general conclusions:

1 Courts resolve conflicts through special legal procedures and special doctrines called law. Their functions, though, are also profoundly political.

2 There are many courts, all with some policy importance. The Supreme Court is the most constantly visible in part because it has the most policy importance. But it does not have a monopoly on judicial policymaking.

3 Courts have become involved in a vast range of social policies. Therefore, their potential for impact has grown over time.

4 The politics of bargaining, small-group decision making, and influence seeking characterize the be-

havior of persons in and around the federal court system. Judges bargain with each other individually. And courts collectively interact with the president, bureaucrats, legislators, and interest groups in arriving at decisions.

5 Courts are responsive, in the long run, to broad trends of public opinion. The content of court decisions changes over time. It often follows changes in dominant public opinion and successful political coalitions. The weight of precedent helps slow change but does not prevent it.

6 Court opinions on fundamental policy issues are often unclear. The phrases judges use and interpret are as imprecise as the phrases in presidential speeches and acts of Congress.

7 There is no correct answer to the question of how active courts should be. That question itself is a matter of ongoing political debate and will never be settled.

FURTHER READING

ABRAHAM, HENRY J. (1984) The Judicial Process, 5th ed. New York: Oxford University Press. An examination of decision making in U.S. courts, especially the Supreme Court, with comparative materials on courts in Great Britain, the Soviet Union, and France.

BAUM, LAWRENCE (1985) The Supreme Court. 2d ed. Washington, D.C.: Congressional Quarterly Press. An assessment of the policymaking function of the Supreme Court.

GOLDMAN, SHELDON, and THOMAS P. JAHNIGE (1985) The Federal Courts as a Political System. 3d ed. New York: Harper & Row. An in-depth examination of the federal courts, including district courts and courts of appeal.

WOODWARD, BOB, and SCOTT ARMSTRONG (1979) The Brethren: Inside the Supreme Court. New York: Simon & Schuster. An "inside" look at decision making in the Supreme Court, 1969–1976.

PART 5

Political Processes
and Public Policy

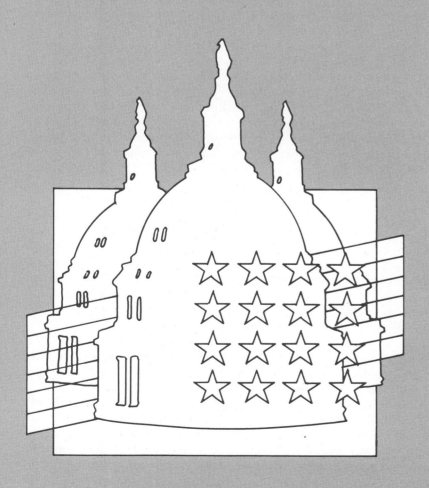

13
Liberties
and Rights

As dawn broke over the white-pillared U.S. Supreme Court one day last week, more than 100 spectators were already clustered on the granite steps, huddled in bed rolls or stamping their feet to ward off the autumn chill. By midmorning the crowd had doubled and doubled again, stretching across the court plaza all the way to First Street. Photographers maneuvered to capture celebrities as they arrived, including Senators Robert Griffin and Thomas Eagleton, and Mrs. Earl Warren, widow of the Chief Justice who presided over the historic school desegregation decision of 1954. As the crowds pressed forward, young demonstrators waved picket signs and chanted slogans.

Inside the court, every seat was taken by the time the principals began arriving. Archibald Cox, Harvard law professor, former solicitor general and special Watergate prosecutor, was resplendent in black cutaway, striped tie and a matching grey crew cut. So was Wade McCree, in the solicitor general's traditional morning coat. At precisely 10 that Wednesday morning, the court clerk intoned "Oyez, oyez," and the nine black-robed Justices suddenly appeared from behind red velvet curtains and settled into their seats at the elevated bench. The stage was set for what could turn out to be the most important civil rights case in a generation, *Regents of the University of California* v. *Allan Bakke*.

Time, October 24, 1977, p. 95. Copyright 1977 Time Inc. All rights reserved. Reprinted by permission from TIME.

* * * * *

Thus began an account of the oral argument before the U.S. Supreme Court of a case that raised a thorny issue: What measures can public institutions constitutionally take to redress the effects of past discrimination against racial minorities. Can these institutions act positively in favor of such minorities now? Or is that constitutionally banned discrimination too?

The Bakke case was only one event—one that attracted a great deal of attention, to be sure—in an ongoing fight over defining minority rights and their limits. It, and thousands of other events in the history of that process, were enmeshed in politics. Liberties and rights in this country are all matters of political debate and political decision.

The framers of the Constitution, in the preamble, stated reasons for forming this nation. Among the expected benefits of the new government were "justice" and "the blessings of liberty." Federal courts play a central role in defining the meaning of *justice* and *liberty*. Those terms are constantly changing with changing times. In earlier chapters we showed how certain ideas of liberty and justice were part of the philosophy of the early settlers. We looked at how our

Bakke becomes a doctor. Allan Bakke graduates from medical school in 1982. He was admitted to medical school only because of a Supreme Court ruling that he had been discriminated against in favor of less qualified minority candidates for admission.

430

basic beliefs impinge on the changing meanings of liberty and justice. We examined how various freedoms and liberties have waxed and waned as our political culture developed. We looked at how all our basic government institutions are involved in defining and maintaining rights and liberties. And we looked at how nongovernment actors such as interest groups play a role, too.

We will pay much attention to court decisions in this chapter. But those decisions alone are only one set of events in a broader political debate.

Our whole history has been marked by political debate and controversy over what civil liberties mean. In recent years there has been special focus on minority—racial, ethnic, and sexual—liberties that are called civil rights. In the last few decades, the debate—in and out of the courts—has focused on the concepts of *personal rights* and *equality.* In looking at personal rights, we will focus on free speech and assembly, free press, freedom of religion, privacy, and crime and punishment. In dealing with equality, we will examine aspects of racial, sexual, and political equality. We will also look at limits placed on some impacts of economic inequalities.

This chapter is not a complete catalog of liberties and rights. Neither is it a history of them. Nor is it an analysis of all the twists and turns of legal doctrine. The chapter is an attempt to deal with some important liberties and rights that have been matters of political debate in the last few decades and will, in various forms, continue to be debated. We will look at a bit of historical context when essential; we will refer to a few of the leading legal doctrines. But, above all, our intent is to give you a sense of how liberties and rights result from political processes. They are subjects of controversy and can and do change over time. They are dynamic, not static.

Four major sections follow. First, we briefly set the context for understanding liberties and rights in this nation. Second, we explore some personal rights. Third, we look at aspects of equality. Fourth, we offer a few brief thoughts on the future of our liberties and rights.

Opposition to Bakke's claim. Demonstrators in Detroit oppose Bakke's position that it is unconstitutional to give preference to minorities in matters such as admission to professional schools. The Court admitted Bakke but also left room for affirmative action programs.

THE CONTEXT OF LIBERTIES AND RIGHTS

The general nature of liberties and rights

Rights and *liberties* are two terms used a great deal in political debate. In general, in the United States, a *liberty* (also called a civil liberty) is some act or class of acts that cannot be infringed on by governments. Right is the stronger term. In a broad sense, it includes more than just the common modern meaning of civil rights for minorities. It is a claim, ideally backed by law and government action, to certain protections, guarantees, or benefits. Government is not only barred from interfering with rights; it also, ideally, is obliged to obtain and guard these rights and to prevent others from limiting them. So free speech is both a liberty and a right. It is a liberty because governments cannot, in principle, interfere with it. But it is also a right because government has to stop nongov-

ernment actors from interfering with it. Backers of abortion argue that women should have the liberty to control their own bodies. When they have argued that such liberty should become a right, fierce political debate has ensued. Government protection of a right to abortion can take several forms. It can be court decisions that make it unconstitutional for states to prevent abortions. (Those women who can afford abortions can have them.) Or it can make government pay for abortions for women who cannot afford them.

The definition and protection of both liberties and rights are very special in most societies, especially so in ones that see themselves as "open" and want to remain so. The United States prides itself on being open, free, and democratic. So a broad range of liberties and rights must be defined and maintained, even in the face of challenge.

Liberties and rights are of special and paramount importance in the United States. But that neither says they are absolute nor that they do not change, either by being narrowed or by being broadened. As with other political issues, their meaning is always shifting; and they are subject to constant pressures from many directions and actors as real instances of definition, protection, expansion, or restriction arise. Liberties and rights are immersed in politics.

Competing claims cause controversies and debates over specific liberties and rights. Sometimes both sides make plausible moral arguments. In the late 1970s in the largely Jewish suburb of Skokie, Ill., the American Nazi party wanted to hold a parade. The residents of Skokie, some of whom had survived the Holocaust in Europe, opposed granting the parade permit on very solid moral grounds. The Nazis and their lawyers, joined by the American Civil Liberties Union, made a competing moral claim. Free speech means allowing even the most vile points of view to be expressed. (And the parade was viewed to be a symbolic act equivalent to speech.) The courts upheld the Nazis' right to a permit.

Or take the case of obscenity. Local governments and citizens can make a plausible case: "adult" book stores and movie theaters near residential areas are threats to the morals of their children. The store and theater owners can also make a case: their activities and businesses are protected by the First Amendment guarantees of free speech and by extension, free expression. There is a benefit in banning smut-pushers from the neighborhood, but that benefit must be balanced against the value of the right of free expression. Rights, in theory, are not subject to balances or limitations supported by the will of the majority. In practice, however, courts do balance them and approve some limitations.

In many cases, of course, the moral and even constitutional arguments are just window dressing for other interests, often economic. Pornographers are not likely to be civil libertarians but are instead out to make quick bucks. Segregationists bitterly opposed the expansion of rights for blacks in a host of ways. They often used "moral" claims based on how they interpreted freedom of association. (That is, they only wanted to associate with whites in certain activities.) This counterbalanced the claims of blacks and their allies that equality went across color lines. Segregationist claims were often based on a mixture of economic motives and strong fear and hatred. They feared, in the end, economic competition from a newly upwardly mobile black community. And they simply disliked blacks, at least those claiming to be equal.

It is wise to be skeptical of moral assertions. One should not swallow whole moral platitudes issued by either side in a controversy over rights and liberties. Neither side wants to compromise its view of its own "rights and liberties." In fact, in the normal way of doing political business in our nation, compromise is usually the solution to controversies. And, as in other areas, one day's compromise becomes the next day's controversy. Argument quickly breaks out that may well lead to yet another compromise. This does not mean, of course, that there is anything inevitable about expanding rights and liberties. They can also be diminished and sometimes are. Contending forces push in many directions and have varying strength at different times. And government, inevitably a participant and sometimes a referee in such controversies, will itself take different positions at different times. The same is true of the courts.

The relation of the federal government to liberties and rights

All parts of the federal government—not just courts—are involved in defining rights and liberties in the abstract and, more important, in practice. They can all threaten rights and liberties; they can all expand them; or they can bargain and negotiate compromises.

Ideally, of course, the government should protect rights and liberties. But government can also violate them. It has used the Federal Bureau of Investigation (FBI), the Internal Revenue Service (IRS), and other agencies to spy on American citizens; this has been done in blatantly illegal and highly offensive ways from the post–World War II period up until the last few years. (We make the happy assumption the activities have stopped, but that may be inaccurate.) This spying was ordered by presidents, carried out by bureaucrats, and probably known about and approved by some members of Congress.

The government also put about 110,000 people of Japanese ancestry (two thirds of them U.S. citizens) in what amounted to concentration camps for most of World War II. Here, there was nothing secret. It was ordered by President Franklin Roosevelt and carried out by many federal and state authorities. It was approved by the vast majority of Congress in legislation that gave the president power to take such action. And it was finally sanctioned by the courts in decisions on suits brought by those affected. The government's claims were powerful enough to convince even Supreme Court justices noted for their de-

Court-approved violation of civil rights. Japanese-Americans arrive at an inland relocation camp in 1942 after being removed from the West Coast. The Supreme Court found the removal constitutional in 1944.

votion to civil liberties. Hugo Black, usually a friend of civil liberties in his 34 years on the Court (1937–71), delivered the opinion in the case of *Korematsu* v. *United States* (1944). (Korematsu was an American citizen convicted for failure to leave as ordered.)

> It is said that we are dealing here with the case of imprisonment of a citizen in a concentration camp solely because of his ancestry, without evidence or inquiry concerning his loyalty and good disposition towards the United States. . . . Regardless of the true nature of the assembly and relocation centers—and we deem it unjustifiable to call them concentration camps with all the ugly connotations that term implies—we are dealing specifically with nothing but an exclusion order. To cast this case into outlines of racial prejudice, without reference to the real military dangers which were presented, merely confuses the issue. . . . Congress, reposing its confidence in this time of war in our military leaders—as inevitably it must—determined that they should have the power to do just this [that is, exclude people of Japanese ancestry and concentrate them away from the West Coast].

Robert Jackson, one of the justices who dissented, pointed out that *only* those of Japanese ancestry were excluded (despite citizenship). German or Italian aliens were not excluded, nor were citizens convicted of treason but out on parole. West Coast whites eagerly seized Japanese-American property at ridiculously low prices. This revealed, no doubt, one of the side benefits of the action from the point of view of the majority of residents.

There are similar examples of the government restricting rights. Congress passed the Sedition Act in the 1790s. Midnight deportations were arranged by the attorney general during the "red scare" just after World War I.

States and localities have an equally spotty record. After all, state law in the South was what officially kept blacks "in their place" for so long.

Governments, of course, are not the only threat to liberties and rights. Private individuals and groups often infringe on each other. Ku Klux Klan members used to lynch black men for alleged rapes of white women. Right and wrong are not hard for most of us to see in such an incident. But a group of feminist protesters closing a theater showing pornographic movies is a more complex example. Many of us can sympathize and support the feminist view. We would agree that films portraying women in a subservient, "sexual plaything" role are disgusting and also reinforce dangerous stereotypes. On the other hand, the precedent of letting any group prevent some other group from engaging in "free expression" is very disturbing. Suppose a church or the "moral majority" demands that theaters showing movies with explicit sexual themes be closed. What if they make that demand by forcibly preventing entry into the theater? Or suppose the same crowd enters a library or a school textbook warehouse and destroys books it finds offensive—those on evolution, for instance. The point is that your own values help you to identify "good" and "bad" persons in such situations. But ultimate "right" and "wrong" in the sense of protecting a free society are harder to pinpoint.

The government is not always committed to the expansion and protection of rights. The desired role for all parts of the federal government can be seen as:

Refraining from actions that threaten rights and liberties.

Preventing other governments (states and localities) from engaging in such actions.

Conferring and supporting specific rights and liberties by positive action.

Protecting people against the actions of others that restrict rights and liberties.

In some ways the Supreme Court—some of the time—has played a special role in defining liberties and rights. But, as noted in Chapter 12, the Court cannot guarantee that other actors will adopt their view in practice. Some have suggested that the federal courts should pay special heed to the claims of disadvantaged groups—the poor and racial or ethnic minorities. This view may be attractive in many ways, but it is controversial. Under Chief Justice Earl Warren, the Court did, in fact, play some part of this role. The Court under Warren Burger has retreated from it. Even when the Supreme Court chooses this role, the disadvantaged must still fight for their causes in many political arenas. Reliance on the courts alone is not a wise strategy. The courts are weak reeds in terms of power. And they are inconsistent in terms of doctrine.

The "Red scare." This cartoon attacks Attorney General A. Mitchell Palmer for arranging mass deportations of suspected radicals in 1919. The rights of those deported received no protection.

Local government units threaten free speech. Books recently banned or under attack by various school boards.

Liberties, rights, and the general policy process

Though liberties and rights are special in some senses, both involve *policy* and the *allocation of values*. Individuals and groups argue and fight over these and—some of the time—reach compromises thought to be workable at least for the time being. The meanings of rights and liberties expand and contract, in line with some of the general policy patterns and processes discussed in subsequent chapters.

The actors who determine the meaning of liberties and rights are numerous. The large role given courts and lawyers is somewhat different, but only in degree. Courts and lawyers are involved in many policy areas. And many non-legal and nonjudicial actors are involved in defining rights and liberties—interest groups, bureaucracies, Congress, the president, state and local governments, and the general public.

PERSONAL RIGHTS: THE MEANING OF A FREE SOCIETY

Free speech, press, assembly, and petition

In part, the First Amendment says that "Congress shall make no law . . . abridging the freedom of speech, or of the press; or of the right of the people peaceably to assemble, and to petition the Government for a redress of grievances." What has this prohibition come to mean in practice? Let's look first at the general meaning attached by the Supreme Court to freedom of speech. We include instances in which "national security" is claimed. Second, we will look briefly at obscenity as a specific form of speech or expression. It, too, has claims to some protection. Third, we will look at freedom of the press and what it means in practice.

The general meaning and pattern of protection for speech The First Amendment puts limits on government action. It encompasses *almost* any kind of expression that can be imagined: public speeches, private conversation, printed materials of all kinds, and radio and television broadcasts. It also includes picketing and demonstrating, wearing armbands and buttons, slogans on car license plates, and artistic presentations and entertainment of all kinds. It has also been extended to apply to the creation and maintenance of political organizations, questions involving loyalty oaths and other programs aimed against subversion, and the right to travel abroad freely. However, the definition of speech does not include *all* expression. In 1982, the Supreme Court excluded pornography involving children from protection under the First Amendment. The Court hasn't ever held that all speech is absolutely protected under all conditions, and has upheld a number of restrictions as constitutionally approved.

The Supreme Court has applied the doctrine that the 14th Amendment—aimed explicitly at the states—includes guarantees in the Bill of Rights; these originally applied only to the national government. The Court has applied most of those guarantees one at a time under the doctrine of **selective incorporation.** The First Amendment prohibition against government action "abridging the freedom of speech" was extended to state and local governments in 1925. Only then did the Court begin to strike down government actions in this area.

The Court has sought a doctrine of when speech can be suppressed and when it can proceed unhampered. The first attempt at a general doctrine came in 1919;

the Court declared that speech could be restricted if it created "a clear and present danger" that "substantive evils that Congress has a right to prevent" would be brought about. In a 1927 case, the Court elaborated: "In order to support a finding of clear and present danger it must be shown either that immediate serious violence was to be expected or was advocated, or that past conduct furnished reason to believe that such advocacy was then contemplated." In short, the Court looked for a link between speech and action that could be banned. Merely supporting ideas was not enough to restrict speech; there had to be a great likelihood that illegal or violent action would follow.

The doctrine of clear and present danger has had to be interpreted case by case. Over time the Court added a second concept; society's interests in guarding free speech had to be "balanced" against society's interests in preventing unwanted or illegal action. This doctrine was used, for instance, in a 1972 case. The Court ruled that a newspaper reporter could not refuse to appear before a grand jury investigating crime because the reporter wanted to protect confidential sources vital to news gathering. The Court stated that the social interest in investigating crime was greater than the social interest in guarding the reporter's sources.

In assessing limits on speech in the name of "national security" or preventing "subversion," the Court has restrained the government. But it has rarely branded such activity as totally unconstitutional. Thus, it upheld federal statutes banning membership in the communist party, forbidding support for overthrow of the government by force and violence, and requiring the communist party to file membership lists. At the same time, it has imposed limits making it either very hard or impossible to enforce the statutes.

Likewise, the Supreme Court has upheld federal security programs. But it has required fairly strict safeguards during implementation. Statutes designed to prevent "subversives" from traveling abroad by denying them a U.S. passport have not been overturned directly; instead they have been interpreted to make them largely unenforceable.

The Court has also shied away from direct confrontation with Congress over inquiries into subversive activities. Here again, though, it has set some limits on what congressional committees can do.

In dealing with state statutes, inquiries, and loyalty and security programs aimed at subversion, the Supreme Court has not only imposed procedural requirements but has also felt freer to rule some of these statutes and activities unconstitutional.

In another area—criticism of public officials—the Supreme Court has effectively developed a doctrine that people are almost immune from libel or slander prosecution for anything they say or write about public officials.

"THAT'S TO TAKE CARE OF OBSCENITY CASES"

Obscenity   Government limits on the publication and distribution of material alleged to be obscene or pornographic offer another example in which doctrine has been unclear. Decisions have wavered between allowing restrictions and ruling them unconstitutional.

The Supreme Court first addressed the issue in 1957. In the *Roth* case, the justices agreed that obscene materials were not protected by the First Amendment. They defined "obscene material" as that "which deals with sex in a manner appealing to prurient interest." If the average person, applying contemporary community standards, found that the main theme of the material taken as a whole appealed to prurient interests, then the material was not constitutionally

What's pornography? What can be banned? Pickets with opposing views in Chicago. Courts often have to rule on such conflicting values.

protected. This standard was open to all kinds of interpretation. The Court, though, was generally reluctant to use it to support censorship until the mid-1960s.

In 1966, the Supreme Court further confused its own doctrine by moving in two directions at once. It became more restrictive in two ways. It made the motives of those selling allegedly obscene material a factor. And it ruled that material designed specifically to appeal to the prurient interests of sexual deviants was not constitutionally protected. It became more liberal, though, by ruling that if the material had *any* redeeming social value, then the Constitution protected it.

In 1973, the Supreme Court chose the more conservative path on obscenity. But it still left confusion about what its decisions would mean in future cases. In the case of *Miller* v. *California,* the Court defined "hard-core pornography," which was not constitutionally protected, in three steps:

1. Whether the average person, applying contemporary standards, would find that the work, taken as a whole, appeals to prurient interests.
2. Whether the work, taken as a whole, lacks serious literary, artistic, political, or scientific value.
3. Whether the work depicts or describes, in a patently offensive way, sexual conduct specifically defined by the applicable state law.

The Court explicitly endorsed the idea that different states and localities could apply different standards: "It is neither realistic nor constitutionally sound to read the First Amendment as requiring that the people of Maine or Mississippi accept public depiction of conduct found tolerable in Las Vegas or New York City. . . . People in different states vary in their tastes and attitudes, and this diversity is not to be strangled by the absolutism of imposed uniformity."

Adding to the already great confusion, the Court gave examples of material that might be repressed: "patently offensive representations or descriptions of ultimate sexual acts, normal or perverted, actual or simulated, or patently offensive representations or descriptions of masturbation, excretory functions, and lewd exhibition of the genitals."

Despite the thrashing about of the Court in this area, there is evidence that the pronouncements have had little impact on those dealing with such material. Enforcement of these vague statements has been uneven, largely because the statements are vague. Perhaps Justice Potter Stewart gave the real rule the justices were using in a concurring opinion in a 1964 case. He agreed that neither he nor the Court might ever be able to offer a single understandable definition of hard-core pornography. But, he said, "I know it when I see it."

Free press In protecting the press from censorship, the Supreme Court has generally reacted negatively to what the justices see as "prior restraint." In 1971, the *New York Times* and the *Washington Post* secured copies of the so-called *Pentagon Papers;* these contained secret information on the war in Vietnam. The federal government tried to block publication, claiming that national security would be compromised. The court ruled in favor of the newspapers by a vote of 6 to 3. The newspapers were allowed to publish the material. But the doctrine under which the decision was made was less than clear. All nine justices wrote their own opinions. Six agreed with the overall position of the newspapers; three agreed with the government. But the justices disagreed on many

Pentagon Papers. Dr. Daniel Ellsberg, who gave secret material to the *New York Times.* The federal government tried to halt publication but the Supreme Court ruled against the government.

Television coverage of trials? Which value should prevail: the media's right to cover public proceedings or the accused persons' right to privacy? Here a California murder trial takes place with cameras in the courtroom.

points of doctrine. Most in the majority also noted that in some circumstances they might approve prior restraint.

A good example of the Court seeming to stress different meanings of the free press clause can be seen in two recent decisions. The earlier one is generally thought to be restrictive. The later one is generally hailed as reversing trends toward restriction and perhaps even creating a new right.

In the case of *Gannett* v. *De Pasquale* (1979), the Court ruled that representatives of the press had no right to attend a pretrial hearing on evidence. If the judge and the lawyers for both sides agreed to it, such exclusion was allowed. The case was decided 5 to 4. But no single opinion was signed by all five justices in the majority. There were several majority opinions and all used somewhat different reasoning.

There was a general outcry in the press against this ruling. Later, Chief Justice Burger gave an interview in which he stressed his own view: this ruling did not apply to trials themselves. A large number of trial court judges had begun to close trials after the Court ruling in Gannett; Burger was suggesting they were wrong to do so. Justice Lewis Powell made public comments in the same vein. He had voted with the majority in the Gannett case, but he said that the press may have an independent First Amendment right to attend trials.

In 1980, the Court ruled in the case of *Richmond Newspapers, Inc.* v. *Virginia.* This time it did hold, 7 to 1, that the press has a First Amendment right to attend trials. Chief Justice Burger, speaking for the Court, said "We hold that the right to attend criminal trials is implicit in the guarantees of the First Amendment." Justice John Paul Stevens, in a concurring opinion, said he thought the Court had created a new right under the First Amendment. It was a right not just to make information public (upheld in the *Pentagon Papers* case) but also to collect it. Some newspaper columnists were quick to underscore this claim. But a more sober judgment was given in another concurring opinion by Justice Potter Stewart: "This does not mean that the First Amendment right of members of the public and representatives of the press to attend civil and criminal trials is absolute. Just as a legislature may impose reasonable time, place and manner restrictions upon the exercise of First Amendment freedoms, so may a trial judge impose reasonable limitations upon the unrestricted occupation of a courtroom by representatives of the press and members of the public."

Religion

The First Amendment also says, "Congress shall make no law respecting an establishment of religion, or prohibiting the free exercise thereof." As with the guarantees of speech, press, assembly, and petition, the provisions on religion have been interpreted to apply to all levels of government. Note that there are two provisions: governments cannot "establish" religions (that is, they cannot give state aid to create state favoritism); and they cannot restrict its free exercise. The intent of the framers was to keep government neutral on matters of religion, neither to support nor restrict it.

In practice the deceptively simple language of the Constitution on establishment can have many interpretations. It has been interpreted to approve and to disapprove various forms of public aid to religious schools. When the Supreme Court has approved such aid in the form of free busing, textbooks, and public health measures for students at religious schools, it has argued that these children as individuals are the objects of the programs. They, not the religious institutions, benefit. In 1983, the Court approved a Minnesota statute that allowed parents of students in both public and private schools, including church schools, to deduct some costs of education from their state income tax returns.

A federal district judge ruled in 1982 Arkansas was unconstitutionally promoting religion. The ruling involved a law requiring balanced treatment in the classroom of evolution and creationism. The judge concluded that the latter had no scientific merit; state intervention on its behalf "was simply and purely an effort to introduce the biblical version of creation into the public school curricula."

In March 1984, the Supreme Court ruled that the city of Pawtucket, Rhode Island, could fund a public nativity scene at Christmas without violating the establishment clause. Chief Justice Burger, writing for the five-justice majority, said that such a scene did not endorse a specific religion; but it "engenders a friendly community spirit of good will in keeping with the season."

Justice Brennan, joined by three other justices, dissented vigorously, saying, in part:

> Contrary to the Court's suggestion, the crèche is far from a mere representation of a "particular historic religious event." It is, instead, best understood as a mystical re-creation of an event that lies at the heart of Christian faith. To suggest, as the Court does, that such a symbol is merely "traditional" and therefore no different from Santa's house or reindeer is not only offensive to those for whom the crèche has profound significance, but insulting to those who insist for religious or personal reasons that the story of Christ is in no sense a part of "history" nor an unavoidable element of our national "heritage."

SUPREME COURT OF THE UNITED STATES

No. 82–1256

DENNIS LYNCH, ETC., ET AL., PETITIONERS *v.*
DANIEL DONNELLY ET AL.

ON WRIT OF CERTIORARI TO THE UNITED STATES COURT OF
APPEALS FOR THE FIRST CIRCUIT

[March 5, 1984]

THE CHIEF JUSTICE delivered the opinion of the Court.
We granted certiorari to decide whether the Establishment Clause of the First Amendment prohibits a municipality
from including a crèche, or Nativity scene, in its annual
Christmas display.

I

Each year, in cooperation with the downtown retail merchants' association, the City of Pawtucket, Rhode Island,
erects a Christmas display as part of its observance of the
Christmas holiday season. The display is situated in a park
owned by a nonprofit organization and located in the heart of
the shopping district. The display is essentially like those to
be found in hundreds of towns or cities across the Nation—
The

Constitutional crèche. The Pawtucket display that won a stamp of approval from the Supreme Court and the first page of the Court's majority opinion in the case.

A 1980 case involved New York State reimbursement to private schools, including religious ones, for certain educational tasks. The Court upheld the state
program by a 5 to 4 vote. Justice Byron White wrote the majority opinion, and
he was unusually candid about the fuzzy nature of the issues:

> This is not to say that this case, any more than past cases, will furnish a litmus-
> paper test to distinguish permissible from impermissible aid to religiously ori-
> ented schools. But Establishment Clause cases are not easy; they stir deep feel-
> ings; and we are divided among ourselves, perhaps reflecting the different views
> on this subject of the people of this country. What is certain is that our decisions
> have tended to avoid categorical imperatives and absolutist approaches at either

end of the range of possible outcomes. This course sacrifices clarity and predictability for flexibility.

The Supreme Court has ruled that religious observances and instruction may not take place on public school property. But students may be released from school to go to such rites and classes elsewhere. In 1962, the Court ruled that public prayers and Bible reading in public schools were an unconstitutional breach of the wall that theoretically divides church and state. Since that ruling, there has been continuous controversy. It shows few signs of abating. In fact, school boards and teachers intent on prayer have devised many local practices to evade the Court's ruling.

School prayer. Despite Supreme Court rulings school children, including these in Boston, pray in the public schools. One child who chooses not to pray remains seated at her desk.

Both sides demonstrate. Anti-abortion and pro-abortion rallies in Washington. Addressing the pro-choice rally is U.S. Representative Pat Schroeder of Colorado.

Privacy and abortion

The Constitution does not mention privacy as such; it does contain implicit references. In 1965, a constitutional right to privacy was first proclaimed by the Supreme Court. Since then, the courts have spelled out their interpretation of this right (Grossman and Wells, 1980: 1315–25). One of the most controversial applications came in 1973 when the Court voted 7 to 2 to prevent any state from making abortion illegal. Since that time, there have been other court decisions, and much legislative action, both in Congress and the states. Much of

---

THE DEVELOPMENT OF THE ABORTION ISSUE, 1973–1983

January 22, 1973 The Supreme Court (in *Roe* v. *Wade*) rules that abortion must be legal nationwide and that facilities cannot be restricted.

July 1, 1976 The Supreme Court rules that husbands cannot veto abortions by their wives and that parents cannot veto abortions by unmarried daughters.

September 30, 1976 Congress passes the Hyde Amendment. It is a strict restriction on the use of federal medicaid money for abortions.

October 22, 1976 A federal district judge (John Dooling) rules that the Hyde Amendment is unconstitutional.

June 20, 1977 The Supreme Court rules that states have no legal obligation to pay for "nontherapeutic" abortions. The Court does not define that term, though.

June 29, 1977 The Supreme Court tells Judge Dooling to restudy his decision in light of the June 20 decision. The congressional spending restriction resumes in August.

July 2, 1979 The Supreme Court opens the door for states to require either parental consent *or* an alternative procedure (such as consent of a judge) in abortions for unmarried minor females.

January 15, 1980 After many months of elaborate proceedings, Judge Dooling again declares the Hyde Amendment unconstitutional.

June 30, 1980 The Supreme Court reverses Judge Dooling's decision. It holds the Hyde Amendment constitutional. In doing so it says that neither the federal government nor the states are obliged to pay for any abortions, even those that are medically necessary.

June 15, 1983 The Supreme Court, by a vote of 6 to 3, reaffirms its 1973 decision. The three youngest justices dissent; restriction is supported by the Solicitor General of the United States, an official of the Reagan administration.

June 28, 1983 The Senate, by a vote of 49 to 50, defeats a proposed constitutional amendment stating that "the right to an abortion is not secured by this constitution." (Passage of the amendment would have required a two-thirds favorable vote.)

Source: Adapted from the *New York Times*, July 1, 1980, for events through 1980. © by *The New York Times Company*. Reprinted by permission. Updated by authors.

the controversy has focused on public funding for abortions, which no doubt helps increase abortion rates among poor women (Hansen, 1980). Abortion is an issue that involves all branches and levels of government, as well as vigorous interest groups on both sides.

In June 1980, the Court decided by a 5 to 4 vote that poor women have no constitutional right to public funding for abortions. Congress's ban on federal funding of most abortions was upheld. In a companion case, a state ban was also found constitutional. The members of the Court, in their opinions, disagreed strongly and explicitly over the constitutional and social meaning of their ruling.

In June 1983, the Supreme Court again spoke, this time in a 6 to 3 opinion. It struck down a specific city ordinance in Akron, Ohio, dealing with abortion. More important, the majority specifically and unequivocally endorsed the general principle of the 1973 decision:

> These cases come to us a decade after we held in *Roe* v. *Wade* that the right of privacy, grounded in the concept of personal liberty guaranteed by the Constitution, encompasses a woman's right to decide whether to terminate her pregnancy. Legislative responses to the Court's decision have required us on several occasions, and again today, to define the limits of a state's authority to regulate the performance of abortions. And arguments continue to be made, in these cases as well, that we erred in interpreting the Constitution. Nonetheless, the doctrine of *stare decisis* [that precedent should be sustained], while perhaps never entirely persuasive on a constitutional question, is a doctrine that demands respect in a society governed by the rule of law. We respect it today, and reaffirm *Roe* v. *Wade*.

Crime and punishment

The Bill of Rights details the rights of suspects or accused persons. The framers spelled out a number of guarantees. These safeguards had developed in English law and were embedded in the Constitution. The Fourth Amendment prohibits "unreasonable searches and seizures." The Fifth Amendment prohibits trying a person twice for the same crime and protects against self-incrimination. The Sixth Amendment guarantees jury trial and representation by an attorney. And the Eighth Amendment prohibits "cruel and unusual punishments." Over the years the Supreme Court has also ruled that under the 14th Amendment these guarantees at the federal level, and some others, as well, apply equally to the states.

The Warren Court was very active in defining and extending the rights of suspects and accused persons. The Burger Court has modified a number of those rulings in a more conservative direction. But it has not retreated completely to the pre-Warren doctrines. The best known of the Warren Court's decisions was in *Miranda* v. *Arizona* in 1966. The Court had earlier ruled that improperly seized material could not be used as evidence in state criminal trials. In this case, the Court disallowed confessions gained without proper protections:

> The prosecution may not use statements . . . stemming from custodial interrogation of the defendant unless it demonstrates the use of procedural safeguards effective to secure the privilege against self-incrimination. . . . Prior to any questioning, the person must be warned that he has a right to remain silent, that any statement he does make may be used as evidence against him, and that he has a

Chief figure in extension of rights to accused criminals. Ernesto Miranda was the plaintiff in the landmark case in which the Supreme Court broadly defined the rights of persons accused of crimes. In the last few years the Court has restricted those rights.

THE CLASH OF JUDICIAL OPINION: THE SUPREME COURT SPEAKS ON PUBLIC FUNDING OF ABORTIONS

Justice Potter Stewart for the majority

In *Roe* v. *Wade*, 1973, this Court held unconstitutional a Texas statute making it a crime to procure or attempt an abortion. But the Court in *Wade* also recognized that a state has legitimate interests during a pregnancy in both insuring the health of the mother and protecting potential human life.

The Hyde Amendment . . . places no governmental obstacle in the path of a woman who chooses to terminate her pregnancy, but rather, by means of unequal subsidization of abortion and other medical services, encourages alternative activity deemed in the public interest.

But, regardless of whether the freedom of a woman to choose to terminate her pregnancy for health reasons lies at the core or the periphery of the due process liberty recognized in *Wade* it simply does not follow that a woman's freedom of choice carries with it a constitutional entitlement to the financial resources to avail herself of the full range of protected choices. . . .

Although government may not place obstacles in the path of a woman's exercise of her freedom of choice, it need not remove those not of its own creation. Indigency falls in the latter category. The financial constraints that restrict an indigent woman's ability to enjoy the full range of constitutionally protected freedom of choice are the product not of governmental restrictions on access to abortions but rather of her indigency.

Although the liberty protected by the due process clause affords protection against unwarranted government interference with freedom of choice in the context of certain personal decisions, it does not confer an entitlement to such funds as may be necessary to realize all the advantages of that freedom. To hold otherwise would mark a drastic change in our understanding of the Constitution.

Justice Harry Blackmun, dissenting

There is condescension in the Court's holding "that she may go elsewhere for her abortion"; the Government punitively impresses upon a needy minority its own concepts of the socially desirable, the publicly acceptable and the morally sound. There truly is another world "out there," the existence of which the Court, I suspect, either chooses to ignore or fears to recognize.

Justice William Brennan, dissenting

The proposition for which these cases [earlier abortion decisions] stand thus is not that the State is under an affirmative obligation to ensure access to abortions for all who may desire them; it is that the State must refrain from wielding its enormous power and influence in a manner that might burden the pregnant woman's freedom to choose whether to have an abortion. The Hyde Amendment's denial of public funds for medically necessary abortions plainly intrudes upon this constitutionally protected decision, for both by design and in effect it serves to coerce indigent pregnant women to bear children that they would otherwise elect not to have.

[T]he Hyde Amendment is a transparent attempt by the Legislative Branch to impose the political majority's judgment of the morally acceptable and socially desirable preference on a sensitive and intimate decision that the Constitution entrusts to the individual. Worse yet, the Hyde Amendment does not foist that majoritarian viewpoint with equal measure upon everyone in our Nation, rich and poor alike; rather, it imposes that viewpoint only upon that segment of our society which, because of its position of political powerlessness, is least able to defend its privacy rights from the encorachments of state-mandated morality.

Source: from opinions delivered in the case of *Harris* v. *McRae* (1980).

right to the presence of an attorney, either retained or appointed. . . . If . . . he indicates in any manner and at any stage of the process that he wishes to consult with an attorney before speaking, there can be no questioning. Likewise, if the individual is alone and indicates in any manner that he does not wish to be interrogated, the police may not question him.

Decisions about what evidence may be used in a trial directly affect police behavior: Evidence obtained by illegal searches or intimidation of suspects cannot be used; police must therefore stop such activity or their work will be useless in court. Denying suspects the right to talk with an attorney is grounds for dismissing a case; police must thus take care to inform suspects of their rights.

More recently, the Court has also been concerned with the rights of prisoners. It has decided cases involving censorship of prisoners' mail, their access to legal materials and assistance, and protection when they are charged with violation of prison rules. In all these cases, it has strengthened prisoners' rights. It has not, though, always gone as far as advocates for the prisoners wished. A number of lower federal courts have gone further, ruling that overcrowded prisons are a direct violation of the Eighth Amendment provision against "cruel and unusual punishments."

The rights of suspects, prisoners, and accused criminals are like all other areas of the law: doctrine in any one case cannot provide full and complete answers to what the courts will do in later cases. The courts are engaged in political debate that is often masked in legal terminology.

Cases dealing with crime and police behavior are always sensitive political issues. They also stir passionate feelings on the part of the judges. For example, the Supreme Court ruled in 1979 that it was not unconstitutional to put two people detained before trial in a cell designed for one. Justice Thurgood Marshall dissented along with three colleagues. After the ruling he took the unusual step of criticizing his colleagues in public. He accused the majority of showing no sensitivity for defendants too poor to afford bail. He said they preferred "instead to provide us with such enduring legal homilies, as, 'There is no one man, one cell principle lurking in the due process clause.'" He added, "For a prisoner in jail, that ain't funny" (*New York Times,* May 28, 1979).

In 1972, the Supreme Court struck down the death penalty *as then applied* as "cruel and unusual punishment." But a majority of the justices were unwilling to say that the death penalty is unconstitutional in all cases. The Court struck down the mandatory death penalty and the penalty's application to rape. But it has allowed executions if the states provide for consideration of aggravating and mitigating circumstances and for thorough appeals in each case. The issue remains complex. Each state's laws are likely to be brought before the Court as the states seek to carry them out. The federal courts now virtually decide life and death for each individual sentenced to execution. And, just to complicate matters, murderers of white victims are much more likely (seven times more likely, according to a *New York Times* report of January 5, 1984) to be sentenced to death than the murderers of black victims. This may become a factor in future court decisions.

Sentenced to death. The U.S. Supreme Court has held that death sentences for first-degree murder which are *required* by state laws are unconstitutional. But the death penalty may still be imposed by judges in many states, as it was for this man waiting on death row in North Carolina's Central Prison for the U.S. Supreme Court to decide his fate.

EQUALITY: THE MEANING OF A JUST SOCIETY

What is equality? How much of it should there be and in what form? These are matters that involve both political and legal debate and controversy. The Constitution contains language at least implying that individuals should be treated equally (Grossman and Wells, 1980: 409–15). The 14th Amendment, adopted after the Civil War, was intended to protect the newly freed blacks from legal discrimination. It provides that no state can "deny to any person within its jurisdiction the equal protection of the laws." The phrase "equal protection of the laws" has become the basis for many legal debates. A number of important Supreme Court rulings have been based on it. Even though the 14th Amendment speaks of banning state action, it has been applied both to private action that requires state support and, through the 5th Amendment, to the federal government. The broader struggle over equality, of course, may involve the Supreme Court little or not at all. Instead, it involves contending political forces trying to get ratification of their own ideas of desirable equality versus desirable or at least allowable inequality. Each wants its views to be the basis of the law.

The following pages on equality, of necessity, only touch on a few aspects of this vital area. We deal first with some aspects of racial and ethnic equality. Second, we look at sexual equality. Third, we note one policy affecting political equality—"one person, one vote." Finally, we briefly address legal attention paid to the impact of economic inequalities on other matters.

Racial and ethnic equality

Our society has always made racial and ethnic distinctions in practice. Most often they have hurt minorities. Almost all minorities—especially those that are black, brown, yellow, or red—have been or still are subject to debilitating and shameful discrimination. All have also sought redress, and have often formed political movements to achieve their goals. The struggle for equality is long and painful. Success comes slowly and rarely does it come fully. Some oppressed minorities, especially blacks, have made special use of lawsuits, particularly those based on constitutional interpretation, in pressing their case. In the following sections, we can only allude to the general political struggle for equality by blacks and other minorities. Earlier chapters have drawn many examples from these political struggles. Here we will pay close attention to the legal and constitutional status of some aspects of equality for minorities.

In general, the Supreme Court is suspicious of classifications of people by race. It wants to give such classifications "strict scrutiny" when they appear; this simply means that the Court will examine the classifications with extra care. Yet other classifications (such as income for setting up tax brackets) only have to be "reasonable." Recall though, Court scrutiny of actions affecting the status of the 110,000 persons of Japanese ancestry living in the United States during World War II. It led the majority to approve their removal from their homes and relocation in what amounted to concentration camps. "Strict scrutiny," as with all invented legal phrases, has no magic protective powers. The Court is likely to alter its test to fit its desired results.

Black Americans   The Supreme Court has played both a formative and endorsing role in racial equality. It helped generate the government's agenda in dealing with racial discrimination in public education, other public facilities, and voting. It has since made legitimate wide-ranging federal statutes. These laws have aimed at banning discrimination in housing and employment as well as in education, public facilities, and voting.

The Court's role in public education is best known because of its dramatic decision of 1954 in *Brown* v. *Board of Education.* This decision held that an 1896 precedent approving separate but equal public facilities for blacks and whites was not applicable to education. The Court held that separateness in and of itself caused inequality. This decision had been anticipated a few years earlier

25th anniversary of *Brown* decision. Linda Brown, whose case led the Supreme Court to declare racial segregation in public schools unconstitutional in 1954, participates in ceremonies in 1979. With her is Benjamin Hooks, executive director of the National Association for the Advancement of Colored People, an organization that was the principal force behind the original lawsuit.

in cases involving graduate education and legal education. After the *Brown* decision, the Supreme Court ruled that discrimination based on race in a number of public facilities, such as swimming pools, beaches, and golf courses, was unconstitutional.

After the *Brown* decision, federal judges at all levels took action. They struck down various local schemes designed to delay or avoid true school desegregation. In many cases federal district judges became intimately involved in drafting and approving the details of desegregation plans.

As early as 1915 the Supreme Court began to rule against various attempts in southern states to keep blacks from voting. Congress began to act in this area in 1957. It strengthened federal protection of voting rights in subsequent years, particularly in the Voting Rights Act of 1965.

Congress passed major legislation in 1964 and 1968 attacking discrimination in public accommodations, employment, and housing. The Supreme Court has upheld the provisions of these acts that have been tested judicially.

Blacks' struggle for equality is, of course, a long and complicated story. The background of the *Brown* decision alone fills a large and fascinating volume (Kluger, 1976). Here we want to allude to only a few dimensions of recent government involvement—by both courts and other agencies. We will pay some attention to school desegregation in the South, to busing to achieve school integration in the North, and to affirmative action (what opponents label "reverse discrimination").

School desegregation in the south As mentioned, the *Brown* case had a long and complex history. After the decision, there was more waiting for something to happen. The Court spoke, but most southern school systems—the decision was, in effect, aimed at them—did little or nothing to comply. Many instead began deliberately to evade and stall. By 1964, only 2 percent of black children in southern schools attended class with whites.

In that year, Congress passed an important civil rights act after a struggle between highly visible and resourceful forces (see Sundquist, 1968: Chapter 6). President Lyndon Johnson was both the symbolic head and a very forceful participant in the drive for this legislation.

Among its many provisions, the Civil Rights Act of 1964 included Title VI: "No person in the United States shall, on the basis of race, color, or national origin, be excluded from participation in, denied the benefits of, or be subjected to discrimination under, any program or activity receiving federal financial assistance." Public schools received such assistance. Thus, the federal government now had an explicit weapon in pursuing the Court's decision of 10 years earlier; it could withdraw financial support.

For the first few years, major enforcement of Title VI in education came from the commissioner's office in the Office of Education (in the Department of Health, Education, and Welfare.) In 1967, though, an Office for Civil Rights (OCR) was formed in HEW (see Rabkin, 1980; and Bullock, 1980). Both the commissioner and OCR wrote broad regulations to apply Title VI prohibitions against racial discrimination in southern public schools. Then they moved swiftly to carry out those regulations. The target was clear. OCR did not need to rely on a field staff; it conducted few on-site inspections. Instead, it simply let figures and past history throughout the South suffice to prove discrimination. Efforts were either supported by Congress and the President or at least were not hampered. Local school systems were, predictably, often hostile; the weapon of cutting off federal funds was too strong to resist in most cases. It was also supplemented with additional pressures in some cases (Rodgers and Bullock, 1976).

The results of Title VI as implemented in southern systems are impressive. In 1964, as noted, more than 98 percent of black public school students attended all-black schools. By 1968, this figure had dropped to 68 percent. And by 1972, it had dropped to less than 9 percent. This change was achieved with some opposition. But it was done without massive nationwide controversy.

In 1983, the Supreme Court showed it was still concerned with upholding the notion that government action could not sanction racial discrimination in education. It ruled that the Internal Revenue Service properly denied tax-exempt status to Bob Jones University in South Carolina and to Goldsboro Christian Schools in North Carolina because both practiced discrimination.

Busing for the purpose of integration   OCR, the federal government, and the courts turned their attention to segregation in northern school systems (even though it had never been formally established by law). Here, they faced a much tougher battle. Now the political opposition—both government and public opinion—was much more widespread. The debate over desegregation orders often focused on busing to achieve integration. In 1971 the Supreme Court approved busing where other methods seemed not to work. The Court has not approved all specific instances, but has continued to approve many lower court orders that mandate busing. In 1982, the Court held that the people of Washington State could not prevent busing to achieve racial balance, as they had attempted through a statewide initiative and referendum. However, at the same time, the Court held that the City of Los Angeles could, again through a referendum of its citizens, retreat from a probusing policy that exceeded constitutional standards of nondiscrimination. The new policy in L.A. still met the federal standard. Busing remains politically controversial.

Perhaps even more important, demographic trends work against true racial integration in big cities in the North. There are two major factors: whites flee the cities; and birth rates for both blacks and Hispanics are high. Therefore, school systems in the North have increasingly fewer white children. Courts must approve or, more to the point, mandate busing schemes that cross municipal lines to encompass whole counties or metropolitan areas; otherwise, legal action to achieve integration seems doomed to fail (see Orfield, 1978). In 1974, in a Detroit case, the Supreme Court rejected such a plan—unless it could be shown that suburban districts also had discriminated against minorities. The Court has refused to disturb some cross-district busing plans in other cities. It has held, in short, that integration is not required by the Constitution, though racial discrimination is prohibited.

Affirmative action   One of the most controversial government policies in the 1970s was **affirmative action.** This is aimed at overcoming long-time discrimination against minorities and women. Those opposed called it **reverse discrimination.** White males made legal claims that such rules meant discrimination against them. The Supreme Court spoke—with somewhat mixed and unclear voices—in four cases in 1978, 1979, 1980, and 1984; these involved the relation of affirmative action programs to constitutionally defined equality.

In 1978, the Court decided the *Bakke* case. In effect, it made two rulings. The narrow ruling was that Bakke had been illegally barred from the University of California at Davis medical school because that school had explicitly set aside some of its slots only for minorities. Five justices took this view. At the same time, though, five justices stated that the Constitution permits some attention to race and past discrimination in forming affirmative action programs in higher education.

The *Bakke* decision was unclear in some ways and very narrow in its applications. It has had little impact on either government-set or university-adopted affirmative action programs. Explicit quotas for minorities are now generally avoided. But both federal institutions and various universities have found other ways to achieve the same ends. Ten months after the *Bakke* ruling, the HEW secretary said that, after a careful review of all HEW programs, only one small program for drug abusers had to be changed at all (*Washington Post*, April 22, 1979). The Davis medical school admitted Allan Bakke. It dropped formal racial quotas for minorities in its admissions procedures, but left room for considering race at all stages of the new admissions process.

In 1979, a year after the *Bakke* case, the Supreme Court decided the case of *United Steelworkers of America* v. *Weber*. It upheld 5 to 2 a voluntary affirmative action program sponsored jointly by a union and a company; the program was challenged by a white worker. This ruling was based on the majority interpretation of that part of the Civil Rights Act of 1964 forbidding racial discrimination. The majority concluded that the act did not ban this particular voluntary plan. But it did not set guidelines for future plans. Again it made it clear that, in effect, each plan would have to be tested on its own. This plan was designed "to eliminate a manifest racial imbalance," was temporary, and would not really hurt white workers in the Court's view. Therefore, it was not prohibited.

In 1980, the Court again upheld a consideration of race in trying to right past wrongs. Six to three, the Supreme Court ruled that Congress did not violate the Constitution when it passed a bill setting aside 10 percent of 1977 Public Works Employment Act funds for minority businesses. The majority said that "the Congress has not sought to give select minority groups a preferred standing in the construction industry, but has embarked on a remedial program to place them on a more equitable footing with respect to public contracting opportunities."

In June 1984, the Court, in a six to three decision warmly applauded by the Reagan Administration, ruled that seniority overweighed affirmative action in determining the order in which layoffs must occur. Since affirmative action programs mean that many of the minorities (and women) hired are likely to be the newest employees, this decision opened the way to some reestablishment of mostly white (and mostly male) groups of employees in some occupations and locations. The decision itself involved the fire department in Memphis.

Hispanic Americans and American Indians   Constitutional decisions by the courts involving two other large minorities—Hispanics and Native Americans—are not numerous. In one of those few rulings, the Supreme Court upheld the Bureau of Indian Affairs in giving Indians preference in hiring. It based the ruling on a congressional statute.

Blacks made use of the courts and lawsuits as a central strategy in their struggle for equality. Hispanics and American Indians have not relied as heavily on a legal strategy. In part, this may be because the discrimination they face is not usually written into law—at least not as often as it was for blacks. The political activities of leaders of these two ethnic minorities are, of course, visible. And they are of major importance as the nation continues to grapple with

Loser in "reverse discrimination" claim. Brian Weber at his place of employment. He claimed that a voluntary affirmative action program agreed on between his company and a union violated his constitutional rights, but his claim was rejected by the Supreme Court in a 1979 decision.

Direct action by American Indians. Indians have long relied more heavily on direct lobbying and direct action than on legal maneuvers as they have pursued grievances. The 1924 photo (*top*) shows Osage Indians seeking compensation for land with President Coolidge. The 1972 photo (*bottom*) was taken during an Indian takeover of the Bureau of Indian Affairs in Washington.

Pre-1982. A Mexican child receives instruction from a volunteer in El Paso because he was not allowed to enroll in the public schools. A 1982 Court decision required free public education for such children of illegal immigrants.

what equality means in a multiracial and multiethnic society (see Garcia and de la Garza, 1977; and Kickingbird and Kickingbird, 1977).

For Indians courts are active in determining their rights and benefits under old treaties, which are quite important to individual tribes. For example, the Supreme Court in 1980 awarded $105 million to the Sioux nation. But these cases do not involve constitutional questions about equality.

In 1982, the Court decided a case brought on behalf of Mexican children in Texas, although the principle established is not limited to Hispanics. In this case, the Court ruled 5 to 4 that children who are illegal aliens have a constitutionally protected right to free public education.

Asian Americans   There have long been many Americans of Chinese and Japanese descent. In recent years, a large number of Filipinos and Vietnamese have also come to this country. Discrimination against Chinese was tested in some Supreme Court cases in the late 1800s. The Court ruled at that time against blatantly discriminatory state or local action. But much discrimination never reached the courts and remained intact for a long time. A great deal of discrimination remains; it is probably most intense for the newest immigrants. Some of these groups are only starting to organize politically. Lawsuits thus far have not been central to their strategies for gaining equal treatment.

Sexual equality

Women   Women have also been active in seeking equal treatment and the rights due them, and rely on many political tactics and strategies. The proposed Equal Rights Amendment has been a focal point of debate for the last decade. Those seeking sexual equality are also active in the legal arena. Thus, in the past decade or so the Supreme Court (and other courts as well) have paid special attention to what are collectively called "women's rights."

RECENT ANTIEQUALITY SEX DISCRIMINATION DECISIONS IN THE SUPREME COURT

1974   California law set up disability insurance for disabled private employees not covered by Workmen's Compensation; it excluded coverage for normal pregnancy and was upheld as a rational state decision.

1975   Federal laws providing for a guarantee of longer service for women than men in the U.S. Navy despite nonpromotion was upheld.

1976   Private employers with plans for compensating employees temporarily unemployed because of disability are not required to include pregnancy as one of the disabilities covered.

1979   A Georgia law that lets the mother of an illegitimate child sue for the wrongful death of the child but bans such suits by fathers of such children if they have not made the child legitimate was upheld.

1979   A provision of the Social Security Act that denied "mother's insurance benefits" to mothers of illegitimate children who never married the wage-earner father was upheld.

1981   A California law punishing men but not women for "statutory rape" was upheld on the ground that a state legislature may take notice of the special problems of women.

1981   A congressional statute establishing draft registration for men only was upheld.

1984   The federal law from 1972 barring sex discrimination in schools and colleges receiving federal aid was interpreted narrowly so that only individual programs within a school or college proved to be discriminatory would be denied federal money. Previously, aid to the entire institution was at stake.

SUPREME COURT OF THE UNITED STATES

No. 82–940

ELIZABETH ANDERSON HISHON, PETITIONER
v. KING & SPALDING

ON WRIT OF CERTIORARI TO THE UNITED STATES COURT OF
APPEALS FOR THE ELEVENTH CIRCUIT

[May 22, 1984]

CHIEF JUSTICE BURGER delivered the opinion of the Court.

We granted certiorari to determine whether the District Court properly dismissed a Title VII complaint alleging that a law partnership discriminated against petitioner, a woman lawyer employed as an associate, when it failed to invite her to become a partner.

A blow for equality. The Court ruled that private law firms may not discriminate on the basis of sex, race, religion, or national origin in 1984. The specific case involved a woman lawyer in Atlanta.

The Court has seemed to invent a new middle position between the "strict scrutiny" given racial categories for discrimination and the much looser "reasonableness" standard given other categories (Ducat and Chase, 1983: 871). In effect, it has wobbled between the two.

The Court has also wobbled in terms of commitment to gender equality (Goldstein, 1979, 1981). It has surely not always pleased advocates of women's rights. Cases in the last decade have seemed generally to push either in an antiequality direction or in the direction of greater equality. The Court is active in deciding questions about gender equality, but, as with many socially sensitive areas in recent years, has tended to be divided on these issues. Thus "winners" and "losers" in individual cases are hard to predict in advance.

RECENT PROEQUALITY SEX DISCRIMINATION DECISIONS IN THE SUPREME COURT

1977   The provision that widowers had to show they had been dependent on their spouses before being allowed to collect social security benefits was struck down; widows did not have to prove the same dependence.

1977   The legal provision that women can exclude three more lower earnings years than men in calculating social security benefits was upheld. It was seen as a permissible remedy to offset some of the effects of past discrimination in employment.

1978   A Los Angeles rule that female employees make a larger contribution to pension plans because they live longer than men was struck down. It was seen as an impermissible discrimination.

1979   An Alabama law that provided that husbands, but not wives, could be required to pay alimony was struck down. It was based on stereotypes about the earning power of the sexes.

1979   A Missouri law granting women automatic exemption from jury duty upon request was struck down. It was based on invalid assumptions about the relation of women to family needs.

1979   A New York law that allowed an unwed mother, but not an unwed father, to block adoption of an illegitimate child was struck down.

1980   A Missouri law requiring a widower to prove financial dependence on his wife to collect benefits from her work-related death but that did not require such proof from a widow was struck down.

1982   A state university in Mississippi policy of admitting only women to its nursing school was struck down in part because it perpetuated stereotypes about what occupations are appropriate for women.

1983   The Pregnancy Discrimination Act of 1978, an Amendment to the Civil Rights Act of 1964, was interpreted by the Court to require that employer health insurance plans cover pregnancy costs for workers' spouses.

1983   The Court interpreted federal law against sex discrimination to prohibit pension plans that pay unequal retirement benefits to men and women because women tend to live longer. (However, the Court refused to order back payments, a ruling that disappointed advocates of equal treatment for women.)

1984   The Court ruled unanimously that Title VII of the 1964 Civil Rights Act prohibits discrimination among their employees by law firms on the basis of sex, race, religion, or national origin. The case involved a woman lawyer denied a partnership at a prestigious Atlantic law firm.

It is worth underscoring at this point that strides toward gender equality are probably much more dependent on laws passed through normal legislative and political processes than on court decisions.

Homosexuals   Homosexuals have long faced not only social ostracism and discrimination, but also many legal restrictions on their rights. In the 1970s, various groups were formed to push for equal rights for homosexuals. They met with some success and some setbacks. Some local campaigns over ordinances received national publicity and thus became "media events." The issues were quite genuine, though.

Groups supporting homosexual rights (or gay rights, as they are often called) have been active in bringing lawsuits that challenge various laws and practices. State courts and lower federal courts have ruled in both directions in these cases; sometimes homosexual rights were favored; sometimes restrictions on them were backed. To date, the Supreme Court has often ducked the issue, usually by refusing to take cases. The Court, though, has sustained some "crimes against nature" statutes. Thus, rights for homosexuals continue to vary from state to state and city to city.

Political equality

The Supreme Court has ruled since the early 1960s that legislative district boundaries—for both houses of state legislatures and the House of Representatives—must be drawn so that the populations of districts are equal. This is the famous "one person, one vote" principle. The point of these rulings is, of course, to help guarantee equal representation for individuals; or, put the other way, to guarantee that state legislatures cannot draw districts that favor one set of interests over others. In many state legislatures, before the decisions, rural districts regularly had smaller populations than urban districts. Thus, cities were greatly underrepresented in state legislatures. Congressional districts in many states were also drawn to overrepresent rural areas.

Throughout the 1960s, court decisions got stricter about the amount of variance allowed. The rulings pushed for a standard as close to literal equality in numbers as possible. Lower federal courts were deeply involved in redistricting.

With the Burger Court of the early 1970s, standards loosened somewhat. The Court still held to the general principle of equality, but was willing to tolerate more deviation, at least for state legislative districting. Often it ruled that states could respect subdivision boundaries (such as county lines or town lines in New England) for legislative districts. For state districts, the Court seemed willing to accept deviations of up to 10 percent between the most and least populous. The Court would also carefully look at deviations of up to 20 percent; automatic approval was not expected, though. For congressional seats, however, the Court stuck to a policy of strict numerical equality. This was reaffirmed in a 1983 case in which the Court held that New Jersey congressional districts would have to be drawn again, even though the numerical difference in the largest district (527,472) and the smallest district (523,798) was tiny.

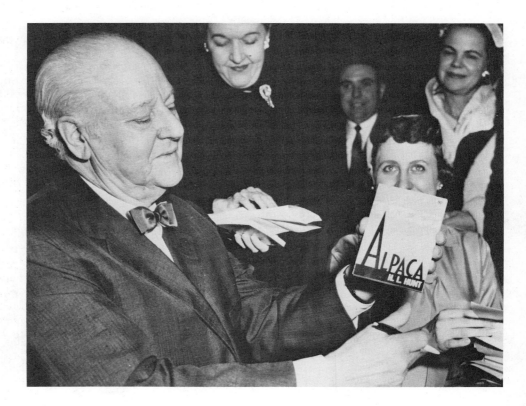

Political and economic inequality. Some favor increased inequality. The late H. L. Hunt, Texas multimillionaire, wrote a utopian novel in 1960 advocating political rule by the rich.

Limiting the impact of economic inequality

For a period in the 1960s, during the heyday of the Warren Court, the Supreme Court appeared to flirt with the idea that economic inequality was a "suspect classification." That is, it would require "strict scrutiny" for possible violation of the equal protection of the laws clause of the Constitution. That flirtation came to a halt in the Burger Court. The Court now seems quite willing, indeed eager, to leave debates over the treatment of the poor to legislative and political processes.

Debate over the treatment and distribution of wealth, how much equality to legislate, and the amount of inequality to leave has often been central to our politics. It surfaced in the 1930s and again in the 1960s. At other times, this issue is less in the limelight. A number of examples and discussions in this book have dealt with aspects of that ongoing debate.

For a long time, the Supreme Court was willing to let states legislate against the poor in many ways, often indirect (Grossman and Wells, 1980: 649–56). Only in the 1960s did the Court even make sure that poor people got proper legal representation when charged with crimes. Also at that time, the Court began

---

THE SUPREME COURT SPEAKS ON THE RELATION OF WEALTH TO EQUAL PROTECTION

Justice Lewis Powell, for the majority

The system of alleged discrimination and the class it (the Texas school financing system) defines have none of the traditional indicia of suspectness: the class is not saddled with such disabilities, or subjected to such a history of purposeful unequal treatment, or relegated to such a position of political powerlessness as to command extraordinary protection from the majoritarian political process. . . . To the extent that the Texas system of school finance results in unequal expenditures between children who happen to reside in different districts, we cannot say that such disparities are the product of a system that is so irrational as to be be invidiously discriminatory. . . . The Texas plan is not the result of hurried, ill-conceived legislation. It certainly is not the product of purposeful discrimination against any group or class.

Justice Potter Stewart, concurring with the majority

The method of financing public schools in Texas, as in almost every other state, has resulted in a system of public education that can fairly be described as chaotic and unjust. It does not follow, however, and I cannot find, that this system violates the Constitution of the United States. . . . I am convinced that any other course would mark an extraordinary departure from principled adjudication under the Equal Protection Clause of the Fourteenth Amendment. . . . Unlike other provisions of the Constitution, the Equal Protection Clause confers no substantive rights and creates no substantive liberties.

Justice Thurgood Marshall, dissenting

In my judgment, the right of every American to an equal start in life, so far as the provision of a state service as important as education is concerned, is far too vital to permit state discrimination on grounds as tenuous as those presented by this record. Nor can I accept the notion that it is sufficient to remit these appellees to the vagaries of the political process which . . . have proven singularly unsuited to the task of providing a remedy for this discrimination. I, for one, am unsatisfied with the hope of an ultimate "political" solution sometime in the indefinite future while, in the meantime, countless children unjustifiably receive inferior educations. . . . Thus, I believe that the wide disparities in taxable district property wealth inherent in the local property tax element of the Texas financing scheme render that scheme violative of the Equal Protection Clause.

Source: from opinions delivered in the case of *San Antonio Independent School District* v. *Rodriguez*.

to examine welfare systems, which were challenged in various cases. The Court looked at conditions attached to the receipt of welfare, eligibility for welfare, due process considerations, and limits on the amount of welfare grants. On the last point, the Warren Court seemed headed for requiring equality to the extent of setting a subsistence level for everyone. The Burger Court has continued to oversee eligibility standards; but it has basically given states a free hand in setting benefits where federal law gives them that prerogative.

The death knell for treating wealth as a "suspect classification" open to strict scrutiny came in the case of *San Antonio School District* v. *Rodriguez* in 1973. In this case, decided 5 to 4, the method of school funding in Texas was challenged; the Court did not hold unequal funding to be unconstitutional. Like most states each school district takes care of most of its own public school funds; some supplements comes from state and federal funds. Thus, as in most of the country, rich neighborhoods and areas have more money for education than poor areas. However, the majority and minority views in this case are very different. Justice Lewis Powell wrote the opinion for the majority; Justice Potter Stewart wrote a concurring opinion; and Justice Thurgood Marshall wrote a dissenting opinion. The different legal and social philosophies show the kind of political disagreements in which justices engage as they tell the nation what they think the Constitution means.

THE FUTURE OF LIBERTIES AND RIGHTS

There is no sure way to predict the future of liberties and rights in the nation. Their content is, inevitably, the subject of a great deal of political debate and controversy. Thus, there will be shifts in that content depending on the success of contending coalitions. Three general points are relevant in thinking about the future of liberties and rights. First, there must be public concern for their preservation or extension. Second, the federal courts clearly have a special role in maintaining liberties and rights; but that role is itself subject to debate and change. Third, there is nothing automatic that makes this country first among the world's nations in terms of liberties and rights for its people. If we aspire to such a lofty status, we must work for it.

Public opinion, liberties, and rights

In Chapter 3 we made two important points about public opinion in terms of free expression and racial equality. First, the American people support liberties and rights more in the abstract than in concrete situations involving those liberties and rights. Second, the American people in recent decades have become more supportive of liberties and rights, including equality for minorities.

However, fluctuations in such opinion are still possible. Negative attitudes among the public in general or even in critical sectors of the public could create situations in which specific liberties and rights might erode. Courts and other government agencies are ultimately both pushed and limited in what they do about liberties and rights by the context of opinion.

A major recent study of American beliefs about civil liberties (McClosky and Brill, 1983: 437–38) concluded with a succinct statement that seems absolutely true:

Civil liberties are fragile and susceptible to the political climate of the time. Hard-won civil rights and liberties are not eternally safeguarded, but are highly vulnerable to assaults by strategically placed individuals and groups who find certain rights or liberties morally offensive, dangerous to safety and stability, and devitalizing to the political order. Such assaults become especially threatening when the civil liberties under attack do not enjoy widespread popular support. This . . . is often the case, a result in great part of the failure of large segments of the population to have effectively internalized the libertarian norms to which the American political culture, from the beginning, has been dedicated.

The federal courts as guardians of liberties and rights

As we noted in Chapter 12, courts also have constituencies and reflect political trends. This is true in part at the federal level because presidents have appointive power and Senates have the power to ratify presidential choices. But courts can certainly move more slowly in responding to what might be temporary political trends than can presidents, their appointees, and legislatures, which are more exposed politically than courts.

Some argue that courts have a special role as guardians of liberties and rights. The Supreme Court is thought to have a particular duty here. Others are willing to concede some special role for the Supreme Court, especially in guarding traditional First Amendment liberties. But they are much more reluctant to see the Supreme Court and other federal courts take a guardian role with regard to other liberties and rights. These include wealth and privacy. In part, this argument reflects the general argument, discussed in Chapter 12, over how active courts should be. But it is also partly a different debate. That is, some will say that courts should restrain their overall activism but should be particularly diligent about liberties and rights. This debate will, of course, likely never be settled definitively. New spokespersons for different positions will continue to emerge and make their cases. This an area of political as well as philosophical disagreement.

Liberal and conservative judges themselves seem to agree on one matter: the Supreme Court can and should protect existing liberties and rights from new incursions by government. And most are also willing to grant that the courts can sometimes act legitimately in new areas. The disagreement is over what those new areas should be and how aggressive the Court should be. The dominant members of the Warren Court were quite willing to define liberties and rights broadly. The dominant members of the Burger Court take a more limited view. However, there is complexity in relying on the courts; and courts also recognize some special role in the liberties and rights area. Quotes from various representatives of the judiciary indicate the complexity. Justice Lewis Powell is generally thought to be fairly conservative. Yet he is quite willing to be aggressive in the segregation area. Judge J. Skelly Wright has been long known as one of the most liberal and activist federal judges. He makes the case for a special role for the federal courts in protecting the politically powerless and disadvantaged. But he also is willing to note some limits on judicial activism. Shirley Hufstedler points out the practical limits of relying on courts to settle broad social issues.

THE COURTS, LIBERTIES, AND RIGHTS: THREE VIEWS OF A COMPLEX RELATIONSHIP

Justice Lewis Powell, in an interview at Kenyon College, reported in the *Washington Post*, August 12, 1979 © Associated Press:

> The views taken by the court in one era do not necessarily survive a different era. . . . Our independence does give the court a freedom to make decisions . . . that the legislative branch may be reluctant to make. . . . The court's peculiar responsibility is to decide what the Constitution means. . . . [In relation to the *Brown* decision in 1954] One would have to strain to find an intention on the part of the Congress . . . to provide that there should be integration in education. . . . The Court cannot rely solely on what the founding fathers intended, or even on congressional intent when the Fourteenth Amendment was adopted. The court . . . undoubtedly has made decisions that should have been considered and acted upon by the legislative branch. . . . A role sometimes viewed as legislative . . . is thrust upon us.

Judge J. Skelly Wright, chief judge of the U.S. Court of Appeals for the District of Columbia, in a 1967 ruling when he was a district judge:

> Judicial deference to [legislative] judgments is predicated in the confidence courts have that they are just resolutions of conflicting interests. This confidence is often misplaced when the vital interests of the poor and of racial minorities are involved. For these groups are not always assured of a full and fair hearing through the ordinary political processes, not so much because of the chance of outright bias, but because of the abiding danger that the power structure—a term which need carry no disparaging or abusive overtones—may incline to pay little heed to even the deserving interests of a politically voiceless and invisible minority.

Judge Wright, in a 1979 speech to the Harvard Law School, reported in the *Washington Post*, October 17, 1979:

> Judges do not have a roving commission as agents of the Congress to oversee the implementation of legislation by the bureaucracy. [But in the area of civil rights the courts should be increasingly active] because in my view giving life and breath to the equal protection clause is the noblest mission of the federal judiciary.

Shirley M. Hufstedler, then a Court of Appeals Judge in Los Angeles, in an article in the *Washington Post*, January 1, 1978:

> The decision-making process is individualized and personal. Federal judges have no bureaucracies to tap and, with trivial exceptions, no experts to help them who are not supplied by the litigants as witnesses. The average personal staff of a federal judge is one secretary and two law clerks. Supreme Court justices have two secretaries and as many as four law clerks. Since the chief justice of the United States and the chief judges of the lower courts have additional administrative duties, they are given slightly larger personal staffs. . . .
>
> Americans have expectations about what courts can do that cannot be fulfilled. Courts are primarily deciders, not supervisors or social problem solvers. Judges know, for instance, that when they decide that a school system must be integrated, they are not "solving" racial hatreds; when judges grant divorces, they are not "solving" matrimonial problems. Evils do not vanish with the wave of a court decree.

U.S. rights and liberties in a world context

U.S. citizens often become quite smug about their liberties and rights in contrast to those in some other countries. Certain assumptions are often made: We are unique among the world's countries in offering such a wide array of liberties and rights; there is something in the natural order of the universe that guarantees that situation will continue forever. This smugness is not justified.

First, a number of other countries do a good job of protecting basic liberties. One survey (Gastil, 1979) lists nations in seven categories, "most free" to "least

U.S. JUDGE ORDERS WIDER SAFEGUARDS AGAINST CITY SPYING

A federal judge yesterday ordered that every city agency—and not just the Police Department—must be scrutinized by outside management auditors to guard against political spying.

U.S District Court Judge Susan Getzendanner also directed police to set up central supervision of two activities with the greatest potential for political spying abuses.

They are the investigations conducted of "public gatherings"—such as demonstrations and rallies—and preparations made for protecting visiting dignitaries, which often include checking out protesters and other dissidents.

Getzendanner's action was an outgrowth of the so-called "police spying" and "Red Squad" suits.

The Police Board was ordered to hire an independent firm to audit city compliance with the order and ferret out signs of improper spying.

The firm of Touche-Ross & Co. conducted the first audit, in late 1982, and made 92 recommendations for improved compliance.

Eventually the department complied with all but two of the recommendations: That all city agencies that might do any kind of "political spying" be subjected to the audit, and that "public gathering" and "dignitary protection" probes be centrally supervised, not spread throughout the department as now occurs.

Attorneys for plaintiffs in the spying suits then asked Getzendanner to order police to also follow the last two recommendations, and yesterday she did.

free." In terms of civil liberties, 18 nations were in the top category. The United States is, to be sure, one of those 18, but it does not sit by itself, superior to all "those foreigners." The foreigners include 11 countries in Western Europe, one other in North America (Canada), three other former British possessions (Australia, New Zealand, and Barbados), one in Asia (Japan), and one in Central America (Costa Rica).

Second, the United States does compare well in a number of specific areas concerning liberties and rights. But it surely does not always come out "on top." (See a number of the specific studies in Claude, 1976.) One study of the right to privacy compares the United States, Great Britain, and India. It concludes that India does best, then Great Britain, then the United States. This is despite the fact we have the greatest number of laws on the subject. A 1972 ranking of freedom of the press put the United States tied for seventh with Finland behind four West European countries, Canada, and Peru (Taylor and Hudson 1972:51–53).

In other areas, the United States compares well: in free expression (compared to Japan); in the status of women (compared to Scandinavia); in the rights of children (compared to Scandinavia). But we do no better than the other countries. And both here and in the other countries, some problem areas are identified.

We are not suggesting that the United States does a poor job with liberties and rights. But it is a mixed record. Depending on one's political values, other societies do as well or better in some specific areas. The phrase "depending on one's political values" is, of course, critical. Liberties and rights are subjects of political debate and decision making just as are other areas of policy.

Third, the strong role of the courts in our system of government clearly is not enough to maintain, let alone expand, liberties and rights. Other government units, in addition to courts, must also be concerned with liberties and rights or these rights will surely be defined narrowly. And, of greatest importance, there must be some widely shared values that support a structure of liberties and rights.

CONCLUSIONS

In this chapter, we looked at liberties and rights in the United States as subjects of both political and legal disagreement. They are subject to the same political processes as other policies. There is nothing automatic about maintaining liberties and rights. Both political action and legal decisions can expand, contract, or leave liberties and rights as they are. Earlier chapters dealt with some aspects of political struggles over liberties and rights. In this chapter, we alluded to those struggles. But we have been mainly concerned with the legal standing of liberties and rights as interpreted by the courts. This survey leads us to certain conclusions:

1 The status of liberties and rights is absolutely critical in a society that aspires to be open, free, and democratic.

2 Liberties and rights change their meaning in relation to changing circumstances and as the result of political controversy.

3 Ideally, the federal government should be a particular friend to liberties and rights. It should guarantee them. But it does not always play such a role.

4 Federal courts, especially the Supreme Court, can play a special role in protecting liberties and rights. But their aggressiveness in this direction varies and, ultimately, they cannot do the job alone.

5 The most important liberties and rights in the United States in the 1980s involve two sets of matters—personal rights such as free speech and privacy, and aspects of equality such as race, ethnicity, gender, and wealth. The specific content of these liberties and rights is constantly changing.

FURTHER READING

ABRAHAM, HENRY J. (1982) Freedom and the Court: Civil Rights and Liberties in the United States. 4th ed. New York: Oxford University Press, A summary of the work of the Supreme Court in several important substantive areas, including due process, free speech, freedom of religion, and civil rights for minorities.

BULLOCK, CHARLES S. III, and CHARLES M. LAMB, eds. (1984) Implementation of Civil Rights Policy. Monterey, Calif.: Brooks/Cole Publishing. Examines conditions associated with progress toward equality in implementation in specific areas of civil rights: housing, voting, education, and employment.

KLUGER, RICHARD (1976) Simple Justice: The History of *Brown* v. *Board of Education* and Black America's Struggle for Equality. New York: Alfred A. Knopf. A detailed history of civil rights for blacks in the United States, with special focus on the long legal proceedings leading to *Brown* v. *Board of Education* in 1954.

LEWIS, ANTHONY (1964) Gideon's Trumpet. New York: Random House. A case study of the Supreme Court's major decision on the right of all persons to be represented by a lawyer in criminal proceedings.

14

Policymaking and the Federal System

On a single day in 1985 all of the following took place:

The president and secretary of labor met. The latter urged the president to support expanded subsidies to private businesses for worker training. At the same time, the secretary urged increasing the percentage of workers who did not have to be disadvantaged in the traditional sense of the term to be eligible for training.

In the Washington headquarters of the Department of Labor—presumably run by the secretary of labor—a few civil servants met and began planning for next year's training programs at the same level and with the same regulations as this year's programs.

In the Denver, Dallas, and Atlanta regional offices of the Department of Labor, prohibitions against stipends during training were being waived for local Service Delivery Areas requesting such waivers. In the New York, Boston, and Seattle regional offices, the same requests were being denied.

Meetings were going on in 17 different state bureaucracies about what regulations to draft and what reports to require from local Service Delivery Areas. By the end of the day, 17 different patterns of answers had begun to emerge.

In Service Delivery Areas all over the country, there was a sense of confusion among professional staff about what they could and could not do and to whom and what they had to report when about what they did do.

The staff of the member of Congress who chairs the Employment Opportunities Subcommittee of the House Committee on Education and Labor was preparing a bill that would add a major new component to the federal employment and training law. This component would be run directly by the federal government and would be targeted exclusively at the poor.

The staff of the U.S. Senator who chairs the Employment and Productivity Subcommittee of the Committee on Labor and Human Resources was preparing an amendment to the existing statute that would wipe out all eligibility requirements for trainees. Anyone chosen by local businesses would be eligible.

The staff of the National Association of Counties was preparing draft legislation that would return some aspects of the program now under state control to local units. They called staff members in the United States Conference of Mayors and the National League of Cities to get support.

The staff of the National Governors Association was preparing a draft that would further strengthen the role of the states in training programs.

The staff of the National Alliance of Business was discussing ways of giving local business people organized in Private Industry Councils mandated by federal law more control over local decision making in training programs.

* * * * *

What's going on here? Who's in charge of what? What will happen to the substance of policy? Is the policy process always so confused and complex? Everyone seems to be running in different directions. How do these people get together?

Obviously, policymaking, as the examples indicate, is complex. But luckily, there are patterns in the policy process. Not every policymaking story is unique. We can make some general statements.

This chapter will explore the major patterns of policymaking. First, it will focus on the stages of the policy process. Second, it will describe the major types of policy. Third, it will comment on subgovernments in different policy areas. Fourth, it will look at stability and change in the content of policy. Finally, it will look at the nature and importance of federalism in policymaking.

THE POLICY PROCESS

Policy is the government's official statements about its goals and planned actions in handling a perceived problem or activity. To have any potential for impact, policy must be carried out through concrete actions, usually in the form of programs.

There are three main stages in forming and carrying out policies. First, the government must decide what problems or areas to look at. This is **agenda setting.**

Second, government must say what it will do. This involves adopting goals and methods for reaching those goals. It also involves decisions about which goals and methods will be ratified—legitimizing some goals and programs. This stage is **policy and program formulation and legitimation.**

Third, the government must take concrete actions to reach its goals. This is the **program implementation** stage.

Policy actions have some impact on society. What differences do such actions make? This is surely an important question. Policymakers should address it by appraising policy impact as they decide on the future of any policy and program.

This view of the policy process is shown in diagram form in Figure 14–1. A short discussion of each of the three main stages in the policy process follows as do a few preliminary words about policy impact.

Setting the agenda

The topics on which government focuses at any given time are the agenda. The agenda changes. Sometimes it does so quickly, sometimes slowly. After the post–Civil War attention paid the rights of newly freed slaves abated, it was almost another century before minority civil rights won a permanent place on the agenda. At the other extreme, the question of child pornography came onto the agenda almost overnight in 1977. Foreign events, such as the hostage sei-

The President helps set the agenda. Ronald Reagan addresses a joint session of Congress in February 1981 as Vice President George Bush and House Speaker Thomas O'Neill applaud.

zure in Iran in late 1979 or Israel's invasion of Lebanon in 1982 immediately put some issues on the agenda.

How does an item get on the agenda? And how does it stay there long enough to be acted on? First, the item must interest enough people to be visible. If an item concerns only a handful, it is not likely to be on the agenda. Many people are worried about cancer; therefore, cancer easily stays on the agenda. Allergies mainly concern the much smaller number of people who suffer severely from them; they are thus much harder to get or keep on the agenda.

Second, a potential agenda item cannot seem to threaten most of the population. Civil rights were therefore kept off the agenda for a long time because many white people thought any move toward racial equality threatened their own place in society. When civil rights were restored to the agenda, it was because some whites joined new black leaders to counteract the fears and prejudices of other whites.

Third, a potential agenda item must win the attention and support of people in high positions; this includes the president, some members of the House and Senate, and leaders of major corporations, unions, or interest groups.

Even a government as large and active as ours cannot watch all potential problems. Therefore, the agenda is always changing. What problems should receive how much attention from which actors and institutions? At one time, energy may top the list. At another time, poverty may be deemed most important. At still another, foreign policy questions may overshadow all other issues. And there are times when no single problem looms largest.

Problems first have to be seen and defined. Then support must be mobilized to include the problems on the agenda or increase their priority. Many are in-

FIGURE 14–1

An Overview of the Policy Process

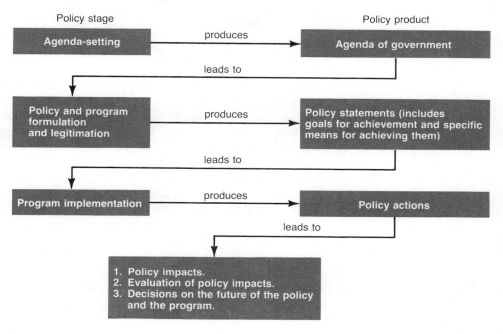

volved, both inside and outside government. They all compete for the attention of government bodies and participants to create the agenda.

The exact origins of changes in the government agenda are usually hard to pinpoint (Cobb and Elder, 1983). Actors both in and out of government may be important. There are many routes to gaining a place on the agenda. Some problems get attention because of scholars and popular writers. In the early 1960s, poverty was rediscovered as a problem worthy of attention. In part this was because of works by economist Robert Lampman and popular writer Michael Harrington.

A long-time agenda item bears fruit. President Harry S Truman dedicates a dam in Kentucky in 1945. The dam, part of the system of the Tennessee Valley Authority, fulfilled part of the dream of Nebraska Senator George Norris to establish the TVA as a model federal government program for flood control, reclamation, and the production of electric power.

Some problems are noticed because skillful lawyers bring them to the courts and force a decision that sparks later action. For instance, NAACP lawyers pressed the cases that led to the 1954 *Brown* decision that declared segregated public schools unconstitutional. This helped set a major agenda item for succeeding decades.

Some problems get attention because they are highly visible—they are automatically seen as problems. Examples include the Soviet launch of the Sputnik satellite in 1957, energy shortages in the last few years, and the massive federal debt in the 1980s.

Some problems are noticed because government officials themselves take the lead. Senator George Norris of Nebraska pressed for decades to have the government look at the problems of the Tennessee River basin. Senator Paul Douglas of Illinois worked for nearly 10 years to get government to look at economically depressed regions.

No single document or speech contains the agenda of the national government. It is not in the State of the Union message; neither is it in the president's vest pocket. It is a composite of all the items that government agencies are looking at at any given time. Because of the size and fragmented and complex nature of the government, the agenda is very large and always in flux. Priorities are hard to pinpoint. And, of course, at any one time, different people have different priorities. The budget is perhaps the best single source of the agenda. Comparing changes in the budget over time gives some clues to changing priorities.

At the agenda-setting stage, broad goals may be adopted by many actors. Sometimes a generally agreed-on goal emerges: for instance, that poverty should be reduced or inflation curbed. Sometimes a number of goals are adopted and some may be at odds with each other. Often an item may be added to the agenda without clear goals or with multiple competing goals.

Formulating and legitimating policies and programs

Policy formulation is developing alternatives for what should be done in addressing an agenda item. Legitimation or adoption involves ratifying one alternative or a compromise between several alternatives.

Some proposed alternatives are not legitimated; instead, they are either largely or wholly rejected. The processes of formulation and legitimation are entwined: as alternatives come up during formulation, they may be immediately legitimated or not.

In a single field, numerous alternatives may be formulated and even legitimated in a short period of time. Take, for example, the tangled history of energy policy since 1972. Groups in Congress, interest groups, the president and his advisers, and various parts of the bureaucracy all groped to solve the problem. Over a few years, many alternatives were proposed: deregulate natural gas; regulate natural gas more; break up oil companies; subsidize oil companies to increase exploration efforts; penalize car makers for making inefficient cars; penalize car owners through taxes on gas guzzlers; suspend air pollution control laws to allow the burning of coal; subsidize research on removing pollutants from coal. Some of these choices got temporary legitimation but were canceled later.

During formulation and legitimation, four things take place: information is

Modern Stonehenge? One of many energy alternatives is solar power, pictured here in California. No coherent energy policy has been adopted in the United States.

collected, analyzed, and distributed; alternatives are developed; coalitions in support of various alternatives are formed; and a decision is made.

Collecting, analyzing, and distributing information involve a look at the scope of the problem and at possible ways to deal with it. Not all data on the problem and its solutions are available. Not all the available data are collected. Analysis is selective. Information is distributed to serve specific ends. It is not neutral.

While developing and choosing alternatives, the actors focus on a few possible solutions. Sometimes only one is seriously considered, but all possibilities are never considered.

At some point, only one or a few alternatives are left. Then supporters of those solutions make their cases where they think they will most pay off. Sometimes, most or all of the advocates agree on one solution and unite in pushing it. Usually, two or more alternatives get serious, meaningful, and potentially successful backing.

Finally, a decision is made. One alternative may be adopted. No alternative may have enough support to win approval; so the decision may be not to do anything. Sometimes a symbolic decision is made. A good example is the Communist Control Act of 1954. Liberal Democrats sponsored this act to protect themselves from charges of being "soft on communism"; but they hoped no president would really try to use the act. Its design was so sloppy that it was unworkable and probably unconstitutional.

There are two facets to policy statements that are approved: a general goal, such as "We will wipe out poverty"; and specific means to achieve the goal, such as setting up community action programs. At the national level, policy statements are most often made in statutes. But they may also be made in speeches or executive orders, statements by bureaucrats, agency regulations in the *Federal Register*, and court decisions. Some policy statements are highly vis-

Agencies are involved in formulating and legitimating policies and programs. Secretary of Agriculture John Block testifies before a House committee in 1983.

ible; others are more hidden. A major statute is easy to spot; a regulation buried in the *Federal Register* is hardly noticed. Different actors may make different policy statements in the same area. Or they may view the same statute, regulation, or court decision quite differently.

Numerous actors help make and approve decisions. Formally, such decisions tend to be made by the executive branch and Congress. But different layers of those branches get involved, along with a number of nongovernment and judicial bodies and actors.

There are some patterns to institutional influences on making and approving policy. Collecting, analyzing, and distributing information are dominated by the bureaucracy. Congress, the president, and interest groups have less input in this area. Alternatives are usually developed and chosen through bargaining between the bureaucracy, Congress, and the president, with smaller input from interest groups. The president and his advisers and appointees can have the most sway in advocacy. But their limited resources force them to focus on just a few issues. Congress also has much influence in advocacy; there is less input from the bureaucracy and interest groups. The president and Congress dominate final decisions on policy statements.

Implementing programs

What does the government do? Once a policy statement has been made, there are many decisions about the details of implementation. *Implementation* is the actions by which public and private actors try to reach policy-statement goals (Van Meter and Van Horn, 1975). The government may, for instance, declare a "war on poverty." But unless actions are aimed at better economic conditions for the poor, nothing much will happen. Good will and symbolic statements are not implementation.

Implementing includes giving out funds, assigning personnel, developing and issuing regulations (often a minilegislative process in the bureaucracy), enforcing those regulations, collecting and distributing information, writing and signing contracts, and setting up organizational subunits, such as field offices, coordinating committees, and task forces. For instance, when the Social Security Administration writes checks for retired people, it is an implementing action. Building a Veterans' Administration hospital begins the process of implementing a statute providing medical care for veterans.

The same things that take place in forming and approving policy occur in implementation decisions: information is collected, analyzed, and distributed; alternatives are developed and chosen; advocacy occurs; and a decision is made.

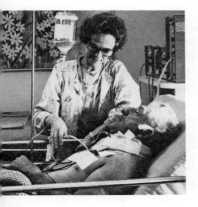

Implementing medical care for veterans. A veteran recovers from surgery at a Veterans Administration hospital.

The impact of policies

What differences do government actions make? Many policies are assumed to have some planned results. They are also apt to have results that were not foreseen or planned.

The reaction of people meant to be helped may partially determine a program's impact. Splendid health clinics may be built. If no one uses them, they have no impact. The clinics may be too far from bus routes. Or people may not want to get mixed up with any public agency.

Both government and outside organizations examine policies and programs.

Many aspects can be judged: for example, design, implementation, and impact. The impact of policies on society is the most important evaluation element. It is also the most difficult to judge.

SUBSTANTIVE TYPES OF POLICY

In different policy situations different interests are at stake. Different people and groups stand to win or lose. What is at stake affects political relationships among those backing the policies they favor. It also determines which actors will have the most force and impact in the debate.

Types of domestic policies

Domestic policies are meant to affect what happens *within* the country. There are four types: distributive, competitive regulatory, protective regulatory, and redistributive. Each has distinct political patterns that appear during decision making.

Distributive policies   These policies and programs promote specific, desired private actions. Society as a whole wants these actions, and at least in theory, they would not or could not be done without government intervention. Such policies and programs provide subsidies for private actions by individuals, groups, and corporations. A **subsidy** is a payment of some kind meant to induce desired behavior. Many policies turn out to be subsidies, even if they do not seem so at first glance. Examples of distributive domestic policies are:

Land grants to railroads used to promote settlement.

Land grants for railroad companies and homesteaders in the 1800s to induce developing and settling the West.

Building the interstate highway system.

Direct cash payments to purchase certain farm products (feed grains, wheat, rice, dairy products, soybeans, honey, cotton, oils, tobacco, peanuts, sugar, wool, and mohair). Price supports for the same products. Direct loans for farm improvements—for animal and equipment purchase, soil and water conservation, or insurance. Tax subsidy (through deductions) for farming. Insurance against crop failure.

Grants for scientific research.

Grants for airport construction and improvement, hospital construction, sewage systems, and mass transit.

Grants of patents to companies and inventors to promote invention.

Development of water resources (dam building, diversion) by the Army Corps of Engineers, the Bureau of Reclamation, and the Soil Conservation Service.

Tax deductions for interest on home loans and local property taxes to promote homeownership.

Special benefits for veterans.

Low-cost permits for grazing on public lands.

Revenue sharing with states and local governments.

Subsidies for merchant marine construction and operation.

Competitive regulatory policies These policies and programs limit the number of people or groups who can supply or deliver certain goods and services. Some potential deliverers who want the business win, some lose. Some decisions allocate scarce resources that cannot be divided, such as TV channels and radio frequencies. Some decisions limit competition in the supply of goods and services. Only certain deliverers can supply them; others are excluded. Some decisions regulate the quality of services delivered by setting standards of performance. If those standards are not met, a new deliverer can be chosen. This type of policy is a hybrid. It subsidizes the winning competitors. But it also tries to regulate the delivery in the public interest. Examples of competitive regulatory policies are:

Granting and reviewing licenses to run TV and radio stations.

Authorizing certain airlines to operate certain routes.

Authorizing certain trucking companies to haul named products over set routes.

In recent years, national policy has decreased competitive regulation by reducing the federal role in airlines, railroads, truck lines, and even some aspects of communications.

Protective regulatory policies These policies and programs protect the public by setting conditions for various private activities. Conditions thought to be harmful (air pollution, false advertising) are banned; conditions thought to be helpful (publishing interest rates on loans) are required. Examples include:

The rule that banks, stores, and other grantors of credit disclose their true interest rates.

Certification of commercial airplanes and licensing of pilots.

Licensing of drugs before they can be sold.

Setting rates for airlines, truck lines, railroads, barge lines, and pipelines.

President Woodrow Wilson battles the trusts in this 1913 cartoon.

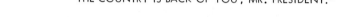

"THE COUNTRY IS BACK OF YOU, MR. PRESIDENT."

Bans on unfair business and labor practices, and business combinations that restrain competition.

Penalties on the owners and makers of cars that emit more than a set level of pollutants.

Minimum wage and maximum hour limits for workers in some industries.

Limits on strip mining and rules for restoring the land after mining.

Control of private power rates through competing, publicly produced power.

Wage and price controls.

Bans on harmful food additives.

Ad campaigns about the dangers of smoking.

High taxes to reduce the use of scarce resources such as oil.

Coffin nails. In the interest of protecting public health, the federal government requires that cigarette packages and advertising carry the warning of the U.S. surgeon general that "smoking is dangerous to your health."

The Reagan administration has pushed for substantial deregulation in the protective area, but with very limited success in terms of changing statutes. The administration, however, has relaxed enforcement of many protective regulations.

Redistributive policies   These policies and programs distribute wealth, property rights, or some other value among social classes or racial groups. They are called **redistributive** because the policies transfer some value to one group *at the expense of* another group. Thus, the more well off sometimes see themselves as losers in a program that helps the less well off. Whites sometimes see themselves as losers in programs that give special help to minorities.

Redistribution runs in several directions. Some programs redistribute items of value from the less well off to the more well off or from minorities to whites. But usually these programs are not seen as redistributive by the public. Thus, redistribution, as debated publicly, almost always involves programs intended to benefit the disadvantaged in society. Examples include:

Limited redistribution. Free federal cheese is given to a needy person.

Progressive personal income tax rates—richer people pay a higher percentage of their incomes.

Income maintenance through a negative income tax or tax credits that return money to some poor people who pay no taxes.

Prohibition of racial discrimination in housing, public accommodations, and education.

Affirmative action in hiring women and minorities by federal contractors.

Employment and training programs mainly for the poor.

Food stamps for the poor.

Special legal services for the poor.

Government-sponsored health insurance for the elderly.

Types of foreign and defense policies

Foreign and defense policies are intended to affect the behavior of other nations and also provide security for the United States and its allies. (They will be discussed in greater detail in Chapter 16.) There are three types of such policies: structural, strategic, and crisis. Each involves a distinct political pattern during the decision-making process.

Structural policies   Structural policies and programs procure, locate, and organize military personnel and materiel. They are made within the guidelines of previous strategic decisions. Since the government competes with no one in this field, defense is totally subsidized. But how that subsidy is given out varies greatly. Examples of structural defense policies are:

Defense procurement decisions, some of which involve some competition between manufacturers.

Placement, size, and closing of military bases and other facilities.

Decisions on new weapons systems (types of aircraft, ships, tanks).

Size of reserve military forces.

Programs that send surplus farm products overseas.

Strategic policies   Through strategic policies and programs, our basic military and foreign-policy stance is revealed and carried out. Examples include:

The basic mix of military forces: the ratio of offensive to defensive weapons; the ratio of ground-based missiles to submarine-based missiles to manned bombers; the ratio of combat troops to support troops.

Foreign trade: the conditions under which import tariffs and quotas will be assigned.

Sales of arms to foreign nations. Should we arm Israel? Should we arm Saudi Arabia? How much? At what price? With what types of weapons?

Foreign aid: the amount and use of both economic and military aid; the ratio of military aid to Israel and the Arab nations; the use of aid to reward or punish other nations for their policies.

The number and location of U.S. troops overseas.

The extent of U.S. involvement, if any, in certain military-political situations overseas: Vietnam, Cambodia, Laos, Angola, Zaire, Rhodesia, El Salvador, Iran, Lebanon, Nicaragua.

Levels of immigration into the United States.

A response to crisis. When Japanese forces attacked Pearl Harbor, Hawaii, in 1941, President Franklin D. Roosevelt went before Congress to recommend a declaration of war. Behind him are Vice President Henry Wallace and House Speaker Sam Rayburn.

Crisis policies   Crisis policies are short-run responses to immediate problems that are perceived as serious, have burst on the agenda with little or no warning, and demand immediate action. Examples are the U.S. response to:

Japan's attack on Pearl Harbor in 1941.

France's collapse in Southeast Asia in 1954.

The attack by Britain and France on the Suez Canal in 1956.

The Soviet Union's placement of missiles in Cuba in 1962.

North Korea's seizure of a U.S. naval ship in 1968.

Cambodia's seizure of a U.S. merchant ship in 1975.

Iran's seizure of hostages in 1979.

The Soviet Union's invasion of Afghanistan in 1979.

The Soviet Union's threat to invade Poland in late 1980 and early 1981.

Israel's invasion of Lebanon in 1982.

The deteriorating military situation in Lebanon in 1984.

General comments on policy type

The sections above outline broad types of policies. They are based on the distinct patterns of political interaction connected with each type of policy. Specific differences in the patterns will be discussed in Chapter 15.

Over time, a policy or program may move from one area to another. The Model Cities program of the mid-1960s started with a clearly redistributive goal. It offered more services to those in the poorest parts of inner cities. But it quickly became partly distributive by offering subsidies to local governments. And it was partly regulatory. It focused on managing relations between Washington agencies and local governments and among the Washington agencies that delivered the service.

Special revenue-sharing or block-grant programs were begun in the areas of employment and training in 1973 and in community development in 1974. They show the movement of programs from redistributive to distributive. Before the special revenue-sharing programs began, programs were aimed at the poorest people. Many employment and training programs were aimed at parts of the poorest groups: youth, older workers, and minorities. Community development projects aimed at those parts of cities and towns where the poorest people lived. In the newer programs, some eligibility restrictions were dropped or loosened. There was a broader group of potential clients. But Congress gave the programs the same or somewhat less money. How the money was parceled out to states and localities quickly became the focus of debate. Policymakers were mainly concerned with distribution to government bodies. Redistribution to social classes did not interest them. For both programs, much of the debate at the local level was over what groups got the contracts for local service delivery, not over what services would be delivered or who would get them.

The most common shift in domestic programs is toward distribution. The politics of subsidy decisions are easier. This is because direct head-to-head confrontations are rare. And most of the time, all parties seem to come out winners. When there is a shortage or scarcity, redistribution is more likely. Policymakers who consider redistribution to the disadvantaged normally court political controversy.

POLICY SUBGOVERN-MENTS

Policies and programs are produced and carried out by groups of actors and institutions that work with each other. Not all those who can affect decisions do so. Sometimes, they choose not to. They have only so many resources and use these on the matters they care about most. Sometimes they are excluded by other, stronger actors and institutions.

In general, those with the most at stake in any given policy decision are the most influential in making it. Those with the most at stake usually come from several bodies: the executive branch, Congress, and the private sector. The dominant group of these people from different bodies can be thought of as a *subgovernment* (Cater, 1964). This is a notion we introduced at the end of Chapter 7 on interest groups.

Subgovernments are clusters of people who make most of the routine decisions in a policy area. Any subgovernment is a group of mostly like-minded people. They come from key parts of Congress (usually subcommittees), the executive branch (usually bureaus running specific programs), and the private sector (most often industries or producer-oriented interest groups).

Typical people in a national subgovernment include a few members of the House and Senate and a few key staff members; one or a few representatives of the executive branch, such as a bureau chief; and a few lobbyists for companies, unions, or other groups that are most affected. Given the vast and complex nature of the government, it is easy to see how subgovernments run quietly. They work without much publicity or attention from outsiders. The press, the president, and Congress often ignore them. Subgovernments are dominant in distributive domestic policies and structural foreign and defense policies. They are also important in competitive regulatory questions; they try to turn regulation into self-regulation. They sometimes poke into redistributive domestic policies or strategic foreign and defense policies.

The rules of the game blur the line between the government and nongovernment bodies. And any line between the two is easily crossed; usually this is thought proper. It is customary for the most affected people and groups to be in almost constant contact with officials during policymaking (Lowi, 1979).

HOW THE FARMERS GET WHAT THEY WANT: SELF-GOVERNING POLICY SYSTEMS

The politics within each system is built upon a triangular trading pattern involving the central agency, a Congressional committee or subcommittee, and the local district farmer committees (usually federated in some national or regional organization). Each side of the triangle complements and supports the other two.

The Extension Service, for example, is one side of the triangle completed by the long-tenure "farm bureau" members of the Agriculture Committees in Congress and, at the local level, the American Farm Bureau Federation with its local committees. Further group support is provided by two intimately related groups, the Association of Land Grant Colleges and Universities and the National Association of County Agricultural Agents.

Another such triangle unites the Soil Conservation Service, the Agriculture subcommittee of the House Appropriations Committee, and the local districts organized in the energetic National Association of Soil Conservation Districts. Further support comes from the Soil Conservation Society of America (mainly professionals) and the former Friends of the Land, now the Izaak Walton League of America.

Probably the most complex of the systems embraces the parity program. It connects the Agricultural Stabilization and Conservation Service with the eight (formerly ten) commodity subcommittees of the House Agriculture Committee and the dozens of separately organized groups representing the various commodities. (Examples: National Cotton Council, American Wool Growers Association, American Cranberry Growers Association.) These groups and congressmen draw support from the local price-support committees wherever a particular commodity is grown. . . .

These systems have a vigorous capacity to maintain themselves and to resist encroachment. They have such institutional legitimacy that they have become practically insulated from the three central sources of democratic political responsibility. Thus, within the Executive branch, they are autonomous. Secretaries of agriculture have tried and failed to consolidate or even to co-ordinate related programs. Within Congress, they are sufficiently powerful to be able to exercise an effective veto or create a stalemate. And they are almost totally removed from the view, not to mention the control, of the general public.

Source: Theodore J. Lowi, "How the Farmers Get What They Want." *Reporter*, May 21, 1964, p. 36.

Former Secretary of Labor Ray Marshall expressed this view in 1977 in discussing wage and price controls:

> I think that in a society like ours, any system to be effective has to have overwhelming support from the parties involved. And I think that's a general proposition. We're not going to impose any kind of system on unions and employers—and make it effective. If it works, whatever we do, it's going to be because they agree with what we're doing, and have participated in it.

The importance of subgovernments is strengthened by the constant flow of people between positions in Congress (including staff), the executive branch, and private groups. For instance, of the 101 members of seven regulatory agencies between 1961 and 1975, 11 once worked for the regulated industry; 26 were

SUPPORT FOR INDIAN POLICIES IN THE 1850s: CONTINUITY OF SUBGOVERNMENT IMPORTANCE

Agents and other field employees of the Indian Bureau usually owed their appointments to a member of Congress. All too often this patronage spawned a three-way alliance that fed on the annuity system. Senators and representatives placed their protégés in official posts, and they in turn, in league with local traders, contractors, and other claimants, pursued schemes for harvesting the appropriations that their mentors in Washington assiduously cultivated. All three profited, often spectacularly. The Indian lost, often spectacularly.

Source: Robert M. Utley, *The Indian Frontier of the American West 1846–1890* (Albuquerque, N.M.: University of New Mexico Press, 1984), p. 46.

lawyers who had practiced before the agencies; 20 once were federal civil servants working in the same area; 10 had been on congressional staffs; and 6 had been in Congress. Only 28 at most did not come from subgovernment roles. The other 73 were working with the same people, policies, and ideas they had dealt with for many years. Small wonder that subgovernments have been called "incest groups" (Lewis, 1977).

Do not assume subgovernments make all policies. National subgovernments are strongest in making and approving three kinds of policy: distributive, competitive regulatory, and structural. Their importance is low in protective regulatory policy and strategic policy. It is very low in redistributive policy. It is nonexistent in crisis policy.

STABILITY AND CHANGE IN POLICY

Policies and programs usually change slowly. Only special circumstances cause dramatic changes.

A political system in which compromise and bargains are needed to make decisions promotes slow policy change. Those who take part in such a system do not want to upset these bargains by raising basic issues again and again. Thus, the first bargains tend to be supported and reaffirmed over time. This means that the basic shape of most policies and programs stays the same for a long time.

The way policymakers think also promotes slow policy change. When they approach a problem, they usually do not think it through from scratch. They would prefer to make some changes in existing programs and policies rather than design new ones. They are wary of new approaches. A problem never faced before or a crisis may be analyzed from scratch, but these are exceptional cases.

Another reason for slow change is that people cannot see all sides of a problem or amass all relevant data (Lindblom, 1959). Because of this, problems are only partly analyzed; alternatives usually do not stray very far from policy as it stands.

There are some institutional conditions that promote innovation. An aggressive president and aggressive congressional leaders of the president's party promote more innovation. If control is weak in executive branch agencies, then subordinates in those agencies feel more free to float new ideas.

In making budget decisions, bureaucrats and members of Congress, especially those on appropriations committees, think in terms of small changes from a base budget figure. But the actual budget decisions are not always just small changes.

THE NATURE AND IMPORTANCE OF FEDERALISM IN POLICYMAKING

The United States is a federal system. Its 50 states have important policy powers that are used along with national powers. The states are important actors in many policy areas. And the states have formed many local government units that have their own importance in public policy. In 1982, in addition to 1 national government and 50 state governments, there were over 3,000 counties, over 19,000 municipalities, almost 17,000 townships and towns, over 15,000 school districts, and almost 29,000 special districts for sanitation, transportation, and other specific functions. About 17 of every 20 of these (about 70,000

Crumbling streets and highways. Which parter—nation, state, or locality— has how much responsibility for repairing Fifth Avenue in New York City or Interstate 70 in western Pennsylvania? The answer is complicated.

of close to 83,000 units of government) had the power to levy taxes, in some cases only with the approval of voters in a referendum.

Federalism appears and reappears both in policy processes and in policies themselves. Representation in Congress is, in spirit, a federalistic device. Federal, state, and local bureaucrats mix their functions to carry out programs. State and local courts are vital in the total judicial system.

In the present section we will first describe how federalism developed. Second, we will comment on its workings. Third, we will focus on how national, state, and local governments carry out programs together.

The development of federalism

During our first 100 years, people thought the federal government and the states were clearly divided and had separate powers and duties (Sundquist, 1969). Relations between federal and state governments were formal and distant. National purposes had national laws and programs; state and local purposes had state and local laws and programs.

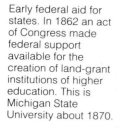

Early federal aid for states. In 1862 an act of Congress made federal support available for the creation of land-grant institutions of higher education. This is Michigan State University about 1870.

Starting in 1887, the federal government began to give grants-in-aid (money) to state governments for specific uses. The first such grants were for agriculture. These grants grew slowly in number and volume for close to 50 years; during the depression, their use and size mushroomed. After World War II, the rapid growth resumed. Until the 1960s, though, the grants were given for

purposes set by the states. Only vague national purposes were stated. But in the 1960s, the grant-in-aid programs changed in two ways. First, the number and size of grants expanded dramatically. Second, statutes explicitly stated that major national purposes were to be reached through these programs.

One added feature marked grant-in-aid programs in the 1950s, '60s, and '70s. They no longer handled everything through state governments. The federal government now dealt more and more with local governments; at first, mostly with cities, then, more and more, with counties, school districts, and other special districts. They also dealt with private, nonprofit groups such as community action agencies. In some programs, the role of the states was minor. But in others, including the most costly, the state role remained central (Epstein, 1978). The Reagan administration made some headway in restoring an even more central role for the states in the grant system.

The main grant-in-aid programs are now called **categorical** grants. They are aimed at specific purposes. A federal agency provides the money and keeps a high degree of control over spending, planning, operations, evaluation, and standards. There were almost 500 such programs by the late 1970s (Advisory Commission on Intergovernmental Relations, 1979). Many of these programs overlapped. In 1977, for instance, 15 programs were for child nutrition; 23 were for elementary and secondary education; and 20 were for health care. One count was made in 1979 of federal aid programs for local fire departments. It showed that 49 federal units were involved in what has always been thought of as a purely local function (Stanfield, 1981). An employee of the Advisory Commission on Intergovernmental Relations took two months just to find the agencies. Even after that work, she could not find out how much money was spent in all the programs. By 1981, there were 361 federal grant programs. By 1984, this number had shrunk to 259. In both years, over 85 percent of all spending was concentrated in 25 programs.

Categorical grants made up 98 percent of all federal aid to states and localities in 1968. Since then, general purpose grants (general revenue sharing) and block grants (special revenue sharing and broad-based grants) have reduced that percentage. From 1976 through 1987 (the latter year is, of course, an estimate) the percentage has fluctuated only between 77 and 81. The Reagan administration, despite its goals, has not been able to reduce federal centralization of categorical programs.

The creation of general revenue sharing and some block grants did not end the dominance of categorical aid. But it did represent an important development in federal-state-local relations. During the 1960s, officials at all three levels began to move toward a concept of partnership. Intergovernmental cooperation meant moving further away from **dual federalism,** which involved separate government entities each going their own way. This new concept took various names; the most descriptive was **cooperative federalism.** In terms of programs, various measures were taken to make relationships in grant-in-aid programs smoother.

General revenue sharing started in 1972. It provided about $30 billion to almost 39,000 units of local government over five years (Nathan, et al., 1975). The program was renewed in 1976 for a 45-month period—January 1977 through September 1980. It gave out $25.5 billion during that time. Through 1980, the annual amount of general revenue sharing was about $7 billion. The New York and California state governments get about $600 million each year; some small

The federal government aids New York City. *Left*, New York Governor Hugh Carey and U.S. Treasury Secretary Michael Blumenthal reach agreement on measures to deal with New York City's financial crisis. *Right*, Governor Mario Cuomo, Mayor Edward Koch, and President Reagan pose with a symbolic check for $85 million as partial payment toward a highway in Manhattan.

"I HEREBY DECLARE THIS CORNERSTONE..."

local governments get only a few dollars. There are few restrictions on how states and localities use this money.

In late 1980, Congress reauthorized general revenue sharing through September 1983. Local governments were given $4.6 billion a year for the three years. States were, in effect, dropped from the program after 1980. In late 1983 Congress passed a simple three-year extension of revenue sharing at the same annual cost of $4.6 billion. This newest extension will expire on September 30, 1986.

States and localities used little of the money for new social programs. Instead, a large amount went to reduce taxes or to avoid new local taxes. Despite provisions in the statute for citizen participation, such participation did not amount to much.

In block grants states and localities get federal funds for a broad purpose. Then they can decide themselves how to use that money to fulfill the aim. Since the mid-1960s, there have been many proposals for block-grant programs. Only five had been created by 1981: (1) the Partnership for Health Act of 1966; (2) the Safe Streets Act of 1968, which created the Law Enforcement Assistance Administration; (3) the Comprehensive Employment and Training Act of 1973; (4) the community development block grant part of the Housing and Community Development Act of 1974; and (5) Title XX of the Social Security Act, added in 1974. Each of these programs has had its own problems. But on balance, they are more efficient in distributing federal aid than the endlessly growing and overlapping categorical programs.

The Reagan administration sought to increase the use of block grants but had only marginal success. Nine new block grants were created by Congress in 1981, but only a few of them had much importance. Most proposals were rebuffed by Congress. In 1982, Congress replaced the Comprehensive Employment and Training Act of 1973 with another employment and training block grant, the Job Training Partnership Act.

There are several reasons that cooperative federalism has developed. First, the grant-in-aid programs grew too quickly in number, scope, cost, and regulations. Giant muddles often resulted. Overlap, redundancy, and confusion marked federal, state, and local attempts to carry out these programs. The clients of the programs had even more reason to be confused. Service delivery became a major problem. People did not know about the programs for which they were eligible. And policymakers of all political hues agreed there were problems.

Second, the states and localities were becoming very large as government bodies. They now had the muscle to demand a larger share of authority and duties. In spending and especially in employing civilians, state and local growth has been much greater than federal growth in the last three decades.

Third, the states and localities set up interest groups of their own in Washington. The most important groups became more and more skillful at getting results. They were also more committed to increasing the autonomy of state and local governments. The U.S. Conference of Mayors, the National League of Cities (formally joined with the mayors for a number of purposes), the National Association of Counties, and the National Governors Association all began to speak with persuasive voices.

Jimmy Carter expressed his commitment to cooperative federalism during his 1976 presidential campaign. It came in part from his tenure as governor of Georgia. (He was the first governor to become president since Franklin Roosevelt in 1933.) Some efforts were made by the Carter White House to improve federal-state-local relations and to coordinate programs better. But nothing much happened.

Ronald Reagan, another former governor, came to office talking about "new federalism." Most of the Reagan proposals aimed at restructuring the federal system have also gone nowhere, however. Rather, the essence of the Reagan new federalism in practice has involved fairly sizable cuts in federal spending through grant-in-aid programs, especially those targeted for poor people. State and local governments and their interest groups have united to oppose these initiatives. At the same time, they have not been either willing or able to compensate for cuts in aid programs for the more disadvantaged classes in society.

The Reagan administration, with significant support from Congress, has told the states and local governments that they will have less money with which to undertake more responsibilities. The states and localities have not been pleased and have worked hard to restore federal funding.

The dynamics of federalism

The federal system is an important context in making and carrying out policy decisions. The system involves a complex set of relationships between its many units. These relationships have much to do with what policies get adopted and how they are carried out (Leach, 1970). In these relationships, it is often hard to sort out the actors. Federal, state, and local participants are mixed in terms of goals, payment of salaries, and program duties.

How government units interact has little order, routine, or pattern. Patterns have grown in some areas, mostly in the allocation of funds by formula, as with general or special revenue sharing. But there is still much more disorder than order. This means that how the system processes policy problems differs from problem to problem.

As with any complex system with many actors there are difficulties. It is hard to reach coordinated decisions on policy or process. Action is not automatic. The incentive for action may come from many sources. No one source routinely leads on the federal level, though the president comes closest to leading. In some fields, nongovernment actors may be mostly responsible.

It is no surprise that problems are attacked piecemeal. National policies that are coherent and really national are very rare. Early in his first year in office, President Carter called for "an urban and regional policy" for the nation. In fact, when he left office, the country was no closer to such a policy than it had been before he took office. The lack of a policy that focuses on aspects of regional growth is striking. The United States was the only developed democracy in the world that did not have any policy in this area (Sundquist and Mields, 1979). At the end of Carter's term, a commission suggested that the United States subsidize the flow of people to the South and West from the Northeast and Midwest. This triggered new outbursts from interests in the Frostbelt and the Sunbelt.

Despite the rhetoric about cooperative federalism and even its reality in some fields, there is still a lot of energy spent blocking initiatives. In short, the main relationship between the federal government in Washington and its field offices, 50 state governments, and local governments is still **bargaining.** Bargaining is evident in almost any issue. Governors, especially those in the West, have been fighting for larger roles in energy and in water development and control. The new broad-purpose or block-grant programs in areas such as employment and training or community development have given rise to involved bargaining (Van Horn, 1979; Williams, 1980; Nathan and Dommel, 1978). Many people argue that the federal government is too powerful and intrudes too much in state and local government business. Sometimes these arguments are political; mayors and governors take the lead. The Advisory Commission on Intergovernmental Relations has buttressed the arguments with facts (Advisory Commission on Intergovernmental Relations, 1980).

Growth and change in federal assistance to states and localities

Federal aid to state and local governments has grown greatly since World War II. Table 14–1 shows figures from 1950 through 1987. Table 14–2 shows the changing nature of federal aid to state and local governments between 1960 and 1987.

Administrative problems   A number of complex, hard-to-solve management problems have come up. Major problems developed in the 1950s and '60s as federal aid grew. There were too many administrative requirements. The federal government did not react to changes in state and local priorities. Washington offices of federal agencies did not let field offices make decisions. There were too many programs in the same area. Regulations were often complex and confusing.

Despite some attempts to create cooperation between the federal government and the states and localities, problems remain (Kettl, 1983; Walker, 1981). States and localities still have a hard time getting information from the federal government on grants. The government releases money in an irregular way. Thus, states and localities have a hard time planning their expenditures. Federal administrative processes are still complex. Federal programs still overlap and are redundant.

TABLE 14–1

The Growth of Federal Grants-in-Aid to State and Local Governments, 1950–1987

Fiscal year	Amount (millions of dollars)	Federal aid as a percent of	
		Total federal outlays	State-local expenditures
1950	$ 2,253	5	10
1960	7,020	8	15
1970	24,014	12	19
1980	91,472	16	26
1987 (est.)	107,939	10	NA

NA: Not available.

Source: *Special Analyses, Budget of the United States Government, Fiscal Year 1985* (Washington, D.C.: U.S. Government Printing Office, 1984), p. H-16.

TABLE 14–2

Percentage Distribution of Federal Grants-in-Aid Programs, by Program Area, 1960–1987

Program area	1960	1970	1980	1987 (estimated)
Natural resources and environment	2	2	6	3
Agriculture	3	4	1	1
Transportation	43	19	14	18
Community and regional development	2	5	7	4
Education, training, employment, and social services	7	27	24	16
Health	3	16	17	26
Income security	38	24	20	24
General purpose fiscal assistance	2	2	9	6
Other	*	1	2	2

*Less than 0.5 percent.

Source: *Special Analyses, Budget of the United States Government, Fiscal Year 1985* (Washington, D.C.: U.S. Government Printing Office, 1984), p. H-14.

The federal government assists cities. The Chicago Department of Public Works is helped by the federal Economic Development Administration to provide jobs for unemployed people.

Aid from the local perspective: increasing dependence   How much and what kind of federal aid comes either through state or local governments or straight to local citizens? This is seemingly a simple question. But it is extremely hard to answer because of the vast array of programs and the various ways of spending.

FEDERAL AID IN ARLINGTON COUNTY, VIRGINIA

Arlington got $24.2 million in federal funds in fiscal 1983, ended last June 30, representing 12% of the county's total expenditures of $206 million. The federal inflow was $6 million less than the year before—partly because of the Reagan cutbacks—but close to what the county collected in fiscal 1980 and 1981.

A big chunk of the funds last year—around $11.3 million—went for means-tested programs in which the county acts as a conduit for federal help to the poor and near poor. Arlington does have its needy, with 7.2% of the population below the official poverty level in the 1980 census. Among the various programs means-tested were Indo-Chinese refugee assistance ($2,876,600), rent subsidies from the Department of Housing and Urban Development ($2,049,267), and low-level jobs and job training under the Comprehensive Employment and Training Act ($1,403,974).

Most of the remaining $12.9 million that Arlington received last year, however, benefited people who on average have distinctly above-average incomes. A big chunk of the money was general revenue sharing, which Washington disburses to almost every county and city— $4.6 billion this year. Arlington got $2,617,463 in fiscal 1983. It all went to the fire department—an odd use for federal funds, it might seem, but Arlington was well within its rights. . . .

Education also gets generous federal help. Arling-

ton's schools—19 elememtary, four intermediate, and three high schools—received $4,140,466 last year from the Department of Education under 22 programs. One of the largest programs was impact aid, which cost the U.S. Treasury $512,869. Impact aid is meant to compensate localities for the cost of educating the offspring of military personnel, who presumably do not support the schools through taxes. Every Administration since Eisenhower's has tried to eliminate the program, only to run into implacable congressional resistance. Military personnel who live off post do pay real estate taxes, so their children certainly should be excluded from the head count that determines the amount paid. Even when soldiers do not pay property taxes, a military base confers considerable economic benefits on a community.

Last year the Department of Education's grants to Arlington schools supported programs that ranged from vocational education ($850,827) to bilingual education ($102,936) to adult basic education ($77,180) to "expository writing" ($32,528) to a special program for "gifted and talented" children ($49,083). This year the school authorities spent $34,000 in discretionary federal money to buy 20 microcomputers for elementary schools.

Source: Irwin Ross, "One County's Pipeline to the Treasury." *Fortune*, February 20, 1984, pp. 50–52. © 1984 Time Inc. All rights reserved.

FEDERAL AID IN SANTA BARBARA COUNTY, CALIFORNIA

GOLETA, Calif.—The president of the United States lives near this coastal town that hugs the edge of the Santa Ynez Mountains. While no one has ever seen dollar bills flutter down from his passing helicopter, Ronald Reagan's government has been dispensing checks here, even as he chops wood and plots budget cuts up at his ranch.

Goleta, a Santa Barbara suburb of fast-food stops, think tanks and avocado groves, supports 66,075 residents who share much of their famous neighbor's distaste for waste, taxes and overregulation.

But as the federal government brings about $1 billion to them and the other 240,000 residents of Santa Barbara County each year, they and their president are finding the federal largess so woven into their daily lives that they seem willing to accept the taxes and triplicate forms that go with it. . . .

Defense installations in Santa Barbara County received $965,224,000 in fiscal 1982, most of it going to Vandenburg Air Force Base. For fiscal 1984, the county government got $9,185,124 in welfare under aid to families with dependent children, $1,767,032 for wel-

fare administration, $683,377 for food stamps, and $475,000 for airport work. And county assistant administrative officer David Elbaum said the sheriff has been guaranteed at least $210,000 over several years for the trouble of providing extra protection for President Reagan.

The county will receive $3,220,932 in federal revenue sharing this fiscal year, 30 percent of which has been alloted to a bewildering array of local public service groups. The Blue Jacket Teen Age Club got $500, Afro-American Community Services $5,200, the Goleta Valley Girls' Club Inc. $5,000, and the Lompoc Rape Crisis Center $8,800.

Gary Gleason, general manager of the Santa Barbara transit district, is far more willing to accept the demands of federal regulation in exchange for $560,000 in operating funds—about 16 percent of his budget—and $2,220,000 in capital funds to help him buy 20 new buses.

Source: Jay Mathews, "Federal Largess is Blossoming in Reagan Back Yard," *Washington Post*, February 2, 1984.

Federal, state, and local purposes—as carried out through programs using public funds—are inextricably mixed. They cannot help but affect one another.

In the 1970s, states and localities depended on the federal government for about one fourth of all their spending. In the 1980s, that proportion shrank to about one fifth. States and localities—mostly the latter—became agents to carry out federal programs, mainly in the social services. But they did not have direct access to the tax base that supported those programs. And they did not have complete control over the means of carrying them out. Congress and the federal bureaucracy controlled the purse strings and set the conditions for carrying out programs. Yet people depended on nonfederal bureaucrats to run the programs. This led some city officials to conclude that they were not really responsible for the poor. They were only agents for programs that the "feds" mandated. As Mayor Margaret Hance of Phoenix said: "The poor are a federal, not a local, responsibility. If Washington cannot afford these programs, we certainly can't. Local people do not feel that welfare programs should be financed by local taxes" (*New York Times*, December 21, 1980). Since President Reagan was able to deliver on his promises to cut federal programs for the poor, those individuals have an increasingly tough time finding any level of government to sustain programs for them.

CONCLUSIONS

In this chapter we summarized the major patterns of policymaking in the United States. We also focused on Federalism as it affects policymaking. Several broad conclusions are warranted.

Big city mayor wants federal government to take care of the poor. Former Phoenix Mayor Margaret Hance and two views of her city. One shows poverty conditions at close range. The other shows the more well-off side of the city: freeways, traffic jams, and tall buildings.

1 The federal government is enormously complex. Yet there are patterns in how policy is made. First, agendas are set. Second, policies and programs are created and approved. Third, policies and programs are carried out.

2 Policymaking becomes more regular because who is involved becomes more important depending on what is at stake. Subgovernments dominate policymaking in distributive and competitive regulatory policy. They also dominate in structural foreign and defense policy. The more controversial areas of domestic policy—protective regulatory and redistributive—allow a larger role for Congress as a whole, for the president and the presidency, and for national interest groups. Strategic foreign and defense policy also give a major role to the president and Congress as a whole. The president dominates crisis foreign and defense policy.

3 Policy is generally quite stable. It is hard to make policy changes.

4 The federal nature of our government adds another enormously complicating and fragmenting dimension to making and carrying out policy. In many areas, reaching national goals requires state and local government action as well as action by the federal government.

FURTHER READING

COBB, ROGER W., and CHARLES D. ELDER (1983) Participation in American Politics: The Dynamics of Agenda-Building. 2d ed. Baltimore, Md.: Johns Hopkins University Press. An interesting treatment of how governmental agendas are formed.

JONES, CHARLES O. (1984) An Introduction to the Study of Public Policy. 3d ed. Monterey, Cal.: Brooks/Cole Publishing. A short, but both thorough and thoughtful, treatment of the flow and analysis of public policies.

LOWI, THEODORE J. (1979) The End of Liberalism. 2d ed. New York: W. W. Norton. An interesting argument that the dominance of pluralism in American policymaking has resulted in policy with no integrity.

SUNDQUIST, JAMES L. (1969) Making Federalism Work. Washington, D.C.: Brookings Institution. A careful treatment of the development of federalism and how it can be used to foster effective programs.

WALKER, DAVID B. (1981) Toward a Functioning Federalism. Cambridge, Mass.: Winthrop. A general analysis of the American federal system by a long-time Assistant Director of the Advisory Commission on Intergovernmental Relations.

15

Domestic Policies

Now that the last obstacles to the Tennessee-Tombigbee Waterway have been cleared away, local civic boosters, state officials and businessmen all along its course are rushing to position themselves for the cash and commerce they say will surely follow the tow barges down the long network of canals and locks.

The unfinished $2 billion project, which will connect the Tennessee and Tombigbee Rivers to provide an alternative inland water route from the Tennessee and Ohio Valleys to the Gulf of Mexico, is scheduled to open in September 1985.

In July, President Reagan ended more than a decade of political struggle by signing legislation that assures the final $202 million necessary to complete the 234-mile navigation system, the largest single public works project ever undertaken by the Army Corps of Engineers.

A legal struggle had ended two months earlier, when the last remaining parties to a series of lawsuits seeking to block the project dropped out of the fight, conceding that further challenges to the waterway, which was begun in 1971 and is now more than 90 percent complete, appeared futile. . . .

Opponents say whatever benefits the waterway will provide are not worth its $2 billion price tag.

In either case, the decision to complete the Tenn-Tom helps mark the end of an era, as one of the last remaining vast Federal water development projects in the Southeast. . . .

Until construction began on the waterway in 1971, the Tombigbee was a picturesque if unremarkable river, meandering lazily through the poor cotton fields and depressed rural landscape near the Alabama-Mississippi border. In the spring it often ran at flood tide. In the late summer it was mostly mud flats and barely carried enough water to float a rowboat.

Through the construction of five dams and 10 locks along the course of the river, Army engineers have turned the river into a 300-foot-wide, nine-foot-deep industrial channel. They have also cut a canal through the rocky Appalachian foothills in far northeastern Mississippi in order to connect the waterway with the Tennessee River, which at that point flows north on its way to the junction with the Ohio and Upper Mississippi River systems in western Kentucky.

Much of the initial opposition to the waterway came from the Louisville & Nashville Railroad, which initiated litigation aimed at blocking the project. Among other things, the railroad argued that by financing the waterway, the Federal Government was discriminating against alternative means of transportation.

Later, environmentalists joined the lawsuit, saying the waterway would, in effect, convert a free-flowing river into an industrial channel and flood 40,000 acres of forested bottomland.

Meanwhile, in Washington, a coalition of Congressional leaders from the Northeast and Middle West sought to block further funds for the Tenn-Tom, describing it as a $2 billion boondoggle and a grievous example of pork-barrel politics. But the project also had powerful backers, like Mississippi Senator John C. Stennis.

Studies commissioned by the Corps of Engineers say the waterway offers potential cost savings to shippers in 14 states, as far away as Minnesota and Pennsylvania. The corps predicts the waterway will handle some 28 million tons of cargo after it opens in 1985.

William E. Schmidt, "Southern River Project Stirs Economic Hopes," New York Times, September 28, 1983. © 1983 by The New York Times Company. Reprinted by permission.

Unless Congress enacts legislation to prevent it, on April Fool's Day, the nation's bankruptcy court will cease to exist. And indeed we all may be the fools, victims of extraordinary lobbying efforts by special interest groups that have held up legislation that would establish a new court because of their selfish demands for unrelated bankruptcy amendments. How did the bankruptcy court system come to be so threatened?

The question involving the courts stems from a major change included in the Bankruptcy Code enacted by Congress in 1978, one that permitted the bankruptcy courts to judge disputes between bankruptcy trustees and other parties related to a bankruptcy case. Under former practice, a bankruptcy trustee almost always had to sue a third person in a nonbankruptcy Federal court.

But on June 28, 1982, the Supreme Court ruled that this broader jurisdiction could constitutionally be given only to judges who had life appointments and were free from the political influences of upcoming elections. Unfortunately, the bankruptcy judges under the 1978 Bankruptcy Code had 14-year terms. As a remedy, a new, though simple, law had to be enacted by Congress. Yet, the simple procedure of changing a 14-year term of office to life tenure became a matter of cheap political barter.

Consideration of H.R. 3, proposed by Representative Peter Rodino, chairman of the House Judiciary Committee and Representative Hamilton Fish, the committee's ranking Republican, a bill that would handle this situation simply by having the bankruptcy judges appointed for life, has been held up by its sponsors. They fear that the House Rules Committee will allow a package of amendments to be tacked onto their bill that would change the 1978 code as it relates to consumer bankruptcy.

A majority of Rules Committee members, however, support directly or indirectly H.R. 1800, a bill that contains a group of highly controversial amendments supported by the consumer finance industry. And complicating matters more is a push by the A.F.L.-C.I.O. for amendments on either H.R. 1800 or H.R. 3 that would prohibit corporate use of bankruptcy to sever their labor-management agreements, as was ruled acceptable by the Supreme Court last month.

Amidst all this clutter of special-interest amendments and proposals, we have a clear constitutional crisis. The Supreme Court has found an element of the 1978 Bankruptcy Code to be unconstitutional. The Court has given the Congress ample time to respond; but the game of politics has prevented it from doing so.

The consumer credit industry lobbyists have convinced half of the members of the House of Representatives that if their special interest legislation cannot be joined to a bill responding to a constitutional directive from one branch of Government to another, then the crisis should continue.

Lawrence P. King, "Bankruptcy Courts on the Brink: The Plague of Special Interest Groups," New York Times, March 4, 1984. © 1984 by The New York Times Company. Reprinted by permission.

* * * * *

Both of these stories graphically portray the complicated nature of the federal government's involvement in policy. In both there was initial legislation. In both it was followed by government action aimed at implementing the legislation. In both lawsuits and courts were involved. In both the initial legislation was not sufficient to accomplish the purposes desired by supporters; additional laws were required. In both a variety of interest groups displayed their clout. Finally, a variety of compromises were necessary for action.

We begin this chapter on shaping and implementing domestic policy with some expectations about the major features of these activities. These expectations stem from many sections of previous chapters. We can expect that policies will take a long time to shape through the formulation and legitimation processes. We can also expect that they will take a long time to implement. In all of these processes—formulation, legitimation, and implementation—competing interests and ideas, coalition building among competitors, negotiation between competitors, and final compromise between competitors will characterize much of what happens.

Most policies in the United States have unclear goals. Different supporters of a policy have different goals and, to build a winning coalition, vague and broad goals are stated. Even competing goals are sometimes contained in the same policy. Clear goals thus do not emerge from formulation and legitimation. And this has a variety of consequences, especially for implementation. As a result, those who implement programs may head in several directions at once. And, of course, they may simply be confused about what they are supposed to achieve. Ultimately, evaluators of programs will also have problems trying to figure out the goals against which program progress should be measured.

In looking at domestic formulation and legitimation (which together constitute the shaping of policy) we will examine aspects of access to decision making, coalition building, and compromise. In looking at implementation—how the federal government carries out policies and programs—we will first explore its meaning. Next we will summarize patterns of influence in the implemen-

A major project is legislated and implemented. The Tennessee-Tombigbee Waterway was in the midst of controversy for most of the 14 years (1971–85) it took to develop. Glover Wilkins, shown with a U.S. Army Corps of Engineers official, heads the local development authority sponsoring the project. The advertisement promoting business is in Japanese, as the aspirations of the developers are to draw world trade through the waterway (location of the waterway is shown in dots). Senator John Stennis of Mississippi (*below, left*) was a vigorous and effective supporter of the project in Washington. Senator Daniel Patrick Moynihan of New York (*below, right*) labeled the project a ''cloning'' of the Mississippi River.

tation of different kinds of policies. After that we will briefly consider budgeting, a major aspect of implementation in most programs. Finally, we will examine several recent examples of implementation to illustrate its complexity.

ACCESS TO DECISION MAKING IN THE SHAPING OF POLICIES

Who makes policy decisions? The answer has much to do with the substance of the decisions made. Many actions in politics come from self-interest. Those who have access to the processes, institutions, and people through which decisions are made are apt to use that access to push for policies that promote their own interests.

Both policy formulation and approval are competitive. This means that a single elite does not make all decisions. The system is ''porous''; many people and groups can gain access to important processes and thus develop some influence over the outcome. But some people and groups have more access and influence than others.

Why cannot anyone gain access to the processes? There are several reasons. One is that there are formal rules for some of the main aspects of decision making. Some people have routine access to official bodies. Thus, a member of Congress has much influence over decisions that need congressional statutes; a concerned person in Seattle with no official standing has little. A president has more access to decision making than do taxpayers in Des Moines. *But* the person in Seattle or the taxpayers in Des Moines can have some indirect impact. With a lot of energy and luck, they may not be completely shut out.

There is another reason for different levels of access and influence. Different people and groups have different levels of knowledge about the processes, issues, and timetables involved.

A lot of policy formulation and legitimation is invisible except to those most directly affected. Others may have an interest in a decision, but if they do not know it is being made, they cannot gain influence or access. Those in an organized group will recognize their interests more quickly than nonmembers because the group will tell its members what is at stake.

Still another reason for different levels and amounts of access is that some groups have more resources than others. Groups with money can run large lobbying campaigns with lots of booklets and personal visits to Washington. Poorer groups or unorganized people cannot afford this. Large groups can also run voter registration drives that affect elected policymakers.

Access and influence are different. People or groups with *access* have the

Organized groups get access. Organized farm workers picket in Chicago as a means of getting access to policymaking.

chance to be a part of some phases of policy formulation and approval even though the results may not be to their liking. People or groups with *influence* will see at least some of their preferences become part of an approved policy. Access is necessary for influence, but does not always guarantee it.

Channels of access

Channels of access between those inside and outside the government run in two directions—from the officials back into society and from society to the officials. Figures 15–1 and 15–2 show these channels.

Several aspects of the figures should be stressed. First, there are many potential channels in both directions. Second, people within society try to affect each other as well as officials. Third, no one group can always monopolize access to the exclusion of other groups. Neither is any one group always the captive of the officials.

Another way to view access is to think about its potential in terms of the specific actions during formulation and legitimation at the national level. What institutions and actors are likely to dominate which actions? What differences will this dominance likely make?

Federal bureaucracies do most of the collecting, analyzing, and distributing of information, since they have many more resources to do this than other main actors (Congress, the president, and interest groups). The other actors can only try to influence the kind of information obtained and provide some marginal

FIGURE 15–1

Channels of Access from the Public to Officials

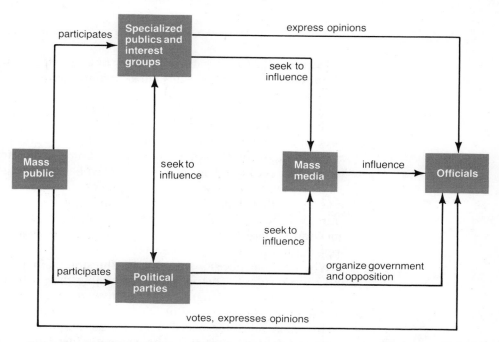

Source: Randall B. Ripley and Grace A. Franklin, eds., *National Government and Policy in the United States* (Itasca, Ill.: F. E. Peacock Publishers, 1977), p. 6.

FIGURE 15—2

Channels of Access from Officials to the Public

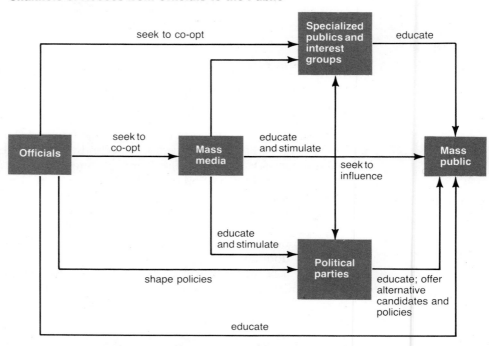

Source: Randall B. Ripley and Grace A. Franklin, eds., *National Government and Policy in the United States* (Itasca, Ill.: F. E. Peacock Publishers, 1977), p. 7.

data. But, if the bureaucracy is doing its job, it will develop information on its own.

Because information gathering comes first, it helps shape the choices. Though the bureaucracy's access fades later, its impact continues because of its initial importance in information gathering.

The stages of developing and choosing alternatives and advocating positions are highly competitive. In the former, Congress, the president, and the bureaucracy all have a great deal of access. Interest groups have somewhat less access, though they can have some importance. On controversial policy, alternatives can get kicked all over Washington before choices are made.

Advocacy is the most competitive process of all; everyone involved has a lot of access at this stage. The president can, on a few chosen issues, mobilize resources to be the most visible advocate. But actors in Congress, the bureaucracy, and interest groups also have many resources and powers to support or oppose the president's preferences.

When formal decisions are made, the dominant participants are Congress and the president. This is so for the simple reason that policies usually need legislation, and it is Congress and the president that, in the end, have the power to make formal decisions. But what has gone on in the first three stages limits what comes out at the decision stage. Last-minute changes can be made; Congress and the president at this point are not just ratifying foregone conclusions. But their options are few. The compromises, agreements, and bargains that have

been struck, usually over a long period of time, shape much of what results in this last formal stage.

When all four activities are viewed together, interest groups are the least important institutional actors. But they compete fully with the official participants at the advocacy stage. They may also have unusual impact on any one formulation and legitimation debate. And, as we shall see in the next section, they have special access to high officials in some types of policy. This can also magnify their importance.

Patterns of influence in shaping domestic policies

Different clusters of actors and institutions have more or less access and influence depending on what policies are at stake. Figure 15–3 summarizes the most important relationships in terms of the basic policy types we introduced in Chapter 14.

For both distributive and competitive regulatory policymaking, subgovernments dominate. The president and central bureaucracy have much less influence. Congress as a whole also has very little influence but instead typically supports the decisions of subcommittees. Subgovernments treat these areas of policy as their private preserve, and for the most part, they are left alone.

The top level of the executive branch and Congress play a more important role in protective regulatory policies. Congress and these top layers bargain with each other and with those parts of the private sector to be regulated. But agencies and subcommittees can and do get involved.

In redistributive policy decisions the most important bargaining takes place among the top level of the executive branch, Congress, and peak associations in the private sector. (*Peak associations* are conglomerates of other groups. Examples include the U.S. Chamber of Commerce and the AFL-CIO.) Bureaus and subcommittees are much less involved in the final decision that they are in the other areas, but sometimes congressional committees break deadlocks and suggest compromises. Bureaus rarely get involved in the final compromise process, but may have helped shape some of the debate and its outcome. This is true because they are so important in collecting, analyzing, and distributing the information that all actors use.

FIGURE 15—3

The Relative Importance of Relationships for Determining Policy Statements, by Policy Type

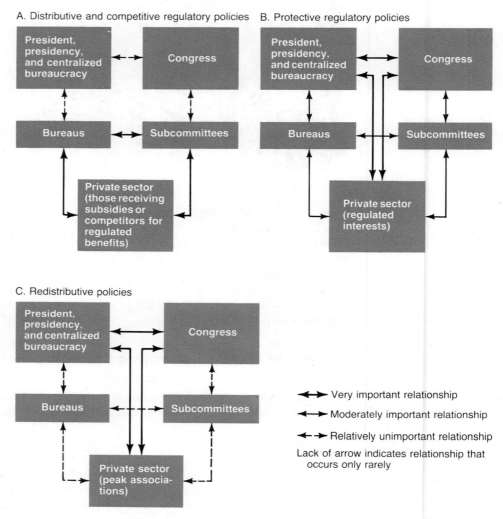

A. Distributive and competitive regulatory policies

B. Protective regulatory policies

C. Redistributive policies

↔ Very important relationship

← Moderately important relationship

←- -→ Relatively unimportant relationship

Lack of arrow indicates relationship that occurs only rarely

Examples of access and influence

Water policy Early in 1977, President Jimmy Carter said he wanted to spend less for water development projects, so he took steps to cut a number of projects from the budget for fiscal year 1978. Water development projects are among the purest examples of distributive policies. Yet Carter thought he could intrude. He tried to make these projects a matter of national priority and arrive at a more rational use of public resources.

The policy formulation phase of the debate began on February 21 when the president named 19 projects he wanted to cut from his budget. Later, he added more projects to his "hit list," and the total grew to 32. On April 18, the president ended this phase of the debate by announcing the outcome of his review of the 32 projects.

That final outcome was instructive: the president suggested that funding for 18 of the 32 projects be stopped. (He left the door open, though, to restoring 3 of the 18.) Funding for five would be reduced. And funding for nine would stay the same. The projects that were kept in whole or in part were mostly the largest projects, the ones with the most active political support, and those closest to being finished. A president can make a dent in decision making about subsidies, but, in fact, it is only a dent.

Also instructive is the harvest of ill will that Carter reaped by trying to intrude in a matter not normally in his province. Some of his supporters in Congress were angry over his approach and over his failure to consult with them. The Senate Majority Leader, Robert C. Byrd (D-W. Va.), described a Senate vote opposing the president as "a clear signal to the White House that this Congress expects to be consulted [on] matters which come within the responsibility of the legislative branch." He also called the president's handling of the water project review "a serious aberration" (*Washington Post*, March 12, 1977).

In an exchange on the Senate floor, Warren G. Magnuson (D-Wash.) and J. Bennett Johnston, Jr. (D-La.) captured the essence of distributive policy formulation: everyone with something at stake supports everyone else so that all can gain what they want.

Mr. Magnuson: I could go on for quite a while about this so-called move that is going on downtown on the water projects.

Mr. Johnston: Nobody is going to be doing anything but trying to restore their water projects. I can tell the Senate that I am not. We can let the rest of this jobs bill go. We are going to drop everything to try to get these water projects on stream again. I do not doubt that we are going to win the fight.

Mr. Magnuson: In the long run, we will win it. We can override the president's veto in the long run.

Mr. Johnston: That is right.

Mr. Magnuson: But it stops everything. . . . Can the senator from Louisiana imagine a senator from Washington going to his state and holding a hearing on the benefits or demerits of Grand Coulee Dam?

[*Laughter*]

They would hang me from a tree if I were to hold a hearing on it, after this has been established for years.

This is absolutely incredible. I know about the projects that the senator from Louisiana has there. This is the lifeblood of the economy in some of those areas.

It is the best thing we can do. There are other things we can do, but it is the best single thing we can do to revive our economy, to keep these projects moving, because we are going to have something of value to show for it when they are done.

President Reagan was much less disposed to attack water projects than was Carter. However, Reagan wanted less spending and more local cost sharing than was the general preference in Congress. The pork-barrel instincts of most members of Congress remained keen.

Energy policy   The energy initiative taken by President Carter in April 1977 was much more complex than his water policy. The package he proposed had distributive and also both competitive regulatory and protective regulatory aspects. In the protective regulatory area in particular, the president is expected to play a large role.

Carter made up his proposals with help only from his closest advisers. But,

A maverick member of Congress loses. Appropriately disguised for the occasion, Representative Silvio Conte (R–Mass.) appears at a news conference in late 1983 to protest a "pork-barrel" water projects bill. Said Conte, "The congressmen have their nostrils right in the trough and they're slurping it up for their districts at the expense of all the taxpayers." The bill passed by voice vote.

once he made his package public, many other people had access to formulation. Despite the secrecy of Carter's deliberations, lobbyists still found out who was critical to early decision making and made themselves heard.

Before Carter announced his package in late April, oil industry lobbyists got some technical decisions made in their favor that would probably give them hundreds of millions of dollars more in revenues in the next few years. The *Washington Post* said in late April that the "oil companies and industry trade associations such as the American Petroleum Institute have had an intense lobbying effort under way. It began before Carter's inauguration, and reached saturation level in recent weeks. One aide to presidential energy adviser James R. Schlesinger said, 'We've been under carpet bombing by lobbyists of every stripe.' "

The lobbyists influenced important technical details. For example, Carter was first going to propose that to be exempt from price controls, oil would have to come from new wells drilled at least five miles from an old well. This would prevent new wells from tapping into the same oil pool as an old well, just to get the oil exempted from price control. Over the last weekend before the proposals were made public, the distance was reduced to 2.5 miles. In explaining how the oil industry got to the proposal drafters, one high oil official said, "Somebody tapped somebody on the shoulder."

A list was made by the *Washington Post* (April 23, 1977) of those in the "energy establishment"—the key parties in the formulation and legitimation actions set off by the president's April 1977 proposals. It included:

> Five major environmental and/or consumer groups.
>
> Seven major oil companies.
>
> Five major oil, gas, and coal associations.
>
> Six law firms representing the oil industry (and one firm listed as "antiestablishment").
>
> Eight lobbyists for oil and gas companies and associations.
>
> Four senators and five representatives in critical spots in the Senate and House, such as the chairmen of the Senate Finance Committee, the House Ways and Means Committee, and the Senate and House Interior committees.
>
> Eight key figures in the administration in addition to the president (people such as the Chairman of the Council of Economic Advisers, the energy adviser, the Secretary of the Treasury, the head of the Office of Management and Budget, and the Secretary of the Interior).
>
> Thirteen member nations of the Organization of Petroleum Exporting Countries (OPEC).

Energy problems continued throughout Carter's term. Some bills were passed, some were defeated. No really "comprehensive" legislation resulted. One of Carter's worst defeats in Congress—at least symbolically—concerned energy. In 1981, Carter vetoed a bill that killed an import fee he had put on foreign oil to promote conservation. Then, for the first time since 1952, a Democratic Congress overrode the veto of a Democratic president.

President Reagan wanted to rely on the market to regulate energy matters and so proposed only a reduction of government activities, including deregulation of natural gas and abolition of the Department of Energy. He had not achieved these goals by mid-1984, however.

Housing policy   In housing policy, many influential forces have emerged. They routinely have access to formulation and legitimation. In the late 1960s, this list (Wolman, 1971) included:

> Ten Senators primarily on the Housing Subcommittee of the Senate Banking and Currency Committee and the Appropriations Subcommittee responsible for housing matters.
>
> Nine Representatives primarily on the Housing Subcommittee of the House Banking and Currency Committee and on the Appropriations Committee.
>
> Seven House and Senate staff assistants.
>
> Fourteen officials at the Department of Housing and Urban Development.
>
> Eight people in and around the White House.
>
> Mayors of three major cities who were officers in groups representing large cities.
>
> Seventeen other people mostly representing interest groups such as the U.S. Conference of Mayors, the National Association of Housing and Redevelopment Officials, the National Association of Home Builders, the Urban League, and the AFL-CIO.

The most important interest groups in the housing subgovernment were representatives of home builders, cities and municipalities, local housing officials, and mortgage bankers. There were no major groups representing the presumed clients—poor people living in inadequate housing. The poor had limited access. But those who stood to gain financially (home builders and mortgage bankers) or from jobs created for officials (city and local housing officials) had excellent access. This makes it almost impossible to draft a redistributive housing bill. Because of the pattern of access, subsidies to home builders, mortgage bankers, and city officials will almost surely be built into any housing policy.

The following examples from 1980 show the continuing power of producer interests and the weakness of the poor.

Congress helped the housing industry, which was caught in one of its worst slumps in years because of the sluggish economy and soaring mortgage rates. It raised the limits on home prices and loans set in the 1974 Emergency Home Purchase Act. The change helped the housing industry by increasing subsidies for mortgages.

The administration, with approval from Congress, used funds from a program for low-income home buyers to provide more subsidized mortgages for middle-income home buyers. Interest rates and price ceilings were also raised. HUD officials guessed that diverting these funds to the middle classes would help stimulate the building of 100,000 single-family homes for moderate-income families. In the crunch, help for the low-income home buyer was dropped in favor of keeping housing contractors in business.

Congress came close to shifting emphasis in the rental area from the poor to the middle class, but failed at the last minute. Perhaps as part of the price they had to pay for scuttling the plan to divert low-income rental assistance to the middle class, the representatives of the poor could not stop the weakening of a bill to guard tenants' rights. This bill was aimed in part at protecting displaced tenants.

Congress failed to strengthen federal authority to end housing discrimination. The 1968 Fair Housing Act had only provided for the Department of

Housing and Urban Development (HUD) to mediate housing disputes. The proposed legislation, which ultimately died in the Senate after a conservative filibuster, would have given HUD the power to bring suit in such cases.

COALITION BUILDING AND COMPROMISE IN THE SHAPING OF POLICIES

"IT MIGHT BE THEIR SOLUTION TO THE UNEMPLOYMENT PROBLEM"

Consider the following. The president has announced in the strongest terms that he favors a new national health insurance program to be funded out of general tax revenues. Benefits would be available to all, but extra help would go to the poor in the form of routine medical and dental checkups. The chairman of the House Ways and Means Committee, which will handle the bill, supports the idea except for the extra help for the poor. The chairman of the Senate Finance Committee, which will also handle the bill, is opposed to funding the scheme out of general tax revenues. This would make the more well off pay for more of the benefits for everyone. Instead, he favors a special flat payroll assessment that would tax all wage earners equally on the first $10,000 of their income. The American Medical Association is opposed to the whole idea. The organization behind the largest health insurance companies says it will support the president *only* if the statute guarantees the private insurance industry all of the business at profitable rates. Other groups and people have taken a variety of positions on the details of the program.

How does anything concrete ever emerge from such a situation? Is so much disagreement not fatal to a new program?

There may or may not be action. A new policy may or may not be approved. The key to success is twofold. *Coalitions* supporting and opposing the proposal must be built, and *compromises* must occur so that one coalition is strong enough to prevail. Without coalitions—clusters of people and groups that can agree at least for a while on a desirable outcome—few policy initiatives would ever succeed. And compromise is what holds coalitions together. It lets them add one or more former opponents to their side at the last minute to cement victory.

Throughout policy formulation and legitimation, coalitions have to be built and rebuilt. They are rarely permanent. During the formulation phase, coalitions need not contain a majority. They must, however, be large enough to persuade others that their proposal should be considered for final approval. During legitimation majorities must be fashioned not just once, but many times, to keep a solution moving toward formal adoption. In Congress alone, majorities are needed in subcommittees and then in full committees in both the House and Senate; they are needed on the floor not just for final passage, but also for major amendments and major procedural motions. Majorities are again needed in each of the delegations from both the House and Senate that meet as the conference committee and again in both the full House and Senate to pass the conference report.

One technique often used to build a winning coalition is to exempt certain groups from the negative effects of a proposed policy (Leman, 1979). This lessens or eliminates their reasons for opposition. When minerals other than coal were exempted, a winning coalition was built for a strip mine bill in 1977. Tobacco is not under the jurisdiction of the Food and Drug Administration. This was done to neutralize the strong political opposition of the tobacco industry, which would surely come into play if its interests were threatened. Many bills include what is called a *hold harmless* clause when they cut benefits or change

Presidents get involved in coalition building. John Kennedy in the White House and Lyndon Johnson in his plane use the phone to help build coalitions for their policies.

programs. Hold harmless means that those who currently benefit will keep getting their aid, or at last a high percentage of it, no matter what the law might say in general. In 1973, part of the price for passing the Comprehensive Employment and Training Act (CETA) was to guarantee all localities at least 90 percent of the funds they got in the last pre–CETA year, no matter what the new funding formula gave them. Likewise, there was a seven-year hold harmless clause (with declining percentages) attached to the Community Development Block Grant program of 1974.

The need for constant coalition building has at least four results. First, it takes a long time to approve a policy. Second, compromise is a must to form and reform coalitions and majorities and to hold them together. Third, given the time span and the many compromises that are made, policies often change a great deal during formulation and legitimation. Backers may wind up with a product quite different from what they originally wanted. Fourth, since it is so difficult to get action, it is usually easier not to act than to act.

Four examples of major policies follow to illustrate these points. (Analysis of minor policies confirms the same points. See Redman, 1973; Reid, 1980.)

The development of federal aid formulas

One of the easiest areas in which to show compromise and coalition building is in the devising of formulas for distribution of federal aid. Senator Abraham Ribicoff (D-Conn.) summed up the essence of the process in the Senate. In speaking about the formula for giving out about $4 billion for public works jobs he said, "Day in and day out on this floor all of us get these sheets of paper [with various proposed formulas], and everybody fiddles around with a formula to find out . . . whether it will give a dollar more to 26 states, and then you become a winner—and then the national interest is forgotten." Senator Howard Metzenbaum (D-Ohio) voiced the view of the individual senator in the same debate: "Sure I want to be a broad United States Senator, with national concerns, but charity begins at home" (*New York Times,* March 20, 1977).

The details of formulas for distributing federal aid are usually complex. But such technical details have a lot to do with what areas get how much money and, in the end, with how much money and services are available for what people. For example, in putting together the formula for general revenue-sharing funds lack of plumbing was included, but lack of adequate heating was not. Because of housing patterns and climate in different parts of the country, this sent more money to the South than to the colder Northeast.

Similarly, in the federal aid to elementary and secondary education program welfare payments are counted as income. This cuts the proportion of the population labeled impoverished in a number of Northeastern cities. Thus, it cuts those cities' share of federal aid. In the congressional decisions that created the revenue-sharing and aid-to-education formulas the representatives of big Northeastern cities were not trying to help poor Southerners at the expense of their own constituents. They just lacked the votes and the vital positions in Congress needed to get their way. At decision time, theirs was a minority coalition on formula details. So, to have a program at all, they had to agree to some features they did not like.

CETA was a special revenue-sharing or block-grant program passed in late 1973. It replaced a large number of categorical programs in the employment and training field. The formula used to disburse funds under the program shifted resources from the South to the West and North, and away from central cities toward the suburbs (Mirengoff and Rindler, 1976). This happened mostly because of the weight given to unemployment and poverty in the formula and because a formula was used at all. In the bargaining that led to the formula for CETA, the coalition of suburban interests was stronger than the one for central cities. Likewise, southern interests were outnumbered. So urban and southern interests were shortchanged. These interests had to accept unfavorable compromises to have a program at all.

The formula for distributing general revenue-sharing money is also very complex. It, too, resulted from a geographic compromise during policy formulation and approval. A major study (Nathan, Manvel, and Callkins, 1975: 18) sums up how the formula came about:

> The greatest challenge to the revenue-sharing conference committee lay in reconciling the complicated and quite different House and Senate versions of the distributional formulas for state-by-state allocations. The House version favored high-population, industrialized states, the Senate version, low-income, rural states. The Solomon-like compromise that was reached retained both formulas and allowed each state's allocation to be determined according to the formula most favorable to it. The Senate formula was retained for intrastate distribution.

It is hardly by chance that the House formula favored populous states (the House is based on population). Nor is the more rural Senate formula a surprise (all states have two Senate seats, regardless of population). In this case, the two coalitions were equally strong—one was dominant in the House and the other in the Senate. So the compromise gave both coalitions most of what they wanted.

Federal regulation of strip mining

Congress took 10 years to decide on federal regulation of strip mining. The process stretched from 1968 to mid-1977. In 1968, the Senate began by holding hearings on the first specific bill on the subject. In 1971, President Nixon proposed a bill, and in 1972 the House passed a bill; but the Senate did not act. In 1973, the Senate passed a bill. In 1974, the House passed a bill and went to

Strip mining in
Wyoming. Congress
passed regulatory
legislation in 1977.

conference with the Senate on its 1973 bill. After long talks, Congress passed a
bill. But President Ford pocket vetoed it, thus stopping an attempt to override
the veto. By mid-March 1975, Congress again presented a bill to the president,
who again vetoed it. The attempt to override was delayed until July because of
dwindling support in the House. When the attempt came, it failed by three
votes.

In late 1975 attempts were made in the House Interior Committee to revive
the bill. They failed, largely because another successful Ford veto was anticipated. In 1976 the Rules Committee twice prevented bills from reaching the
House floor.

In 1977 an important actor changed: Jimmy Carter replaced Gerald Ford in
the White House. The coalition in favor of strip-mining regulation had been
patiently built for 10 years. Now it could pass a bill that would get the president's OK. But the rules of the game in 1977 were the same as always: compromise was still a must to keep a winning coalition in place. The following is
a glimpse of the coalitions on both sides and the compromises made in 1974
and 1977.

In 1974 the basic controversy was whether there should be a federal law at
all and, if so, how strong it should be. Coal producers and most electric companies that are main coal users wanted no bill at all. They claimed coal com-

panies would willingly reclaim strip-mined land and that state laws were sufficient. Their argument stressed two points. First, federal controls would reduce output, thereby reducing our chances of cutting dependence on foreign oil for energy. Second, controls would raise the price of coal, which would also work against its use.

Those favoring the bill were led by environmentalists outside Congress and a few leading Democrats in Congress, especially Representative Morris Udall of Arizona. They argued that, without strict regulation, strip mining would ravage the country. The companies would leave new areas looking like the most depressed parts of Appalachia. The bill's backers claimed that states lacked the power or will to regulate strip mining effectively. They also disputed the claim that coal production would suffer with regulation.

In 1974 a large number of organized groups had access to decision making in the House subcommittee and full committee and in the conference committee. These included environmental groups, coal, steel, and electric companies, the U.S. Chamber of Commerce, and the United Mine Workers union (UMW). Many executive-branch agencies also lobbied hard for some provisions.

The coalitions on both sides were broad-based but unstable. The legislation was complex; many features could be considered separately. Some coalition members only had one narrow interest to protect. And, as long as they got their way on that one interest, they would stay with their coalition. The UMW was most concerned with an amendment to tax strip-mined coal more than deep-mined coal. The former was mined mostly in the West, where the UMW is weak. The latter was mined mostly in the East, where it is strong. Some Pennsylvania interests supported the bill mainly because they wanted to ensure an exemption for anthracite coal, which is found only in Pennsylvania.

Executive-branch agencies were badly divided over the bill. Despite the White House's well-known position, officials and agencies disagreed both in public and in private. When the bill finally came to President Ford, his two top energy officials gave him conflicting advice.

By 1977 the proponents had a supportive president eager to sign a bill, but they had lost some strength in Congress. They had to engage in yet more compromise to keep a winning coalition together.

The first compromise made by backers was to limit the bill almost exclusively to coal mining. Earlier bills had covered, for example, copper. But the chance of a strong negative coalition being formed by a number of the interests targeted for regulation led to the focus on coal.

As in 1974 issues were not settled quietly and finally in subcommittee and committee. Rather, decisions made there were reexamined, debated, and extensively changed on both the House and Senate floors. And some issues remained to be resolved in the conference committee.

In general terms, the House committee produced a moderately strong bill in late April. It was strengthened even more on the House floor and passed a week later. In the Senate, the outcome was different. The committee produced a moderately strong bill in early May, but a few weeks later the bill was weakened greatly on the Senate floor. The net result exempted owners of small mines from some provisions and reduced some environmental provisions.

The conference committee bill, reported in July, was somewhere between the two versions. Mining interests gained several concessions. Both houses passed the bill, and the president signed it in early August.

Medicare

Government-sponsored health insurance has been on the national agenda in a serious way since 1935 (Marmor, 1973). But the policy was only legitimated in 1965 when Medicare was passed. It set up a federal medical insurance program for the aged under the umbrella of social security.

The main feature of the medicare story involves two ideologically based stands. They were used as focal points by two large coalitions directly opposed to each other. The debate between the two was mostly unchanging; the same arguments were stated by the same actors year after year. Opponents found many levers in Congress to stop action, and they succeeded. The public favored medicare long before a coalition was able to win approval of the idea.

The dam broke at last when an aggressive political majority emerged in the executive branch and Congress, including the relevant committees, that allowed medicare to pass in 1965. But the backers' final success was achieved only with a lot of bargaining. Many compromises were needed among House and Senate members and between House and Senate members and high-level members of the administration.

THE DEVELOPMENT OF MEDICARE, 1935–1965

1935 The Roosevelt administration explores compulsory national health insurance as part of the Social Security Act, but no legislation is recommended to Congress.

1943 Three Democratic senators cosponsor a bill to broaden the Social Security Act. It would include compulsory national health insurance paid for with a payroll tax. No legislative action results.

1945 In his health message, President Truman proposes a medical insurance plan for those of all ages. It would be paid for through a social security tax.

1949 The Truman proposal is considered and hotly contested in congressional hearings. No legislative action results.

1954 President Eisenhower opposes the concept of national health insurance as "socialized medicine." He suggests an alternative: reimburse private insurance companies for heavy losses on private health insurance claims. No action is taken on this proposal.

1957 Representative Forand introduces the "Forand bill." It provides hospital care for needy elderly social security beneficiaries, to be financed through increased social security taxes. No action is taken by Congress. Heavy AFL-CIO lobbying, though, generates public interest.

1960 The Forand bill is defeated by the House Ways and Means Committee (17-8). Chairman Mills opposes the bill.

1960 As a substitute for the Forand bill, Congress enacts the Kerr-Mills bill. It is designed to encourage the states to help older, needy persons (those not poor enough to qualify for Old Age Assistance but too poor to pay their medical bills).

1960 Health care is an issue in the presidential campaign; Kennedy vows support.

1961–64 President Kennedy's version of the Forand bill is submitted each year in the House and Senate, but the House Ways and Means Committee defeats it.

1962 The Senate defeats an amendment to a public welfare bill that includes the Kennedy proposal (52-48).

1964 The Senate passes (49-44) a medicare plan similar to Kennedy's proposal. It is in the form of an amendment to the Social Security Act. The plan dies when House conferees (from the Ways and Means Committee) refuse to allow its inclusion.

January 1965 The 1964 elections bring many new Democrats to Congress. The makeup of the Ways and Means Committee is changed to give it a majority of medicare supporters.

January 1965 President Johnson makes medical care his number one legislative priority.

July 1965 The medicare bill is signed into law after passage in both houses by generous margins.

Source: Adapted from material in *Congressional Quarterly Almanac*, 1965, pp. 236–47.

Medicare. Members of the Senior Citizens Forum supported passage of the federal medicare legislation in their parade down the boardwalk in Atlantic City, N.J., in 1964.

Federal aid to education

Since World War II, debate over federal aid to education has been complex and tangled (Bendiner, 1964; Eidenberg and Morey, 1969; Munger and Fenno, 1962; Sundquist, 1968). Right after the war, the federal government began to increase its special-purpose aid to education at all levels. But a logjam formed on the question of broad general aid—especially to elementary and secondary schools. It was broken only by shifting the form and aim of general-purpose aid. Aid-to-education measures seen as helping many special segments of the population or defined geographic areas were much easier to pass than broad, general-purpose measures that were seen as shifting aid from one racial or religious group to another. The final breakthrough on a form of general-purpose aid came in 1965. It was possible only because the focus was shifted from race and religion to poverty, and because subsidy features were stressed. The compromise was based on changing the definition of the benefits to be provided.

Through all the debates House and Senate members and a few people at both the White House and HEW were important. They framed initiatives, attempted compromises, and shifted the debate until the most controversial questions were muted. Generally, those involved were subcommittee chairmen, ranking House and Senate members, and HEW officials at the assistant secretary level or above. But because of the broad involvement of many groups and interests, agreement at this level was never enough to generate policy decisions. Large organizations such as the National Education Association, civil rights groups, and Catholic and Protestant groups also got involved. And the highest levels of the executive branch—usually including the president—got involved, too.

General aid to school districts failed for more than 20 years because of hostility toward federal control of a traditionally local function. After 1954, some felt aid would be used as a lever to force public school integration. There was also the issue of whether private, especially Roman Catholic, schools would get aid. Combinations of these three issues again and again killed general aid in Congress. The proaid coalition in the Senate was formed early, and the Senate passed bills in 1948, 1949, 1960, and 1961. But in the House, the antiaid coalition kept control either of the whole House or at least of the Education and Labor Committee or the Rules Committee from 1943 through 1964. The full House killed bills on the floor in 1956, 1957, and 1961. In 1960 the Rules Committee killed a bill that had passed both houses but required a conference committee. It prevented action in a number of other years. The Education and Labor Committee was very hostile from 1943 through 1955.

The logjam was broken in 1965. Liberal Democrats made sweeping gains in the House in the 1964 election as a result of President Johnson's landslide. But even more important, the effort to achieve general-purpose aid was compromised in favor of a special-purpose approach. Both backers and opponents of general-purpose aid decided at last that some aid was better than none. The different sides in the fight over the status of religious schools compromised; they allowed those schools to share in some, but not all, of the aid given to public schools. The successful program was aimed at poor children, not at school systems as such. So it looked like special-purpose aid. A number of special-purpose programs had passed since the end of World War II and the new program, though far larger than any before, followed those precedents. Thus, the proaid coalition was finally able to enact at least part of the education program it wanted.

WHAT IS IMPLEMENTATION?

Implementation is what governments do and cause to be done after policy statements of intent are made. These actions are set in the midst of the general flow of policy activities summarized in Figure 15–4. They are preceded by formulation and legitimation activities, which lead to statements of policy intent and specific program designs. Many factors affect and help shape implementation. These include the kind of communications between those responsible for implementation, the kind of enforcement activities undertaken to ensure that goals are met, the types of agencies responsible for implementation, and general political, economic, and social conditions. In turn, implementation activities lead to program performance, which helps shape the impact of the program.

Core implementation activities

There are four kinds of government actions in implementation (see Jones, 1984: Chapter 8). The first is *acquisition*. Responsible agencies amass the needed resources, including personnel, equipment, land, raw materials, and—above all—money. Second is *interpretation*. The agencies put the language of statutes into concrete directives and regulations. Third is *organization*. Bureaucratic subunits and routines are created. Fourth is *application*. Agencies extend aid to or restrict

FIGURE 15—4

The Flow of Policy Activities

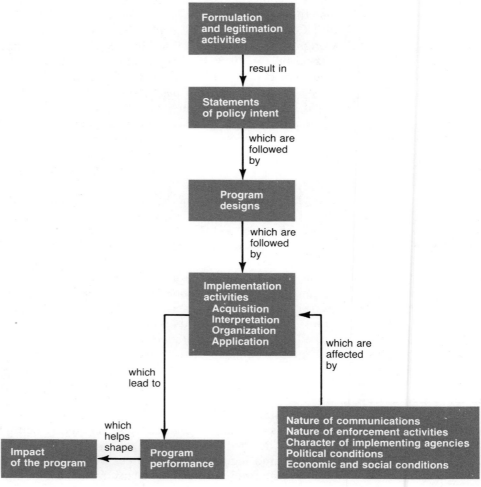

their clientele. They provide services, payments, limits on activity, or whatever else has been agreed on as their tangible product.

Let's use a concrete case to illustrate. In 1977 Congress created a Young Adult Conservation Corps (YACC). The purpose of this program was to create work for jobless youths on conservation projects. The program was also supposed to provide training and other support services so that alumni of the corps would be better able to compete for jobs in the real labor market. Day-to-day operations were directed by the Departments of Agriculture and the Interior under the general guidance of the Department of Labor.

To begin the program these three departments had to *acquire* staff. This meant transferring some people and hiring others. They also acquired sites for YACC camps, equipment (shovels, axes, Jeeps, food, furniture), raw materials (seedling trees, fertilizer), and dollars to pay for all this.

The departments had to *interpret* the law by making regulations that are

"No madam, we don't get after teenagers to clean up their rooms."

published in the *Federal Register*. These regulations are issued in draft, and any interested parties may review and comment on them for a month or two. A final version was published after the departments agreed on what changes, if any, to make on the basis of the comments received. The regulations covered such items as eligibility standards and how to determine them, allowable expenses, accounting methods, records needed on both fiscal and nonfiscal matters, and required reports.

The departments had to *organize*. Each assigned internal responsibilities and developed forms for processing paperwork. Also, because of the joint nature of the venture, they had to form interdepartmental committees to oversee the entire program and reach agreement on various issues.

Finally, they were ready to *apply* their programs to the target population. They enrolled participants, put them to work, paid them, and helped them get permanent jobs when their time in the YACC was over.

The context of implementation

The relation of implementation to formulation, legitimation, and impact Formulation and legitimation are intertwined with implementation. Policy is constantly being made and approved during implementation. This means that implementation details may change with new developments. Policymaking and administration are intertwined. Those who implement policy often try to anticipate changes before they occur or while they are being debated. This means that several sets of goals are being pursued at the same time. Sometimes they are not compatible. For example, a mental health program is open to everyone, but legislation is pending to restrict it to the poor. So the implementing agency may start moving toward such restrictions even before they are approved. The agency tries to outguess Congress.

At the other end of the process, implementation mingles with impact. Im-

Regulations. The *Federal Register* comes out every business day. Note that between January 1 and February 4, 1983, it had already printed more than 5,500 pages.

plementation determines a first and most important policy impact: who gets what in the way of benefits.

Society and implementation Implementation of many programs has a social aspect. In some programs recipients must take some positive action before they can benefit. They may have to apply for benefits, enroll in a program, prove they qualify, or show up at a facility. An agency may build, equip, and staff a health clinic. But if neighborhood people do not use it, then implementation of the community health program is incomplete.

Budget actions and implementation One of the most important implementing actions involves the budget. Budget actions in both the executive branch and Congress often involve further refinement of policy. The budget provides the basic resource—money—without which no program can be mounted. De-

Society and implementation. Recipients of free food must come in person or the food is not distributed.

cision making on budgets is elaborate and time-consuming and often involves important policy disputes.

Program goals and implementation   Implementation goals are often murky and usually changing. They may also be diffuse and implicit. Goals often come out only in implementation. They may have been hidden or unexpressed before. Thus, those implementing policy shape goals as well as pursue goals stated by others. Implementation is neither neutral nor automatic.

Whether or not goals are clearly stated, the process may change the actual goals being pursued. Such changes may happen for many reasons, including changing conditions and personal preferences. One such change involved the Model Cities program in the late 1960s. The program was supposed to focus federal funds on the poorest parts of cities so as to attack problems in a unified way. But it seemed to act mainly as a means to experiment with smoothing administrative processes between federal and city agencies and among federal agencies. The goal of helping those in the inner city was replaced by the goal of helping bureaucratic agencies try out various modes of coordination.

Another goal change involved Title II of the Comprehensive Employment and Training Act of 1973. Its aim was to provide public service jobs with local government units for the chronically unemployed. When a major economic recession developed in late 1974 and 1975, that aim was quickly changed. The focus shifted to those who were just unemployed for the time being, even if they were not disadvantaged in terms of being poor, uneducated, or a member of a racial or ethnic minority.

Bureaucratic characteristics and implementation One feature of most bureaucracies explains some of the slips between program intent and actual results. Policymakers are usually quite separate from those responsible for day-to-day operations. Those who work with the White House, Congress, and major interest groups to set broad program goals are not the same people who make routine decisions about what goals are actually pursued. And those in-

---

THE REAGAN BUREAUCRACY SLOWS REGULATORY ENFORCEMENT

In 18 months the Environmental Protection Agency has reduced the number of cases referred for enforcement action by more than 70 percent. Inspections for clean air violations fell by 65 percent. Since January 1981, the enforcement division has been reorganized four times, and three enforcement chiefs have been fired (two appointed *and* fired by Gorsuch). According to internal memoranda, the enforcement section is faced with the loss of 43 percent of its field staff.

At the Occupational Safety and Health Administration, created to protect workers, Auchter quickly eliminated unannounced inspections for 80 percent of manufacturing firms. The number of violations cited fell 49 percent, inspections declined 10 percent, follow-up inspections dropped 55 percent, and fines imposed for violations fell 77 percent. Heavy fines—over $10,000—plummeted 90 percent. Auchter has proposed to forgive penalties for violations that are later corrected, thus removing one incentive to correct hazards before they are discovered by inspectors.

At the Food and Drug Administration, charged with protecting us from dangerous and mislabeled foods, drugs, cosmetics, medical devices, and man-made radiation, citations over 18 months dropped 88 percent, and seizures of dangerous products fell 65 percent.

In 1980, the National Highway Traffic Safety Administration, enforcer of auto safety, initiated 118 engineering analyses of possible defects. Last year 19 analyses were begun.

The enforcement staff of the Consumer Product Safety Commission—responsible for protecting the public from hidden hazards in toys, appliances, power equipment, household chemicals and hundreds of other products—has been reduced 46 percent since the Reagan administration took office. Recalls have been cut 60 percent.

The Interior Department's Office of Surface Mining (OSM) is supposed to regulate coal mining and enforce land reclamation requirements. In six Eastern states, the number of inspections fell 38 percent between 1980 and 1982, while violations charged fell 62 percent. In six Western states where OSM oversees state-administered programs, OSM was required by law to conduct 162 inspections, but it conducted only 40 and charged only three violations.

Source: Jonathan Lash, "Don't Like a Law. Don't Enforce It," *Washington Post,* October 10, 1982.

volved in daily administration never take part in policy decisions. So, the latter are confronted with vague policy statements they do not understand and did not help shape. It is small wonder their decisions redirect programs away from the goals policymakers had hoped for.

Policy and program designers must assess the abilities of agencies that will carry out their programs. Otherwise, problems are sure to arise.

Few agencies, however, check their capabilities against requirements. For instance, a policy may require critical activities by the field offices of a federal agency. But those field offices may be staffed by people untrained for the task at hand. Under such conditions, failure, or at least severe problems, may result.

Bureaucracies also have a great deal of discretion in how they choose to implement a law and what parts of it they choose to implement. Under Reagan, a number of agencies reduced their enforcement of provisions not favored by the administration, even though Congress had not acted. A much lower level of activity also characterized enforcement of civil rights laws in various bureaucracies during Reagan's presidency (Wines, 1982).

The example of the Office of Surface Mining in the Department of Interior was explored at considerable length by a political scientist (Menzel, 1983). He found that the Reagan administration had successfully redirected implementation of the 1977 strip-mining law from what it had been in the Carter administration. Formal regulations were rewritten to be more lax and, at the same time, enforcement style became much more hospitable to coal-mining companies. Secretary of the Interior James Watt had promised such changes in his first week in office in January, 1981 (*The Wall Street Journal*, January 30, 1981):

> "There will be major changes in the management (of the office) soon," Mr. Watt vowed at a briefing of agency officials earlier this week. "Some of you will be excited about the changes," he said, but others, who disagree with the new stance, "won't find it comfortable" being part of the department. He warned that he might encourage them "to seek other opportunities."

His agency delivered on his promises.

The actors in implementation   Many people and groups are involved in implementation. The primary responsibility usually falls on bureaucrats, but other officials and people outside the government also participate. Legislators get involved when formulation and legitimation cross paths with implementation. This is especially true in decisions about tangible physical benefits, such as those involving the size and location of military bases. The courts get involved by both requiring and banning certain activities. Private citizens and groups—particularly the latter—also get involved through requests for benefits or by seeking to influence implementation details.

The existence of the federal system and its heavy use for implementing much domestic policy add more complexities and actors (Van Horn and Van Meter, 1976). Even when state and local officials have no formal powers, they may well have informal powers or access to implementation decisions. This could come through their interest groups in Washington (for example, the U.S. Conference of Mayors, the National Governors Association, or the National Association of Counties). Or it could come through their representatives in Congress. In other programs, they have formal roles ranging from advising to full decision making.

At any one time, there are apt to be several modes of state and local participation in a federal department's implementation decisions. For instance, state and local officials can have an impact in the U.S. Department of Agriculture in three different ways (Talbot and Hadwiger, 1968). In one set of programs, such as those of the Commodity Exchange Authority, the Consumer and Marketing Service, and the Agricultural Research Service, state and local influence is mostly sporadic and informal. These are federal programs with federal responsibility, though decentralized to federal field offices in many cases. In a second set of programs, such as those of the Federal Extension Service, the Cooperative State Research Service, and state experiment stations, the national government supervises but leaves most administrative decisions to state and local levels. Substantial funds and most personnel decisions are also at those levels. A third set, such as the programs of the Agricultural Stabilization and Conservation Service, the Rural Electrification Administration, the Soil Conservation Service, and the Farmers Home Administration, is midway between the first two. They have more federal supervision than programs in the second set. But state and local officials have more influence here than over programs in the first set.

The fact that most federal agencies are decentralized can lead to problems in implementation. Most domestic agencies have some sort of field structure and delegate different tasks to their field units. Often the gap between the policy layer and the operations layers falls along geographic lines. The entire policy layer is in Washington. The workers in the field offices are all in the operations layer. Such a situation reinforces the potential for slips between policy intent and service delivery.

Table 15–1 lists many of the actors implementing nominally federal programs. All three government levels are shown. Many people and groups get a crack at influencing how programs are carried out.

TABLE 15–1

Actors in Implementation

Executive officials and organizations	Legislative officials and organizations	Bureaucratic officials and organizations	Nongovernmental individuals and organizations	Judicial officials and organizations
Federal level: President Executive Office of the President staff	Congress Congressional staff and support agencies	Department and agency heads Staff—civil servants (in Washington, in field offices)	Corporations Labor unions Interest groups Advisory bodies Media (all with national focus and impact)	Federal judges (3 levels). Law clerks Marshals Masters, Experts Federal attorneys
State level: Governor Governor's staff	State legislature Staff and support agencies for legislatures	Department and agency heads Staff—civil servants (in state capital, in field offices)	Same as above (with state focus and impact)	State judges, Law clerks. Miscellaneous state judicial officials
Local level: Mayor; County commissioners; etc. Staff	City councils, etc. Staff	Department and agency heads Staff—civil servants (in central office, in field offices)	Same as above (with local focus and impact)	Local judges Law clerks Miscellaneous local judicial officials

PATTERNS OF INFLUENCE IN DOMESTIC PROGRAM IMPLEMENTA- TION

Different subsets of actors typically are most heavily involved in implementing different types of policy (Ripley and Franklin, 1982). Figure 15–5 summarizes the patterns of involvement and influence in the four types of domestic policy discussed. Note particularly that these diagrams take into account the many levels of bureaucracy involved: federal bureaucracy in Washington, federal field offices, and a variety of state and local bureaucracies.

Distributive policies and programs

In distributive programs the main actors come from layers of federal, state, and local bureaucracies, the beneficiaries of the programs (chiefly producer interests), and Congress. The recipients and the bureaucracies are closely linked. Influence flows both ways when detailed decisions are made about implementation. Recipients also have some influence on Congress regarding such deci-

FIGURE 15–5

Patterns of Influence in Implementation of Different Types of Policies and Programs

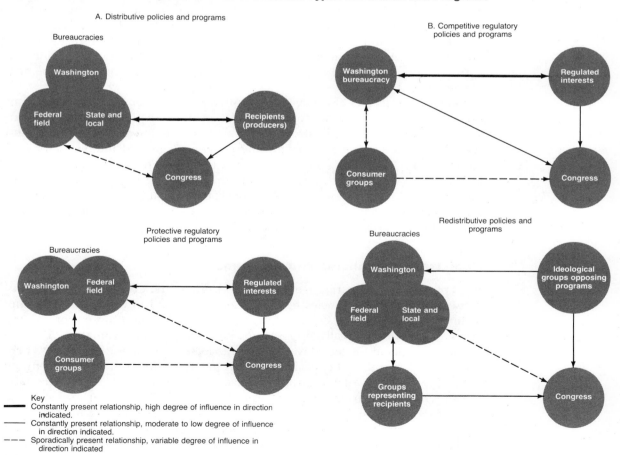

sions. And Congress and the federal part of the bureaucracy interact on occasion. Each can influence the other.

Competitive regulatory policies and programs

Competitive regulatory implementation has four main actors—the Washington federal bureaucracy, regulated interests, Congress, and, sometimes, consumer groups (who are recipients). The main two-way relationship with a lot of mutual influence is between the bureaucrats and the regulated interests. This does not imply that the regulated interests always capture the regulators. It does imply that the regulators and the regulated develop mutually defined interests, though they may continue to disagree on some matters. One relationship of secondary importance is between the regulated interests and Congress. The former exerts some influence over the latter. Another is between Congress and the bureaucracy. Consumer groups are only sporadically active. They have limited influence on Congress and a limited relationship with the bureaucracy. In the latter, influence flows in both directions.

Protective regulatory policies and programs

There are four main actors in protective regulatory implementation. They are the federal bureaucracy both in Washington and in the field, regulated interests, Congress, and consumer groups. Here, the most important relationships are within the bureaucratic cluster. There is an important two-way relationship between bureaucrats and regulated interests, but that relationship may be hostile much of the time.

Regulated interests also have much influence with Congress. In turn, Congress carries on a sporadic two-way relationship with the bureaucrats. Consumer groups have a fairly strong two-way relationship with bureaucrats, and they can influence Congress from time to time. Regulated interests and consumer groups are at odds most of the time. Both have ties to Congress and the bureaucracy, which they use to promote their differing views. The three nonbureaucratic forces disagree with and push the bureaucrats from different directions at once. This puts the bureaucrats in a stressful situation. But it also allows them to pick and choose among possible options.

Redistributive policies and programs

In implementing redistributive policies and programs, the chief actors are bureaucracies—federal agencies both in Washington and in the field, and many state and local agencies. Other actors are the recipients and those representing them, people ideologically opposed to the programs, and Congress. Bureaucrats, especially at the local level, have wide leeway in making decisions. There are no cozy, mutually beneficial, two-way relationships. But the recipients, *if organized*, can have a fairly strong two-way relationship with the bureaucrats. Those who are opposed on ideological grounds, *if organized*, can pressure the bureaucracies to restrict the program. Or they can pressure for change by moving the program toward distributive rather than redistributive ends. They can also put the same kind of pressure on Congress. Beneficiary groups also have access to Congress, however, and thus compete for congressional attention and favor. Congress, in turn, intervenes in redistributive bureaucratic activity only occasionally.

BUDGETING AS THE FIRST STEP

Without money, government can do nothing. Decisions about what agencies and programs get how much are very important. Money does not solve problems. But without, it implementation cannot start.

Budgeting is the heart of modern government. It sets priorities. It provides limits for government action. It is a tangible expression of where government hopes to have an impact. Politically, it provides a highly visible focus for competition between varying interests both in and out of government.

Budget growth and change

TABLE 15—2

Budget Outlays of the United States Government (selected years, 1930—1989)

Fiscal year	Outlays (billions of dollars)
1930	$ 3.3
1940	9.5
1950	42.6
1960	92.2
1970	195.7
1980	576.7
1983	796.0
1986 (est.)	992.1
1989 (est.)	1,183.7

Source: *Budget of the United States Government, Fiscal Year 1985* (Washington, D.C.: U.S. Government Printing Office, 1984), p. 9-62.

The size of the budget has grown with the size of government. In 1792, the entire federal government spent only $5 million. The war year of 1917 was the first time the federal government spent over $1 billion. Table 15–2 summarizes the size of total federal budget outlays in current dollars from 1930 through a projection for 1989. It should be noted, however, that if inflation is taken into account, growth is less than it appears. For example, when spending for 1960 and 1982 is compared in terms of current dollars, the increase is almost eightfold. However, when the two budgets are put in constant dollars (with inflation taken into account), the ratio of spending in the latter to the former year drops to just over 2.3.

The federal government estimates that three fourths of its spending each year is "uncontrollable." This figure has been stable since the early 1970s and is projected to continue. Uncontrollable spending is necessitated by previous commitments. Veterans' benefits, pensions for federal employees, social security, and medicare are examples. But no spending is really uncontrollable. Congress could change basic laws or even renege on these obligations. But because of political realities some spending is, in fact, fixed. Congress is not apt to cut social security payments, for example.

A long-time recipient of benefits from an entitlement program. A Vermont woman, 95, who received the very first check issued by the social security system in 1940 is congratulated by an official on the 35th anniversary of the program.

One analyst of the federal budget thinks that even the official estimate of 75 percent uncontrollable spending is too low (LeLoup, 1978). About 90 to 95 percent of any year's spending seems to be "locked in over the short run."

Congress decided in the 1960s and '70s that more people should be *entitled* to benefits and not dependent on annual action by Congress and the president. These **entitlement programs** are a big part of uncontrollable spending. For 1980, for example, nine programs involved at least $10 billion each in spending required by law. These included almost $100 billion for old age and survivors insurance, $36 billion for medicare hospital insurance and supplementary insurance (two programs), $17 billion for disability insurance, $16 billion for unemployment insurance, $22 billion for civil servants' retirement benefits, $12 billion for military retirement benefits, $14 billion for medicaid, and $11 billion for veterans' compensation and benefits. Most of these programs were exempted from the appropriations process; instead they had what are called permanent appropriations. Even when Congress technically kept the annual appropriations process, there was really no choice. Interest on the national debt required another $68 billion, and here, too, there was no choice. There were also many entitlement programs with required outlays of less than $10 billion.

In one department alone, Health and Human Services, entitlement-program spending grew from about $44 billion in 1970 to $96 billion by 1975, $180 billion by 1980, and about $300 billion by 1985. These figures represented 92 percent of the department's total spending in 1970 and grew to about 96 percent by 1985.

The proportion of uncontrollable expenditures varies from function to function and from agency to agency. For example, for 1976, most income security payments were uncontrollable. But only about half of spending on education, manpower, and social services was uncontrollable. The same is true of agriculture, national resources, energy, and the environment. Only one third of defense spending was uncontrollable (LeLoup, 1980: 74).

Changes in budget patterns reflect changing priorities. Table 15–3 breaks down selected budgets from 1960 through 1985 into four major categories of spending in percentage terms. Several points can be made in looking at these summary figures. Until Reagan's presidency, the percentage of spending on national defense was going down (although dollars spent were increasing) and the percentage for payments to individuals was going up. The Reagan administration reversed both trends. Also under Reagan, as the federal deficit seemed to get

SURVIVAL OF THE FATTEST

TABLE 15–3

Federal Budget Outlays by General Purpose (selected years, 1960–1985)

Year	Percentage of total federal outlays				
	National defense	Payments to individuals	Net interest	Aid to state and local governments	Other
1960	49	26	7	8	10
1970	40	32	7	12	9
1980	24	47	9	16	4
1985 (proposed)	29	42	13	11	5

Source: *Statistical Abstract of the United States, 1982–83* (Washington, D.C.: U.S. Government Printing Office, 1982), p. 247, for 1960, 1970, and 1980. *Budget of the United States Government, Fiscal Year 1985* (Washington, D.C.: U.S. Government Printing Office, 1984), p. M-2, for 1985.

out of control and approach $200 billion annually for at least the rest of the 1980s, the net-interest percentage went up substantially. This represents what it costs the federal government to borrow money. The Reagan administration also reduced the percentage of spending on aid to state and local governments, which had grown over the preceding two decades.

Budgeting for specific agencies: building support

Budget figures show broad general trends. But within those trends and on a year-to-year basis there is a constant battle between various agencies and their supporters for their share of the pie. Agencies develop grand strategies for building external support from interest groups and other clients. They also try to build support in congressional subcommittees for their year-to-year budget. A large part of their budget may come automatically because it is uncontrollable. But that fact dims. The struggle is over what is controllable and can be changed (Wildavsky, 1979).

Agency strategy consists of building support and trust with key figures in and out of government. Both have an impact on their budgetary success. In general, assertive agencies do better than passive ones. The agencies that ask for more will get more (LeLoup, 1980: Chapter 4).

The complex interaction of agencies and congressional appropriations subcommittees helps determine the yearly budget figure. Here, the subcommittee members make a major input into the details of agency policy and program implementation. The main importance of this interaction may be not so much final dollar figures as more substantive decisions. These might be what rules to make, where to place facilities, and what key people to put in responsible positions. Thus, the appropriations committees are involved in agency implementation.

GOVERNMENT IN ACTION: CASES OF IMPLEMENTATION

We conclude this chapter with some examples of implementation. We will not load you down with needless detail. But we think it important that you have some sense of the reality of government implementing efforts. We have chosen cases that show the government at work in different policy areas. We also have chosen cases that show varying degrees of success or failure. Success in implementation means simply that things are going about as planned; it does not necessarily mean the policy is desirable. Likewise, failure means that a lot of things seem to be going wrong. The policy itself may be good or bad.

Many implementation problems show up in these cases; they involve such internal matters as fuzzy goals and poor management. They also show poor coordination between layers of government, unpredicted reactions from private-sector actors, and insufficient political support at all levels.

Maritime industry subsidies: smooth implementation in the distributive area

There are many specific subsidy programs for the merchant shipping and maritime industries (Lawrence, 1965; Jantscher, 1975). The principal ones are:

An operating subsidy that offsets the higher operating costs of American shipping lines compared to foreign lines.

A construction subsidy to shipyards so they can reduce prices and make their products more competitive with foreign-built ships.

Cabotage laws requiring ocean commerce between U.S. points to be carried in ships built and registered in the United States. These provisions added about $3 billion to the cost of shipping between 1950 and 1970. They were paid by consumers of the goods in the form of higher prices.

Tax subsidies that provide what amount to interest-free loans to shipowners to buy ships and equipment from U.S. manufacturers.

Requirements for using U.S. rather than foreign ships for certain kinds of overseas shipments.

This package of subsidies has been in place for decades and has changed little, except for additions. Political support for the basic laws wards off any attempt at change, even if change is proposed. Under these conditions, implementation is free of controversy and almost automatic. A number of interests—shipowners, shipbuilders, maritime unions, relevant bureaucrats, and relevant House and Senate members—dominate the creation and continuation of the laws. These interests also work together easily and naturally to make sure that the aid is distributed swiftly and without a hitch. Some subsidy provisions are self-executing. Tax write-offs only need to be used by accountants for the affected companies. But where a government agency must act, controversy is rarely involved. The action pleases the recipients of the goodies and is not attacked by anyone else.

Federal aid to education: distribution is easy; redistribution is difficult

In 1965 President Johnson and Congress broke a 20-year logjam over a number of sticky issues, and a very large federal aid to education bill became law. The bill had five major programs in five separate titles.

The following discussion focuses on implementation of Title I from its inception in 1965 through 1972 (Murphy, 1971, 1973; Bailey and Mosher, 1968). During that time, the annual cost of that single title grew from $1 billion to $1.6 billion. Its central purpose was to aid disadvantaged students. Two very complex formulas were used to distribute the money. The first determined how much money would go to each county in the country. The second determined how the money would be divided among school districts within each county. Title I tried to give more money to schools with the poorest and most disadvantaged children. The money was for specific projects aimed at compensatory education. The states were to approve projects by applying federal standards. The school districts, though, got their money automatically as a matter of right through the two formulas. The U.S. Office of Education (USOE) was supposed to accept or reject local assurances that the law would be followed in spending the money. And it was supposed to offer guidance in administering the program at state and local levels.

From 1965 until 1970, the program did not work as planned. The money was allocated according to the formula. But little effort was made to see that it was spent as provided in the law. Audits of abuses, for example, were delayed or not carried out. In many ways, the program was treated simply as general aid

Federal aid for education. Grant programs of the federal government have poured billions of dollars into the local public school systems.

to elementary and secondary education. Local school districts had virtual autonomy in deciding how the money should be spent. Some school districts may have made a real effort to focus on the most disadvantaged, but that was almost a matter of chance. In 1970 and 1971, a few concerned people caused a flurry of activity. But that activity subsided.

What explains these disappointing outcomes?

The people who had helped produce what they assumed to be a reform of the educational system were not the people responsible for implementing the reform. There was virtually no overlap between the two groups. The reformers had come from Congress, the high levels of the executive branch, and a few leading interest groups. The implementers were housed in the USOE, an old and small bureaucracy that was greatly expanded to handle the new chores. Those mainly responsible for implementation were long-time civil servants who had well-defined and long-held views about how to proceed—views hostile to the reformers' goals.

The program's goals were murky, the inevitable result of putting together a winning coalition to pass the bill. Coalitions often bring together groups with different views of the legislation's purpose. In this case, some really wanted to help the disadvantaged. Others were much more interested in what amounted to general federal aid to public secondary and elementary education.

The USOE was badly understaffed. It was very small, almost a century old, and had never done anything very innovative. Now it was called on to carry out a huge innovative program very quickly. Some valiant efforts were made, but past shortcomings plagued its efforts. Likewise, state education agencies, which had a critical role, were for the most part ill-prepared for anything needing innovation or a high degree of competence.

The basic distribution of administrative powers in the program created problems. Much power was simply given to state education agencies and local school districts. But even the power kept by the USOE was not used in any direct or forceful way. For example, the office was authorized to accept or reject assurances submitted by each state that the law would be followed. Rejection of a state's assurances meant that funds would be withheld. But the USOE always accepted the assurances without assessing their meaning or sincerity. The authority to withhold money is likely to be politically unworkable. Any such action would bring instant protests from members of Congress, local governments, and national interest groups for state and local governments.

The Office of Education was also given power to develop basic criteria for state and local governments. Again, in form, the final sanction of withholding funds was possible. But even during passage of the law, a loud minority in Congress made it clear that they would object to USOE efforts to use this power. In fact, the USOE never tried very hard.

The norm of home rule in public education was strongly entrenched. The system constantly fought anything focusing on the poor and disadvantaged. Both the USOE and the state agencies deferred in word and deed to the local school districts. They were reluctant to monitor, criticize, or enforce. Good relations among professional educators required that none hassle the others and that local autonomy be respected.

Finally, there was no strong, sustained pressure from reformers that Title I programs focus explicitly on the poor. This pressure might have kept the USOE and state and local groups moving toward that goal, even if slowly. The outburst of such activity in 1970 and 1971 had some impact. But that impact was temporary because the outburst itself was temporary.

Few would argue that implementing Title I of the Elementary and Secondary Education Act has done no good. Local school systems have received funds that they would not have gotten otherwise. But whether the program was used to help poor children is a different question. In the first seven years, the answer seems to be no.

Antitrust implementation in the department of justice, 1973—1976: a protective regulatory agency revives

The Antitrust Division of the Department of Justice has had its ups and downs. It can never escape criticism altogether. Either some parts of private business will be unhappy, or "trustbusters" in Congress or law schools will be unhappy. But in the early 1970s, the division's application of antitrust laws reached a low point. In 1972, a crisis arose over how the division and the Department of Justice had handled a case against International Telephone and Telegraph. ITT had simply used campaign funds to bribe the government not to prosecute vigorously.

Following the ITT debacle, new leadership set out to prove that the division could carry out the major intent of various antitrust laws. In the next four years, much progress was made. This case shows how capable managers can reinstitute implementation that seems faithful to statutory intent.

Some changes were procedural. For instance, until 1973 the attorney general had to approve every antitrust action. This usually put political considerations into the question of whom to prosecute. In 1973, this practice was changed so that the assistant attorney general in charge of the division could proceed on his or her own.

The new leadership of the division looked more at price fixing and dramatically increased the number of criminal prosecutions in such cases. The new leaders also used more division resources in entering proceedings before other federal agencies. They felt they could avoid needless subsequent prosecutions by earlier persuading other agencies to make rulings that they favored. For example, they filed papers with the Civil Aeronautics Board supporting requests for fare reductions by commercial airlines.

The division's success in reasserting itself as a credible agency was enhanced by added funds from Congress. These allowed increases in staff size.

In this case, then, there was active support for the course set by the new leadership. The members of the small staff agreed with the general direction sought by the new leaders. The whole staff was housed in the same building in Washington, so that chances of misunderstanding were reduced. Under these favorable conditions, an agency came back from disgrace and performed well in implementing its central programs.

New communities: a flawed experiment in redistribution

In 1968 and 1970, Congress passed laws to create a New Communities Program (Evans and Rodwin, 1979). By the mid-1970s, according to the program's former administrator, it had been "reduced to a salvage operation." It was scrapped completely in 1978. At the end of 1977, a few thousand people lived in 14 forlorn remnants of the 16 started projects. Backers had dreamed of 100 new starts on such projects annually, with the resulting towns someday inhabited by millions of people. What went wrong?

Congress provided a variety of federal funds and loan guarantees to induce private developers to build specific new communities outside central cities. The projects were supposed to house growing urban populations; use more efficient and less costly designs for housing, heating, and transportation; provide social services for residents on a planned basis; and give minorities and the disadvantaged a chance to move from central cities.

Six major problems quickly turned the program into a fiasco.

First, the financial details were faulty. Design problems were worsened by Department of Housing and Urban Development (HUD) employees. They distrusted real estate developers and lacked experience in dealing with such development.

Second, the new communities had no local constituency to watch out for their interests. They were built with vague promises of good things to come. But too few people were getting anything in the short run to produce support for the kind of financing and attention needed. Their existence did, however, arouse some opposition. Mayors of large cities were desperate for funds to revive inner-city areas. They viewed this program as competitive and a threat to their own chances for federal aid.

Third, federal officials did not take the right steps to gain state and local government support. Yet state and local officials were absolutely critical. They had to provide such facilities as roads, schools, and water and sewage plants that make communities—old or new—livable.

Fourth, people thought that because Congress had spoken in the 1968 and 1970 legislation, the rest of the federal bureaucracy would support HUD's efforts. Such was not the case. Other parts of the federal establishment, in particular the Office of Management and Budget, worked to sabotage the program.

Fifth, the program was built on the assumption that the national economy would be stable. This assumption was false. First an energy crisis and then a severe recession from 1973 to 1975 coincided with the period during which the projects had their last chance to avoid collapse.

Finally, HUD relied mainly on private developers to carry out the projects' broad social purposes—such as more housing for minorities. The developers made profit their number one goal and gave short shrift to other goals. HUD made an implementation error in thinking that developers would behave differently.

Implementation of desegregation in housing and schools

Public housing in Chicago, 1963–1971: the triumph of local power   In Chicago's public housing program in the early 1950s, local priorities overshadowed federal priorities on almost all issues. The federal agency was mainly a funnel for money to help the city do what it liked in the housing field. This was especially true in the area of race. The city used federal money to foster increased or continued segregation in housing for blacks.

The 1960s was a time of civil rights ferment and some important national policy statements. A 1962 executive order and civil rights statutes in 1964 and 1968 made it illegal for a local public housing agency using federal funds to practice racial discrimination.

How did these provisions affect public housing programs at the local level—specifically in Chicago? Basically, they did not (Lazin, 1973). Throughout the 60s, Chicago used its federally funded program to promote racial segregation. Chicago may have been atypical. The visible national political clout of its mayor, Richard Daley, was greater than that of any other local official in the country. But, in fact, many problems caused the outcome and probably would have promoted it no matter who had been mayor. The basic patterns of local control over a federal program continued and were strengthened by federal actions. Thus, it would be a mistake to think the federal government struggled valiantly to uphold the law only to be thwarted by a crafty, determined, and politically savvy local government. In fact, the feds and the locals worked together to promote racially segregated housing despite formal, legally binding statements to the contrary by the president and Congress.

The authority under which HUD could have pursued racial desegregation in housing was itself murky. The executive order and two civil rights acts referred to above did not really define such key terms as *racial discrimination* and *affirmative action*. Neither did HUD regulations. In fact, HUD regulations were unclear and often did not really make discrimination illegal.

Both nationally and locally, HUD operated under norms that stressed deference to local wishes. It bargained with local officials. It worked for good relations with local officials to get local support for its other programs and for its existence in general. HUD did not question local assurances that the city was doing all it could to get rid of racial discrimination and segregation in housing, even when such assurances were obviously untrue.

Few took a different view from the official city position in dealing with HUD. The one persistent local legal challenge to the Chicago Housing Authority actions paid off modestly only in 1984 through a decision by a federal judge.

The public housing program probably helped provide better housing for some poor people in Chicago and elsewhere. But despite national policy, the program did not help reduce segregation in housing. In fact, at least in Chicago, it was used to increase segregated housing.

Housing segregation. Racial groups are still segregated in much of Chicago's public housing.

HEW's office for civil rights and schools: southern success and northern problems   In 1964, Congress passed the Civil Rights Act. Among other things, this prohibited racial discrimination in any program getting federal money. Local public schools were a natural target for federal actions since they all received federal aid. At first, implementation came from the office of the commissioner of education in the Department of Health, Education, and Welfare (HEW). In 1967, an Office for Civil Rights (OCR) was created in HEW (Rabkin, 1980; Bullock, 1980). One of its prime concerns has been segregation in public schools.

The OCR record is mixed. It moved well and successfully in dealing with racial segregation in public schools in the South (see Chapter 13). But in dealing with the same problem elsewhere, its record is not impressive. In the South, OCR appeared to move with determination. In the North, OCR engaged in weak and spotty enforcement despite broad verbal claims. The two different results of OCR can be linked to some systematic differences in implementation in the South and elsewhere.

First, in the South, the target was quite clear and progress was easy to measure. All-black and all-white schools needed to be changed. Segregation was clearly the result of years of state law and so could be easily shown as violating the 1964 Civil Rights Act. In the North, though, segregation was not the result of law. Illegal segregation had to be proved in each case. Therefore, field work and investigation consumed a lot of time and energy.

Second, the mandate for OCR in the South was clear. The law was broad, but OCR and its legislative and bureaucratic leaders were all willing and anxious to focus it on the southern schools. In cases elsewhere, however, both Congress and bureaucrats have ceased being helpful. OCR is left to flounder with broad and vague laws.

Third, in the southern case, Congress and several presidents supported OCR efforts. But elsewhere they were either hostile or gave only occasional support. No one was consistently supportive. Some high legislative and bureaucratic officials supported some efforts, were bitterly critical of others, and were simply not interested in many.

In addition, hitting the southern target was easy. OCR could rely on its Washington staff to do most of the work. This meant that instructions to OCR bureaucrats could be followed easily and only a small number of people would be involved. Elsewhere, OCR had to create and rely on a large field staff for enforcement. This increased internal coordination problems.

OCR was also clearly committed—both in word and deed—to southern desegregation. Commitment elsewhere is high verbally, but its depth beyond that is in question.

Finally, in the South, local forces opposed to desegregation were weak and isolated by the late 1960s and 70s. Elsewhere, local forces opposed to desegregation were more numerous and much stronger. They also had a lot of political clout at the national level.

CONCLUSIONS

In this chapter we examined the complex ways domestic policy gets made and implemented in the United States. Our exploration leads us to the following observations:

1   Access to decision-making processes is the prerequisite for influencing decisions. Those with the best access shape more policy to their liking than do those with less access.

2 Access channels are partially open in the United States. This creates meaningful competition over the nature of public policy in many areas.

3 There are regular patterns in terms of who is most important in making different kinds of decisions. Entrenched interests with the most at stake are hard to displace.

4 Shaping public policy requires building coalitions. Those who fashion what turns out to be the winning coalition must make many compromises. The goals of programs become very murky in this process.

5 Money is essential to implementation. But success depends on many other factors. Throwing money at problems without careful attention to other details often results in wasting some of that money.

6 Implementation is likely to be smoother in distributive policy areas than in other areas. Here all involved stand to gain something tangible. Therefore each has an incentive to reach the specified goals without delay.

7 Implementation is likely to be most difficult when redistribution is at stake. In such cases, some groups see themselves as losers if implementation is smooth. Thus, they have great incentives to seek allies who will help them slow or subvert implementation.

8 No implementation is apt to be problem-free. But the problems can be identified and solved, at least in part. The political patterns underlying some problems are strong and persistent. But they do not inevitably produce program failure, as some critics of government assert. Rather, they produce pitfalls and dangers. Dedicated implementers need to know about these and try to avoid them as best they can.

9 Miracles cannot be expected from government units. They must necessarily engage in implementation activities that are complex and that require both will and some luck to bring everything together as planned.

10 Very little about formulation, legitimation, or implementation of American public policy is ever final. As soon as policies that have been made and approved are in place, questions about their content are raised. Congress usually considers amendments to major bills within a year after passage. It often adopts major changes within a year or two. There is always a tentative and unsettled quality to public policy. The first stages of making a public policy may take a very long time. Even if approval is not achieved for a long time, formulation goes on as coalitions form, dissolve, and reform. When approval is reached, coalitions begin to push for specific changes, for continuation of the basic policy without change, or for the end of the policy. Implementation is also open to competing interests. And implementation decisions, which also constantly change, can alter important parts of domestic policy without formal legislation.

FURTHER READING

Le LOUP, LANCE T. (1980) Budgetary Politics, 2d ed. Brunswick, Ohio: King's Court. A short but comprehensive analysis of federal budgeting.

REDMAN, ERIC (1973) The Dance of Legislation. New York: Simon & Schuster. An interesting story of how a bill becomes a law, in this case the Emergency Health Personnel Act of 1970.

REID, T. R. (1980) Congressional Odyssey: The Saga of a Senate Bill. San Francisco: W. H. Freeman. Another good bill-becomes-a-law book, this one focused on a waterway-user-charge bill that passed in 1978.

RIPLEY, RANDALL B., and GRACE A. FRANKLIN (1982) Bureaucracy and Policy Implementation. Homewood, Ill.: Dorsey Press. An analysis of the implementation of different types of domestic policies and programs in the United States.

RIPLEY, RANDALL B., and GRACE A. FRANKLIN (1984) Congress, the Bureaucracy, and Public Policy. 3d ed. Homewood, Ill.: Dorsey Press. A basic analysis of the relationships between Congress, the bureaucracy, the presidency, and organized interest groups in the shaping of federal laws.

SUNDQUIST, JAMES L (1968) Politics and Policy. Washington, D.C.: Brookings Institution. A classic analysis of federal policymaking in the 1950s and 1960s.

16
Foreign and Defense Policy

At 2:27 Sunday morning in Augusta, Georgia, President Reagan's phone rang. National Security Adviser Robert C. McFarlane told him that an explosion had ripped through a building housing U.S. Marines in Beirut, Lebanon. About 45 were thought to have died (the eventual figure was 240).

The phone call capped the fateful weekend of October 21–23, 1983. Originally, the president had gone to the Augusta National Golf Club to relax and reassure his host, Secretary of State George P. Shultz, that he had the president's ear and was in charge of foreign policy. The trip also proved a useful "cover" for planning a military venture under consideration: invasion of the Caribbean island of Grenada to dislodge a leftist coup.

That weekend, the president got little rest and played little golf. The first afternoon, a gunman smashed onto the course and demanded to speak to the president, who was on the 16th fairway; two hours later, the man surrendered, after holding several people hostage in the pro shop. Secretive huddles were held on the Grenada situation. Then came the phone call about the Beirut disaster. The presidential party decided to return to Washington—not only for the symbolic message that the president was in charge, but also as a continuing cover for the Grenadan planning.

Four hours after the phone call, the presidential helicopter landed on the White House south lawn in a pouring rain. Standing with Mrs. Reagan, Shultz, and McFarlane, the president called the Beirut bombers "bestial" (Williams, 1983). Over the next three days, Reagan consulted on steps to protect the Marines in Lebanon, issued statements, gave final approval to the Grenadan invasion, and met privately with congressional leaders. Tuesday morning he announced the invasion to the nation; two days later, he delivered a stirring prime-time speech on the twin crises.

These events dramatically showed both the reach and limits of our foreign policy. As a major world power, the United States is sooner or later affected by nearly everything that happens around the world. For strategic reasons, we have been involved for decades in the Middle East, among other things aiding the fragile regime of Lebanese President Amin Gemayel and even joining a multinational "peacekeeping" force. Long-standing Caribbean concerns were aroused by the possibility that the island airport on Grenada could be used to ship arms and troops to destabilizing forces in other Central American countries.

Yet U.S. forces anywhere are targets of criticism—and terrorist strikes. Within a few months, the United States and its peacekeeping allies had quit Beirut, leaving Lebanon to an uncertain fate. The Grenadan exercise, while a military

Grenada briefing. [Left] Admiral Wesley McDonald, Atlantic fleet commander, briefs reporters, who were barred from the scene.

Grenada oversight. [Right] Rep. Louis Stokes (D–Ohio) shares C-rations with soldier during fact-finding tour of Grenada.

success, was strictly small potatoes; and in any event, U. S. troops soon left because of the need to still international criticism.

The Lebanon and Grenada situations—though both classic international crises allowing wide presidential discretion—also showed the thin line separating foreign and domestic affairs. American lives were at stake: not only troops, but embassy personnel and civilians (including 1,000 medical students in Grenada). And though leading Democratic presidential contenders briefly halted their campaign schedules during the crisis, it wasn't long before the president's handling of foreign policy, especially the Lebanon disaster, became prime topics of the 1984 presidential campaign.

* * * * *

Foreign and defense policymaking and implementation are the subjects of this chapter. We will discuss the nation's foreign policy and security goals, and the resources needed to pursue them. We will emphasize the political backdrop for such policies. We hope to dispel the notion that foreign policy is something apart, far removed from the rest of American policy. The chief policymakers—the president and Congress—are described. So are the bureaucracies, especially the State and Defense departments and intelligence agencies, that play powerful rules in shaping the policies they implement.

WHAT IS FOREIGN POLICY?

Foreign policy is the sum total of decisions and actions guiding a nation's dealings with other nations. The chief factors are *national goals* and *resources* to achieve them. Statecraft is the art of putting the two together. Every nation, regardless of size or strength, must adjust goals and resources so they balance.

Setting goals

Competing goals　Deciding foreign policy goals is not simple. "Great debates" have often resulted from conflicting objectives: examples involve ties to Old World powers such as England and France during our nation's first years, high versus low tariffs, American expansionism abroad, and military involvement in foreign wars. Conflict over the Vietnam War, for example, caused rioting, draft evasion, and loss of confidence in policymakers.

Any issue can offer many competing goals; some are unattainable, others mutually exclusive. Nations and their people often embrace incompatible objectives at the same time. Few see how these objectives mesh, or how pursuing one may place another out of reach.

In the Lebanese case, Americans wanted to deal harshly with terrorist tactics and governments that condoned or tolerated them. Yet reprisals against the terrorists, mainly Islamic splinter groups, were a two-edged sword: They could anger Arab governments in the region, making President Gemayel's position even more precarious.

Changing conditions　Foreign policy objectives are hard to pin down because they cannot be universally applied. People sometimes talk as if they expect foreign policy to be consistent. But conditions vary so that consistency is rarely feasible. The stance the nation takes toward the Soviet Union may not be right for Zimbabwe.

Changing times, too, demand frequent reassessment. According to the old saying, generals tend to prepare for fighting the previous war; diplomats, too, tend to define problems in terms of prior crises.

The lesson of World War II seemed to be that the United States could not afford isolationism, that we should answer threats to liberty wherever they occur. "Appeasement" was frowned upon; leaders sought to avoid the fate of British Prime Minister Neville Chamberlain, who compromised with Hitler in a vain quest for "peace in our time."

During the 1950s and 60s, this "lesson" steered us into conflicts like Korea and Vietnam. But conditions were far different from what they had been in Europe. It was one thing to side with Britain or France against the Nazis; it was quite another to intrude in less-developed countries with strong nationalistic social movements and little tradition of democratic government. At home, it was one thing to wage all-out war; pursuing limited political wars at less than full capacity was a different story.

The lesson of Vietnam, paid for with 56,000 American lives and untold billions of dollars, was caution in foreign involvement. But is this a reliable guide for some future crisis involving other issues? When new problems arise—as in Lebanon or El Salvador—policymakers must decide what lessons apply.

Means and ends　Even if foreign policy goals are agreed on, it is not always clear what action to take. The human rights campaign of the 1970s is an example. It struck a responsive chord with those dedicated to the principles of the Declaration of Independence. What tactics, though, are most apt to enhance the rights of other nations' citizens? Criticisms of human-rights violations may influence world opinion; but they are just as likely to harden the relevant nations' actions toward dissidents. The white-dominated regime of South Africa poses such a dilemma. Which is more effective—boycotting South Africa or keeping ties and pressuring for better treatment of blacks? The answers are rarely simple.

In sum, it is no easier to identify our foreign policy goals than to define our policy on housing or abortions. Foreign policy goals, like those of domestic policy, are many and often in conflict. They shift with circumstances. And they must be applied with care and flexibility.

Resources for world power

A nation attains its foreign policy goals by allocating *resources*. Like goals, resources vary. The notion of resources is kin to the concept of *power*, applied here to sovereign states rather than to individuals or groups. Broadly defined, power is a nation's ability to influence other nations in directions that favor its interests.

Power is an elusive concept. People often equate it with military force. But military resources are not always relevant for solving foreign policy problems. Abundant natural, human, or economic resources are just as vital in the international sweepstakes. Nations also draw strength from the legitimacy or stability of their political regimes and from the loyalty of their people. Power, in other words, is many sided, changing, and relative to the problem at hand.

Geopolitics   The U.S. course in the world arena is decisively shaped by its resources. One resource is geographic position. Advocates of geopolitics (a form of geographic determinism) hold that this factor, more than any other, decides a nation's fate in world affairs. Geography, argued Nicholas Spykman (1942: 41), "is the most fundamental factor in the foreign policy of states because it is the most permanent."

Geographic position has dictated much of our foreign policy. Separated from Europe by a broad ocean, America has been free from military incursions since 1814, when the British sacked the capital. Long, unprotected boundaries to the north and south were a threat when unfriendly powers ruled adjoining land. But even this threat was removed over time. Border security meant our country could develop free from the threat of outside aggression.

Agribusiness. U.S. farm products are the leading export commodities.

This seeming remoteness fueled an isolationist philosophy—aloofness from other nations' affairs. In his 1796 farewell address, George Washington warned against "entangling alliances" with other nations. Every year on his birthday, the address is recited in both chambers of Congress. However, his isolationist spirit became obsolete with the advent of global economic ties, not to mention intercontinental missiles and nuclear weapons.

By any count, America is blessed by geography. It commands a continental domain with abundant natural resources to aide its rise to world leadership. It is the world's leading or near-leading producer of most minerals—iron, copper, lead, zinc, and precious metals. Despite its energy deficit, it produces 65 percent of the world's natural gas, a fourth of its crude petroleum, and a fifth of its coal. It is the world's premier manufacturing nation, leading in most classes of manufactured goods. It is also the world's greatest agricultural power: half of the world's corn, a fourth of its oats and meat products, a fifth of its cotton and dairy products, and 15 percent of its wheat come from the United States. The country's commanding position flows largely from self-sufficiency in many classes of raw materials and manufactured goods.

Economic development It has become more and more obvious that a nation's power—including its capacity to wage war—is built on its economic base. By almost every sign, our economic resources are vast and resilient. The gross national product (GNP) is more than $3.5 trillion. Even when growth and productivity lag, the country compares well with other major industrial nations.

Educational and technological capacity is a paramount resource. The productivity of our labor force of more than 100 million is high because of training and automated equipment. Research laboratories contribute basic knowledge; they also offer many inventions and technological refinements to raise productivity and living standards.

A striking example of the potential of science, technology, industry, and organization was the U.S. space thrust. When in 1961 President Kennedy voiced the goal of landing on the moon, it seemed remote. But eight years and $24 billion later, Apollo 11 astronauts did just that.

The power generated from such resources is awesome. We rely on tax rates no higher than those of comparable industrial countries (and lower than some); but our country supports many domestic social programs and global aid. Since World War II, it has spent some $150 billion in foreign economic, military, and technical aid. Its military arsenal can kill every person on earth many times over. It has even borne the brunt of major military efforts without quickly destroying its domestic economy: the Korean War was waged with 14 percent of the GNP; the Vietnam War at its height involved only 8 percent of the GNP.

The limits of power

Yet there are severe limits to what the resources of even the world's strongest nation can achieve. American power is awesome but not infinite.

Interdependencies Many problems flow from economic interdependence. Like other developed nations, our country relies on abundant, cheap raw materials for a sophisticated economy and comfortable living standards. It has vast natural resources to support its economy. Yet there are crucial gaps.

Less-developed nations with critical raw materials—like oil—can force concessions from developed countries. They can resort to the time-honored practices of controlling supplies and prices. Whether this can tilt the world's balance of power, only time will tell. Many of the very poorest nations also lack valuable raw materials to use in bargaining.

The other side to interdependence is that industrial nations need outlets for their manufactured goods or services. Between 1965 and 1982, U.S. exports as a percent of GNP have doubled. Despite vast internal markets, American firms are looking outward and concerning themselves with trade barriers and the ability of other nations to buy goods.

Policies beyond price Some policy goals are unattainable at any price. Or they are so costly that no nation would rationally use the resources they require. As seen, the nation's might offered no way to insure by force Lebanon's security. Economic sanctions and military thrusts could be tried; full-scale military invasion was out of the question. The Vietnam War was another lesson in the limits of power. True, it was not an all-out effort. Sensing the public would not support that, presidents Johnson and Nixon took pains to contain the effort and hide its impact from the average person. Yet by all usual standards, the effort was massive; at its height, it involved 800,000 American troops.

Economic clout. Broker at the Paris stock exchange records dollar's value against the French franc. The world's leading currency, the dollar fluctuates with the nation's economic strength.

Limits of power. Vietnamese flee village bombing.

The real challenge of Vietnam was not military, however. One of the war's bitterest foes, Senator J. William Fulbright (D-Ark.), questioned (1966: 15) whether even the United States could "go into a small, alien, undeveloped Asian nation and create stability where there is chaos, the will to fight when there is defeatism, democracy where there is no tradition of it, and honest government where corruption is a way of life." The United States wanted to halt the advance of international communism. So it helped an ill-supported, corrupt regime stave off a popular movement. Supporters of that movement drew strength from the cause of national liberation and military aid from communist allies. It was, in short, a civil war which outside military help could affect but not decide. Our armed forces could defoliate the country, but they could not create a viable regime where none existed.

This lesson in the limits of power should come as no surprise to those with a sense of history. Two hundred years earlier, the world's strongest power, Great Britain, lost 13 colonies under like circumstances. The colonies were shaken by civil strife, and the outcome was by no means certain. Had Parliament chosen to throw more military resources into the fray, it might have tilted the victory to the loyalists. But Parliament was divided; it would not strip its defenses in other parts of the world. Even if England had won militarily, would that have ensured loyalty and peace in the colonies? Probably not. Certain objectives, in short, are so costly they are beyond the practical reach of even the most richly endowed nation.

TYPES OF FOREIGN AND DEFENSE POLICIES

Bearing in mind the dilemma of balancing goals and resources, it helps to think of several types of foreign and defense policies. (A similar breakdown of domestic policy is given in Chapter 15.) These are **crisis policies,** reactions to direct challenges to the nation's security; **strategic policies,** advancing the nation's interests by military force or otherwise; and **structural policies,** involving economic interests or deployment of resources or personnel.

Crisis policies

Self-preservation is not the only goal of foreign or military policy; but when it is directly threatened, other goals must be cast aside. One definition of an international crisis is a sudden challenge to the nation's safety and security. Examples range from the Japanese attack on Pearl Harbor in 1941 to the attack on the Marines in Lebanon in 1983.

Crises engage policymakers at the highest levels. These are the president, the secretaries of state and defense, the National Security Council, and the Joint Chiefs of Staff. During a crisis, policymakers keep a tight rein on information flowing upward from line officers. Indeed, crisis management is so important (see Chapter 9) that President Reagan insisted on a White House team led by Vice President Bush for that function.

Public and media attention rivet on crises. People tend to support whatever course the decision makers choose. Patriotism runs high, as people hasten to "rally 'round the flag" (Mueller, 1973: 208–13).

Most foreign and defense policymaking is aimed at deterring crises; it tries to prevent direct challenges to the nation. Yet, with public attention and support at their highest levels, crisis politics given officials unique chances for leadership. Thus, leaders sometimes promote a crisis atmosphere in the hope of mobilizing public support. President Carter sought vainly to raise public consciousness on the energy crisis by calling it "the moral equivalent of war." His failure to keep a crisis atmosphere during the prolonged Iranian hostage affair helped cause his loss of support.

Strategic policies

Strategic policies embrace most of what are thought of as foreign policy questions. Decision makers must plan strategies toward other nations while guarding interests at home. Examples include the basic mix of military forces and weapons systems; arms sales to foreign powers; trade inducements or limits; economic, military, and technical aid to less-developed nations; major treaties with other nations; and our basic stance toward such global bodies as the UN and world banking agencies.

Strategic policies engage not only top-level executive decision makers, but also committees of Congress and middle-level executives. The State Department is an agency for strategic decision making, as is the office of the secretary of defense. The individual uniformed services may also become involved.

Strategic policies engage ideological, racial, ethnic, or economic interests. At times, they command widespread public and media attention. The Panama Canal Treaty debate of 1978, the Soviet grain embargo of 1980–81, and the sale of AWACS planes to Saudi Arabia in 1981 are examples. Increasingly, these questions involve structural (distributive) politics; interests compete for strategic policies that will benefit them—for example, arms sales and grain sales.

Structural policies

Foreign and military programs call for vast resources—millions of employees and billions of dollars each year. Deploying these resources is structural policymaking. These policies include weapons systems and procurement, location of military installations, weapons and surplus food sales to foreign countries, and trade restrictions to protect domestic industries.

Structural policymaking is about the same for foreign and defense issues as for domestic issues. It straddles both domains, as do distributive policies.

Structural decisions engage a wide span of political groups. Defense contracts and installations, for instance, are hotly sought by business firms, labor unions, local communities, and their political representatives in Washington. The Defense Department's strength flows mainly from the large volume of structural decisions it controls. In contrast, the State Department makes few such decisions. This hampers its dealings with domestic interest groups.

PRESIDENTIAL LEADERSHIP

Those making foreign policy face an environment that both limits and helps their actions. They cannot ignore public opinion (or inattention), the media, interest groups, or electoral politics. But these forces, no matter how strong, cannot manage our relations with other nations. That is the task of the president, Congress, and the bureaucracy.

Constitutional powers

In foreign and military affairs, the president has the burden of leadership. His constitutional powers are impressive. He appoints ambassadors and other U.S. emissaries; he receives representatives of other nations; he negotiates treaties. "The president," declared John Marshall in 1799, "is the sole organ of the nation in its external relations, and its sole representative with foreign nations."

The president is solely responsible for day-to-day relations with foreign powers. In calling the president the "sole organ" of foreign affairs, Marshall was surely referring mainly to communication with other governments (Corwin 1957: 178).

The broader task of making foreign policy, however, is shared with Congress. The Senate must confirm ambassadors and ratify treaties. Although the president is commander-in-chief, Congress has the power to declare war, raise and equip military forces, and finance commitments.

Foreign policy is also subject to interpretation by the courts. Normally the courts give wide berth to presidential powers. To free 52 U.S. citizens held hostage in Iran, Carter in 1981 waived all pending claims by U.S. citizens against that country. Although the action was highly controversial, Carter was upheld. In a 1984 ruling (*Regan* v. *Wald),* the Supreme Court, by a 5-to-4 vote, even upheld a questionable executive order forbidding most Americans to spend money on travel to Cuba. "It did so," remarked commentator Anthony Lewis (1984), "by taking a worshipful view of executive power—by virtually assuming that anything the executive branch does under the label 'foreign policy' is lawful."

Yet presidents do not have unlimited leeway; even in global crises, they cannot circumvent procedures established by Congress (*Youngstown Sheet and Tube Co.* v. *Sawyer,* 1952). But in the crunch, judges are very, very hesitant to limit presidents.

War powers As with other sovereign powers, the president and Congress share so-called war powers. Congress has exclusive authority to "declare war" (Article I, Section 8); the president is commander-in-chief of the military (Article II, Section 2).

The United States has formally declared war five times: the War of 1812 (1812–14), the Mexican War (1845–48), the Spanish-American War (1898), World War I (1917–18), and World War II (1941–45). Only once did Congress actually delve into the merits of waging war, and that was in 1812, when the vote was rather

Imperial adventure. The sinking of the U.S. battleship *Maine* in Havana harbor plunged the nation into the brief, successful Spanish-American War of 1898. (Theodore Roosevelt, right, poses with his "Rough Riders" after capturing San Juan Hill.

close. In every other case, Congress overwhelmingly supported going to war, though the declarations themselves merely acknowledged that a state of war already existed. (In two cases—the Mexican and Spanish-American conflicts—it later regretted its action.)

The power to declare war is unreliable. Although war has been declared five times, our country has used military force on foreign soil nearly 200 times (Fisher, 1972: 177). Most of these actions were authorized by presidents on the pretext of protecting life or property abroad.

In the post–World War II era, our country was bound by a network of treaties and agreements pledging mutual assistance if signatory nations were attacked. Thus, President Johnson was told by his advisers that no declaration of war was required in Vietnam. They said he already had ample powers under the 1964 Gulf of Tonkin Resolution, the now-defunct Southeast Asia Treaty Organization (SEATO) treaty, and his "inherent powers."

Eight times since World War II, presidents have cloaked foreign intervention under the rationale of protecting American lives and property abroad. These included Lebanon in 1958, the Dominican Republic in 1965, the Cambodian "incursion" of 1970, the South Vietnamese invasion of Laos in 1971, the *Mayagüez* incident of 1975, the Iranian rescue mission of 1980, and Lebanon and Grenada in 1983. The Korean (1950–53) and Vietnam (1965–73) wars were justified on the grounds of treaty obligations and "inherent powers" derived from the broad notion of executive authority.

Backlash over the Vietnam War spawned the War Powers Resolution (P.L. 93–148), which became law in 1973 over Nixon's veto. Under it, the president must (1) consult with Congress before introducing U.S. troops into hostilities; (2) report any commitment of troops to Congress within 48 hours; and (3) terminate the use of forces within 60 days if Congress does not declare war, extend the period by law, or is unable to meet. (The president may extend the period to 90 days, if necessary.)

The War Powers Resolution has proved an awkward compromise. While it may have deterred some actions, the resolution has not kept presidents from intervening in emergencies. In some cases, members of Congress sat on the sidelines, only later questioning the actions. Other cases were debated at length. When President Reagan committed forces to the Lebanon peacekeeping mission, he initially declined to adhere precisely to the resolution. He feared that the timetable set in motion by the resolution would limit his flexibility and might encourage hostile factions to delay coming to the bargaining table. The impasse was resolved when Congress, led by House Speaker Thomas P. O'Neill, passed a resolution authorizing deployment of troops for 18 months (extending beyond the 1984 elections). When the Lebanon mission later collapsed, both the White House and congressional leaders sought to spread the blame.

Further clouding the War Powers Resolution was the Supreme Court's 1983 decision striking down so-called "legislative vetoes" (*INS* v. *Chadha*; see Chapter 11). Experts disagree, but it seems likely that the resolution's major provisions would survive the Court's scrutiny. Whether they will survive political warfare is less clear. Presidents will continue to seek flexibility and resist congressional "meddling." Members of Congress will still ask to be consulted; they will also strive to control the use of troops abroad.

Dulles and Kissinger. Two secretaries of state who dominated foreign policy were John Foster Dulles (1953–59) and Henry Kissinger (1973–77). Dulles, left, personified Cold War policies of containing Communism and challenging Russian power. Kissinger, shown on the right talking to then-Israeli Prime Minister Golda Meir, reflected post-cold war pragmatism and closer relations with such Communist powers as the USSR and China.

Presidential advisers

Presidential primacy in foreign affairs rests in part on the fact that the president is a single individual who can call upon various expert advisers in formulating policies. The quality of the president's advisory system is nowhere more important than in foreign and defense matters.

The secretary of state   Over time, the president's prime foreign policy adviser has been the secretary of state—the senior cabinet official and, in earlier times, a presidential contender in his own right.

This post has drawn some of the nation's most distinguished public servants. A few were more noteworthy than the presidents who appointed them; some forged policies of lasting importance. John Quincy Adams (1817–25) was the true author of the Monroe Doctrine, which proclaimed opposition to foreign intervention in the Americas. George C. Marshall (1947–49), the grand military strategist of World War II, drew up postwar policies of global alliances and aid to war-torn and less-developed countries.

Contemporary secretaries of state may or may not be major foreign policy architects; they may or may not be close personal advisers of the president. Two who were both were John Foster Dulles (1953–59) and Henry Kissinger (1973–77). Their power flowed not from their cabinet post but from their unique relationship with the president.

The National Security Council   A potential instrument for White House coordination is the National Security Council (NSC), created by the National Security Act of 1947. NSC is to advise the president on "domestic, foreign, and military policies relating to the national security."

As a presidential instrument, the NSC has been used differently by each one. Eisenhower repeatedly used it. But after 1961, it fell into disuse, though it was on occasion used to ratify decisions reached through informal negotiations.

In 1969, Nixon reestablished the NSC as "the principal forum for presidential consideration of foreign policy issues." Under national security adviser Kissinger, NSC committees and aides began to multiply once more, as they had under Eisenhower. The basic NSC structure remained in place under later presidents. Its size and importance varies with the presidents' personal style and relations with key advisers.

White House versus State Department?   Since the 1960s, presidents have tended to seek advice from White House staffs, not the State Department. NSC staff directors like Kissinger (until he went to the State Department) and Zbigniew Brzezinski (1977–81) tended to outshine the secretaries of state. This downgraded the department's influence.

Reagan and his original foreign policy adviser, Richard V. Allen, declared their intention of restoring the secretary of state as principal foreign policy adviser. Even so, quarrels over White House–State Department powers soon broke out and led to Alexander Haig's resigning as secretary of state. New personnel (George Shultz as secretary of state; William Clark and then McFarlane as national security adviser) eased the tensions, but did not remove institutional rivalries.

The imperial presidency

Constitutional powers aside, presidents draw facts and advice from diverse executive agents, making the foreign policy role the main source for growth of what has been called "the imperial presidency" (Schlesinger, 1973). Many think that presidents should play a dominant role in foreign policy. They offer the "energy, speed, and dispatch" that legislative bodies lack.

The Vietnam War challenged presidential domination in foreign affairs. It pointed out the dangers of this doctrine: biased information, rigidity, intragroup conformity, and blind loyalty to prior commitments. It cast doubt on the propriety of presidential leadership; and it stiffened the will of Congress to make itself heard.

As the Vietnam era recedes from view, critics wonder whether the presidency has been too tightly restrained by new congressional controls. Certainly all presidents since Nixon have thought this. Congress typically lacks the organization or the consensus to act decisively in foreign affairs; but the Constitution gives Congress most of the trump cards. If it has the will, Congress can

Diplomacy. President Kennedy and Soviet Foreign Minister Andrei Gromyko in "photo opportunity" during White House negotiations.

halt a president in his tracks; even if it is divided, it can insert itself and frustrate the president's wishes.

CONGRESS AND FOREIGN POLICY

No matter how forceful a president's foreign policy initiatives, they must have the support of Congress. All foreign policy programs entail congressional participation at some stage.

Congressional involvement in foreign policy is flowing, not ebbing. The lines between foreign and domestic policy are growing more and more obscure. Major foreign policies now carry large dollar amounts for trade, aid, or military help. These bring into play Congress's cherished power of the purse. Since the 1970s, there have been strong reassertions of initiative in Congress, especially when major national commitments are at stake.

Constitutional powers

The Constitution makes Congress an equal partner in foreign policy. Though the president is expected to manage day-to-day foreign relations, Congress can influence those relations in ways both large and small.

Treaty power   The Constitution (Article II, Section 2) provides that the president "shall have power, by and with the advice and consent of the Senate, to make treaties, provided two thirds of the senators present concur." This power, not shared with the House, lends the Senate special prestige and tradition in this area.

The Senate may accept or reject a treaty. However, treaties are rarely rejected outright. (Only 19 were between 1789 and 1982.) More often, the Senate attaches reservations, amends the treaty, or simply delays action. This can render the treaty inoperative or force the president to renegotiate all or part of it.

Treaty powers. President Carter signs Panama Canal Treaty, later ratified by the Senate after heated debate.

One study (Crabb, 1983: 104) found that between 1789 and 1963, the Senate had approved without change 944 treaties, or 69 percent of those submitted.

The Senate's active role in ratification was shown during the 1977–78 debate over the Panama Canal treaty. The public opposed the "giveaway" of the canal to the Panamanians, so the treaty was unpopular. Senate floor debate dragged over two and a half months—the longest such debate since the Treaty of Versailles was considered in 1919 (Crabb and Holt, 1984: 73). Half the senators went to Panama to check the situation. No less than 192 changes in the treaty, some major, were proposed. In the end, the treaty was ratified, 68 to 32, but with several Senate-imposed amendments.

Over time, treaties have been a vital part of our relation with foreign powers. When made and duly ratified, they are the law of the land. But not all are self-executing; often statutes are needed to carry out their terms. Congress may or may not pass these.

Today, presidents use **executive agreements** to reach accords of the type formerly reserved for treaties. Such agreements have no formal status in the Constitution. But they have been used six times more often than treaties, and by every president since Washington. These agreements have become the standard method for dealing with foreign powers. During our first half century, 60 treaties and 27 executive agreements were signed. As of January 1, 1983, there were 966 treaties and 6,571 executive agreements in force.

Congress may or may not be taken into the president's confidence when executive agreements are reached. From time to time, a constitutional amendment requiring Senate ratification of these agreements has been pushed. Since the Vietnam War, the Senate Foreign Relations Committee has shown renewed vigor in reviewing them.

Senate confirmation powers   A second senatorial prerogative (Article II, Section 2) is confirming presidential appointment of ambassadors, ministers, and consuls; appointments and promotions in the foreign service; and appointments to high-level posts. The Senate Foreign Relations Committee now studies thousands of appointments, most of Foreign Service officers. FSOs work under a merit system, apart from but similar to that for other federal workers.

Appointees to foreign posts are normally confirmed; the theory is that presidents have the right to pick their own teams. In the past, this allowed rewarding large campaign donors with key ambassadorial posts. Lately, the practice has come under attack; pressure is growing for presidents to choose career diplomats or qualified private citizens. Confirmation proceedings are often used to air views on the president's foreign policy rather than to probe the candidate's fitness. In 1981, a Reagan State Department choice, Ernest Lefever, caused a storm of controversy over his human-rights views; finally, he withdrew his name.

The power of the purse   Until World War II, foreign operations required little money. This changed radically after the war. America became a major provider of economic, military, and technical aid. We also contributed to international and regional development banks and to various types of loan programs.

The yearly debate over such aid allows Congress to influence foreign policy, for better or worse. Congress can place "strings" on foreign aid; it can restrict or prohibit funds for countries that do not conform with certain conditions. Presidents and aides usually deplore these as limiting their dealings with other

Presidential initiative. Reagan and Chinese President Li Xiannian in Peking.

countries. They feel restrictions are more apt to cause resentment than conformity to congressional directives.

In the final analysis, no major foreign or military enterprise can be sustained unless Congress provides the money. Presidents may be able to conduct an operation for a time using existing funds and supplies, as Johnson did at first with Vietnam. But sooner or later, the issue of funding must be confronted. Our role in South Vietnam finally ended when Congress refused to provide emergency aid funds. Funding decisions limited the Reagan administration's Central American activities.

Foreign and defense policies increasingly involve economic resources. This has served to heighten Congress's leverage. It has also equalized the role of the House in comparison to the Senate, because of the historic taxing and funding role of the House.

Other congressional powers   Congress holds other high cards in the foreign policy game. It has power over interstate and foreign commerce, a critical function in these days of worldwide trading. Exercise of normal legislative powers can shape foreign policy. Statutes and joint resolutions (such as the Gulf of Tonkin Resolution during the Vietnam War) help define foreign policy; they empower or limit executive policymakers. Congressional committees oversee foreign policy activities, sometimes through investigations but more often through routine hearings and informal consultations. When considering critical actions, presidents often confide in congressional leaders.

Who speaks for Congress?

A subject as widespread as foreign affairs causes a huge jurisdictional tangle among Capitol Hill committees. Of the standing committees, 16 of the 22 in the House and 12 of the 16 in the Senate consider foreign policy issues. In each chamber, foreign affairs, armed services, and appropriations committees bear the major duties.

The Senate Foreign Relations Committee has a distinguished history because it considers treaties and nominations of foreign policy officials. Normally it sees itself as a partner and adviser to the president. During the height of dispute on the Vietnam War, in the late 1960s and early 1970s, the committee, led by Senator J. William Fulbright (D-Ark.), was a forum for antiwar debate. Since then, the committee has resumed a more supportive role.

For most of its history, the House Foreign Affairs Committee worked in the shadow of its Senate counterpart. At one time, in the 1920s, the most momentous issue before the committee was a $20,000 authorization for an international poultry show in Tulsa, Oklahoma (Martin, 1960: 49). All this changed after World War II; foreign aid programs thrust the House—with its unique powers of the purse—into virtual parity with the Senate (Carroll, 1966: 20). Today, the annual foreign aid bill remains the centerpiece of the panel's workload, although it ranges over the whole spectrum of foreign policy issues.

The Senate and House Armed Services Committees straddle the national security arena. They annually authorize Pentagon spending for research, development, and procurement of all weapons systems; construction of military facilities; and civilian and uniformed personnel.

Armed Services Committee members are less interested in global strategy than

Arms. Military spending tends to be attractive locally.

in structural matters—force levels, military installations, and defense contracts (Huntington, 1961). Thus, military policy is in many ways an extension of constituency politics.

The two committees have tended to attract members favorable to military spending and home-district installations. One junior member branded the House committee as "the Pentagon's lobby on the Hill." But the committees reflected Capitol Hill skepticism over the magnitude of Reagan administration defense spending in the mid-1980s; and they are fond of Pentagon "whistle blowers" and critics of waste.

Other congressional panels get into the act. Defense spending is the largest controllable segment of the yearly federal budget; therefore, appropriations committees and subcommittees exert detailed control over foreign and defense policies. Two overseeing committees review intelligence activities. Tariffs and other trade regulations are the province of the taxing committees (House Ways and Means, Senate Finance). Banking committees handle international financial and monetary policies. And so on.

The ebb and flow of power

If the Constitution invites the president and Congress to struggle over control of policy, nowhere is that fight more overt than in foreign affairs. Relations between the two branches have been volatile. One scholar (Bax, 1977) identifies no less than five patterns of legislative-executive relations since World War II: *accommodation, antagonism, acquiescence, ambiguity,* and *acrimony.* We will examine the historical occurrence of these patterns.

The Cold War era   The closing years of World War II and the first postwar years (1943–50) were marked by *accommodation;* "Close cooperation was initiated between high-level executive officials and the committee and party leaders of Congress" (Bax, 1977). This made for a consistent postwar policy. It permitted speedy approval of unprecedented American treaty and aid pledges; it kept foreign policy out of partisan politics. This was the era of bipartisanship. Capitol Hill statesmen Senators Arthur H. Vandenberg (R-Mich.) and Tom Connally (D-Tex.) both chaired the Senate Foreign Relations Committee during that time.

During the period of *antagonism* (1950–53), partisan squabbling broke out over the "loss" of China to the Communists, the Korean War, and Truman's dismissal of World War II hero General Douglas MacArthur.

With Eisenhower's election (1953), a period of *acquiescence* set in. A national consensus favored the policy of containment—keeping communism within its existing borders. Congress got into the habit of ratifying the president's plans; it cut marginal amounts from program budgets but generally supported presidential initiatives. The period lasted beyond Eisenhower's terms and into the 1960s. The high-water mark occurred in 1964, when Johnson persuaded Congress to approve the Gulf of Tonkin Resolution, a vague grant of authority to act in Southeast Asia. The next year, Johnson began escalating the Vietnam effort without further consultation with Congress.

Controversy over Vietnam brought a period of *ambiguity* (1967–70), with questioning and uneasiness. Nixon's invasion of Cambodia in 1970, done without consulting Congress, launched a period of *acrimony* (1970–76), marked by disputes over Vietnam and almost every other phase of foreign policy.

The post-Vietnam era   In 1975, American participation in the Vietnam War was halted by action of Congress. Since then, Congress has shown little desire to follow blindly wherever the president leads. I. M. Destler (1981: 167) described the 1970s changes:

> The congressional revolution against presidential foreign policy dominance began as a revolt against the people, ideas, and institutions held responsible for the Vietnam War debacle. In terms of its objectives, this revolution was highly successful. Congress reined in the president and constrained the use of military and paramilitary power. It also elevated policy goals the executive had neglected, such as human rights and nuclear nonproliferation.

Some observers—especially those in the White House—think Congress acts too strongly, hampering the development of coherent, consistent foreign policy. Too many scattered power centers on Capitol Hill, some think, get in the president's way and prevent swift, concerted action (Cutler, 1980).

Even so, presidents have not been afraid to act in emergencies. Ford rescued the captured U.S. ship *Mayagüez;* Carter sent an Iranian rescue mission; Reagan launched the Grenada invasion. These acts were authorized swiftly and without the prior consultation envisioned in the 1973 War Powers Act. Also, Congress went along with many major thrusts of the Carter and Reagan administrations—from the Panama Canal Treaty and the Egypt-Israel Camp David accords to the sale of nuclear materials to India and AWACs to Saudi Arabia.

When pressed by circumstances, presidents tend to act as they see fit; they hold Congress at arm's length and hope success will stifle its criticism. On the other side, Congress is unwilling to yield its renewed powers. Thus, the delicate balance of power continues.

THE POLITICAL BACKDROP

Makers of foreign policy are not totally free to set the nation's course with other nations. The basic goals and resources, as we outlined, are the raw materials from which foreign policy is fashioned. Policymakers are also held back by factors from the political arena: public attitudes, media coverage, interest-group actions, and electoral politics.

Public opinion and foreign policy

International relations are not solely the province of professional diplomats. Regardless of government forms, diplomacy takes place in a context of public tolerance or disapproval. People will not commit resources or make sacrifices unless they understand overall goals. Policies gain added support if they are seen as right and legitimate. Proclaiming the reasons for forming a new nation, the Declaration of Independence was written "with a decent respect to the opinions of mankind"; today public opinion plays an even greater role in global politics.

Lack of information   Public attitudes toward foreign and military affairs are less structured or informed then those on domestic matters. The average person pays less attention to *all* issues than pure democratic ideals might dictate. This is doubly true of foreign and military affairs. Many consider them remote or unrelated to their daily lives.

U.S. stakes. Fear of Soviet influence in Nicaragua (1927 cartoon).

"The majority of Americans," according to a respected study (Katz et al., 1954: 35), "are not interested in foreign affairs as such, as they appear to take an interest only in those problems clearly affecting their own interests." Recent studies verify that citizens show more interest in local or national events than in events in other countries, or even in U.S. relations with those countries. Top foreign policy problems, as seen by citizens, are those that strike at the home front: protecting American workers' jobs, keeping up the dollar's value, and maintaining energy supplies. Lagging somewhat behind are such goals as worldwide arms control, containing communism, combating world hunger, and defending our allies (Reilly, 1983: 8–13).

A general feeling exists to "keep the country out of war" while at the same time "maintaining a strong defense posture." Although a majority of people support the country's active involvement in world affairs, this commitment to internationalism has eroded since the post–World War II period (Reilly, 1983: 11–14). Beyond that, most people have scant understanding of the techniques, methods, or issues of foreign policy.

To the extent that people view foreign events, they tend to do so simplistically. Lacking historical background, they tend to see events as episodic, as separate and unrelated happenings. They think events are caused by individuals who are good or evil: the work of a Stalin or a Churchill, a Kissinger or an Ayatollah Khomeini. They see the nation's vital interest resting with countries most visible to them: Japan, Canada, Great Britain, Saudi Arabia, West Germany, Israel and Mexico (Reilly, 1983: 16–17).

Volatility   Because of inattention and scanty information, Americans' foreign policy views are subject to changes in mood (Almond, 1960). Even during global crises, private and domestic affairs—for example, jobs, inflation, and crime—have a strong pull on public attention and loyalty. Mass publics lack personal experience or stable beliefs to anchor their commitments. So they are susceptible to guidance from the president or other visible foreign policy leaders. Many people seem disposed to follow American policy wherever it may lead: "My country, right or wrong."

Longing for leadership   Lacking stable foreign policy views, the average person tends to be a passive receiver of cues from leaders. During most of the Cold War period, this meant deference to strong presidents who could articulate the nation's policy and make their ideas prevail even against opposing views. Three fourths of the respondents to one survey (Sigel, 1966: 125) thought the president, if he felt it necessary, should send troops abroad despite public opposition.

Since the Vietnam War, people no longer automatically assume "the president knows best" on foreign policy. They now seem to feel the public and Congress should be partners in policymaking. Also, leaders should be candid and open.

Foreign policy elites   Mass opinion may be unstable, but the views of informed elites, attentive publics, are given disproportionate weight by decision makers (Almond, 1960). The White House and the State Department cannot ignore mass opinion. Yet, on a daily basis, they deal mainly with elites.

Elites are roughly defined as those who inform themselves about world developments; they regularly read the *New York Times* or some major metropolitan journal; they belong to such organizations as the Council on Foreign Relations (a New York–based group with numerous local chapters) or the League of Women Voters; they travel abroad or attend conferences on global questions; they have business or professional stakes in worldwide developments; they perceive a wider range of pressing international issues than the general public and are far more committed to internationalism. Most important, they express their views in letters or statements to newspapers, journals, Congress, and other key groups.

At the heart of foreign policy elite groups is a fairly well-defined bipartisan group of business people, lawyers, and scholars. They are centered in but not limited to, the international trading centers of the Northeast and the West Coast. A majority of high-level diplomats and makers of foreign policy come from these groups. Nearly every secretary of state since World War II, regardless of party, has come from this source.

As in so many phases of American life, the foreign policy elite is becoming broader and more diverse. Diplomats are no longer picked from the upper social stratum or a few selective schools. Those from centrist, establishment groups like the Council on Foreign Relations are being matched by representatives of "think tanks" (scholarly research organizations) from the left and right wings, and by grass-roots groups like the nuclear freeze movement. As the Council's president recently conceded, "It's no longer the case where you can get everybody important in foreign policy together in one room in New York" (Bernstein, 1982: 29).

Foreign affairs in the mass media

Communications media help shape foreign policy views. However, most newspapers, journals, and electronic media give less time or space to foreign developments than to news closer to home. They assume readers or viewers prefer it that way. Moreover, foreign stories are very costly to gather and relay; despite advances in recent years, most news outfits are understaffed in foreign capitals. Vast areas of the world are untouched by news gatherers. Television, on which a majority of people rely for news, is especially thin in this area. A common complaint of critics is that "television news only does stories about foreign countries when there's a war or some other violent crisis going on" (Bedell, 1982).

As a result, reporting tends to be episodic—focused on specific events. It pays little attention to long-range trends or developments (Cohen, 1965). Anyone who follows international affairs through the mass media gains a strobelight view of the world—people and events are seen in a jerky, uncoordinated way.

Lacking adequate resources for covering foreign news, the media normally rely on official news sources—the president, the secretaries of state and defense, and other government sources. The "official line" thus forms the basis for most stories on foreign and military matters.

Media people, who admire the ideal of crusading journalism, point with pride to the success of a few investigative reporters. The *New York Times'* David Halberstam roamed the Vietnamese countryside to report the failure of the military's vaunted village "pacification" program. Seymour Hirsch exposed the My Lai massacre by U.S. troops. True, they won Pulitzer prizes; but they struggled with official hostility and their colleagues' scorn in digging out the real story of the Vietnam War (Halberstam, 1972). Like most events that take place overseas, the Vietnam War was covered mainly from the official press briefing rooms.

Reporting also relies on *stereotypes* to help public understanding. These simplified views of reality sometimes distort the truth. Some less-developed nations, for instance, think western media convey negative images of their countries, so they have imposed strict limits on news coverage of their affairs.

Interest-group involvement

The powerful groups that dominate domestic policymaking are increasingly vocal in foreign affairs. That is because the bread-and-butter issues that motivate their members are now ensnared by world economic, social, and political developments. Thus, structural issues—trade, finance, arms sales, weapons procurement—involve business, labor, and professional lobbies much as do domestic areas. In crisis or strategy issues, however, fewer groups speak out.

Structural issues   Interest groups are ever more alert to structural (distributive) aspects of foreign relations. When global affairs impinge upon their jobs or profits, they are vocal and determined. In industries hard pressed by foreign competition—shoes, textiles, steel, electronics, and automobiles—business and labor band together to lobby for quotas or other restrictions. A centerpiece of current labor union policy, for example, is support for so-called "domestic content" laws that would require certain proportions of autos and other products to be manufactured in the United States.

In contrast, firms that want to sell goods and services overseas generally favor lower trade barriers. In the 1960s, such firms led lobbying for the nation's policy of reducing trade restrictions (Bauer, Pool, and Dexter, 1963). Today, the president's trade representative and other officials expend much effort opening foreign markets for American investment and sales.

Major defense and aerospace contracting firms favor higher defense spending and are active salespersons for the weapons systems they build. Unions in such industries usually agree with management, because jobs are at stake.

Another source of income for such firms is international arms sales (called "transfers"). These are often more lucrative than sales to the government. Hence, industry has a lively interest in arms sales, often financed by U.S. aid or loans (Sampson, 1977). U.S. firms are also vigorous lobbyists in foreign capitals, using a variety of tactics, including bribery, to sell their wares.

Ethnic and racial politics   Ethnic groups are another potent force in foreign policy. The United States is a nation of immigrants, with citizens from almost every nation it deals with. And this has a policy impact. For example, groups representing Eastern European nationals—Poles, Czechs, Slovenians, and others—observe patriotic days and support publicity efforts, such as Captive Nations Week, which oppose Soviet rule of this area. President Ford remarked in the second TV debate of the 1976 campaign that Eastern Europe was not under Soviet rule; ethnic groups were among the first to protest. Greek interests, led by friendly members of Congress, succeeded for a time in cutting off foreign aid to Turkey because of Turkey's incursion in Cyprus.

America's support of Israel since its creation in 1948 flows from many factors. A major one is the presence of active Jewish communities in large cities, especially in such key states as New York, Illinois, and California. Politicians in these areas understand Jewish support for Israel. New York mayors have been known to snub Arab visitors. The 1984 Democratic presidential race featured a flap over candidate Jesse Jackson's supposed ethnic slurs directed at Jews, not to mention a bidding war among the candidates over whether to move the U.S. embassy from Tel Aviv to Israel. Behind these gestures lies the fact that Democratic candidates covet Jewish financial support and (in key states) votes.

Racial consciousness also has foreign policy overtones. Jesse Jackson's presidential bid, for example, stressed domestic concerns but also touched on such issues as sanctions against South Africa, heightened attention and aid to Third World countries, and more regard for Arab nations of the Middle East.

Ethnic and racial groups exert influence insofar as they can mobilize domestic support for their interests abroad. "The 'secret weapon' of ethnic interest groups," writes Senator Charles McC. Mathias, Jr. (R-Md.) (1981: 996), "is . . . the ability to galvanize for specific objectives the strong emotional bonds of large numbers of Americans to their cultural or ancestral homes."

Strategic issues   With all these groups focusing on specific policies, what groups pay attention to the larger issues of global or military strategy? The answer is, not many. Some organizations study problems and issue reports. Examples are the Council on Foreign Relations and the League of Women Voters. Scholarly specialists keep track of issues within their frame of reference; they are sometimes called upon to advise the government. In the 1970s, a group called the Trilateral Commission was created. It is sponsored by New York business interests and has members from Europe, Japan, and the United States (hence the name). It is a forum for policy papers and talks on foreign policy problems affecting economically developed nations.

Some feel such groups make up a kind of "foreign policy establishment" representing right-of-center interests of multinational business and banking firms. The scholars, lawyers, and business people in this group often become presidential appointees in the State and Defense departments, regardless of party. There is little public, press, or interest-group involvement in strategic or global issues; thus, such elite circles can wield great influence on foreign policy.

Electoral politics and foreign policy

Foreign policy issues often affect election outcomes. Eisenhower's 1952 campaign was helped by dislike of the Korean War and Truman's "appeasement" of communism. A military man, Eisenhower promised, "I shall go to Korea" to inspect the situation. He inspired confidence and acted quickly to end the war. Campaigning for the presidency in 1960, Kennedy charged the Republican White House had lagged behind the Russians in weapons, causing a dangerous "missile gap." He promised to "get America moving again"; he meant action on stalled Democratic domestic proposals as well as stronger, more varied military planning.

Eight years later, Democrats lost out largely because of the Vietnam War; this split the party, forced Johnson to retire, and helped elect Kennedy's former opponent, Nixon. Carter's failure to end the Iranian hostage crisis helped cause his falling public ratings and his 1980 defeat.

Bipartisanship   *Bipartisanship* in foreign policy has always had its advocates; occasionally it approached being official policy. According to the canon of bipartisanship, "politics stops at the water's edge." To ensure unity in dealing with foreign powers, it is argued, leaders of both parties should support the president's initiatives; and they should not question major foreign policy tenets in political campaigns.

Incumbent presidents and their advisers are especially fond of bipartisanship. After a bruising campaign in which the foreign policy of Truman and his secretary of state, Dean Acheson, had been scorched, the new secretary, John Foster Dulles, said (Harsch, 1956: 29):

> Under our Constitutional system we have a general election every four years. . . . one side presents his case, as two lawyers do when they go into court. At that stage the two parties are not judges and they are not judicial. In my opinion they should not be. . . . but when that time is past, then I believe we should try to work together on a bipartisan basis.

Bipartisanship. Senators Arthur Vandenberg (R–Mich.) and Tom Connally (D–Tex.), leaders of the Foreign Relations Committee, testify for NATO alliance, 1949.

Bipartisanship flourished in the post–World War II years; Truman consulted such GOP stalwarts as Senator Arthur H. Vandenberg (R-Mich.) on the United Nations and such postwar aid programs as the Marshall Plan and Point Four. Bipartisanship broke down in the 1950–53 period. Blamed for this were the Korean War, reverses in China, and propaganda by the GOP's right wing, mainly Senator Joseph R. McCarthy (R-Wis.). After Eisenhower's 1952 election, bipartisanship was again the order of the day. Democratic leaders such as Senator Walter F. George (D-Ga.) played Vandenberg's role of "loyal opposition."

Bipartisanship was one of the Vietnam War's many casualties. The war escalated while its purposes or outcomes were still obscure. Bitter debates broke out between the two parties and within Johnson's own party. People asked whether post–World War II bipartisanship had not blurred controversy and kept dissenting views from being aired.

In fact, bipartisanship has through the years been the exception, not the rule. In almost every generation there have been bitter foreign policy debates. These involved war and peace, tariffs, relations with major powers, neutrality or intervention, and many other issues. Except for World War II, all of our declared wars (plus undeclared ones such as the Civil War, Korea, and Vietnam) have been as bitterly fought in political arenas as on the battlefields.

Local issues   In local campaigns, broad-scale strategic issues intrude only on occasion. Yet structural issues often come up. These involve government spending, location of facilities or personnel, or ethnic or racial problems. In this area, foreign and defense policies blend with domestic policies.

In ethnic or racial enclaves, politicians learn to stress the hopes of local groups. At public functions in ethnic neighborhoods, New York City candidates are seen eating dollops of Polish, Greek, Mideastern, and other ethnic specialities. They down such traditional dishes as knishes and blintzes, tamales, ham hocks and chitlings, and pizza and ices. More important, international concerns of ethnic and racial groups are voiced by their elected representatives.

Elective officials whose districts have defense plants or major contractors boost measures that will assure jobs and prosperity. The late L. Mendel Rivers (D-S.C.), chairman of the House Armed Services Committee, whose hometown included the Charleston Navy Yard among other defense facilities, used to campaign on the slogan, "Rivers Delivers!"

Not all projects are welcomed with open arms. Installations with adverse environmental, esthetic, or security effects are increasingly scrutinized by local communities. The major drawback of the MX missile, in fact, was an awkward basing mode that no one wanted near their communities; finally, it was decided to adapt existing missile silos to accommodate the MX—a questionable compromise.

THE FOREIGN POLICY BUREAU-CRACIES

Day-to-day policy emissaries are neither in the White House nor on Capitol Hill. They are in the "permanent government," agencies with ongoing missions for implementing policy. With blurred lines between foreign and domestic policy, almost every federal agency gets into the act sooner or later. The chief foreign policy actors are found in the White House, the Department of State, the defense establishment, and the intelligence community.

We can learn much from watching the push and pull of various foreign policy bureaucracies; each has different traditions, missions, and information sources (Allison, 1971). Some analysts believe bureaucratic rivalry is all there is to executive-branch foreign policy; they think there is no single, identifiable foreign policy for the country (Allison and Halperin, 1972). Yet the bureaucracies work in an atmosphere affected, if not controlled, by the president, Congress, and public opinion. It matters not how vague these public's preferences may be on specific foreign policy problems.

The Department of State

The nation's foreign office is the Department of State. Its yearly budget ($2 billion) and size (fewer than 24,000 employees) rank it among the smaller cabinet departments. Yet it oversees relations with more than 150 independent nations and 50 international organizations. Couriers hand carry documents some 10 million miles a year among almost 300 diplomatic outposts overseas. The command post is on the seventh floor of its huge Washington headquarters. From there, the secretary and aides scan incoming cables, communicate with foreign posts, and monitor crises as they unfold.

How State is organized   The department is organized both by geography

State Department. Headquarters in Washington's "Foggy Bottom" neighborhood

and by function. Basic operations are handled by five regional bureaus: African Affairs, European Affairs, East Asian and Pacific Affairs, Inter-American Affairs, and Near Eastern and South Asian Affairs. (A separate bureau works with international organizations.) Within each bureau, a country desk keeps contact with each nation in its region.

The chain of command for a country such as India starts with the ambassador and the country team in our embassy in the capital, New Delhi. From there it moves to Washington: First it goes to the "Indian desk," then to the assistant secretary, the secretary, and finally to the president.

Superimposed upon this traditional organization is a trend toward functional bureaus and offices that cut across geographic lines. These include Educational and Cultural Affairs, Economic and Business Affairs, Politico-Military Affairs, Security and Consular Affairs, Protocol, and Congressional Relations. The Policy Planning Staff provides overall strategic and policy advice.

The Foreign Service   The heart of the State Department's staff is the diplomatic corps—more than 12,000 Foreign Service Officers (FSOs). Created in 1924, the Foreign Service was for many years a small, elite corps of high-status people. In 1954, FSOs were integrated with allied civil service workers. However, professional diplomats are still trying to shake their image as timid, striped-pants people.

Embassies   Ambassadors are the president's representatives to foreign governments. Three fourths of all ambassadors are FSOs; the rest are private citizens or wealthy campaign contributors who can afford the high cost of diplomatic society in foreign capitals.

Since foreign policy spills over into domestic affairs, many agencies keep counselors or aides in foreign countries, often attached to the mission. Military attachés are normally assigned to the mission; so are labor and agricultural attachés, and so forth. Forty-four of our government agencies have aides in the U.S. embassy in London. At one point, 700 civilians were attached to the embassy in New Delhi; only 100 of these worked for the State Department.

Intelligence officers, masked by innocuous titles, collect information and cultivate contacts in the host country. Most of their activities are harmless; others, like espionage and covert operations, are the equivalent of a different brand of foreign policy. While ambassadors voice our stated policies, covert activities at variance with those policies may emanate from their own embassy without their knowledge.

A department without a constituency   The State Department is a constant target for critics. They snipe at State's bureaucratic complexity, convoluted procedures, slow responses, and excessive caution. Successive presidents have despaired of getting prompt, decisive action. "Damn it, Bundy, I get more done in one day in the White House than they do in six months at the State Department," Kennedy once said. "They never have any ideas over there . . . never come up with anything new" (Schlesinger, 1965: 406).

At the heart of the problem is lack of a strong domestic constituency. Unlike other federal departments, State has not forged strong ties with major domestic interest groups.

Clienteles are really the host governments with which State deals abroad. State is absorbed in the daily challenges of comprehending and coping with these governments. So its officers tend to view U.S. policy in terms of its impact or reaction abroad. A key part of a diplomat's job is conveying to superiors the likely impact of proposed policies. "Because of its traditional role in diplomacy, the State Department has come to be regarded as spokesman more for foreign viewpoints than the national interests" (Irish and Frank, 1975: 231).

Giving other nations' viewpoints will not win thanks from policymakers who want quick answers and fret about domestic interest groups and public opinion. This does not mean the State Department is disloyal—a familiar charge during the McCarthy era of the early 1950s. Rather, it acknowledges a shaky political base, a fate it shares with foreign offices the world over.

George P. Shultz. Secretary of State (1982–   ).

Other agencies

Several independent agencies handle key parts of our foreign policy, guided by the president and secretary of state.

Foreign aid   The International Development Cooperation Agency is an umbrella agency; it is responsible for development aid to other nations. Its major component is the Agency for International Development (AID). AID gives out nonmilitary assistance—economic, technological, agricultural, and humanitarian—to foreign countries. Another component is the *Overseas Private Investment Corporation* (OPIC). This helps Americans make profitable investments in about 80 developing countries.

The *Peace Corps,* created by Kennedy in 1961, dispatches motivated, trained volunteers to help developing nations. Its 5,200 volunteers work in 62 countries—in teaching, farming, medicine, community development, and technical jobs. Originally a separate agency, the Peace Corps is now part of ACTION, an umbrella agency for both overseas and domestic volunteer programs. Early Peace Corps workers were often enthusiastic and idealistic. Today, they are more apt to be technicians.

Propaganda   The U.S. Information Agency (USIA) promotes U.S. policies by distributing information. On one hand, it informs the rest of the world about our country; on the other, it manages cultural exchanges between the United

Peace Corps. Arts instructor from Massachusetts works with Costa Rican children.

Voice of America technician prepares program for foreign broadcast.

States and other countries. USIA cannot give out information at home. But it has considerable autonomy; under it, the government's information apparatus has been centralized for the first time.

USIA has branches in more than 100 countries, with libraries and information centers. It produces and distributes motion pictures and other materials. Its Voice of America broadcast network beams entertainment, news, and features in 36 languages throughout the world. Its job is to portray American society and policy to its listeners. Its editorial commentaries are no longer subject to prior censorship; but they are reviewed by USIA after transmission. USIA often seeks guidance from the state department in explaining foreign policies.

Two other radio networks inform people of developments not likely to be reported by their own press. Radio Free Europe broadcasts in six languages to five East European countries. Radio Liberty broadcasts to the Soviet Union in 16 languages. Based in Munich, these networks were launched in the early 1950s by the Central Intelligence Agency; they were divorced from it in 1971. Commentaries must follow guidelines and should avoid agitation or propaganda. They are closely monitored by officials, including a watchdog Board of International Broadcasting.

As a government propaganda outlet, USIA walks a tightrope. It cannot thwart government policy; yet to retain credibility with audiences, it must give balanced reporting. The content of broadcast and other communications media is a source of lively controversy. Policymakers want to use them to spread official policies; journalists see them as avenues of information and resent controls. A trend toward more independent programming was halted by the Reagan administration, whose controversial USIA Director, Charles Z. Wick, emphasized pro–United States and anti-Soviet themes.

Foreign trade Promoting international trade carries such high priority that the United States Trade Representative is a cabinet-level post with the rank of ambassador and a staff located in the Executive Office of the President. Under Reagan, the post was filled by William E. Brock, a former U.S. Senator and Republican party chairman. The trade representative, who reports directly to the president, directs all U.S. trade negotiations and formulates overall trade policy.

The U.S. International Trade Commission is a six-person body charged with making investigations and hearing complaints about practices under customs, tariffs, and trade laws. In recent years, the commission and its staff of some 400 have been deluged with complaints from U.S. firms (now about 200 a year) about unfair competition from foreign goods—for example, because the goods are subsidized by a foreign government or are "dumped" on the U.S. market at bargain prices. If the commission finds such practices, the president may take steps to protect the domestic industry: import duties may be increased, quotas established, or "adjustment assistance" given to harmed workers, firms, or communities.

Overall responsibility for promoting trade and assisting U.S. businesses entering international markets lies with the Department of Commerce. Its International Trade Administration, headed by an under secretary, runs a number of programs to publicize U.S. goods and advise firms. To strengthen the government's trade role, a "beefed-up" Department of Commerce and Trade has been proposed.

Arms control The *Arms Control and Disarmament Agency* is a quasi-independent body under the aegis of the State Department. It makes and carries out arms control programs and staffs U.S. negotiations with other nations. One such was the Strategic Arms Limitation Talks (SALT) with the Soviet Union. Its director reports to the president through the secretary of state. Needless to say, this agency's status rises and falls with the administration's interest in arms negotiations.

THE DEFENSE ESTABLISH-MENT

Military preparedness is a pivotal foreign policy resource. In times of crisis, it may push aside all other foreign policy considerations. In peacetime, it is a tool for bargaining with foreign powers.

The Department of Defense

Across the Potomac River from the nation's capital stands the Pentagon. This nerve center of the defense establishment houses some 23,000 employees. It is so huge that messengers ride electric carts along its halls. Like the Pentagon, everything about the Department of Defense (DOD) is big. Its budget approaches $300 billion annually. It is the nation's largest employer, with 1 million civilian and more than 2 million military employees.

Overseas, the Pentagon supervises 359 U.S. military bases. U.S. military presence in all corners of the world affects the global balance of power, both economic and military.

The DOD structure   Actually, DOD is a relatively young agency. After more than 150 years of separate existence, the uniformed services were brought under the control of a single secretary of defense by the National Security Act of 1947 (amended in 1949). The office of the secretary of defense handles procurement, intelligence, personnel, research, logistics and installations, and financial and systems analysis. Its foreign policy arm is the Office of International Security Affairs (ISA). It also has two intelligence organizations, the Defense Intelligence Agency (DIA) and the National Security Agency (NSA).

Another portion of the central defense apparatus is the Joint Chiefs of Staff,

Joints Chiefs of Staff.

appointed by the president for four-year terms. These include the chiefs of staff of the three armed services and the commandant of the Marine Corps. The chairman of the joint chiefs is appointed by the president to a two-year term, with one renewal. The staff is drawn equally from the various services.

The joint chiefs have two overall roles. One is giving military advice to the president, the secretary of defense, the National Security Council, and Congress. The other is supervising the four combatant commands—in readiness, capabilities, and planning. The challenge for the joint chiefs and their staff is to speak for the whole military and resist the strong pull of their individual services. Reformers would like to strengthen the joint chiefs and their staffs and underscore their independence from the individual services.

Interservice rivalries   Within DOD, the independent services are represented through separate departments of the Army, Air Force, and Navy (including the Marine Corps). Each department is headed by a civilian secretary and assistant secretaries. Military operations are the responsibility of the respective chiefs of staff.

The history of DOD has been a struggle to coordinate the various services. Each is operationally separate, with unique combat missions and cherished traditions. Each is jealous of its uniforms, equipment, and installations. Thus, the military has four tactical air forces—one for each service. If a plane is designed for the Navy, it is not apt to suit the Air Force or the Army. The Army prefers to have its own aircraft provide air support for its ground forces, rather than rely on the Air Force, with its airborne mission. Hence the Army boasts the world's second largest air force (the Air Force is the largest). It provided the bulk of support for ground soldiers in Vietnam (Bergerson, 1980).

Military-civilian relations   Another aspect of DOD's management problem is the relation between military officers and civilians. Our country is dedicated to civilian control, exercised by the president as commander-in-chief and transmitted through the secretary of defense and other presidential appointees.

Truman's dismissal of World War II hero General Douglas MacArthur for insubordination during the Korean War spectacularly illustrated this principle. At the time, surveys showed that twice as many people supported MacArthur as supported Truman. Early in his term, Jimmy Carter recalled and reassigned

Commander in chief. President Truman meets General Douglas MacArthur on Wake Island in 1950 to lay down strategy for conducting the Korean War.

two Army generals for making statements that went beyond administration policies.

Nevertheless, military officers are at the vortex of the defense establishment. They are, of course, experts in combat techniques and weapons capabilities. They are looked to as experienced military tacticians. An unmistakable mystique surrounds people who have fought an enemy on a battlefield and who display the brass and ribbons to prove it. Many armchair warriors in the Pentagon and in Congress are bedazzled by military brass. They sometimes adopt positions more favorable to the military than those advocated by the officers themselves. Service and veterans' groups also promote the military viewpoint within the bureaucracy, and sometimes in public arenas.

The military-industrial complex

The vast bulk of defense spending goes for structural policies or programs. Defense has about $100 billion to spend on procurement each year—a figure that is escalating in the 1980s. The rest of the defense budget goes mostly for personnel.

"IS THERE ANY KIND OF GAS THAT WILL GIVE PEOPLE NERVE?"

Defense spending, in other words, is tightly linked to the nation's economy. Supporters of such spending include firms with defense contracts; labor unions in defense industries; towns benefiting from contracts or installations; and congressmen from those locales.

Seldom do localities resist defense spending in their backyards. If the installation is disruptive or potentially harmful, local groups may urge that it be located elsewhere. (Utah and Nevada citizens worried about proposed MX missile sites.) Typically, though, defense spending is welcomed because it yields jobs and profits.

In his farewell speech, President Eisenhower, a five-star general himself, warned against the "unwarranted influence" of the "military-industrial complex." Said Eisenhower (1961: 616): "The conjunction of an immense military establishment and a large arms industry is new in the American experience. The total influence—economic, political, even spiritual—is felt in every city, every statehouse, every office of the federal government."

Defense influence has not slackened since then. Military budgets are several times what they were in the 1950s. Defense spending carries an aura of urgency and necessity that makes it hard to oppose. After the Vietnam war, the defense share of the federal budget went down some. Lacking a "hot" war, or fears brought on by the Cold War, military preparedness lost some of its urgency. By the 1980s, a bipartisan consensus favored defense spending hikes to close gaps and meet threats around the world; but President Reagan's hikes were so steep that many legislators, fearing the effect on deficits, forced somewhat slower growth.

THE INTELLIGENCE COMMUNITY

"Nothing is more necessary and useful for a general than to know the intentions and projects of the enemy," wrote Niccolò Machiavelli in *The Prince*, a 16th century tract on politics. Covert efforts to pinpoint enemy plans and resources have always played a part in military strategy. Washington organized a spy system during the Revolutionary War; spies have been vital in every war

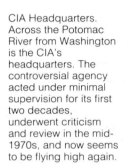

CIA Headquarters. Across the Potomac River from Washington is the CIA's headquarters. The controversial agency acted under minimal supervision for its first two decades, underwent criticism and review in the mid-1970s, and now seems to be flying high again.

since then. During World War II, President Roosevelt created the Office of Strategic Services (OSS). It was a cloak-and-dagger outfit that performed a whole range of covert activities—espionage, sabotage, intelligence, and counterintelligence.

The central intelligence agency

The Central Intelligence Agency (CIA), successor to the wartime OSS, was formed by the National Security Act of 1947, as amended in 1949. Its "charter," or mandate, was vague, an omission seen in retrospect as regrettable. It was planned to coordinate the various intelligence agencies, including those of State, Defense, and the Atomic Energy Commission.

The CIA's heyday   Under a series of tough-minded directors, the CIA became a prime instrument of the Cold War crusade against communism. As it turned out, the agency was also conducting its own brand of foreign policy. At times, this was at variance with stated U.S. policy and often outside the boundaries of the agency's own charter.

The CIA employs about 15,000 people and spends several billion a year. Its headquarters stand in a wooded area near Langley, Virginia, across the Potomac from Washington. Its *Intelligence Directorate* conducts research and collects overt information. Its *Operations Directorate* collects information secretly (espionage). It has also engaged in secret political warfare, which has brought the CIA controversy and notoriety.

The CIA enjoys unusual autonomy and freedom from outside scrutiny, even though it is responsible to the National Security Council and thence to the president (who appoints the CIA's director and deputy director). Until the late 1970s, it was virtually exempt from congressional oversight. Irish and Frank (1975: 487) state: "From its inception, the CIA has operated on its own terms with minimum public exposure and congressional oversight. The agency does whatever it does silently and secretly. It never publicizes, admits, or denies the range of its activities. Its budget is buried in numerous departmental estimates and its personnel are covertly dispersed through various front organizations."

Doubts and reversals   Nothing in the CIA's charter suggests that it was to intervene in affairs of foreign countries, much less conduct covert military operations. By the 1960s, however, spotty reports of its activities began to surface in the press. In some foreign countries, the CIA became a sinister symbol of U.S. power. Kennedy's aide, Arthur M. Schlesinger, Jr. (1965: 427), wrote that by the mid-1960s the CIA budget exceeded the state department's by 50 percent; CIA operatives outnumbered State's in many embassies. "The root fear," explained Roger Hilsman (1967: 64–65), "was that the CIA represented . . . a state within a state, and certainly the basis for fear was there."

By the mid-1970s, revelations of CIA operations had damaged its credibility. It had sponsored a series of thrusts at foreign powers, including overthrow of some regimes. Assassination plots against foreign leaders were uncovered.

The CIA had also spied on American citizens at home. This violated its charter's prohibition of domestic activities. It had infiltrated antiwar and other dissident groups; it used dozens of foundations and private groups as fronts, subsidizing even the National Students Association (Wise, 1976).

It was further revealed that the CIA had helped a White House group later dubbed the "plumbers" (because they fixed leaks). They burglarized a psychiatrist's office to obtain records on Daniel Ellsberg, a former NSC aide who had turned against the Vietnam War and leaked the secret Pentagon Papers to the press. Later, Nixon tried to enlist the CIA in his efforts to stop the FBI from probing the Watergate burglary, which involved breaking into Democratic headquarters during the 1972 presidential campaign.

These revelations, special inquiries by House and Senate committees, and a high-level executive report, caused President Ford to revise CIA procedures in 1976. Two years later, Carter sought to rehabilitate the agency. He gave it a coordinating role within the intelligence community, and he permitted CIA spying. The latter was to be done only with specific approval.

Unleashed again   In the 1980s, the CIA's fortunes turned again. As the Cold War warmed up and Soviet-U.S. relations cooled off, concern over the nation's intelligence capacity grew. Stronger CIA directors were appointed; many of the 1970s restrictions on its activities were relaxed. There was public furor when it was learned that the CIA had helped mine harbors to aid the administration's drive against a leftist government in Nicaragua.

The outcome of the 1970s reforms is thus elusive. New restrictions and reporting requirements were meant to focus the agency's mission and increase control. The agency, for example, was to keep the House and Senate Intelligence Committees "fully and currently informed" about its activities; but apparently this was not always honored. As one Hill staffer remarked, the CIA director "wouldn't tell you if your coat was on fire—unless you asked him" (Lardner, 1984). Most important, the long-promised revision of the CIA's charter never took place. Like other agencies, the CIA prospers or suffers with the political climate.

Other agencies

The CIA is the keystone of the intelligence community; but it is by no means the only participant. In fact, 40 or more government agencies do intelligence work.

Under a 1978 reorganization, the 11 chief members of the intelligence community are, in addition to the CIA: the National Security Agency (NSA); the Defense Intelligence Agency (DIA); Army, Navy, and Air Force intelligence operations; the State Department's Bureau of Intelligence and Research; the Federal Bureau of Investigation; the Drug Enforcement Administration; and the Treasury and Energy departments.

Intelligence is a minor part of some of these in dollars or personnel. Yet their concerns—from terrorism to nuclear safety to narcotics traffic—are important in terms of the government's overall responsibilities. The agencies are supposed to cooperate with one another; how much overlap or duplication results, no one knows for sure.

The intelligence dilemma

The exposés of the 1970s did not resolve the question of the proper scope of intelligence. The dilemma arises from conflicting goals.

On the one hand, most people concede that such work is needed. The CIA was formed in part because policymakers wanted to avoid intelligence failures like the one resulting in Pearl Harbor (Crabb and Holt, 1984: 24–25). In 1979, a sizable Soviet military force was belatedly found in Cuba; that same year, the United States (and most other countries) were caught by surprise when the Iranian monarchy fell.

Covert operations, on the other hand, are more controversial. Intelligence leaders, like former CIA Director Allen Dulles (1963), argue they are needed to protect the United States from a hostile world. Critics counter that they cause distrust of our policies and often do far more harm than good.

Secret agencies like the CIA have other drawbacks. Much of their information comes from conventional sources; but they are sometimes tempted to rely on tips from dissidents or spies in foreign countries. This puts them at the mercy of people whose view of the world may be biased or distorted. For instance, reports from Cuban refugees led the CIA to tell Kennedy an invasion of Cuba would be met by an anti-Castro uprising which would liberate the island. Partly on this basis, Kennedy in 1961 proceeded with the planned Bay of Pigs invasion—an action he bitterly regretted.

A more serious problem for secret agencies is their "closed" character. They lack adequate review of their plans; obviously no public debate is involved. Hence, leaders are prone to overshoot their missions; they launch shoddy or ill-advised projects of little value. Intelligence agencies are especially vulnerable to this form of "group think" (Janis, 1983). Their operatives (and the people with whom they deal) walk in a kind of political netherworld. They have their own constricted picture of what makes the world tick.

FOREIGN POLICY IN A DEMOCRACY

The debate over intelligence activities points up a larger dilemma: Can foreign policy be carried on effectively by a free and open society?

Through history, affairs between nations were carried out by a small cadre of professional diplomats acting on behalf of their chiefs of state. Elites dominated international affairs. The reason was that matters of negotiation or information gathering could not involve large numbers of people. They require speed, confidence, and coherence. Also, foreign policy can demand that national resources be diverted from consumption or services to other uses with less immediate benefits. A war can mean the sacrifice of a nation's treasure or the lives of its citizens.

Some people feel foreign policymaking is not compatible with open, discursive policy debates. Diplomatic realists feel broad discussion hampers leaders from pursuing the nation's best interests. Hence, few of them admire former President Woodrow Wilson's goal of "open covenants openly arrived at."

No one can prove these beliefs one way or the other. They are matters of faith, not empirical propositions. The Vietnam War era was not, by and large, kind to elite theorists of foreign policymaking. The war itself was a failure; executive officers convinced themselves and each other of the correctness of their promises and the viability of their methods. In theory, policymakers should tap all relevant information and select rational options. In fact, decision makers are often prisoners of biased or false data, sometimes deliberately twisted to fit the aims of those in the top posts.

A good case can be made for "multiple advocacy" in foreign policy. Here a variety of outlooks and specialized skills are brought to bear on tough problems (George, 1972). Closed decision systems are best suited for limited objectives that are fully agreed upon. But broad foreign policy objectives are by no means self-evident or easily agreed upon. The marketplace of ideas, in short, is a proper setting for foreign policymaking; the policies themselves are open to debate and contention.

CONCLUSIONS

In this chapter we explained foreign and defense policies. We also identified the major policymakers. Such policies are closely tied to domestic problems, though often thought to be remote from them. Also, many foreign and military issues are structural (distributive). They involve allocations of personnel and material that are not very different from those required for domestic politics.

1 Foreign policy, which embraces this nation's dealings with other nations, involves the pursuit of national goals and the use of national resources. Whether or not the nation realizes its goals depends on the abundance of its resources and its willingness to use them. Some goals are so costly that they are out of even the richest nation's reach.

2 Presidents are the chief agents in foreign affairs; they conduct diplomatic negotiations and manage day-to-day relations with other powers; they are commanders-in-chief of the armed forces. Their aides must distill the viewpoints of various foreign policy agencies into usable policy advice.

3 Congress shares foreign policy powers with the president. It advises and consents to appointments and treaties; it declares war; it provides funds; and it oversees executive activities. After a period of executive dominance, Congress has, since the Vietnam War, been more active in overseeing foreign and defense policies.

4 Makers of foreign policy work against a backdrop of public opinion, media coverage, interest-group activity, and electoral politics.

5 The State Department is the prime implementer of foreign policy. It lacks a vigorous domestic constituency. Thus, it has the thankless job of conveying foreign powers' reactions to U.S. policies.

6 The defense establishment has many ties to powerful domestic groups—business, labor, and political officials. It is not a unified community. But its economic importance lends it irresistible political leverage.

7 Intelligence agencies carry out an alternative mode of foreign policy. Although most people agree intelligence gathering is needed, many question the advisability of covert activities.

FURTHER READING

AMBROSE, STEPHEN E. (1980) Rise to Globalism: American Foreign Policy, 1938–1980. 2d ed. New York: Penguin Books. A readable account of recent U.S. diplomatic history.

CRABB, CECIL V., JR., and PAT M. HOLT (1984) Invitation to Struggle: Congress, the President and Foreign Policy. 2d ed. Washington: Congressional Quarterly Press. An examination of recent presidential and congressional foreign-policy making, with case studies.

FALLOWS, JAMES (1981) National Defense. New York: Random House. A critical review of U.S. defense policy by a prominent neoliberal and former Carter speech writer.

FRANK, THOMAS, and EDWARD WEISBAND (1979) Foreign Policy by Congress. New York: Oxford University Press. A study of Congress's expanded role in foreign policy, emphasizing the 1973 War Powers Resolution, lobby groups, and congressional staff growth.

NATHAN, JAMES A., and JAMES K. OLIVER (1983) Foreign Policymaking and the American Political System. Boston: Little Brown. A good standard treatment of the politics of foreign policy.

17

The Impact of Government

On October 29, 1980, candidate Ronald Reagan posed his now famous question: ". . . ask yourself are you better off than you were four years ago." The question was good politics but bad economics for it assumed economic events during 1977–80 flowed from President Carter's policies.

The facts are less heroic. Economic progress depends on a President's policies but it also depends on influences outside the President's control: the economy he inherits, rainfall in the midwest, movements in the price of oil, state and local government decisions, and so on. These influences, moreover, have lives of their own so that economic periods do not neatly coincide with Presidential administrations.

The years 1981–84 are a case in point. Politically, they represent President Reagan's first term in office. Economically, they represent the second through fifth years of a period that began with the 1979 fall of the Shah of Iran and a major round of OPEC price increases. The history of this economic period—rapid inflation, deep recession, recovery and no net growth in family incomes—parallels the events that followed the first major OPEC price increases in 1973–74.

During this period President Reagan's policies have been important in determining the balance between deeper recession and higher inflation. His policies have also served to increase income inequality. But even with respect to inequality the President's policies have been less important than inflation and other forces beyond any single person's control.

> *Frank Levy and Richard C. Michel," The Way We'll Be in 1984: Recent Changes in the Level and Distribution of Disposable Income." (Discussion Paper, The Urban Institute, Washington, D.C., November 1983).*

* * * * *

The most important aspect of government in any society is the impact of its policies on its people. If the government happens to be of a nation as important and powerful as the United States, then the impact of those policies extend worldwide.

But, as the comments above suggest, government is only one force in determining what happens in any single nation and throughout the world. A host of other forces, many completely beyond the reach of government influence, let alone control, are enormously important.

This does not mean that citizens should not take seriously their responsibilities for pushing their government in ways they favor through participation in the political system. Nor does it mean that what government does makes no

The changing fortunes of war. American self-confidence was at a high point when the Japanese surrendered to General Douglas MacArthur on September 2, 1945, in Tokyo Bay. It was quite low by the time American marines took down the flag in Beirut, Lebanon, as they evacuated after a failed mission in early 1984.

difference. Citizens should compete in the political arena for policies they favor; but they should do so with a balanced sense of what government can and cannot reasonably be expected to do or affect.

Americans came out of the period of World War II victory and the enormous growth and prosperity in the years following with beliefs that America, Americans, and the American government could do almost anything. The "American century" was proclaimed. A series of shocks began to make these beliefs appear outmoded; the breaking of the American nuclear monopoly by the Soviet Union in 1949 was critical early in the process of disillusionment. Other key events surely include the American debacle in Vietnam in the 1960s and early 70s; and the putrid mess known as "Watergate" that exposed corruption in many senses at the very highest levels of our government in the early 1970s. In the late 1970s and early 80s, a variety of events guaranteed that the myth of American invincibility was dead. These include humiliation over the hostages in Iran; collapse of industries we used to regard as peculiarly American such as steel or automobiles; and the "redeployment" or "retreat" in Lebanon of the U.S. Marines. Our triumphs were reduced to the scale of invasion of the tiny island of Grenada in the fall of 1983; one critic said this "proved that the United States could conquer a golf course."

The shocks piled up. A number of Americans reacted by becoming unusually cynical about and mistrustful of their government. In increasing numbers they withdrew from the political process. This is an understandable response. But we don't think it is a healthy response. Government is limited in what it can achieve, to be sure. But in areas where it can have impact—and they are still many and some are vital—there are important values to debate. The best way citizens can join those debates is through informed participation. Nothing that most Americans value—security, prosperity, liberty—is automatic or guaranteed. Participation by informed citizens does not guarantee achieving these values either; it can increase the positive impact of government in seeking them.

In this chapter we focus on some important questions about the impact of American government and the policies it adopts and implements. First, we explore the limits of what government can achieve. Second, we comment on the meaning of **policy impact.** Third, we provide concrete examples of the impact of a few major domestic policies. Fourth, we briefly address the question of how impact is evaluated. Finally, we deal with the vital question of the responsiveness of the American national government to public expectations.

THE LIMITS ON WHAT GOVERNMENT CAN ACHIEVE

Government agencies do not have an easy time with the impacts of their programs. One main reason could be that implementation is flawed. Therefore the program will not have the desired results. Another reason may be that the desired results are not clearly stated or thought out. Or the goals may be clear and the implementation effective, but the resources allocated (mostly personnel and money) are insufficient. Even if the war on poverty had not had other problems, it was not realistic to hope poverty would be eliminated with a budget of $1 billion a year. Goals may be clear and carried out well with adequate resources; the impact may not be nearly as great as desired or expected. The conditions faced by a government agency or agencies may be insurmountable, at least in any reasonable period of time. Or those conditions may so limit what can be done that whatever is achieved is minor compared to the original goals.

The government faces some unusually tough challenges. Dramatic changes within the United States, for example, have profound impacts on society. In many cases all the government can do is to try to adjust to those changes. Typically, it cannot direct them in any meaningful way. In recent years there

Policy must react to events and forces partially or wholly beyond the control of policymakers. These pictures show examples. *Left:* French soldiers are shown in Vietnam just before the French collapse at Dien Bien Phu in 1954. American policymakers contemplated a nuclear attack in support of the French but decided not to intervene at all at that time. *Right:* two blast furnaces in Youngstown, Ohio, are demolished in 1982. They were built early in the century when American steel was dominant worldwide. Now the world, even much of the United States, looks elsewhere for its steel. Policymakers have had to react to this development.

have been changes such as the aging of our population; the shift of the work force from blue-collar to white-collar and service occupations; and the radical drop in the number of farmers needed both to feed ourselves and still retain a healthy capacity for exporting food. All have been major factors limiting policy responses.

Challenges from abroad are even more clearly outside the control of the United States. Nationalism, revolution, and anti-Americanism in numerous countries throughout the Third World are simply facts of life to be faced by American policymakers.

Some problems get worse despite government efforts. Even problems created by humans begin to seem insoluble, as welfare programs in recent years show (Steiner, 1971). There was a vast spending increase in programs aimed at the "welfare class." These included aid to families with dependent children, medicaid, food stamps, housing, supplementary security income, aid to elementary and secondary education, basic opportunity grants for education, Head Start, and job training and antipoverty programs. Yet the problems of the "welfare class" have not eased much.

In many cases, government only works around the margins of basic problems. A Department of Energy report pointed out that its forecasts about energy supply, consumption, and prices for the next 10 years did not vary much, whatever the government did. The forces governing such matters are simply beyond the scope of government in the short run. And 10 years is a short run in this case. What government does or does not do can matter. Even marginal changes can be important, at least symbolically. But claims that government can solve a major problem in a short time should not be blindly believed. For instance, some say the nation is headed toward an "economy of scarcity" to replace its traditional "economy of abundance." If so, government can deal with only limited aspects of the fallout from that huge change and can probably do little to slow the change.

There is, of course, an ongoing political debate over how much and what government should attempt. That debate in various forms has provided many of the most lively political issues throughout our history. Some want government to undertake new enterprises and expand present ones. Others are content with present government programs and do not want new ones added. Still others want the scope of government activity reduced and the size of remaining programs pared down.

The number of people who receive some government aid, however, is huge. For 1977 the Commerce Department estimated the figure at 53.5 percent of all Americans. In 1985, the government estimated that five major social programs each had clienteles of 10,000,000 or more. Social Security topped the list with almost 37 million. Then came medicare with about 30 million, medicaid with 23 million, food stamps with 20 million, and aid to families with dependent children with more than 10 million.

People may preach against government spending and government programs in general, *but* when it comes to the program that aids them, their attitude suddenly shifts. Some have the image that only the poor drain government resources. In fact, all layers of society feed "at the trough" in many ways. Many well-off people get tangible benefits from the government such as tax write-offs or farm price support. And some corporations are either temporary or semipermanent government wards. Chrysler, Lockheed, and Conrail are recent giants with begging bowls.

Causality: the direct and indirect impact of government actions

Direct links between government actions and their impact on people and society are very hard to prove. This is especially so with large-scale programs.

In 1965, a special federal program was created to focus on the problems of Appalachia (Branscome, 1977; Ripley, 1972: Chapter 4). After two decades, the most program officials could claim was that some economic indicators for the region had improved. But they could not show that the program had caused those improvements or that the improvements would not have happened anyway. Many of the program's investments were in human resources and were aimed mainly at long-term impact (a generation or more). Claims of early "success" were unfounded. In fact, it will always be hard to "prove" whether better medical and health facilities, highways, and vocational education really raised the quality of life in Appalachia.

The problems of turning plans into impact in a region as vast and problem-ridden as Appalachia were captured well by a government official (Branscome, 1977: 6): "Doing something in Washington to help the people down in the hills is sort of like making love through an innerspring mattress. The planning is baffling. The execution is painful. The results are frustrating, and both parties are left in despair."

Some kinds of impact are easier to prove. The federally imposed 55-mile-per-hour speed limit has cut traffic deaths. The federal government threatened to cut off funds before some states adopted the limit. Ironically, the government pushed for the lower limit to save energy. It seems to have done little to save gas; it has saved lives.

Highly visible results the public thinks are linked to government action can bring rapid public reaction and policy change. For example, in the fall of 1975 Congress passed year-round daylight savings time to help save fuel. In the winter of 1976 several children were killed by cars in the predawn dark as they trudged to school. There was widespread public feeling that these deaths would not have happened under standard time since it would have been light then. Congress quickly got the message; year-round daylight savings time was ended.

Some broad changes in society may or may not be impacts of specific federal actions. They can be caused in part by forces outside government control, in part by government activity. Deciding what causes what is often impossible. For instance, over the last 50 years, the gap in per capita income between the poorest and richest states has greatly decreased. People from the South, the plains, the Southwest, and the mountain West have become better off; those in the Northeast and on the West Coast have become worse off, though the latter are still better off than the former. Since the 1930s a whole range of federal programs has pushed toward greater regional equality. But the movement of industry to sources of cheaper labor and better tax incentives probably had even more to do with shrinking regional differences in income.

Some effects are direct results of programs. For instance, as mentioned, traffic deaths dropped after speed limits were lowered. Likewise, food stamps may help improve the diets of the poor. If as a result of that improved diet, children are absent less and more attentive in school, and learn more, these are secondary, or indirect, impacts.

Not all indirect impacts are favorable. Some are seen as favorable by certain people and as unfavorable by others, depending on their values and points of

Lifesaver. The 55-miles-per-hour speed limit required by federal law was intended to conserve gasoline consumption, but its main consequence has been to reduce highway deaths.

Progress? The top picture shows Appalachia in the 1930s. The bottom picture shows a 1980s family after 50 years of federal efforts to help.

Renewing Hartford, Connecticut. A federal urban renewal program razed much of downtown Hartford, Connecticut, and replaced the old structures with modern office buildings. But the former residents of the urban renewal area had little to say in this development.

view. Federal housing programs (Federal Housing Administration mortgage insurance, Veterans Administration mortgage insurance, and urban renewal and public housing programs) indirectly strengthened or created patterns of racial segregation in housing (Lowi, 1979: Chapter 9).

Some indirect impacts seem planned. The intended direct impact of the War on Poverty of the 1960s was getting rid of poverty. A secondary impact was helping the poor speak for themselves and present their needs effectively in political debate. The basic goal of the Model Cities program was improving the economic base and the quality of life in inner-city slums. A secondary goal was to urge city governments to hire more people from those neighborhoods.

Causality in foreign affairs is particularly hard to track. Under what conditions do U.S. actions have the desired impacts on other nations? When dealing with small and weak nations perhaps the direct impact is obvious. In the case of Grenada, the government we did not like vanished. But even in such a case impacts on the behavior and attitudes of other governments—those in Latin America or Great Britain, in this case—are much more difficult to prove. And, of course, much of the time we are not seeking to influence the behavior of a Grenada through direct military intervention, but to influence the behavior of Japan, or the Soviet Union, or the People's Republic of China, or West Germany through much more subtle means.

Intended and unintended impact

Some impacts are intended or expected; others are unintended or unexpected. It is often hard to tell them apart. The people who design programs have different motives. A racist congressman could support public housing because, in time, such programs might promote racial segregation. But a liberal would not want this result. The goals for most programs are extremely general and often unclear and contradictory; this causes added problems in sorting out intended and unintended results. Unintended impacts range from trivial to massive.

In early 1981 the Department of Agriculture reported on the effects of policies and programs meant to protect small- and medium-sized farms. In fact, the report showed, they had helped large farms and the demise of small- and medium-sized farms.

Medicare was created in the 1960s to help the elderly with medical bills. By 1979, it was paying only 30 percent of their doctor bills. Some doctors even raised their fees just to collect more insurance money.

There are programs for opening educational opportunity to the less advantaged. These gave aid through basic educational opportunity grants, supplemental economic opportunity grants, national direct student loans, and the federal work-study program. But they were also being used by proprietary schools (for example, for beauticians) to make a lot of money. A number of schools depended on the programs for their success.

Programs to improve inner-city housing have displaced many poor people who have no place else to go.

In the 1970s we pushed the Shah of Iran to democratize more rapidly. One side effect of his acquiescence may have been his downfall and the eventual rise of the Ayatollah Khomenei and his associates. Surely we did not intend this result.

Policies always have side effects. If policymakers could account for those side effects in advance, they could make better and more informed choices. But often they focus so much on one effect that they ignore side effects, even though the effects can be predicted.

The visibility of impact

Sometimes impacts are not seen even by those directly affected. Others are visible to many people because they are very "hot topics." Thus, the effects of

570

Government impact on stock brokers. The federal Securities and Exchange Commission's policies affect the work of stockbrokers, such as these at the American Stock Exchange.

busing students to achieve racially mixed schools are debated by many people who have never seen a school bus, let alone had a child bused anywhere for racial balance.

Some effects are visible to those affected but almost invisible to the rest of us. For example, in 1975 the Securities and Exchange Commission, which regulates the stock market and securities dealers, banned fixed brokerage commission rates. The practice had begun in 1792 in the organization that was to become the New York Stock Exchange. In 1975 brokerage houses, for the first time, had to compete for customers in terms of the prices they charged. This move by the SEC had a number of effects. Most of them were only felt by brokerage firms and related businesses. Many firms went out of business or merged with larger ones. The competition was too much for them. Between late 1974 and late 1976, almost 300 brokerage firms closed. Related companies that did research on securities almost all folded. Large investors such as insurance companies, pension funds, and mutual funds now pay much lower commission fees. Small investors still pay the pre-1975 fees.

Even in the foreign and defense field visibility varies a great deal. Naturally, military action as in Lebanon or Grenada has almost universal and instantaneous visibility once the mass media can cover the story. However, changes in tariff policy or immigration policy are visible only for a short time, and that visibility differs in different locations. A change in the tariff on steel would be big news in Pittsburgh or Gary or Cleveland but would not be of much interest to anyone in Scottsbluff, Nebraska, or Tyler, Texas. Changes in the law regarding undocumented workers or the implementation of anti–illegal immigration measures by the border patrol would get front-page coverage in San Diego or El Paso but would be close to invisible in Minneapolis or Knoxville.

Special publics might find certain policies visible but in different ways. In 1983, for example, a variety of U.S. policies helped keep the value of the American dollar very high and increasing when compared to the other major currencies. This fact delighted American tourists or would-be tourists, although they probably had no real knowledge of the U.S. policies that had helped lead to this result. But the same fact depressed American exporters who had a hard time selling their expensive goods to overseas buyers.

Anticipated impact and political salesmanship

Claims about expected impact are often used in formulation and approval debates. They are rarely based on fact, but rather on hope or assertion. President Johnson and the first director of the Office of Economic Opportunity, Sargent Shriver, claimed in 1964 and 1965 that the War on Poverty would end poverty by the bicentennial in 1976. It sounded good, but it was not based on analysis. Almost all our social programs are "oversold." They are supposed to be *the* solution to whatever problem is addressed. Such claims almost always produce disappointment. And to attract broad support, they are almost always out of reach. Sometimes the claims in nonsocial fields are more valid. To get support for a major space program, President Kennedy promised a manned moon landing by the end of the 1960s. That goal was achieved.

Exaggerated claims also typify debate on foreign and defense policy. In 1983 and 1984 the administration claimed that increased aid to Nicaraguan rebels or to the government in El Salvador was essential if Central America was not to go communist. But if such aid was granted, communist governments could have emerged anyway. Or aid could have been denied and the governments could have remained noncommunist. The point is that to make any firm claim about the black-and-white impact of one amount of U.S. aid versus some competing amount is probably unreasonable, although politically understandable.

Claims of impact are also used at a much less visible level during formulation and legitimation debates. For example, those pushing distributive programs often issue detailed projected impact statements. The statements show money flowing to congressional districts and states to get support for programs. Often the executive-branch agency that supports such a program sends out summaries and computer printouts to all congressional offices to get support. Lobbyists for favored groups, companies, or unions do the same. Sometimes, though rarely, an independent group will check the validity of the claimed effect. And sometimes such checks show the claims to be faulty. A good example is the efforts of Rockwell International to sell Congress on continuing the B-1 bomber program. Congressman John Seiberling from the Akron, Ohio, area had been assured by Rockwell that the program would provide $70.5 million in contracts to the area. Implied, of course, was that this would all add to the economy. But Seiberling calculated that the taxes paid by his constituents as their share of the program cost would be about $84 million, well over the promised benefits.

A government agency will occasionally not oversell its program but begin with realistic expectations. In 1977, the Office of Youth Programs of the Employment and Training Administration in the Department of Labor issued "A Planning Charter for the Youth Employment and Demonstration Projects Act of 1977." This did not promise a complete cure for the problems of youth unemployment; instead, it took a realistic look at the constraints the program faced. Then it specified attainable goals for the first two years. The Office of Youth

Programs identified four major constraints. First, funds were limited. Second, the program had to be integrated with a complex set of existing programs. Third, there were few knowledgeable Department of Labor staff members to help implement the program. And fourth, the nature of specific parts of the program included in the act by Congress was diverse. The specific statements about "attainable goals" were not excessive. This is admirable, but rare, behavior.

EXAMPLES OF DOMESTIC IMPACT: WHO PAYS AND WHO BENEFITS?

We have picked a few examples to explore impacts, but we can only scratch the surface. We hope to show the many kinds of impacts—and a few general trends—that can be credited to some specific government efforts. We have purposely chosen areas marked by heated, continuing political debate.

Paying for government: the impact of tax policy

The phrase **tax policy** implies a master scheme to distribute the tax load. In fact, there is no such scheme. All levels of government make decisions about taxes without coordinating them. So the tax system looks like a crazy quilt. Presidents often talk about basic tax reform at the federal level but are almost always last seen sinking into the morass of the Internal Revenue Code with little to show for their good intentions. Despite the lack of a coordinated planning system, the nation's pattern of taxation does have some broad social impacts. Taxation is the prelude to almost all other government activity. Therefore, it is worthwhile to sketch the general outlines of some of those impacts.

Who pays? Surely you have looked at a paycheck and wondered why you are being paid $200 a week but receive only $140. A large part of the reason for the "missing" $60 is income taxes. They are withheld for the federal government, probably for the state government, and perhaps for a city government. But the missing money is only part of the taxes you pay. You also pay state

"I'm afraid we can't allow you to deduct last year's tax as a bad investment, Mr. Willoughby."

and local sales taxes, local property taxes (directly if you own the property, indirectly if you rent), and social security taxes.

When the impacts of all these taxes are viewed together, almost everyone pays about the same percentage of income in taxes. That percentage hovers around 25 percent, whether income is $5,000, $15,000 or $50,000 (Pechman, 1977: 5–6; Le Loup, 1980: 234–35). This means that the total U.S. tax system has a *proportional* impact. Everyone pays about the same proportion of income.

The federal personal income tax is the one moderately *progressive* tax in the system. People with higher incomes pay a higher percentage of their income in taxes. A significant reduction in the progressive features of the federal personal income tax was made in 1981.

State and local personal income taxes are mildly progressive in some jurisdictions and proportional in others. Sales taxes, property taxes, and federal social security payroll taxes are generally *regressive*. Those with higher incomes pay a lower percentage of income in taxes.

The total impact of the two principal federal taxes—personal income and social security payroll—are also close to proportional. In 1982, families of four with the median family income paid 25 percent of their income in these two taxes. Those with twice the median income (the relatively well off) paid only 26 percent. And those with half of the median income (the relatively poor) paid 20 percent. This represented a substantial change—both in amounts and in relative percentages—from 1955, when those with the median income paid 9 percent, those with twice the median income paid 12 percent, and those with half the median income paid 4 percent. By 1982, everybody was taxed more heavily, but the difference in rates of taxation for people earning different amounts shrank.

Where does the federal government get its money?   The government gets some money by borrowing (through means such as the sale of bonds and Treasury certificates). Borrowing represented one dollar of every five dollars needed by federal government in 1985.

Most of the money comes from taxes. There are four major categories:

Personal income taxes.

Social insurance taxes and contributions. These include social security and railroad retirement taxes, unemployment taxes and deposits from employers, contributions by federal employees to their retirement system, and payments for extra medical insurance under the medicare program.

Corporate income taxes.

Other taxes. These include excise taxes on a variety of products, services, and activities (such as airport and airway use, telephone bills, and gasoline and other fuels), estate taxes, gift taxes, and tariffs on foreign imports.

"HE WANTS TO BUY THE TAX DEDUCTIONS OF THESE PEOPLE WHO AREN'T USING THEM"

Over time, government reliance on different categories has changed. Until World War I, the largest source of money was tariffs. Before the Civil War, 90 percent of federal money came from this source. Currently, tariffs provide only about 1 percent of federal money.

In the last few decades, the government has relied much less on taxing corporate income, and much more on social insurance taxes. Individual income taxes have remained the largest source of federal revenue (corporations can sell unused tax benefits to each other). Figure 17–1 shows the recent mixes of federal tax receipts. Federal tax laws are very complex. They have many loopholes

FIGURE 17–1

The Source of Federal Tax Revenue, 1960–1985 (amounts from different sources for every $1 in federal tax revenue)

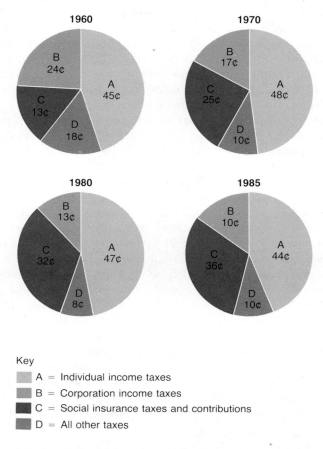

Key

A = Individual income taxes

B = Corporation income taxes

C = Social insurance taxes and contributions

D = All other taxes

Sources: Calculated from *Statistical Abstract of the United States, 1982–83* (Washington, D.C.: U.S. Government Printing Office, 1982), p. 247, for 1960, 1970, and 1980; *The Budget of the United States Government, Fiscal Year 1985* (Washington, D.C.: U.S. Government Printing Office, 1984), p. 4-3, for 1985 estimate.

that let people and corporations legally avoid certain taxes. Most people do not benefit from these loopholes. The main beneficiaries are high-income people and corporations.

Attacking poverty

Starting with the War on Poverty in 1964, the federal government increased spending to help poor people. Poverty is officially defined as less than a certain income level. In 1982, if a family of four had an income of less than $9,862, it was in poverty.

The percentage of the population below the poverty level has varied over time. It also varies depending on how income is measured. Does it include only cash income? Or should it also include the market value of noncash benefits such as food stamps, school lunches, public housing, medicaid, and medicare?

FIGURE 17–2

Extent of Poverty, 1959–1982 (all people, whites, blacks, those of spanish origin)

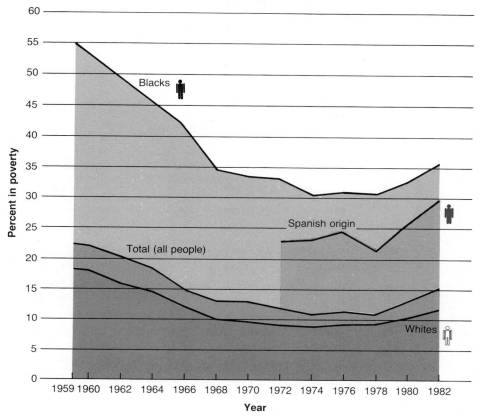

Source: Based on data in the *New York Times*, February 24, 1984, for 1982; *Statistical Abstract of the United States, 1968*, p. 329, for 1962 and 1964; and *Statistical Abstract of the United States, 1982–83*, p. 440, for the rest.

Cash income already includes cash benefits from some government programs such as aid to families with dependent children (the most common kind of "welfare") and supplemental security income.

The overall changing poverty rate (the percentage of the total population with income below the poverty level) is pictured in Figure 17–2. In this graph income is defined as cash income (including cash benefits from government social programs). In addition, the different rates for whites, blacks, and persons of Spanish origin are portrayed. Several general observations can be made. First, all of the lines show a general decline until the late 1970s and then begin to rise. The rates are not as high in the early 1980s as they were in the late 1950s or early 1960s. Second, the black poverty rate has consistently been at least three times the white poverty rate. Third, the poverty rate for persons of Spanish origin has hovered around 2.5 times the white rate.

How can these patterns be explained? Changes over time are both a function of the general state of the economy and of the state of federal programs aimed at the poor. When the economy is growing and healthy, poverty declines. When the economy is on the rocks, poverty increases. Similarly, when programs aimed

TABLE 17–1

Percentage of American Population and Selected Subgroups in Poverty Using Two Definitions of Income

	1979		1982	
	Official poverty definition	Alternative definition	Official poverty definition	Alternative definition
Total	11.7%	6.8%	15.0%	10.0%
White	9.0	5.6	12.0	8.3
Black	31.0	14.9	35.6	21.5
Hispanic	21.8	12.0	29.9	20.5
Elderly	15.2	4.3	14.6	3.5
Families headed by women	34.9	16.6	40.6	24.8

Notes: Official poverty definition counts only cash income. Alternative definition counts cash income and the market value of noncash benefits such as food stamps, school lunches, public housing, medicaid, and medicare. The figure for families headed by women counts individuals rather than family units.

Source: Data from the U.S. Bureau of the Census; adapted from a table in the *New York Times*, February 24, 1984. © by The New York Times Company. Reprinted by permission.

"SUPPOSE WE TRY SETTING IT ON THE GROUND"

at the poor are growing, the desired impact of reducing poverty can be observed. When those programs are cut, poverty increases. The Congressional Budget Office has documented that the social program cuts initiated under the Reagan Administration have hurt the poor the most (see summary in Rich, 1983; see also Havemann, 1982; Demkovich and Havemann, 1982). Problems of the poor in the first few years of the 1980s were compounded because of a deteriorating economy.

How much impact do alternative definitions of poverty (including the market value of noncash benefits) have? Table 17–1 summarizes the comparative situation between 1979 and 1982 and also compares the two different measures in those years for poverty rates among the total population, whites, blacks, Hispanics, the elderly, and families headed by women. Inspection shows that noncash benefits reduce poverty dramatically among the elderly and substantially for blacks and families headed by women. They are not as effective in reducing poverty for whites and Hispanics.

The percentages reported mean that in 1982, 34.4 million Americans were living below the poverty level using the definition of cash income. This number is still 22.9 million if the expanded definition of income is used.

Do the same people remain poor over time? It used to be assumed that there was a "culture of poverty" in which poor parents bred poor children and few people or families moved out. However, a study released in early 1984 (Duncan, 1984) challenges this conventional wisdom. It presents data showing that about one of every four Americans was in poverty status for some time during the 1970s and that only a little over two percent of the population stayed in poverty throughout the entire decade. If this study is correct, then economic mobility—both upward and downward—is, in fact, prevalent in the United States.

In addition to taking millions out of poverty, at least on a year-by-year basis, what other impacts do government transfer programs have? Do they equalize income? Table 17–2 shows the share of total U.S. income for different groups before and after the impact of government programs *and* taxes. The population has been divided into fifths on the basis of income. The lowest fifth is the 20

TABLE 17–2

Income Shares of American Households, 1976

Income categories	Percentage share of income	
	Before government transfers and taxes	After government transfers and taxes
Lowest 20 percent	0.3	7.2
Medium low 20 percent	7.2	11.5
Middle 20 percent	16.3	16.6
Medium high 20 percent	26.0	23.4
Highest 20 percent	50.2	41.3
Total	100.0	100.0

Source: Adapted from Congressional Budget Office, *Poverty Status of Families under Alternative Definitions of Income* (Washington, D.C.: U.S. Government Printing Office, 1977), p. 26.

percent with the lowest incomes. The highest fifth is the 20 percent with the highest incomes. If there was an equal distribution of incomes, each fifth would have 20 percent of the country's total income. The table shows that taxes and social programs are, on the whole, redistributive from the two highest fifths to the two lowest and mostly from the highest to the lowest. But it also shows that even with the impact of government programs, there is inequality in the distribution of income. This basic pattern has not changed much since World War II. The distribution of economic classes has been quite stable for the last four decades.

A recent study looked at changes in the distribution of disposable income

Direct federal impact on standard of living. A New York City consumer exchanges federal food stamps for groceries.

TABLE 17–3

Distribution of Disposable Income by Income Category

Year	Income category				
	Lowest 20%	Medium Low 20%	Middle 20%	Medium High 20%	Highest 20%
1979	7.1	13.2	18.5	24.2	37.0
1984	6.6	13.0	18.4	24.4	37.6

Source: Data taken from Frank Levy and Richard C. Michel, "The Way We'll Be in 1984: Recent Changes in the Level and Distribution of Disposable Income" (Discussion Paper, Urban Institute, Washington, D.C., November 1983), p. 36.

between 1979 and 1984 (Levy and Michel, 1983). The concept of "disposable income" took into account all federal, state, and local taxes and both cash and noncash benefits. Table 17–3 shows the percentage of total national disposable income available to each income class in both 1979 and 1984. The table shows roughly the same distribution reported in Table 17–2. The movement between 1979 and 1984 was very small, but in the direction of decreasing income shares at the lower end of the scale and increasing them at the upper end.

What is the quality of social programs' impact on people? Do the programs rob them of the incentive to work? Or do beneficiaries become more self-sufficient when relieved of the worries of survival? Does decent nutrition, housing, education, and health help them to work more efficiently and to better their jobs and incomes?

There are no complete answers to these questions, but there are partial ones. Upward Bound, a program designed to spark the interest of the disadvantaged in higher education, did work. Seventy-one percent of those taking part, mostly members of minority groups, entered some sort of school after completing high school. This compares to 47 percent of nonparticipants with the same kinds of social, racial, and economic backgrounds. Upward Bound participants are mostly high school students between their junior and senior years. They spend about two months in the summer on college campuses going to formal courses, informal meetings, and counseling sessions. When they return to high school, they continue to get special counseling. Twenty-four percent more of them seek higher education of some kind than would usually be the case. Between 15,000 and 20,000 taken part each year since the program began in 1965. So the net impact of the program has been to induce about 3,000 to 5,000 young people (80 percent of whom are black or Hispanic) to go on to higher education each year. These people should be more economically self-sufficient in the future with added schooling. Some of you reading this may be in college now because of Upward Bound.

Another study of the effects of income support and social welfare programs between 1950 and the mid-1970s (Danziger, Haveman, and Plotnick, 1980) found that poverty was reduced by 50 to 60 percent and that the desire of the recipients to work was reduced by 3 to 7 percent.

Housing programs

Federal housing programs in the 1960s and early 70s had some successes and some failures (Downs, 1974; Levitan and Taggart, 1976). Many were effective in keeping housing production high, providing financing, attracting private investment, and creating new neighborhoods of good quality. These programs

Slums? Tax policies affect the housing of a community. When tax laws discourage renovating old housing, houses can deteriorate.

Suburbs? Often tax policies, in discouraging the renovation of older houses, promote new home construction in suburbs. This can contribute to suburban sprawl.

were somewhat effective in promoting economic stabilization, assisting low- and middle-income families, and encouraging home ownership. But the same programs were most ineffective in reducing housing costs and improving conditions in decaying inner-city neighborhoods. They were somewhat ineffective in stabilizing the level of housing production, which fluctuated a lot.

When housing programs for the poor are examined, it seems they had moderate success in providing assistance for low- and middle-income families. But inner-city neighborhoods continued to decay despite efforts to the contrary.

Federal tax laws have had a largely unplanned impact on development patterns in cities. Tax law allows for much faster depreciation of investments in new construction than for investments of equal size in renovating old buildings; this promotes investment of funds in new buildings. People will therefore help finance new suburban housing developments, plants, and shopping centers on vacant land rather than use their money to help rebuild central cities. Consciously or not, those who wrote the tax law over the years have helped produce urban sprawl and the loss of jobs and decent housing in central cities.

More biases in the tax code have also favored building single-family, owner-occupied houses over multifamily rental units.

So the tax code that has favored suburban developers and investors has also helped shape the face of modern America, with beltways, long commutes, and dying central cities.

EVALUATING IMPACT

The worth of government programs is judged in terms of what they accomplish. This may be a comparison of program performance with stated goals. But many goals are vague, and comparison is often impossible. Different people and groups interpret even a clear goal in different ways. Those who assess them look for different things and make different judgments.

There is also formal evaluation involving more technical analytic activity. Usually it is conducted by social scientists either inside the government or from the outside but with government funding. What social scientists do in these studies is basically what individuals, interest groups, or consumer groups do when they rate a program: they ask how it stacks up against some standards they set for it.

The objects of evaluation

Formal and informal judgments of many aspects of government behavior, including program impact, are made. Evaluative questions often include some of the following:

Are enough resources provided for the program?

Is the program being carried out according to preexisting standards?

Do intended beneficiaries search out and get the intended goods and services.

Is the program being run according to traditional standards of efficiency and economy? Is the money being spent well, honestly, and correctly?

Are the processes used in making decisions about the program fair, open, and procedurally correct?

Has the program achieved its intended impact on the beneficiaries?

Has the program had impacts other than those specified in the goals?

Has the program had broad impacts on society or on people other than the direct recipients?

What did the program achieve even if its goals were largely unclear?

The political nature of evaluation

All evaluations are political. Some are political in their primary intent. Others try to be more objective (formal and technical) but are used for political purposes, either by the evaluators or others.

Formal-technical evaluations are rigorous. They *specify* clearly what is to be evaluated; they *measure* the features of the program to be judged as logically as possible, using data about the program; and they *analyze* data to reach concrete conclusions (Jones, 1984: Chapter 9). Those who do such evaluations, though, may have preformed notions that help shape their findings.

The results of any analysis can fuel political debate. In recent years, evaluations of Head Start (aimed at disadvantaged preschool children) and of the educational impact of racial integration have become hot topics of political debate. This is true even though the evaluations were done by social scientists who presumably had no ax to grind. When evaluations touch sensitive political nerves they are likely to become the subject of charges and countercharges about their validity. It may be, in fact, that their validity can fairly be attacked or their results interpreted in several different ways. Attacks on the quality of research may really be attacks on the values the research seems to espouse or on researcher advice that may threaten certain interests.

Evaluations sometimes show very little. Or they may produce contradictory findings. Political debate may still take place over fragmentary findings. For example, many large-scale studies of what promotes learning in public schools have shown very little. The findings are either mixed or of no consequence on a number of elements. Yet those who debate programs such as aid to education make confident claims about what will and will not work and what is needed to improve the quality of public education.

The final decision about accepting an evaluation is political. Congress may expand a program because it accepts a positive evaluation. The president may recommend ending a program because he is convinced it does not work. Nixon supported many arguments for killing or drastically cutting most of the Great Society programs of president Johnson with evaluation results. He halved the Job Corps budget, for example, based on two evaluations. The first was a public report by the General Accounting Office. It concluded that the Job Corps had only limited impact and was too costly for what it produced. The second was a private report from the secretary of labor to Nixon detailing a number of shortcomings in the program and suggesting major cuts in its size and cost.

All actors in the policy process can and do get involved in political evaluation and evaluative argument. Most formal-technical evaluation is done either in the bureaucracy or by outsiders with bureaucracy blessing and funding. The amount of technical evaluation varies greatly from agency to agency. Some agencies have a rather long history of supporting a lot of evaluation by outsiders, a good deal of which is of high quality. Other agencies have experimented with high quality formal evaluation in-house. A number of agencies have never shown any interest in formal evaluation. A bureaucracy confronted with an evaluation that questions its basic assumptions is likely to ignore the evaluation and proceed with "business as usual" (Frieden, 1980).

Congress is at the center of political evaluation debates. In recent years, it has shown interest in developing some evaluation capacities of its own. Most important was formation of the Congressional Budget Office in connection with the Budget Act of 1974. The office is by law politically neutral. It has produced a series of competent and important evaluative statements about policy options facing Congress. Its performance was vastly enhanced by its first director, Alice Rivlin, from the Brookings Institution. She was also involved in evaluation as an assistant secretary of HEW in the late Johnson years. She coupled her commitment to good evaluation with good judgments in appointments and in

An evaluation pioneer. Alice Rivlin, former director of the Congressional Budget Office, made that agency a major source of program evaluation.

how to get along with Congress in a politically sensitive role. Her leadership helped set up a creative and innovative organization. It produced work that was taken quite seriously by many congressional members, subcommittees, and communities.

Congress has also received some help in evaluating programs from the General Accounting Office, the Congressional Research Service, and the Office of Technology Assessment.

Above all, Congress is interested in political evaluations. This normal pattern is shown by a Senate Committee on Veterans Affairs hearing at which one of the authors testified in mid-1979. The hearing focused on "Oversight of Veterans' Employment Programs", of which there were many. The hearing lasted for over four hours, and more than 20 people appeared. Only one formal evaluative effort was presented in that whole time (by the hardworking author!). All other presentations involved opinion, and some were just self-praise based on no particular evidence. Committee members often focused on trivial and marginal issues. Sometimes they asked questions about important aspects of the programs. But only one witness (who appeared for 15 minutes—a 5-minute statement and 10 minutes responding to questions) could answer with hard evidence.

It should also be noted that data are not neutral or objective. In the late 1970s, there was a substantial debate among both experts and politicians on how to measure inflation. Some measures make inflation look worse, others make it look not so bad. A person's best measure depends on his or her political stake in which measure is used. The same kind of debate took place over how to measure unemployment. Even technical evaluations can be called into question on the very basic matters of definition and measurement.

THE RESPONSIVENESS OF GOVERNMENT TO PUBLIC NEEDS

The meaning of responsiveness

The notion of government responsiveness has at least three dimensions. First, a responsive government will act on matters that are widely viewed as problems and as proper subjects for government action. Second, it will be prompt, efficient, and effective when it does act. Third, it will show respect for the people with whom it deals and use fair, open, and efficient procedures.

But judgments about responsiveness, like others about government institutions and behavior, are political. People will disagree over whether any one government is responsive at any one time. Different people have different values; and those values shape judgments about responsiveness.

In general, it seems that our national government is likely to change its policies slowly. People who demand quick change are apt to be disappointed and to consider the government unresponsive. Those who are content with current policies are more apt to see the government as responsive enough.

Slow change is most likely in distributive policy. Government aid tends to be given to a number of special publics without sudden change. Competitive regulatory policy is most often shaped to reduce real competition in favor of peace between the government and the regulated interests. Therefore, it looks much like distributive policy. Protective regulatory policy moves by fits and starts.

There are occasional new bursts of government activity, but they are usually tempered by weakening amendments or interpretations almost as soon as the policy is enacted. Redistributive policy only rarely results in profound redistribution. The lot of the poor is enhanced only marginally, though that margin may be very important.

In the realm of foreign and defense policy, change in structural matters is slow. Change in strategic matters is fitful. Responses to crises are unpredictable and may or may not result in longer run policy changes.

Our political system maximizes the amount of decision making processed in a way that minimizes the potential for change in policy. Most change is by small steps. Those who decide about even small steps of change are politicians and bureaucrats. Very little systematic analysis of policy is done in this setting. Far fewer decisions involving small change are processed in settings in which policy analysts have impact and can use formal analytic methods. A few large changes are made when outside conditions (such as an economic collapse) let advocates push policy along the lines they believe in (Braybrooke and Lindblom, 1963).

Present processes, institutions, practices, and substantive policies were basically formed during a period of great economic abundance. That period appears to be ending. Threats to our environment, our economy, and the energy on which so much of our economic strength is based give a glimpse of a grim future. In such a future the United States, like most of the world, will work with an economy of scarcity, not abundance. The processes, institutions, practices, and policies that worked well with abundance may not work well with scarcity. But they are very difficult to change. The dismemberment of President Carter's effort to deal with the energy problems facing the nation in 1977 is symptomatic of the wrenches the system is likely to go through before needed changes are made. Again, though, the question of responsiveness depends on point of view. To a person most concerned with keeping a big car, nonaction on a very high gasoline tax is responsive behavior. But to an energy economist, nonaction is nonresponsiveness.

The most important expectations

Citizens of the United States have, in a variety of ways, for several centuries, pressed their government to be trustworthy, competent, and support and expand a political system based, at important points, on citizen participation and access. They have also expected policies that further personal liberty, equality of individuals, and accommodation of a wide diversity of people, beliefs, and values. Some of these expectations are about the system of self-government and some are about the policies promoted by that system. The expectations overlap and are interwoven. They, like all matters involving values in a free society, have been the subject of sharp debates and political struggles throughout our history.

Americans expect a political system worthy of *trust*. Both those who govern and the institutions within which they work must be viewed as proceeding free of corruption and in honorable and fair ways. When revelations during Watergate made it clear that the trust had been violated in many important ways, public confidence in government plummeted. Such confidence can be rebuilt

A member of Congress seeks trust. Jim Leach, an Iowa Republican, chats with two farmers in his district. Trust in individuals and trust in "the system" are interrelated.

slowly and painstakingly. There is an inherent streak of suspicion of government, officials, and politicians in the American population. When events confirm the suspicions, a cynical view can result.

Americans also expect a *competent* government. No government encourages cynicism and hostility more than one led by fools or with institutions incapable of being effective. In a democratic society a competent government does essentially what its leaders promise it will do. Wise leaders do not promise what cannot be delivered. A competent government does what it can do as effectively as possible. But it neither tries to do everything nor promises beyond its means. A competent American government does its best within the framework of what is appropriate for government to undertake in a free society. And it does its work openly to discourage the view that results are rigged in advance.

Americans expect a government that encourages political *participation* rather than suppressing it. Participation goes well beyond the formal act of voting in elections in which there are real choices—although that seemingly straightforward and undeniable right is denied to a great majority of the world's people. Participation extends to allowing and even encouraging other expressions of policy preferences and opinion. It also includes the notion that citizens should have direct access to the officials who govern them. Officials are not supposed to be aloof "rulers" more appropriate to a 17th-century monarchy or a modern authoritarian or totalitarian state.

Americans have long prized personal *liberty*. They have been keen to insist that government not restrict liberty more than absolutely necessary. Jefferson's language about inalienable rights captured what our ancestors believed in the 17th and 18th centuries and what we have continued to believe throughout the 19th and 20th centuries. Individual liberty is well entrenched in the United States, although it is also threatened by both government and private action. The rights to believe what you wish, express those beliefs, live where you wish, travel when you want to, and work at whatever occupation you choose are enormously valuable. We take them for granted. In fact, citizens have a responsibility to make sure their national government pursues liberty and squashes threats to it. This does not mean that political debate over the meaning of individual rights will not or should not occur. It will and it should.

Liberty. The right to travel outside the United States is highly prized by Americans, although subject to some controversial restrictions.

Americans have shown a capacity to grow in terms of a belief in *equality* and an accompanying demand that government promote equality. The importance of equality as an ideal has grown over the course of American history. The practical effects of a number of policies have also expanded the meaning of equality. The widespread beliefs of Americans in equality (or at least equal opportunity) with regard to education, employment, upward economic mobility, benefits of government programs, voting and other forms of political participation, and health are clear. Even though some of the worst inequalities have been corrected, at least in part, a variety of inequalities continue to blot our record. Many opportunities for the poor, women, racial and ethnic minorities such as blacks, Hispanics, recent Asian immigrants, and the aged are not equal to those of the more privileged in society. Political debate and struggle over the concrete meaning of equality will continue.

Finally, Americans can expect their government to play a leading role in promoting forms of *accommodation* in society allowing people who are diverse in terms of racial, ethnic, and cultural backgrounds and beliefs to reach agreements peacefully. Ours is a vast country geographically and in terms of the heterogeneity of peoples and beliefs. Inevitably, this has also helped foster competing and diverse economic interests. A monumental task of politics, government, and political leaders in a society such as ours is accommodating divergent interests and demands so that conflicts can be peacefully resolved without violence or lingering fear and hatred. Politics and government service are noble callings when they are filled by people promoting principled compromises that make possible a prosperous, peaceful, and—above all—free nation.

CONCLUSIONS

In this chapter we dealt with a few central aspects of the impact of American government and its policies. Several concluding statements seem appropriate.

1 Any government, particularly a government in a society that values liberty, is limited in what it can achieve. Some limits are present specifically to make sure government does not threaten liberty. Other limits simply result from the fact that important trends and events are beyond government control or influence.

2 Government has great trouble in creating a major desired impact in a short time even in areas in which it has undoubted influence. Government appears powerful to the citizenry. But when it seeks to act, it often faces even more powerful social forces, traditions, and practices.

3 It is often very hard to prove that government action did or did not have some specific result. Nevertheless, political debate proceeds on the basis of confident assertions about both the past and future impacts of government actions.

4 Many government impacts are not intended. Predicting all the important results of government activity is difficult. It is an art that has not been mastered and probably never can be.

5 The evaluation of program impact is largely political. More objective formal-technical evaluation is in its infancy. And the results of such evaluation are usually overshadowed by political considerations. Much of the time people make decisions about future policies without knowing much about the results of past policies.

6 The value of specific government programs and actions will inevitably be assessed differently by different people because the values and interests of these people conflict.

7 American citizens can and should expect that their government will merit trust, be competent, encourage political participation, and work to aid society in seeking liberty, equality, and peaceful solutions of differences of opinion through accommodation of the immense diversities that characterize the United States and its people.

586

FURTHER READING

BUDGET OF THE U.S. GOVERNMENT. This yearly document, published, usually in February, by the U.S. Government Printing Office in Washington, is both a political statement by the incumbent administration and a valuable collection of information about government agencies and programs and the overall importance of government in society.

LEVITAN, SAR A., and ROBERT TAGGART (1976) The Promise of Greatness. Cambridge, Mass.: Harvard University Press. An analysis of a great number of Great Society programs that suggests that they had the desired impact in most cases.

PECHMAN, JOSEPH A. (1983) Federal Tax Policy. 4th ed. Washington, D.C.: Brookings Institution. A careful analysis of the nature and impact of federal tax laws.

PECHMAN, JOSEPH A., ed. (1984) Setting National Priorities: The 1985 Budget. Washington, D.C.: Brookings Institution. This is a yearly interpretation of the proposed budget, usually available in the spring after the president presents the budget.

SCHWARZ, JOHN E. (1983) America's Hidden Success: A Reassessment of Twenty Years of Public Policy. New York: W. W. Norton. An examination of American domestic policy from 1960 to 1980 which concludes that, overall, these policies succeeded.

APPENDIX

APPENDIX A

The Declaration of Independence in Congress, July 4, 1776

*The unanimous Declaration
of the thirteen united States of America,*

When in the Course of human events, it becomes necessary for one people to dissolve the political bands which have connected them with another, and to assume among the Powers of the earth, the separate and equal station to which the Laws of Nature and of Nature's God entitle them, a decent respect to the opinions of mankind requires that they should declare the causes which impel them to the separation.

We hold these truths to be self-evident, that all men are created equal, that they are endowed by their Creator with certain unalienable Rights, that among these are Life, Liberty and the pursuit of Happiness. That to secure these rights, Governments are instituted among Men, deriving their just powers from the consent of the governed. That whenever any Form of Government becomes destructive of these ends, it is the Right of the People to alter or to abolish it, and to institute new Government, laying its foundation on such principles and organizing its powers in such form, as to them shall seem most likely to effect their Safety and Happiness. Prudence, indeed, will dictate that Governments long established should not be changed for light and transient causes; and accordingly all experience hath shown, that mankind are more disposed to suffer, while evils are sufferable, than to right themselves by abolishing the forms to which they are accustomed. But when a long train of abuses and usurpations, pursuing invariably the same Object evinces a design to reduce them under absolute Despotism, it is their right, it is their duty, to throw off such Government, and to provide new Guards for their future security.—Such has been the patient sufferance of these Colonies; and such is now the necessity which constrains them to alter their former Systems of Government. The history of the present King of Great Britain is a history of repeated injuries and usurpations, all having in direct object the establishment of an absolute Tyranny over these States. To prove this, let Facts be submitted to a candid world.

He has refused his Assent to Laws, the most wholesome and necessary for the public good.

He has forbidden his Governors to pass Laws of immediate and pressing importance, unless suspended in their operation till his Assent should be obtained; and when so suspended, he has utterly neglected to attend to them.

He has refused to pass other Laws for the accommodation of large districts of people, unless those people would relinquish the right of Representation in the Legislature, a right inestimable to them and formidable to tyrants only.

He has called together legislative bodies at places unusual, uncomfortable, and distant from the depository of their Public Records, for the sole purpose of fatiguing them into compliance with his measures.

He has dissolved Representative Houses repeatedly, for opposing with many firmness his invasions on the rights of the people.

He has refused for a long time, after such dissolutions, to cause others to be elected; whereby the Legislative Powers, incapable of Annihilation, have returned to the People at large for their exercise; the State remaining in the mean time exposed to all the dangers of invasion from without, and convulsions within.

He has endeavoured to prevent the population of these States; for that purpose obstructing the Laws for Naturalization of Foreigners; refusing to pass others to encourage their migrations hither, and raising the conditions of new Appropriations of Lands.

He has obstructed the Administration of Justice, by refusing his Assent to Laws for establishing Judiciary Powers.

He has made Judges dependent on his Will alone, for the tenure of their offices, and the amount and payment of their salaries.

He has erected a multitude of New Offices, and sent hither swarms of Officers to harass our people, and eat out their substance.

He has kept among us, in times of peace, Standing Armies without the Consent of our legislatures.

He has affected to render the Military independent of and superior to the Civil Power.

He has combined with others to subject us to a jurisdiction foreign to our constitution, and unacknowledged by our laws; giving his Assent to their acts of pretended Legislation:

For quartering large bodies of armed troops among us:

For protecting them, by a mock Trial, from Punishment for any Murders which they should commit on the inhabitants of these States:

For cutting off our Trade with all parts of the world:

For imposing taxes on us without our Consent:

For depriving us in many cases, of the benefits of Trial by Jury:

For transporting us beyond Seas to be tried for pretended offences:

For abolishing the free System of English Laws in a neighbouring Province, establishing therein an Arbitrary government, and enlarging its Boundaries so as to render it at once an example and fit instrument for introducing the same absolute rule into these Colonies:

For taking away our Charters, abolishing our most valuable Laws, and altering fundamentally the Forms of our Governments:

For suspending our own Legislatures, and declaring themselves invested with Power to legislate for us in all cases whatsoever.

He has abdicated Government here, by declaring us out of his Protection and waging War against us.

He has plundered our seas, ravaged our Coasts, burnt our towns, and destroyed the lives of our people.

He is at this time transporting large armies of foreign mercenaries to compleat the works of death, desolation and tyranny, already begun with circumstances of Cruelty & perfidy scarcely paralleled in the most barbarous ages, and totally unworthy the Head of a civilized nation.

He has constrained our fellow Citizens taken Captive on the high Seas to bear Arms against their Country, to become the executioners of their friends and Brethren, or to fall themselves by their Hands.

He has excited domestic insurrections amongst us, and has endeavoured to bring on the inhabitants of our frontiers, the merciless Indian Savages, whose known rule of warfare, is an undistinguished destruction of all ages, sexes and conditions.

In every stage of these Oppressions We have Petitioned for Redress in the most humble terms: Our repeated Petitions have been answered only by repeated injury. A Prince, whose character is thus marked by every act which may define a Tyrant, is unfit to be the ruler of a free people.

Nor have We been wanting in attentions to our British brethren. We have warned them from time to time of attempts by their legislature to extend an unwarrantable jurisdiction over us. We have reminded them of the circumstances of our emigration and settlement here. We have appealed to their native justice and magnanimity, and we have conjured them by the ties of our common kindred to disavow these usurpations which, would inevitably interrupt our connections and correspondence. They too have been deaf to the voice of justice and of consanguinity. We must, therefore, acquiesce in the necessity, which denounces our Separation, and hold them, as we hold the rest of mankind, Enemies in War, in Peace Friends.

We, therefore, the Representatives of the united States of America, in General Congress, Assembled, appealing to the Supreme Judge of the world for the rectitude of our intentions, do, in the Name, and by authority of the good People of these Colonies, solemnly publish and declare, That these United Colonies are, and of Right ought to be Free and Independent States; that they are Absolved from all Allegiance to the British Crown, and that all political connection between them and the State of Great Britain, is and ought to be totally dissolved; and that as Free and Independent States, they have full power to levy War, conclude Peace, contract Alliances, establish Commerce, and to do all other Acts and Things which Independent States may of right do. And for the support of this Declaration, with a firm reliance on the Protection of Divine Providence, we mutually pledge to each other our Lives, our Fortunes and our sacred Honor.

APPENDIX B

The Constitution of the United States

We the People of the United States, In Order to form a more perfect Union, establish Justice, insure domestic Tranquility, provide for the common defense, promote the general Welfare, and secure the Blessings of Liberty to ourselves and our Posterity, do ordain and establish this Constitution for the United States of America.

ARTICLE I

Section 1. All legislative Powers herein granted shall be vested in a Congress of the United States, which shall consist of a Senate and House of Representatives.

Section 2. The House of Representatives shall be composed of members chosen every second Year by the People of the several States, and the Electors in each State shall have the Qualifications requisite for Electors of the most numerous Branch of the State Legislature.

No Person shall be a representative who shall not have attained to the Age of twenty five Years, and been seven Years a Citizen of the United States, and who shall not, when elected, be an Inhabitant of that State in which he shall be chosen.

Representatives and direct Taxes shall be apportioned among the several States which may be included within this union, according to their respective Numbers, which shall be determined by adding to the whole Number of free Persons, including those bound to Service for a Term of Years, and excluding Indians not taxed, three fifths of all other Persons. The actual Enumeration shall be made within three Years after the first Meeting of the Congress of the United States, and within every subsequent Term of ten Years, in such Manner as they shall by Law direct. The Number of Representatives shall not exceed one for every thirty Thousand, but each State shall have at Least one Representative; and until such enumeration shall be made, the State of New Hampshire shall be entitled to chuse three, Massachusetts eight, Rhode-Island and Providence Plantations one, Connecticut five, New York six, New Jersey four, Pennsylvania eight, Delaware one, Maryland six, Virginia ten, North Carolina five, South Carolina five, and Georgia three.

When vacancies happen in the Representation from any State, the Executive Authority thereof shall issue Writs of Election to fill such Vacancies.

The House of Representatives shall chuse their speaker and other Officers; and shall have the sole Power of Impeachment.

Section 3. The Senate of the United States shall be composed of two Senators from each State, chosen by the Legislature thereof, for six Years; and each Senator shall have one Vote.

Immediately after they shall be assembled in Consequence of the first Election, they shall be divided as equally as may be into three Classes. The Seats of the Senators of the first Class shall be vacated at the Expiration of the second Year, of the second Class at the Expiration of the fourth Year, and of the third Class at the Expiration of the sixth Year, so that one third may be chosen every second Year; and if Vacancies happen by Resignation, or otherwise, during the Recess of the Legislature of any State, the Executive thereof may make temporary Appointments until the next Meeting of the Legislature, which shall then fill such Vacancies.

No Person shall be a Senator who shall not have attained to the Age of thirty Years, and been nine Years a Citizen of the United States, and who shall not, when elected, be an Inhabitant of that State for which he shall be chosen.

The Vice President of the United States shall be President of the Senate, but shall have no Vote, unless they be equally divided.

The Senate shall chuse their other Officers, and also a President pro tempore, in the Absence of the Vice President, or when he shall exercise the Office of the President of the United States.

The Senate shall have the sole Power to try all Impeachments. When sitting for that Purpose, they shall be on Oath of Affirmation. When the President of the United States is tried, the Chief Justice shall preside: And no Person shall be convicted without the Concurrence of two thirds of the Members present.

Judgment in Cases of Impeachment shall not extend further than to removal from Office, and disqualification to hold and enjoy any Office of honor, Trust or Profit under the United States: but the Party convicted shall nevertheless be liable and subject to Indictment, Trial, Judgment and Punishment, according to law.

Section 4. The Times, Places and Manner of holding Elections for Senators and Representatives, shall be prescribed in each State by the Legislature thereof; but the Congress may at any time by Law make or alter such Regulations, except as to the Places of chusing Senators.

The Congress shall assemble at least once in every Year, and such Meeting shall be on the first Monday in December, unless they shall by Law appoint a different Day.

Section 5. Each House shall be the Judge of the Elections, Returns and Qualifications of its own Members, and a Majority of each shall constitute a Quorum to do Business; but a smaller Number may adjourn from day to day, and may be authorized to compel the Attendance of absent Members, in such Manner, and under such Penalties as each House may provide.

Each House may determine the Rules of its Proceedings, punish its Members for disorderly Behaviour, and, with the Concurrence of two thirds, expel a Member.

Each House shall keep a Journal of its Proceedings, and from time to time publish the same, excepting such Parts as may in their Judgment require Secrecy; and the Yeas and Nays of the Members of either House on any question shall, at the Desire of one fifth of those Present, be entered on the Journal.

Neither House, during the Session of Congress, shall, without the Consent of the other, adjourn for more than three days, nor to any other Place than that in which the two Houses shall be sitting.

Section 6. The Senators and Representatives shall receive a Compensation for their Services, to be ascertained by Law, and paid out of the Treasury of the United States. They shall in all Cases, except Treason, Felony and Breach of the Peace, be privileged from Arrest during their Attendance at the Session of their respective Houses, and in going to and returning from the same; and for any Speech or Debate in either House, they shall not be questioned in any other Place.

No Senator or Representative shall, during the Time for which he was elected, be appointed to any civil Office under the Authority of the United States, which shall have been created, or the Emoluments whereof shall have been encreased during such time; and no Person holding any Office under the United States, shall be a Member of either House during his Continuance in Office.

Section 7. All Bills for raising Revenue shall originate in the House of Representatives; but the Senate may propose or concur with Amendments as on other Bills.

Every Bill which shall have passed the House of Representatives and the Senate, shall, before it become a Law, be presented to the President of the United States; If he approve he shall sign it, but if not he shall return it, with his Objections to that House in which it shall have originated, who shall enter the Objections at large on their Journal, and proceed to reconsider it. If after such Reconsideration two thirds of that House shall agree to pass the Bill, it shall be sent, together with the Objections, to the other House, by which it shall likewise be reconsidered, and if approved by two thirds of that House, it shall become a Law. But in all such Cases the Votes of both Houses shall be determined by Yeas and Nays, and the Names of the Pesons voting for and against the Bill shall be entered on the Journal of each House respectively. If any Bill shall not be returned by the President within ten Days (Sundays excepted) after it shall have been presented to him, the Same shall be a Law, in like Manner as if he signed it, unless the Congress by their Adjournment prevent its Return, in which Case it shall not be a Law.

Every Order, Resolution, or Vote to which the Concurrence of the Senate and House of Representatives may be necessary (except on a question of Adjournment) shall be presented to the President of the United States; and before the Same shall take Effect, shall be approved by him, or being disapproved by him, shall be repassed by two thirds of the Senate and House of Representatives, according to the Rules and Limitations prescribed in the Case of a Bill.

Section 8. The Congress shall have Power To lay and collect Taxes, Duties, Imposts and Excises, to pay the Debts and provide for the common Defence and general Welfare of the United States; but all Duties, Imposts and Excises shall be uniform throughout the United States;

To borrow Money on the credit of the United States;

To regulate Commerce with foreign Nations, and among the several States, and with the Indian Tribes;

To establish an uniform Rule of Naturalization, and uniform Laws on the subject of Bankruptcies throughout the United States;

To coin Money, regulate the Value thereof, and of foreign Coin, and fix the Standard of Weights and Measures;

To provide for the Punishment of counterfeiting the Securities and current Coin of the United States;

To establish Post Offices and post Roads;

To promote the Progress of Science and useful Arts, by securing for limited Times to Authors and Inventors the exclusive Right to their respective Writings and Discoveries;

To constitute Tribunals inferior to the supreme Court;

To define and punish Piracies and Felonies committed on the high Seas, and Offences against the Law of Nations;

To declare War, grant Letters of Marque and Reprisal, and make Rules concerning Captures on Land and Water;

To raise and support Armies, but no Appropriation of Money to that Use shall be for a longer Term than two Years;

To provide and maintain a Navy;

To make Rules for the Government and Regulation of the land and naval Forces;

To provide for calling forth the Militia to execute the Laws of the Union, suppress Insurrections and repel Invasions;

To provide for organizing, arming, and disciplining, the Militia, and for governing such Part of them as may be employed in the Service of the United States, reserving to the States respectively, the Appointment of the Officers, and the Authority of training the Militia according to the discipline prescribed by Congress;

To exercise exclusive Legislation in all Cases whatsoever, over such District (not exceeding ten Miles square) as may, by Cession of particular States, and the Acceptance of Congress, become the Seat of the Government of the United States, and to exercise like Authority over all Places purchased by the Consent of the Legislature of the State in which the Same shall be for the Erection of Forts, Magazines, Arsenals, dock-Yards, and other needful Buildings;-And

To make all Laws which shall be necessary and proper for carrying into Execution the foregoing Powers, and all other Powers vested by this Constitution in the Government of the United States, or in any Department or Officer thereof.

Section 9. The Migration or Importation of such Persons as any of the States now existing shall think proper to admit, shall not be prohibited by the Congress prior to the Year one thousand eight hundred and eight, but a Tax or duty may be imposed on such Importation, not exceeding ten dollars for each Person.

The Privilege of the Writ of Habeas Corpus shall not be suspended, unless when in Cases of Rebellion or Invasion the public Safety may require it.

No Bill of Attainder or ex post facto Law shall be passed.

No Capitation, or other direct, Tax shall be laid, unless in Proportion to the Census or Enumeration herein before directed to be taken.

No Tax or Duty shall be laid on Articles exported from any State.

No Preference shall be given by any Regulation of Commerce or Revenue to the Ports of one State over those of another: nor shall Vessels bound to, or from, one State be obliged to enter, clear, or pay Duties in another.

No Money shall be drawn from the Treasury, but in Consequence of Appropriations made by Law; and a regular Statement and Account of the Receipts and Expenditures of all public Money shall be published from time to time.

No Title of Nobility shall be granted by the United States:

And no Person holding any office of Profit or Trust under them, shall, without the Consent of the Congress, accept of any present, Emolument, Office, or Title, of any kind whatever, from any King, Prince, or foreign States.

Section 10. No State shall enter into any Treaty, Alliance, or Confederation; grant Letters of Marque and Reprisal; coin Money; emit Bills of Credit; make any Thing but gold and silver Coin a Tender in Payment of Debts; pass any Bill of Attainder, ex post facto Law, or Law impairing the Obligation of Contracts, or grant any Title of Nobility.

No State shall, without the Consent of the Congress, lay any Imposts or Duties on Imports or Exports, except what may be absolutely necessary for executing its inspection Laws: and the net Produce of all Duties and Imposts, laid by any State on Imports or Exports, shall be for the Use of the Treasury of the United States; and all such Laws shall be subject to Revision and Controul of the Congress.

No State shall, without the Consent of Congress, lay any Duty of Tonnage, keep Troops, or Ships of War in time of Peace, enter into any Agreement or Compact with another State, or with a foreign Power, or engage in War, unless actually invaded, or in such imminent Danger as will not admit of delay.

ARTICLE II

Section 1. The executive Power shall be vested in a President of the United States of America. He shall hold his Office during the Term of four Years, and, together with the Vice President, chosen for the same term, be elected, as follows.

Each State shall appoint, in such Manner as the Legislature thereof may direct, a Number of Electors, equal to the whole Number of Senators and Representatives to which the State may be entitled in the Congress: but no Senator or Representative, or Person holding an office of Trust or Profit under the United States, shall be appointed an Elector.

The Electors shall meet in their respective States, and vote by Ballot for two Persons, of whom one at least shall not be an Inhabitant of the same State with themselves. And they shall make a List of all the Persons voted for, and of the Number of Votes for each; which List they shall sign and certify, and transmit sealed to the Seat of the Government of the United States, directed to the President of the Senate. The President of the Senate shall, in the Presnce of the Senate and House of Representatives, open all the Certificates, and the Votes shall then be counted. The Person having the greatest Number of Votes shall be the President, if such Number be a Majority of the whole Number of Electors appointed; and if there be more than one who have such Majority, and have an equal Number of Votes, then the House of Representatives shall immediately chuse by Ballot one of them for President: and if no Person have a Majority, then from the five highest on the List the said House shall in like Manner chuse the President. But in chusing the President, the Votes shall be taken by States, the Representation from each State having one Vote; A quorum for this Purpose shall consist of a Member or Members from two thirds of the States, and a Majority of all the States shall be necessary to a Choice. In every Case, after the Choice of the President, the Person having the greatest Number of Votes of the Electors shall be the Vice President. But if there should remain two or more who have equal Votes, the Senate shall chuse from them by Ballot the Vice President.

The Congress may determine the Time of chusing the Electors and the Day on which they shall give their Votes; which Day shall be the same throughout the United States.

No Person except a natural born Citizen, or a Citizen of the United States, at the time of the Adoption of this Constitution, shall be eligible to the Office of President; neither shall any person be eligible to that Office who shall not have attained to the Age of thirty five Years, and been fourteen Years a Resident within the United States.

In Case of the Removal of the President from Office, or of his Death, Resignation, or Inability to discharge the Powers and Duties of the said Office, the Same shall devolve on the Vice President, and the Congress may be Law provide for the Case of Removal, Death, Resignation or Inability, both of the President and Vice President, declaring what Officer shall then act as President, and such Officer shall act accordingly, until the Disability be removed, or a President shall be elected.

The President shall, at stated Times, receive for his Services a Compensation, which shall neither be encreased nor diminished during the Period for which he shall have been elected, and he shall not receive within that Period any other Emolument from the United States, or any of them.

Before he enter on the Execution of his Office, he shall take the following Oath or Affirmation:- ''I do solemnly swear (or affirm) that I will faithfully execute the Office of President of the United States, and will to the best of my Ability, preserve, protect and defend the Constitution of the United States.''

Section 2. The President shall be Commander in Chief of the Army and Navy of the United States, and of the Militia of the several States, when called into the actual Service of the United States; he may require the Opinion, in writing, of the principal Officer in each of the executive Departments, upon any Subject relating to the Duties of their respective Offices, and he shall have power to grant Reprieves and Pardons for Offences against the United States, except in Cases of Impeachment.

He shall have Power, by and with the Advice and Consent of the Senate, to make Treaties, provided two thirds of the Senators present concur; and he shall nominate, and by and with the Advice and Consent of the Senate, shall appoint Ambassadors, other public Ministers and Consuls, Judges of the supreme Court, and all other Officers of the United States, whose Appointments are not herein otherwise provided for, and which shall be established by Law; but the Congress may by Law vest the Appointment of such inferior officers, as they think proper, in the President alone, in the Courts of Law, or in the Heads of Departments.

The President shall have Power to fill up all Vacancies that may happen during the Recess of the Senate, by granting Commissions which shall expire at the End of their next Session.

Section 3. He shall from time to time give to the Congress Information of the State of the Union, and recommend to their Consideration such Measures as he shall judge necessary and expedient; he may, on extraordinary Occasions, convene both Houses, or either of them, and in Case of Disagreement between them, with Respect to the Time of Adjournment, he may adjourn them to such Time as he shall think proper; he shall receive Ambassadors and other public Ministers; he shall take Care that the Laws be faithfully executed, and shall Commission all of the officers of the United States.

Section 4. The President, Vice President and all civil Officers of the United States, shall be removed from Office on Impeachment for, and Conviction of, Treason, Bribery, or other High Crimes and Misdemeanors.

ARTICLE III

Section 1. The judicial Power of the United States, shall be vested in one supreme Court, and in such inferior Courts as the Congress may from time to time ordain and establish. The Judges, both of the supreme and inferior Courts, shall hold their Offices during good Behaviour, and shall, at stated Times, receive for their Services, a Compensation, which shall not be diminished during their Continuance in Office.

Section 2. The judicial Power shall extend to all Cases, in Law and Equity, arising under this Constitution, the Laws of the United States, and Treaties made, or which shall be made, under their Authority;- to all Cases affecting Ambassadors, other public Ministers and Consuls;-to all Cases of admiralty and maritime Jurisdiction;-to Controversies to which the United States shall be a Party;-to Controversies between two or more States; between a State and Citizens of another State;-between Citizens of different States;-between Citizens of the same State claiming Lands under Grants of different States, and between a State, or the Citizens thereof, and foreign States, Citizens or Subjects.

In all Cases affecting Ambassadors, other public Ministers and Consuls, and those in which a State shall be Party, the supreme Court shall have original Jurisdiction. In all the other Cases before mentioned, the supreme Court shall have appellate Jurisdiction, both as to Law and Fact, with such Exceptions, and under such Regulations as the Congress shall make.

The Trial of all Crimes, except in Cases of Impeachment, shall be by Jury; and such Trial shall be held in the State where the said Crimes shall have been committed; but when not committed within any State, the Trial shall be at such Place or Places as the Congress may be Law have directed.

Section 3. Treason against the United States, shall consist only in levying War against them, or in adhering to their Enemies, giving them Aid and Comfort. No Person shall be convicted of Treason unless on the Testimony of two Witnesses to the same overt Act, or on Confession in open Court.

The Congress shall have Power to declare the Punishment of Treason, but no Attainder of Treason shall work Corruption of Blood, or Forfeiture except during the Life of the Person attainted.

ARTICLE IV

Section 1. Full Faith and Credit shall be given in each State to the public Acts, Records, and judicial Proceedings of every other State. And the Congress may by general Laws prescribe the Manner in which such Acts, Records and Proceedings shall be proved, and the Effect thereof.

Section 2. The Citizens of each State shall be entitled to all Privileges and Immunities of Citizens in the several States.

A Person charged in any State with Treason, Felony, or other Crime, who shall flee from Justice, and be found in another State, shall on Demand of the executive Authority of the State from which he fled, be delivered up, to be removed to the State having Jurisdiction of the Crime.

No Person held to Service or Labour in one State, under the Laws thereof, escaping into another, shall, in Consequence of any Law or Regulation therein, be discharged from such Service or Labour, but shall be delivered up on Claim of the Party to whom such Service or Labour may be due.

Section 3. New States may be admitted by the Congress into this Union; but no new State shall be formed or erected within the Jurisdiction of any other State; nor any State be formed by the Junction of two or more States, or Parts of States, without the Consent of the Legislatures of the States concerned as well as of the Congress.

The Congress shall have Power to dispose of and make all needful Rules and Regulations respecting the Territory or other Property belonging to the United States; and nothing in this Constitution shall be so construed as to Prejudice any Claims of the United States, or of any particular State.

Section 4. The United States shall guarantee to every State in this Union a Republican Form of Government, and shall protect each of them against Invasion; and on Application of the Legislature, or of the Executive (when the Legislature cannot be convened) against domestic Violence.

ARTICLE V

The Congress, whenever two thirds of both Houses shall deem it necessary, shall propose Amendments to this Constitution, or, on the Application of the Legislatures of two thirds of the several States, shall call a Convention for proposing Amendments, which, in either Case, shall be valid to all Intents and Purposes, as Part of this Constitution, when ratified by the Legislatures of three fourths of the several States, or by Conventions in three fourths thereof, as the one or the other Mode of Ratification may be proposed by the Congress; Provided that no Amendment which may be made prior to the Year One thousand eight hundred and eight shall in any Manner affect the first and fourth Clauses in the Ninth Section of the first Article; and that no State, without its Consent, shall be deprived of its equal Suffrage in the Senate.

ARTICLE VI

All Debts contracted and Engagements entered into, before the Adoption of this Constitution, shall be as valid against the United States under this Constitution, as under the Confederation.

This Constitution, and the Laws of the United States which shall be made in Pursuance thereof; and all Treaties made, or which shall be made, under the Authority of the United States, shall be the supreme Law of the Land; and the Judges in every State shall be bound thereby, any Thing in the Constitution or Laws of any State to the Contrary notwithstanding.

The Senators and Representatives before mentioned, and the Members of the several State Legislatures, and all executive and judicial Officers, both of the United States and of the several States, shall be bound by Oath or Affirmation, to support this Constitution; but no religious Test shall ever be required as a Qualification to any Office or public Trust under the United States.

ARTICLE VII

The Ratification of the Conventions of nine States, shall be sufficient for the Establishment of this Constitution between the States so ratifying the Same.

Done in Convention by the Unanimous Consent of the States present the Seventeenth Day of September in the Year of our Lord one thousand seven hundred and Eighty seven and of the Independence of the United States of America the Twelfth. In witness whereof We have hereunto subscribed our Names.

[The first 10 Amendments were ratified December 15, 1791, and form what is known as the Bill of Rights.]

AMENDMENT 1

Congress shall make no law respecting an establishment of religion, or prohibiting the free exercise thereof; or abridging the freedom of speech, or of the press; or the right of the people peaceably to assemble, and to petition the Government for a redress of grievances.

AMENDMENT 2

A well regulated Militia, being necessary to the security of a free State, the right of the people to keep and bear Arms, shall not be infringed.

AMENDMENT 3

No Soldier shall, in time of peace be quartered in any house, without the consent of the Owner, nor in time of war, but in a manner to be prescribed by law.

AMENDMENT 4

The right of the people to be secure in their persons, houses, papers, and effects, against unreasonable searches and seizures, shall not be violated, and no Warrants shall issue, but upon probable cause, supported by Oath or affirmation, and particularly describing the place to be searched and the persons or things to be seized.

AMENDMENT 5

No person shall be held to answer for a capital, or otherwise infamous crime, unless on a presentment or indictment of a Grand Jury, except in cases arising in the land or naval forces, or in the Militia, when in actual service in time of War or public danger; nor shall any person be subject for the same offence to be twice put in jeopardy of life or limb; nor shall be compelled in any criminal case to be a witness against himself, nor be deprived of life, liberty, or property, without due process of law; nor shall private property be taken for public use, without just compensation.

AMENDMENT 6

In all criminal prosecutions, the accused shall enjoy the right to a speedy and public trial, by an impartial jury of the State and district wherein the crime shall have been committed, which district shall have been previously ascertained by law, and to be informed of the nature and cause of the accusation; to be confronted with the witnesses against him; to have compulsory process for obtaining witnesses in his favor, and to have the Assistance of Counsel for his defence.

AMENDMENT 7

In Suits at common law, where the value in controversy shall exceed twenty dollars, the right of trial by jury shall be preserved, and no fact tried by a jury, shall be otherwise reexamined in any Court of the United States, than according to the rules of the common law.

AMENDMENT 8

Excessive bail shall not be required, nor excessive fines imposed, nor cruel and unusual punishments inflicted.

AMENDMENT 9

The enumeration in the Constituion, of certain rights, shall not be construed to deny or disparage others retained by the people.

AMENDMENT 10

The powers not delegated to the United States by the Constitution, nor prohibited by it to the States, are reserved to the States respectively, or to the people.

AMENDMENT 11

[Ratified February 7, 1795]

The Judicial power of the United States shall not be construed to extend to any suit in law or equity, commenced or prosecuted against one of the United States by Citizens of another State, or by Citizens or Subjects of any Foreign State.

AMENDMENT 12

[Ratified July 27, 1804]

The Electors shall meet in their respective states and vote by ballot for President and Vice-President, one of whom, at least, shall not be an inhabitant of the same state with themselves; they shall name in their ballots the person voted for as President, and in distinct ballots the person voted for as Vice-President, and they shall make distinct lists of all persons voted for as President, and of all persons voted for as Vice-President, and of the number of votes for each, which lists they shall sign and certify, and transmit sealed to the seat of the government of the United States, directed to the President of the Senate; The President of the Senate shall, in the presence of the Senate and House of Representatives, open all the certificates and the votes shall then be counted;-The person having the greatest number of votes for President, shall be the President, if such number be a majority of the whole number of Electors appointed; and if no person have such majority, then from the persons having the highest numbers not exceeding three on the list of those voted for as President, the House of Representatives shall choose immediately, by ballot, the President. But in choosing the President, the votes shall be taken by states, the representation from each state having one vote; a quorum for this purpose shall consist of a member or members from two-thirds of the states, and a majority of all the states shall be necessary to a choice. And if the House of Representatives shall not choose a President whenever the right of choice shall devolve upon them, before the fourth day of March next following, the Vice-President shall act as President, as in the case of the death or other constitutional disability of the President.-The person having the greatest number of votes as Vice-President, shall be the Vice-President, if such number be a majority of the whole number of Electors appointed, and if no person have a majority, then from the two highest numbers on the list, the Senate shall choose the Vice-President; a quorum for the purpose shall consist of two-thirds of the whole number of Senators, and a majority of the whole number shall be necessary to a choice. But no person constitutionally ineligible to the office of President shall be eligible to that of Vice-President of the United States.

AMENDMENT 13

[Ratified December 6, 1865]

Section 1. Neither slavery nor involuntary servitude, except as a punishment for crime whereof the party shall have been duly convicted, shall exist within the United States, or any place subject to their jurisdiction.

Section 2. Congress shall have the power to enforce this article by appropriate legislation.

AMENDMENT 14

[Ratified July 9, 1868]

Section 1. All persons born or naturalized in the United States, and subject to the jurisdiction thereof, are citizens of the United States and of the State wherein they reside. No State shall make or enforce any law which shall abridge the privileges or immunities of citizens of the United States; nor shall any State deprive any person of life, liberty, or property, without due process of law; nor deny to any person within its jurisdiction the equal protection of the laws.

Section 2. Representatives shall be appointed among the several States according to their respective numbers, counting the whole number of persons in each State, excluding Indians not taxed. But when the right to vote at any election for the choice of electors for President and Vice President of the United States, Representatives in Congress, the Executive and Judicial Officers of a State, or the members of the Legislature thereof, is denied to any of the male inhabitants of such State, being twenty-one years of age, and citizens of the United States, or in any way abridged, except for participation in rebellion, or other crime, the basis of representation therein shall be reduced in the proportion which the number of such male citizens shall bear to the whole number of male citizens twenty-one years of age in such State.

Section 3. No person shall be a Senator or Representative in Congress, or elector of President and Vice President, or hold any office, civil or military, under the United States, or under any State, who, having previously taken an oath, as a member of Congress, or as an officer of the United States, or as a member of any State legislature, or as an executive or judicial officer of any State, to support the Constitution of the United States, shall have engaged in insurrection or rebellion against the same, or given aid or comfort to the enemies thereof. But Congress may by a vote of two-thirds of each House, remove such disability.

Section 4. The validity of the public debt of the United States, authorized by law, including debts incurred for payment of pensions and bounties for services in suppressing insurrection or rebellion, shall not be questioned. But neither the United States nor any State shall assume or pay any debt or obligation incurred in aid of insurrection or rebellion against the United States, or any claim for the loss or emancipation of any slave; but all such debts, obligations and claims shall be held illegal and void.

Section 5. The Congress shall have power to enforce, by appropriate legislation, the provisions of this article.

AMENDMENT 15

[Ratified February 3, 1870]

Section 1. The right of citizens of the United States to vote shall not be denied or abridged by the United States or by any State on account of race, color, or previous condition of servitude.

Section 2. The Congress shall have power to enforce this article by appropriate legislation.

AMENDMENT 16

[Ratified February 3, 1913]

The Congress shall have power to lay and collect taxes on incomes, from whatever source derived, without apportionment among the several States, and without regard to any census or enumeration.

AMENDMENT 17

[Ratified April 8, 1913]

The Senate of the United States shall be composed of two Senators from each State, elected by the people thereof for six years; and each Senator shall have one vote. The electors in each State shall have the qualification requisite for electors of the most numerous branch of the State legislatures.

When vacancies happen in the representation of any State in the Senate, the executive authority of such State shall issue writs of election to fill such vacancies: *Provided,* That the legislature of any State may empower the executive thereof to make temporary appointments until the people fill the vacancies by election as the legislature may direct.

This amendment shall not be so construed as to affect the election or term of any Senator chosen before it becomes valid as part of the Constitution.

AMENDMENT 18

[Ratified January 16, 1919]

Section 1. After one year from the ratification of this article the manufacture, sale, or transportation of intoxicating liquors within, the importation thereof into, or the exportation thereof from the United States and all territory subject to the jurisdiction thereof for beverage purposes is hereby prohibited.

Section 2. The Congress and the several States shall have concurrent power to enforce this article by appropriate legislation.

Section 3. This article shall be inoperative unless it shall have been ratified as an amendment to the Constitution by the legislatures of the several States, as provided in the Constitution, within seven years from the date of the submission hereof to the States by the Congress.

AMENDMENT 19

[Ratified August 18, 1920]

The right of citizens of the United States to vote shall not be denied or abridged by the United States or by any State on account of sex. Congress shall have the power to enforce this article by appropriate legislation.

AMENDMENT 20

[Ratified January 23, 1933]

Section 1. The terms of the President and Vice President shall end at noon on the 20th day of January, and the terms of Senators and Representatives at noon on the 3d day of January, of the years in which such terms would have ended if this article had not been ratified; and the terms of their successors shall then begin.

Section 2. The Congress shall assemble at least once in every year, and such meetings shall begin at noon on the 3d day of January, unless they shall by law appoint a different day.

Section 3. If, at the time fixed for the beginning of the term of the President, the President elect shall have died, the Vice President elect shall become President. If a President shall not have been chosen before the time fixed for the beginning of his term, or if the President elect shall have failed to qualify, then the Vice President elect shall act as President until a President shall have qualified; and the Congress may by law provide for the case wherein neither a President elect nor a Vice President elect shall have qualified, declaring who shall then act as President, or the manner in which one who is to act shall be selected, and such person shall act accordingly until a President or Vice President shall have qualified.

Section 4. The Congress may by law provide for the case of the death of any of the persons from whom the House of Representatives may choose a President whenever the right of choice shall have devolved upon them, and for the case of the death of any of the persons from whom the Senate may choose a Vice President whenever the right of choice shall have devolved upon them.

Section 5. Sections 1 and 2 shall take effect on the 15th day of October following the ratification of this article.

Section 6. This article shall be inoperative unless it shall have been ratified as an amendment to the Constitution by the legislatures of three-fourths of the several states within seven years from the date of its submission.

AMENDMENT 21

[Ratified December 5, 1933]

Section 1. The eighteenth article of amendment to the Constitution of the United States is hereby repealed.

Section 2. The transportation or importation into any State, Territory, or Possession of the United States for delivery or use herein of intoxicating liquors, in violation of the laws thereof, is hereby prohibited.

Section 3. This article shall be inoperative unless it shall have been ratified as an amendment to the Constitution by conventions in several States, as provided in the Constitution, within seven years from the date of the submission hereof to the States by the Congress.

AMENDMENT 22

[Ratified February 27, 1951]

Section 1. No person shall be elected to the office of the President more than twice, and no person who has held the office of President, or acted as President, for more than two years of a term to which some other person was elected President shall be elected to the office of the President more than once. But this Article shall not apply to any person holding the office of President when this Article was proposed by the Congress, and shall not prevent any person who may be holding the office of President, or acting as President, during the term within which this Article becomes operative from holding the office of President or acting as President during the remainder of such term.

Section 2. This article shall be inoperative unless it shall have been ratified as an amendment to the Constitution by the legislatures of three-fourths of the several States within seven years from the date of its submission to the States by the Congress.

AMENDMENT 23

[Ratified March 29, 1961]

Section 1. The District constituting the seat of Government of the United States shall appoint in such manner as the Congress may direct:

A number of electors of President and Vice President equal to the whole number of Senators and Representatives in Congress to which the District would be entitled if it were a state, but in no event more than the least populous State; they shall be in addition to those appointed by the States, but they shall be considered, for the purposes of the election of President and Vice President, to be electors appointed by a State; and they shall meet in the District and perform such duties as provided by the twelfth article of amendment.

Section 2. The Congress shall have power to enforce this article by appropriate legislation.

AMENDMENT 24

[Ratified January 23, 1964]

Section 1. The right of citizens of the United States to vote in any primary or other election for President or Vice President, for electors for President or Vice President, or for Senator or Representative in Congress, shall not be denied or abridged by the United States or by any State by reason or failure to pay any poll tax or other tax.

Section 2. The Congress shall have power to enforce this artilce by appropriate legislation.

AMENDMENT 25

[Ratified February 10, 1967]

Section 1. In case of the removal of the President from office or of his death or resignation, the Vice President shall become President.

Section 2. Whenever there is a vacancy in the office of the Vice President, the President shall nominate a Vice President who shall take office upon confirmation by a majority vote of both House of Congress.

Section 3. Whenever the President transmits to the President pro tempore of the Senate and the Speaker of the House of Representatives his written declaration that he is unable to discharge the powers and duties of his office, and until he transmits to them a written declaration to the contrary, such powers and duties shall be discharged by the Vice President as Acting President.

Section 4. Whenever the Vice President and a majority of either the principal officers of the executive department or of such other body as Congress may by law provide, transmit to the President pro tempore of the Senate and the Speaker of the House of Representatives their written declaration that the President is unable to discharge the powers and duties of his office, the Vice President shall immediately assume the powers and duties of the office as Acting President.

Thereafter, when the President transmits to the President pro tempore of the Senate and the Speaker of the House of Representatives his written declaration that no inability exists, he shall resume the powers and duties of his office unless the Vice President and a majority of either the principal officers of the executive department or of such other body as Congress may by law provide, transmit within four days to the President pro tempore of the Senate and the Speaker of the House of Representatives their written declaration that the President is unable to discharge the powers and duties of his office. Thereupon Congress shall decide the issue, assembling within forty-eight hours for that purpose if not in session. If the Congress, within twenty-one days after receipt of the latter wirtten declaration, or, if Congress is not in session, within twenty-one days after Congress is required to assemble, determined by two-thirds vote of both Houses that the President is unable to discharge the powers and duties of his office, the Vice President shall continue to discharge the same as Acting President; otherwise, the President shall resume the powers and duties of his office.

AMENDMENT 26

[Ratified June 30, 1971]

Section 1. The right of citizens of the United States, who are eighteen years of age or older, to vote shall not be denied or abridged by the United States or by any State on account of age.

Section 2. The Congress shall have the power to enforce this article by appropriate legislation.

EQUAL RIGHTS FOR WOMEN

[*Proposed March 22, 1972*]

Section 1. Equality of rights under the law shall not be denied or abridged by the United States or by an State on account of sex.

Section 2. The Congress shall have power to enforce, by appropriate legislation, the provisions of this article.

Section 3. This amendment shall take effect two years after date of ratification.

DISTRICT OF COLUMBIA REPRESENTATION

[*Proposed August 22, 1978*]

Section 1. For purposes of representation in the Congress, election of the President and Vice President, and article V of this Constitution, the District constituting the seat of government of the United States shall be treated as though it were a State.

Section 2. The exercise of the rights and powers conferred under this article shall be by the people of the District constituting the seat of government, and as shall be provided by the Congress.

Section 3. The twenty-third article of amendment to the Constitution of the United States is hereby repealed.

Section 4. This article shall be inoperative, unless it shall have been ratified as an amendment to the Constitution by the legislatures of three-fourths of the several States within seven years from the date of its submission.

APPENDIX C
Presidents of the United States

	Party	Term
1. George Washington (1732–99)	Federalist	1789–1797
2. John Adams (1735–1826)	Federalist	1797–1801
3. Thomas Jefferson (1743–1826)	Democratic-Republican	1801–1809
4. James Madison (1751–1836)	Democratic-Republican	1809–1817
5. James Monroe (1758–1831)	Democratic-Republican	1817–1825
6. John Quincy Adams (1767–1848)	Democratic-Republican	1825–1829
7. Andrew Jackson (1767–1845)	Democratic	1829–1837
8. Martin Van Buren (1782–1862)	Democratic	1837–1841
9. William Henry Harrison (1773–1841)	Whig	1841
10. John Tyler (1790–1862)	Whig	1841–1845
11. James K. Polk (1795–1849)	Democratic	1845–1849
12. Zachary Taylor (1784–1850)	Whig	1849–1850
13. Millard Fillmore (1800–74)	Whig	1850–1853
14. Franklin Pierce (1804–69)	Democratic	1853–1857
15. James Buchanan (1791–1868)	Democratic	1857–1861
16. Abraham Lincoln (1809–65)	Republican	1861–1865
17. Andrew Johnson (1808–75)	Union	1865–1869
18. Ulysses S. Grant (1822–85)	Republican	1869–1877
19. Rutherford B. Hayes (1822–93)	Republican	1877–1881
20. James A. Garfield (1831–81)	Republican	1881
21. Chester A. Arthur (1830–86)	Republican	1881–1885
22. Grover Cleveland (1837–1908)	Democratic	1885–1889, 1893–1897
23. Benjamin Harrison (1833–1901)	Republican	1889–1893
24. William McKinley (1843–1901)	Republican	1897–1901
25. Theodore Roosevelt (1858–1919)	Republican	1901–1909
26. William Howard Taft (1857–1930)	Republican	1909–1913
27. Woodrow Wilson (1856–1924)	Democratic	1913–1921
28. Warren G. Harding (1865–1923)	Republican	1921–1923
29. Calvin Coolidge (1871–1933)	Republican	1923–1929
30. Herbert Hoover (1874–1964)	Republican	1929–1933
31. Franklin Delano Roosevelt (1882–1945)	Democratic	1933–1945
32. Harry S Truman (1884–1972)	Democratic	1945–1953
33. Dwight D. Eisenhower (1890–1969)	Republican	1953–1961
34. John F. Kennedy (1917–63)	Democratic	1961–1963

35. Lyndon B. Johnson (1908–73)	Democratic	1963–1969
36. Richard M. Nixon (b. 1913)	Republican	1969–1974
37. Gerald R. Ford (b. 1913)	Republican	1974–1977
38. Jimmy Carter (b. 1924)	Democratic	1977–1981
39. Ronald W. Reagan (b. 1911)	Republican	1981–

APPENDIX D
The 1984 Presidential Election

The 1984 presidential election, pitting incumbent Republican President Ronald Reagan and Vice President George Bush against Democratic challengers Walter F. Mondale and Geraldine A. Ferraro, was an impressive win for President Reagan. He captured 53,355,081 popular votes (59 percent), while Mondale won only 36,884,702 (41 percent). Former Vice President Mondale won in only one state—his home state of Minnesota—and in the District of Columbia. Consequently, Mondale won only 13 electoral votes (Minnesota's 10 electoral votes, and the 3 votes of Washington, D.C.), while Reagan captured 525 electoral votes. President Reagan piled up large popular-vote majorities in many southern states, formerly Democratic bastions, as well as garnering large vote margins in the sunbelt and western states. Mondale made his best showing in the midwestern and northeastern states, and his ticket won overwhelmingly in the nation's capitol. Table D–1 provides the state-by-state results, showing popular votes, percentages of popular votes, and electoral votes won by both presidential election tickets.

The election featured the contest between the Reagan-Bush and Mondale-Ferraro tickets, but other candidates' names appeared on the ballot in every state. A total of 15 parties presented candidates in at least one state. David Bergland, presidential candidate of the Libertarian party, was on the ballot in 38 states, the most for a minor party candidate in 1984. Other minor party candidacies included: Lyndon LaRouche, Jr., who conducted a television campaign for the Democratic party nomination (accusing Mondale and former Secretary of State Henry Kissinger of being Soviet agents), and then ran for president as an independent; Olympic pole-vaulter Bob Richards, running as a Populist party candidate; and Sonia Johnson, Citizen party candidate, who had been excommunicated by the Mormon Church for her active efforts in behalf of the Equal Rights Amendment. Other parties on the ballot in a few states included the Communist, the Socialist Worker, the Workers' World and Workers' League, the Prohibition and the Independent Alliance. These minor party candidates added some interest to the election, but they attracted only a miniscule proportion of the presidential vote.

The Reagan-Bush ticket won majorities of voters in a variety of demographic categories, as Table D–2 shows. The major exceptions were blacks, nearly 90 percent of whom voted for the Mondale-Ferraro ticket, and Jews, more than two thirds of whom voted Democratic. In addition, 55 percent of persons in the lowest income category (less than $10,000 per year) voted for Mondale-Ferraro. Notably, the Democrats lost their historic support among young voters and Catholics in 1984.

The Reagan sweep at the presidential level was accompanied by mixed results in congressional and state races. The Republicans lost ground in Senate races, giving the Democrats a net gain of two Senate seats. At the same time, Republican Senate winners chalked up unusually large margins—12 of 17 Republican winners got 60 percent or more of the vote, compared to only 8 of 16 Democratic Senate winners. And Republican gains in the election of members of the House of Representatives were unusually small as against the large presidential vote for the Republican incumbent.

Despite some reshuffling in the state governorships, the 1984 election left things much as they had been in the gubernatorial lineup—with 16 Republican governors and 34 Democratic governors, only one more Republican than before. Democrats retained control of both houses of the state legislatures in 28 states, down from 33 before the election. Only in Connecticut was there a complete reversal, where both houses changed from Democratic to GOP majorities. In four states—Delaware, Minnesota, Nevada, and Ohio—the Republicans picked up majorities in each for one state legislative chamber.

In general, the 1984 election was a successful experience for incumbents of both political parties. An unusually high proportion of incumbents was running for return to office at all levels, and few were denied another term of office. This element of stability reflected in the election results did not prevent interpretation of what happened on election day as a "realignment" of the major political parties. There was widespread ticket-splitting, with voters choosing the candidate of one party for president, and the candidates of the other party for Congress, governor, or the state legislature. Such wholesale division of voters' choices beclouds claims of lasting electoral realignment, but the election outcome certainly did give encouragement to the efforts of the Republican party and precipitated reappraisal and reflection among Democrats. And, many activists in both parties, if not rank-and-file voters, found solace and promise for 1988 in the 1984 election results.

TABLE D–1

1984 Presidential Election Results

State	Reagan-Bush Republican			Mondale-Ferraro Democratic		
	Popular vote	Percent of popular vote	Electoral vote	Popular vote	Percent of popular vote	Electoral vote
Alabama	851,609	60	9	545,925	39	—
Alaska	115,390	67	3	51,169	30	—
Arizona	676,524	66	7	330,771	33	—
Arkansas	529,756	61	6	336,406	39	—
California	5,305,434	58	47	3,815,992	42	—
Colorado	768,711	63	8	434,560	36	—
Connecticut	883,461	61	8	561,387	39	—
Delaware	151,494	60	3	100,632	40	—
District of Columbia	26,805	13	—	172,459	87	3
Florida	2,582,980	65	21	1,397,097	35	—
Georgia	1,060,680	60	12	701,605	40	—
Hawaii	185,050	55	4	146,654	44	—
Idaho	296,687	73	4	108,447	27	—
Illinois	2,687,112	57	24	2,066,580	43	—
Indiana	1,332,681	62	12	814,659	38	—
Iowa	700,779	54	8	603,810	46	—
Kansas	675,366	67	7	332,476	33	—
Kentucky	816,580	60	9	535,559	40	—
Louisiana	1,030,091	61	10	648,040	39	—
Maine	336,113	61	4	212,190	39	—
Maryland	836,395	52	10	759,205	47	—
Massachusetts	1,297,737	51	13	1,226,490	49	—
Michigan	2,247,058	60	20	1,528,558	40	—
Minnesota	1,024,631	50	—	1,039,904	50	10
Mississippi	585,052	62	7	351,677	38	—
Missouri	1,268,408	60	11	838,599	40	—
Montana	214,269	60	4	135,071	38	—
Nebraska	447,810	71	5	184,058	29	—
Nevada	188,794	67	4	91,654	32	—
New Hampshire	255,140	69	4	116,284	31	—
New Jersey	1,914,942	60	16	1,255,115	40	—
New Mexico	304,323	60	5	200,703	39	—
New York	3,553,762	54	36	3,021,719	46	—
North Carolina	1,340,274	62	13	821,364	38	—
North Dakota	199,352	66	3	103,957	34	—
Ohio	2,655,395	59	23	1,805,845	40	—
Oklahoma	861,757	69	8	384,918	31	—
Oregon	639,755	56	7	508,516	44	—
Pennsylvania	2,572,472	54	25	2,213,429	46	—
Rhode Island	204,450	52	4	191,914	48	—
South Carolina	561,963	64	8	316,746	36	—
South Dakota	198,119	63	3	114,967	37	—
Tennessee	1,002,722	59	11	705,820	41	—
Texas	3,351,589	64	29	1,897,190	36	—
Utah	467,214	75	5	155,098	25	—
Vermont	134,252	58	3	94,518	41	—
Virginia	1,338,378	63	12	798,553	37	—
Washington	945,052	56	10	736,260	44	—
West Virginia	400,261	55	6	324,073	45	—
Wisconsin	1,198,379	55	11	992,807	45	—
Wyoming	132,073	70	3	53,272	28	—
Total	53,355,081	59	525	36,884,702	41	13

TABLE D–2

Democratic Characteristics of the Republican and Democratic Vote in 1984

Characteristic	Percent of total vote	Percent of the vote for:	
		Republicans	Democrats
All voters	100	59	41
Men	50	63	37
Women	50	56	44
Whites	82	63	37
Blacks	12	11	89
Hispanics	4	47	53
East	25	59	41
South	28	58	42
Midwest	29	59	41
West	18	59	41
Southern whites	22	73	27
Nonsouthern whites	60	64	36
Protestants	62	61	39
Catholics	8	59	41
Jews	3	32	68
"Born-again" white Protestants	14	80	20
Age: 18–24	13	59	41
25–29	13	61	39
30–39	26	57	43
40–49	17	59	41
50–59	14	62	38
60+	17	60	40
Family income:			
Below $10,000	16	45	55
$10,000–20,000	25	56	44
$20,000–30,000	24	61	39
$30,000–40,000	18	66	34
Over $40,000	17	68	32
Union households	30	48	52
Nonunion households	70	64	36
Didn't finish high school	8	48	51
High school graduate	29	56	44
Some college	29	62	38
College graduate	21	63	37
Postgraduate	14	52	48
Democrats	34	16	84
Independents	36	67	33
Republicans	30	97	3
Liberals	30	32	68
Moderates	34	59	41
Conservatives	36	82	18
1980 vote:			
Reagan (Republican)	45	90	10
Carter (Democratic)	31	20	80
Anderson (Independent)	5	32	68
Did not vote	15	58	42
Registered:			
Before 1981	84	60	40
In 1984	8	61	39
In 1981–83	8	51	49

Sources: *National Journal,* vol. 16 (November 10, 1984), p. 2132; and ABC News–*Washington Post* exit polls published in the *Washington Post,* November 8, 1984, p. A48.

References

CHAPTER 1

BAILYN, BERNARD (1968) The Origins of American Politics. New York: Vintage Books.

BOLES, JANET K. (1979) The Politics of the Equal Rights Amendment. New York: Longman.

BOWEN, CATHERINE DRINKER (1966) Miracle at Philadelphia. Boston: Little, Brown.

BURNETT, EDMUND CODY (1964) The Continental Congress. New York: W. W. Norton.

COOPER, JAMES FENIMORE (1956) The American Democrat. New York: Vintage Books (first published in 1838).

ELAZAR, DANIEL J. (1972) American Federalism: A View from the States. 2d ed. New York: Thomas Y. Crowell.

HARTZ, LOUIS (1955) The Liberal Tradition in America. New York: Harcourt Brace Jovanovich.

HARTZ, LOUIS (1964) The Founding of New Societies. New York: Harcourt Brace Jovanovich.

HENDERSON, H. JAMES (1974) Party Politics in the Continental Congress. New York: McGraw-Hill.

HYNEMAN, CHARLES S., and GEORGE W. CAREY (1967) A Second Federalist: Congress Creates a Government. New York: Appleton-Century-Crofts.

KURTZ, STEPHEN G., and JAMES H. HUTSON, eds. (1973) Essays on the American Revolution. Chapel Hill: University of Carolina Press.

LIPSET, SEYMOUR MARTIN (1963) The First New Nation. New York: Basic Books.

MERRITT, RICHARD L. (1966) Symbols of American Community, 1735–1775. New Haven, Conn.: Yale University Press.

MITCHELL, WILLIAM C. (1962) The American Polity. New York: Free Press.

MORISON, SAMUEL ELIOT (1965) The Oxford History of the American People. New York: Oxford University Press.

PARRINGTON, VERNON L. (1954) Main Currents in American. Thought, Vol I: The Colonial Mind, 1620–1800. New York: Harcourt Brace Jovanovich. (first published in 1927).

PLUMB, J. H. (1963) Men and Centuries. Boston: Houghton Mifflin.

ROCHE, JOHN P. (1961) "The Founding Fathers: A Reform Caucus in Action." American Political Science Review 55 (December): 799–816.

WAHLKE, JOHN C., ed. (1973) The Causes of the American Revolution. 3d ed. Lexington, Mass.: D. C. Heath.

WOOD, GORDON S. (1969) The Creation of the American Republic, 1776–1787. New York: W. W. Norton.

YOUNG, JAMES S. (1966) The Washington Community, 1800–1828. New York: Columbia University Press.

CHAPTER 2

BELL, RUDOLPH M. (1973) Party and Faction in American Politics. Westport, Conn.: Greenwood Press.

BENSON, LEE (1964) The Concept of Jacksonian Democracy. New York: Atheneum Publishers.

BINDER, LEONARD, et al. (1971) Crises and Sequences in Political Development. Princeton, N.J.: Princeton University Press.

BURNHAM, WALTER DEAN (1965) "The Changing Shape of the American Political Universe." American Political Science Review 59 (March):7–28.

BURNHAM, WALTER DEAN (1970) Critical Elections and the Mainsprings of American Politics. New York: W. W. Norton.

CHAMBERS, WILLIAM NISBET, and WALTER DEAN BURNHAM, eds. (1975) The American Party Systems. 2d ed. New York: Oxford University Press.

CONVERSE, PHILIP E. (1972) "Change in the American Electorate," in The Human Meaning of Social Change. Edited by Angus Campbell and Philip E. Converse. New York: Russell Sage Foundation, pp. 263–337.

CRONIN, THOMAS E. (1975) The State of the Presidency. Boston: Little, Brown.

ELAZAR, DANIEL J. (1972) American Federalism: A View from the States. 2d ed. New York: Thomas Y. Crowell.

FENNO, RICHARD F. JR., (1959) The President's Cabinet. New York: Vintage Books.

GAMSON, WILLIAM A. (1975) The Strategy of Social Protest. Homewood, Ill.: Dorsey Press.

GOODMAN, PAUL (1967) "The First American Party System," in The American Party Systems: Stages of Political Development. Edited by W. N. Chambers and W. D. Burnham. New York: Oxford University Press, pp. 56–89.

GREELEY, ANDREW M. (1974) Ethnicity in the United States. New York: John Wiley & Sons.

HOFSTADTER, RICHARD (1972) The Idea of a Party System. Berkeley: University of California Press.

HOLCOMBE, ARTHUR N. (1950) Our More Perfect Union. Cambridge, Mass.: Harvard University Press.

HUNTINGTON, SAMUEL P. (1968) Political Order in Changing Societies. New Haven, Conn.: Yale University Press.

JEWELL, MALCOLM E., and SAMUEL C. PATTERSON (1977) The Legislative Process in the United States. 3d ed. New York: Random House.

LADD, EVERETT C., JR. (1970) American Political Parties, New York: W. W. Norton.

LANE, ROBERT E. (1959) Political Life. Glencoe, Ill.: Free Press.

LIPSET, SEYMOUR MARTIN (1960) Political Man. Garden City, N.Y.: Doubleday Publishing.

LOWI, THEODORE J. (1971) The Politics of Disorder. New York: Basic Books.

McCLOSKEY, ROBERT G. (1960) The American Supreme Court. Chicago: University of Chicago Press.

McCORMICK, RICHARD P. (1967) "Political Development and the Second Party System," in The American Party Systems: Stages of Political Development. Edited by W. N. Chambers and W. D. Burnham. New York: Oxford University Press, pp. 90–116.

PESSEN, EDWARD (1969) Jacksonian America. Homewood, Ill.: Dorsey Press.

REAGAN, MICHAEL D., and JOHN G. SANZONE (1981) The New Federalism. 2d ed. New York: Oxford University Press.

ROOSEVELT, THEODORE (1927) Theodore Roosevelt: An Autobiography. New York: Charles Scribner's Sons.

SEARS, DAVID O., and JOHN B. McCONAHAY (1973) The Politics of Violence. Boston: Houghton Mifflin.

SKOWRONEK, STEPHEN (1982) Building a New American State. Cambridge: Cambridge University Press.

STOHL, MICHAEL (1976) War and Domestic Political Violence. Beverly Hills, Calif.: Sage Publications.

STOKES, DONALD E. (1975) "Parties and the Nationalization of Electoral Forces," in The American Party Systems. Edited by William N. Chambers and Walter Dean Burnham. New York: Oxford University Press, pp. 182–202.

SUNDQUIST, JAMES L. (1983) Dynamics of the Party System. Rev. ed. Washington, D.C.: Brookings Institution.

THUROW, LESTER C. (1975) Generating Inequality: Mechanisms of Distribution in the U.S. Economy. New York: Basic Books.

YOUNG, JAMES S. (1966) The Washington Community, 1800–1808. New York: Columbia University Press.

CHAPTER 3

ABERBACH, JOEL D., and JACK L. WALKER (1973) Race in the City. Boston, Mass.: Little, Brown.

ALMOND, GABRIEL A. (1950) The American People and Foreign Policy. New York: Harcourt Brace Jovanovich.

ALMOND, GABRIEL A., and SIDNEY VERBA (1963) The Civic Culture. Princeton, N.J.: Princeton University Press.

BARTLEY, NUMAN V., and HUGH D. GRAHAM (1975) Southern Politics and the Second Reconstruction. Baltimore, Md.: Johns Hopkins University Press.

BASS, JACK, and WALTER DeVRIES (1976) The Transformation of Southern Politics. New York: Basic Books.

BLAKE, JUDITH (1971) "Abortion and Public Opinion: The 1960–1970 Decade." Science (February): 540–49.

BRYCE, JAMES (1907) The American Commonwealth, 2 vols. New York: Macmillan.

CITRIN, JACK (1974) "The Political Relevance of Trust in Government." American Political Science Review 68 (September): 973–88.

CROTTY, WILLIAM J., ed. (1971) Assassinations and the Political Order. New York: Harper & Row.

CURRY, RICHARD O., and THOMAS M. BROWN, eds. (1972) Conspiracy: The Fear of Subversion in American History. New York: Holt, Rinehart & Winston.

DAVIS, JAMES A. (1975) "Communism, Conformity, Cohorts, and Categories: American Tolerance in 1954 and 1972–73." American Journal of Sociology 81 (November): 491–513.

DAWSON, RICHARD E., KENNETH PREWITT, and KAREN S. DAWSON. Political Socialization. 2d ed. Boston, Mass.: Little, Brown.

DEVINE, DONALD J. (1972) The Political Culture of the United States. Boston: Little, Brown.

DUNNE, FINLEY PETER (1898) Mr. Dooley in Peace and War. Boston: Scholarly Books.

EASTON, DAVID, and JACK DENNIS (1969) Children in the Political System. New York: McGraw-Hill.

ELAZAR, DANIEL (1970) Cities of the Prairie. New York: Basic Books.

ELAZAR, DANIEL, and JOSEPH ZIKMUND II, eds. (1975) The Ecology of American Political Culture. New York: Thomas Y. Crowell.

EPSTEIN, BENJAMIN R., and ARNOLD FORSTER (1967) The Radical Right. New York: Vintage Books.

ERIKSON, ROBERT S., and NORMAN R. LUTTBEG (1973) American Public Opinion: Its Origins, Content, and Impact. New York: John Wiley & Sons.

ERSKINE, HAZEL (1970) "The Polls: Freedom of Speech." Public Opinion Quarterly 34 (Fall): 483–96.

FREE, LLOYD A., and HADLEY CANTRIL (1967) The Political Beliefs of Americans. New Brunswick, N.J.: Rutgers University Press.

GARCIA, F. CHRIS (1973) Political Socialization of Chicano Children. New York: Praeger Publishers.

GASTIL, RAYMOND D. (1975) Cultural Regions of the United States. Seattle: University of Washington Press.

GITHENS, MARIANNE, and JEWEL L. PRESTAGE, eds. (1977) A Portrait of Marginality: The Political Behavior of the American Woman. New York: David McKay.

GREELEY, ANDREW M. (1947) Ethnicity in the United States. New York: John Wiley & Sons.

GREENBERG, BRADLEY S., and EDWIN B. PARKER, eds. (1965) The Kennedy Assassination and the American Public. Stanford, Calif.: Stanford University Press.

GREENBERG, EDWARD S. (1969) "Children and the Political Community: A Comparison across Racial Lines." Canadian Journal of Political Science 2 (December): 471–92.

GREENSTEIN, FRED I. (1974) "What the President Means to Americans," in Choosing the President. Edited by James

D. Barber. Englewood Cliffs, N.J.: Prentice-Hall, pp. 121–47.

GREENSTEIN, FRED I. (1975) "The Benevolent Leader Revisited: Children's Images of Political Leaders in Three Democracies." American Political Science Review 69 (December): 1371–98.

HESS, ROBERT D., and JUDITH V. TORNEY (1967) The Development of Political Attitudes in Children. Chicago: Aldine Publishing.

HODGE, ROBERT W., PAUL M. SIEGEL, and PETER H. ROSSI (1964) "Occupational Prestige in the United States, 1925–63." American Journal of Sociology 70 (November): 286–302.

HOFSTADTER, RICHARD (1965) The Paranoid Style in American Politics. New York: Alfred A. Knopf.

JACKMAN, ROBERT W. (1972) "Political Elites, Mass Publics, and Support for Democratic Principles." Journal of Politics 34 (August): 753–73.

JACOBS, PAUL, and SAUL LANDAU (1966) The New Radicals. New York: Vintage Books.

JAHODA, GUSTAV (1963) "The Development of Children's Ideas about Country and Nationality." British Journal of Educational Psychology 33 (February): 143–53.

JENNINGS, M. KENT, and RICHARD G. NIEMI (1974) The Political Character of Adolescence: The Influence of Families and Schools. Princeton, N.J.: Princeton University Press.

JENNINGS, M. KENT, and RICHARD G. NIEMI (1981) Generations and Politics. Princeton, N.J.: Princeton University Press.

KIRKPATRICK, JEANE J. (1974) Political Woman. New York: Basic Books.

LANE, ROBERT E. (1962) Political Ideology: Why the American Common Man Believes What He Does. New York: Free Press.

LIPSET, SEYMOUR MARTIN, and EARL RAAB (1970) The Politics of Unreason. New York: Harper & Row.

LIPSET, SEYMOUR MARTIN, and WILLIAM SCHNEIDER (1983) The Confidence Gap. New York: Free Press.

McCLOSKY, HERBERT, and ALIDA BRILL (1983) Dimensions of Tolerance. New York: Russell Sage Foundation.

MILLER, WARREN E., and TERESA E. LEVITIN (1976) Leadership and Change: The New Politics and the American Electorate. Cambridge, Mass.: Winthrop.

NIEMI, RICHARD G. (1974) How Family Members Perceive Each Other. New Haven: Yale University Press.

NIEMI, RICHARD G., and HERBERT F. WEISBERG, eds. (1976) Controversies in American Voting Behavior. San Francisco: W. H. Freeman.

NUNN, CLYDE Z., HARRY J. CROCKETT, JR., and J. ALLEN WILLIAMS, JR. (1978) Tolerance for Nonconformity. San Francisco, Calif.: Jossey-Bass.

ORREN, KAREN, AND PAUL PETERSON (1967) "Presidential Assassination: A Case Study in the Dynamics of Political Socialization." Journal of Politics 29 (May): 388–404.

ORUM, ANTHONY M., and ROBERTA S. COHEN (1973) "The Development of Political Orientations among Black and White Children." American Sociological Review 38 (February): 62–74.

PETERS, JOHN G., and SUSAN WELCH (1980) "The Effects of Charges of Corruption on Voting Behavior in Congressional Elections." American Political Science Review 74 (September): 697–708.

STOUFFER SAMUEL A. (1966) Communism, Conformity, and Civil Liberties. New York: John Wiley & Sons.

WOLFENSTEIN, MARTHA, and GILBERT KILMAN, eds. (1965) Children and the Death of a President. Garden City, N.Y.: Doubleday Publishing.

WRIGHT, JAMES D. (1976) The Dissent of the Governed: Alienation and Democracy in America. New York: Academic Press.

CHAPTER 4

ALMOND, GARBIEL A., and SIDNEY VERBA (1963) The Civic Culture. Princeton, N.J.: Princeton University Press.

BARNES, SAMUEL H. and MAX KAASE (1979) Political Action: Mass Participation in Five Western Democracies. Beverly Hills, Calif.: Sage Publications.

BRODY, RICHARD A. (1978) "The Puzzle of Political Participation in America," in The New American Political System. Edited by Anthony King. Washington, D.C.: American Enterprise Institute, pp. 287–324.

BULLITT, STIMSON (1977) To Be a Politician, rev. ed. New Haven, Conn.: Yale University Press.

KATZ, DANIEL, BARBARA A. GUTEK, ROBERT L. KAHN, and EUGENIA BARTON (1975) Bureaucratic Encounters. Ann Arbor, Mich.: Institute for Social Research.

KIRKPATRICK, JEANE (1976) The New Presidential Elite: Men and Women in National Politics. New York: Russell Sage Foundation.

LANE, ROBERT E. (1959) Political Life: Why People Get Involved in Politics. Glencoe, Ill.: Free Press.

MILBRATH, LESTER W., and M. L. GOEL (1977) Political Participation. 2d ed. Chicago: Rand McNally.

NIE, NORMAN H., and SIDNEY VERBA (1975) "Political Participation," in Handbook of Political Science. Edited by Fred I. Greenstein and Nelson W. Polsby. Reading, Mass.: Addison-Wesley, Publishing, vol. 4, pp. 1–74.

VERBA, SIDNEY, and NORMAN H. NIE (1972) Participation in America. New York: Harper & Row.

CHAPTER 5

ABRAMSON, PAUL R. (1975) Generational Change in American Politics. Lexington, Mass.: D. C. Heath.

ABRAMSON, PAUL R., JOHN H. ALDRICH, and DAVID W. ROHDE (1982) Change and Continuity in the 1980 Elections. Washington, D.C.: Congressional Quarterly Press.

ASHER, HERBERT 3d (1984) Presidential Elections and American Politics. 3d ed. Homewood, Ill.: Dorsey Press.

AXELROD, ROBERT (1972) "Where the Votes Come From: An Analysis of Electoral Coalitions, 1952–1968." American Political Science Review 66 (March): 11–20.

BAIN, HENRY M., and DONALD S. HECOCK (1957) Ballot Position and Voter's Choice. Detroit: Wayne State University Press.

BEST, JUDITH (1975) The Case against Direct Election of the President. Ithaca, N.Y.: Cornell University Press.

BURNHAM, WALTER DEAN (1970) Critical Elections and the Mainsprings of American Politics. New York: W. W. Norton.

BURNHAM, WALTER DEAN (1982) The Current Crisis in American Politics. New York: Oxford University Press.

CAMPBELL, ANGUS, PHILIP E. CONVERSE, WARREN E. MILLER, and DONALD E. STOKES (1960) The American Voter. New York: John Wiley & Sons.

CASSEL, CAROL A. (1979) "Changes in Electoral Participation in the South." Journal of Politics 41 (August): 907–17.

CONVERSE, PHILIP E. (1972) "Change in the American Electorate," in The Human Meaning of Social Change. Edited by Angus Campbell and Philip E. Converse. New York: Russell Sage Foundation, pp. 263–337.

CROTTY WILLIAM J. (1977) Political Reform and the American Experiment. New York: Thomas Y. Crowell.

GLASS, DAVID, PEVERILL SQUIRE, and RAYMOND WOLFINGER (1984) "Voter Turnout: An International Comparison." Public Opinion 6 (December/January): 49–55.

GLENN, NORVAL D. (1972) "Sources of the Shift to Political Independence: Some Evidence from a Cohort Analysis." Social Science Quarterly 53 (December): 494–519.

GREEN, PAUL M. (1983) "Washington's Victory: Divide and Conquer." Illinois Issues 9 (April): 15–20.

LONGLEY, LAWRENCE D., and ALAN G. BRAUN (1975) The Politics of Electoral College Reform. 2d ed. New Haven, Conn.: Yale University Press.

MILLER, WARREN E., and TERESA A. LEVITIN (1976) Leadership and Change: The New Politics and the American Electorate. Cambridge, Mass.: Winthrop.

NIE, NORMAN H., SIDNEY VERBA, and JOHN R. PETROCIK eds. (1979) The Changing American Voter. Enlarged ed. Cambridge, Mass.: Harvard University Press.

NIEMI, RICHARD G., and HERBERT F. WEISBERG, eds. (1976) Controversies in American Voting Behavior. San Francisco: W. H. Freeman.

PATTERSON, SAMUEL C., and GREGORY A. CALDEIRA (1983) "Getting Out the Vote: Participation in Gubernatorial Elections." American Political Science Review 77 (September): 675–89.

PEIRCE, NEAL R., and LAWRENCE D. LONGLEY (1981) The People's President. Rev. ed. New Haven, Conn.: Yale University Press.

PHILLIPS, KEVIN P., and PAUL H. BLACKMAN (1975) Electoral Reform and Voter Participation. Washington, D.C.: American Enterprise Institute for Public Policy Research.

PEIRCE, NEAL R., and LAWRENCE D. LONGLEY (1981) The People's President. Rev. ed. New Haven, Conn.: Yale University Press.

PHILLIPS, KEVIN P., and PAUL H. BLACKMAN (1975) Electoral Reform and Voter Participation. Washington, D.C.: American Enterprise Institute for Public Policy Research.

POLSBY, NELSON W., and AARON WILDAVSKY (1984) Presidential Elections. 6th ed. New York: Charles Scribner's Sons.

POMPER, GERALD M. (1975) Voters' Choice: Varieties of American Electoral Behavior. New York: Dodd, Mead.

RUSK, JERROLD G. (1976) "The Effect of the Australian Ballot Reform on Split Ticket Voting: 1876–1980," in Controversies in American Voting Behavior. Edited by Richard G. Niemi and Herbert F. Weisberg. San Francisco: W. H. Freeman, pp. 484–513.

SAYRE, WALLACE S., and JUDITH H. PARRIS (1970) Voting for President: The Electoral College and the American Political System. Washington, D.C.: Brookings Institution.

SMOLKA, RICHARD G. (1977) Election Day Registration. Washington, D.C.: American Enterprise Institute for Public Policy Research.

TUFTE, EDWARD R. (1973) "The Relationship between Seats and Votes in Two-Party Systems." American Political Science Review 67 (June): 540–54.

WHITE, THEODORE H. (1961) The Making of the President 1960. New York: Atheneum.

WOLFINGER, RAYMOND E., and STEVEN J. ROSENSTONE (1980) Who Votes? New Haven, Conn.: Yale University Press.

YUNKER, JOHN H., and LAWRENCE D. LONGLEY (1976) The Electoral College: Its Biases Newly Measured for the 1960s and 1970s. Sage Professional Papers in American Politics 3, 04-031. Beverly Hills, Calif.: Sage Publications.

CHAPTER 6

AMERICAN ASSEMBLY (1982) The Future of American Political Parties. New York: American Assembly of Columbia University.

BIBBY, JOHN F. (1980) "Party Renewal in the National Republican Party," in Party Renewal in America. Edited by Gerald M. Pomper. New York: Praeger pp. 102–115.

BIBBY, JOHN F., CORNELIUS P. COTTER, JAMES L. GIBSON, and ROBERT L. HUCKSHORN (1983) "Parties in State Politics," in Politics in the American States. 4th ed., Edited by Virginia Gray, Herbert Jacob, and Kenneth N. Vines. Boston: Little, Brown, pp. 59–96.

CONVERSE, PHILIP E. (1966) "The Concept of the Normal Vote," in Angus Campbell, Philip Converse, Warren E. Miller, and Donald E. Stokes, Elections and the Political Order. New York: John Wiley & Sons.

COTTER, CORNELIUS P., and BERNARD C. HENNESSY (1964) Politics without Power: The National Party Committees. New York: Atherton Press.

COTTER, CORNELIUS P., and JOHN F. BIBBY (1980) "Institutional Development of Parties and the Thesis of Party Decline." Political Science Quarterly 95 (Spring): 1–27.

DEMOCRATIC NATIONAL COMMITTEE (1982) Report of the Commission on Presidential Nomination. Adopted by the Democratic National Committee (March 26).

DENNIS, JACK (1966) "Support for the Party System by the Mass Public." American Political Science Review 60 (September): 600–15.

DOWNS, ANTHONY (1957) An Economic Theory of Democracy. New York: Harper & Row.

DUVERGER, MAURICE (1954) Political Parties. New York: John Wiley & Sons.

EHRENHALT, ALAN (1984) "How Not to Pick a Presidential Candidate." Congressional Quarterly Weekly Report 42 (January 28): 167.

EPSTEIN, LEON D. (1967) Political Parties in Western Democracies. New York: Praeger Publishers.

FARNEY, DENNIS (1984) "Policy Debate within GOP to Heat Up Whether or Not Reagan Seeks Reelection." The Wall Street Journal (January 28): 58.

GIBSON, JAMES L., CORNELIUS P. COTTER, JOHN F. BIBBY, and ROBERT J. HUCKSHORN (1982) "Whither the Local Parties?" Paper delivered before the Western Political Science Association meeting (March).

GIBSON, JAMES L., CORNELIUS P. COTTER, and JOHN F. BIBBY (1983) "Assessing Party Organizational Strength." American Journal of Political Science 27 (May): 193–222.

JACKSON, BROOKS (1984) "Loopholes Allow Flood of Campaign Giving by Business, Fat Cats." The Wall Street Journal (July 5): 1.

JACOBSON, GARY C. (1980) Money in Congressional Elections. New Haven: Yale University Press.

JACOBSON, GARY C. (1984) "Money in the 1980 and 1982 Congressional Elections," in Money and Politics in the United States. Edited by Michael J. Malbin. Chatham, N.J.: Chatham House, pp. 38–69.

JOHNSTON, MICHAEL (1979) "Patrons and Clients, Jobs and Machines: A Case Study of the Uses of Patronage." American Political Science Review 73 (June): 385–393.

JONES, CHARLES O. (1964) "Inter-Party Competition for Congressional Seats." Western Political Quarterly 17 (September): 461–76.

KEY, V.O., JR. (1964) Politics, Parties and Pressure Groups. 5th ed. New York: Thomas Y. Crowell.

KIRKPATRICK, JEANE J. (1976) The New Presidential Elite. New York: Russell Sage and Twentieth Century Funds.

"Kirkpatrick's Speech Delights Party" (1984) The New York Times (August 22): A16.

LADD, EVERETT CARLL (1983) "A Party Primer." Public Opinion 6 (October–November): 20–58.

LARDNER, GEORGE, JR. (1983) "Democratic Contenders Woo House." Washington Post (July 14): A2.

LONGLEY, CHARLES H. (1980) "Party Reform and Nationalization: The Case of the Democrats," in The Party Symbol. Edited by William J. Crotty. San Francisco: W. H. Freeman.

MALBIN, MICHAEL J. (1979) "Campaign Financing and the 'Special Interests.' " The Public Interest 56 (Summer): 21–42.

MAYHEW, DAVID R. (1966) Party Loyalty among Congressmen. Cambridge, Mass.: Harvard University Press.

MAYHEW, DAVID R. (1974) "Congressional Elections: The Case of the Vanishing Marginals." Polity 6 (Spring): 295–317.

McCLOSKY, HERBERT, PAUL J. HOFFMAN, and ROSEMARY O'HARA (1960) "Issue Conflict and Consensus among Party Leaders and Followers." American Political Science Review 54 (June): 406–27.

MITOFSKY, WARREN, and MARTIN PLISSNER (1981) "The Making of the Delegates, 1968–1980." Public Opinion 3 (October–November): 37–43.

MOREHOUSE, SARAH McCALLY (1980) "The Effect of Preprimary Endorsements on State Party Strength." Paper presented at the American Political Science Association convention (August).

NIE, NORMAN, H., SIDNEY VERBA, and JOHN R. PETROCIK (1976) The Changing American Voter. Cambridge, Mass.: Harvard University Press.

NIEMI, RICHARD G., and HERBERT F. WEISBERG, eds. (1984) Controversies in American Voting Behavior. 2d ed. Washington, D.C.: CQ Press.

PATTERSON, THOMAS E., and ROBERT D. McCLURE (1976) The Unseeing Eye. New York: G. P. Putnam's Sons.

PERRY, JAMES M. (1984) "Democrats Must Play Game of Rules." The Wall Street Journal (January 18): 58.

PLISSNER, MARTIN, and WARREN MITOFSKY (1981) "Political Elites." Public Opinion 4 (October–November): 47–50.

POLSBY, NELSON W. (1983) Consequences of Party Reform. Oxford: Oxford University Press.

POLSBY, NELSON W., and AARON WILDAVSKY (1984) Presidential Elections. 6th edition. New York: Charles Scribner's Sons.

POMPER, GERALD M. (1968) Elections in America. New York: Dodd, Mead.

RANNEY, AUSTIN (1974) "Changing the Rules of the Nominating Game," in Choosing the President. Edited by James D. Barber. Englewood Cliffs, N.J.: Prentice-Hall, pp. 71–93.

RANNEY, AUSTIN (1976) "Parties in State Politics," in Politics in the American States. 3d ed. Edited by Herbert Jacobs and Kenneth Vines. Boston: Little, Brown, pp. 61–99.

RANNEY, AUSTIN (1977) Participation in American Presidential Nominations, 1976, Washington, D.C.: American Enterprise Institute.

RASKIN, A. H. (1984) "Labor's Gamble on Mondale." New York Times Magazine (January 20): 30 ff.

ROSENSTONE, STEVEN J., ROY L. BEHR, and EDWARD LAZARUS (1984) Third Parties in America. Princeton, N.J.: Princeton University Press.

SABATO, LARRY J. (1981) The Rise of Political Consultants. New York: Basic Books.

SHOGAN, ROBERT (1977) "Fund Raiser a Political Maverick—Brings Millions into Conservative Coffers." Los Angeles Times (December 19): II, 10.

SOULE, JOHN W., and WILMA E. McGRATH (1975) "A Comparative Study of Presidential Nominating Conventions: The Democrats 1968 and 1972." American Journal of Political Science 19 (August): 501–18.

SORAUF, FRANK J. (1984) Party Politics in America. 5th ed. Boston: Little, Brown.

STONE, WALTER J., and ALAN I. ABRAMOWITZ (1983) "Winning May Not Be Everything, But It's More than We Thought: Presidential Party Activists in 1980." American Political Science Review 77 (December): 945–956.

WEAVER, PAUL H. (1976) "Captives of Melodrama." New York Times Magazine (August 29): 6 ff.

WHITE, JOHN KENNETH, and DWIGHT MORRIS (1984) "Shattered Images: Political Parties in the 1984 Election." Public Opinion 6 (December–January): 44–48.

CHAPTER 7

BAUER, RAYMOND A., ITHIEL DE SOLA POOL, and LEWIS ANTHONY DEXTER (1963) American Business and Public Policy. New York: Atherton Press.

BERRY, JEFFREY (1977) Lobbying for the People. Princeton, N.J.: Princeton University Press.

CIGLER, ALLAN J., and BURDETT A. LOOMIS (1983) "The Changing Nature of Interest Group Politics," in Interest Group Politics. Edited by Allan J. Cigler and Burdett A. Loomis. Washington: Congressional Quarterly Press, pp. 1–30.

CLOSE, ARTHUR C., ed. (1983) Washington Representatives 1983. Washington, D.C.: Columbia Books, Inc.

COOK, MARY ETTA, and ROGER H. DAVIDSON (1984) "Deferral Politics," in Public Policy and the Natural Environment. Edited by Helen Ingram. Greenwich, Conn.: JAI Press.

COWAN, EDWARD (1982) "Carlton Group Spurns Lobbying Limelight." New York Times (March 18): D 1.

CRITTENDEN, ANN (1982) "A Stubborn Chamber of Commerce." New York Times (June 27): F 4–5.

HAIDER, DONALD H. (1974) When Governments Come to Washington. New York: Free Press.

HAMMOND, SUSAN WEBB, ARTHUR G. STEVENS, JR., and DANIEL P. MULHOLLAN (1983) "Congressional Caucuses: Legislators as Lobbyists," in Interest Group Politics. Edited by Allan J. Cigler and Burdett A. Loomis. Washington, D.C.: Congressional Quarterly Press, pp. 275–297.

HAYES, MICHAEL T. (1981) Lobbyists and Legislators. New Brunswick, N.J.: Rutgers University Press.

HECLO, HUGH (1978) "Issue Networks and the Executive Establishment," in The New American Political System. Edited by Anthony King. Washington, D.C.:American Enterprise Institute:

JOHNSON, LYNDON B. (1971) The Vantage Point. New York: Holt, Rinehart & Winston.

KELLER, BILL (1983) "Lowest Common Denominator Lobbying: Why The Banks Fought Withholding." Washington Monthly 15 (May): 32–39.

LIPSET, SEYMOUR M., et al. (1956) Union Democracy. Glencoe, Ill.: Free Press.

LIPSKY, MICHAEL (1968) "Protest as a Political Resource." American Political Science Review 62 (December): 1144–1158.

LOWI, THEODORE J. (1969) The End of Liberalism. New York: W. W. Norton.

McCONNELL, GRANT (1967) Private Power and American Democracy. New York: Alfred A. Knopf.

MICHELS, ROBERT (1915) Political Parties. New York: Dover Publications (1959 ed.).

MILBRATH, LESTER, and M. L. GOEL (1977) Political Participation. 2d ed. Chicago: Rand McNally.

MOE, TERRY M. (1980) The Organization of Interests. Chicago: University of Chicago Press.

OLSON, MANCUR, JR. (1965) The Logic of Collective Action. Cambridge: Harvard University Press.

ORNSTEIN, NORMAN J., and SHIRLEY ELDER (1978) Interest Groups, Lobbying and Policymaking. Washington: Congressional Quarterly Press.

PIKA, JOSEPH A. (1983) "Interest Groups and the Executive." In Interest Group Politics. Edited by Allan J. Cigler and Burdett A. Loomis. Washington: Congressional Quarterly Press: 298–323.

RIGGS, FRED W. (1950) Pressures on Congress: A Study of the Repeal of Chinese Exclusion. New York: King's Crown Press.

SALISBURY, ROBERT H. (1983) "Interest Groups: Toward a New Understanding," in Interest Group Politics. Edited by Allan J. Cigler and Burdett A. Loomis. Washington, D.C.: Congressional Quarterly Press: 354–70.

SANSWEET, STEPHEN J. (1980) "Political-Action Units at Firms are Assailed by Some over Tactics." The Wall Street Journal (July 24): 1.

SCHATTSCHNEIDER, E. E. (1942) Party Government. New York: Holt, Rinehart & Winston.

SCHATTSCHNEIDER, E. E. (1960) The Semi-Sovereign People. New York: Holt, Rinehart & Winston.

SCHLOZMAN, KAY LEHMAN, and JOHN T. TIERNEY (1983) "More of the Same: Washington Pressure Group Activity in a Decade of Change." Journal of Politics 45 (May): 351–377.

TAYLOR, STUART, JR. (1983) "Justice System Stifled by Its Costs and Its Complexity, Experts Warn." New York Times (June 1): A 1 ff.

TRUMAN, DAVID B. (1971) The Governmental Process. 2d ed. New York: Alfred A. Knopf.

U.S. HOUSE OF REPRESENTATIVES, COMMISSION ON ADMINISTRATIVE REVIEW (1977) Final Report. H. Doc. 95–272 (December 31): Vol. 2.

VERBA, SIDNEY, and NORMAN H. NIE (1972) Participation in America. New York: Harper & Row.

WALKER, JACK L. (1983) "The Origins and Maintenance of Interest Groups in America." American Political Science Review 77 (June): 390–406.

ZEIGLER, L. HARMON, and G. WAYNE PEAK (1972) Interest Groups in American Society. 2d ed. Englewood Cliffs, N.J.: Prentice-Hall.

CHAPTER 8

BAGDIKIAN, BEN H. (1971) The Information Machines: Their Impact on Men and the Media. New York: Harper & Row.

BERELSON, BERNARD, PAUL LAZARSFELD, and WILLIAM McPHEE (1954) Voting. Chicago: University of Chicago Press.

BONAFEDE, DOM (1980a) "The Press Makes News in Covering the 1980 Primary Election Campaign." National Journal 12 (July 12): 1132–35.

BONAFEDE, DOM (1980b) "The New Political Power of the Press." Washington Journalism Review 2 (September): 25–27.

BRODER, DAVID S. (1981) "New Life for an Old Forum." Washington Post (February 4): A 17.

COMSTOCK, GEORGE, STEVEN CHAFEE, NATAN KATZMAN, MAXWELL McCOMBS, and DONALD ROBERTS (1978) Television and Human Behavior. New York: Columbia University Press.

CROUSE, TIM (1973) The Boys on the Bus. New York: Ballantine Books.

DAVIDSON, ROGER H., and WALTER J. OLESZEK (1985) Congress and its Members. 2d ed. Washington, D.C.: Congressional Quarterly Press.

DE FLEUR, MELVIN L., and SANDRA BALL-ROKEACH (1975) Theories of Mass Communication. 3d ed New York: David McKay.

DE FRANK, THOMAS M. (1982) "Fine-Tuning the White House Press Conference." Washington Journalism Review 4 (October): 27–29.

DREW, ELIZABETH (1976) "A Reporter in Washington, D.C.: Winter Notes—II." The New Yorker (May 31): 54–99.

ERICKSON, ROBERT S. (1976) "The Influence of Newspaper Endorsements in Presidential Elections: The Case of 1964." American Journal of Political Science 20 (May): 207–33.

FAGAN, RICHARD (1966) Politics and Communication. Boston: Little, Brown.

FRIENDLY, JONATHAN (1983) "Reporter's Notebook: Surprising Profile of a Journalist." New York Times (May 13): A 16.

GRABER, DORIS A. (1984) Mass Media and American Politics. 2d ed. Washington, D.C.: Congressional Quarterly Press.

GREY, DAVID C. (1968) The Supreme Court and the News Media. Evanston, Ill.: Northwestern University Press.

HEARD, ALEXANDER (1966) "The Organization and Functions of Campaigns," in American Party Politics: Essays and Readings. Edited by Donald G. Herzberg and Gerald M. Pomper. New York: Holt, Rinehart & Winston, pp. 321–30.

HESS, STEPHEN (1981) The Washington Reporters. Washington, D.C.: The Brookings Institution.

HESS, STEPHEN, and MILTON KAPLAN (1975) The Ungentlemanly Art: A History of American Political Cartoons. Rev. ed. New York: Macmillan.

KATZ, ELIHU (1957) "The Two-Step Flow of Communication: An Up-to-Date Report on an Hypothesis." Public Opinion Quarterly 21 (Spring): 61–78.

KATZ, ELIHU and JACOB J. FELDMAN (1962) "The Debates in the Light of Research. A Survey of Surveys," in The Great Debates. Edited by Sidney Krause. Bloomington, Ind.: Indiana University Press, pp. 173–223.

KRAUS, SIDNEY, and DENNIS DAVIS (1976) The Effects of Mass Communication on Political Behavior. University Park, Penn.: Pennsylvania State University Press.

LASSWELL, HAROLD D. (1948) "The Structure and Function of Communication in Society," in The Communication of Ideas. Edited by L. Bryson. New York: Harper & Row, pp. 37–51.

LAZARSFELD, PAUL, BERNARD BERELSON, and HAZEL GAUDET (1944) The People's Choice. New York: Columbia University Press.

MINOW, NEWTON N., JOHN BARTLOW MARTIN, and LEE M. MITCHELL (1973) Presidential Television. New York: Basic Books.

NADER, RALPH (1977) "The Labor Press: Let Them Eat Puffery." Los Angeles Times (October 6): II, 7.

PATTERSON, THOMAS E. (1980) The Mass Media Election: How Americans Choose Their President. New York: Praeger Publishers.

PATTERSON, THOMAS E., and ROBERT G. McCLURE (1976) The Unseeing Eye. New York: G. P. Putnam's Sons.

PETERS, CHARLES (1976) "The Ignorant Press." Washington Monthly 8 (May): 55–57.

RANNEY, AUSTIN (1983) Channels of Power: The Impact of Television on American Politics. New York: Basic Books.

ROBINSON, JOHN P. (1977) Changes in Americans' Use of Time, 1965–1975. Cleveland, O.: Cleveland State University Report (August).

ROBINSON, MICHAEL J. (1977) "The TV Primaries." The Wilson Quarterly (Spring): 80–83.

ROBINSON, MICHAEL JAY, and MAURA CLANCEY (1984) "Teflon Politics." Public Opinion 7 (April–May): 14–18.

ROSHCO, BERNARD (1975) Newsmaking. Chicago: University of Chicago Press.

SCHWARTZ, TONY (1984) "The Major TV Networks' Dwindling Audiences." New York Times (January 14): C 20.

SEARS, DAVID O. (1977) "The Debates in the Light of Research: An Overview of the Effects." Paper presented at the annual meeting of the American Political Science Association, Washington, D.C. (September 1–4).

SHAW, DONALD L., and MAXWELL E. McCOMBS (1977) The Emergence of American Political Issues: The Agenda-Setting Function of the Press. St. Paul, Minn.: West Publishing.

SHALES, TOM (1984) "Bringing Him Back Live." Washington Post (January 4): D 1.

WASHINGTON POST WRITERS GROUP (1976) Of the Press, by the Press, for the Press, and Others, Too. Boston: Houghton Mifflin.

CHAPTER 9

BARBER, JAMES DAVID (1977) Presidential Character. 2d ed. Englewood Cliffs, N.J.: Prentice-Hall.

CORWIN, EDWARD S. (1957) The President, Office and Powers. New York: New York University Press.

CRONIN, THOMAS E. (1980) The State of the Presidency. 2d ed. Boston: Little, Brown.

DAVIDSON, ROGER H., and WALTER J. OLESZEK (1985) Congress and Its Members. 2d ed. Washington, D.C.: Congressional Quarterly Press.

EDWARDS, GEORGE C., III (1983) The Public Presidency. New York: St. Martin's Press.

FISHER, LOUIS (1975) Presidential Spending Power. Princeton, N.J.: Princeton University Press.

FORD, HENRY JONES (1898) The Rise and Growth of American Politics. New York: Da Capo Press (1967 ed.).

GREENSTEIN, FRED I. (1974) "What the President Means to Americans: Presidential 'Choice' Between Elections," in Choosing the President. Edited by James David Barber. Englewood Cliffs, N.J.: Prentice-Hall, pp. 121–47.

GROSSMAN, MICHAEL B., and MARTHA J. KUMAR (1981) Portraying the President: The White House and the News Media. Baltimore, Md.: Johns Hopkins University Press.

HECLO, HUGH (1977) A Government of Strangers. Washington: Brookings Institution.

HESS, STEPHEN (1976) Organizing the Presidency. Washington, D.C.: Brookings Institution.

KAMEN, AL (1984) " 'Great Little Law Firm' Is Troubleshooter for the President." The Washington Post (September 4): A1.

KERNELL, SAMUEL (1978) "Explaining Presidential Popularity." American Political Science Review 72 (June): 506–22.

KESSEL, JOHN (1974) "The Parameters of Presidential Politics." Social Science Quarterly 55 (June): 8–24.

KESSEL, JOHN (1975) The Domestic Presidency. North Scituate, Mass.: Duxbury Press.

LIGHT, PAUL C. (1982) The President's Agenda. Baltimore, Md.: Johns Hopkins University Press.

MINOW, NEWTON N., JOHN BARTLOW MARTIN, and LEE M. MITCHELL (1973) Presidential Television. New York: Basic Books.

MUELLER, JOHN E. (1973) War, Presidents, and Public Opinion. New York: John Wiley & Sons.

NATHAN, RICHARD P. (1983) The Administrative Presidency. New York: John Wiley & Sons.

NEUSTADT, RICHARD E. (1954) "The Presidency and Legislation: The Growth of Central Clearance." American Political Science Review 48 (September): 641–71.

NEUSTADT, RICHARD E. (1955) "The Presidency and Legislation: Planning the President's Program." American Political Science Review 49 (December): 980–1021.

NEUSTADT, RICHARD E. (1976) Presidential Power: The Politics of Leadership. Rev. ed. New York: John Wiley & Sons.

PRITCHETT, C. HERMAN (1982) "The President's Constitutional Position," in Rethinking the Presidency. Edited by Thomas E. Cronin. Boston: Little, Brown, pp. 117–38.

REEDY, GEORGE E. (1970) The Twilight of the Presidency. New York: New American Library.

SCHLESINGER, ARTHUR M., JR. (1973) The Imperial Presidency. Boston, Mass.: Houghton Mifflin.

SCIGLIANO, ROBERT (1971) The Supreme Court and the Presidency. New York: Free Press.

STIMSON, JAMES A. (1976) "Public Support for American Presidents: A Cyclical Model." Public Opinion Quarterly 40 (Spring): 1–21.

WAYNE, STEPHEN J. (1982) "Expectations of the President," in The President and the Public. Edited by Doris A. Graber. Philadelphia, Pa.: Institute for the Study of Human Issues, pp. 17–38.

WILSON, WOODROW (1908) Constitutional Government in the United States. New York: Columbia University Press (1961 ed.).

CHAPTER 10

BULLOCK, CHARLES S. (1973) "Committee Transfers in the United States House of Representatives." Journal of Politics 35 (February): 85–117.

CONGRESSIONAL RECORD (1984) 98th Congress, 2d Session (May 15): H3843.

DAVIDSON, ROGER H. (1969) The Role of the Congressman. Indianapolis, Ind.: Bobbs-Merrill.

DAVIDSON, ROGER H., and WALTER J. OLESZEK (1977) Congress against Itself. Bloomington, Ind.: Indiana University Press.

EHRENHALT, ALAN (1981) "The 'Juniority' System in Congress." Congressional Quarterly Weekly Report 39 (March 21): 535.

FENNO, RICHARD F., JR. (1973) Congressmen in Committees. Boston: Little, Brown.

FENNO, RICHARD F., JR. (1975) "If, as Ralph Nader Says, Congress Is 'The Broken Branch,' How Come We Love Our Congressmen So Much?" in Congress in Change. Edited by Norman J. Ornstein. New York: Praeger Publishers, pp. 277–87.

FENNO, RICHARD F., JR. (1978) Home Style. Boston: Little, Brown.

FOX, HARRISON W., JR., and SUSAN WEBB HAMMOND (1977) Congressional Staffs. New York: Free Press.

FROMAN, LEWIS A., and RANDALL B. RIPLEY (1965) "Conditions for Party Leadership." American Political Science Review 69 (March): 52–63.

GERTZOG, IRWIN N. (1984) Congressional Women: Their Recruitment, Treatment, and Behavior. New York: Praeger Publishers.

GREEN, MARK J., J. M. FALLOWS, and DAVID R. ZWICK (1972) Who Runs Congress? New York: Bantam-Grossman.

HAMMOND, SUSAN WEBB, ARTHUR G. STEVENS, JR., and DANIEL P. MULHOLLAN (1983) "Congressional Caucuses: Legislators as Lobbyists," in Interest Group Politics. Edited by Allan J. Cigler and Burdett A. Loomis. Washington, D.C.: Congressional Quarterly Press, pp. 275–297.

HUITT, RALPH K. (1961) "Democratic Party Leadership in the Senate." American Political Science Review 55 (June): 333–45.

HUNT, ALBERT R. (1980) "Teachers Tie Election Cash to Single Issue." The Wall Street Journal (October 17): 33.

KINGDON, JOHN W. (1981) Congressmen's Voting Decisions. 2d ed. New York: Harper & Row.

MALBIN, MICHAEL J. (1980) Unelected Representatives: Congressional Staffs and the Future of Representative Government. New York: Basic Books.

MANLEY, JOHN F. (1973) "The Conservative Coalition in Congress." American Behavioral Scientist 17 (December): 223–47.

MATSUNAGA, SPARK M., and PING CHEN (1976) Rulemakers of the House. Urbana, Ill.: University of Illinois Press.

MATTHEWS, DONALD R. (1960) U.S. Senators and their World. Chapel Hill, N.C.: University of North Carolina Press.

MAYHEW, DAVID (1974) Congress: The Electoral Connection. New Haven, Conn.: Yale University Press.

MILLER, WARREN E., and DONALD E. STOKES (1963) "Constituency Influence in Congress." American Political Science Review 57 (March): 45–56.

MOSHER, FREDERICK C. (1979) The GAO: The Quest for Accountability in American Government. Boulder, Colo.: Westview Press.

ORNSTEIN, NORMAN J, ROBERT L. PEABODY, and DAVID W. ROHDE (1981) "The Contemporary Senate: Into the 1980s," in Congress Reconsidered. 2d ed., Edited by Lawrence C. Dodd and Bruce I. Oppenheimer. Washington, D.C.: Congressional Quarterly Press, pp. 13–30.

PARKER, GLENN R. (1974) Political Beliefs about the Structure of Government. Congress and the Presidency. Sage Professional Papers in American Politics, vol. 2, no. C4-018. Beverley Hills, Calif.: Sage Publications.

PARKER, GLENN R., and ROGER H. DAVIDSON (1979) "How Come We Love Our Congressmen So Much More than Our Congress?" Legislative Studies Quarterly 4 (February): 53–61.

POLSBY, NELSON W. (1968) "The Institutionalization of the U.S. House of Representatives." American Political Science Review 62 (March): 144–68.

RIPLEY, RANDALL B. (1967) Party Leaders in the House of Representatives. Washington, D.C.: Brookings Institution.

ROTHMAN, DAVID J. (1966) Politics and Power: The United States Senate, 1869–1901. Cambridge, Mass.: Harvard University Press.

SCHICK, ALLEN (1980) Congress and Money. Washington, D.C.: Urban Institute.

SCHNEIDER, JERROLD E. (1979) Ideological Coalitions in Congress. Westport, Conn.: Greenwood Press.

SHEPSLE, KENNETH A. (1978) The Giant Jigsaw Puzzle: Democratic Committee Assignments in the Modern House. Chicago: University of Chicago Press.

SMITH, STEVEN S., and CHRISTOPHER J. DEERING (1984) Committees in Congress. Washington, D.C.: Congressional Quarterly Press.

SUNDQUIST, JAMES L. (1981) The Decline and Resurgence of Congress. Washington, D.C.: Brookings Institution.

TURNER, JULIUS, and EDWARD SCHNEIER (1971) Party and Constituency: Pressures on Congress. Baltimore, Md.: Johns Hopkins University Press.

WILSON, WOODROW (1885) Congressional Government. Baltimore, Md.: Johns Hopkins University Press (1980 ed.).

YOUNG, JAMES S. (1966) The Washington Community, 1800–1828. New York: Columbia University Press.

CHAPTER 11

ABERBACH, JOEL D., ROBERT D. PUTNAM, and BERT A. ROCKMAN (1981) Bureaucrats and Politicians in Western Democracies. Cambridge, Mass.: Harvard University Press.

BERMAN, LARRY (1979) The Office of Management and Budget and the Presidency, 1921–1979. Princeton, N.J.: Princeton University Press.

BROWN, DAVID S. (1972) "The Management of Advisory Committees: An Assignent for the '70's." Public Administration Review 32 (July/August): 334–42.

COLE, RICHARD L., and DAVID A. CAPUTO (1979) "Presidential Control of the Senior Civil Service: Assessing the Strategies of the Nixon Years." American Political Science Review 73 (June): 399–413.

DOWNS, ANTHONY (1967) Inside Bureaucracy. Boston, Mass. Little, Brown.

DREW, ELIZABETH B. (1970) "Dam Outrage: The Story of the Army Engineers." Atlantic (April): 51–62.

FENNO, RICHARD F., JR. (1966) The Power of the Purse: Appropriations Politics in Congress. Boston, Mass.: Little, Brown.

FIORINA, MORRIS P. (1977) Congress—Keystone of the Washington Establishment. New Haven, Conn.: Yale University Press.

FIORINA, MORRIS P. (1979) "Control of the Bureaucracy: A Mismatch of Incentives and Capabilities," in The Presidency and the Congress: A Shifting Balance of Power. Edited by William Livingston, Lawrence Dodd, and Richard Schott. Austin, Tex.: Lyndon B. Johnson School of Public Affairs and Lyndon Baines Johnson Library.

FRIED, ROBERT C. (1976) Performance in American Bureaucracy. Boston, Mass.: Little, Brown.

HECLO, HUGH (1975) "OMB and the Presidency—The Problem of 'Neutral Competence.' " Public Interest (Winter): 80–98.

HECLO, HUGH (1977) A Government of Strangers. Washington, D.C.: Brookings Institution.

JONES, CHARLES O. (1975) Clean Air: The Policies and Politics of Pollution Control. Pittsburgh, Pa.: University of Pittsburgh Press.

KAISER, FREDERICK M. (1980) "Congressional Action to Overturn Agency Rules: Alternatives to the 'Legislative Veto.' " Administrative Law Review 32 (Fall): 667–712.

KATZ, DANIEL, BARBARA A. GUTEK, ROBERT L. KAHN, and EUGENIA BARTON (1975) Bureaucratic Encounters. Ann Arbor: Institute for Social Research, University of Michigan.

KATZMANN, ROBERT A. (1980) Regulatory Bureaucracy: The Federal Trade Commission and Antitrust Policy. Cambridge, Mass.: Harvard University Press.

KAUFMAN, HERBERT (1976) Are Government Organizations Immortal? Washington, D.C.: Brookings Institution.

LOWI, THEODORE J. (1979) The End of Liberalism. 2d. ed. New York: W. W. Norton.

MEIER, KENNETH J. (1979) Politics and the Bureaucracy: Policymaking in the Fourth Branch of Government. North Scituate, Mass.: Duxbury.

MOE, RONALD C. (1975) "Senate Confirmation of Executive Appointments: The Nixon Era," in Congress against the President. Edited by Harvey Mansfield. New York: Praeger Publishers, pp. 142–52.

MOSHER, LAWRENCE (1983) "Despite Setbacks, Watt is Succeeding in Opening up Public Lands for Energy." National Journal (June 11): 1230–34.

NATHAN, RICHARD P. (1983) The Administrative Presidency. New York: John Wiley & Sons.

NEUSTADT, RICHARD E. (1973) "Politicians and Bureaucrats," in Congress and America's Future. 2d. ed. Edited by David B. Truman. Englewood Cliffs, N.J.: Prentice-Hall, pp. 118–40.

NEWLAND, CHESTER A. (1983) "A Mid-Term Appraisal— The Reagan Presidency: Limited Government and Political Administration." Public Administration Review 43 (January/February): 1–21.

OGUL, MORRIS S. (1976) Congress Oversees the Bureaucracy: Studies in Legislative Supervision. Pittsburgh, Pa.: University of Pittsburgh Press.

RIPLEY, RANDALL B., and GRACE A. FRANKLIN (1984) Congress, the Bureaucracy, and Public Policy, 3d ed. Homewood, Ill.: Dorsey Press.

ROTHMAN, STANLEY and S. ROBERT LICHTER (1983) "How Liberal Are Bureaucrats?" Regulation (November/December): 16–22.

ROURKE, FRANCIS E. (1976) Bureaucracy, Politics, and Public Policy. 2d ed. Boston, Mass.: Little, Brown.

SEIDMAN, HAROLD (1980) Politics, Position, and Power: The Dynamics of Federal Organization. 3rd ed. New York: Oxford University Press.

TAYLOR, TELFORD (1955) Grand Inquest. New York: Simon & Schuster.

WILENSKY, HAROLD L. (1967) Organizational Intelligence. New York: Basic Books.

WILSON, JAMES Q. (1975) "The Rise of the Bureaucratic State." The Public Interest (Fall): 77–103.

WYNIA, BOB L. (1974) "Federal Bureaucrats' Attitudes toward a Democratic Ideology." Public Administration Review 34 (March/April): 156–62.

CHAPTER 12

ABRAHAM, HENRY J. (1975) Justices and Presidents: A Political History of Appointments to the Supreme Court. New York: Penguin Books.

ABRAHAM, HENRY J. (1980) The Judicial Process. 4th ed. New York: Oxford University Press.

BALL, HOWARD (1980) Courts and Politics: The Federal Judicial System. Englewood Cliffs, N.J.: Prentice-Hall.

BASS, JACK (1981) Unlikely Heroes. New York: Simon & Schuster.

BAUM, LAWRENCE (1981) The Supreme Court. Washington, D.C.: Congressional Quarterly Press.

BOND, JON R. and CHARLES A. JOHNSON (1982) "Implementing a Permissive Policy: Hospital Abortion Services after *Roe* v. *Wade*." American Journal of Political Science 26 (February): 1–24.

CARP, ROBERT A., and C. K. ROWLAND (1983) Policymaking and Politics in the Federal District Courts. Knoxville, Tenn.: University of Tennessee Press.

CASPER, JONATHAN D. (1976) "The Supreme Court and National Policy Making." American Political Science Review 70 (March): 50–63.

COOK, BEVERLY B. (1977) "Public Opinion and Federal Judicial Policy." American Journal of Political Science 21 (August): 567–600.

COOK, BEVERLY B. (1979) "Judicial Policy: Change Over Time." American Journal of Political Science 23 (February): 208–14.

CRAIG, BARBARA HINKSON (1983) The Legislative Veto: Congressional Control of Regulation. Boulder, Col.: Westview Press.

DAHL, ROBERT A. (1957) "Decision-Making in a Democracy: The Supreme Court as a National Policy-Maker. Journal of Public Law 6 (Fall): 279–95.

EISENSTEIN, JAMES (1978) Counsel for the United States. Baltimore: Johns Hopkins University Press.

GILES, MICHEAL W., and THOMAS G. WALKER (1975) "Judicial Policy-Making and Southern School Segregation." Journal of Politics 37 (November): 917–36.

GLAZER, NATHAN (1975) "Towards an Imperial Judiciary?" Public Interest (Fall): 104–23.

GOLDMAN, SHELDON (1975) "Voting Behavior on the United States Courts of Appeals Revisited." American Political Science Review 69 (June): 491–506.

GOLDMAN, SHELDON (1983) "Reagan's Judicial Appointments at Mid-term: Shaping the Bench in His Own Image." Judicature 66 (March): 334–47.

GOLDMAN, SHELDON, and THOMAS P. JAHNIGE (1976) The Federal Courts as a Political System. 2d ed. New York: Harper & Row.

HOROWITZ, DONALD L. (1977) The Courts and Social Policy. Washington, D.C. Brookings Institution.

JACOB, HERBERT (1984) Justice in America: Courts, Lawyers, and the Judicial Process. 4th ed. Boston: Little, Brown.

KRITZER, HERBERT M. (1979) "Federal Judges and Their Political Environments: The Influence of Public Opinion." American Journal of Political Science 23 (February): 194–207.

McCLOSKEY, ROBERT G. (1960) The American Supreme Court. Chicago: University of Chicago Press.

MILNER, NEAL A. (1971) The Court and Local Law Enforcement: The Impact of Miranda. Beverly Hills: Sage Publications.

MUIR, WILLIAM (1968) Prayer in the Public Schools. Chicago: University of Chicago Press.

MURPHY, BRUCE ALLEN (1982) The Brandeis/Frankfurter Connection: The Secret Political Activities of Two Supreme Court Justices. New York: Oxford University Press.

NAGEL, STUART S. (1961) "Political Party Affiliation and Judges' Decisions." American Political Science Review 55 (December): 843–50.

O'CONNOR, KAREN and LEE EPSTEIN (1983) "The Rise of Conservative Interest Group Litigation." Journal of Politics 45 (May): 479–89.

RICHARDSON, RICHARD J., and KENNETH N. VINES (1970) The Politics of Federal Courts. Boston: Little, Brown.

ROHDE, DAVID W., and HAROLD J. SPAETH (1976) Supreme Court Decision Making. San Francisco: W. H. Freeman.

ROWLAND, C. K., and ROBERT A. CARP (1980) "A Longitudinal Study of Party Effects on Federal District Court Policy Propensities." American Journal of Political Science 24 (May): 291–305.

SARAT, AUSTIN, and JOEL B. GROSSMAN (1975) "Courts and Conflict Resolution: Problems in the Mobilization of Adjudication." American Political Science Review 69 (December): 1200–17.

SCHMIDHAUSER, JOHN (1959) "The Supreme Court: A Collective Portrait." Midwest Journal of Political Science 3 (August): 1–57.

SCIGLIANO, ROBERT (1971) The Supreme Court and the Presidency. New York: Free Press.

SHAPIRO, MARTIN (1978) "The Supreme Court: From Warren to Burger," in The New American Political System. Edited by Anthony King. Washington, D.C.: American Enterprise Institute.

SLOTNICK, ELLIOT E. (1979) "Who Speaks for the Court? Majority Opinion Assignment from Taft to Burger." American Journal of Political Science 23 (February): 60–77.

WASBY, STEPHEN L. (1976) Small Town Police and the Supreme Court. Lexington, Mass.: Lexington Books.

WOODWARD, BOB, and SCOTT ARMSTRONG (1979) The Brethren: Inside the Supreme Court. New York: Simon & Schuster.

CHAPTER 13

BULLOCK, CHARLES S., III (1980) "The Office for Civil Rights and Implementation of Desegregation Programs in the Public Schools." Policy Studies Journal 8 (Special Issue No. 2): 597–616.

CLAUDE, RICHARD P., ed. (1976) Comparative Human Rights. Baltimore, Md.: Johns Hopkins University Press.

DUCAT, CRAIG R. and HAROLD W. CHASE (1983) Constitutional Interpretation: Cases—Essays—Materials. 3d ed. St. Paul, Minn.: West Publishing.

GARCIA, F. CHRIS and RUDOLPH O. de la GARZA (1977). The Chicano Political Experience. North Scituate, Mass., Duxbury.

GASTIL, RAYMOND D. (1979) Freedom in the World. New York: Freedom House.

GOLDSTEIN, LESLIE FRIEDMAN (1979) The Constitutional Rights of Women. New York: Longman.

GOLDSTEIN, LESLIE FRIEDMAN (1981) "The Constitutional Status of Women: The Burger Court and the Sexual Revolution in American Law." Law and Policy Quarterly 3 (January): 5–28.

GROSSMAN, JOEL B., and RICHARD S. WELLS (1980) Constitutional Law and Judicial Policy Making. 2d ed. New York: John Wiley & Sons.

HANSEN, SUSAN B. (1980) "State Implementation of Supreme Court Decisions: Abortion Rates Since Roe v. Wade." Journal of Politics 42 (May): 372–95.

KICKINGBIRD, LYNN, and KIRKE KICKINGBIRD (1977) Indians and the U.S. Government. Washington, D.C.: Institute for the Development of Indian Law.

KLUGER, RICHARD (1976) Simple Justice: The History of Brown v. Board of Education and Black America's Struggle for Equality. New York: Alfred A. Knopf.

McCLOSKY, HERBERT and ALIDA BRILL (1983) Dimensions of Tolerance: What Americans Believe about Civil Liberties. New York: Russell Sage Foundation.

ORFIELD, GARY (1978) Must We Bus? Washington, D.C.: Brookings Institution.

RABKIN, JEREMY (1980) "Office for Civil Rights," in The Politics of Regulation. Edited by James Q. Wilson. New York: Basic Books.

RODGERS, HARRELL R., JR., and CHARLES S. BULLOCK, III (1976) Coercion to Compliance. Lexington, Mass.: D. C. Heath.

SUNDQUIST, JAMES L. (1968) Politics and Policy. Washington, D.C.: Brookings Institution.

TAYLOR, CHARLES LEWIS, and MICHAEL C. HUDSON (1972) World Handbook of Political and Social Indicators. 2d ed. New Haven, Conn.: Yale University Press.

CHAPTER 14

ADVISORY COMMISSION ON INTERGOVERNMENTAL RELATIONS (1979) "A Catalog of Federal Grant-in-Aid Programs to State and Local Governments: Grants Funded FY 1978. Report A-72. Washington, D.C.: ACIR.

ADVISORY COMMISSION ON INTERGOVERNMENTAL RELATIONS (1980) The Federal Role in the Federal System: The Dynamics of Growth. Report A-77. Washington, D.C.: ACIR.

CATER, DOUGLASS (1964) Power in Washington. New York: Random House.

COBB, ROGER W., and CHARLES D. ELDER (1983) Participation in American Politics: The Dynamics of Agenda-Building. 2nd ed. Baltimore: Johns Hopkins University Press.

EPSTEIN, LEON D. (1978) "The Old States in a New System," in The New American Political System. Edited by Anthony King. Washington, D.C.: American Enterprise Institute.

KETTL, DONALD F. (1983) The Regulation of American Federalism. Baton Rouge: Louisiana State University Press.

LEACH, RICHARD H. (1970) American Federalism. New York: W. W. Norton.

LEWIS, EUGENE (1977) American Politics in a Bureaucratic Age: Citizens, Constituents, Clients, and Victims. Cambridge, Mass.: Winthrop.

LINDBLOM, CHARLES E. (1959) "The Science of 'Muddling Through.'" Public Administration Review 19 (Spring): 79–88.

LOWI, THEODORE J. (1979) The End of Liberalism. 2d ed. New York: W. W. Norton.

NATHAN, RICHARD P., ALLEN D. MANVEL, SUSANNAH E. CALKINS, and Associates (1975) Monitoring Revenue Sharing. Washington, D.C.: Brookings Institution.

NATHAN, RICHARD P., and PAUL R. DOMMEL (1978) "Federal-Loan Relations Under Block Grants." Political Science Quarterly 93 (Fall): 421–42.

STANFIELD, ROCHELLE L. (1981) "What Has 500 Parts, Costs $83 Billion and Is Condemned by Almost Everybody?" National Journal (January 3): 4–9.

SUNDQUIST, JAMES L. (1969) Making Federalism Work. Washington, D.C.: Brookings Institution.

SUNDQUIST, JAMES L., and HUGH MIELDS, JR. (1979) "Regional Growth Policy in the United States," in Balanced National Growth. Edited by Kevin Allen. Lexington, Mass.: Lexington Books.

VAN HORN, CARL E. (1979) Policy Implementation in the Federal System. Lexington, Mass.: Lexington Books.

VAN METER, DONALD S., and CARL E. VAN HORN (1975) "The Policy Implementation Process: A Conceptual Framework." Administration and Society 6 (February): 445–88.

WALKER, DAVID B. (1981) Toward a Functioning Federalism. Cambridge, Mass.: Winthrop.

WILLIAMS, WALTER (1980) Government by Agency: Lessons from the Social Program Grants-in-Aid Experience. New York: Academic Press.

CHAPTER 15

BAILEY, STEPHEN K., and EDITH K. MOSHER (1968) ESEA: The Office of Education Administers a Law. Syracuse, N.Y.: Syracuse University Press.

BENDINER, ROBERT (1964) Obstacle Course on Capitol Hill. New York: McGraw-Hill.

BULLOCK, CHARLES S., III (1980) "The Office for Civil Rights and Implementation of Desegregation Programs in the Public Schools." Policy Studies Journal 8 (Special Issue No. 2): 597–616.

EIDENBERG, EUGENE, and ROY D. MOREY (1969) An Act of Congress. New York: W. W. Norton.

EVANS, HUGH, and LLOYD RODWIN (1979) "The New Towns Program and Why It Failed." The Public Interest, (Summer): 90–107.

JANTSCHER, GERALD R. (1975) Bread upon the Waters: Federal Aids to the Maritime Industries. Washington, D.C.: Brookings Institution.

JONES, CHARLES O. (1984) An Introduction to the Study of Public Policy. 3d ed. Monterey, California: Brooks/Cole.

LAWRENCE, SAMUEL A. (1965) United States Merchant Shipping Policies and Politics. Washington, D.C.: Brookings Institution.

LAZIN, FREDERICK A. (1973) "The Failure of Federal Enforcement of Civil Rights Regulations in Public Housing, 1963–1971: The Co-optation of a Federal Agency by Its Local Constituency." Policy Sciences 4 (September): 263–73.

Le LOUP, LANCE T. (1978) "Discretion in National Budgeting: Controlling the Controllables." Policy Analysis 4 (Fall): 455–75.

Le LOUP, LANCE T. (1980) Budgetary Politics. 2d ed. Brunswick, Ohio: King's Court.

LEMAN, CHRISTOPHER (1979) "How to Get There from Here: The Grandfather Effect and Public Policy." Policy Analysis 6 (Winter): 99–116.

MARMOR, THEODORE R. (1973) The Politics of Medicare. Rev. ed. Chicago: Aldine.

MENZEL, DONALD C. (1983) "Redirecting the Implementation of a Law: The Reagan Administration and Coal Surface Mining Regulation." Public Administration Review 43 (September/October): 411–20.

MIRENGOFF, WILLIAM, and LESTER RINDLER (1976) The Comprehensive Employment and Training Act: Impact on People, Places, Programs. Washington, D.C.: National Academy of Sciences.

MUNGER, FRANK J., and RICHARD F. FENNO, JR. (1962) National Politics and Federal Aid to Education. Syracuse, N.Y.: Syracuse University Press.

MURPHY, JEROME T. (1971) "Title I of ESEA: The Politics of Implementing Federal Education Reform." Harvard Educational Review 41 (February): 35–63.

MURPHY, JEROME T. (1973) "The Education Bureaucracies Implement Novel Policy: The Politics of Title I of ESEA, 1965–72," in Policy and Politics in America: Six Case Studies. Edited by Allan P. Sindler. Boston: Little, Brown, pp. 160–98.

NATHAN, RICHARD P., ALLEN D. MANVEL, SUSANNAH E. CALKINS, and Associates (1975) Monitoring Revenue Sharing. Washington, D.C.: Brookings Institution.

RABKIN, JEREMY (1980) "Office for Civil Rights," in The Politics of Regulation. Edited by James Q. Wilson. New York: Basic Books.

REDMAN, ERIC (1973) The Dance of Legislation. New York: Simon & Schuster.

REID, T. R. (1980) Congressional Odyssey: The Saga of a Senate Bill. San Francisco: W. H. Freeman.

RIPLEY, RANDALL B., and GRACE A. FRANKLIN (1982) Bureaucracy and Policy Implementation. Homewood, Ill.: Dorsey Press.

RIPLEY, RANDALL B., and GRACE A. FRANKLIN (1984) Congress, the Bureaucracy, and Public Policy. 3d ed. Homewood, Illinois: Dorsey Press.

SUNDQUIST, JAMES L. (1968) Politics and Policy. Washington, D.C.: Brookings Institution.

TALBOT, ROSS B., and DONALD F. HADWIGER (1968) The Policy Process in American Agriculture. San Francisco: Chandler.

VAN HORN, CARL E., and DONALD S. VAN METER (1976) "The Implementation of Intergovernmental Policy," in Public Policy Making in a Federal System. Edited by Charles O. Jones and Robert D. Thomas. Beverly Hills, Calif.: Sage Publications, pp. 39–62.

WILDAVSKY, AARON (1979) The Politics of the Budgetary Process. 3d ed. Boston: Little, Brown.

WINES, MICHAEL (1982) "Administration Says It Merely Seeks a 'Better way' to Enforce Civil Rights." National Journal (March 27): 536–41.

WOLMAN, HAROLD (1971) Politics of Federal Housing. New York: Dodd, Mead.

CHAPTER 16

ALLISON, GRAHAM T. (1971) The Essence of Decision: Explaining the Cuban Missile Crisis. Boston: Little, Brown.

ALLISON, GRAHAM T., and MORTON H. HALPERIN (1972) "Bureaucratic Politics: A Paradigm and Some Policy Implications." World Politics 24 (supplement): 40–79.

ALMOND, GABRIEL (1960) The American People and Foreign Policy. New York: Praeger Publishers.

BAUER, RAYMOND A., ITHIEL de SOLA POOL, and LEWIS ANTHONY DEXTER (1963) American Business and Public Policy: The Politics of Foreign Trade. New York: Atherton Press.

BAX, FRANS R. (1977) "The Legislative-Executive Relationship in Foreign Policy: New Partnership or New Competition?" Orbis (Winter): 881–904.

BEDELL, SALLY (1982) "Why TV News Can't be a Complete View of the World." New York Times (August 8): Section 2, p. 1.

BERGERSON, FREDERIC A. (1980) The Army Gets an Air Force. Baltimore, Md.: Johns Hopkins University Press.

BERNSTEIN, RICHARD (1982) "An Elite Group on U.S. Policy is Diversifying." New York Times (October 30): 29.

CARROLL, HOLBERT N. (1966) The House of Representatives and Foreign Affairs. Rev. ed. Boston: Little, Brown.

COHEN, BERNARD C. (1965) The Press and Foreign Policy. Princeton, N.J.: Princeton University Press.

CORWIN, EDWARD S. (1957) The President: Office and Powers. 4th ed. New York: New York University Press.

CRABB, CECIL V., JR. (1983) American Foreign Policy in the Nuclear Age. 4th ed. New York: Harper & Row.

CRABB, CECIL V., JR, and PAT M. HOLT (1984) Invitation to Struggle: Congress, the President and Foreign Policy. 2nd ed. Washington, D.C.: Congressional Quarterly Press.

CUTLER, LLOYD N. (1980) "To Form a Government." Foreign Affairs 59 (Fall): 126–43.

DESTLER, I. M. (1981) "Dateline Washington: Congress as Boss?" Foreign Policy 42 (Spring): 167–80.

DULLES, ALLEN (1963) The Craft of Intelligence. New York: Harper & Row.

EISENHOWER, DWIGHT D. (1961) Public Papers of the Presidents. Washington, D.C.: U.S. Government Printing Office.

FISHER, LOUIS (1972) President and Congress: Power and Policy, New York: Free Press.

FULBRIGHT, J. WILLIAM (1966) The Arrogance of Power. New York: Random House.

GEORGE, ALEXANDER L. (1972) "The Case for Multiple Advocacy in Making Foreign Policy." American Political Science Review 66 (September): 751–85.

HALBERSTAM, DAVID (1972) The Best and the Brightest. New York: Random House.

HARSCH, JOSEPH C. (1956) "John Foster Dulles: A Very Complicated Man." Harper's Magazine 213 (September): 29.

HILSMAN, ROGER (1967) To Move a Nation: The Politics of Foreign Policy in the Administration of John F. Kennedy. Garden City, N.Y.: Doubleday Publishing.

HUNTINGTON, SAMUEL P. (1961) The Common Defense. New York: Columbia University Press.

IRISH, MARIAN, and ELKE FRANK (1975) U.S. Foreign Policy: Context, Conduct, Content. New York: Harcourt Brace Jovanovich.

JANIS, IRVING L. (1983) Groupthink. Boston: Houghton Mifflin.

KATZ, DANIEL, et al., eds. (1954) Public Opinion and Propaganda. New York: Holt, Rinehart & Winston.

KENNAN, GEORGE F. (1952) American Diplomacy, 1900–1950. New York: New American Library.

LARDNER, GEORGE, JR. (1984) "Will We Ever Harness Our Rogue Agency?" Washington Post (April 22): D5.

LEWIS, ANTHONY (1984) "Royal Prerogative (1)" New York Times (July 2): A15.

MARTIN, JOE (1960) My First Fifty Years in Politics. New York: McGraw-Hill.

MATHIAS, CHARLES McC., JR., (1981) "Ethnic Groups and Foreign Policy." Foreign Affairs 59 (Summer): 975–98.

MUELLER, JOHN E. (1973) War, Presidents, and Public Opinion. New York: John Wiley & Sons.

REILLY, JOHN E., ed. (1983) American Public Opinion and U.S. Foreign Policy 1983. Chicago: Chicago Council on Foreign Relations.

SAMPSON, ANTHONY (1977) The Arms Bazaar: From Lebanon to Lockheed, New York: Viking Press.

SCHLESINGER, ARTHUR M, JR. (1965) A Thousand Days: John F. Kennedy in the White House. Boston: Houghton Mifflin.

SCHLESINGER, ARTHUR M., JR. (1973) The Imperial Presidency. Boston: Houghton Mifflin.

SIGEL, ROBERTA A. (1966) "Image of the American Presidency—Part II of an Exploration into Popular Views of Presidential Power." Midwest Journal of Political Science 10 (Februrary):125.

SPYKMAN, NICHOLAS J. (1941) America's Strategy in World Politics. New York: Harcourt Brace Jovanovich.

WILLIAMS, JUAN (1983) "Reagan's Days Off Erupt in Crisis." Washington Post (October 24): A14.

WISE, DAVID (1976) The American Police State. New York: Random House.

CHAPTER 17

BRANSCOME, JAMES (1977) The Federal Government in Appalachia. New York: Field Foundation.

BRAYBROOKE, DAVID, and CHARLES E. LINDBLOM (1963) A Strategy of Decision. New York: Free Press.

DANZIGER, SHELDON, ROBERT HAVEMAN, and ROBERT PLOTNICK (1980) "Retrenchment or Reorientation: Options for Income Support Policy." Public Policy 28 (Fall): 473–90.

DEMKOVICH, LINDA E., and JOEL HAVEMANN (1982) "The Poor and the Near Poor May Be Bearing the Brunt." The National Journal (October 23): 1796–1800.

DOWNS, ANTHONY (1974) "The Successes and Failures of Federal Housing Policy." The Public Interest (Winter): 124–45.

DUNCAN, GREG J. (1984) Years of Poverty, Years of Plenty: The Changing Economic Fortunes of American Workers and Families. Ann Arbor, Mich.: Survey Research Center, The University of Michigan.

FRIEDEN, BERNARD J. (1980) "Housing Allowances: An Experiment that Worked." The Public Interest (Spring): 15–35.

HAVEMANN, JOEL (1982) "Sharing the Wealth: The Gap Between Rich and Poor Grows Wider." The National Journal (October 23): 1788–95.

JONES, CHARLES O. (1984) An Introduction to the study of Public Policy. 3d ed. Monterey, Calif.: Brooks/Cole.

Le LOUP, LANCE T. (1980) Budgetary Politics. 2d ed. Brunswick, Ohio: King's Court.

LEVITAN, SAR A. and ROBERT TAGGART (1976) The Promise of Greatness. Cambridge, Mass.: Harvard University Press.

LEVY, FRANK, and RICHARD C. MICHEL (1983) "The Way We'll Be in 1984: Recent Changes in the Level and Distribution of Disposable Income." Discussion paper, Washington, D.C.: The Urban Institute.

LOWI, THEODORE J. (1979) The End of Liberalism. 2d ed. New York: W. W. Norton.

PECHMAN, JOSEPH A. (1977) Federal Tax Policy. 3d ed. Washington, D.C.: Brookings Institution.

RICH, SPENCER (1983) "Poor Hurt Most by Social Cuts, CBO Study Says." Washington Post (August 26).

RIPLEY, RANDALL B. (1972) The Politics of Economic and Human Resource Development. Indianapolis, Ind.: Bobbs-Merrill.

STEINER, GILBERT Y. (1971) The State of Welfare. Washington, D.C.: Brookings Institution.

Illustration Credits

CHAPTER 8

CHAPTER 9

316 James Schlesinger, *courtesy Georgetown Censer for Strategic and International Studies*
317 Cartoon, by *Powell for the Raleigh News and Observer*
318 Kennedys and Shah of Iran, *United Press International Photo*
320 George Bush, *Official White House Photo*
321 The Reagan Cabinet, *Bill Fitz-Patrick/The White House*

CHAPTER 10

327 Rep. Walker, House chamber, Rep. O'Neill, *courtesy C-Span;* Rep. Gingrich, *Wide World Photos.*
331 Cartoon, *copyright 1978 by Herblock in* The Washington Post
335 Select panel, *Wide World Photos*
337 Senate Foreign Relations Committee, *courtesy Sen. Charles Percy*
338–39 Legislators: Byrd, Cranston, Dellums, Fascell, Gonzalez, Hatfield, Kassebaum, Pepper, Rostenkowski, *courtesy* their respective offices.
340 Senators Kennedy and Hatch, *United Press International Photo*
342–43 Henry Clay, Thomas B. Reed, Joseph G. Cannon, *Historical Pictures Service, Chicago;* Tip O'Neill, *Wide World Photos*
345 Cartoon *by Jeff MacNelly; reprinted by permission: Tribune Media Services, Inc.*
346 Black, Hispanic caucuses, *Wide World Photos*
353 Huey Long, *Wide World Photos;* William Roth, *UPI/Bettmann Archive*
355 Phil Gramm, *Wide World Photos*
359 James Jones and Pete Domenici, *Wide World Photos*
361 David Stockman, *Wide World Photos*
363 Hill intern, *courtesy Sweet Briar College*
363 Personal staffers, *courtesy Rep. Dan Glickman*
365 Washington, D.C., *Air Photographics, Inc.*
367 Cartoon, *by Breathed, reprinted by permission of International Creative Management, Inc. Copyright © 1983 The Washington Post Company*
369 Watergate Committee, *Pictorial Parade*

CHAPTER 11

373 Pilot, *courtesy U.S. Air Force;* teacher, *courtesy National College of Education*
374 Unemployment line, *Russell Rief, Pictorial Parade;* welfare worker, *courtesy ACTION*
375 Government forms, *Frank O. Williams/The Bookworks, Inc.*
381 Mail sorting, *courtesy U.S. Postal Service*
381 Beef grading, *USDA;* JFK and Frances Kelsey, *United Press International Photo*
382 Volunteer attorney, *courtesy VISTA*
383 Cartoon, *from Herblock Through the Looking Glass (W. W. Norton & Co., 1984)*
384 Land fill hearing, *United Press International Photo*
385 Caspar Weinberger, *Wide World Photos*
387 Army-McCarthy hearings, *United Press International Photo*
388 Harry Truman, *Historical Pictures Service, Chicago*
389 Senator Proxmire and press release, *courtesy his office*
390 Edwin Meese, *Wide World Photos*
390 Impeachment ticket, *Historical Pictures Service, Chicago*
391 Soviet ship, *United Press International Photo*
391 Cartoon, *from Herblock Through the Looking Glass (W. W. Norton Co., 1984)*
392 James Watt, Ann Gorsuch, *United Press International Photos*
393 President Reagan with David Stockman, *United Press International Photo*
394 Disaster assistance, *courtesy Federal Emergency Management Agency*
396 Cecil Andrus, *courtesy Mr. Andrus*

Index

This book has been set VIP in 10 and 9 point Palatino, leaded 2 points. Chapter numbers and titles are 27 point Helvetica Black. Part numbers are 18 point Helvetica Black and part titles are 27 point Helvetica Black. The size of the type page is 39 by 52 picas.